Management Accounting

Visit the *Management Accounting* Companion Website at
www.pearsoned.co.uk/weetman to find valuable **student** learning
material including:

- Multiple choice questions to help test your learning
- Extensive links to valuable resources on the web
- An online glossary to explain key terms

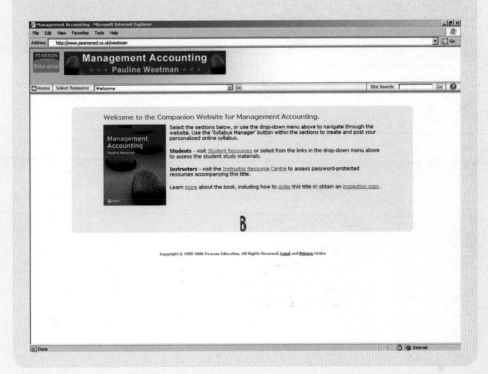

Management Accounting

PAULINE WEETMAN

Professor of Accounting, University of Strathclyde

FT Prentice Hall

FINANCIAL TIMES

An imprint of **Pearson Education**

Harlow, England • London • New York • Boston • San Francisco • Toronto • Sydney • Singapore • Hong Kong
Tokyo • Seoul • Taipei • New Delhi • Cape Town • Madrid • Mexico City • Amsterdam • Munich • Paris • Milan

To my parents,
Harry and Freda Weetman

Pearson Education Limited

Edinburgh Gate
Harlow
Essex CM20 2JE

and Associated Companies throughout the world.

Visit us on the World Wide Web at:
www.pearsoned.co.uk

ISBN-13: 978-0-273-70199-6
ISBN-10: 0-273-70199-1

British Library Cataloguing-in-Publication Data
A catalogue record for this book is available from the British Library

Library of Congress Cataloging-in-Publication Data
A catalog record for this book is available from the Library of Congress

10 9 8 7 6 5 4 3 2 1
10 09 08 07 06

Typeset in 9.5/12pt Palatino by 35
Printed and Bound by Mateu-Cromo Artes Graficas, Spain

The publisher's policy is to use paper manufactured from sustainable forests.

Contents

Chapter 3   Materials and labour costs

Chapter 4   Overhead costs

Chapter 8   Process costing   181

Part 2   DECISION MAKING

Chapter 9   Short-term decision making   206

Part 3   PERFORMANCE MEASUREMENT AND CONTROL

Chapter 15 Standard costs   363

Chapter 16 Performance evaluation and feedback reporting   400

Chapter 17   Divisional performance   428

Part 4   FINANCIAL MANAGEMENT AND STRATEGIC PLANNING

Chapter 18   Financial management: working capital and business plans   452

Chapter 19   Business strategy and management accounting   476

Appendix I   Quick check list: A glossary of management accounting terms   499

Appendix II   Solutions to numerical and technical questions in Management Accounting   507

Supporting resources

Visit **www.pearsoned.co.uk/weetman** to find valuable online resources

Companion Website for students
- Multiple choice questions to help test your learning
- Extensive links to valuable resources on the web
- An online glossary to explain key terms

For instructors
- Student handouts containing a skeleton outline of each chapter
- PowerPoint slides that can be downloaded and used as OHTs
- Suggested discussion answers to real world case studies
- Solutions to questions in the text
- Additional multiple choice questions and further graded questions in application of knowledge and in problem solving

Also: The Companion Website provides the following features:
- Search tool to help locate specific items of content
- E-mail results and profile tools to send results of quizzes to instructors
- Online help and support to assist with website usage and troubleshooting

For more information please contact your local Pearson Education sales representative or visit **www.pearsoned.co.uk/weetman**

Preface

Introduction

This book is written for the first and second levels of undergraduate degree study in accounting and business studies, or equivalent introductory accounting courses where an understanding of accounting is a basic requirement. It is based on the author's experience in providing a first level management accounting text and takes account of helpful suggestions from reviewers of three successive editions of that text. In particular, it has taken some of the newer costing techniques into mainstream discussion, reflecting their increasing acceptance in management accounting practice. Business strategy and competitive position are recurring themes.

An accompanying website at www.pearsoned.co.uk/weetman provides the lecturer with a complete resource pack for each chapter comprising: student handouts containing a skeleton outline of each chapter, leaving slots for students to complete; overhead-projector masters that match the lecture handouts, suggested discussion answers to real-world cases, solutions to text book questions in addition to those given at the end of the book, additional multiple-choice questions and further graded questions in application of knowledge and in problem solving.

End-of-chapter questions are graded according to the skills being assessed. There are tests of understanding, tests of application of knowledge in straightforward situations and tests of problem solving and evaluation using the acquired knowledge in less familiar situations.

Overall the aim of this text book is to provide a knowledge and understanding of management accounting which establishes competence in the key areas while engaging the interest of students and encouraging a desire for further specialist study. It also contributes to developing the generic skills of application, problem solving, evaluation and communication, all emphasised as essential attributes by potential employers.

Subject coverage

Managers have access to a wealth of detailed financial information and have a responsibility for the careful management of the assets and operations of the organisation. The way in which the managers of an organisation use financial information is very much contingent on the purpose for which the information is intended. Management accounting is a specialist area of study within accounting more generally. Ideally, management accounting and financial accounting would coalesce if the external users could be given access to all internal information, but that might damage the competitive position of the business and would probably swamp the external users in detail.

The text book chapters indicate two levels of study, corresponding to the first and second years of degree courses in accounting. First-level degree courses in accounting are increasingly addressed to a broad base of potential interest and this book seeks to provide such a broad base of understanding in chapters 1 to 4, 9, 11, 13 and 16. Second-level degree courses reinforce the ability to apply management accounting techniques in situations of decision making, control and problem solving. This book provides those features in chapters 5 to 8, 10, 12, 14, 15, 17, 18 and 19.

Aim of the book

The book aims to establish a firm understanding of the basic techniques, while recognising the growth of more recent developments in management accounting. A contingency approach is adopted which emphasises that the selection of management accounting techniques is conditional on management's purpose. To meet this purpose, the management accountant performs the roles of directing attention, keeping the score and solving problems. Strategic management accounting is emphasised from the outset so that students are aware that management accounting must take an outward-looking approach. These themes are reiterated throughout, concluding with an explanation of the role of management accounting in business strategy, including e-business in the new economy. A student who has completed this study of management accounting at first and second levels will be aware of many of the day-to-day practices of management accounting in business and the relevance of those practices.

In particular

- *Concepts* of management accounting are presented in Chapters 1 to 4 and applied consistently thereafter.
- *User needs* are discussed by including first-person commentary from a professional consultant who gives insight into the type of interpretative comment which students of management accounting often find difficult.
- *Real world cases* ask questions based on extract from newspapers, annual reports and promotional material. They provide practical illustration through specific examples in each chapter and in the case studies discussed by the consultant. Reinforcement is provided by end-of-chapter cases which encourage discussion of scenarios.
- *Interpretation* is a feature of all the management accounting chapters where the use of first-person commentary by the consultant allows more candid discussion than would be appropriate in the usual dispassionate style of the academic text.
- *What the researchers have found* is a section running through the chapters explaining a selection of academic papers and other resource sources that are helpful in understanding how management accounting is developing in practice. Each paper is summarised to show why it may be of interest. The wide range of source journals used shows that management accounting techniques are of interest in many different forms of business and public-benefit organisation.
- *Future developments* – an emphasis throughout on strategic management accounting, with its focus on benchmarking against competitors, culminates in a final chapter on business strategy and its application in e-business and e-commerce. Lean accounting, target costing, value chain analysis and total quality management are described and illustrated. Activity-based costing is dealt with as part of the normal approach to overhead costing; benchmarking and the balanced scorecard are described in the performance measurement chapter, and the impact of advanced manufacturing technologies is assessed in the investment appraisal chapters.
- *Self-evaluation* is encouraged throughout each chapter. Activity questions are placed at various stages of the chapter, while self-testing questions at the end of the chapter may be answered by referring again to the text. Further end-of-chapter questions provide a range of practical applications. Answers are available to all computational questions, either at the end of the book or on the website. Group activities are suggested at the end of each chapter with the particular aim of encouraging participation and interaction.

Flexible course design

There was once a time when the academic year comprised three terms and we all knew the length of a typical course unit over those three terms. Now there are semesters, trimesters, modules and half-modules so that planning a course of study becomes an exercise in critical path analysis. This text is written for two 12-teaching-week semesters but may need selective guidance to students for modules of lesser duration.

The chapters are designated 'level one' and 'level two' to indicate a structure for using the book with first and second year students. The level one chapters provide a broader overview of the subject area, with greater depth provided in the level two chapters. The book could be useful where a course contains a broadly based first year class with an option for second year study by those members of the class intending greater specialisation.

The plan of the book also recognises the wide variety of course design. Some lecturers prefer to focus on decision making in depth while others prefer a broad coverage of decision making and control. Some management accounting courses include investment appraisal and capital budgeting while others leave this to a finance course. The arrangement of the chapters allows flexibility in content and sequence of the course programme.

In teaching and learning management accounting, various combinations are possible, depending on course design and aims. Chapters 1 to 4 provide an essential set of basic tools of analysis but thereafter some flexibility is feasible. For a focus on product costing, Chapters 5 to 8 provide a range of material. For concentrating on decision making, short term and longer term, Chapters 9 and 11 are recommended at level one, followed by Chapters 10 and 12 at level two. For concentrating on planning and control, Chapters 13 and 16 give students a first level understanding, with Chapters 14, 15 and 17 providing more detail on the variety of techniques in use. The final section on financial management and strategic planning shows in Chapter 18 how the management accountant can support financial management of working capital, while Chapter 19 reviews some of the many developing techniques available for integrating management accounting with broader management initiatives.

Approaches to teaching and learning

Learning outcomes

Learning outcomes are measurable achievements for students, stated at the start of each chapter. The achievement of some learning outcomes may be confirmed by Activities set out at the appropriate stage within the chapter. Others may be confirmed by end-of-chapter questions.

End-of-chapter questions are graded and each is matched to one or more learning outcomes. The grades of question are:

Test your understanding (Series A questions)

The answers to these questions can be found in the material contained in the chapter.

Application (Series B questions)

These are questions that apply the knowledge gained from reading and practising the material of the chapter. They resemble closely in style and content the technical material of the chapter. Confidence is gained in applying knowledge in a situation that is very similar to that illustrated. Answers are given at the end of the book or in the Resources for Tutors available on the companion website.

Problem solving and evaluation (Series C questions)

These are questions that apply the knowledge gained from reading the chapter, but the style of each question is different. Problem-solving skills are required in selecting relevant data or in using knowledge to work out what further effort is needed to solve the problem. Evaluation means giving an opinion or explanation of the results of the

Plan of the book

Part 1 DEFINING, REPORTING AND MANAGING COSTS			
LEVEL 1	**Chapter 1** What is management accounting?	**Chapter 2** Classification of costs	**Chapter 3** Materials and labour costs	**Chapter 4** Overhead costs
LEVEL 2	**Chapter 5** Absorption costing and marginal costing	**Chapter 6** Job costing	**Chapter 7** Recording transactions in a job costing system	**Chapter 8** Process costing

Part 2 DECISION MAKING		
LEVEL 1	**Chapter 9** Short-term decision making	**Chapter 11** Capital investment appraisal
LEVEL 2	**Chapter 10** Relevant costs, pricing and decisions under uncertainty	**Chapter 12** Capital budgeting applications

Part 3 PERFORMANCE MEASUREMENT AND CONTROL		
LEVEL 1	**Chapter 13** Preparing a budget	**Chapter 16** Performance evaluation and feedback reporting
LEVEL 2	**Chapter 14** Control through budgeting	**Chapter 15** Standard costs	**Chapter 17** Divisional performance

Part 4 FINANCIAL MANAGEMENT AND STRATEGIC PLANNING	
LEVEL 2	**Chapter 18** Financial management: working capital	**Chapter 19** Business strategy and management accounting

problem-solving exercise. Some answers are given at the end of the book but others are in the Resources for Tutors available on the website for use in tutorial preparation or class work.

Website

A website is available at www.pearsoned.co.uk/weetman by password access to lecturers adopting this textbook. The Resources for Tutors contain additional problem questions for each chapter, with full solutions to these additional questions as well as any solutions not provided in the textbook. The website includes basic tutorial guidance, student notes and overhead-projector or powerpoint displays to support each chapter.

Target readership

This book is targeted at programmes which have first and second level management accounting classes where there is a benefit from having one text book to cover the two levels of study. The split of level one and level two chapters is suitable for a broad-ranging business studies type of first-level degree course followed by a more specific second level degree class. The book has been written with undergraduate students particularly in mind, but may also be suitable for professional and postgraduate business courses where management accounting is taught at first and second levels.

Support material for lecturers

As institutions come under increasing scrutiny for the quality of the teaching and learning experience offered, a textbook must do more than present the knowledge and skills of the chosen subject. It must make explicit to the students what targets are to be achieved and it must help them to assess realistically their own achievements of those targets. It must help the class lecturer prepare, deliver, explain and assess the knowledge and skills expected for the relevant level of study.

The Resources for Tutors provide a table of learning outcomes (knowledge and skills) tested by each question. The general skills tested are application of techniques, problem solving and evaluation and communication. This will be helpful for lecturers who seek to demonstrate how their teaching and assessment matches external subject benchmark statements and learning and skills frameworks.

Acknowledgements

I am particularly appreciative of the helpful and constructive comments and suggestions received from reviewers as this text progressed. I am also grateful to academic colleagues for their feedback and to undergraduate students of five universities who have taken my courses and thereby helped in developing an approach to teaching and learning the subject. Professor Graham Peirson and Mr Alan Ramsay of Monash University provided a first draft of their text based on the conceptual framework in Australia which gave valuable assistance in designing the predecessor of this book. Ken Shackleton of the University of Glasgow helped plan the structure of the management accounting chapters. The Institute of Chartered Accountants of Scotland gave permission for use of the end-of-chapter case study questions. I am grateful to those at Pearson Education, namely, Matthew Smith and Sarah Wild for support and encouragement in developing this text from earlier work and to Colin Reed for the text design.

Guided tour of the book

Chapter contents provide a quick and easy reference to the following section.

Key terms and **definitions** are emboldened where they are first introduced, with a definition box to provide concise explanation where required.

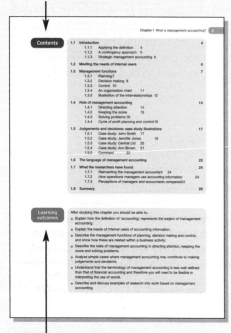

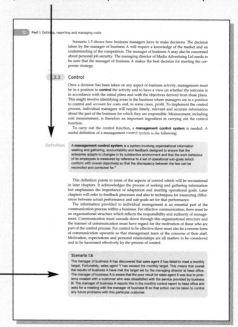

Scenarios throughout the text are excerpts from the industry that provide practical illustrations of specific aspects of the subject.

Learning outcomes at the start of each chapter show what you can expect to learn from that chapter, and highlight the core coverage.

Activities appear throughout each chapter to encourage self-evaluation and help you to think about the application of the subject in everyday life.

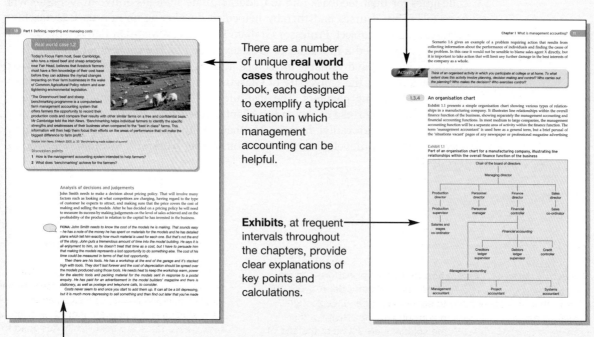

There are a number of unique **real world cases** throughout the book, each designed to exemplify a typical situation in which management accounting can be helpful.

Exhibits, at frequent intervals throughout the chapters, provide clear explanations of key points and calculations.

The **Professional Consultant** is a first-person commentary which appears at intervals throughout the text to provide a valuable insight into the type of interpretative comment which you may find more taxing. This commentary by the consultant, Fiona McTaggart, allows a more candid discussion of issues and problems within the subject.

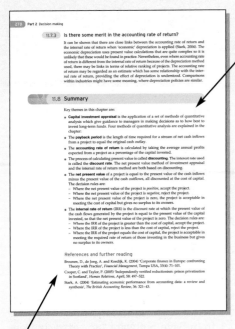

Each chapter ends with a **'bullet point' summary**. This highlights the material covered in the chapter and can be used as a quick reminder of the main issues.

Test your understanding (Series A) questions are short questions to encourage you to review your understanding of the main topics covered in each chapter.

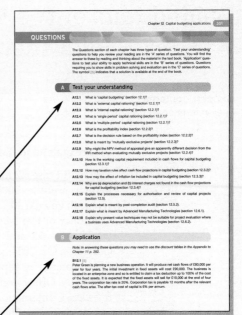

References and further reading provides full details of sources of information referred to in the chapter.

Application (Series B) questions are questions that ask you to apply the knowledge gained from reading and practising the material in the chapter, and closely resemble the style and content of the technical material. Answers are given at the end of the book or in the Resources for Tutors section on the Companion Website at **www.pearsoned.co.uk/weetman**.

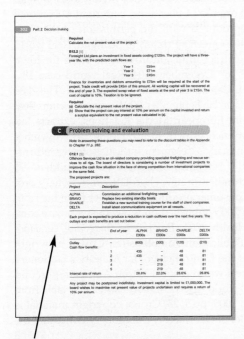

Problem solving and evaluation (Series C) questions require problem solving skills to select relevant data in order to work out what further effort is needed to solve the problem. Evaluation questions ask for your opinion surrounding the results of the problem solving exercise. Some solutions are found at the end of the book but others are in the Resources for Tutors section on the Companion Website at **www.pearsoned.co.uk/weetman**, for use in tutorial preparation or class work.

In the **Case studies** section at the end of each chapter there are short exercises relating to the real world cases, as well as additional case studies and a relevant individual or group task. These tasks are specifically designed to help you apply the management accounting skills and knowledge that you have acquired from the chapter to the real world.

Publisher's acknowledgements

We are grateful to the following for permission to reproduce copyright material:

Real world case 3.2 from Royal Association of British Dairy Farmers, extract taken from the RABDF website 2005; Text extract on p.103 (Case 4.6) from NHS costing manual, www.dh.gov.uk, 2005, Crown copyright material is reproduced with the permission of the Controller of Her Majesty's Stationery Office and the Queen's Printer for Scotland; Real world cases 5.1 and 5.3 from Department of Health Reference Costs 2005 Collection – Guidance, Oct 2004, p.66 and para. 156 downloaded from www.dh.gov.uk, Crown copyright material is reproduced with the permission of the Controller of Her Majesty's Stationery Office and the Queen's Printer for Scotland; Exhibit 5.17 from IAS 2 (2003) *Inventories*, International Accounting Standards Board, © 2003 International Accounting Standards Committee Foundation, All rights reserved. No permission granted to reproduce or distribute; Real world cases 6.3 and 7.1 from Sage Software Inc., extracts from www.bestosoftware.com and www.sage.com; Real world case 8.2 (including images) from www.swisswater.com/decaf/process/lesson3. Swiss Water Decaffeinated Coffee Company, located at 3131 Lake City Way, Burnaby, B.C., Canada USA 3A3. SWISS WATER Process coffees are available through Caffé Nero; Real world case 10.1 from Newsquest (Herald & Times) Ltd, an article 'Time for a regime change if things can only get BETTA' by Alf Young published in *The Herald* 20th January 2005; Real world case 12.3 from Economic analysis of the design, cost and performance of the UK Renewables Obligation and the capital grants scheme, www.nao.org.uk/publications, copyright © National Audit Office, Crown copyright material is reproduced with the permission of the Controller of Her Majesty's Stationery Office and the Queen's Printer for Scotland; Real world case 13.3 from The North Devon Journal, an extract from 'Improvement plans for town allotments' published in *North Devon Journal* 16th December 2004; Real world case 18.3 from PARS International Corporation and REL Consultancy.com, extracts from 'The 2004 Working Capital Survey' published in *CFO Magazine* September 2004 www.cfo.com, Real world cases 11.3, 15.1, 15.3, 19.1 and 19.2 from European Media Relations, extracts 'ntl Incorporated third quarter results led by continued growth in ntl: Home' 3rd November 2004, 'Anooraq Resources Corporations: preliminary assessment indicates strong returns' 9th March 2005, 'IDS Scheer announces ARIS™ reference model for home builders' 9th November 2004, 'Research and markets: opportunities for new chocolate confectionary products examined' 21st February 2005 and 'Top consumer products companies form board to review supply chain best practices' 15th March 2005 published on www.businesswire.com; Real world case 14.3 from Department of Health 2004, *Programme Budgeting Guidance Manual*, downloaded from www.dh.gov.uk/PublicationsAndStatistics, Crown copyright material is reproduced with the permission of the Controller of Her Majesty's Stationery Office and the Queen's Printer for Scotland; Real world case 16.3 from Annual report and accounts 2003–04, DSA, www.dsa.gov.uk; Real world case 17.3, short extract and table from the Wolseley plc Annual Report and Accounts 2005; pp.5, 25, Crown copyright material is reproduced with the permission of the Controller of Her Majesty's Stationery Office and the Queen's Printer for Scotland.

We are grateful to the Financial Times Limited for permission to reprint the following material:

Real world case 3.3 Budapest, the next Bangalore? New EU members join the outsourcing race, © *Financial Times*, 21 September 2004; Real world case 6.1 Why a monster hit did not make giant profits, © *Financial Times*, 15 February 2005; Real world case 10.2

Motor maker that reversed expectations, © *Financial Times*, 28 September 2004; Real world case 13.2 UK Coal (UKC) from *Investor's Chronicle UK*, 11 March 2005; Real world case 17.1 Kerry Foods hit by Quest charges, © *Financial Times*, 2 March 2005; Real world case 17.2 Chief who turned a ragbag into a silk purse, © *Financial Times*, 1 March 2005; Real world case 18.2 'Legislation' has failed to curb late payments, © *Financial Times*, 18 February 2004.

We are grateful to the following for permission to reproduce photographs:

Real world case 1.1 Alamy/ImageState; Real world case 1.2 Alamy/Art Kowalsky; Real world case 1.3 Rex Features; Real world case 2.1 Alamy/Renee Morris; Real world case 2.2 Corbis/Melanie Acevedo/PictureArts; Real world case 2.3 Alamy/The Photolibrary Wales; Real world case 3.1 Alamy/Comstock Images; Real world case 3.2 Alamy/The Photolibrary Wales; Real world case 3.3 Alamy/Photofusion Picture Library; Real world case 4.1 The Scotsman Publications Ltd.; Real world case 4.2 Corbis/Charles Gupton; Real world case 4.3 Alamy/Photofusion Picture Library; Real world case 5.1 Alamy/The Photolibrary Wales; Real world case 5.2 Alamy/Photofusion Picture Library; Real world case 5.3 Alamy/Jack Sullivan; Real world case 6.1 Alamy/ImageState; Real world case 6.2 Alamy/ImageState; Real world case 6.3 Alamy/Richard Levine; Real world case 7.1 Alamy/Oote Boe; Real world case 7.2 Alamy/SCPhotos; Real world case 7.3 Corbis/Paul Edmonson; Real world case 8.1 Corbis/Ashley Cooper; Real world case 8.3 Corbis/Sally A Morgan/Ecoscene; Real world case 9.1 courtesy of Flying Brands; Real world case 9.2 Corbis/Bo Zaunders; Real world case 9.3, courtesy of Delta Airlines; Real world case 10.1 Corbis/Steve Terill; Real world case 10.2 Science Photo Library/Sheila Terry; Real world case 10.3 Corbis/Mark E. Gibson; Real world case 11.1 Alamy/Dominic Burke; Real world case 11.2, courtesy of Punch Taverns; Real world case 11.3, courtesy of NTL; Real world case 12.1 Alamy/Photofusion Picture Library; Real world case 12.2 from Tate and Lyle Annual Report 2004; Real world case 12.3 Alamy/Ace Stock Ltd.; Real world case 13.1 Alamy/Photofusion Picture Library; Real world case 13.2 Alamy/Robert Harding Picture Library Ltd.; Real world case 13.3 Alamy/The Photolibrary Wales; Real world case 14.2 Corbis/Helen King; Real world case 14.3 Alamy/Photofusion Picture Library; Real world case 15.1 Alamy/ImageState; Real world case 15.2 Department of Defense/Cpl. Brian A. Jaques, U.S. Marine Corps; Real world case 15.3 Corbis/Vince Streano; Real world case 16.1 Corbis/Philip Gould; Real world case 16.2, courtesy of Punch Taverns; Real world case 16.3 Alamy/Dominic Burke; Real world case 17.1, courtesy of Kerry's Wall's Brand; Real world case 17.2 Alamy/Howard Harrison; Real world case 17.3 Sant Media/Photographersdirect.com; Real world case 18.1 Anthony Blake Picture Library/Ming Tang-Evans; Real world case 18.2 Corbis/Bob Abraham; Real world case 18.3, courtesy of Dell Inc.; Real world case 19.1 Alamy/Photofusion Picture Library; Real world case 19.2 Anthony Blake Picture Library/Robert Lawson; Real world case 19.3 Corbis/Alan Schein Photography;

In some instances we have been unable to trace the owners of copyright material, and we would appreciate any information that would enable us to do so.

DEFINING, REPORTING AND MANAGING COSTS

Management accounting takes us inside an organisation. It could be a private sector business organisation, or it could be a public sector service provider. The common feature is that managers need information to help them with planning, decision making and control. Management accounting will provide information that directs attention, keeps the score and solves problems. Chapter 1 explains these functions of management and of management accounting.

Inside the business there is information available in great detail. Costs of all types are recorded and analysed to evaluate performance. Chapter 2 explains how costs can be classified according to how they behave in relation to activity levels. It also shows that some costs relate to products and output while other costs relate to the passage of time. The type of classification used depends on the purpose for which costs are needed.

The costs of manufacturing goods or providing a service can be grouped as costs of materials, costs of labour and other costs of output. The costs that are not directly identified to a unit of output are called overhead costs. Chapters 3 and 4 explain how costs of materials, labour and overhead are recorded and analysed.

The definitions explained in Chapters 2, 3 and 4 are applied in Chapter 5 to show that different treatments of overhead costs give different measures of profit when inventory levels are changing. Absorbing all costs into products means that unsold inventory carries its share of overheads to the profit of the period when it is eventually sold. Treating overheads as a cost of the period means that these costs fall into the profit of the period of manufacture or service provision.

Chapter 6 explains how the cost of a job is calculated. Chapter 7 shows the system for recording job costs. Chapter 8 describes the approach to be used when a process is continuous so that separate jobs cannot be distinguished.

Part 1 DEFINING, REPORTING AND MANAGING COSTS			
LEVEL 1	**Chapter 1** What is management accounting?	**Chapter 2** Classification of costs	**Chapter 3** Materials and labour costs	**Chapter 4** Overhead costs
LEVEL 2	**Chapter 5** Absorption costing and marginal costing	**Chapter 6** Job costing	**Chapter 7** Recording transactions in a job costing system	**Chapter 8** Process costing

What is management accounting?

This case study describes the role of the management accountant. Read it now, but only attempt the discussion points after you have finished studying the chapter.

The day of the 'bean counter' has gone forever.

Line managers responsible for the day-to-day profitability of their business operations use sophisticated software to analyse the financial consequences of their decisions. Financial record-keeping and analysis are automated. And financial accountability has become a key part of every executive's job description.

Meanwhile, to maintain the growth rates that capital markets demand, business leaders are compelled to make increasingly risky decisions. They look to their finance people to support and participate in these decisions to help them understand the risks and likely consequences and to help manage the rapid change that their organisations must then undergo.

This means that management accountancy skills influence every area of a business, are internationally recognised and are valued in every business and industry sector.

Source: 'Your career', website of the Chartered Institute of Management Accountants, 2005, www.cimaglobal.com/main/prospective/career/

Discussion points

1 What does the phrase 'bean counter' mean?

2 How do line managers and business leaders use management accountants to help them in their management activities?

Contents

Learning outcomes

After studying this chapter you should be able to:

- Explain how the definition of 'accounting' represents the subject of management accounting.
- Explain the needs of internal users of accounting information.
- Describe the management functions of planning, decision making and control, and show how these are related within a business activity.
- Describe the roles of management accounting in directing attention, keeping the score and solving problems.
- Analyse simple cases where management accounting may contribute to making judgements and decisions.
- Understand that the terminology of management accounting is less well defined than that of financial accounting and therefore you will need to be flexible in interpreting the use of words.
- Describe and discuss examples of research into work based on management accounting.

1.1 Introduction

Accounting has been defined as follows:

Definition

> **Accounting** is the process of identifying, measuring and communicating financial information about an entity to permit informed judgements and decisions by users of the information.[1]

Many would argue that those who manage an organisation on a day-to-day basis are the foremost users of accounting information about that organisation. The description **management** is a collective term for all those persons who have responsibilities for making judgements and decisions within an organisation. Because they have close involvement with the business, they have access to a wide range of information (much of which may be confidential within the organisation) and will seek those aspects of the information which are most relevant to their particular judgements and decisions. **Management accounting** is a specialist branch of accounting which has developed to serve the particular needs of management.

Activity 1.1

Imagine that you are in charge of a cycle hire business in a holiday resort. You have 50 cycles available for hire. Some customers hire cyles for one day; others take them for up to one week. Write down any three decisions that you might make as a manager, where accounting information would be helpful in making the decision.

1.1.1   Applying the definition

Consider the following three scenarios which are typical of comments in the 'Management' section of the financial press. As you read each scenario, think about how it relates to the definition of 'accounting' given at the start of this section. Then read the comment following the scenario and compare it with your thinking.

> **Scenario 1.1**
>
> In the 12 months to June 30, net profits dropped from £280m to £42m, depressed by hefty investments, increased paper costs and poor advertising spending . . . The chief executive has explained the company's plans for improving its margins to the average level for the industry. The directors are also committed to getting the assets to work creatively together. [*Report on a magazine publishing company*]

Scenario 1.1 indicates decision making related to **profit margins** and the effective use of **assets**. The profit margins will be improved either by improving **sales** or by controlling **costs**, or through a mixture of both. Assets will be used more effectively if they create more **profit** or higher sales. Achieving these targets requires a range of managerial skills covering sales, **production** and asset management. Identifying the relevant costs and **revenues**, measuring the achievement of targets and communicating the outcomes within the organisation are all functions of management accounting. The chief executive will need to form a judgement on whether the decisions taken are likely to satisfy investors and maintain their confidence in the management team.

Scenario 1.2

Salespersons at a car manufacturer's dealership noticed business was slow in April. They reacted by encouraging customers to take more time in deciding whether to buy a car. What was the reason? They were paid a monthly bonus when sales exceeded a specified target. They could see that the April sales would not reach the target and so encouraged customers to wait until May, to increase the likely volume of May sales. In a brewing company the sales manager set a low sales target, in the hope of exceeding it easily. This caused the company to reduce production, so that when demand for beer rose to a higher level because of good weather, the company could not provide adequate supplies. [*Journalist's comment on how unrealistic targets can distort achievement of company objectives.*]

Scenario 1.2 shows that at some point in the past a decision was taken to create employee incentives by setting quantifiable targets. Unfortunately this has led to a narrow focus on measuring the achievement of the targets. There was a problem in allowing the employees too much freedom to influence either the setting of the target or the achievement of the target. There was no judgement about the best interests of the company. A further decision is now required to balance the motivation of the employees against the best interests of the company. Communication is an important feature of getting the decision right.

Scenario 1.3

Engineers are challenging the assumption that companies are run by 'number-crunchers' . . . The hidden skill of engineers is their ability to be analytical and numerate. As someone who has to evaluate and sit on the boards of information technology and software development companies, I have the ability to understand the basics of their business. [*Managing director of a venture capital company, qualified engineer.*]

The term 'number-cruncher' tends to be used as a somewhat uncomplimentary description of an accounting specialist. The engineer quoted in Scenario 1.3 has related to the measurement aspect of accounting and has identified the need to make judgements ('evaluate') using analytical skills. However, this quotation has made no mention either of communication or of decision making. There is an increasing expectation that the management accountants in an organisation will work with the engineers or other technical specialists, try to understand the nature of the business and ensure that the judgements are communicated to the experts so that cost-effective decisions can be made.

1.1.2   A contingency approach

The word 'contingency' means 'condition'. The contingency theory of management accounting describes the process of creating a control system for a given set of purposes. This is sometimes described in terms of a **'contingency theory'** of management accounting. The management accounting approach is conditioned by ('contingent upon') the situation.

The idea for thinking about management accounting in terms of contingency theory comes from a study of management and the ways in which management structures are created. Researchers have shown that management structures depend on factors such as the size of the organisation, the production technology and the competitiveness of the industry. These are the contingencies (conditions) that shape the management structure.

In management accounting, control systems have been shown to depend on the external environment of the business, the production technology, the size of the organisation and the corporate strategy.[2]

Management accounting methods have been developed within particular industries. In the UK economy, approximately 75 per cent of output is provided by service industry with only 25 per cent of output being provided by manufacturing industry. However, management accounting began to develop in the twentieth century at a time when manufacturing industry dominated. As the service sector has grown, management accounting has developed to meet its particular needs. What remains of the manufacturing sector has moved from being labour intensive to being capital intensive. In some parts of the world, manufacturing remains labour intensive. The agricultural sector may be stronger in developing economies. All these differences lead to different judgements and decisions, and hence different approaches to identifying, measuring and communicating accounting data. The following chapters will explain management accounting techniques that have been developed to meet particular needs in making judgements and decisions.

1.1.3   Strategic management accounting

The traditional approach to management accounting has been to regard internal decision makers as inward looking. This has led to developing techniques for identifying, measuring and communicating costs where only internal comparisons have been thought relevant. Those techniques remain useful in some cases and are sufficiently widely used to justify studying them in an introductory course. However, the later years of the twentieth century brought an increasing awareness that company managers must be outward looking. They must form a strategy for their business that has regard to what competitors are achieving. This requires management accounting to identify, measure and communicate data on the company relative to data for other similar companies. Managers must consider competitive forces such as the threat of new entrants, substitute products or services, rivalry within the industry and the relative bargaining strength of suppliers and customers. Managers must also consider how their organisation adds value in creating its product. There is a flow of business activity from research and development through production, marketing, distribution and after-sales support. This chain of activities creates costs which must be compared with the value added by the organisation. The term '**strategic management accounting**' applies to the identification, measurement and communication of cost data in all these situations where the organisation is being judged against the performance of competitors.

1.2   Meeting the needs of internal users

Although the definition of accounting remains appropriate for internal reporting purposes, its application will be different because internal users need to form judgements and make decisions that are different from those of external users. External users form judgements on the overall performance of the entity and make decisions about their relationship with it. Their decisions are of the type: 'Shall I invest money in this business?', 'Shall I continue to be an investor in this business?', 'Shall I supply goods to this business?', 'Shall I continue to supply goods to this business?', 'Shall I become a customer of this business?', 'Shall I continue to be a customer of this business?'

The internal users make different types of judgement and different types of decision. They may have to judge the performance of the various products of the organisation as compared with those of competitors. They may have to judge the performance of different divisions within the organisation. Their decisions are of the type: 'Shall I invest in manufacturing more soap powder, or do I switch resources into toothpaste?', 'Shall I continue offering a television repair service as support for my sales of televisions?', 'Is it cost effective to have three separate locations at which my tenants can pay their rent?', 'Will this investment in a new factory pay for itself over the next ten years?' There is great variety in the judgements and decisions made by those who manage the business. Their needs are so wide ranging that management accounting has developed as a separate discipline, within the overall 'accounting' umbrella, in order to serve the particular needs of management.

The use of accounting as a tool which will assist in the management of a business raises two significant questions:

1   What types of informed judgement are made by management and about management?
2   What types of decision are made by management?

It is presumed that many of those reading this text for the first time may not have a great deal of experience of the types of judgement and decision made in business. This chapter therefore devotes space to four case study illustrations of management situations where management accounting will have a contribution to make. The case studies are uncomplicated so that the management accounting applications are intuitively obvious. After each case study outline there is a comment on the management accounting aspects. You will then meet Fiona McTaggart, a management accounting consultant, who explains how she sees the management accountant's contribution to the management issues raised in each of the four case studies.

Before exploring the case studies, this chapter sets out, in section 1.3, some basic categories of management functions and then outlines, in section 1.4, the role of management accounting in helping to meet the information needs of those management functions.

1.3   Management functions

This section describes three management functions: planning, decision making and control.

To be effective, each of these functions requires the application by management of communication and motivation skills. To ensure that the entity's operations are effective, those who work in the entity must be persuaded to identify with its objectives. Managers require the skills to motivate those for whom they are responsible, creating a sense of teamwork. The communication process is a vital part of creating a sense of teamwork and ensuring that all the players understand the role they play in achieving targets. They must also be motivated to want to achieve the targets. Management accounting has a particularly important role in that process of communication and motivation.

1.3.1   Planning

'**Planning**' is a very general term which covers longer-term strategic planning and shorter-term operational planning. These two types of planning differ in the time scale that they cover. **Strategic planning** involves preparing, evaluating and selecting *strategies* to achieve objectives of a long-term plan of action. **Operational planning** relates to the detailed plans by which those working within an organisation are expected to meet the short-term objectives of their working group.

Strategic planning is based on objectives set by those who manage the entity at a senior level. If the entity is a legal entity such as a limited liability company or a public sector corporation, objectives will be set for the corporate entity which will require high level **corporate strategic planning**. Within the company or corporation there will be major divisions of activities into key business areas, each with their own objectives requiring **business strategic planning**. The corporate entity may contain many different businesses and those who manage the corporate entity as a whole must manage the entire collection of businesses. They must decide which businesses to develop in the corporate interest, which to support when in temporary difficulties, and which to dispose of as no longer contributing to the corporate well-being. Business strategic planning focuses on each of the separate businesses, which have to consider not only their position within the corporate group of businesses but also their position within the industry or sector to which the business belongs.

Shorter-term operational planning is also referred to as **functional strategic planning**. It concentrates on the actions of specific functions within the business. Although these functions may have a longer-term existence they must also plan their activity in shorter-term periods so that achievement of targets may be monitored regularly.

At a practical level, managers find that they have to plan ahead in making major decisions on such things as sales, production and **capital expenditure**. Such planning is required for the immediate future and for the longer term. Businesses will typically make a detailed plan for the year ahead and a broader plan for a two- to five-year period. Plans for sales require decisions on which products to sell, which markets to target and what price to charge. Plans for production require decisions on the mix of resources, including labour, the source of raw materials or component parts, the level of stock of raw materials and finished goods to hold and the most effective use of productive capacity. Plans for capital expenditure require a longer-term perspective, taking into account the expected life of the capital equipment acquired. As well as investing in **fixed assets**, the business will need **working capital** as a base for a new project. Decisions will be required on the level of working capital which is appropriate. If the enterprise is to move ahead, plans must lead to decisions.

Scenario 1.4 shows some of the planning stages for Media Advertising Company. This is a company which earns profit by selling advertising space on television, internet and mobile phone texts. Each of these three businesses is organised separately. The managing director of the company has a corporate strategy of achieving returns for shareholders based on all three businesses. The managing director has worked with the business managers to set an overall strategy for each of the three businesses which will help to meet the corporate strategy. If any one of the businesses does not meet its strategic target it might be restructured or even closed down. The managers of each business then put in place their own operational planning to ensure that they meet the business strategy. The scenario shows the operational planning for the television sales business. The managers of the other two businesses will set similar operational plans.

1.3.2 Decision making

Decision making is central to the management of an enterprise. The manager of a profit-making business has to decide on the manner of implementation of the objectives of the business, at least one of which may well relate to allocating resources so as to maximise profit. A non-profit-making enterprise (such as a department of central or local government) will be making decisions on resource allocation so as to be economic, efficient and effective in its use of finance. All organisations, whether in the private sector or the public sector, take decisions which have financial implications. Decisions will be about resources, which may be people, products, services or long-term and short-term investment. Decisions will also be about activities, including whether and how to undertake them. Most decisions will at some stage involve consideration of financial matters, particularly cost. Decisions may also have an impact on the working conditions and employment prospects of employees of the organisation,

Scenario 1.4 Planning

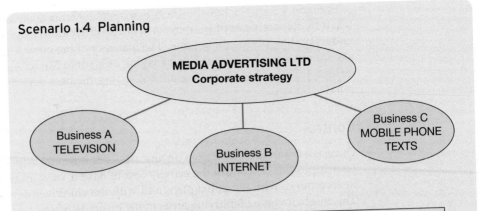

Corporate strategic planning

Prepared by: managing director, Media Advertising Ltd

We intend to operate in three business areas with an overall return of 12% per annum on shareholders' funds for the next 3 years

Business strategic planning

Prepared by: managing director in consultation with business managers A, B and C

We will expand profits of all three businesses by 15% over three years

We will maintain profit margins in A and B at 40% but increase margin in C to 45%

We will increase the sales of business A to 12% of the industry sector total

We will reduce labour costs in business B by outsourcing all administrative work.

Operational planning – Business A

Prepared by: business manager, A

We need £2m capital expenditure in new equipment over 3 years

Our sales mix will be 60% home and 40% export

We will reduce overtime working to 5% of total wages cost

We will hold stock levels to cover 10 days' sales

so that cost considerations may, in making a final decision, be weighed against social issues. Where the owners are different persons from the manager (e.g. shareholders of a company as separate persons from the directors), the managers may face a decision where there is a potential conflict between their own interests and those of the owners. In such a situation cost considerations may be evaluated in the wider context of the responsibility of the managers to act in the best interests of the owners.

Scenario 1.5 Decision making

In Media Advertising Ltd the manager of business A has a problem. The sales mix was planned as 60% home and 40% export. The export sales have not met expectations because the home currency has become stronger during the year and overseas buyers now think the advertising charges are too high. The manager has two choices:

1 Reduce the price charged to overseas buyers and risk complaints from home customers.
2 Accept the lower volume of export sales and try to increase home sales by reducing the price charged to home customers.

Scenario 1.5 shows how business managers have to make decisions. The decision taken by the manager of business A will require a knowledge of the market and an understanding of the competition. The manager of business A may also be concerned about personal job security. The managing director of Media Advertising Ltd needs to be sure that the manager of business A makes the best decision for meeting the corporate strategy.

1.3.3   Control

Once a decision has been taken on any aspect of business activity, management must be in a position to **control** the activity and to have a view on whether the outcome is in accordance with the initial plans and with the objectives derived from those plans. This might involve identifying areas in the business where managers are in a position to control and account for costs and, in some cases, profit. To implement the control process, individual managers will require timely, relevant and accurate information about the part of the business for which they are responsible. Measurement, including cost measurement, is therefore an important ingredient in carrying out the control function.

To carry out the control function, a **management control system** is needed. A useful definition of a management control system is the following:

Definition

A **management control system** is a system involving organisational information seeking and gathering, accountability and feedback designed to ensure that the enterprise adapts to changes in its substantive environment and that the work behaviour of its employees is measured by reference to a set of operational sub-goals (which conform with overall objectives) so that the discrepancy between the two can be reconciled and corrected for.[3]

This definition points to some of the aspects of control which will be encountered in later chapters. It acknowledges the process of seeking and gathering information but emphasises the importance of adaptation and meeting operational goals. Later chapters will refer to feedback processes and also to techniques for measuring differences between actual performance and sub-goals set for that performance.

The information provided to individual management is an essential part of the communication process within a business. For effective communication, there must be an organisational structure which reflects the responsibility and authority of management. Communication must cascade down through this organisational structure and the manner of communication must have regard for the motivation of those who are part of the control process. For control to be effective there must also be a reverse form of communication upwards so that management learn of the concerns of their staff. Motivation, expectations and personal relationships are all matters to be considered and to be harnessed effectively by the process of control.

Scenario 1.6

The manager of business A has discovered that sales agent X has failed to meet a monthly target. Fortunately, sales agent Y has exceed the monthly target. This means that overall the results of business A have met the target set by the managing director at head office. The manager of business A is aware that the poor result for sales agent X was due to problems created with a customer who was dissatisfied with the service provided by business B. The manager of business A reports this in the monthly control report to head office and asks for a meeting with the manager of business B so that action can be taken to control any future problems with this particular customer.

Scenario 1.6 gives an example of a problem requiring action that results from collecting information about the performance of individuals and finding the cause of the problem. In this case it would not be sensible to blame sales agent X directly, but it is important to take action that will limit any further damage in the best interests of the company as a whole.

Activity 1.2

Think of an organised activity in which you participate at college or at home. To what extent does this activity involve planning, decision making and control? Who carries out the planning? Who makes the decision? Who exercises control?

1.3.4 An organisation chart

Exhibit 1.1 presents a simple organisation chart showing various types of relationships in a manufacturing company. It illustrates line relationships within the overall finance function of the business, showing separately the management accounting and financial accounting functions. In most medium to large companies, the management accounting function will be a separate area of activity within the finance function. The term 'management accountant' is used here as a general term, but a brief perusal of the 'situations vacant' pages of any newspaper or professional magazine advertising

Exhibit 1.1

Part of an organisation chart for a manufacturing company, illustrating line relationships within the overall finance function of the business

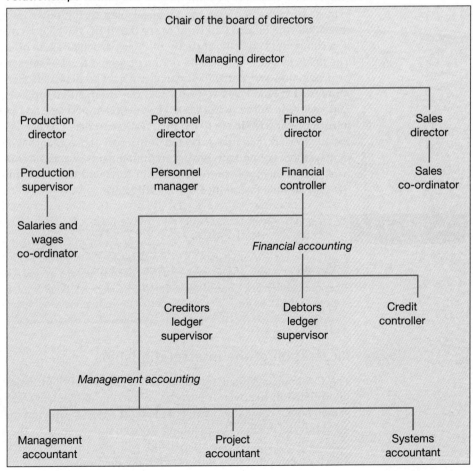

accountancy posts would indicate the range of titles available and the versatility expected. Two other functions have been shown in the chart as 'project accountant' and 'systems accountant'. Such specialists have specific roles in the internal accounting process within the enterprise which are relevant, although not exclusive, to the management accounting function.

The organisation chart shows individual people, each with a different job to do. Each person has a specialisation indicated by the job title, but he or she also has responsibilities to others higher in the structure and with authority over others lower in the structure. In the interests of the business as a whole, individuals must communicate up and down the line relationships and also across the horizontal relationships.

Taking one line relationship as an example, the finance director must make plans for the year ahead which are communicated to the financial controller. The financial controller must consult the systems accountant to ensure that the accounting systems are in place to record and communicate these plans within the organisation. The financial controller must also consult the project accountant to ensure that there is an evaluation of any capital investment aspects of the finance director's plans. The management accountant will prepare accounting statements showing how the plans will be implemented. The financial controller will bring together the details supplied by each person, summarising and evaluating the main factors so that the results may be relayed to the finance director.

Horizontal relationships can be more difficult when communications channels are being planned, because there are so many potential combinations. It is a responsibility of management to decide which horizontal relationships have the greatest communication needs. Continuing the planning theme, the finance director will be expected to communicate the financial plan to the other members of the board of directors, who in turn will want to see that it fits the board's overall strategy and that it is compatible with the capacity of their particular areas of activity in the business. The financial plan will depend on the projected level of sales and will reflect strategy in production and personnel management. The plan will therefore need to be communicated to the sales co-ordinator, the production supervisor and the personnel manager. The sales co-ordinator, production supervisor and personnel manager will in turn provide feedback to the financial controller. The detailed analysis of the plans for the period, and the expected impact of those plans, will be evaluated by the management accountant, project accountant and systems accountant. They will report back to the financial controller who in turn will channel information to the finance director and the rest of the board of directors.

Activity 1.3

Think again about the organised activity which you identified in Activity 1.2. Prepare an organisation chart to include all the persons involved in the activity. Draw green lines with arrows to show the direction of communication. Draw red lines with arrows to show the direction of responsibility. What does the pattern of red and green lines tell you about communication and co-ordination in the organisation? What is the mechanism for motivation? Does it use the green lines of the communication network?

1.3.5 Illustration of the interrelationships

The three management functions of planning, decision making and control are all interrelated in the overall purpose of making judgements and decisions. Exhibit 1.2 shows how a company owning a chain of shops supplying motorcycle spares might go about the business of planning to open a new shop in the suburbs of a city. The shop will sell motorcycle spares and will also provide advice on basic repair work which motorcyclists can safely undertake themselves.

Exhibit 1.2
Managing a decision on the location of a new business

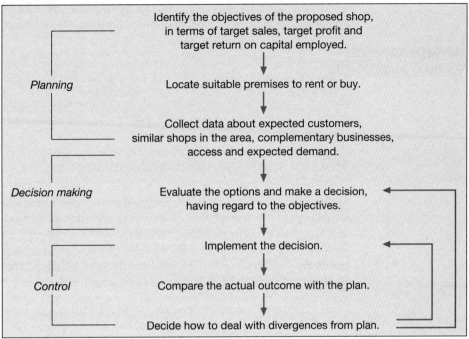

The shop's objectives will be concerned with achieving target sales and profit, and with making an adequate return on the capital invested in establishing the shop. Because of the desire to offer an advice service as well as selling spare parts, there will be non-financial objectives expressed in terms of customer satisfaction. These non-financial objectives will have indirect financial implications because satisfied customers will lead to increased sales and increased profits. The location of the shop, other types of shop close by, hours and days of opening and approach to stock control are all factors which are considered in the planning process. The choice of shop premises will depend upon the rent to be paid, any costs associated with the property, such as refurbishment and repairs, access for delivery and collection, and security. If the shop is to trade successfully there will need to be parking facilities, good access by road and preferably public transport backup for those who need spare parts but whose motor cycles are too much in need of repair to be used as transport to the shop. Location requires careful consideration. Is it preferable to have the shop in a neighbourhood where a high proportion of residents own motor cycles or to locate it on a main road along which they travel to work? Evaluation for decision-making purposes will require information about planned costs and revenues, although non-cost factors may also influence the decision.

Knowing the objectives and planning to meet those objectives will result in a decision, but the decision to start up the shop is not the end of the story. There has to be a continuing judgement as to whether the shop is successful and, eventually, there may be another decision on expanding or contracting the shop's activity. The continuing exercise of judgement will require a management accounting information outcome of the judgement. Any future decision to expand or contract will similarly include a requirement for information on planned costs and revenues.

Planning, decision making and control are shown on the diagram in Exhibit 1.2 as separate parts of the total activity. Communication is shown by arrows from one stage to the next. Motivation is not easily shown on a diagram, so there is no attempt to do so, but it remains an important part of the communication process. The greater the number of communication trails built into the process, the more effective will be the understanding and motivation of those who carry out the work of the business at various levels of management. Ideally, the diagram would be criss-crossed with communication trails so that all participants are well informed.

Activity 1.4

Imagine that you want to set up a business as a travel agent booking low-cost holidays with the emphasis on good value. List two activities that you might carry out in each of the stages of planning, decision making and control.

1.4 Role of management accounting

In the previous illustration of planning where to open a new shop, there is work for the management accountant: first, in **directing attention** to accounting information which is relevant to making plans and taking the decision; second, in **keeping the score** for making judgements on the effectiveness of decisions; and third, in helping to **solve problems** which arise when the results of decision making do not work out as expected. So there are three roles that management accounting could play in this exercise that will be found to be general features of any decision-making situation encountered by management. These are: directing attention, keeping the score and solving problems.

1.4.1   Directing attention

Directing attention is a matter of being able to answer questions such as 'Who should take action?' or 'Whose responsibility is this loss?' or 'Who is to be congratulated on this favourable result?' Managers are busy people. They do not always have time to consider every detail of cost information about the operation or process they control. They look to the management accountant to direct their attention to the exceptional points of interest, be these good or bad. One way of carrying out that function is to highlight those costs which have departed from expectations – provided everyone understands at the outset what the expectations are. Words such as *fairness* and *timeliness* are almost bound to be involved in attention-directing processes.

Managers are also sensitive people. They do not like being blamed unjustly for something they see as being beyond their control. So the management accounting information has to be presented in such a way as to relate to the level of responsibility and degree of authority held by the manager concerned. On the other side of the coin, managers enjoy being praised for achievements and may welcome management accounting information which helps them to demonstrate their accountability for the resources entrusted to them.

In any organisation emphasising strategic management, it will be part of the role of management accounting to direct the attention of management towards information about competitors. Competitive forces include: the threat posed by new entrants to the industry, the emergence of substitute products or services, the relative strength of suppliers and customers in controlling prices and conditions in the industry, and the intensity of rivalry within the industry. Such information is often well known on an anecdotal basis. The management accountant may be required to collect and present information in a useful and focused manner.

The role of management accounting in directing attention will therefore depend on how managers wish their attention to be directed. A business which retains an inward-looking approach to management will expect management accounting to direct attention inwards. A business which is thinking strategically about its position in the market for goods and services will expect management accounting to include an outward-looking perspective.

Strategic management accounting has been defined as follows:

Definition

Strategic management accounting is the provision and analysis of financial information on the firm's product markets and competitors' costs and cost structures and the monitoring of the enterprise's strategies and those of its competitors in these markets over a number of periods.[4]

The practical effects of the different types of management accounting approaches are summarised in Exhibit 1.3 which contrasts the potential limitations of an inward focus with the benefits claimed for an outward focus.

Exhibit 1.3
Contrasting an inward and outward focus of management

Possible limitations of an inward focus for management	Benefits of an outward focus for management
A risk of placing too much emphasis on evaluating past actions.	Management accounting includes a prospective element evaluating the potential outcomes of various strategies.
A risk of focusing on the business entity alone.	Management accounting sets information about the business entity in the context of other businesses in the sector.
A tendency to focus on a single reporting period.	Management accounting sets the results of one period in a longer-term analysis.
Directing attention towards separate single issues of decision making.	Management accounting directs attention towards sequences and patterns in decision making.
Directing attention to the outcome of the manufacturing or service activity of the particular organisation.	Management accounting directs attention to the competition for the manufacturing or service activity.
A tendency to concentrate on existing activities.	Management accounting is expected to look also to prospective activities.
Risk of not considering linkages within the organisation or potential for effective linkages beyond.	Management accounting is expected to direct attention to effective linkages which will improve competitive position.

1.4.2 Keeping the score

Keeping the score is very much a case of being able to answer the questions 'How much?' or 'How many?' at any point in time. It requires careful record keeping and a constant monitoring of accounting records against physical quantities and measures of work done. The emphasis is on *completeness* but also on *fairness*. Questions such as 'How much?' may involve sharing, or allocating, costs. Accounting is concerned with allocations of various types, all concerned with aspects of *matching*. That could require matching costs to a time period, matching costs to an item of output, or matching costs against revenue for the period. For this matching process to be effective, information must be complete and the basis of allocation must be fair.

For the business which has a strong emphasis on strategic management, score keeping will include being able to answer questions such as 'How much of the market share?' or 'How many compared to our competitors?' Questions of fairness of allocation within the business may be important but it may be even more important to understand the performance of the business in relation to others. Such questions will be answered by both financial and non-financial measures.

1.4.3   Solving problems

Solving problems involves a different type of question. It might be 'Why did that plan go well?' or 'Why did that action fail?' or 'Which of these three choices is the best to take?' In solving problems of this type, *relevance* is an important issue. People who have taken a decision are often reluctant to admit that it has not turned out as expected and may continue to make mistakes unless someone points out that past events are of little or no relevance to decisions on future action. Where choices are concerned, those choices will involve people, each of whom may have different motives for preferring one choice above others. Management accounting information may have a role in providing an objective base for understanding the problem to be solved, even where at the end of the day a decision is based on non-accounting factors.

Some problems resemble making a jigsaw, or perhaps deciding which piece of the jigsaw has gone missing. Other problems are like solving crosswords where the answers must interlock but some of the clues have been obliterated. In solving any problem of that type, logical reasoning is essential. No one can memorise the answer to every conceivable question which might arise. You will find that management accounting tests your powers of logical reasoning in that every problem you encounter will never entirely resemble the previous one.

1.4.4   Cycle of profit planning and control

Exhibit 1.4 illustrates a combination of the management accounting functions of directing attention, keeping the score and solving problems. It shows the cycle of profit planning and control, starting with the measurement of existing performance, which is an example of the score-keeping aspects of management accounting. From

Exhibit 1.4
Stages in the cycle of profit planning and control

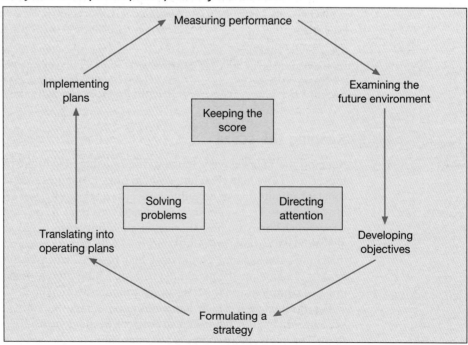

the measurement of existing performance the cycle moves through an examination of the future environment of the business, where techniques of economic analysis would be used. In developing objectives, the management accountant would provide accounting information on targets to be achieved. Formulating a strategy is a management task but the management accountant is then expected to provide detailed budgets which translate that strategy into operating plans. When the plans are implemented the management accountant must be ready to measure the results and compare these with the outcome expected when the operating plans were set. From there the cycle is repeated.

Activity 1.5

Look back to your list from Activity 1.4 for planning, decision making and control in setting up a travel agency business. Make another list of ways in which management accounting will help in directing attention, keeping the score and solving problems.

1.5　Judgements and decisions: case study illustrations

You are now presented with four cases where there is a need for decisions and for judgements. After each case study there is a brief analysis of the decisions and judgements that will arise in each.

These four cases indicate areas where management accounting could serve as a tool to provide information which is relevant to decision making and to the formation of judgement at all levels within an organisation. Hopefully, you will have recognised some situations in each case where accounting information will be of help.

The organisation chart in Exhibit 1.1 includes an expert management accountant. It has already been explained that most medium to large companies include specialist management accountants on their staff. However, from time to time a consultant may be called in to give a wider and more frank appraisal than might be feasible for a paid employee. In this and subsequent chapters you will meet Fiona McTaggart, a freelance management accountant, who is prepared to offer advice on a variety of case study situations. In practice, the management accountant within the organisation might provide similar advice, but this text uses the management consultant so that her comments are not unduly constrained by existing limitations within the business.

Fiona explains what she could offer from her management accounting experience in each of these four case study situations. Read her explanations and in each case identify the places where she is hinting at directing attention, keeping the score or solving problems.

Activity 1.6

Read the text of each case study (set out in the box at the beginning of each case) and then make a note of the way in which you think management accounting may help each person. Compare your answer with the discussion which follows each case.

1.5.1　Case study: John Smith

John Smith has taken early retirement at the age of 50 in order to develop his hobby of model shipbuilding into a full-time business. He has several models already assembled and has advertised in the model builders' weekly journal. Interested enquiries are starting to come in and he realises that he does not know what price to charge for the models.

Real world case 1.2

Today's Focus Farm host, Sean Cambridge, who runs a mixed beef and sheep enterprise near Fair Head, believes that livestock farmers must have a firm knowledge of their cost base before they can address the myriad changes impacting on their farm businesses in the wake of Common Agricultural Policy reform and ever tightening environmental legislation.

'The Greenmount beef and sheep benchmarking programme is a computerised farm management accounting system that offers farmers the opportunity to record their production costs and compare their results with other similar farms on a free and confidential basis.' Mr Cambridge told the *Irish News*. 'Benchmarking helps individual farmers to identify the specific strengths and weaknesses of their business when compared to the "best in class" farms. This information will then help them focus their efforts on the areas of performance that will make the biggest difference to farm profit.'

Source: *Irish News*, 8 March 2005, p. 30 'Benchmarking made subject of summit'

Discussion points

1 How is the management accounting system intended to help farmers?

2 What does 'benchmarking' achieve for the farmers?

Analysis of decisions and judgements

John Smith needs to make a decision about pricing policy. That will involve many factors such as looking at what competitors are charging, having regard to the type of customer he expects to attract, and making sure that the price covers the cost of making and selling the models. After he has decided on a pricing policy he will need to measure its success by making judgements on the level of sales achieved and on the profitability of the product in relation to the capital he has invested in the business.

FIONA: *John Smith needs to know the cost of the models he is making. That sounds easy – he has a note of the money he has spent on materials for the models and he has detailed plans which tell him exactly how much material is used for each one. But that's not the end of the story. John puts a tremendous amount of time into the model building. He says it is all enjoyment to him, so he doesn't treat that time as a cost, but I have to persuade him that making the models represents a lost opportunity to do something else. The cost of his time could be measured in terms of that lost opportunity.*

Then there are his tools. He has a workshop at the end of the garage and it's stacked high with tools. They don't last forever and the cost of depreciation should be spread over the models produced using those tools. He needs heat to keep the workshop warm, power for the electric tools and packing material for the models sent in response to a postal enquiry. He has paid for an advertisement in the model builders' magazine and there is stationery, as well as postage and telephone calls, to consider.

Costs never seem to end once you start to add them up. It can all be a bit depressing, but it is much more depressing to sell something and then find out later that you've made a loss. I could help John work out his costs and make sure the price he charges will leave a profit so that he builds up his investment in the business.

Making the decision on selling price would not be the end of my involvement. I would continue to measure costs each month and compare these with sales. I would give John reports on profit and cash flow and warnings if working capital was starting to build up. If he gives credit he'll need to keep an eye on the level of debtors, and there will always be a stock, either of raw materials or of finished goods or of both. Trade creditors will fund some of the stock but working capital mismanagement has been the downfall of many a business which tried to expand too fast.

I will also need to keep John down to earth in ensuring that what has until now been a hobby can become a successful business. I will direct his attention to professional business reports for this kind of specialist service. I will encourage him to subscribe to information services and I will incorporate such information in my reports to John so that he can take a realistic view of his performance compared with what might be expected in the general business of special craft work.

In advising John Smith, Fiona McTaggart will direct attention to the costs which are relevant to the pricing decision, she will keep the score by calculating profits once the business is in production and will help solve problems by monitoring the working capital position.

1.5.2 Case study: Jennifer Jones

Jennifer Jones has been operating a small hairdressing business for several months. She would like to expand by employing an assistant and by purchasing new dryers and washing equipment. She cannot decide whether the investment would be justified.

Analysis of decisions and judgements

Jennifer Jones will be taking a longer-term view in making a decision about investing in new equipment. That equipment must generate cash flows over its expected life. Jennifer's decision to invest will take into account the number of customers she expects, the prices she is able to charge them, and the cost of paying the proposed assistant, projected ahead for several years. It will also take into account the percentage return expected on the capital invested in the equipment.

If she decides to invest, she will need to monitor the success of that investment by making judgements on the profitability of the product in relation to the capital she has invested in it, and on whether the **return on the investment** is adequate in the light of having expanded the business.

FIONA: *Jennifer Jones needs help in taking a longer-term perspective. To assess the profitability of the new equipment and the assistant, I'll first of all need Jennifer to tell me how many customers she can realistically expect and what she will be able to charge them. I'll need those estimates over the life of the equipment, which will probably be around five years.*

Once I have the estimates of cash inflows from customers over the five years, I can set against that the cash outflows in terms of payments for all the costs of providing the service, including the wages of the intended assistant. Then I will apply to those cash flows a factor which makes an allowance for uncertainty in the future and also takes account of the rate of interest Jennifer could earn if she invested her money in financial markets rather than hairdryers. I'll then compare the expected cash flows with the initial cost of acquiring the equipment, to see whether it's a good idea. Of course, if Jennifer gets the cash flow estimates wrong, then the answer won't mean very much, but that's not my problem.

If Jennifer makes the decision to invest, I'll be needed after that to monitor the success of the project. I can measure the cash flows after the event and give an indication of how well they met expectations. I can compare the cost of the assistant with the revenue generated by the extra work available.

Problems might arise if there is a change of fashion and everyone decides they prefer short straight hair. That could cause chaos in the hairdressing industry and might make some of the washing equipment surplus to requirements. There is a great temptation in such situations to hang on to the past because of the cash which was sunk into it. That's often the wrong thing to do because it brings disaster ever closer. It may be better to cut off the activity altogether and limit the losses. I can give a dispassionate view based on cost rather than sentiment and emotion.

Fiona McTaggart will provide information which is relevant to the investment decision by drawing attention to the cost in comparison with the expected cash inflows. She will keep the score on the cash inflows and outflows once the project is established and she will help in problem solving by evaluating the losses arising if an unsuccessful project continues in operation.

1.5.3 Case study: Central Ltd

> Central Ltd is a small business manufacturing and assembling plastic components for use in car manufacture. It has been drawn to the attention of the financial controller that one of the plastic components could be purchased elsewhere at a price less than the cost of manufacture. What action should the production director take?

Analysis of decisions and judgements

The production director of Central Ltd needs to decide whether to continue manufacturing the component within the business or to cease production and buy the component elsewhere. To make that decision requires a knowledge of the full cost of manufacture and reassurance that the cost has been calculated correctly. It also depends on the relative aims and objectives of the financial controller and the production director, who may be in conflict and who may be putting their own point of view at the expense of the overall good of the business. Costs of ceasing manufacture will also need to be taken into account. Beyond the accounting costs there are human costs and business risks. Is there alternative employment for the staff released from this internal production? Will there be redundancy costs? Is it safe to rely on this outside supplier? What are the risks to Central Ltd if supplies dry up?

Whatever decision is taken, there will be a subsequent need for judgement in monitoring the effectiveness of the decision and its impact on profitability. In the decision and in the subsequent judgements of the effectiveness of that decision, there will be a need for communication and interaction between the financial controller and the production director.

FIONA: *Central Ltd is an example of the football game situation where sometimes the players in a team forget that they are on the same side. I saw a game last week when the home team won on the away team's own goals. The same thing could happen for Central. When people have a defined role in an organisation they can be too closely involved in their own work to see the bigger picture. The financial controller sees the costs of manufacturing and assembling the parts and has identified a cost saving based on a simple comparison. It's hard for the production director to fight the logic of that argument but I can see he's worried.*

What I can do is turn his worries into cost arguments which should be considered alongside the direct make-or-buy comparison. The costs may not be capable of such precise calculation but I'll give estimates of the risk to the business and the sensitivity of the situation. I'll pay particular attention to the quality issues and to the risk of disruption of supply. It's more than likely that the financial controller and the production director will still not agree even when they have the information, so I'll present my information in a way which the board of directors can relate to the overall objectives and strategy of the company. Whatever decision is taken, I'll establish a monthly reporting system, to be operated by the financial controller, which will give the earliest possible warning of whether the decision remains in the best interests of the company.

That is the traditional management accounting role which I am happy to provide. However, I will also indicate, in conversation with the financial controller and the production director, that it would be important to discover first of all what their competitors are doing about this problem. The competitors will not answer the question directly but potential suppliers of the components may be willing to indicate that there is a similar demand emerging elsewhere. If the problem here is that production costs are too high in relation to the rest of the industry then perhaps the board of directors has to focus on cost reduction rather than external purchase. If the price is lower externally, someone somewhere has apparently found a better approach to cost control.

Fiona McTaggart will provide information directly relevant to the make-or-buy decision. She will help in problem solving by setting out the information in such a way that others in the organisation can be satisfied that a decision will be in the best interests of the company as a whole. Finally, she will establish a score-keeping system which continues to monitor the effectiveness of the decision taken.

1.5.4 Case study: Ann Brown

> Ann Brown is a hospital manager having responsibility for ensuring that the cost of treatment is recovered in full by invoicing the patient or the appropriate organisation which is financing the patient care. Pricing policy is dictated at a more senior level.

Analysis of decisions and judgements

Ann Brown has no direct decision-making responsibility but the information she collates and the records she keeps, in relation to identifying costs and charging these costs to patients, will be used in the decision-making process at a more senior level. It will also be used as a tool of judgement on the effectiveness of the hospital's cost control and charging policy for the various treatments and services provided. In this case the criteria for the judgement may be rather different in that there may be less emphasis on profitability and more on the quality of service in relation to the cost of providing that service.

FIONA: *Ann Brown doesn't have direct decision-making responsibility. She is a small cog in a large machine. However, the efficiency with which she carries out her job will have a direct impact on the performance of the hospital and will have an impact on future decision making at a more senior level. Charging out to patients the cost of their care is a difficult matter and requires very careful record keeping. Patients who are ill don't question their treatment at the time, but when they are convalescing they have lots of time to look through the bill, especially if the medical insurance company is asking questions. Some patients may be paid for via the health service but at the end of the line there is a fundholder who wants to ensure that the funds are used to best advantage.*

The cost of, say, major surgery can be the least difficult to work out because the time in theatre will be known, the staff on duty will be listed and their salary costs can be apportioned over the time taken. But when the patient is back on the ward recovering, there have to be records kept of the type of nursing care, the specialist equipment and supplies, food costs and the hotel-type services associated with providing a bed. Then there have to be charges to cover the overhead costs of heating, maintaining and cleaning the buildings.

Ann Brown needs an effective recording system which is accurate in terms of care for each patient but is not so cumbersome to apply that the nurses' time is entirely taken up with clerical recording. Many costs can be applied to patient care on a pre-determined charge-out rate based on previous experience. A computerised cost recording system, with a carefully thought out coding system for each cost, is essential. Of the four cases I have considered here, this will be the most time-consuming to set up, but it will give satisfaction all round when it is working and seen to be fair to patients in terms of individual charge-out costs as well as giving the hospital reassurance that all costs are being recovered.

The cost-recording system will provide information for the decision-making process in relation to future pricing policy and also for the more difficult decisions as to which specialised medical functions at the hospital are cost effective and which functions do not fully cover costs. There are bound to be problems within the hospital if decisions are needed on expanding or cutting back. Everyone hates the accountant at those times, but at least I can design a system which provides an objective starting point even though non-financial factors are eventually the determining factor.

Fiona McTaggart is describing here the score-keeping aspects of management accounting. That score keeping will be used as information for the decision-making process and may also have a problem-solving aspect if disputes arise where medical decisions have a cost impact.

1.5.5 Comment

These case study discussions have given some insight into how the management accountant has a role to play in contributing to the management of an organisation. Three general themes have been explored, namely keeping the score, directing attention and solving problems. The case studies have shown that within each of these three themes there are many different approaches to be taken, depending on the circumstances. By way of illustration of the scope of management accounting activity, Fiona McTaggart has the following list of special studies she has undertaken, as an adviser on management accounting, where problem-solving skills have been required:

- product cost comparisons
- evaluation of product profitability
- alternative choices of resource usage
- asset management
- labour relations
- capital investment
- investigation on behalf of customer for contract pricing purposes
- directing attention to the activities of competitors.

All of these, and other problem situations, will be encountered in subsequent chapters. This chapter ends with a warning that there will be some new terminology to learn and a review of the role of the management accountant.

Real world case 1.3

The Chartered Institute of Public Finance and Accounting (CIPFA) is the leading accountancy body for public services, whether in the public or private sectors. Many existing members occupy positions of influence in Local Authorities, NHS Trusts, Central Government, Housing, Education, Water, Electricity and Gas companies and private sector organisations such as Nationwide Building Society, IBM, Marks and Spencer and the World Bank. CIPFA members are also employed by all of the top accounting firms.

Source: www.cipfa.org

Discussion points

1 How might management accounting in public services differ from management accounting in profit-making organisations?

2 Why would the Nationwide Building Society and Marks and Spencer be listed as 'public service' providers?

1.6 The language of management accounting

Management accounting is not a difficult subject but it requires a logical mind to understand it. To be successful, methods of management accounting must reflect a reasoned approach to a judgement on a situation problem and a logical basis for making decisions. If reason and logic are strong, then it should not be difficult to understand the approach.

Unfortunately, as with most specialist subjects, management accounting has developed a language of its own, which is helpful to those who work closely with the subject but can sometimes cause problems at the outset for newcomers. This chapter has avoided using specialist terminology, relying on intuitive ideas. However, any progress in understanding management accounting will be limited without the use of that terminology, so subsequent chapters will introduce the technical terms, each of which will be explained. End-of-chapter questions will help you to test your understanding of new terminology before you move on to each new chapter.

One important difference from financial accounting is that there is no official regulatory process governing management accounting. This is very different from the framework of company law, accounting standards and other regulatory processes which are found throughout financial reporting to external users. Consequently there is relative freedom in management accounting to tailor the accounting process to the management function. That does not mean that management accounting is any less rigorous professionally than other forms of accounting reporting. In the UK there is a professional body, the Chartered Institute of Management Accountants (CIMA), which provides guidance to its members on good practice in management accounting. That guidance includes a wide range of publications ranging from definitions of terminology to reports on newly emerging techniques. Similar professional bodies having a management accounting specialism exist in other countries.

1.7   What the researchers have found

This section describes three research papers. The first describes how the nature of 'management accounting' has been reinvented to meet the needs of business operations. The second describes the perceptions of the operations managers towards management accounting. The third compares the perceptions of managers and accountants regarding information supplied by the management accounting function.

1.7.1   Reinventing the management accountant

Parker (2002) reviewed the driving forces that constitute the environment of management accounting and the changing skills demanded of management accountants. He concluded that management accountants need to take on the role of both advising and leading business development. He recommended reinvention 'on a grand scale'. Management accountants would need a more broadly developed knowledge base including areas such as operations, product and process technology, systems, marketing and strategic management. The focus must switch from historical stewardship to strategic planning and forward control. In future, management accountants would be expected to contribute to strategic management, knowledge management, risk management, environmental management and change management. The trends that Parker describes are already established, so Parker's 'grand scale' recommendation is effectively for extending an existing development.

Burns and Yazdifar (2001) surveyed members of the Chartered Institute of Management Accountants (CIMA) to produce 'top 10' lists of features in the changing role of management accountants. The top three tasks for management accountants by 2005 were business performance evaluation (58%), cost control or financial control (40%) and interpreting/presenting management accounts (35%). The top three skills expected of management accountants by 2005 were analytical/interpretive (61%), IT/system knowledge (47%) and broad business knowledge (44%).

1.7.2   How operations managers use accounting information

Van der Veeken and Wouters (2002) carried out a case study observation of a large building company in the Netherlands over a period of two years. They asked:

- What strategies do managers use to achieve planned financial project results?
- In what way does accounting information contribute to these strategies?
- Which factors explain the use of accounting information?
- What are the implications for the design of accounting information systems?

They found that higher level managers used accounting information to help identify poorly performing projects. The foremen in charge of projects observed work on the building site and measured progress by the amount of resources (such as building materials) used. They did not use cost information directly but the cost outcome was not surprising because it reflected their judgement in managing the project. They were also able to deal with uncertainties and unexpected events based on their experience rather than based on accounting information. The researchers concluded that it is more important that local managers can respond to uncertainties and changes than that they can carry out a precise plan based on cost estimates. The accounting information is more relevant to overall judgements by higher-level managers as to whether satisfactory performance has been achieved on a project.

1.7.3   Perceptions of managers and accountants compared

Pierce and O'Dea (2003) visited 11 companies to meet the management accountant and a senior manager in each area of production and in sales or marketing. They put the same questions about use of techniques to the management accountants and the managers. They found some examples of management accounting information that were used by managers less frequently than the management accountants believed, but they also found particular items of information that were used by managers more frequently than the management accountants believed. The main demands of managers were for information that is more timely, broad, flexible and in a better format. When asked about the future role of management accountants, the main theme of managers was to describe the management accountant as a business partner. Interaction, location in the working environment, teamwork and understanding the business were all seen as important characteristics for the effective management accountant.

1.8 Summary

You have seen from the discussion in section 1.1.3 and the case studies that management accounting should direct attention towards strategic issues of surviving and prospering in a competitive environment. The remaining chapters of this book will introduce the various techniques that have been developed in management accounting for keeping the score, directing attention and solving problems. The traditional techniques are described, with current thinking and developments explained and contrasted as relevant.

Key themes in this chapter are:

- **Management accounting** is concerned with reporting accounting information within a business, for management use only.

- **Management** takes its widest meaning in describing all those persons (managers) responsible for the day-to-day running of a business.

- The managers of a business carry out functions of **planning**, **decision making** and **control**.

- Management accounting supports these management functions by directing attention, keeping the score and solving problems.

- The **contingency theory** of management accounting explains how management accounting methods have developed in a variety of ways depending on the judgements or decisions required.

- **Strategic management accounting** pays particular attention to the provision and analysis of financial information on the firm's product markets and competitors' costs and cost structures, and the monitoring of the enterprise's strategies and those of its competitors in these markets over a number of periods.

References and further reading

Burns, J. and Yazdifar, H. (2001) 'Tricks or treats?' *Financial Management*, March: 33–35.

CIMA (2000) *Management Accounting Official Terminology*, CIMA Publishing.

Parker, L. (2002) 'Reinventing the management accountant', CIMA address delivered at Glasgow University, March, available on www.cimglobal.com

Pierce, B. (2001) 'Score bores', *Financial Management*, May: 41.

Pierce, B. and O'Dea, T. (2003) 'Management accounting information and the needs of managers: perceptions of managers and accountants compared', *British Accounting Review*, 35(3): 257–90.

Van der Veeken, H.J.M. and Wouters, M.J.F. (2002) 'Using accounting information systems by operations managers in a project company', *Management Accounting Research*, 13: 345–70.

QUESTIONS

The Questions section of each chapter has three types of question. 'Test your understanding' questions to help you review your reading are in the 'A' series of questions. You will find the answers to these by reading and thinking about the material in the text book. 'Application' questions to test your ability to apply technical skills are in the 'B' series of questions. Questions requiring you to show skills in problem solving and evaluation are in the 'C' series of questions.

A   Test your understanding

A1.1   Define 'management accounting' (section 1.1).

A1.2   Explain why management decisions will normally require more than a management accounting input (section 1.1.1).

A1.3   What is meant by a 'contingency theory' of management accounting (section 1.1.2)?

A1.4   Why is management accounting required to take on an outward-looking role of contributing to business strategy by identifying, measuring and communicating financial information about a wider business community (section 1.1.3)?

A1.5   Explain the needs of internal users for management accounting information (section 1.2).

A1.6   Explain, giving a suitable example in each case, what is meant by the management functions of:
(a) planning (section 1.3.1);
(b) decision making (section 1.3.2); and
(c) control (section 1.3.3).

A1.7   Explain, giving a suitable example in each case, how management accounting may serve the purposes of:
(a) directing attention (section 1.4.1);
(b) keeping the score (section 1.4.2); and
(c) solving problems (section 1.4.3).

A1.8   Describe, and explain each stage of, the cycle of profit planning and control (section 1.4.4).

A1.9   In the chapter there are four case studies where Fiona McTaggart explains what she is able to offer in four situations, using her management accounting experience. Her advice is primarily inward looking and based on the traditional approaches to planning, control and decision making. Add two sentences to each of Fiona's explanations in order to present a more strategic awareness of the activities of competitors (section 1.5).

A1.10   Suggest reasons for the lack of an agreed set of standard terminology of management accounting (section 1.6).

A1.11   How has the role of the management accountant been 'reinvented' in recent years (section 1.7.1)?

A1.12   How do high-level managers and lower-level managers use accounting information in different ways (section 1.7.2)?

A1.13   How do managers differ from management accountants in their view of accounting information (section 1.7.3)?

B   # Application

B1.1

(a) Imagine you are the finance director of a company which is planning to open a new super-market chain. Prepare a chart similar to that shown in Exhibit 1.2 which sets out key aspects of the planning, decision making and control.

(b) Give two examples of financial objectives and two examples of non-financial objectives which you might expect of the sales manager of the new supermarket chain.

(c) Explain how management accounting skills would be required in providing product costs comparisons when the supermarket chain becomes operational.

B1.2

A record company is planning to launch an internet music service. Subscribers who pay £15 per month will be allowed to download 100 songs per month to a personal computer. If the sub-scription lapses, access to the music will be lost. The quality of the file transfer is guaranteed to be high. Legal advice has been obtained to confirm that the arrangement is within copyright regulations. Royalties will be paid to recording artistes based on the number of times that a song is requested.

(a) Identify the judgements and decisions to be made here.

(b) Explain how management accounting may help in directing attention, keeping the score or solving problems.

B1.3

A group of doctors operates a joint surgery. They are planning to provide a private clinic where minor surgery can be performed on a day basis (no overnight facilities will be offered). The pro-ject will require investment in a new building and operating theatre. Three theatre nurses will be required and three healthcare assistants will be employed. Admissions will be dealt with by the existing medical secretaries. The fees charged will cover costs plus a profit percentage based on cost.

(a) Identify the judgements and decisions to be made here.

(b) Explain how management accounting may help in directing attention, keeping the score or solving problems.

B1.4

A recently retired police officer has received a lump sum award and a pension. She has a hobby of making soft toys which have for some years been sold to friends and colleagues at a price to cover the cost of materials. She now wishes to turn this into a commercial venture and to sell them through a children's clothing shop, which has agreed to provide shelf space for the sale of 20 toys per month. She is not concerned initially about making a high profit and will be satisfied with covering costs. The shop will take a fee of 5% of the sale price of each toy sold.

(a) Identify the judgements and decisions to be made here.

(b) Explain how management accounting may help in directing attention, keeping the score or solving problems.

C   # Problem solving and evaluation

C1.1

You have been invited to write a proposal for the development of a new production line to process dog food. The production of dog food will take up space previously devoted to cat food. Write 250 words (approx.) explaining how management accounting would be used to justify any decision by the production manager to replace cat food with dog food in the pro-duction process.

C1.2

Chris and Alison Weston have been manufacturing and selling children's toys from a workshop attached to their house. Alison has carried out the manufacturing activity and Chris has provided the marketing and financial support. The scale of customers' orders has reached a point where they must make a decision about renting a production unit on a nearby trading estate and employing two assistants. One assistant would be required to help make the toys and the other would carry out routine record keeping, allowing Chris to spend more time on marketing. Write 250 words (approx.) explaining (a) the main judgements and decisions which will arise; and (b) the kind of advice that could be offered by a management accounting expert

C1.3

Set out below is a selection of advertisements for posts in management accounting. Read the text of the advertisement and relate the specified requirements to the three management accounting roles set out in this chapter, namely:

(a) directing attention;
(b) keeping the score; and
(c) solving problems.

PLANNING AND REPORTING CONTROLLER

Reporting to the group finance director, your key task will be to drive a step change in all areas of corporate reporting and planning and provide analytical impetus to the development of business strategy. Responsibilities will include:

- Ownership and control of the quality of reporting and forecasting throughout the business
- Managing the group's quarterly strategic business unit review, forecasting and annual planning cycles
- Managing the day-to-day Treasury processes including cash-flow forecasting
- Supporting the finance director in all corporate activities including financing, acquisitions, presentations and *ad hoc* projects as required.

This is a high profile role which interfaces directly with directors, shareholders, advisers, banks, head office functions and divisions.

The ideal candidate will be an ambitious graduate qualified accountant with a minimum of four years post-qualification experience. First class communication skills and good systems knowledge will complement your proven technical expertise.

HEAD OF MANAGEMENT INFORMATION

Reporting to the financial director, you will be responsible for:

- Developing and automating the production of management accounts and contract cash reporting
- Implementing and managing a robust process for all contract valuations
- Managing all aspects of budgeting, forecasting and group reporting
- Developing relationships with operational teams to improve controls and increase commercial awareness
- A review of financial processes and implementation of new systems and controls.

The successful candidate will be commercially minded and profit-motivated with the ability to manage a strong team.

MANAGEMENT ACCOUNTANT

This is a major support services organisation, supplying services and products to government agencies and commercial businesses worldwide. Working closely with the commercial teams, you will provide them with full financial support at every stage of the contract life cycle. Main responsibilities include:

- Assisting with the compilation of new bids and tenders
- Ongoing contract monitoring including budgeting and forecasting
- Development of key performance indicators for the business
- Production of monthly management accounts, analysis and commentary

You will need to have excellent business acumen and highly developed communication skills.

MANAGEMENT ACCOUNTANT
(*Charitable organisation*)

This is a leading charity providing safe, secure and affordable housing for young people and working with homeless young people to provide safe shelter. Reporting to the head of finance, the role involves working closely with various departments identifying areas of concern and solutions.

Key responsibilities include:
- Reviewing of trial balance, and generation and review of management accounts; identifying and resolving any issues and offering a business support function
- Attending committee meetings to present the accounts to the trustees
- Identifying trends in the management accounts and advising management as to recommendations
- Development of budgets and forecasts
- Investigating and improving financial performance in the operations of the residential centres

This role would suit an individual who is looking to shape the continuing development of the work of the charity.

HEAD OF MANAGEMENT ACCOUNTS
(*The finance office of a university*)

You will be responsible for the setting, monitoring, control and reporting on budgets and the regular production of management accounts. In addition, you will ensure the provision of a comprehensive payroll service and be responsible for arranging and accounting for capital finance.

PRINCIPAL MANAGEMENT ACCOUNTANT
(*Public sector organisation*)

This is one of the most successful police forces in the country. With 2,000 employees and an annual budget of over £80 million, it is essential that the organisation has appropriate and well-maintained financial management and information systems to support the demands of modern policing.

We now require a dynamic team leader to ensure the continued development of these systems and to provide a comprehensive financial advice/support service to senior managers.

The successful candidate will be closely involved in the production of medium-term financial plans, annual budgets and financial information systems upgrades as well as the training and development of non-technical staff on financial management.

You will be self-reliant and able to work to tight deadlines whilst maintaining high standards, be capable of clearly communicating financial concepts in a persuasive and effective manner and have a suitable professional qualification with three years' experience in financial management.

Case studies

Real world cases

Prepare short answers to Case studies 1.1, 1.2 and 1.3.

Case 1.4 (group case study)

Form a study group of four to six persons who are to act out the role of the finance director and related staff on the accounting team of a company which is planning to open a new super-market chain at an out-of-town location. Give a ten-minute presentation to the rest of the class explaining the major issues you will be expected to deal with in making a contribution to the decision and the subsequent monitoring of that decision.

Case 1.5 (group case study)

Form a study group of four to six persons who are to negotiate the development of a new pro-duction line to process canned peas. The canned peas will replace an existing product, canned carrots. Half of the team will argue on behalf of the canned peas while the other half will argue on behalf of the canned carrots. Give a ten-minute presentation to the class (five minutes for each half of the team) explaining how management accounting information will help you to justify the decision you propose and to monitor the implementation of the decision.

Notes

1. AAA (1966) *A Statement of Basic Accounting Theory*, American Accounting Association, Evanston, Illinois, p. 1.
2. Otley, D. (1995) 'Management control, organisational design and accounting information systems', chapter 3 in Ashton, D., Hopper, T. and Scapens, R. (eds.) *Issues in Management Accounting* (2nd edn), Prentice Hall.
3. Lowe, E. A. (1971) 'On the idea of a management control system', *Journal of Management Studies*, **8** (1), pp. 1–12.
4. Bromwich, M. (1990) 'The case for strategic management accounting: the role of accounting informa-tion for strategy in competitive markets', *Accounting, Organizations and Society*, **15** (1/2), pp. 27–46.

Chapter 2

Classification of costs

This case study shows a typical situation in which management accounting can be helpful. Read the case study now, but only attempt the discussion points after you have finished studying the chapter.

This extract is taken from an article describing the expansion of the farmed area devoted to the growing of borage, whose oil is used in the health food market to alleviate a number of human disorders.

All borage grown by contracted farmers in the Driffield area is now dried at Inn Carr Farm. There are two other drying plants, based at Bishop Burton, near Beverley, and at Aughton, near Bubwith, Selby. Oil extracted at the New Holland plant is sold to encapsulators to produce products for the health food market.

Mr Voase said: 'Last year's harvest was difficult because of the wet weather in August. But we still managed to achieve three hundredweight of cleaned seed per acre.

'The crop fetched £288 per acre and after variable costs of £87 per acre, including fertiliser and chemical inputs also swathing, drying, cleaning and storage we were left with a margin of £201 per acre.

'This season the contract price is £1,800 per tonne. It is a very low-input crop and Glafield [seed company] provide the seed free of charge. A four tonne per acre crop of feed wheat selling at £60 per tonne gives on average gross output of £240 leaving a margin of £125 per acre compared with £201 for borage.'

Source: *Yorkshire Post*, 29 January 2005, 'Healing herb that's at top of the crops.'

Discussion points

1 What are the variable costs of growing this crop?
2 Why does the farmer prefer growing borage to growing wheat?

Contents

Learning outcomes

After reading this chapter you should be able to:

- Define 'cost'.
- Explain the need for cost classification.
- Define 'activity' and 'output'.
- Explain and distinguish variable costs and fixed costs.
- Explain and distinguish direct costs and indirect costs.
- Explain and distinguish product costs and period costs.
- Explain how cost classification can be developed to be relevant to the circumstances of planning, decision making and control.
- Explain and devise a cost coding system.
- Explain how costs may be selected and reported for the type of activity required (cost unit, cost centre, profit centre or investment centre).

2.1 Definition of a cost

A **cost**, in its widest meaning, is an amount of expenditure on a defined activity. The word 'cost' needs other words added to it, to give it a specific meaning. This chapter explains some of the basic classifications that give meaning to the word 'cost' in management accounting.

The cost of an item of input or output may be analysed in terms of two measurements:

1 a physical quantity measurement
multiplied by
2 a price measurement.

Where a production process uses 100 kg of material which has a price of £5 per kg, the cost is £500. Where a production process uses 200 hours of labour time at a rate of £4 per hour, the cost is £800. That may appear to be a statement of the obvious, but the breaking down of cost into physical quantity and price is frequently essential for the application of management accounting methods where the physical flow of inputs and outputs may sometimes be recorded separately from the unit price. The analysis of the separate elements of quantity and price will be dealt with in more detail in Chapter 15.

2.2 The need for cost classification

Cost classification systems in practice are as varied as the businesses they serve. In Chapter 1 the functions of management are described as: planning, decision making and control. For purposes of classification, it is convenient to take planning and control as a combined function because the classifications required by each are similar. For decision making, particular care has to be taken to use classifications of cost which are relevant to the decision under consideration.

This chapter will first explain three *traditional* types of cost classification:

1 **variable costs** and **fixed costs** (section 2.4);
2 **direct costs** and **indirect costs** (section 2.5); and
3 **product costs** and **period costs** (section 2.6).

Each of these cost classifications will then be related to the management functions of planning, decision making and control (section 2.7). It is important to emphasise here that the three types of cost classification are *different* ways of looking at costs. Any particular item of cost could have more than one of these classifications attached to it, depending on the purpose of the classifications being used.

Finally, the chapter will explain the importance of correct coding of costs in a computer-based system (section 2.8), and will show how costs are selected and reported according to the unit of the business for which information is required (section 2.9).

2.3 The meaning of 'activity' and 'output'

The word **'activity'** will be used in this textbook as a general description to cover any physical operation that takes place in an enterprise. In a business providing bus transport for schoolchildren the activities will include driving the bus, cleaning the bus, making telephone calls to check routes and times, and ensuring that the administrative requirements, such as insurance and licences, are in place. In a local government department providing assistance to elderly persons, the activities will include sending out home helps, paying the home helps, telephoning the clients to arrange visits and checking that spending is within the budget allowed. In a manufacturing business providing floor cleaning machines the activities will include ordering parts, assembling parts, delivering the finished products to shops for sale, taking in returns for repair under warranty, paying employees and checking on the quality of the goods produced. These are all activities and they all cause costs to be incurred. The idea of activities causing costs ('driving costs') is central to much of the classification of costs and the collection of costs relating to a specific activity. You will find later that the phrase 'activity-based costing' has been created to recognise that management accounting is most effective when it links costs to the activities of the business.

Activities have to be measured. For the soap manufacturer the measure of activity is the number of cartons of washing powder sold. For the retail store it could be the number of items of clothing sold, or it could be the value of clothing sold. Selling a large number of small-value items causes higher staffing costs than does selling a small number of high-value items. For the road haulage business the measure of activity could be the hours worked by drivers or the number of miles driven. Hours worked takes no account of whether the drivers are on the road or waiting at the depot. Miles driven are a better measure of productive activity but do not distinguish full loads from empty trucks. Fuel costs are higher for a full load than for an empty truck. Activity might be measured using a combined unit of kilogram-miles.

Throughout the following chapters the word 'activity' will be used and measures of activity will be described. You will be expected to show your analytical skills in thinking about the meaning of the word and the relevance of the measure of activity to cost classification and cost behaviour.

Output is a particular kind of activity. It is the product or service provided by the enterprise or by one of its internal sections. The output of a soap manufacturer is washing powder; the output of a retail store is the clothing that it sells; the output of a service engineer might be the repair of washing machines; the output of a garden centre is pot plants grown from from seed; the output of a road haulage business is the loads delivered by its drivers; the output of a refuse disposal company is the service of emptying household dustbins; the output of an airline is the passenger loads carried; the output of a school is the successful education of its pupils.

Activity 2.1

(This is another use of the word 'activity' where you are asked to pause and think actively about what you have read.) Think about any activity that you carry out during the week (e.g. travel to college, eating meals, washing clothes). How would you measure the volume of that activity in a week? How might the cost of the activity be affected by the volume of activity? For example, could you share some travel costs; would one large meal cost more or less than two small meals; would one large wash cost more or less than two small washes?

2.4 Variable costs and fixed costs

Costs behave in different ways as the level of activity changes. Some costs increase in direct proportion to the increased level of activity. These are called variable costs. Some costs do not vary, whatever the level of activity. These are called fixed costs. Some show elements of both features. These are called semi-variable costs. Fixed costs that increase in steps are called step costs.

2.4.1 Variable costs

Definition

> A **variable cost** is one which varies directly with changes in the level of activity, over a defined period of time.

Examples of **variable cost** are:

- materials used to manufacture a unit of output or to provide a type of service
- labour costs of manufacturing a unit of output or providing a type of service
- commission paid to a salesperson
- fuel used by a haulage company.

Exhibit 2.1 shows the costs of clay used by a pottery company for various levels of output of clay vases for garden ornaments. The clay required for each vase costs £10.

Exhibit 2.1
Costs of clay related to activity levels

Output (number of vases)	100	200	300
Cost (£s)	1,000	2,000	3,000

The **total cost** increases by £10 for every vase produced, and is described as *variable*. The **unit cost** (the cost of one unit of output) is £10 per vase and is *constant*. Sometimes students find it a little confusing at this point to decide whether they should be thinking about the total cost or the unit cost. It may help you to think of yourself as the owner of the business manufacturing the vases. If you are the owner, you will be most interested in the total cost because that shows how much finance you will need in order to carry on production. You will only recover the cost of buying the clay when you sell the finished goods to the customers. Until then you need finance to buy the clay. The more you produce, the more finance you will need. If you approach the bank manager to help you finance the business you will be asked 'How much do you need?', a question which is answered by reference to total cost.

Exhibit 2.2 shows, in the form of a graph, the information contained in Exhibit 2.1.

Exhibit 2.2
Graph of variable cost measured as activity increases

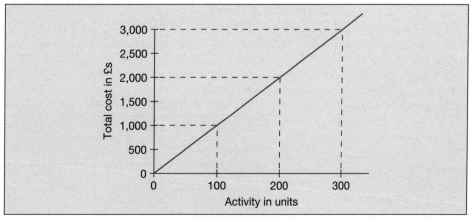

It plots activity level (number of vases produced) on the horizontal axis and total cost on the vertical axis. The graph reinforces the idea that the total cost is a variable cost. It shows a straight line moving upwards to the right. The fact that the line is straight, rather than curving, means that the total cost increases in direct proportion to the increase in activity (that is, total cost increases by £10 for every unit of output).

2.4.2   Fixed costs

Definition

> A **fixed cost** is one which is not affected by changes in the level of activity, over a defined period of time.

Examples of **fixed costs** are:

- rent of buildings
- salary paid to a supervisor
- advertising in the trade journals
- business rates paid to the local authority
- depreciation of machinery calculated on the straight-line basis.

A fixed cost is by definition unchanged over a period of time, but it may vary in the longer term. Rent, for example, might be fixed for a period of one year, but reviewed at the end of every year with the possibility of an increase being imposed by the landlord.

Continuing our illustration based on a pottery company, Exhibit 2.3 shows the cost of renting a building in which to house its kiln and other production facilities. The total cost remains *fixed* at £3,000 irrespective of how many vases are produced. The unit cost is *decreasing* as output increases, as shown in Exhibit 2.4, because the fixed cost is spread over more vases. Here again, it is more important usually to think about total cost because unless the pottery can pay its rent it cannot continue in business. This type of cost is therefore described as a fixed cost. The cost of rent is shown in graphical form in Exhibit 2.5.

Exhibit 2.3
Costs of rental related to activity levels

Output (number of vases)	100	200	300
Cost (£s)	3,000	3,000	3,000

Exhibit 2.4
Unit cost of the pottery rental

Output (number of vases)	Unit cost (£)
100	30
200	15
300	10

Exhibit 2.5
Illustration of fixed cost

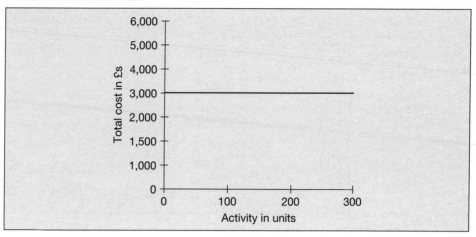

2.4.3 Semi-variable costs

Definition

A **semi-variable cost** is one which is partly fixed and partly varies with changes in the level of activity, over a defined period of time.

Examples of **semi-variable cost** are:

- office salaries where there is a core of long-term secretarial staff plus employment of temporary staff when activity levels rise
- maintenance charges where there is a fixed basic charge per year plus a variable element depending on the number of call-outs per year.

Exhibit 2.6 sets out the costs incurred by a telephone sales company which pays a fixed rental of £2,000 per month and a call charge of £1 per telephone sale call. This total cost has a mixed behaviour, which may be described as semi-variable. It has a *fixed* component of £2,000 and a *variable* component of £1 per telephone sale.

Exhibit 2.6
Telephone rental costs

Activity (number of calls)	100	200	300
Cost (£s)	2,100	2,200	2,300

The graph of this semi-variable cost is shown in Exhibit 2.7. The fixed cost is shown by the point where the line of the graph meets the vertical axis. The *variable* component is shown by the *slope* of the graph. The *slope* of the graph shows the total cost increasing by £1 for every extra unit of activity. The *fixed* component of £2,000 is shown as the point where the line of the graph meets the vertical axis.

Exhibit 2.7
Illustration of semi-variable cost

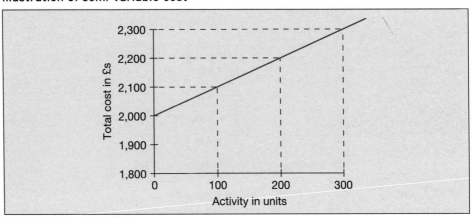

2.4.4   Step costs

A fixed cost that increases in steps is called a **step cost**.

The **cost** is fixed over a specified level of activity but then increases as a further amount of fixed cost is incurred. One example is the cost of renting storage space. The rent is unchanged while the output can be fitted into one store but, as soon as a second store has to be rented, the total cost increases. Another example is the cost of paying a supervisor of a team of employees. Suppose one supervisor can manage up to 20 employees. Cost of supervision will be fixed for the level of activity from 1 to 20 employees. Beyond that level a second supervisor will be needed, causing a sudden increase in fixed cost.

Exhibit 2.8 shows a step cost of rent increasing annually over five years. The rental starts at £1,000 and increases by £100 each year.

Exhibit 2.8
Step cost for five-year period, with annual increase

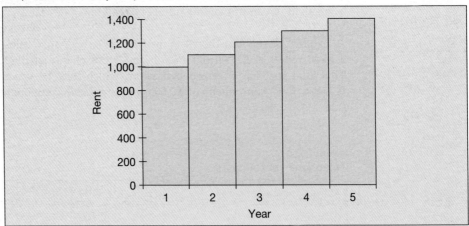

The graph in Exhibit 2.8 is different from those shown earlier in the chapter because the horizontal axis measures time rather than activity. However, it is also possible to estimate the activity levels expected over the five-year period. Whatever the expected activity level, the relationship between total cost and activity level will be more complex than the simple fixed, variable and semi-variable relationships already shown. For the purposes of the rest of this textbook all the costs you meet will be simplified as fixed, variable or semi-variable, within a defined period of time.

2.4.5   Importance of the time period chosen

The extent to which a cost varies with activity depends on the period of time chosen. In manufacturing picnic tables, the cost of the plastic frame and the table top are variable costs, as is the labour cost of assembly. The annual rent of the warehouse where the tables are assembled is a fixed cost for the year, but will be increase in steps (a step cost) over a period of several years if there is a rent review each year.

Activity 2.2

At this point, be sure that you are comfortable with the idea of variable costs, fixed costs and semi-variable costs. These will appear frequently in later chapters and it is important to understand them. If you are not familiar with graphs, go back through the section and try to draw each graph from the data presented.

Real world case 2.2

The following extract is describing the problems of a company which manufactures high quality glass and china pottery.

Waterford Wedgwood, the luxury goods company, has warned it may have to cut jobs after experiencing a slump in sales since the start of the year.

Redmond O'Donoghue, the chief executive of the group which bought Royal Doulton for £40m earlier this year, warned that annual profits will miss expectations and that the company was being forced to cut costs to improve profitability.

'The demand for our type of products is softer than it has been. Although we are still maintaining our leading market share, the size of the sector is falling. In this position, we have to accept that our sales will be lower than we would have hoped and instead attack our fixed cost base,' he said, adding that job losses were possible.

Source: *The Independent*, 15 March 2005, 'Fresh Waterford Wedgwood warning sparks job fears', Rachel Stevenson.

Discussion points

1 What kinds of fixed cost might be expected at a company which manufactures glass and china goods?

2 Why are fixed costs a problem when demand is falling?

2.5 Direct costs and indirect costs

The costs of a business activity can also be classified as direct and indirect costs. **Direct costs** are those which are directly related to a particular object (such as a product which has been manufactured) or a particular service (such as a repair job completed) or a particular location (such as a department within the organisation).

Indirect costs are those which *cannot* be directly related to a particular object or service or location and therefore have to be apportioned on a basis which is as fair as can be devised.

The first question you should ask, whenever you see the words 'direct' or 'indirect' is 'Direct or indirect in which respect?' This will remind you that the words have no meaning in isolation. An item which is a direct cost for a department could be an indirect cost for the units of output produced by the department. Take the example of electricity consumed in a department. If the department has a meter, then the amount of electricity used may be identified directly with the department. However, if all items produced within the department share the benefit of the electricity supply, then the cost will need to be shared among them as an indirect cost so far as products are concerned.

Definitions

The definition of direct and indirect costs depends on the purpose for which the cost will be used.

Direct costs are directly traceable to an identifiable unit, such as a product or service or department of the business, for which costs are to be determined.

Indirect costs are spread over a number of identifiable units of the business, such as products or services or departments, for which costs are to be determined. Indirect costs are also called overhead costs.

Overhead costs are the costs which cannot be identified directly with products or services.

Fiona McTaggart gives an example of how she would distinguish direct costs and indirect costs in a particular situation.

FIONA: *I was working recently with a publishing firm about to bring out a new children's magazine series based on a popular cartoon programme. The publisher had already incurred market research costs in respect of the new magazine series and it looked like a good idea.*

The magazine is to be produced in a department where there are already ten other magazines in production. Writers work freelance and are paid fees on a piecework basis for each item they write. Graphic artists are employed full-time in the department, producing designs and drawings for all the magazines. Once the magazine production is completed, it is sent for external printing at another company which charges on the basis of volume of output. I was asked to help design a monthly cost analysis statement for the new magazine.

I pointed out that some costs were easy to identify because they were directly traceable to the product. Working back from the end of the story, the external printer's charge would be a direct cost of the new magazine because it is directly related to that specific output. The work of the freelance writers is also a direct cost of the new magazine because it is easy to make a list of fees paid to them in respect of particular work on the new magazine.

The work of the graphic artists is an indirect cost so far as the product is concerned, because their time is spread over all magazines produced. They do not keep detailed records of every design they produce. Many designs can be used in more than one magazine title. I suggested that a fair basis of allocation would be to share their cost across all magazines in proportion to the number of illustrated pages in each. That turned out to be a bad idea because some illustrated pages may contain full-size pictures while others may contain a quarter-page design, so it was eventually decided to apply a factor to each page depending on whether it was fully illustrated or partly illustrated.

Although the graphic artists are an indirect cost so far as the product is concerned, they are a direct cost for the department, because they don't work in any other department. I suggested that the full cost of the new magazine would only be known when it was also carrying its share of the direct costs and indirect costs of the department as a whole. Direct costs for the department could include heat and light, maintenance of the operating equipment, machine depreciation and supervisor's salary, while indirect costs could include a share of administration costs and a share of rent and business rates. It is not easy to ensure that all costs are included for purposes of planning and control.

In her explanation, Fiona has repeatedly used the words 'direct' and 'indirect', but at the start of the explanation she is referring to the direct and indirect costs of the new *magazine* while at the end she is referring to the direct and indirect costs of the whole *department*. The departmental costs, taken together, are all indirect costs so far as the products of the department are concerned.

Activity 2.3

Think of some activity observed in your everyday life where costs are involved. (It could, for example, be travelling on a bus, watching the sales assistant in a shop, or asking the television repair service to call.) Write down five costs which might be incurred in that activity. How would you decide which costs are direct and which are indirect?

2.6 Product costs and period costs

Another way of looking at the cost of a unit of output of a business is to distinguish product costs and period costs. **Product costs** are those which are identified with goods or services intended for sale to customers. These costs belong to the products and stay with them until they are sold. If goods remain unsold, or work-in-progress remains incomplete, then the product costs stay with the unsold goods or work-in-progress under the heading of inventory (stock). **Period costs** are those costs which are treated as expenses of the period and are not carried as part of the inventory (stock) value.

Definitions

Product costs are those costs associated with goods or services purchased, or produced, for sale to customers.

Period costs are those costs which are treated as expenses in the period in which they are incurred.

Product costs include direct *and* indirect costs of production. Exhibit 2.9 sets out a statement of product cost that includes direct and indirect costs. The total of direct costs is described as the **prime cost of production**.

Exhibit 2.9 uses the words **production overhead** to describe the total of the indirect costs of production. Examples are:

● depreciation of machinery
● insurance of the factory premises
● rental of warehouse storage space for raw material.

There are many other types of **overhead costs** which you will encounter in your progress through later chapters. They all consist of indirect costs, with the type of cost determining the particular name given to the overhead cost.

Exhibit 2.9
Statement of product cost

	£	£
Direct materials		XXX
Direct labour		XXX
Other direct costs		XXX
Prime cost		XXX
Indirect materials	XXX	
Indirect labour	XXX	
Other indirect costs	XXX	
Production overhead		XXX
Total product cost		XXX

Definitions

Prime cost of production is the total of direct materials, direct labour and other direct costs.

Production overhead cost comprises indirect material, indirect labour and other indirect costs of production.

Example of product costs and period costs in a service business

A financial adviser provides each client with three hours' consultation prior to arranging a pension plan. The cost of the adviser's time is estimated at £500 per hour. Advertising costs £2,000 per month. The client is charged £2,100 commission on completion of the three-hour sequence of consultation. During one week the financial adviser provides 20 hours of consultation. The statement of costs would be:

		£
Product cost	Labour: 20 hours at £500 per hour	10,000
Period cost	Advertising	2,000

Suppose that the consultations are complete for six clients (18 hours) but unfinished for one client, who has been provided with only two hours' consultation by the end of the week. The incomplete consultation is described as work-in-progress. There was no work-in-progress at the start of the week. The calculation of profit would be:

		£	£
Product cost	Sales (commission) 6 clients at £2,100 each		12,600
	Labour: 20 hours at £500 per hour	10,000	
	Less work-in-progress 2 hours at £500 per hour	(1,000)	
	Product cost of goods sold		(9,000)
Period cost	Advertising		(2,000)
	Operating profit		1,600

Example of product costs and period costs in a manufacturing business

A toy manufacturer produces hand-crafted rocking horses. During one week six rocking horses are completed. The direct materials costs of wood and leather materials amount to £180 per completed horse. The indirect materials cost of glue and paint amount to £20 per completed horse. The direct labour cost for craft working is £150 per completed horse. The indirect labour cost of handling within the production department is £50 per completed horse. Advertising amounted to £1,200 per week.

Five completed rocking horses are sold for £1,000 each. There were none in inventory (stock) at the start of the week. The statements of costs would be:

		£
Product cost	Direct materials, wood & leather, 6 @ £180	1,080
	Indirect materials, glue & paint, 6 @ £20	120
	Direct labour: craft work, 6 @ £150	900
	Indirect labour: handling 6 @ £50	300
Period cost	Advertising	1,200

The calculation of profit would be:

		£	£
Product cost	Sales: 5 completed rocking horses		5,000
	Direct materials, wood & leather, 6 @ £180	1,080	
	Indirect materials, glue & paint, 6 @ £20	120	
	Direct labour: craft work, 6 @ £150	900	
	Indirect labour: handling 6 @ £50	300	
		2,400	
	Less unsold inventory (stock), 1 × (180 + 20 + 150 + 50)	(400)	
	Product cost of 5 horses sold		(2,000)
Period cost	Advertising		(1,200)
	Operating profit		1,800

In each of these examples the product cost of completed services and of goods sold is matched against sales revenue of the week. The product cost of work-in-progress and of unsold goods is carried in the valuation of inventory (stock) to be matched against sales revenue of a future week. The period costs are all matched against sales revenue of the week.

In a service organisation, all costs incurred up to the point of completion of the service are regarded as product costs. Any costs incurred beyond the act of service, such as advertising the service or collecting cash from customers, would be a period cost.

In a manufacturing organisation, all manufacturing costs are regarded as product costs. This will include the direct and indirect costs of manufacturing. Chapter 4 will explain the methods of calculating the indirect manufacturing costs for each product item. Costs incurred beyond the completion of manufacture, such as the costs of administration and selling, are period costs. The valuation of unsold inventory (stock) is based on the product cost.

2.7 Cost classification for planning, decision making and control

Sections 2.4, 2.5 and 2.6 have described fixed and variable costs, direct and indirect costs and product and period costs. Each of these may have a role to play in planning, decision making and control. The idea of contingency theory, explained in Chapter 1, is important here; the classification is chosen to suit the intended use.

2.7.1 Planning

Planning involves looking forward and asking questions of the 'what if . . . ?' type. Exhibit 2.10 gives examples of planning questions and sets out the cost classifications that may be appropriate to each.

Exhibit 2.10
Cost classification for planning purposes

Planning question	Cost classification
1 What is the cost impact of a change in levels of production over a period of time?	Fixed and variable costs. Fixed costs will not be affected by production levels; variable costs will alter proportionately.
2 What is the cost effect of planning to expand operations by opening a new outlet in a separate location?	Direct and indirect costs, in relation to the location. The direct costs will include the rental and running costs of the chosen location; indirect costs will be that location's share of the general running costs of the business.
3 What is the cost impact of remaining open for longer hours to improve on existing client services?	Fixed and variable costs. The new service will incur variable costs. Will it cause any step increase in fixed costs?

2.7.2 Decision making

Decision making involves asking questions of the type 'Should we do . . . ? Exhibit 2.11 gives examples of decision-making questions and sets out the cost classifications that may be appropriate to each.

For decision-making purposes, the key word is **relevance.** The costs used in the decision-making process must only be those which are *relevant* to the decision. In this respect, the classification into variable and fixed costs is particularly important. That is because, in the short term, little can be done by a business in relation to fixed costs, so that the need for a decision may focus attention on the variable costs. Fiona McTaggart explains how she would use such a classification to present information for decision making.

Exhibit 2.11
Cost classification for decision-making purposes

Decision-making question	Cost classification
1 Should the company produce components in this country or produce them overseas?	Fixed and variable costs. The variable costs of production should be compared for each country. Fixed costs are not relevant to the decision if they are incurred regardless of the location. Fixed costs are relevant if they can be avoided by changing location.
2 Should the company continue to provide a service when demand is falling?	Fixed and variable costs. The price paid by customers must at least cover the variable costs. In the longer term there must be sufficient revenue to cover variable and fixed costs.

FIONA: *The Garden Decor Company is thinking of making two garden ornaments, gnomes and herons. The variable cost of making a gnome would be £24 and the variable cost of making a heron would be £14. Market research indicates that garden ornaments of similar types are selling in the shops for around £20 each. Output up to the level of 20,000 garden ornaments, in any combination of output of each, would lead to fixed rental and insurance costs of £6,000.*

My recommendation would be that the company should not even contemplate the garden gnomes because the expected selling price of £20 will not cover the variable cost of £24 per unit. The company will make a loss as it produces each item. The selling price of the herons would cover their variable cost and make a contribution of £6 each (£20 minus £14) to the fixed cost. If they can sell 1,000 herons or more, the £6 contribution from each will cover the £6,000 additional fixed costs and any further herons sold will give a profit clear of fixed costs.

Fiona has used the word '**contribution**' in this discussion. You can probably guess its meaning from the context in which it is used, but you will meet the word again as a technical term in Chapter 9.

2.7.3   Control

Control involves looking back and asking questions of the 'how and why . . . ?' type. Exhibit 2.12 gives examples of control questions and sets out the cost classifications that may be appropriate to each.

Exhibit 2.12
Cost classification for control purposes

Control question	Cost classification
1 How closely do the costs of each product match the targets set?	Direct and indirect costs in relation to the product. If the direct costs do not match the targets set then questions must be asked about the product itself. If the indirect costs do not match the targets then questions must be asked about the control of those costs and the method of apportioning (sharing) them across the products.
2 How closely do the costs of a service department match the budget set for the department?	Direct and indirect costs related to the department. The direct costs are closely under the control of the departmental manager, who should explain any deviations. The indirect costs are shared across several departments and so questions may be asked about the basis of apportioning (sharing) those costs.
3 Is the value of the stock of unsold goods stated correctly?	Product costs and period costs. The unsold stock should be carrying its share of the product costs.

Activity 2.4

Imagine you are the manager of a department store in the centre of town. Write down one planning question, one decision-making question and one control question that you might ask and suggest a cost classification that would provide management accounting information relevant to the question.

2.7.4   Cost classification to meet changing circumstances

Chapter 1 noted the contingency approach to management accounting which emphasises that management accounting should be flexible to meet changing circumstances of planning, decision making and control. Some of the changes of recent years, to which management accounting practices have been adapted, are:

- The need to identify more closely the costs incurred in a business with the activities which drive those costs.
- The introduction of new technologies in which labour costs have diminished in relation to the cost of operating flexible computer-based operating systems.
- The reduction in inventories (stocks) of raw materials and finished goods as the business has linked up with suppliers and customers to ensure that items are delivered just at the time when they are needed.
- The emphasis on managing the quality of output and the cost of achieving that quality.
- Comparing the cost structures of the business with those of others in the industry.

These have led particular businesses to develop management accounting practices which suit their particular needs. Observers of those new practices, particularly academic writers, have identified new patterns of management accounting to which they have given titles such as:

- activity-based costing (see Chapter 4)
- just-in-time purchasing (see Chapter 18)
- cost of quality (see Chapter 19)
- benchmarking costs (see Chapter 16).

These approaches reflect dissatisfaction with the traditional approach in particular instances, but they do not indicate that the traditional approach has entirely failed. Consequently it remains necessary to study the traditional approach while having regard to continuing developments.

Real world case 2.3

In rural Wales it has been estimated that walkers spend £55m a year, which creates 3,000 full- and part-time jobs. Mountaineering in area such as Snowdonia adds £22m in terms of annual spending and another 1,200 jobs. Tourism and leisure is the fastest growing global industry and it accounts for 10% of the Welsh workforce. Professor Midmore said, 'The potential of walking as a means of rural economic regeneration is currently under exploited but could contribute significantly. An extension of rights of way would offer significant income and job creation potential.'

According to the professor's research, creating a job via the mechanism of improving and promoting facilities for walkers in Wales would be £433 per job in contrast to the direct and indirect costs of supporting a job in agriculture which is almost 10 times the cost at £4,227.

Source: *Western Mail*, 5 February 2005, 'Gower to feel the power of walkers', Robin Turner.

Discussion points

1 What might be the direct and indirect costs of supporting a job in agriculture?

2 Should this cost information be used as a basis for a decision to no longer support jobs in agriculture?

2.8 Cost coding

We will now look in more detail at an approach to cost recording that allows classification systems to be applied accurately and speedily.

Most costing systems are computerised. In a computerised system every cost item is given a **cost code** number which allows the cost to be traced through the computerised system. For these, the coding is critical to effective use of the cost information. Computers allow selective retrieval of information quickly, but only if the coding is correctly designed to suit the needs of the organisation.

A cost code must be unique to the cost which it identifies. The code should be as short as possible and it is preferable to have a code structure which creates consistent images in the mind of the user. The code may be entirely numerical or may have a mixture of letters and numbers (an *alphanumeric* code).

Definition

A **cost code** is a system of letters and/or numbers designed to give a series of unique labels which help in classification and analysis of cost information.

The design of the coding system and the assignment of code numbers should be carried out centrally so that the system is consistent throughout the organisation. The code system may have built into it the structure of the organisation, so that the code starts by specifying a major unit of the organisation and gradually narrows down to a particular cost in a particular location. Here is Fiona McTaggart to explain a cost coding system she has recently designed.

FIONA: *This company, producing and selling books, has 15 different departments. Within each department there are up to six cost centres. There are three different types of book – reference, academic and leisure. The list of costs to be coded contains 350 items, down to detail such as bindings purchased for special strength in reference works.*

The coding is based on a six-digit alphanumeric code. The department is represented by the first digit of the code, taking one of the letters A to Z (except that the company decided not to use letters I and O because of the confusion with numerical digits). Each cost centre has a letter code, which appears in the second position. (Again the letters I and O are not used.) The next digit is the letter R, A or L depending on whether the book is reference, academic or leisure. The last three digits are numbers taken from a cost code list which covers all 350 items but which could in principle expand up to 999 items in total. Within those three digits, there is further grouping of costs by code – for example, 100 to 199 are reserved for fixed asset items; 200 to 399 are various types of material cost; 400 to 599 are various types of labour cost; 600 to 899 are a whole range of production overhead costs; and 900 to 999 are administration and selling costs.

So, under code number HCA246, it would be possible to find the cost of paper used in printing an academic textbook on the new printing machine. Working backwards through the code, item 246 is paper, letter A is an academic book, letter C denotes the new printing machine (which is itself a cost centre) and letter H indicates the printing department.

Activity 2.5

Create a six-digit coding system which would allow you to classify all the items of expenditure you make in a year. (You will need to write down the items of expenditure first of all and then look for patterns which could be represented in a code.) To test your code, ask a friend to write down three transactions, converting them to code. Then use your knowledge of the code to tell your friend what the three transactions were.

2.9 Cost selection and reporting

Once the costs have been coded, a computerised accounting system can be programmed to retrieve the costs in a systematic manner for reporting purposes. The code structure must include alphanumeric characters that cover each of the purposes for which cost is required.

The code structure outlined by Fiona McTaggart above would allow classification of cost by reference to items of output and would allow classification of cost by reference to **cost centre**. This is only one of the units into which an organisation is subdivided for cost collection purposes. Two others are a **profit centre** and an **investment centre**. The chapter ends with definitions of the following terms that will be encountered in subsequent chapters in relation to cost selection and reporting: cost centre, profit centre and investment centre.

2.9.1 Cost centre

A **cost centre** is a unit of the organisation in respect of which a manager is responsible for costs under his or her control. A cost centre could be a location (e.g. a department) or a function (e.g. the manufacture of a product), or it could even be a production machine or group of similar machines. One essential feature of a cost centre is that it must be a homogeneous unit carrying out a single form of activity. A second essential feature is that it must correspond to an identifiable managerial responsibility.

Identification of a cost centre with managerial responsibility leads to a further type of cost classification, namely **controllable costs** and **non-controllable costs**. Costs allocated to a cost centre should be classified according to whether they are controllable or non-controllable by the manager of that cost centre.

Definitions

A **cost centre** is a unit of the organisation in respect of which a manager is responsible for costs under his or her control.

A **controllable cost** is one which is capable of being managed by the person responsible for the cost centre, profit centre or investment centre to which the cost is reported.

2.9.2 Profit centre

A **profit centre** is a unit of the organisation in respect of which a manager is responsible for revenue as well as costs. In practice an operating division would be a profit centre if it produced output whose selling price could be determined in some manner. The selling price could be based on an internal transfer between departments at an agreed price. It would not necessarily require a sale to a third party outside the business entity.

A profit centre is similar to a cost centre in that it must relate to an area of managerial responsibility, although the activity may be less homogeneous than that of a cost centre. The profit centre, though, is likely to contain more than one cost centre.

Definition

A **profit centre** is a unit of the organisation in respect of which a manager is responsible for revenue as well as costs.

2.9.3   Investment centre

An **investment centre** is a unit of the organisation in respect of which a manager is responsible for **capital investment** decisions as well as revenue and costs. These decisions could be related to such matters as purchase and disposal of equipment or acquisition of premises. The investment centre will be undertaking business activity in such a way that it will probably carry out an operation which is significant to the overall profit-earning capacity of the organisation. As is the case with a profit centre, the investment centre must relate to an area of managerial responsibility, but the activities of the investment centre need not be homogeneous. There will probably be a number of cost centres and profit centres *within* the investment centre.

Definition
> An **investment centre** is a unit of the organisation in respect of which a manager is responsible for capital investment decisions as well as revenue and costs.

2.10   Summary

Key themes in this chapter are:

- Costs may be classified using one or more of the following pairs of definitions
  - **Fixed/variable costs**
  - **Direct/indirect costs**
  - **Product/period costs**
- The choice of cost classification should be matched to the management function of planning, decision making or control.
- **Cost coding** is essential to make the cost classification system operational in a computer-based recording system.
- Cost classification must be relevant to the responsibility level for which the costs are reported, which may be a cost centre, a profit centre or an investment centre.

The chapter has set out the basic terminology of cost classification to be used throughout the book. In later chapters you will meet more detailed classifications such as controllable/non-controllable and avoidable/unavoidable in Chapter 16.

References and further reading

The following references are provided so that you may delve more deeply into any of the cost aspects outlined in this chapter. You should, however, be aware that there is no standard terminology in the field of management accounting, so every author will have a slightly different form of wording to define a given concept.

CIMA (2000) *Management Accounting Official Terminology*, CIMA Publishing.

Innes, J. (ed.) (2004) *The Handbook of Management Accounting*, 3rd edn, CIMA Publishing.

QUESTIONS

The Questions section of each chapter has three types of question. 'Test your understanding' questions to help you review your reading are in the 'A' series of questions. You will find the answers to these by reading and thinking about the material in the text book. 'Application' questions to test your ability to apply technical skills are in the 'B' series of questions. Questions requiring you to show skills in problem solving and evaluation are in the 'C' series of questions. The symbol [S] indicates that a solution is available at the end of the book.

A Test your understanding

A2.1 Explain what is meant by 'cost' (section 2.1).

A2.2 Explain the meaning of 'activity' and 'output' (section 2.3).

A2.3 [S] For each of the following cost classification terms, give a definition and give one example of how the definition applies in practice to a person providing car repairs from a rented garage:
(a) variable cost (section 2.4.1);
(b) fixed cost (section 2.4.2);
(c) semi-variable cost (section 2.4.3);
(d) step cost (section 2.4.4);
(e) direct cost (section 2.5);
(f) indirect cost (section 2.5);
(g) product cost (section 2.6); and
(h) period cost (section 2.6).

A2.4 [S] Explain how each of the following cost items could be classified under more than one of the headings given in question A2.3:
(a) raw materials to be used in production;
(b) subcontracted labour in a special contract; and
(c) rent of a warehouse for one year to allow temporary expansion of output.

A2.5 Classify each of the following as being primarily a fixed cost or a variable cost, and, if necessary, explain why you think such a classification would be difficult without more information being provided:
(a) direct materials;
(b) factory insurance;
(c) production manager's salary;
(d) advertising of the product;
(e) direct labour;
(f) indirect labour;
(g) depreciation of machinery;
(h) lubricants for machines;
(i) payment of a licence fee for the right to exclusive manufacture; and
(j) canteen manager's salary.

A2.6 What are the component costs of the total cost of production (section 2.5)?

A2.7 State the cost headings which are combined to give each of the following (section 2.6):
(a) prime cost;
(b) production overhead cost;
(c) total product cost.

A2.8 Explain how cost classification must be matched to the purpose of planning, decision making or control (section 2.7).

A2.9 How does cost classification vary to meet particular circumstances (section 2.7.4)?

A2.10 Explain the importance of an unambiguous system of cost coding (section 2.8).

A2.11 What are:
(a) a cost centre (section 2.9.1);
(b) a profit centre (section 2.9.2);
(c) an investment centre (section 2.9.3)?

B	Application

B2.1
Give an example of a management planning question for which it would be useful to classify costs as fixed and variable.

B2.2
Give an example of a management planning question for which it would be useful to classify costs as direct and indirect.

B2.3
Give an example of a management control question for which it would be useful to classify costs as direct and indirect.

B2.4
Give an example of a management control question for which it would be useful to classify costs as period and product costs.

B2.5 [S]
(a) Identify the cost behaviour in each of the following tables as:
(i)   fixed cost; or
(ii) variable cost; or
(iii) semi-variable cost.
(b) Draw a graph for each table to illustrate the cost behaviour.

Cost X

Output (units)	100	200	300	400	500
Total cost (£)	600	600	600	600	600
Unit cost (£)	6.00	3.00	2.00	1.50	1.20

Cost Y

Output (units)	100	200	300	400	500
Total cost (£)	300	600	900	1,200	1,500
Unit cost (£)	3.00	3.00	3.00	3.00	3.00

Cost Z

Output (units)	100	200	300	400	500
Total cost (£)	660	720	780	840	900
Unit cost (£)	6.60	3.60	2.60	2.10	1.80

B2.6 [S]
Oven Pies Ltd plans to buy a delivery van to distribute pies from the bakery to various neighbourhood shops. It will use the van for three years. The expected costs are as follows:

	£
New van	15,000
Trade-in price after 3 years	600
Service costs (every 6 months)	450
Spare parts, per 10,000 miles	360
Four new tyres, every 15,000 miles	1,200
Vehicle licence and insurance, per year	800
Fuel, per litre*	0.70

*Fuel consumption is 1 litre every five miles.

(a) Prepare a table of costs for mileages of 5,000, 10,000, 15,000, 20,000 and 30,000 miles per annum, distinguishing variable costs from fixed costs.
(b) Draw a graph showing variable cost, fixed cost and total cost.
(c) Calculate the average cost per mile at each of the mileages set out in (a).
(d) Write a short commentary on the behaviour of costs as annual mileage increases.

B2.7 [S]

During the month of May, 4,000 metal towel rails were produced and 3,500 were sold. There had been none in store at the start of the month. There were no inventories (stocks) of raw materials at either the start or end of the period. Costs incurred during May in respect of towel rails were as follows:

	£
Metal piping	12,000
Wages to welders and painters	9,000
Supplies for welding	1,400
Advertising campaign	2,000
Production manager's salary	1,800
Accounts department computer costs for dealing with production records	1,200

(a) Classify the list of costs set out above into product costs and period costs.
(b) Explain how you would value inventory (stock) held at the end of the month.

C Problem solving and evaluation

C2.1

Supermarket checkout operators are paid a weekly wage plus overtime at an hourly rate. One operator has recently resigned from work. The supermarket manager has been asked whether the direct costs of the supermarket operation could be controlled within the annual target by not filling the vacancy created. What should be the reply?

C2.2

Tots Ltd manufactures babies' play suits for sale to retail stores. All play suits are of the same design. There are two departments: the cutting department and the machining department. You are asked to classify the costs listed below under the following headings:

(a) Direct costs for the cutting department.
(b) Direct costs for the machining department.
(c) Indirect costs for the cutting department.
(d) Indirect costs for the machining department.
(e) Direct costs for the play suits.
(f) Indirect costs for the play suits.

List of costs

(i) towelling materials purchased for making the play suits;
(ii) reels of cotton purchased for machining;
(iii) pop-fasteners for insertion in the play suits;
(iv) wages paid to employees in the cutting department;
(v) wages paid to employees in the machining department;
(vi) salaries paid to the production supervisors;
(vii) oil for machines in the machining department;
(viii) rent paid for factory building;
(ix) depreciation of cutting equipment;
(x) depreciation of machines for sewing suits;
(xi) cost of providing canteen facilities for all staff.

Case studies

Real world cases

Prepare short answers to Case studies 2.1, 2.2 and 2.3.

Case 2.4 (group case study)

You are the management team in a business which makes self-assembly kitchen units and sells them to large do-it-yourself stores. One person should take on the role of the financial controller but the rest of the team may take any managerial roles they choose. Each manager will have responsibility for a cost centre. The group should decide, at the outset, on the name and purpose of each cost centre.

In stage 1 of the team exercise, each manager should write down the name of the cost centre and a list of the costs for which the manager expects to have responsibility. A copy of the cost centre name and the list of costs should be supplied to each member of the team.

In stage 2, each manager should separately write down his or her requirements from a company-wide cost coding system, yet to be designed, which has been specified in outline as having six alphanumeric characters. Each manager should also make a note of any costs which are shared with another manager or managers.

While the managers are carrying out the second stage, the financial controller should prepare a cost coding system which would meet the needs as specified on the lists of costs provided by each manager from stage 1.

In stage 3, the group should come together for a management meeting at which the financial controller will provide his or her cost coding system and each manager will respond with his or her ideas. If possible, a mutually agreed solution should be found but, at the very least, the group should identify the areas where further negotiation will be required. Finally, the group should make a five-minute presentation to the class describing the negotiations on the coding system and commenting on the practical problems of such negotiation.

Case 2.5 (group case study)

The group is the management team of a supermarket chain operating ten shops in out-of-town locations. Each member of the group should choose a management role, one of which must be the financial controller. Work together to prepare a proposal for establishing one profit centre, together with three cost centres within the profit centre for which each manager will be responsible, writing a definition of the responsibilities of each profit centre and cost centre.

Then work together further to produce a list of costs for each cost centre, in a table as follows:

Type of cost	Fixed/variable cost	Direct/indirect for the cost centre	Product/period cost

Set out *one* question relating to planning, *one* question relating to control and *one* question relating to decision making. Explain how the table of cost classification will help answer each of these questions.

Chapter 3

Materials and labour costs

This case study shows a typical situation in which management accounting can be helpful. Read the case study now, but only attempt the discussion points after you have finished studying the chapter.

Company buyers across Europe aim to cut the cost of procuring raw materials, goods and services this year by 13%, the highest amount in four years. The aggressive target coincides with the arrival of the purchasing manager – once seen as an administrative function – at the finance director's right hand side. But many of the 225 purchasing heads from financial services and manufacturing companies responding to an annual survey by software company Ariba admitted they had little idea what was being spent by other departments. For instance, 37% said they could account for less than 10% of the amount that their companies spent on services. Instead, to hit their cost saving targets, more buyers than ever said they will rationalise their supplier bases and pressurise those left to deliver more cheaply. They would continue to renegotiate contracts despite admitting that average year-on-year savings from contracted suppliers had fallen from 10% to 7% in the past year, the growing use of non-contracted suppliers based on low-cost countries apparently eroding the previously wide price difference between the two.

Source: *Daily Telegraph*, 24 February 2005, Business2jobs, p. 1, 'Buyers resolve to slash costs'.

Discussion points

1 What is the role of the purchasing manager?

2 What are the limitations of forcing cost savings onto suppliers rather than looking to internal improvements?

Contents

Learning outcomes

After reading this chapter you should be able to:

- Explain how materials costs form part of the total product cost.

- Explain the process of controlling and recording costs of materials.

- Explain the FIFO and LIFO approach to inventory valuation (stock valuation).

- Explain the process of controlling and recording costs of labour.

- Describe and discuss examples of research into management of materials and labour costs.

3.1 Introduction

Some businesses *manufacture* goods, while others perform a *service*. In the UK economy some 75% of gross domestic product (output) is based on service sector companies. The remaining 25% is mainly based on manufacturing. Some businesses manufacture goods, while others perform a service. The service sector is heavily reliant on labour resources. The public sector (health service, education, national and local government departments) is also heavily dependent on labour resources.

Whatever the nature of the business, all will at some stage use materials, employ labour and incur overhead costs. In this chapter you will learn about procedures for recording the costs of materials and costs of labour, and be aware of some of the problems which are encountered. Overhead costs are dealt with in Chapter 4.

A statement of the cost of a unit of output provides a useful starting point for this chapter in setting out a list of items to be explained in more detail (*see* Exhibit 3.1). When the unit of output represents a product or service for a customer the calculation shown in Exhibit 3.1 is called a **job cost**.

Exhibit 3.1
Statement of cost of a unit of output

	£	£
Direct materials		xxx
Direct labour		xxx
Other direct costs		xxx
Prime cost		xxx
Indirect materials	xxx	
Indirect labour	xxx	
Other indirect costs	xxx	
Production overhead		xxx
Total product cost		xxx

Materials and labour are part of the product cost (where products may be goods or services). The direct materials and direct labour are part of the prime cost. The indirect materials and indirect labour are part of the production overhead costs.

Definition

> **Prime cost** is the cost of direct materials, direct labour and other direct costs of production.

Direct and indirect costs are defined in section 2.5. Some materials and labour costs are classified as direct because they can be identified with specific products or services. Some materials and labour costs are classified as indirect because they are spread across a range of products or services. These indirect costs have to be shared in some way across the products as part of the overhead costs. This will be explained in Chapter 4.

Section 3.2 of this chapter describes methods for recording and controlling the costs of materials. The nature of the materials, and the type of output of the enterprise, will lead to classification as direct or indirect costs of materials. Section 3.3 explains the problems of measuring the cost of production when prices of purchased materials are changing. Section 3.4 describes methods for recording and controlling the costs of labour. The nature of the work done, and the type of output of the enterprise, will lead to classification as direct or indirect costs of labour.

Look at some item in the room where you are sitting as you read this chapter (perhaps a table or a desk or a window). What words would you use to describe the cost of materials and labour used in producing that item (e.g. wood, plastic, work in assembly, running costs of workshop)? How would you start to measure the cost of materials and labour used in producing that item?

3.2 Accounting for materials costs

Exhibit 3.2 shows the sequence of **activities** which control the ordering, delivery and safe-keeping of materials, together with the subsequent payment to suppliers. Information that is useful for accounting purposes will be collected from the documentation that is created during these procedures.

Exhibit 3.2
Materials control procedures

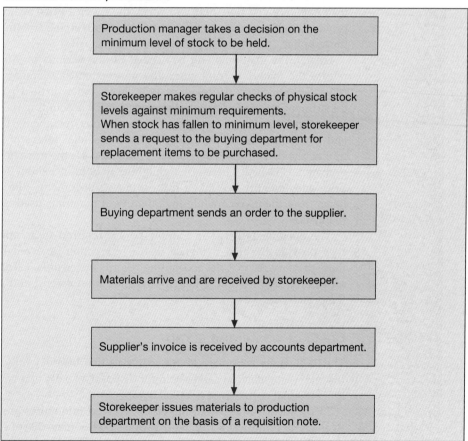

It is not difficult to see that with so many procedures involved there needs to be careful control over materials moving into, and out of, store. Each stage in the process requires a document as evidence that the transaction or process has been completed correctly. Every business has a different system of documentation which suits its particular needs. The following description is typical of the documents encountered in materials handling and control. Italics are used to indicate each document.

Materials handling and control documentation

When the storekeeper notes that the inventory has fallen to the minimum level, triggering a reorder requirement, a *purchase requisition* will be sent to the buying department. The buying department will have a list of items which the production manager wishes to have available in store and the quantity to be reordered. Provided the item is on that list, the buying department will send a *purchase order* to the supplier. In some cases the production manager may have issued a purchase requisition directly because a new item of materials, not previously held in store, is required. It is the responsibility of the buying department to choose a supplier who provides reliable service and a high-quality product at a competitive price. A copy of the purchase order will be sent to the storekeeper as notification that the materials have been ordered.

When the materials arrive from the supplier, the driver of the delivery vehicle will bring a *delivery note* which the storekeeper will sign, after checking against the quantities received and noting any discrepancies. The storekeeper will then prepare a *materials received note*, sending one copy to the buying department and another to the accounts department. Soon after the materials arrive, the accounts department will receive the *supplier's invoice*, showing the quantities of the materials supplied and the price charged for them. The accounts department will check the quantities against the materials received note and will check the invoice price against an agreed price list provided by the buying department. If all is correct, the accounts department will pay the supplier.

Finally, the materials will be needed by the various production departments. To release the materials from store, the production departments will produce a *stores requisition* which the storekeeper will check and will then pass on to the accounts department for use in keeping the management accounting records.

Exhibit 3.3 provides a summary of the various documents, their origin, destination and use for recording purposes. The two essential pieces of information for determining the cost of materials used in production are the price per unit and the quantity of materials issued. These are highlighted in bold in Exhibit 3.3. As you will see, the price and quantity are taken from different documents, the supplier's price being taken from the invoice while the quantity of materials used is taken from the stores requisition.

The documents listed in Exhibit 3.3 are referred to as **primary records** because they provide the first evidence that a transaction or event has taken place. From these primary records the accounting records are created. Clearly, the accuracy of the accounting information is heavily dependent on careful and accurate processing of the primary records.

Costs of waste and scrap

The term **waste** is applied to any materials that have no value, whatever the reason. If some waste material can be sold for disposal, usually at a very low price in relation to its original cost, then it is called **scrap**.

In the ideal situation, all materials received into stores are issued to production. Real life is not always like that, because stores may disappear before they have a chance to be used in the production process. The disappearance may be caused by deterioration or damage in store, the materials may become obsolete or unsuitable for use in production or they may be stolen. Sometimes materials may appear to have gone missing when in reality it is the accounting records which are incorrect because a stores requisition note has been lost or an item has been allocated to the wrong **job cost record**, or perhaps there is a calculation error on a stores list. It is always worthwhile to check the accuracy of the accounting records before assuming that materials have disappeared.

Exhibit 3.3
Documentation in materials control procedures

Document	Origin	Destination	Use
Purchase requisition	Storekeeper or production manager	Buying department	Authority for purchase of materials from supplier
Purchase order	Buying department	1 Supplier 2 Storekeeper	Authority to supply materials Indication that materials will arrive
Delivery note	Delivery driver	Storekeeper	Check on quantity received, in good state
Materials received note	Storekeeper	1 Buying department 2 Accounts department	Confirmation that buying process is complete Evidence of quantities for checking against invoice
Supplier's invoice	Supplier	Accounts department	Shows quantities received and **unit price**
Stores requisition	Production departments	1 Storekeeper 2 Accounts department	Authority to release materials from store Record of **quantities used** in production

For the management accountant the loss of materials creates another cost problem. The cost must be charged somewhere in the system but it cannot appear as a direct cost because the materials never reached the production department. The cost of waste therefore has to be noted as a separate indirect materials cost, to be spread over the cost of all products. If any cash can be recovered by selling for scrap any unwanted obsolete or damaged materials, then the proceeds of sale of scrap may be recorded as reducing the overall cost of wastage. Examples of waste and scrap are shown in Exhibit 3.4.

Exhibit 3.4
Waste and scrap

(a) *Waste*
An advertising agency has 10,000 leaflets to distribute. Envelopes cost 3 pence each. The postal franking machine is faulty and damages 100 envelopes which have to be replaced. The total cost of envelopes used is 10,100 at 3p = £303. The cost of the wastage is 100 envelopes at 3p = £3. The total cost of envelopes is 3.03 pence per leaflet distributed. The cost of waste has been treated as an indirect cost that is spread over the cost of all the service provided.

(b) *Scrap*
A toy manufacturer makes model cars by pressing metal. In one batch, sufficient metal is obtained to manufacture 60 cars. The metal costs £600, or £10 per car. A fault in the manu-facturing process damages 10 cars. These have to be sold for scrap, bringing a total of £30. The cost of each car that is available for sale is as follows:

	£
	£
Cost of material	600
Less cost of scrap	(30)
Net cost	570
Number of good cars is 50	50 cars
Cost per car £570/50	£11.40

3.2.3 Cost classification and materials costs

The cost classification system is required to show whether costs are direct or indirect costs and whether they are fixed or variable costs.

How are direct and indirect materials costs distinguished?

The earlier description of materials costing procedures has shown how multiplying unit price by the quantity of materials used will give a measure of cost, although there may need to be a choice of unit price to be applied (*see* section 3.3). Materials issued to production are usually made available on the basis of a stores requisition, so there should be no problem in identifying direct materials costs for the job in question.

Wherever possible, it is preferable to record materials costs as direct costs, identified with the job. On the other hand, the cost of spending time on keeping records must be weighed against more productive uses of that time.

Some materials costs may be spread over a range of products and activities, each of which must take a share. These are the indirect costs. The case of wastage occurring before the materials are issued to production has already been discussed. Other examples would include transportation costs and all the costs of receiving, issuing and handling stores (such as the storekeeper's wages).

How are fixed and variable materials costs distinguished?

Most materials costs will be variable costs, irrespective of whether they are direct or indirect so far as the job is concerned. If output is not being achieved, then materials will not be used and will be held in store for use in a future period.

To be a fixed cost, the materials would have to be required for use in a period irrespective of whether or not production takes place. That is an unlikely situation in most business operations.

Activity 3.2

You have been employed as a storekeeper at a superstore selling vehicle accessories. Write down the main procedures you would carry out to ensure that:

- *the materials in store are held securely*
- *the accounting records of inventory are accurate and*
- *the materials are issued only to authorised persons.*

3.3 Costs when input prices are changing

One problem faced by the accounts department is that suppliers change their prices from time to time. Materials held in store may have arrived at different times and at different unit prices. How does the accounts department decide on the unit price to be charged to each job when all the materials look the same once they are taken into store? In some cases it may be possible to label the materials as they arrive so that they can be identified with the appropriate unit price. That is a very time-consuming process and would only be used for high-value, low-volume items of materials. In other cases a convenient method is needed which gives an answer which is useful and approximately close to the true price of the units used. Yet another approach is to ignore the effect of changing prices by using a standard cost established for the entire accounting period. (Standard costs are explained in Chapter 15.)

3.3.1   Method of calculation

The usual procedure in the UK is to assume, for pricing purposes, that the first materials to arrive in store are the first ones to leave. This is usually abbreviated to 'FIFO' (first-in-first-out). Some businesses prefer to use the average cost of all items in inventory as the basis for pricing issues. Another possibility is to assume that the last materials to arrive in store are the first ones to leave. This is not used frequently in the UK because it is not accepted by the tax authorities. However, for management purposes, the best method for the purpose should be applied, irrespective of legal requirements. Management accounting escapes the constraints of statute law, accounting standards and tax law which restrict practice in financial accounting.

Exhibit 3.5 compares three options – First-In-First-Out (FIFO), Last-In-First-Out (LIFO) and Average cost. In each case, Exhibit 3.5 takes a very simple approach, not complicated by having inventory at the start of the period. In real life the calculations can be much more tricky.

3.3.2   Approximation when dates are not recorded

In business there may not be time to keep the detailed records shown in the calculations in Exhibit 3.5. In such cases the sales volume is known in total but the dates of sale are not recorded. The calculation then uses the best approximation available,

Exhibit 3.5
Pricing the issue of goods to production

There are three parts to this illustration. Panel (a) contains a table setting out the data to be used in the calculation. Panel (b) defines the three bases of calculation. Panel (c) uses the data from panel (a) to illustrate each of the three bases.

(a) Data

Date	Received	Unit price	Price paid	Issued to production
	units	£	£	units
1 June	100	20	2,000	–
20 June	50	22	1,100	–
24 June	–	–	–	60
28 June	–	–	–	70
Total	150		3,100	130

(b) Bases of calculation

First-In-First-Out (FIFO)
Assume that the goods which arrived first are issued first

Last-In-First-Out (LIFO)
Assume that the goods which arrived last are issued first

Average cost
Assume that all goods are issued at the average price of the inventory held

Exhibit 3.5 **continued**

(c) Calculations

Basis	Date	Quantity and unit price	Issued to production	Held in inventory	Total
FIFO			£	£	£
	24 June	60 units at £20	1,200		
	28 June	40 units at £20 30 units at £22	1,460		
	30 June	20 units at £22		440	
Total			2,660	440	3,100
LIFO			£	£	£
	24 June	50 units at £22 10 units at £20	1,300		
	28 June	70 units at £20	1,400		
	30 June	20 units at £20		400	
Total			2,700	400	3,100
Average			£	£	£
	24 June	60 units at *£20.67	1,240		
	28 June	70 units at *£20.67	1,447		
	30 June	20 units at *£20.67		413	
Total			2,687	413	3,100

*Weighted average [(100 × 20) + (50 × 22)]/150 = £20.67

which usually means working through the costs from the oldest date, for FIFO, or the most recent date, for LIFO, without attempting to match the various batches bought and sold during the year.

3.3.3 Choice of FIFO, LIFO or average cost

Look at panel (c) of Exhibit 3.5 and compare it with panel (a) of that exhibit. You will see from panel (a) that the total amount spent on materials during the month was £3,100. You will see from panel (c) that the total of the cost of goods issued to production, plus the cost of unsold goods, is always £3,100 irrespective of which approach is taken. All that differs is the allocation between goods used in production and goods remaining unsold. Cost can never be gained or lost in total because of a particular allocation process, provided the process is used consistently from time to time. The FIFO approach suffers the disadvantage of matching outdated costs against current revenue. The LIFO approach improves on FIFO by matching the most recent costs against revenue, but at the expense of an inventory value which becomes increasingly out of date. The average cost lies between the two and becomes more intricate to recalculate as more items come into inventory. In practice the choice for internal reporting in management accounting is a matter of finding the best method for the purpose.

There is an effect on profit of the year which may influence management choice. When prices are rising and inventory volumes are steady or increasing, FIFO gives a lower cost of sales and so a higher profit than LIFO. If there were no regulations, companies that wished to show higher profits (perhaps to impress the stock market) might prefer FIFO. Companies that wished to show lower profits (perhaps to reduce tax bills) might prefer LIFO. In the UK, HM Revenue and Customs (tax authorities) do not permit LIFO. Accounting standards point towards FIFO.

3.4 Accounting for labour costs

The cost of any resource used in a business is the product of the amount of resource used and the price per unit of the resource. For the resource of labour, the amount of resource is usually measured in terms of hours worked and the price is usually expressed as a rate paid per hour.

3.4.1 Types of pay scheme

The first problem which the management accountant meets in dealing with labour costs is that different employees are on different pay schemes and there are additional costs imposed on the employer through having employees.

- Some employees receive a *monthly salary*, paid at the end of the month worked. They are expected to work whatever number of hours is necessary to complete the tasks assigned to them. This type of remuneration is most commonly found in the case of administrative staff where the emphasis is on undertaking tasks which are necessary to the overall duties and responsibilities of the post.
- Other employees receive a basic *salary per week*, or *per month*, which is augmented by extra payments depending on output levels or targets achieved. This type of pay scheme has a 'loyalty' element in the basic salary, together with a reward for effort in the output-related extra payments.
- Some employees may be paid an *hourly rate* based on actual hours worked, receiving no payment where no hours are worked. Finally, there may be some employees paid on a piecework basis, receiving a fixed amount for every item produced, regardless of time taken.
- *Benefits in kind.* There may be labour costs of the business which are not paid to the employee in the form of wages or salary. These would include the provision of a car, free medical insurance, clothing allowances, rent allowances, relocation and disruption payments, inducements to join the company and lump sum payments on leaving the company.
- There are also the *employer's labour costs*, such as contributions to national insurance, which are part of the total labour cost as far as the business is concerned.

3.4.2 Incentive pay schemes

There is a view that linking pay to performance will encourage staff to work harder. In a manufacturing-based industry, rewards can be given in pay to reflect the volume of output from each employee. This is called *performance-related pay* ('PRP'). In a service-based industry, and in the public sector, it is more difficult to relate pay to performance. Very often the quality of service is more important than the quantity of service. PRP is used when it is relatively easy to measure output from an individual

Real world case 3.2

Milk producers have been underestimating the real costs of production by more than 20%, according to an industry working party representing production and recording interests.

Initiated by the Royal Association of British Dairy Farmers (RABDF), following industry-wide consultation in August last year, a working party comprising members of ADAS, Promar, the John Easterbrooke Partnership and practical dairy farmers was established to investigate the subject.

One of the main objectives of the group at the start was to ensure that everyone in the dairy food chain understood how much it really costs to produce a litre of milk – given the misinformation prevalent at the time, that producers could make a profit and have enough to reinvest even at a milk price of 16p/litre.

'Having succeeded in drawing the various organisations together for round table discussions, it soon became apparent that fixed costs and farm overheads were problem areas. But the key element was that in most recording schemes' figures the farmer's own remuneration was either underestimated or excluded altogether!' said Tim Brigstocke, RABDF chairman and leader of the working party.

'With margins continuing to be low, or in many cases negative, it is essential that producers don't kid themselves any longer that they can exist and grow at a milk price of 16p or even 18p/litre.

'According to our study, the true costs of production could be as high as 23p/litre, taking account of the farmer's remuneration, family labour costs, pensions and staff development. It is our view that these costs have been underestimated routinely by at least 20% for many years and the time is well overdue for the real situation to be broadcast far and wide.

'It would undoubtedly be in the best interests of the British dairy farmer if all milk recording bodies and all companies involved in dairy management were to adopt the new RABDF guidelines whenever they publish information on the costs of milk production. The guidelines have already been accepted by many of the key companies in this field and the signs are good for industry-wide acceptance.'

Source: Royal Association of British Dairy Farmers, www.rabdf.co.uk (2005)

Discussion points

1 Why is it difficult for self-employed persons to estimate the true cost of labour for their business?

2 How can self-employed persons estimate a labour cost for their work?

employee. *Merit pay* is a form of reward that is based on a judgement of the quality of the employee's work. Merit pay is used when it is more difficult to measure the output of an individual employee. There is no reason why performance-related pay and merit pay should not be used in the public sector, but research has indicated they are less prevalent.[1]

3.4.3 Determining the labour cost in an item of output

The differences outlined in sections 3.4.1 and 3.4.2 all add to the problems of the management accountant in converting the variety of schemes to a uniform basis for costing purposes. Usually, calculating a rate per hour is sufficient to provide such a uniform basis, provided the number of hours worked is known. The cost of labour used on any job may then be determined by multiplying the hourly cost by the number of hours worked.

3.4.4 Cost classification and labour costs

The classification system is concerned with whether costs are direct or indirect and whether they are fixed or variable.

How are direct and indirect labour costs distinguished?

Multiplying unit cost by the number of hours worked is fine provided there is a time record and that time can be allocated exclusively to one product at a time. In some businesses it might be feasible to keep track of specialist labour time spent on each product. This part of the labour cost is regarded as the **direct labour cost**.

Some labour costs may never be allocated directly to a specific job because they are spread over a range of jobs and activities, each of which must take a share (e.g. a supervisor's salary, a cleaner's wages or non-productive time when skilled employees are not able to work because equipment needs attention). This part of the labour cost is called **indirect labour cost**. Indirect labour costs also include holiday pay, bonus payments and overtime pay. That gives the management accountant a further problem – deciding on a fair basis for apportionment of indirect labour costs. Apportionment of indirect costs will be dealt with in Chapter 4 on production overhead costs.

How are fixed and variable labour costs distinguished?

One quite difficult question with labour costs is to decide whether they are fixed or variable costs. If the employee is on a contract which provides a fixed basic salary, then the total salary is a fixed cost for the organisation. The employee will then spend time on producing output and that amount of time will vary depending on the level of output. Thus the direct labour cost attributable to that employee will be a variable cost, depending on level of output. The remaining time, when the employee is not producing output, will be classed as an indirect cost of non-productive labour.

3.4.5 Recording labour costs

The system for recording labour costs must be capable of dealing with the payroll aspects (keeping track of how much is paid to each employee) and with the cost allocation aspect of tracing those payroll costs, together with other labour costs, to the products of the business. That in turn requires a careful recording of the total time worked by the employees each week, analysed into the time spent on each product and the amount of non-productive time.

Direct labour costs will be calculated using hours worked and the hourly rate for each employee. The hours worked will be collected from employee time sheets which show the time spent on each product unit. Hourly rates for each employee will be available from personnel records, based on the cost of employing that particular person.

In practice, it is likely that costing records will be kept on computer, with employees entering data on-line.

Activity 3.3

You are employed in the personnel department of a large organisation. Explain how the records kept by the personnel department would be useful to the accounting department in preparing the monthly payroll.

Real world case 3.3

Diageo, the British drinks group, looked at 19 cities when planning to establish a European business service centre. It chose Budapest for its low costs, good language skills, convenient location and high-quality labour.

Three years later, the centre employs 270 people, speaking 21 languages, in financial and administrative jobs supporting Diageo operations in seven countries. Over the next year the group plans to expand the centre to 500 staff and provide services for several more countries.

. . . Diageo adds that quality is the key to keeping the centre in Hungary in the long run. The group estimates that annual operating costs in Budapest are $23,000 (£12,800) per person. That is less than half the $50,000 annual costs in Dublin – a location often favoured by multinationals before central Europe emerged as an offshore services centre – but costs in Bangalore are lower still, at $12,000. Hungary therefore has to offer higher-quality services than India to maintain its edge.

Source: *Financial Times*, 21 September 2004, p. 19, from 'Budapest, the next Bangalore? New EU members join the outsourcing race'.

Discussion points

1 How does outsourcing help to lower labour costs for UK companies?

2 What are the risks associated with outsourcing?

3.5 What the researchers have found

3.5.1 Outsourcing labour services

Langfield-Smith and Smith (2003) describe and analyse the outsourcing of information technology and telecommunications (IT&T) by an electricity supply business. The reason for outsourcing was to obtain the best quality of IT&T service through competitive tendering. This was thought likely to provide improvements over in-house provision. Initially the price charged for IT&T was based on direct costs, overhead and a profit margin. But after 18 months of operation the payment system was changed to one based on risks and rewards. Direct costs would be covered by the electricity supply company, to which bonuses would be added based on cost, quality and time. So the remuneration package looked very much like the kind of incentive scheme seen for employees inside a business. What this probably indicates is that labour requires incentive-based rewards, whether as employees or as independent contractors. The researchers interpreted the eventual success of the IT&T outsourcing as evidence of the importance of building a relationship of trust between the management of the electricity supply company and the management of the IT&T company. They concluded that trust could be developed in parallel with more stringent accounting controls, despite evidence to the contrary from other sources. It appears from this research that the management needed the formal mechanism of outsourcing to exercise control over a labour cost that could not be obtained by having the IT&T function provided by employees.

3.6 Summary

Key themes in this chapter are:

- **Total product cost** is defined as consisting of direct materials, direct labour and **production overhead cost**.

- **Prime cost of production** is the cost of direct materials, direct labour and other direct costs of production.

- The purchasing, storage and use of materials are controlled by documentation and processes that are designed to safeguard the assets and ensure the accuracy of recording systems.

- FIFO (first-in-first-out) and LIFO (last-in-first-out) are methods of pricing the issue of goods from inventory, and the valuation of inventory, in times when prices are changing.

- Accounting for materials is explained, highlighting the importance of documentation, the distinction between direct and indirect costs of materials and between fixed and variable costs of materials.

- The costs of **waste** and **scrap** are indirect costs that form part of the total production cost. Any cash received for scrap should be deducted from the cost of buying the materials.

- Labour costs are recorded and controlled in a way that ensures employees are paid correctly for work done and labour costs of activities are recorded accurately.

- Accounting for labour costs is explained, highlighting the distinction between direct and indirect labour costs and between fixed and variable costs of labour.

References and further reading

Burgess, S. and Metcalfe, P. (1999) 'The use of incentive schemes in the public and private sectors: evidence from British establishments', CMPO Working Paper Series No. 00/15.

Langfield-Smith, K. and Smith, D. (2003) 'Management control systems and trust in outsourcing relationships', *Management Accounting Research*, 14: 281–307.

QUESTIONS

The Questions section of each chapter has three types of question. 'Test your understanding' questions to help you review your reading are in the 'A' series of questions. You will find the answers to these by reading and thinking about the material in the text book. 'Application' questions to test your ability to apply technical skills are in the 'B' series of questions. Questions requiring you to show skills in problem solving and evaluation are in the 'C' series of questions. The symbol [S] indicates that a solution is available at the end of the book.

A Test your understanding

A3.1   What are the main items in a statement of the cost of production of an item of output (section 3.1)?

A3.2   How may a system of materials control procedures ensure accurate accounting information for job-costing purposes (section 3.2.1)?

A3.3 Which source documents should be used to create the accounting record for direct materials costs (section 3.2.1)?

A3.4 What are the problems of accounting for wastage and scrap (section 3.2.2)?

A3.5 How are direct and indirect materials costs distinguished (section 3.2.3)?

A3.6 How are fixed and variable materials costs distinguished (section 3.2.3)?

A3.7 What is meant by the term 'FIFO', when used in deciding on the cost price of goods issued to production (section 3.3)?

A3.8 What is meant by the term 'LIFO', when used in deciding on the cost price of goods issued to production (section 3.3)?

A3.9 What types of pay scheme may be found (section 3.4.1)?

A3.10 How are direct and indirect labour costs distinguished (section 3.4.4)?

A3.11 How are fixed and variable labour costs distinguished (section 3.4.4)?

A3.12 What conditions may help to make outsourcing of labour successful (section 3.5.1)?

B Application

B3.1 [S]

The following information was recorded during the month of May by the central warehouse of Stores Co. The warehouse issues goods to retail outlets owned by Stores Co. to allow the retail outlets to meet expected demand from customers. The record represents kitchen units, all of the same type.

Date	Received into store	Unit price	Price paid to supplier	Issued to retail outlets
	units	£	£	units
1 May	120	30	3,600	–
19 May	60	34	2,040	–
22 May	–	–	–	80
30 May	–	–	–	70
Total	180		5,640	150

Calculate (i) the cost of goods issued to retail stores during May and (ii) the cost value of goods held in the warehouse at the end of May, under each of:

(a) FIFO
(b) LIFO
(c) average cost.

B3.2 [S]

Explain which document you would expect to find in the records of Chocolate Ltd as evidence of each of the following transactions or events which took place during the month of June:

(a) Evidence that the buying department of Chocolate Ltd had authority to order new supplies of cocoa beans from a supplier.
(b) Evidence that the supplier had the authority to send cocoa beans to Chocolate Ltd.
(c) Evidence that the cocoa beans arrived at the stores of Chocolate Ltd in good condition and in the quantities expected.
(d) Evidence that the amount payable to the supplier is correct in quantities and prices.
(e) Evidence that the storekeeper of Chocolate Ltd had the authority to release cocoa beans to the production unit, for conversion to chocolate.

B3.3 [S]

The Electric Wiring Company employs staff to repair electrical equipment in customers' homes under maintenance contracts. Each job of work is the cost unit for which costs are recorded and monitored. Explain which of the following will be direct labour costs and which will be indirect labour costs for each cost unit:

(a) The hourly rate payable to an employee technician for hours worked on repairing electrical equipment for customers under maintenance contracts.

(b) The hourly rate payable to a cleaner who works in cleaning the head office premises.

(c) The annual salary paid to a supervisor who allocates work to technicians carrying out repair work for customers, and who also checks the quality of the completed work.

(d) The monthly allowance paid to technician employees for being available 'on call' for emergency repairs.

C Problem solving and evaluation

C3.1

You are the newly appointed secretary of a primary school employing 20 teachers and having 300 pupils. The head teacher has asked you to design a system for ordering books and stationery and controlling the issue of books and stationery to teachers. Make a list of the key features that you will recommend for the new system.

C3.2

You have been asked to plan the labour force for a job of work that will require the equivalent of five skilled workers for a period of 30 days. Within that period there is an expectation of 25 days of productive work and five days equivalent of non-productive work relating to rest periods and statutory holiday leave. You have only been able to find three workers of sufficient skill who will work full-time. There are two part-timers who together will cover the equivalent of one further full-time worker. You will need to hire agency staff on an hourly basis to make up the shortfall.

Explain the problems you will face in estimating the labour cost of the job.

Case studies

Real world cases

Write short answers to Case studies **3.1**, **3.2** and **3.3**.

Note

1. Burgess and Metcalfe (1999).

Chapter 4

Overhead costs

Real world case 4.1

This case study shows a typical situation in which management accounting can be helpful. Read the case study now but only attempt the discussion points after you have finished studying the chapter.

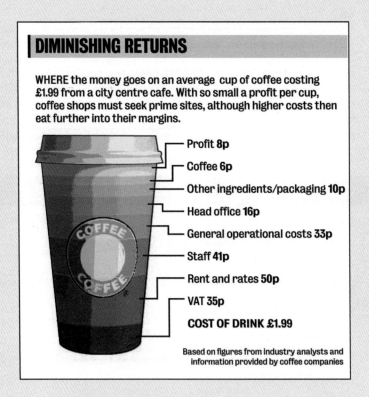

DIMINISHING RETURNS

WHERE the money goes on an average cup of coffee costing £1.99 from a city centre cafe. With so small a profit per cup, coffee shops must seek prime sites, although higher costs then eat further into their margins.

Profit **8p**

Coffee **6p**

Other ingredients/packaging **10p**

Head office **16p**

General operational costs **33p**

Staff **41p**

Rent and rates **50p**

VAT **35p**

COST OF DRINK **£1.99**

Based on figures from industry analysts and information provided by coffee companies

Source: *Scotland on Sunday*, 16 January 2005, p. 12, 'Why does your £2 latte cost such a lot?'.

Discussion points

1 What are the direct costs of this cup of coffee?

2 What are the indirect costs of this cup of coffee?

Contents

Learning outcomes

After reading this chapter you should be able to:

- State the main components of total product cost.

- Explain the traditional approach to allocating and apportioning production overheads to products.

- Explain how cost drivers may be used to allocate overhead costs in activity-based costing.

- Compare and contrast the traditional and activity-based methods of dealing with overhead costs.

- Describe and discuss examples of research into methods of overhead costing.

4.1 Introduction

This chapter begins by outlining traditional procedures for recording the costs of production overheads and indicates some of the problems that are encountered. Many of these procedures remain a cornerstone of present-day management accounting, but some management accountants have looked for new procedures. In particular **activity–based costing (ABC)** has been developed as a new way of recording overhead costs.

A statement of the cost of a unit of output is shown in Exhibit 4.1. It includes the costs of materials and labour, which have been explained and discussed in Chapter 3. This chapter explains how overhead costs are recorded and traced to the output of the organisation. Exhibit 4.2 summarises the way in which costs are traced to products. It relates to a cost centre where the output consists of three different products (goods or services).

Exhibit 4.1
Statement of cost of a production item

	£	£
Direct materials		xxx
Direct labour		xxx
Other direct costs		xxx
Prime cost		xxx
Indirect materials	xxx	
Indirect labour	xxx	
Other indirect costs	xxx	
Production overhead		xxx
Total product cost		xxx

Exhibit 4.2
Tracing costs of Products A, B and C in a single cost centre

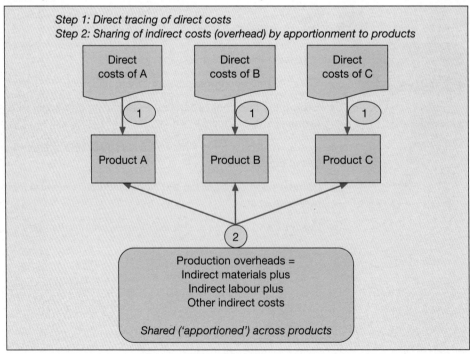

Step 1: Direct tracing of direct costs
Step 2: Sharing of indirect costs (overhead) by apportionment to products

Direct costs of A   Direct costs of B   Direct costs of C

1   1   1

Product A   Product B   Product C

2

Production overheads =
Indirect materials plus
Indirect labour plus
Other indirect costs

Shared ('apportioned') across products

The direct costs in Exhibit 4.2 consist of direct materials, direct labour and any other costs that are directly identifiable with a product. We know how much material is needed for the product, we know how much labour time is worked on the product and we know about any other costs related only to that product. So the arrows flowing downwards in Exhibit 4.2 show the direct costs of each product flowing directly to that product.

Some materials, some labour and some other costs are classified as indirect costs because they are spread across a range of products. These have to be shared in some way across the products. Exhibit 4.2 shows the overhead costs being apportioned ('shared') across products. One debate in management accounting focuses on how to carry out that process of **apportionment.** This chapter presents two approaches in that debate.

Section 4.2 brings together all the indirect costs of production and groups them under the heading production overhead cost. It describes the process of ensuring that overhead costs reach the products, using the **traditional** approach. Section 4.3 sets out an alternative to section 4.2 by sharing out the production overhead costs using an activity-based costing approach. Section 4.4 compares the traditional and the ABC approaches.

Activity 4.1

Think about a journey you have made on public transport. What are the labour costs of operating one journey? What overhead costs are incurred by the organisation providing the transport? How might you find out whether the fares charged to passengers reflect the cost of the transport service?

Real world case 4.2

The acquisition of the international yeast and bakers' ingredients business from Burns Philip was completed after the year end. The bakers' yeast business is market leader in North America, Latin America and Asia and is number 3 in Europe and will trade under the name AB Mauri. The market for bakers' yeast is growing at an overall 3-4% per annum, 1–2% in developed countries but much faster in developing countries such as China, where the growth rate is over 10%. It operates from 42 production sites in 24 countries. The main products of the bakery ingredients business are bread improvers, conditioners, mixes and fats and oils. Combined with Cereform (the group's existing bakery ingredients business), the new business will have coverage of all significant markets, unrivalled market access in developing markets, low cost distribution through sharing of overheads with yeast and leading technology for western style baking.

Source: Associated British Foods Annual Report 2004, p. 23.

Discussion points

1 Why is there a benefit in sharing overheads?

2 What types of overhead might be found in this business?

4.2 Production overheads: traditional approach

Production overheads were defined in Chapter 2 as comprising indirect materials, indirect labour and other indirect costs of production. Indirect materials and indirect labour are explained in Chapter 3. 'Other indirect costs' will include any item which relates to production and which is not a materials cost or a labour cost. The type of indirect cost depends on the nature of the business and, in particular, on whether it is a *manufacturing* business or a *service* business. Examples are:

- (In a manufacturing business): repair of machinery; rent of factory buildings; safety procedures.
- (In a service business): cost of transport to jobs; replacement of tools; protective clothing.

Whatever their nature, all the production overhead costs have to be **absorbed** ('soaked up') into the products.

Normally the management accountant has to devise a scheme of **allocation** and **apportionment**. There are some essential features for any successful scheme. It must be:

- fair to all parties involved in the process of allocation and apportionment
- representative of the benefit each party gains from the shared cost
- relatively quick to apply so that provision of information is not delayed
- understandable by all concerned.

This chapter will use arithmetically simple models for illustrative purposes, although the mechanism for apportionment ('sharing') does not have to be arithmetically simple provided a computer can be used.

The process described here has three stages:

1 allocating and apportioning indirect costs to cost centres;
2 apportioning service department costs over production cost centres;
3 absorbing costs into products.

Definitions

Allocate means to assign a whole item of cost, or of revenue, to a single cost unit, centre, account or time period.

Apportion means to spread costs over two or more cost units, centres, accounts or time periods. (It is referred to by some textbooks as 'indirect allocation'.)

Absorb means to attach overhead costs to products or services.

Allocation, apportionment and absorption in job costing:
- Direct materials are allocated to products.
- Direct labour costs are allocated to products.
- Indirect materials costs and indirect labour costs are allocated and apportioned to cost centres.
- Total indirect costs of service cost centres are apportioned over production cost centres.
- Total overhead costs of production cost centres are absorbed into products.[1]

Exhibit 4.3 provides a diagram to show the three stages in the flow of indirect costs. The calculations are explained in detail in section 4.2.5.

4.2.1 Allocating and apportioning indirect costs to cost centres

There are two main types of cost centre in any business, namely **service cost centres** and **production cost centres**. The production cost centres are those directly involved

Exhibit 4.3
Traditional approach to the flow of indirect costs

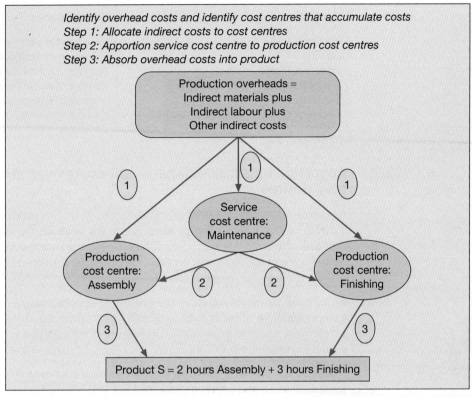

Identify overhead costs and identify cost centres that accumulate costs
Step 1: Allocate indirect costs to cost centres
Step 2: Apportion service cost centre to production cost centres
Step 3: Absorb overhead costs into product

Production overheads =
Indirect materials plus
Indirect labour plus
Other indirect costs

Service
cost centre:
Maintenance

Production
cost centre:
Assembly

Production
cost centre:
Finishing

Product S = 2 hours Assembly + 3 hours Finishing

in the production activity, with the output being either goods or services to customers. The service cost centres are *not* directly involved in the production activity but provide essential backup to the production activity. To sustain long-term profitability, the products of the business must sell at a price which makes a profit after covering the costs of both the service and the production cost centres.

The management accountant will first of all divide the overhead costs into two categories: those which may be allocated as a whole to each cost centre, and those which have to be apportioned (or shared) over a number of cost centres according to how the cost centres benefit from the cost incurred. Exhibit 4.4 sets out some common methods of apportionment where costs are regarded as indirect so far as each cost centre is concerned.

If the records were sufficiently detailed, then most of the costs in Exhibit 4.4 could be turned into items of cost which could be allocated as a whole to each cost centre, avoiding the need for apportionment. For example:

- electricity meters could be installed in each cost centre to measure directly the cost of heating and lighting
- employees could be given tickets for the canteen which could be collected and recorded for each cost centre
- the production supervisor could keep a diary of time spent in each cost centre; depreciation could be calculated for each machine
- the insurance company could be asked to quote a separate premium for each machine.

However, all these procedures would in themselves create a new cost of administration which the business might decide was too high a price to pay for a marginal improvement in the accuracy of allocation of costs.

Exhibit 4.4
Examples of methods of apportionment of costs over cost centres

Cost item	Method of apportionment over cost centres
Rent of building	Floor area of each cost centre
Lighting	Floor area of each cost centre
Power for machines	Number of machines in each cost centre
Production supervisor's salary	Number of employees in each cost centre
Canteen costs	Number of employees in each cost centre
Depreciation and insurance of machinery	Value of machinery in each cost centre

4.2.2 Apportioning service department costs over production cost centres

As explained earlier, service cost centres exist to *support* production but do not make a direct contribution to the product. Once the costs of the organisation have been channelled into the various cost centres, they must be apportioned from service cost centres over production cost centres. The essential features remain the same, namely that the method chosen must be:

- fair to all parties involved in the process of apportionment
- representative of the benefit each party gains from the shared cost
- relatively quick to apply so that provision of information is not delayed
- understandable by all concerned.

Exhibit 4.5 sets out the titles of some service cost centres and gives examples of some methods by which their costs could be apportioned over production cost centres.

Exhibit 4.5
Examples of methods of apportioning total costs of service cost centres across production cost centres

Service cost centre	Method of apportionment over production cost centres
Maintenance department	Number of machines in each cost centre
Employees' restaurant and coffee bar	Number of employees in each cost centre
Stores department	Total value of stores requisitions from each cost centre
Finished goods quality inspection	Value of goods produced by each cost centre
Safety inspectors	Number of employees in each cost centre

Where service departments provide services to each other as well as to the production departments, various methods are possible.

- The **step method** takes the service department with the largest overhead cost first and apportions it across all departments. The service department with the next largest overhead is then apportioned across all departments other than the one already dealt with.
- The **repeated distribution method** involves continuous reapportionment of service department costs across cost centres until the amount remaining in any service department is so small that it can be ignored.
- An algebraic method involves the use of simultaneous equations.

In many cases these give similar answers. The step method, which is the simplest, is illustrated in the following example.

Step method: example

The hospital manager estimates that the services of the wages department and the services of the computer department should be apportioned on the basis of the number of employees in each department. Information is shown in Exhibit 4.6.

Exhibit 4.6
Data for step apportionment of service department costs

	Surgical	Medical	Wages	Computing	Total
Staff numbers	8	4	3	2	
	£	£	£	£	£
Overheads	50,000	40,000	9,000	30,000	129,000

The information in Exhibit 4.6 looks problematic because the computing department provides a service to the wages department and the wages department provides a service to the computing department. A process for apportioning costs from one to the other could continue indefinitely in the absence of a rule to simplify matters. The step apportionment method provides this simplification by taking each department, one step at a time, and apportioning the costs of that department across the remaining departments. The method is shown in Exhibit 4.7.

- *Step 1*: The department with the highest cost, Computing, is apportioned first in the ratio 8:4:3 across the two 'production' cost centres and the remaining service cost centre.
- *Step 2*: The total overhead cost of the second service department, wages, is then apportioned across the two 'production' departments, surgical and medical, but *no* cost is apportioned back to computing.
- *Step 3*: Check the totals of the overhead costs in the two 'production' departments are the same as the totals of the costs at the start of the process.

Exhibit 4.7
Step apportionment of service cost centres

	Production cost centres		Service cost centres		
	Surgical	Medical	Wages	Computing	Total
Staff numbers	8	4	3	2	
	£	£	£	£	£
Overheads	50,000	40,000	9,000	30,000	129,000
Apportion computing 8 : 4 : 3	16,000	8,000	6,000	(30,000)	
Sub-total	66,000	48,000	15,000	–	129,000
Apportion wages 8 : 4	10,000	5,000	(15,000)		
Total	76,000	53,000	–		129,000

Repeated distribution method

Applying the repeated distribution method requires the costs of computing to be apportioned across surgical, medical and wages. Then the costs of wages are apportioned across surgical, medical and computing. This is repeated until the cost remaining in the service department cost centres is very low. For this example it requires seven apportionment calculations. The result is: Surgical £75,878 and Medical £53,122. This is a more accurate answer than that of the step method but the error level of the step method, as a percentage of the repeated distribution method, is 0.1% for Surgical and 0.2% for Medical. That seems sufficiently low to justify using the step method for practical purposes.

4.2.3   Absorbing overhead costs into products

You have now reached the final stage of the process where all the **overhead costs** are collected in the **production cost centres**, ready to be absorbed into products. The essential features, as before, are that the method must be:

- fair to all parties involved in the process of absorption
- representative of the benefit each party gains from the shared cost
- relatively quick to apply so that provision of information is not delayed
- understandable by all concerned.

To absorb a *fair share* of overhead into each product, the method must make use of the *best measure* of work done on a product. The best measure is usually labour hours or machine hours, depending on whether the production process is labour intensive or machine intensive.

Direct labour hours are frequently used because overhead cost is incurred when people are working. The longer they work, the more overhead is incurred. The overhead cost is expressed as '£s of overhead cost per direct labour hour'.

However, sometimes direct labour hours are not the best measure of work performed. In a machinery-intensive environment, machine hours may be preferred to labour hours as a basis for absorbing overhead. The overhead cost is expressed as '£s of overhead cost per machine hour'.

There are occasions when the direct labour hours worked on a job are not known because they are not recorded. In such circumstances an overhead cost *per £ of direct labour* could be applied but it has a disadvantage in that a change in the labour rate could affect the amount of labour cost and hence the allocation of overhead.

Where all products are identical, a *cost per unit* would be sufficient. However, in a job-costing system such identical products are unlikely.

In summary, four possible methods of absorbing overhead costs into products are:

- cost per direct labour hour
- cost per machine hour
- cost per £ of labour cost
- cost per unit.

4.2.4   Overhead cost recovery

The overhead costs are absorbed into products so that all costs may be 'recovered' by charging a selling price that covers costs and makes a profit. The process of absorbing overhead costs into products is also described as **overhead cost recovery**. This is another example of the use of different words to describe the same idea in management accounting. You will find that both descriptions are used.

Overhead cost recovery means absorbing overhead costs into a unit of product so that the overhead costs will eventually be **recovered** in the sale of the product.

4.2.5　Illustration

This section provides an illustration of the allocation and apportionment of overhead costs and shows how the overhead cost is absorbed into products.

Kitchen Units Company assembles and finishes kitchen units to customers' orders. Assembly involves creating the basic units, while finishing involves adding the laminated surfaces and interior fittings as specified by the customer. The machinery and tools required for the work are kept in working order by a maintenance department. The assembly and finishing departments are production departments because they both do work on the product. The maintenance department is a service department because it helps the work of the production departments but does not deal directly with the product.

The illustration in Exhibit 4.8 follows the sequence of Exhibit 4.3. It shows how the overhead costs of one month are allocated and apportioned, and then absorbs the costs to Product S, a kitchen unit which spends two hours in assembly and three hours in finishing.

Table 1 in Exhibit 4.8 sets out the indirect costs incurred by the business. These costs relate to some or all of the three departments and must be shared among them on a fair basis.

Table 2 sets out information about each department which will be helpful in this fair sharing.

Table 3 apportions overhead costs across the three deparments.

Table 4 apportions the costs of the service department to the two manufacturing departments.

Table 5 absorbs overhead costs into a job.

Exhibit 4.8
Illustration of the calculation of an overhead cost rate

Table 1 sets out the indirect costs incurred by the business on behalf of all departments taken together. The costs must be apportioned (shared) over the departments because there is insufficient information to permit allocation of costs as a whole. Table 2 sets out relevant information about each department which will be used in the process of determining an overhead cost rate.

Table 1
Indirect costs incurred by the business

Cost item	Total cost this month
	£
Indirect materials	36,000
Indirect labour	40,000
Rent	1,000
Insurance	1,600
Depreciation	2,000
Total	80,600

Exhibit 4.8 continued

Table 2
Information about each department

	Assembly	Finishing	Maintenance
Direct materials used for production	£400,000	£500,000	not applicable
Number of employees	10	25	5
Floor area	100 sq m	200 sq m	100 sq m
Value of machinery	£30,000	£50,000	£20,000
Number of direct labour hours worked on production	55,000	64,000	not applicable

There are four steps in calculating the overhead cost to be allocated to each job.

Step 1: Apportioning costs over departments, using a suitable method for each cost

In Table 3, each of the cost items contained in Table 1 is shared across the three departments on an appropriate basis chosen from Table 2.

Table 3
Apportioning (sharing) cost items over the three departments

	Total	Assembly	Finishing	Maintenance
	£	£	£	£
Indirect materials[1]	36,000	16,000	20,000	nil
Indirect labour[2]	40,000	10,000	25,000	5,000
Rent[3]	1,000	250	500	250
Insurance[4]	1,600	480	800	320
Depreciation[5]	2,000	600	1,000	400
Total	80,600	27,330	47,300	5,970

Notes:
[1] The cost of indirect materials is likely to be dependent on direct materials so the proportions applied in sharing out the indirect materials costs are 4 : 5. The direct materials are used only in Assembly and Finishing, so the indirect materials will relate only to these two departments.
[2] The cost of indirect labour is likely to be dependent on the total number of employees working in the organisation, so the proportions applied in sharing out the indirect labour costs are 10 : 25 : 5.
[3] Rent costs may be shared out on the basis of floor space occupied by each department, in the proportions 1 : 2 : 1.
[4,5] Insurance and depreciation may both be shared out by reference to the value of the machinery used in each department, in the proportions 3 : 5 : 2.

Step 2: Apportioning service department costs to production departments on the basis of value of machines in each department

The maintenance department provides service in proportion to the machinery used in each department, so it is appropriate to share out the maintenance costs on the basis of value of machinery in Assembly and in Finishing, in the proportions 30,000 : 50,000:

$$\frac{30,000}{80,000} \times 5,970 = 2,239$$

$$\frac{50,000}{80,000} \times 5,970 = 3,731$$

Exhibit 4.8 **continued**

Table 4
Apportioning (sharing) maintenance costs between Assembly and Finishing

	Total	Assembly	Finishing	Maintenance
	£	£	£	£
Total cost per dept (from Table 3)	80,600	27,330	47,300	5,970
Transfer maintenance costs to Assembly and Finishing		2,239	3,731	(5,970)
Total per department	80,600	29,569	51,031	nil

Step 3: Absorbing total overhead costs of each production department into units produced during the period

Dividing the total cost of each department by the number of direct labour hours, we obtain the following overhead cost rates:

      Assembly: £29,569/55,000 hours = 53.76 pence per direct labour hour
      Finishing: £51,031/64,000 hours = 79.74 pence per direct labour hour

Step 4: Finding the overhead costs of any job

Now the overhead cost rate may be used to determine how much overhead cost should be charged to each job. The answer will depend on the number of direct labour hours required in each production department, for any job. Take as an example job S, which spends 2 hours in the assembly department and 3 hours in the finishing department. The overhead cost allocated to job S is calculated as follows:

Table 5
Example of the allocation overhead cost to a job

Department	Calculation	£
Assembly	53.76 pence × 2 hours	1.075
Finishing	79.74 pence × 3 hours	2.392
Total overhead cost		3.46

That's all there is to it. The process of allocation, apportionment and absorption of production overheads takes time because every cost has to be traced through to the product, but it is systematic in that all costs eventually find their way through to a product.

Activity 4.2

Return to the start of Exhibit 4.8 and try to work the example for yourself. It is very important for later chapters that you understand the purpose of Exhibit 4.8 and the method of calculation used. There are some features of the tables in Exhibit 4.8 which are worth noting for future reference. First, it is important to keep totals for each column of figures and a total of all the column totals in order to ensure that there are no arithmetic errors that result in costs appearing from nowhere or disappearing to oblivion. Second, it is important to show working notes at all times because there are so many variations of possible method that the person who reads your calculations will need the working notes to understand the method chosen.

4.2.6 Predetermined overhead cost rates

This chapter has explained methods by which *actual* overhead cost for a period may be absorbed into jobs. However, the calculation of overhead cost rates based on the actual overhead costs incurred during the period means that job cost calculations have to be postponed until the end of the period, because the overhead cost cannot be obtained before that time. This creates practical problems where timely information on job costs is essential if it is to be used for estimating the value of work-in-progress or calculating monthly profit. As a result of this demand for information *before* the actual costs are known, many businesses will use predetermined overhead cost rates, estimated *before* the start of a reporting period. This rate will then be applied to all output of the period. At the end of the period, when the actual overhead is known, there will be an adjustment to bring the estimated overhead cost into line with the actual overhead cost.

Estimating the predetermined overhead rate

How does a manager estimate the predetermined overhead cost rate? The estimate could be based on the known overhead costs of previous periods. It could be a 'best guess' of what will happen in the forecast period. The predetermined overhead cost rate is then applied to the output of the period. This is also described as **overhead cost recovery** because the cost will be 'recovered' when the output is completed and sold.

Estimates abound in accounting and part of the reporting process involves explaining why the actual out-turn did, or did not, match up to the estimate. Provided the estimation process is carried out with care, the benefits of using predetermined overhead costs, in terms of having information early rather than late, by far outweigh the possible negative aspects of having to explain differences between estimated and actual overhead costs charged to products. Chapter 15 introduces the techniques of standard costing and variance analysis, which provide a formal means of analysing and investigating differences between estimated and actual amounts.

Exhibit 4.9 gives the information necessary to calculate a predetermined overhead cost rate. The steps of calculation are then described.

Exhibit 4.9

Calculating a predetermined fixed overhead cost rate

Estimated direct labour hours for normal activity	10,000 hours
Estimated fixed overhead cost in total	£50,000
Predetermined overhead cost rate	£5 per direct labour hour

- *Step 1*: The accounting period is one month. Before the start of the month, the manager estimates that there will be 10,000 labour hours worked, under normal activity conditions, and that fixed overhead of £50,000 will be incurred.
- *Step 2*: The manager calculates the predetermined fixed overhead cost rate as £5 per labour hour (= £50,000/10,000).
- *Step 3*: Throughout the reporting period, as work is done, the manager applies £5 of fixed overhead for every labour hour of each item of output from the business. If exactly 10,000 hours of work are carried out then each item of output will carry its fair share of the overhead. The process of overhead cost recovery is complete.

4.2.7 Under-recovery and over-recovery of overheads

The calculations of overhead cost recovery are not always as neat and tidy as in Exhibit 4.9. This section explains how under-recovery and over-recovery can occur.

Under-recovered overhead: underestimating hours worked

Supposing things do not work out as planned in Exhibit 4.9. The manager finds out at the end of the month that only 8,000 hours were actually worked. In Step 3, a fixed overhead of £5 will be charged to jobs for each hour worked, so £40,000 will be charged in total. We can also say that there is recovery of £40,000. At the end of the month the manager confirms that cash book shows the actual overhead cost incurred is £50,000, corresponding exactly to the estimated amount. The manager has a total fixed overhead cost of £40,000 recovered (charged to jobs) but an actual cost of £50,000 as an expense for the financial profit and loss account. The fixed overhead cost recorded on the job records is said to be **under-recovered**. In the management accounting profit and loss account the fixed overhead element of the cost of goods sold is recorded at £40,000 using the predetermined rate, and a separate cost of £10,000 is recorded as **under-recovered fixed overhead**, so that the total fixed overhead expense of the month equals £50,000.

Under-recovered overhead: underestimating overhead cost

Suppose that the actual hours worked do match the expected hours, so that in Step 3 there is recovery of the full amount of £50,000 (based on 10,000 hours at £5 per hour). However, when the manager checks the cash book, it shows that the actual overhead cost of the month is £55,000 due to an unforeseen rise in fixed service charges. The fixed overhead cost recorded on the job records is again said to be under-recovered. In the management accounting profit and loss account the fixed overhead element of the cost of goods sold is recorded at £50,000 using the predetermined rate, and a separate cost of £5,000 is recorded as under-recovered fixed overhead, so that the total fixed overhead expense of the month equals £55,000.

Definition

> **Under-recovered fixed overhead** occurs when the overhead cost recovered (applied), using a predetermined overhead cost rate, is less than the actual overhead cost of the period. This may be because the actual hours worked are less than the estimate made in advance, or it may be because the actual overhead cost incurred is greater than the estimate of the overhead cost.

Over-recovered overhead: underestimating hours worked

Now suppose an alternative picture. The manager finds out at the end of the month that 11,000 hours were actually worked. In Step 3, a fixed overhead of £5 will be charged to jobs for each hour worked, so £55,000 will be charged in total. We can also say that there is recovery of £55,000. At the end of the month the manager also confirms that cash book shows the actual overhead cost incurred is £50,000, corresponding exactly to the estimated amount. The manager has a total fixed overhead cost of £55,000 recovered (charged to jobs) but an actual cost of £50,000 as an expense for the financial profit and loss account. The fixed overhead cost recorded on the job records is said to be **over-recovered**. In the management accounting profit and loss account the fixed overhead element of the cost of goods sold is recorded at £55,000 using the predetermined rate, and a separate reduction in cost of £5,000 is recorded as **over-recovered fixed overhead**, so that the total fixed overhead expense of the month equals £50,000.

Over-recovered overhead: overestimating overhead cost

Suppose that the actual hours worked do match the expected hours, so that in Step 3 there is recovery of the full amount of £50,000 (based on 10,000 hours at £5 per hour). However, when the manager checks the cash book, it shows that the actual overhead cost of the month is £48,000 due to an unexpected rebate of charges for heating. The fixed overhead cost recorded on the job records is again said to be over-recovered. In the management accounting profit and loss account the fixed overhead element of the cost of goods sold is recorded at £50,000 using the predetermined rate, and a separate reduction in cost of £2,000 is recorded as over-recovered fixed overhead, so that the total fixed overhead expense of the month equals £48,000.

Definition   **Over-recovered fixed overhead** occurs when the overhead cost recovered (applied), using a predetermined overhead cost rate, is greater than the actual overhead cost of the period. This may be because the actual hours worked are greater than the estimate made in advance, or it may be because the actual overhead cost incurred is less than the estimate of the overhead cost.

Effect on profit

If there is over-recovered fixed overhead then too much cost is charged in the management accounts, when compared to the actual cost incurred. The management accounting profit will be too low. To restore the profit to the actual level achieved, the over-recovery must be deducted from the cost charged.

If there is under-recovered fixed overhead, then too little cost is charged in the management accounts, when compared to the actual cost incurred. The management accounting profit will be too high. To restore the profit to the actual level achieved, the under-recovery must be added to the cost charged.

4.2.8   More questions about overhead cost rates

Overhead cost is one of those topics which make you want to ask a new question every time you have an answer to the previous question. Here are some of the questions which might have occurred to you in thinking about overhead cost rates:

1 Is it necessary to have an overhead cost rate for each cost centre or could there be one rate to cover all production?
2 How is it possible to calculate an overhead cost rate per direct labour hour for fixed overhead costs when these do not vary with direct labour hours?
3 What is the best way of ensuring that the process of allocation, apportionment and absorption of costs most closely represents the behaviour of those costs?

The answers to all these questions will be found in thinking about the four conditions for determining a suitable overhead cost rate:

● fair to all parties involved in the process
● representative of the benefit each party gains from the shared cost
● relatively quick to apply so that provision of information is not delayed
● understandable by all concerned.

The answers are therefore as follows.

Is it necessary to have an overhead cost rate for each cost centre or could there be one rate to cover all production?

If there is a wide product range and products spend different amounts of time in different cost centres, it would be undesirable to have one rate to cover all production because that single rate would average out the time spent in the different departments. Thus it is said that blanket overhead cost rates or 'plant-wide rates' should be avoided where possible, or used with great caution. The overhead cost rate to use will be one which can be used with confidence that it meets the four conditions stated earlier.

How is it possible to calculate an overhead cost rate per direct labour hour for fixed overhead costs when, by definition, fixed costs do not vary with direct labour hours?

This question is more difficult to answer and the best starting point is a reminder that accounting is often based on estimates. The fixed overhead costs will have to be absorbed into products eventually. However, this can only be achieved accurately after production is completed. Job cost estimation cannot always wait that long. Therefore, a **predetermined fixed overhead cost rate** is applied to each job on the basis of some measure of work done, such as direct labour hours. If the estimating process is accurate, the estimated hours to be worked will equal the actual hours worked and there will be no problem. If the actual hours are greater than, or less than, the estimate, then there will be a difference, referred to as overapplied or underapplied fixed overhead. (This subject is taken up again in Chapter 5.)

What is the best way of ensuring that the process of absorbing costs into products most closely represents the behaviour of those costs?

This question has aroused considerable excitement in management accounting circles in recent years, as some thinking people realised that too much time had been spent in reading textbooks and theorising. Researchers had omitted to find out whether the actual practice of management accounting was so bad after all. They therefore went out to look and found that some practical management accountants were having some very good ideas, but that those ideas were not finding their way into textbooks.

As a result of those investigations, many articles and books have been written on the importance of **cost drivers**, which are the events that are significant determinants of the cost of an activity. If an oil company has an offshore platform where the supervisor is constantly calling up the helicopter for unplanned visits ashore, the total transport cost for the oil company will rise. The *helicopter flight* is the cost driver and the platform supervisor needs to be aware that the flight cost is part of the cost of running the platform. If a stores department is receiving frequent deliveries of small quantities, the cost driver for the stores department is the *number of deliveries*. Cost drivers are not an earth-shattering discovery in themselves, but they have been built into a description of activity-based costing (ABC) which you will find in section 4.3. Activity-based costing has led many companies to re-examine their approach to allocating overhead costs to products, based on finding a method which most closely models the factors driving the cost.

4.3 Activity-based costing (ABC) for production overheads

Activity-based costing (ABC) is a relatively new approach to allocating overhead costs to products. It focuses on the activities that drive costs (cause costs to occur).

Definition | **Activity-based costing (ABC)** traces overhead costs to products by focusing on the activities that drive costs (cause costs to occur).

The proponents of the subject claim that ABC provides product cost information which is useful for decision making. The claims of ABC will be explored in this chapter by outlining the principles and then examining a case study.

There are five stages to establishing an activity-based costing system. These are:

1 Identify the major activities which take place in an organisation.
2 Identify the factors which most closely influence the cost of an activity. These factors are called the cost drivers and are a direct indication of how the activity demands cost.
3 Create a **cost pool** for each activity and trace costs to cost pools.
4 Calculate a **cost driver rate** as the total costs in a cost pool divided by the number of times that the activity occurs.
5 Allocate costs to products using the demand for each activity.

Exhibit 4.10
Activity-based approach to the flow of overhead costs

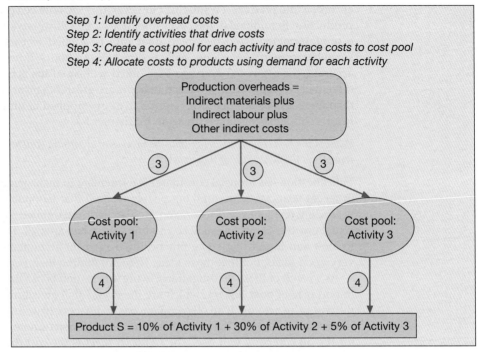

Step 1: Identify overhead costs
Step 2: Identify activities that drive costs
Step 3: Create a cost pool for each activity and trace costs to cost pool
Step 4: Allocate costs to products using demand for each activity

Production overheads =
Indirect materials plus
Indirect labour plus
Other indirect costs

Cost pool:
Activity 1

Cost pool:
Activity 2

Cost pool:
Activity 3

Product S = 10% of Activity 1 + 30% of Activity 2 + 5% of Activity 3

Compare the ABC steps in Exhibit 4.10 with those of the traditional approach in Exhibit 4.3.

4.3.1   Reasons for the development of ABC[2]

In the 1980s, Professors Cooper and Kaplan in the US found the focus on activities and cost drivers in some large US manufacturing businesses which had become dissatisfied with the traditional approach to overhead costing. Cooper and Kaplan wrote up their observations as case studies at Harvard University and then published papers on their findings. The cause of change was that business organisations were changing their nature at the time, with an increase in indirect costs related to changes in processes, new ways of dealing with customers, and new investment in more sophisticated operating systems. There was a swing from variable to fixed overhead costs. Labour resources were replaced to some extent by automation. It became apparent that production volumes were no longer the main drivers of overhead costs. Organisations were looking for a costing system that would be more realistic in tracking the consumption of resources that gives rise to cost.

4.3.2   Nature of an activity

An activity, in its broadest sense, is something which happens in the business. An activity could be using materials to make a physical product or using labour to carry out a service operation. In ABC language, that would be an example of a **unit activity**, which is performed each time a product is produced. Other activities are performed to enable output of products but are not so closely dependent on how many units are produced. These are called **product-sustaining activities**. Examples would be product design, product testing and marketing. Some activities are classified as **batch-related activities** which are fixed for a given batch of products. This would include costs of the buying department, costs of moving stores from the warehouse to the factory floor, and costs of planning a production schedule. Where there are expenses such as rent or insurance which are not driven by making products, they are designated as **facility-sustaining activities** and no attempt is made to allocate these to products. They are charged as a total cost against all products after the separate profit margins on each product are determined.

Example 1

A language college teaches English as a Foreign Language. It has two departments: E (European mother tongue) and A (Asian mother tongue). Information about each is shown in Exhibit 4.11. The overhead cost of cleaning classrooms is £32,000 per year.

Exhibit 4.11
Information for Example 1: departments E and A

Department	E	A
Number of teaching staff	12	18
Annual teaching labour cost	£600,000	£1,000,000
Number of rooms	18	16

The traditional method of allocating cleaning overhead cost to departments has been to apply a rate of two per cent of the labour cost of teaching. This is shown in Exhibit 4.12.

Exhibit 4.12
Traditional treatment of cleaning overhead

	E	A
Overhead cost rate	2% of labour cost	2% of labour cost
Apportionment of cost £32,000	£12,000	£20,000

The head tutor of Department A feels this is unfair because it has fewer classrooms than Department E and so requires less cleaning effort.

Assume that cleaning cost may be regarded as a cost pool and show how activity-based costing can be applied where the number of classrooms is the cost driver for cleaning.

The apportionment of cost by the activity-based method is shown in Exhibit 4.13.

Exhibit 4.13
Activity-based costing for cleaning overhead

	E	A
Cost pool: Cleaning, £32,000		
Cost driver: Fraction of classroom usage	18/34	16/34
Apportionment of cost £32,000	£16,940	£15,060

Comment: The head of Department A will be happier with the use of activity-based costing because it reflects the lower usage of cleaning driven by fewer classrooms. On the other hand, it may be that this is not the best cost driver. For instance, suppose that the head of Department E responds by pointing out that their classrooms are kept tidy and are therefore easier to clean. The debate over cost drivers might take some time to resolve.

Example 2

In the office of a firm of solicitors and estate agents there are overhead costs incurred relating to the cost of office support for the staff preparing legal documentation. There are two departments preparing legal documentation. Department A has dealt with

15 property transactions having an average value of £100,000 each, while Department B has dealt with 5 property transactions having an average value of £1m each.

The total amount of the office overhead costs for the period is £100,000. The traditional approach to overhead cost has been to apportion the amount of £100,000 in proportion to the number of property deals dealt with by each department. They are now asking for an activity-based approach to costing, where the cost driver is the value of transactions in each department, because high value transactions involve more work.

Exhibit 4.14
Traditional treatment of cleaning overhead

	A	B
Cost pool: Office overhead, £100,000		
Cost driver: Number of transactions	15/20	5/20
Apportionment of cost £100,000	£75,000	£25,000
Cost per transaction	£5,000	£5,000

The traditional approach gives the same unit cost regardless of size of transaction.

Exhibit 4.15
Activity-based costing for office overhead

	A	B
Overhead cost rate	1,500/6,500	5,000/6,500
Apportionment of cost £100,000	100,000 × 1.5/6.5 = £23,000	100,000 × 5/6.5 = £77,000
Cost per transaction	£1,530	£15,400

Comment: The activity-based approach puts much more of the overhead cost on to Department B because that one is driving more of the overheads. When the cost per transaction is calculated, the activity-based approach, based on value, loads the cost towards the high-value transaction and so produces a relatively higher cost per unit for these transactions.

4.3.3 Role of the management accountant

Activity-based costing allows the *attention-directing* functions of the management accountant to come to the fore. The management accountant takes a key role in understanding the operation of the business and translating into cost terms the activities *as perceived by those who carry them out*.

Because activity-based costing requires a very thorough analysis of how products drive the costs of various activities, it is not feasible to work through a full illustration here. Instead, one activity, that of purchasing materials for use in a hotel restaurant, will be explored by case study in some detail. Hopefully, that will give you a flavour of the complexity and fascination of ABC and encourage you to read further.

4.3.4 Case study: Glen Lyon Hotel

The Glen Lyon Hotel has two main product lines, with quite different characteristics. In the restaurant, meals are provided on a daily basis to the chef's high standards of perfection. In the conference suite, banquets are arranged for special functions such as weddings. There is a restaurant manager, responsible for restaurant meals, and a functions manager, responsible for banquets. The hotel seeks to offer competitive prices subject to meeting all costs and earning an adequate profit.

The hotel has a purchasing department which purchases the food required by the hotel restaurant and all supplies required for special functions, including crockery and cutlery. The purchasing officer is concerned that the restaurant manager insists on buying food in relatively small quantities, because the chef is very particular about monitoring the continued high quality of supplies. The functions manager also creates problems for the purchasing department because she insists on buying crockery and cutlery in bulk, to save cost, which requires time being taken by the purchasing officer to negotiate the best terms with the supplier. Even the suppliers can create a great deal of work because they are constantly changing their prices and this has to be recorded on the computer system of the purchasing department. The purchasing officer would like to show that these activities are all costly because they drive the amount of work undertaken by the purchasing department.

Fiona McTaggart was called in to help, and she now explains how she went about the task of applying activity-based costing in relation to the activities of the purchasing department.

FIONA: *First of all I asked for a list of all the costs incurred by the department in a year* (see Exhibit 4.16).

Exhibit 4.16
List of costs incurred by resources used in the purchasing department

Resource cost	£
Salary of purchasing officer	15,000
Wages of data processing clerk	9,000
Telephone calls	3,000
Total costs to be allocated	27,000

Identifying the cost drivers

Then I sat down with the purchasing officer for a long meeting during which we talked about how the purchasing process worked. From those discussions I found that a number of activities were driving the work of purchasing and I listed all those (see Exhibit 4.17).

Exhibit 4.17
List of activities in the purchasing department

- Agreeing terms with supplier
- Processing an order
- Updating the price lists
- Updating the supplier records
- Processing queries about invoices.

I explained to the purchasing officer that, although the purchasing department was an identifiable unit of the organisation for staff management purposes, it would no longer be treated as a cost centre under activity-based costing. The purchasing process would be regarded as a set of activities consuming 'resources' such as salaries, wages and telephone calls. Each activity would collect a 'pool' of cost as the resources were used up. The pool of costs would be passed on to those other departments drawing on the services of the purchasing department and from those departments the costs would find their way into products.

Creating the cost pools

The next stage was to decide how much of each resource cost was attributable to the activity driving that cost. This part was quite tricky because the purchasing officer only had a 'feel' for the relative impact in some cases. Take as an example the processing of an order. When the restaurant manager asks for food to be ordered, the purchasing officer first has to phone the supplier to check availability and likely delivery time. Then she checks that someone will be available to open the cold store when the delivery arrives. She is then able to fax the order to the supplier who will phone back to confirm that the goods are available and that delivery will be as requested. Once the goods arrive, the purchasing officer has to check that the delivery note agrees with what was ordered. That whole process takes about 20 minutes for each order.

We carried on talking and I was able to identify, for each resource cost, some measure of how the activity was being driven. The starting point was salaries. We estimated that the purchasing officer spent the equivalent of two days per week agreeing terms with suppliers. The remaining three days were divided equally over the other activities listed. For wages cost, the data processing clerk spent three days per week in processing orders, half a day each week on updating price lists and updating suppliers' records, and one day per week on checking and processing questions from the accounts department about invoices received for payment. The final cost heading was telephone calls. The destination and duration of each call is logged by the telephone system so we took a sample of one week's calls and decided that 60% of telephone calls were routine calls to place an order, 20% were dealing with queries over price changes and the remainder were spread equally over agreeing terms, updating the supplier records and dealing with invoice queries. Following these discussions I sketched a diagram of the ABC approach (see Exhibit 4.18) and then drew up a table showing how each cost item could be allocated to the various activities so that a cost pool is created for each activity (see Exhibit 4.19).

Exhibit 4.18
Sketch of the ABC approach applied to the activity of purchasing

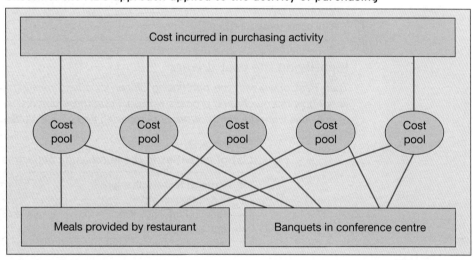

Exhibit 4.19
Creating a cost pool: allocation of resource costs to activities

Resource	Resource cost	Activity cost pools				
		Agreeing terms with supplier	*Processing an order*	*Updating the price list*	*Updating the supplier records*	*Processing invoice queries*
	£	£	£	£	£	£
Salary	15,000	6,000	2,250	2,250	2,250	2,250
Wages	9,000		5,400	900	900	1,800
Telephone	3,000	200	1,800	600	200	200
	27,000	6,200	9,450	3,750	3,350	4,250

Demand for each activity

The next stage was to determine how many times each activity driver was put into action. This involved measuring the volume of each activity, as a measure of the demand for that activity. Agreeing terms with the supplier is not easy to quantify, but we were aware that there are discussions with each supplier at some time during the year, so we took the number of suppliers as the measure of volume driving that activity. It was relatively easy to establish the number of orders processed at the request of the restaurant manager. The price list has to be updated every time the supplier changes the price of any items, and they all change at least twice per month, so we decided that the number of items on the order list was a reasonable measure. Updating supplier records involves changing minor details for existing suppliers but takes more time to record a new supplier. So we used the number of new suppliers as the measure of the volume of that activity. Processing invoice queries depends on the number of such queries.

Cost driver rates

My final accounting statement was a calculation of the cost per activity unit for each activity (see Exhibit 4.20). This was determined by dividing the cost in the pool by the measure of how that activity was being driven by products.

Exhibit 4.20
Calculation of cost per activity unit for each activity

	Activity cost pools				
	Agreeing terms with supplier	Processing an order	Updating the price list	Updating the supplier records	Processing invoice queries
Cost per Exhibit 4.19	£6,200	£9,450	£3,750	£3,350	£4,250
Activity driver	Number of suppliers	Number of orders	Number of items listed	Number of suppliers updated	Number of queries
Activity volume	60	1,600	7,000	60	150
Cost per activity unit	£103.333	£5.906	£0.536	£55.833	£28.333

Using the calculation of cost per activity unit for each activity I was able to explain the benefits of activity-based costing. The purchasing department is providing a service to the rest of the organisation, but at a cost. That cost could be made more visible using activity-based costing because the factors driving the cost could be quantified in their effect. Looking at Exhibit 4.20, it is not difficult to see that the most significant cost drivers are the activities of agreeing terms with suppliers and of updating the suppliers' records. Each new supplier causes a further £159.166 (£103.333 + £55.833) to be incurred at an early stage. The restaurant manager needs to be aware that placing large numbers of low-volume orders causes cost to be incurred on each order. The total cost incurred could be reduced by moving to a lower number of orders, each being of higher volume. (Someone would need to check that that did not create larger new costs in storage of the goods.) The next most costly activity, in terms of cost per unit, is that of answering queries about invoices. The accounts department should be made aware that each enquiry costs £28.333.

I also looked back to the old way of allocating the cost of the purchasing department (see Exhibit 4.21). Before activity-based costing was considered, the organisation charged the purchasing costs to products as a percentage of the value of materials ordered. Looking back to Exhibit 4.19, the total purchasing department costs are shown as £27,000. The purchasing department handles goods to the value of £800,000 in a year. The purchasing department costs were therefore charged to products at 3.375% of cost.

Exhibit 4.21
Previous methods of allocation, based on percentage of value of items requested

	Restaurant manager	Functions manager	Accounts department
	£	£	£
Goods purchased through purchasing department	300,000	500,000	–
3.375% of goods purchased	10,125	16,875	nil

Why was this not the best approach? The answer is that there were two main product lines, having quite different characteristics. One was restaurant meals provided on a routine basis and the other was special banquets for functions such as weddings. My further enquiries revealed that the high-price purchases required for special functions caused relatively few problems in agreeing terms with suppliers and relatively few queries arose over the invoices. Where problems of negotiation and invoicing did arise was in the low-price, high-volume ingredients used routinely in the dining room meals. The information on cost per unit of each activity allowed a much more precise allocation of cost, although I was now in for even more work in tracing the costs from the various activity pools through to the products.

Tracing costs through to products

To trace costs through to products I obtained estimates of the quantity of each activity demanded by the restaurant manager and the function manager (see Exhibit 4.22) and multiplied each quantity by the cost per activity unit calculated in Exhibit 4.20. The result is shown in Exhibit 4.23.

Compare this with the cost allocation under the traditional system which is shown in Exhibit 4.21.

Exhibit 4.22
Quantity of activity demanded by each function

Activity	Demanded by restaurant manager	Demanded by functions manager
Agreeing terms with supplier	10 new suppliers	50 new suppliers
Processing an order	1,200 orders	400 orders
Updating the price list	4,000 items	3,000 items
Updating the supplier records	10 new suppliers	50 new suppliers
Processing invoice queries	All 150 demanded by accounts department	

Exhibit 4.23

Allocation of purchasing cost to restaurant manager, functions manager and accounts department

Activity	Restaurant manager	Functions manager	Accounts department	Total
	£	£	£	£
Agreeing terms with supplier	1,033	5,167		6,200
Processing an order	7,088	2,362		9,450
Updating the price list	2,143	1,607		3,750
Updating the supplier records	558	2,792		3,350
Processing invoice queries			4,250	4,250
Total cost allocated	10,822	11,928	4,250	27,000

My conclusions were that the accounts department had previously been unaware of the costs it was causing the purchasing manager whenever an invoice query was raised. Using activity-based costing would allow the allocation of cost to the accounts department each time a question was raised. Some care might need to be taken to examine the size and significance of the invoice query in relation to the cost allocation. It would not be a good idea for the accounts department to allow a £50,000 error to go unchecked because they feared a charge of £28.33. The implementation of activity-based costing might need to be accompanied by the use of performance measures which show how the benefits of an activity exceed the costs incurred.

The functions manager would incur less overhead cost under the activity-based system than under the previous approach. The recorded cost of functions would therefore decrease. As I explained earlier, the high-priced purchases of food for special functions cause relatively few problems in processing a smaller number of orders. The functions manager seems to have a relatively high number of new suppliers. Cost could be controlled further if fewer suppliers were used for functions. Less purchasing effort would be required.

The restaurant manager experiences little difference in cost under either approach. To improve overhead costs there would need to be a quantum leap in practice, such as reducing the order frequency to the stage where one less person was employed in the purchasing department, or else where a part-time employee could do the work presently undertaken full-time. Merely reducing the order frequency would not be enough if the purchasing staff are still present full-time and the same cost is being spread over a lower volume of activity. Although there is little impact, these figures give the restaurant manager food for thought.

Product costs

In the full application of ABC, the costs would be taken into the final product cost. I have not done that here because the purchasing department's costs are only one small corner of the total business. Activity-based costing creates a lot of work, but a well-coded computerised accounting system can handle that. I spent the best part of one day dealing only with the analysis of the purchasing department costs, so it would take a few weeks of consultancy to cover the entire range of activities which contribute to the cost of the products. My consultancy fees would be another overhead to be allocated, but I believe the hotel would find the effort well worth it in terms of more effective management over a period of years.

Activity 4.3

Imagine you are the owner of a business which rents ice-cream stalls from the local council. You employ persons to run each stall. Write down a list of the costs you would expect to incur. Write another list of the drivers of cost. How could activity-based costing help you understand and control the costs of your business?

4.4 Comparing traditional approach and ABC

4.4.1 Contrasting treatments

Allocating direct costs to products is not a problem. The particular need for activity-based costing lies in the area of absorbing overhead costs into products. The traditional approach to absorbing overhead costs to products was explained in section 4.2. In that section it was shown that, traditionally, costs are first allocated and apportioned to cost centres and then absorbed into products which pass through those cost centres. Activity-based costing follows a different approach to channelling costs towards products. Exhibit 4.24 sets out the contrasting treatments.

Exhibit 4.24
Contrasting activity-based costing and traditional overhead cost allocation

Traditional overhead cost allocation	Activity-based costing
Identify *cost centres* in which costs may be accumulated. Cost centres are determined by the nature of their function (e.g. production or service department cost centres).	Identify the way in which products drive the activity of the business and define suitable *cost pools* for collecting the costs relating to each activity. Activity cost pools are determined by the activities which drive the costs (e.g. obtaining new customers, negotiating customer contracts).
↓	↓
Collect costs in cost centres.	Collect costs in activity cost pools.
↓	↓
Determine an *overhead cost rate* for each production cost centre (e.g. cost per direct labour hour).	Determine a *cost driver rate* for each activity cost pool (e.g. a cost per customer contract, cost per customer order received).
↓	↓
Allocate cost to products using the calculated cost rate and the measure of the *product's consumption of that department's cost* (e.g. number of labour hours required).	Allocate cost to products according to the *product's demand for the activity* which drives cost.

4.4.2 Benefits claimed for activity-based costing

Activity-based costing (ABC) appeared first in the academic literature during the late 1980s. It had reached the professional accountancy journals by the early 1990s and by that time was already being used (or tested) by companies with progressive attitudes.

Real world case 4.3

I. Activity-Based Costing and Management: The Texas Pilot Project

For years, the plumbers, painters, carpenters and maintenance people who worked for the Texas General Services Commission (GSC) shuttled back and forth between the department's administration building, located in Austin's Capitol Complex, and its parts warehouse, about seven miles to the east. While everyone knew this was an inconvenience for the painters and carpenters, what *wasn't* clear was that these trips were costing the agency a considerable amount of money. 'It was a pain to have to constantly drive from one building to the other,' one employee told us, 'but we just assumed that was the way it had to be.'

But it wasn't. And now those 14-mile round trips are gone for good.

In Spring 2000, GSC decided to include the Capitol's maintenance services in an activity-based costing (ABC) analysis to learn the true, fully allocated costs of these activities. The analysis demonstrated, among other things, that the location of the warehouse was costing the department a lot of money that could be spent better elsewhere.

By management estimates, GSC's plumbers, painters and carpenters logged more than 48,000 miles driving between the two locations in 1999. Including salaries for drive times, gasoline, and indirect and administrative costs, the ABC analysis found that GSC could save more than $51,000 a year simply by moving the warehouse to its administration building's basement. Within weeks, GSC did so.

This experience illustrates the benefits the state can realise from ABC. The tremendous opportunities offered by ABC analyses were discussed in the Comptroller's 1999 Texas Performance Review report, *Challenging the Status Quo: Toward Smaller, Smarter Government*. In response to recommendations in that report, the 1999 Legislature adopted Article IX, Section 9-6.43 of the General Appropriations Act, creating an ABC management team of representatives from the Governor's Office of Budget and Planning, State Auditor's Office, Legislative Budget Board and the Comptroller's office. This team was directed to oversee an ABC pilot project and report to the Legislature on its results no later than January 15, 2001. The process followed to fulfill this directive is discussed in detail in this report.

ABC assigns costs to all of the activities in a given process, based on the resources they consume. Activities are the steps necessary to convert resources into a product or service; under ABC, all costs of activities, including overhead, are traced to the product or service for which the activities are performed.

Source: www.window.state.tx.us/specialrpt/abc/costmgmt.html, 2005.

Discussion points

1 What was the benefit of ABC in the situation described here?

2 Why would the state of Texas be so enthusiastic for ABC?

It has not been applied in all cases, but the idea of asking 'what drives cost' is found in many situations. The main benefits claimed are that ABC provides product cost information which, although it includes an allocation of overheads, is nevertheless useful for decision-making purposes. It is useful because the overhead costs are allocated to the products in a way that reflects the *factor driving the cost*. If a product cost is thought to be too high, then it can be controlled by controlling the factors driving the most significant elements of its cost. Attention is directed towards problem areas. Activity-based costing is seen as a valuable management tool because it collects and reports on the significant activities of the business. It is also attractive for service-based organisations which have found that the traditional, manufacturing-based costing methods are not suited to the different nature of the service sector.

You may ask at this point, 'If activity-based costing is the best approach, why has it not replaced the traditional approach to overhead cost apportionment?' The answer to that question is, first, that the technique is still relatively rare in practical application, despite the amount written about it. Second, no allocating mechanism can produce accurate results unless the cost item which is being processed is of high reliability and its behaviour is well understood. The successful application of activity-based costing depends on a thorough understanding of basic principles of cost behaviour and the ability to record and process costs accurately.

Activity-based costing will not solve all problems of forward planning. The analytical method relies on historical data and therefore shares with many other aspects of accounting the disadvantage of being a backward-looking measure which must be used with caution in forward-looking decisions.

Finally, activity-based costing requires detailed accounting records and a well-structured system for **cost coding** so that costs are allocated correctly to cost pools and from there to products. There may need to be a considerable investment in discovering and installing the best information system for the job.

4.5 What the researchers have found

This section describes four research papers. Drury and Tayles (2005) used a postal questionnaire study to show that businesses use a range of practices in overhead absorption, which should be seen as a continuous spectrum of change from traditional to ABC. Soin *et al* (2002) observed the change to ABC in one organisation. Greasley (2001) presents a simulation study of the costing of police custody operations using an ABC framework. Liu (2005) studies the use of ABC in the Crown Prosecution Service.

4.5.1 Range of methods of overhead absorption

Drury and Tayles (2002) reported the results of a postal questionnaire study that examined the range of methods used for overhead absorption. They realised that if a researcher asks a simple question 'Do you use traditional methods or do you use ABC?' then the respondent is forced to make a choice which may not reflect the diversity of what is happening in practice. So Drury and Tayles asked a broader range of questions about the allocation of costs and the identification of cost drivers. From this information they calculated a measure of 'cost system complexity'. The lowest complexity consisted of one cost pool and one cost driver. The highest complexity consisted of more than 50 cost pools and more than 10 cost drivers. The results of the analysis showed that the highest complexity of cost system was associated with, in order of importance, size of sales, finance sector, product diversity, service sector and customisation of products.

The conclusion from this paper is that a range of absorption procedures may be found. Some lie in the 'traditional' area, some are strongly 'ABC-based', but many show a mixture of both approaches, with the use of cost drivers or cost pools.

4.5.2   Research into ABC

Research into the application of ABC usually involves case study work where the researcher observes and analyses the use of ABC. An example of such research may be seen in Soin *et al* (2002). They describe a two-year observation of the implementation of ABC in a clearing bank. This is a service business that does not hold stocks, so the importance of costs lies in decision making and control. The ABC system was introduced by a team of consultants working with the staff of the bank. Introducing ABC requires careful identification of activities which in turn requires observing and talking to employees. This can raise considerable suspicion in the minds of employees, especially if cost savings (meaning loss of jobs) are also part of the plan. The case study brings out some of the complex behavioural problems that arise in a major management accounting change.

The authors concluded that non-accountants in the bank began to appreciate cost data more because the data came from operational knowledge. The ABC accountants also developed a better understanding of the banking operations. The ABC system allowed the financial control department to provide information on various processes and this enhanced the credibility of the financial control process because users started to believe the cost figures. One of the negative aspects, from a management perspective, was that they now knew the 'true' cost of activities and this affected their prices when bidding for new contracts. Competitors were tendering lower prices, perhaps because they did not know the 'true' cost. That raised the question of whether the cost information was useful, if its effect was to lose all contracts.

The authors concluded that the introduction of ABC processes had been a revolutionary activity, but that there remained some reluctance to use the ABC information in strategic management.

4.5.3   Using an ABC framework

Greasley (2001) created a model for the cost of operating a custody system in a police station. The model was built by recording historical data relating to arrests over a 12-month period. The actual costs were not known, but there were records of custody cell utilisation, interview room utilisation, arrest process duration and number of court appearances. The research produced a cost per arrest for different types of offences. Costs were driven by processes (such as booking-in to custody, searching, interview and court appearances) and by resources (such as the number and rank of police staff required to deal with different types offence).

Liu (2005) described a case study to explore the use of ABC in the Crown Prosecution Service, a government agency that decides on prosecuting criminal cases in the courts of law in England and Wales. The system put in place was described as activity-based resource planning (ABRP), building on ABC that had been in place since 1995. The ABRP model reflected the importance of staff as the main cost of the work done and related staff resources and overhead costs to the activities driving work in each area.

4.6 Summary

Key themes in this chapter are:

- **Total product cost** is defined as consisting of direct materials, direct labour and production overhead cost.
- **Production overhead costs** comprise indirect materials, indirect labour and other indirect costs of production.
- **Allocation** of indirect costs to cost centres means that the entire cost item is identified with one cost centre.
- **Apportionment** of indirect costs across cost centres means that the cost item is shared across those cost centres on some basis which is a fair representation of how the cost item is used by each cost centre.
- **Absorption** is the process by which overhead costs are absorbed into units of output, or 'jobs'.
- The processes of **apportionment** and **absorption** are said to be *arbitrary* (meaning 'a matter of choice rather than of strict rules'). To ensure that the best result is obtained, the scheme of apportionment and absorption must be:
  - fair to all parties involved in the process
  - representative of the benefit each party gains from the shared cost
  - relatively quick to apply so that the provision of information is not delayed
  - understandable by all concerned.
- The sequence of **allocate, apportion** and **absorb** is called the **traditional** approach to product costing.
- **Activity-based costing** (ABC) traces overhead costs to products by focusing on the **activities** that **drive** costs (cause costs to occur).
- It also provides a method of spreading overhead costs by asking: what drives each cost?
- Costs are collected in **cost pools** and then spread over products based on cost per unit of activity for the activity in question.
- Costs are then allocated to products on the basis of a cost per unit of activity.
- **Cost drivers** have taken on an increasingly important role in apportioning indirect costs to cost centres.
- Contemporary management accounting practice focuses on the accountant becoming part of the operational team so as to ensure that the job costs derived are understood and reflect the factors that drive the costs to be incurred.

References and further reading

Bjørnenak, T. and Mitchell, F. (2002) 'The development of activity-based costing journal literature, 1987–2000', *The European Accounting Review*, 11(3): 281–508.

CIMA (2000) Management Accounting Official Terminology, CIMA Publishing.

Drury, C. and Tayles, M. (2005) 'Explicating the design of overhead absorption procedures in UK organisations', *British Accounting Review*, 37: 47–84.

Greasley, A. (2001) 'Costing police custody operations', *Policing: an International Journal of Police Strategies and Management*, 24(2): 216–27.

Innes, J. and Mitchell, F. (1995) 'Activity-based costing', Chapter 6 in Ashton, D., Hopper, T., and Scapens, R. (eds) *Issues in Management Accounting*, Prentice Hall.

Liu, L. (2005) 'Activity-based costing', *Financial Management* (UK), March: 29–31.

Soin, K., Seal, W. and Cullen, J. (2002) 'ABC and organizational change: an institutional perspective', *Management Accounting Research*, Vol. 13, 249–71.

QUESTIONS

The Questions section of each chapter has three types of question. 'Test your understanding' question to help you review your reading are in the 'A' series of questions. You will find the answer to these by reading and thinking about the material in the text book. 'Application' questions to test your ability to apply technical skills are in the 'B' series of questions. Questions requiring you to show skills in problem solving and evaluation are in the 'C' series of questions. The symbol [S] indicates that a solution is available at the end of the book.

A   Test your understanding

A4.1   Give three examples of production overheads in each of the following:
(a) a manufacturing business (section 4.2); and
(b) a service business (section 4.2).

A4.2   For each of your answers to the previous question, say whether the cost is a fixed cost or a variable cost (section 4.2 and chapter 2, sections 2.4.1 and 2.4.2).

A4.3   What are the important features of any successful scheme of allocating, apportioning and absorbing indirect costs to products (section 4.2)?

A4.4   [S] For each of the following overhead costs, suggest one method of apportioning cost to cost centres:
(a) employees' holiday pay;
(b) agency fee for nurse at first-aid centre;
(c) depreciation of floor-polishing machines used in all production areas;
(d) production manager's salary;
(e) lighting;
(f) power for desktop workstations in a financial services business;
(g) cost of servicing the elevator;
(h) fee paid to professional consultant for advice on fire regulation procedures.

A4.5   [S] Explain how each of the following service department costs could be apportioned over production centres:
(a) Cleaning of machines in a food-processing business.
(b) Vehicle maintenance for a fleet of vans used by service engineers.
(c) Canteen services for a company operating a large bus fleet.
(d) Quality control department of an engineering business.
(e) Planning department of a bridge-building company.
(f) Research department of a chemical company.

A4.6   State the principles to be applied in absorbing costs into products (section 4.2.3.).

A4.7   Compare the relative merits of calculating overhead costs per unit of products using each of the following methods (section 4.2.3):
(a) Cost per direct labour hour.
(b) Cost per unit of output.
(c) Cost per direct machine hour.
(d) Cost per £ of direct labour.

A4.8   Explain the meaning of overhead cost recovery (section 4.2.4).

A4.9   What are the benefits and what are the possible problems of using predetermined overhead cost rates (section 4.2.6)?

A4.10   Explain what is meant by under-recovery and over-recovery of overhead cost (section 4.2.7).

A4.11   What are the problems of using blanket overhead cost rates (section 4.2.8)?

A4.12   What is meant by 'cost driver' (section 4.3)?

A4.13 What are the four stages in establishing an activity-based costing system (section 4.3)?

A4.14 What is the nature of an activity (section 4.3.2)?

A4.15 What are the main points of difference between traditional overhead cost allocation and activity-based costing (section 4.4.1)?

A4.16 What are the benefits claimed for activity-based costing (section 4.4.2)?

A4.17 What have researchers found about the range of methods of overhead absorption used in practice (section 4.5.1)?

A4.18 How have researchers used a case study in long-term observation of a change to ABC (section 4.5.2)?

A4.19 How can an ABC framework help in modelling the costs of a public service (section 4.5.3)?

B   Application

B4.1 [S]
A factory manufactures garden huts. The production process is classified into two production departments, Assembly and Joinery. There is one service department, the canteen. The relevant forecast information for the year ahead is as follows:

Indirect costs for all three departments in total:

	Total
	£
Indirect labour	90,000
Indirect material	81,000
Heating and lighting	25,000
Rent and rates	30,000
Depreciation	56,000
Supervision	45,000
Power	36,000
Total	363,000

The following information is available about each department:

	Total	Assembly	Joinery	Canteen
Floor space (sq metres)	50,000	20,000	24,000	6,000
Book value of machinery (£)	560,000	300,000	240,000	20,000
Number of employees	150	80	60	10
Kilowatt hours of power	18,000	9,000	8,000	1,000
Direct materials (£)		100,000	50,000	
Direct labour (£)		50,000	42,000	
Maintenance hours		8,000	6,000	
Labour hours		12,640	8,400	

The canteen is used by both production cost centres.

Required
(1) Apportion production overhead costs over the assembly, joinery and canteen departments using a suitable method for each department.
(2) Apportion service department costs over production departments.
(3) For each production department, calculate an overhead cost rate, based on labour hours, which may be used to absorb production overhead cost into jobs.
(4) Find the overhead cost of a job which spends three labour hours in the assembly department and four labour hours in the joinery department.

B4.2 [S]
A company manufactures golf bags. Golf bags have the following manufacturing costs:

	£ per bag
Labour (5 hours at £5.00/hour)	25
Materials	40
Variable production overheads	10

In addition, the company has monthly fixed production overhead costs of £100,000. 5,000 golf bags are manufactured every month.

Required
Prepare a statement of total product cost for a batch of 5,000 golf bags which shows prime cost and production overhead cost as subtotals.

B4.3 [S]
Budgeted information relating to two departments of Rydons Tables Ltd for the next period is as follows:

Department	Production overhead £	Direct material cost £	Direct labour cost £	Direct labour hours	Machine hours
1	270,000	67,500	13,500	2,700	45,000
2	18,000	36,000	100,000	25,000	300

Individual direct labour employees within each department earn differing rates of pay according to their skills, grade and experience.

Required
(a) Rydons Tables intends to use a production overhead cost rate of £6 per machine hour for absorbing production overhead cost into jobs, based on the budget. Write a short note to the managers of the business commenting on this proposal.
(b) During the past year, Rydons Tables has been using a production overhead cost rate of £5.60 per machine hour. During the year overheads of £275,000 were incurred and 48,000 machine hours worked. Were overheads underabsorbed or overabsorbed, and by how much?

B4.4 [S]
A private college has two teaching departments: languages and science. The college also has a library and a staff refectory, both of which provide services to the teaching departments. The library staff also eat in the refectory. The college administrator feels that the benefits of the staff refectory are best measured in proportion to the number of staff in each department. The benefits of the library are best measured in proportion to the number of students in each department. The overhead costs of each department, and other relevant details, are as follows:

	Languages	Science	Library	Refectory	**Total**
Overhead costs allocated (£)	20,000	15,000	12,000	10,000	**57,000**
Number of staff	4	4	2	2	
Number of students	400	300	–	–	

Required
(1) Prepare a cost apportionment of overhead costs using the step method.
(2) Use a computer-based spreadsheet to calculate the apportionment of overheads using the repeated distribution method.

C　Problem solving and evaluation

C4.1

In a general engineering works the following routine has been followed for several years to arrive at an estimate of the price for a contract.

The process of estimating is started by referring to a job cost card for some previous similar job and evaluating the actual material and direct labour hours used on that job at current prices and rates.

Production overheads are calculated and applied as a percentage of direct wages. The percentage is derived from figures appearing in the accounts of the previous year, using the total production overhead cost divided by the total direct wages cost.

One-third is added to the total production overhead cost to cover administrative charges and profit.

You have been asked to draft a short report to management outlining, with reasons, the changes which you consider desirable in order to improve the process of estimating a price for a contract.

C4.2

You have been asked for advice by the owner of a small business who has previously estimated overhead costs as a percentage of direct labour cost. This method has produced quite reasonable results because the products have all been of similar sales value and have required similar labour inputs. The business has now changed and will in future concentrate on two products. Product X is a high-volume item of relatively low sales value and requires relatively little labour input per item. It is largely produced by automatic processes. Product Y is a low-volume item of relatively high sales value and requires considerably more labour input by specially skilled workers. It is largely produced by manual craft processes.

What advice would you give to the owner of the business about allocation of overhead costs comprising:

● the owner's salary for administrative work
● rent paid on the production facilities
● depreciation of production machinery?

Compare the effect of having one overhead recovery rate for all three costs in aggregate, and the effect of identifying the factors which 'drive' each cost in relation to the production process.

Case studies

Real world cases

Prepare short answers to case studies 4.1, 4.2 and 4.3.

Case 4.4 (group case)

As a group you are the senior teaching staff of a school where each subject department is regarded as a cost centre. The direct costs of each cost centre are teachers' salaries, textbooks and worksheets for pupils. The overhead costs of the school administration are charged to each cost centre as a fixed percentage of teachers' salaries in the cost centre. The languages department argues that this is unfair to them as they have a higher ratio of teachers to pupils due to the need for developing spoken language skills. The art department objects to the percentage charge because it includes accommodation costs without recognising that they are housed in portacabins where the roof leaks. The maths department says that they should not have to share the costs of expensive technical equipment when all they need for effective teaching is a piece of chalk. One member of staff has read about 'cost drivers' and the teachers have decided that they would like to meet the school accountant to put forward some ideas about using them. So far they have made a list of the main overhead costs as:

● heating and lighting
● head teacher, deputy heads and office staff salaries
● cleaning

- maintenance
- library
- computing services for staff
- computing labs for pupils
- insurance of buildings and contents.

Allocate among your group the roles of staff in the languages department, art department and maths department. Discuss cost drivers for each of the overhead costs listed and attempt to arrive at an agreement on cost drivers to be presented to the school accountant. What are the problems of agreeing the drivers? What are the benefits?

Case 4.5 (group case)

Two bus companies are competing for passengers on the most popular routes in a major city. The long-established company has strong customer loyalty, provides weekend and evening services as well as frequent day-time services and covers the cost of unprofitable routes from the profits on popular routes. The incoming company has larger resources from which to support a price war and can be selective in running only at peak times on the most popular routes. There are fears that if the incomer wins the bus war, the quality of service provision will diminish in the evenings and at weekends and on unprofitable routes.

As a group allocate the roles of: (1) passenger representatives, (2) the financial controller's department of the long-established company, (3) members of the city council's transport committee, (4) representatives of the police force. In the separate roles discuss the areas where cost savings might be achieved by the long-established company to make it competitive on price. Then come together and negotiate a support package for the company which focuses on improving the financial performance of the company.

Case 4.6

This text book follows the common practice of describing indirect costs as overhead costs. The following extract from the NHS costing manual gives separate definitions to indirect costs and overhead costs. It is an example of costing terminology being adapted to suit the particular circumstances of the organisation.

Key Concepts

2.2.1 Direct, Indirect and Overhead Costs

2.2.1.1 Direct costs are those which can be directly attributed to the particular cost centre.

For example, the cost of drugs incurred by a doctor or paediatrics may be directly attributed by the pharmacy system. Hence, drugs could be a direct cost of paediatrics.

2.2.1.2 Indirect costs are those costs which cannot be directly allocated to a particular cost centre but can usually be shared over a number of them. Indirect costs need to be allocated to the relevant cost centres. For example, there may be no method of directly allocating laundry costs to a particular cost centre and therefore laundry costs are an indirect cost to a number of cost centres.

2.2.1.3 Overhead costs are the costs of support services that contribute to the effective running of a health care provider. Overhead costs may include the costs of business planning, personnel, finance and the general maintenance of grounds and buildings. They need to be apportioned on a consistent and logical basis. Where such services are shared with other parts of the NHS, care should be taken to ensure the relevant proportions are identified to the relevant services. These proportions should be reviewed annually as utilisation of these services will vary.

Source: NHS costing manual www.dh.gov.uk, 2005.

Questions for discussion

1 How does the NHS costing manual distinguish between indirect costs and overhead costs?

2 What warnings are given about the problems of apportioning overhead costs?

Notes

1. CIMA (2000) *Management Accounting Official Terminology,* CIMA Publishing.
2. Innes and Mitchell (1995).

Chapter 5

Absorption costing and marginal costing

Real world case 5.1

This case study shows a typical situation in which management accounting can be helpful. Read the case study now but only attempt the discussion points after you have finished studying the chapter.

The Department of Health publishes guidance to those recording the costs of health service activities. This is an extract from the Guidance manual.

Costing

The principles for costing in the NHS are set out in chapter 2 of the NHS Costing Manual. The fundamental principle is that reference costs should be produced using full absorption costing. This means that each reported unit cost will include the direct, indirect and overhead costs associated with providing that treatment/care.

The costing guidance states that as far as possible costs should be directly allocated to specialty level. Where this is not possible, appropriate apportionment methodology should be used. The costing manual provides guidance on appropriate apportionment methodology and the treatment of indirect and overhead costs. Given maintained audit involvement for 2005, it is vital that decisions and processes undertaken in apportioning costs are defensible.

Source: *Department of Health Reference Costs 2005 Collection – Guidance* October 2004, p. 66 downloaded from www.dh.gov.uk/

Discussion points

1 What problems might be faced in apportioning overhead costs?
2 Why might it be important that decisions and processes used in apportionment are defensible?

Contents

Learning outcomes

After reading this chapter you should be able to:

- Define and explain absorption costing (full costing) and marginal costing (variable costing).

- Illustrate absorption (full) costing and marginal (variable) costing using a simple example.

- Explain and calculate the effect on profit of over-absorbed and under-absorbed fixed overheads.

- Compare profit based on absorption costing with profit based on marginal costing.

- Explain how absorption costing is applied in financial accounting.

- Explain the arguments in favour of absorption costing and marginal costing.

- Describe and discuss examples of research into full costing and marginal costing.

5.1 Introduction

Methods of apportioning (sharing) fixed production overhead costs were explained in detail in Chapter 4. Because of the problems that may arise because of apportionment, there are situations in management accounting where it is preferable to avoid the problem by allocating only variable costs to products. Fixed production overhead costs are regarded as costs of the period rather than costs of the product. The question to be addressed in this section is how the choice between **absorption costing** (which means absorbing all costs into products) and **marginal costing** (which means taking in only the variable costs of production) may be dependent on the purpose to which management accounting is being applied.

Definitions

> In **absorption costing** (*full costing*), all production costs are absorbed into products. The unsold inventory is measured at total cost of production. Fixed production overhead costs are treated as a product cost.
>
> In **marginal costing** (*variable costing*), only variable costs of production are allocated to products. The unsold inventory is measured at variable cost of production. Fixed production overhead costs are treated as a period cost of the period in which they are incurred.

5.2 A note on terminology: marginal or variable?

Some authorities on management accounting refer to 'marginal costing' while others refer to 'variable costing'. The strict interpretation of 'marginal cost' in economics is the additional cost of one more unit of output. From the economists' viewpoint that extra cost could include a stepped increase in fixed cost if capacity has to be expanded to produce one more unit of output or if a new employee is required. For this chapter we assume that the range of activity is narrow so that a marginal change in cost involves variable costs only.

5.3 Illustration of absorption and marginal costing

This example illustrates the application of absorption costing and marginal costing. It uses the same basic data for both illustrations.

5.3.1 Absorption costing

In **absorption costing** (*full costing*), all production costs are absorbed into products. The unsold inventory is measured at total cost of production. Fixed production overhead costs are treated as a product cost.

From the data in Exhibit 5.1, the **budgeted fixed overhead cost rate** is £3 per unit (calculated as £30,000/10,000 units).

The full cost of production per unit is £16 (calculated as variable cost £13 plus fixed cost £3).

The profit and loss statement for July, based on absorption costing is shown in Exhibit 5.2.

Exhibit 5.1
Data for illustration: absorption and marginal costing

Mirror View Ltd produces freestanding magnifying mirrors for use in the home. The budgeted selling price and costs are as follows:

Budget for one unit:

	£
Selling price	20
Direct materials	8
Direct labour	3
Variable production overhead	2
Total variable cost	13

The fixed production overhead cost for one month is budgeted as £30,000. The budgeted production volume is 10,000 units per month. Budgeted sales are expected to equal budgeted production volumes.

For the months of January to June the production and sales were 10,000 per month as budgeted. In the month of July the production was 10,000 but the sales were only 9,600 units, leaving 400 units in inventory (stock) as unsold goods. In the month of August the production was again 10,000 but the sales were 10,400 units. For the months of September to December the production and sales were again 10,000 units as budgeted.

Exhibit 5.2
Profit and loss statement, month of July, based on absorption costing

Month of July	£	£
Sales (9,600 at £20)		192,000
Opening inventory	–	
Costs of production (10,000 at £16)	160,000	
Less closing inventory (400 at £16)	(6,400)	
Cost of goods sold		(153,600)
Profit		38,400

Comment

There is no opening inventory because until the end of June the sales and production were equal. The costs of production are recorded at the full cost of £16 to be absorbed by each unit. The closing inventory is valued at the full cost of production of £16 per unit.

5.3.2 Marginal costing

In **marginal costing** (*variable costing*), only variable costs of production are allocated to products in Exhibit 5.3. The unsold inventory is measured at variable cost of

Exhibit 5.3
Profit and loss statement, month of July, based on marginal costing

Month of July	£	£
Sales (9,600 at £20)		192,000
Opening inventory	–	
Costs of production (10,000 at £13)	130,000	
Less closing inventory (400 at £13)	(5,200)	
Variable cost of goods sold		(124,800)
Contribution to fixed overhead cost		67,200
Fixed overhead costs		(30,000)
		37,200

production. Fixed production overhead costs are treated as a period cost of the period in which they are incurred. The calculations are shown in Exhibit 5.3.

Comment

As in the previous calculation there is no opening inventory because until the end of June, the sales and production were equal. The costs of production are recorded at the variable cost of £13 to be absorbed by each unit. The closing inventory is valued at the variable cost of production of £13 per unit. Sales minus variable costs gives a contribution to fixed overhead costs. (Contribution is discussed in more detail in Chapter 9.) The fixed overhead costs of production are treated as a period cost and reported as a separate line in the profit and loss statement.

5.3.3 Explaining the difference

The difference in profit is £38,400 − £37,200 = £1,200. The profit based on absorption costing is higher in this example because the closing stock of 400 units carries £3 of fixed overhead per unit, as a product cost, to the next accounting period.

Activity 5.1

Now try for yourself to carry out the calculations using absorption costing and marginal costing for the month of August. In August there is an opening stock of 400 units but no closing stock. When you have tried this, check with the next section.

5.3.4 Inventory levels falling

Over the month of August the inventory falls from 400 units at the start of the month to nil at the end of the month (see Exhibits 5.4 and 5.5).

Exhibit 5.4
Profit and loss statement, month of August, based on absorption costing

Month of August	£	£
Sales (10,400 at £20)		208,000
Opening inventory (400 at £16)	6,400	
Costs of production (10,000 at £16)	160,000	
Less closing inventory	–	
Cost of goods sold		(166,400)
Profit		41,600

Exhibit 5.5
Profit and loss statement, month of August, based on marginal costing

Month of August	£	£
Sales (10,400 at £20)		208,000
Opening inventory (400 at £13)	5,200	
Costs of production (10,000 at £13)	130,000	
Less closing inventory	–	
Variable cost of goods sold		(135,200)
Contribution to fixed overhead cost		72,800
Fixed overhead costs		(30,000)
Profit		42,800

Comment

The difference in profit is £42,800 – £41,600 = £1,200. The profit based on absorption costing is lower in this example because the opening inventory of 400 units carries £3 of fixed overhead per unit, as a product cost, from the previous accounting period.

Activity 5.2

Work out how the answers in Exhibit 5.4 and Exhibit 5.5 would change if the inventory levels were rising. Then check with the next section.

5.3.5 Inventory levels rising

Suppose that, over the month of August, the inventory rises from 400 units at the start of the month to 600 at the end of the month (see Exhibits 5.6 and 5.7). Assume the production remains the same at 10,000 units. The sales are therefore 9,800 units.

Exhibit 5.6
Profit and loss statement, month of August, based on absorption costing

Month of August	£	£
Sales (9,800 at £20)		196,000
Opening inventory (400 at £16)	6,400	
Costs of production (10,000 at £16)	160,000	
Less closing inventory (600 at £16)	(9,600)	
Cost of goods sold		(156,800)
Profit		39,200

Exhibit 5.7
Profit and loss statement, month of August, based on marginal costing

Month of August	£	£
Sales (9,800 at £20)		196,000
Opening inventory (400 at £13)	5,200	
Costs of production (10,000 at £13)	130,000	
Less closing inventory (600 at £13)	(7,800)	
Variable cost of goods sold		(127,400)
Contribution to fixed overhead cost		68,600
Fixed overhead costs		(30,000)
		38,600

Comment

The difference in profit is £39,200 – £38,600 = £600. The profit based on absorption costing is higher in this example because the closing inventory of 600 units carries £3 of fixed overhead per unit as product cost while the opening inventory of 400 units carries £3 of fixed overhead per unit, as a product cost, from the previous accounting period. The difference is an increase of 200 units carrying forward £3 of fixed cost per unit, which is £600 in total. This cost of £600 is carried forward to the next period with the unsold inventory.

5.4 Over- and under-absorbed fixed overheads

In Chapter 4 the calculation of over-recovery and under-recovery of fixed overhead costs is explained. This is also called over-absorbed and under-absorbed fixed overheads. The adjustment of costs for over- and under-absorption is made in the cost of sales as shown in this section.

5.4.1 Over-absorbed fixed overhead

Now change the data in Exhibit 5.1 so that the level of production is different from that budgeted. In Exhibit 5.8 the actual production overhead level in July is higher at 10,100 than the budgeted level of 10,000. The actual production level in August is lower at 9,900 than the budgeted level of 10,000. Exhibit 5.9 shows the absorption costing profit for July, while Exhibit 5.10 shows the marginal costing profit for July.

Exhibit 5.8
Data for illustration: absorption and marginal costing

Mirror View Ltd produces freestanding magnifying mirrors for use in the home. The budgeted selling price and costs are as follows:

Budget for one unit:

	£
Selling price	20
Direct materials	8
Direct labour	3
Variable production overhead	2
Total variable cost	13

The fixed production overhead cost for one month is budgeted as £30,000. The budgeted production volume is 10,000 units per month. Budgeted sales are expected to equal budgeted production volumes.

For the months of January to June the production and sales were 10,000 per month as budgeted. In the month of July the production was 10,100 but the sales were only 9,700 units, leaving 400 units in inventory (stock) as unsold goods. In the month of August the production was 9,900 but the sales were 10,300 units. For the months of September to December the production and sales were again 10,000 units as budgeted.

Exhibit 5.9
Profit and loss statement, month of July, based on absorption costing

Month of July	£	£
Sales (9,700 at £20)		194,000
Opening inventory	–	
Costs of production (10,100 at £16)	161,600	
Less over-absorbed overhead (100 at £3)	(300)	
Less closing inventory (400 at £16)	(6,400)	
Cost of goods sold		(154,900)
Profit		39,100

The over-absorbed overhead arises because the actual level of production was 100 units higher than expected. A total cost of £16 was charged to each of the additional units produced. The variable cost element of this charge, at £13 each, was justified because the additional units required additional variable costs of materials and labour. However, the fixed cost element of £3 per unit is not justified because the fixed cost does not increase with additional production. This part of the additional production cost charge must therefore be removed by deducting £300 (100 × £3).

Exhibit 5.10
Profit and loss statement, month of July, based on marginal costing

Month of July	£	£
Sales (9,700 at £20)		194,000
Opening inventory	–	
Costs of production (10,100 at £13)	131,300	
Less closing inventory (400 at £13)	(5,200)	
Variable cost of goods sold		(126,100)
Contribution to fixed overhead cost		67,900
Fixed overhead costs		(30,000)
Profit		37,900

The absorption costing profit is greater than the marginal costing profit. The difference is £1,200 measured as 400 × £3 fixed overhead cost carried forward in closing inventory (with opening inventory nil).

5.4.2 Under-absorbed fixed overhead

For the month of August the information in Exhibit 5.8 shows that the sales are £10,300 units and the production is 9,900 units (see Exhibits 5.11 and 5.12).

Exhibit 5.11
Profit and loss statement, month of August, based on absorption costing

Month of August	£	£
Sales (10,300 at £20)		206,000
Opening inventory (400 at £16)	6,400	
Costs of production (9,900 at £16)	158,400	
Add under-absorbed overhead (100 at £3)	300	
Less closing inventory	–	
Cost of goods sold		(165,100)
Profit		40,900

The under-absorbed overhead arises because the actual level of production was 100 units lower than expected. The lower variable cost is justified by the lower volume. However, the fixed cost element of £3 per unit must be charged on the expected basis of 10,000 units because fixed costs do not decrease when production volume decreases. This part of the production cost charge must therefore be included by adding £300 (100 × £3).

Exhibit 5.12
Profit and loss statement, month of August, based on marginal costing

Month of July	£	£
Sales (10,300 at £20)		206,000
Opening inventory (400 at £13)	5,200	
Costs of production (9,900 at £13)	128,700	
Less closing inventory	–	
Variable cost of goods sold		(133,900)
Contribution to fixed overhead cost		72,100
Fixed overhead costs		(30,000)
Profit		42,100

The absorption costing profit is less than the marginal costing profit. The difference is £1,200 measured as 400 × £3 fixed overhead cost brought forward in the opening inventory with closing inventory nil.

5.5 Case study

This case study compares the effect of carrying fixed production overheads as a product cost or a period cost and also shows the effect of under-absorbed and over-absorbed fixed production overheads.

Casual Tables is a business that manufactures plastic tables for use in pavement cafés and bars. All tables are identical. The planning manager of Casual Tables is planning its operations for the next five months. Data regarding budgeted selling price, budgeted variable cost per unit and fixed production overheads are given in Exhibit 5.13, together with budgeted volumes of production and sales over the next five months. The question to be answered is, 'How much profit is expected for each of the five months?'

Exhibit 5.13
Data for comparing absorption costing and marginal costing

	£
Selling price per unit	20
Variable cost per unit	9
Fixed costs for each period	500

	Month 1 units	Month 2 units	Month 3 units	Month 4 units	Month 5 units
Produced	230	270	260	240	250
Sold	200	210	260	280	300
Held in stock at end of period	30	90	90	50	nil

Under absorption costing the first task is to decide how the fixed production costs for each month should be allocated to products. Where production volume is varying in the manner shown in Exhibit 5.13, a common practice is to base the predetermined overhead cost rate on the **normal level of activity**. There is no precise definition for this, but it would take into account the budgeted level of activity in recent periods, the activity achieved in recent periods, and the expected output from normal working conditions. In this case, it might be reasonable to take a normal level of activity as the average production level, which is 250 units per month. The predetermined fixed overhead cost rate is therefore £2 per unit.

5.5.1 Absorption costing

Using absorption costing, the opening and closing stock is valued at total cost of £11 per unit, comprising variable cost per unit of £9 and fixed cost per unit of £2. Exhibit 5.14 illustrates the absorption costing approach.

The line labelled 'under/(over) absorbed' reflects the absorption of overhead where the production of the months is above or below the base level of 250 units used to calculate the fixed overhead cost rate.

Exhibit 5.14
Expected profit per month under absorption costing

	Month 1	Month 2	Month 3	Month 4	Month 5	Total
	£	£	£	£	£	£
Sales	4,000	4,200	5,200	5,600	6,000	25,000
Production units	230	270	260	240	250	
	£	£	£	£	£	£
Opening inventory at £11	nil	330	990	990	550	nil
Cost of production:						
At £11 per unit	2,530	2,970	2,860	2,640	2,750	13,750
Under/(over) absorbed	40	(40)	(20)	20	–	
Closing inventory at £11	(330)	(990)	(990)	(550)	nil	nil
Cost of goods sold	2,240	2,270	2,840	3,100	3,300	13,750
Profit	1,760	1,930	2,360	2,500	2,700	11,250

In month 1 the production, at 230 units, is 20 units less than the base level of 250. The cost absorbed by 230 units is £460 which is £40 less than the expected fixed overhead cost of £500 for the month. Another way of arriving at the same conclusion is to say that overhead is under-absorbed by £40 (multiplying 20 units by the fixed overhead cost rate of £2 each). In order to increase the absorbed cost of £460 to the expected (or actual) cost of £500, the £40 difference must be added to production cost in calculating the cost of sales.

In month 2 the production level is 270 units, which is 20 units higher than the base level of 250. This means that fixed overhead is over-absorbed by £40 (20 units at £2). The over-absorbed cost must be deducted from the cost of production to arrive at the cost of goods sold.

In month 3 the production level is 260 units, which is 10 units higher than the base level of 250. This means that fixed overhead is over-absorbed by £20 (10 units at £2). The over-absorbed cost is deducted from the cost of production.

In month 4 the production level is 240 units, which is 10 units less than the base level of 250. This means that fixed overhead is under-absorbed by £20 (10 units at £2). The under-absorbed cost is added to the cost of production.

In month 5 the production level is 250 units, equal to the base level. This means that exactly the correct amount of overhead cost is absorbed and no adjustment is needed.

Activity 5.3

Go back to the data of Exhibit 5.13. Cover up the answer in Exhibit 5.14 and then attempt to write out the profit calculation under absorption costing. Add a note of narrative explanation to each line as a means of helping understanding by yourself and others. Make sure that you understand the absorption costing approach fully.

Activity 5.4

Look back at the data of Exhibit 5.13. Before turning to the answer in Exhibit 5.15 attempt to write out the profit calculation under marginal costing. Add a note of narrative explanation to each line as a means of helping understanding by yourself and others.

5.5.2 Marginal costing

Using marginal costing, the stock of unsold output at the end of each month would be valued at the variable cost of £9 per unit. The fixed cost would be regarded as a cost of the month, without allocation to products. Exhibit 5.15 illustrates the marginal costing approach.

Exhibit 5.15
Expected profit per month under marginal costing

	Month 1	Month 2	Month 3	Month 4	Month 5	Total
	£	£	£	£	£	£
Sales	4,000	4,200	5,200	5,600	6,000	25,000
Production units	230	270	260	240	250	
	£	£	£	£	£	£
Opening inventory at £9	nil	270	810	810	450	nil
Cost of production at £9	2,070	2,430	2,340	2,160	2,250	11,250
Closing inventory at £9	(270)	(810)	(810)	(450)	nil	nil
Variable cost of goods sold	1,800	1,890	2,340	2,520	2,700	11,250
Fixed costs of month	500	500	500	500	500	2,500
Total costs	2,300	2,390	2,840	3,020	3,200	13,750
Profit	1,700	1,810	2,360	2,580	2,800	11,250

Comparing Exhibit 5.15 with Exhibit 5.14, it may be seen that there is no under- or over-absorption in the marginal costing example because it treats fixed overhead cost of production as a period cost, not a product cost.

5.5.3 Comparison of profit under each approach

Exhibit 5.16 compares the profit calculated under each approach.

Exhibit 5.16
Comparison of profit, using absorption costing and marginal costing

	Month 1 £	Month 2 £	Month 3 £	Month 4 £	Month 5 £	Total £
Absorption costing	1,760	1,930	2,360	2,500	2,700	11,250
Variable costing	1,700	1,810	2,360	2,580	2,800	11,250
Difference	+60	+120	0	−80	−100	0

In month 1, the absorption costing profit is higher by £60, because there is an increase in inventory of 30 units, carrying a fixed overhead cost of £2 each. The increased inventory carries that cost forward to the next accounting period.

In month 2, the absorption costing profit is higher by £120, because there is an increase in inventory of 60 units, carrying a fixed overhead cost of £2 each.

In month 3, the absorption costing profit and the marginal costing profit are the same, because there is no change in inventory levels.

In month 4, the absorption costing profit is lower by £80, because there is a decrease in inventory of 40 units, bringing an additional fixed overhead of £2 each.

In month 5, absorption costing profit is lower by £100, because there is a decrease in inventory of 50 units, bringing an additional fixed overhead of £2 each.

Over the total period of five months the sales and production are equal, so absorption costing and marginal costing give the same total profit of £11,250.

Activity 5.5

Before reading the rest of this section, write a brief commentary on the most significant features of Exhibit 5.16.

Points to note

1 Over the total period of time, where total production equals total sales, there is no difference in total profit (see Exhibit 5.16). The difference between absorption costing and marginal costing is purely a result of timing of the matching of fixed overhead costs of production with sales.

2 In any period when stock levels are constant, both approaches give the same answer. During month 3, stock levels remain constant and therefore both approaches give the same answer.

3 The differences between the two profit calculations in any period are based entirely on the *change* in volume of stock during the month, multiplied by the fixed overhead cost rate of £2 per unit. During month 1, stock increases by 30 units over the month and, as a consequence, profit under absorption costing is £60 higher than under marginal costing. During month 2, stock increases by 60 units over the month and, as a consequence, profit under absorption costing is £120 higher. During month 4, stock levels decrease by 40 units so that profit under absorption costing is £80 lower. During month 5, stock levels decrease by 50 units and therefore profit under absorption costing is £100 lower.

4 The overall effect of the positive and negative differences over the business life is zero, provided the allocation process is applied consistently. Different allocation processes will cause costs to fall in different time months, but they cannot create or destroy costs in the total.

5 The effect of the change in stock levels may be understood using Exhibit 5.16. Making a general statement from this specific example, it appears safe to say that when stock levels are increasing, profit under absorption costing is higher than it is under marginal costing. That is because a portion of the fixed production cost incurred in the month is carried forward to the next month as part of the closing stock valuation.

6 Generalising further from the analysis, it may be said that when stock levels are decreasing, profit under absorption costing is lower than it is under marginal costing. That is because fixed costs incurred in earlier months are brought to the current month as part of the opening stock, to be sold during the month.

5.6 Why is it necessary to understand the difference?

In Chapter 1 it was shown that management accounting has three major roles in directing attention, keeping the score and solving problems. The particular role which applies in any situation will depend upon the management function which is being served. That management function could relate to the formation of a judgement or to making a decision about a course of action. Chapter 2 showed that the classification of costs very much depends on which of the three management accounting roles is dominant in any specific situation and on the type of management function.

Where the management function relates to planning and control, the management accountant is carrying out a score-keeping function and it is usually necessary to account for fixed overhead costs of production as a part of the product cost. That means absorption costing is the appropriate approach. In this situation there is a strong overlap with financial accounting and with external reporting to stakeholders in a business. If the stakeholders are company shareholders, then the external reporting will be regulated by company law and accounting standards that require fixed costs of production to be treated as product costs and provide guidance on the allocation process. Where the stakeholders are the electorate, in the case of a public sector body, or partners in a business partnership, the rules may be more flexible, but in many cases they conventionally follow the practice recommended for companies.

Real world case 5.2

This extract from a newspaper article comments on comparisons between the public sector National Health Service and the private sector provision of healthcare, quoting the British United Provident Association (BUPA) which owns private hospitals that charge fees to patients.

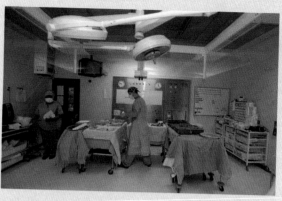

Looking at Tory policies in any detail shows that the party isn't seriously preparing for government. Its health policy, for example, would let private clinics treat National Health Service patients, but only if they can do an operation for the same price or below. Examine the detail, and this policy disintegrates for a simple reason: the official NHS price list is cheaper in every case. BUPA's price list shows £2,100 for a cataract removal, against the NHS's £1,000, and £8,100 for a hip replacement, against the NHS's £4,800.

A fair comparison? Absolutely not, says BUPA; its prices include all costs – building, equipment, capital, sick pay, the works. The NHS price list is not inclusive of overheads – nor, crucially, the phenomenal pensions bill for its one million staff.

For the Tory policy to work, a new and fair NHS tariff must be compiled.

Source: *The Scotsman*, 19 January 2005, p. 24 'Softly-softly Toryism is Howard's big mistake', Fraser Nelson.

Discussion points

1 What is the complaint of the author of the article?

2 How does the complaint in this extract match the information in Real World case 5.1 extracted from the NHS costing guidance?

5.7 Absorption costing in financial accounting

In the valuation of inventory (stock), management accounting interacts with financial accounting. The accounting standards for inventory valuation set out rules which apply principles of absorption costing. This means that a portion of the fixed overheads must be allocated to inventory. If there was total freedom of choice in allocating fixed overheads, some managers would seek to allocate a *high proportion* of fixed overheads to inventory, in order to report the highest possible profit and so maintain stock market confidence, while other managers would seek to allocate a *low proportion* of fixed overheads to inventory, in order to report the lowest possible profit and so reduce the tax bill payable. In order to encourage confidence in the reliability of accounting information, and to reduce opportunities for earnings management, there must be *rules* on the manner of allocating fixed overhead costs of production. The financial reporting standards are also concerned with prudence – meaning that profits should not be overstated. The rules of the International Accounting Standards Board are set out in Exhibit 5.17, with added emphasis to bring out points of particular interest for absorption costing. The requirement for absorption costing is indicated by the wording of paragraph 10. The words '*systematic allocation*' in paragraph 12 are open to interpretation, giving scope for applying management accounting principles. Paragraph 12 also confirms that only production overheads are incorporated in the valuation of inventories, consistent with the condition in paragraph 9 of bringing *the inventories to their present condition and location* (i.e. produced and ready for sale).[1]

Exhibit 5.17
Inventory valuation, IAS 2

9. Inventories shall be measured at the lower of cost and net realisable value.

10. The cost of inventories shall comprise all costs of purchase, costs of conversion and other costs incurred in bringing the inventories to their present location and condition.

11. The costs of purchase of inventories comprise the purchase price, import duties and other taxes (other than those subsequently recoverable by the entity from the taxing authorities), and transport, handling and other costs directly attributable to the acquisition of finished goods, materials and services. Trade discounts, rebates and other similar items are deducted in determining the costs of purchase.

Costs of conversion
12. The costs of conversion of inventories include costs directly related to the units of production, such as direct labour. They also include a *systematic allocation* of fixed and variable production overheads that are incurred in converting materials into finished goods. *Fixed production overheads* are those indirect costs of production that remain relatively constant regardless of the volume of production, such as depreciation and maintenance of factory buildings and equipment, and the cost of factory management and administration. *Variable production overheads* are those indirect costs of production that vary directly, or nearly directly, with the volume of production, such as indirect materials and indirect labour.

13. The allocation of fixed production overheads to the costs of conversion is based on the *normal capacity* of the production facilities. Normal capacity is the production expected to be achieved on average over a number of periods or seasons under normal circumstances, taking into account the loss of capacity resulting from planned maintenance. The actual level of production may be used if it approximates to normal capacity. The amount of fixed overhead allocated to each unit of production is not increased as a consequence of low production or idle plant. Unallocated overheads are recognised as an expense in the period in which they are incurred. In periods of *abnormally high production*, the amount of fixed overhead allocated to each unit of production is decreased so that inventories are not measured above cost. Variable production overheads are allocated to each unit of production on the basis of the actual use of the production facilities.

14. A production process may result in more than one product being produced simultaneously. This is the case, for example, when joint products are produced or when there is a main product and a by-product. When the costs of conversion of each product are not separately identifiable, they are allocated between the products on a rational and consistent basis. The allocation may be based, for example, on the relative sales value of each product either at the stage in the production process when the products become separately identifiable, or at the completion of production. Most by-products, by their nature, are immaterial. When this is the case, they are often measured at net realisable value and this value is deducted from the cost of the main product. As a result, the carrying amount of the main product is not materially different from its cost.

Source: International Accounting Standard IAS 2 (2003) *Inventories*, International Accounting Standards Board.
© 2003 International Accounting Standards Committee Foundation.

Similar principles are applied in the UK accounting standard SSAP 9 (1988) but it gives more detailed guidance on the meaning of 'normal activity'. SSAP 9 contains similar definitions in paragraphs 17 to 21. Appendix 1 'Further practical considerations' contains a section on 'The allocation of overheads' (paras 1 to 10) which gives detailed guidance on the application of absorption costing.

Exhibit 5.18
SSAP 9 and normal level of activity

8. The allocation of overheads included in the valuation of stocks and long-term contracts needs to be based on the company's normal level of activity, taking one year with another. The governing factor is that the cost of unused capacity should be written off in the current year. In determining what constitutes 'normal' the following factors need to be considered:

(a) the volume of production which the production facilities are intended by their designers and by management to produce under the working conditions (e.g. single or double shift) prevailing during the year;
(b) the budgeted level of activity for the year under review and for the ensuing year;
(c) the level of activity achieved both in the year under review and in previous years.

Source: Statement of Standard Accounting Practice SSAP 9 (1988). Stocks and Long-Term Contracts, Accounting Standards Board (UK). Appendix 1.

5.8 Arguments in favour of absorption costing

The arguments put forward in favour of absorption costing are:

1 Since all production costs are incurred with a view to creating a product for sale, all costs should attach to products until they are sold.
2 In the longer term, fixed overhead costs must be recovered through sales if the business is to survive. Setting the stock value by reference to full costs encourages a pricing policy which covers full cost.
3 If fixed production costs are treated as period costs (as happens in marginal costing) and there is a low level of sales activity in a period, then a relatively low profit or loss will be reported. If there is a high level of sales activity, there will be a relatively high profit. Absorption costing smooths out these fluctuations by carrying the fixed costs forward until the goods are sold.
4 Absorption costing helps the 'matching concept' of matching sales with the cost of sales of the same period
5 Where overhead costs are high in relation to direct costs, and fixed overheads are high in relation to variable costs, a marginal costing approach would bring out only a small portion of the total cost picture.
6 Absorption costing can be used in a 'cost plus profit' approach to pricing a contract for a customer.

5.9 Arguments in favour of marginal costing

Where the management accounting role is primarily that of directing attention and the management function is primarily one of decision making, it may be dangerous to regard fixed production costs as product costs. The attractions of using marginal costing in such a situation are as follows:

1 In the short term, relevant costs are required for decision making and fixed overheads are largely non-relevant because they cannot be avoided. They are best seen as a committed cost of the period.
2 Marginal costing avoids the arbitrary allocations of absorption costing, which may be misleading for short-term decision making.
3 Profit calculation is not dependent on changes in stock levels. The Exhibits in this chapter illustrate the practical effect of disentangling fixed costs from stock values.

4 There is no risk of carrying forward in stock an element of fixed production over-head cost which may not be recovered through sales.

5 Allocating all production costs to products and then applying full-cost pricing may result in loss of sales which would have made a contribution to fixed production costs and profit.

6 Where sales volumes are declining but output is sustained, marginal costing pro-vides the profit warning more rapidly than does absorption costing in a situation where attention needs to be drawn urgently to the profit implications.

Activity 5.6

Now that you understand the difference between marginal costing and absorption costing, write a short evaluation of the two approaches.

Real world case 5.3

The Guidance Manual of the NHS, quoted in Real world case 5.1, contains a great deal of detail on how to calculate full absorption costs of activities. This section explains the calculation of the cost of each outpatient's attendance at a clinic providing mental health services, where non-attendance is a problem

156 Due to the particular nature of mental health services, 'DNAs' ('Did Not Attends') utilise considerable mental health resources but, up until now, this activity has not formed part of the reference costs collection. In a change to reporting requirements, outpatient activity for mental health services will require 'DNA' activity to be identified and reported separately as a memorandum item. There is no requirement to submit unit cost data for 'DNAs'. This means that:

● The total cost of a specific outpatient service, calculated using total absorption costing methodology, should be identified for each category of collection, for each of first and follow up outpatient attendances in mental health.

● Activity for the total number of face to face attendances for each of first and follow up attendances should be identified.

● Unit cost for each type of attendance should be calculated by dividing total cost by the total number of face to face attendances for each of first and follow up attendances.

● In addition, total number of 'DNAs' for each of first and follow up attendances should be reported as a memorandum item. This activity must not be included in the total face to face activity reported, nor in the calculation of the unit cost of face to face attendance, as to do so would inappropriately dilute the reported costs.

Source: *Department of Health Reference Costs 2005 Collection – Guidance* October 2004, para 156, downloaded from www.dh.gov.uk/

Discussion points

1 What are the benefits of recommending full absorption costing?

2 What are the benefits and limitations of dividing total cost by number of face to face attendances?

5.10 What the researchers have found

5.10.1 Full costing in the NHS

Northcott and Llewellyn (2003) reported opinions on the UK national reference costing index as a measure of the 'ladder of success' in health care services. The Real world cases 5.1 and 5.3 in this chapter have given a brief insight into the depth of detail of the guidance given on recording costs in the NHS. Northcott and Llewellyn explored views on the way that these costs are aggregated to give a comparative index for hospital costs. They found problems in the absence of a standard against which to compare actual costs, in non-comparability of hospitals featured in the index, and in lack of standardisation of costing practices. The comments made by interviewees included concerns about the process of cost allocation.

Healthcare activities are categorised within healthcare resource groups (HRGs). The costs of these HRGs are calculated retrospectively based on actual costs incurred by hospital trusts. To calculate the HRG costs, the trusts produce 'costed care profiles'. There is no standard approach to working out these costs, so trusts can use different cost pools and different methods of apportionment. Tables are published with the intention that performance can be compared but if the processes are not standardised then the comparisons may not be valid.

The authors recommend separate reporting of direct and indirect costs, more careful definition of clusters of trusts having similar characteristics, target cost outcome for each cluster rather than judging all against the overall average, and a focus on selective comparison rather than coverage of all treatments. However, they also recognise that such changes are unlikely because making the indexes more meaningful could reduce the political power of a single index.

5.10.2 Full cost accounting and environmental resources

Bebbington *et al* (2001) explained the problems of measuring the full cost of production when environmental costs are taken into account. If the full costs are not measured then it is not possible to say whether the activity is sustainable in the longer term. For this exercise 'full cost' has a very broad meaning. It starts with the direct and indirect costs usually associated with production, as explained in Chapters 4 and 5. It then looks for hidden costs of sustaining production, such as monitoring and safety costs. Next come the liabilities to make good environmental damage. Then there are costs and benefits associated with the reputation of the business as good or insensitive to the environment. Finally there are the costs that the organisation would incur if it had a positive attitude towards maintaining and improving the environment. The authors call for a full cost framework based on these ideas. There is no practical framework in place as yet but, given the continued political interest in matters of sustainability, it seems quite likely that the debate on 'full costing' will continue.

5.11 Summary

This chapter has explained the differences between absorption costing and marginal costing.

Key themes in this chapter are:

● In **absorption costing** (*full costing*), all production costs are absorbed into products. The unsold inventory is measured at total cost of production. Fixed production overhead costs are treated as a product cost.

- In **marginal costing** (*variable costing*), only variable costs of production are allocated to products. The unsold inventory is measured at variable cost of production. Fixed production overhead costs are treated as a period cost of the period in which they are incurred.

- Under-absorbed or over-absorbed fixed overhead cost may arise in absorption costing. It is reported in the profit and loss statement as an adjustment to cost of sales.

- Profit under absorption costing *differs* from profit under marginal costing *when inventory levels are changing.* If *total production equals total sales* there is *no difference* in total profit.

- When inventory levels are *falling*, profit under **absorption costing** is *lower* than profit under **marginal costing**. The difference is equal to the *decrease in inventory levels* multiplied by the *fixed overhead cost rate.*

- When inventory levels are *rising*, profit under **absorption costing** is *higher* than profit under **marginal costing**. The difference is equal to the *increase in inventory levels* multiplied by the *fixed overhead cost rate.*

- **Absorption costing** is usually required for inventory valuation in **financial accounting** standards or other regulations. Those using such financial statements need to be aware that reported profit can be affected by the change in the volume of inventory over the period.

- **Marginal costing** may be more useful for **decision making** because it treats fixed production overhead costs as a cost of the period. Reported profit is not affected by the changes in inventory held.

References and further reading

Northcott, D. and Llewellyn, S. (2003) 'The "ladder of success" in healthcare: the UK national reference costing index', *Management Accounting Research*, 14: 51–66.

QUESTIONS

The Questions section of each chapter has three types of question. 'Test your understanding' questions to help you review your reading are in the 'A' series of questions. You will find the answer to these by reading and thinking about the material in the text book. 'Application' questions to test your ability to apply technical skills are in the 'B' series of questions. Questions requiring you to show skills in problem solving and evaluation are in the 'C' series of questions. A symbol [S] means that there is a solution available at the end of the book.

A   Test your understanding

A5.1   Define absorption costing (section 5.3.1).

A5.2   Define marginal costing (section 5.3.2).

A5.3   Explain why absorption costing and marginal costing may lead to different measures of profit in a period (section 5.3.3).

A5.4   When the volume of closing inventory is lower than the volume of opening inventory, which will show the greater profit, absorption costing or marginal costing (section 5.3.4)?

A5.5   When the volume of closing inventory is greater than the volume of opening inventory, which will show the greater profit, absorption costing or marginal costing (section 5.3.5)?

A5.6   When the volume of closing inventory is the same as the volume of opening inventory, which will show the greater profit, absorption costing or marginal costing (sections 5.3.4 and 5.3.5)?

A5.7   What are the requirements of financial reporting with regard to the absorption of fixed overhead costs of production (section 5.7)?

A5.8   Set out the arguments in favour of absorption costing (section 5.8).

A5.9   Set out the arguments in favour of marginal costing (section 5.9).

A5.10   What have researchers found about full costing in the NHS (section 5.10.1)?

A5.11   How is the idea of 'full costing' extended when long-term environmental costs are considered (section 5.10.2)?

B   Application

B5.1 [S]

Bookcases Ltd produces packs of book shelves for self-assembly. The budgeted selling price and costs are as follows:

Budget for one unit:

	£
Selling price	60
Direct materials	36
Direct labour	5
Variable production overhead	3
Total variable cost	44

The fixed production overhead cost for one month is budgeted as £40,000. The budgeted production volume is 5,000 units per month.

In the month of February sales are lower than expected. At the start of March there are 200 unsold units in stock. Production is maintained at 5,000 units in the month of March.

Required

Calculate the profit for March under (a) absorption costing and (b) marginal costing for each of the following situations:

(1) Situation A: sales in March are 4,700 units
(2) Situation B: sales in March are 5,100 units

B5.2 [S]

Playtime Ltd produces jigsaws for sale in model shops. The following information relates to the sales and costs of producing the jigsaws.

Selling price per unit is £20
Variable cost per unit is £10
Fixed costs of the period are £800

Volumes of production and sales are as follows for periods 1, 2 and 3.

	Period 1 units	Period 2 units	Period 3 units
Produced	250	200	180
Sold	210	210	210
Held in stock at end of period	40	30	nil

Required

(a) Using absorption costing, what is the profit of Period 2?

(b) Using marginal costing what is the profit of Period 2?

(c) Compare the profit of Period 1 under absorption costing with that calculated under marginal costing and explain the difference.

(d) Using absorption costing, calculate the value of closing stock at the end of Period 1.

(e) Using marginal costing, calculate the value of closing stock at the end of Period 1.

B5.3

Resistor Ltd manufactures electrical units. All units are identical. The following information relates to June and July Year 5.

(a) Budgeted costs and selling prices were:

	June £	July £
Variable manufacturing cost per unit	2.00	2.20
Total fixed manufacturing costs (based on budgeted output of 25,000 units per month)	40,000	44,000
Total fixed marketing cost (based on budgeted sales of 25,000 units per month)	14,000	15,400
Selling price per unit	5.00	5.50

(b) Actual production and sales recorded were:

	Units	Units
Production	24,000	24,000
Sales	21,000	26,500

(c) There was no stock of finished goods at the start of June Year 5. There was no wastage or loss of finished goods during either June or July Year 5.

(d) Actual costs incurred corresponded to those budgeted for each month.

Required

Calculate the relative effects on the monthly operating profits of applying:

(a) absorption costing;

(b) marginal costing.

B5.4

(a) Explain what is meant by (i) absorption costing; and (ii) variable costing.

(b) Explain the arguments in favour of absorption costing and the arguments in favour of variable costing.

C Problem solving and evaluation

C5.1 [S]

The table below sets out data for the Mobile Phone Manufacturing Company for the four quarters of Year 1.

	£
Selling price per unit	120
Variable cost per unit	70
Fixed overhead production cost for each quarter	20,000

	Qtr 1 units	Qtr 2 units	Qtr 3 units	Qtr 4 units	Total units
Planned production	1,000	1,000	1,000	1,000	4,000
Actual production	1,000	1,000	900	1,100	4,000
Actual sales	900	1,100	900	1,100	4,000

The fixed overhead production cost for each month is based on budgeted production of 1,000 units per quarter. The fixed overhead is absorbed into products on the basis of a predetermined overhead rate of £20 per unit.

Actual production fluctuates in quarters 3 and 4 due to labour problems. Actual sales fluctuate each quarter due to seasonal factors but the company meets its target for production and sales over the year as a whole.

Required

Prepare a statement of quarterly profit for each of the four quarters of Year 1 using:

(a) absorption costing; and
(b) marginal costing.

C5.2

The board of directors of Performance Ltd appointed a new manager to the Southern division of the company at the start of year 6. The expectation was that the manager would improve the gross profit as a percentage of sales, as compared with the results for year 4 and year 5.

Relevant information in respect of the Southern division for each year is as follows:

1. Sales and costs of the division were as follows:

	Year 4	Year 5	Year 6
Sales	10,000 units	11,000 units	12,000 units
Production	9,000 units	10,000 units	15,000 units
Variable cost of production	£5.00 per unit	£6.00 per unit	£7.00 per unit
Variable cost of production	£2.00 per unit	£2.20 per unit	£2.40 per unit
Total fixed costs of production per annum	£210,000	£230,000	£390,000

2. Selling prices each year were based on full unit cost plus a percentage mark-up on cost:

Year 4: Full unit cost plus 25% of cost
Year 5: Full unit cost plus 24% of cost
Year 6: Full unit cost plus 20% of cost

3. There were 4,000 units of finished goods in stock at the start of Year 4. These were valued using costs identical to those incurred during Year 4.

4. The company policy is to value inventories (stocks) on a FIFO basis.

In year 4 and year 5 the company followed its previous practice of valuing inventories (stocks) at variable cost of production for management accounting purposes. The new manager of Southern division has insisted quite strongly that the inventories (stocks) should be valued on a full absorption costing basis, for consistency with external reporting standards.

Required

Prepare a report to the board of directors of Performance Ltd showing how the profit performance of the Southern division in Year 6 compares with that of Year 5 and Year 4 respectively.

Case studies

Real world cases

Prepare short answers to case studies 5.1, 5.2 and 5.3.

Case 5.4 (group case study)

As a group you are planning a garden renovation service to take advantage of the current popularity of television programmes dealing with garden design. Within the group, allocate the following roles:

- Design skills
- Labouring and building skills
- Business planning skills
- Marketing skills.

As a team discuss the approach you would take to estimating the cost of a job for quoting to an intending customer. Discuss also the proposal in a gardening advice magazine that those starting out in a new business should seek only to recover variable costs until the reputation is established. Report back to the rest of the class on:

- The costs to be recorded.
- The extent to which team members agree or disagree on costs to be included.

Your views on the suggestion that only variable costs should be recovered initially.

Note

1. The UK accounting standard SSAP 9 (1988) *Stocks and long-term contracts contracts* contains similar definitions in paragraphs 17 to 21. Appendix 1 'Further practical considerations' contains a section on 'The allocation of overheads' (paras 1 to 10) which gives detailed guidance on the application of absorption costing.

Job costing

This case study shows a typical situation in which management accounting can be helpful. Read the case study now but only attempt the discussion points after you have finished studying the chapter.

The film Monster *was a box office success but, coming from an independent film maker rather than the giant studios of Hollywood, did not bring the early profits that other successes could achieve. This extract explains the problems.*

Monster generated a respectable $34.5m at the US box office, according to Nielsen EDI, the cinema research body. However, because it is riskier for cinemas to show small, niche films instead of mainstream blockbusters, cinema chains tend to keep a larger proportion of the ticket price. Although the figures have yet to be audited, according to Mark Damon, another co-producer on the film, this amounted to about 62% for *Monster*, compared to the typical 45% to 55%. As a result, more than $20m of the box-office revenues stayed with the cinema operators. Some 18% was kept by Newmarket, the film's distributor, leaving behind about $10m.

Then there was the cost of the release campaign, which included posters and television commercials as well as the cost of making celluloid copies and transporting them to different venues. The film industry categorises these costs as 'print and advertising' or P&A. Usually the P&A cost is advanced by the distributors. But, in the case of *Monster*, the producers struggled to find a partner willing to distribute the film.

. . . In total the P&A cost came to about $12m, pushing Monster into a loss of $1.26m at the US box office.

Source: Thomas Clark, *Financial Times*, 15 February 2005, p. 14, 'Why a monster hit did not make giant profits'.

Discussion points

1 Why is a job costing approach suitable for a film production?
2 Why will each job have a different pattern of costs and revenues?

Contents

Learning outcomes

After reading this chapter you should be able to:

- Explain the contents of a job cost record.

- Prepare a job cost record showing direct material, direct labour, other direct costs and production overhead.

- Analyse transactions involved in job costing, using the accounting equation.

- Describe and discuss examples of research into methods of job costing.

6.1 Introduction

In Chapter 3, direct materials and direct labour costs were explained. Chapter 4 explained the accounting treatment of production overheads. This chapter brings together the elements of a job-costing system and explains the procedures for analysing them to calculate the cost of a job undertaken during a period of time. In a job-costing system there will be a job cost record for each job, showing the costs incurred on that job. A job cost record is illustrated in Exhibit 6.1. The transactions of the period are analysed and recorded using the accounting equation.

A **job-costing system** for recording the cost of output is appropriate to a business which provides specialised products or makes items to order, so that each customer's requirements constitute a separate job of work. Job costing is appropriate in manufacturing industries such as shipbuilding, bridge building, construction, property development and craft industries. Job costing would also be used in costing the provision of services by professional persons such as lawyers, doctors, architects and accountants. It could also be used for repair contracts, or specialist service contracts.

Definition

A **job-costing system** is a system of cost accumulation where there is an identifiable activity for which costs may be collected. The activity is usually specified in terms of a job of work or a group of tasks contributing to a stage in the production or service process.

Exhibit 6.1
Illustration of a job cost record

JOB COST RECORD JOB No...........	Customer reference .... Product description		Product code	
DATE	CODE	DETAILS	QUANTITY	£	p
		Direct materials:			
		Type A	kg		
		Type B	kg		
		Type C	litres		
		Direct labour:			
		Employee A	hrs		
		Employee B	hrs		
		Employee C	hrs		
		Other direct costs			
		PRIME COST X			
		Indirect materials			
		Indirect labour			
		Other indirect costs			
		TOTAL PRODUCTION OVERHEAD Y			
		TOTAL PRODUCT COST X + Y			

The **job cost record** shows the costs of materials, labour and overhead incurred on a particular job. The accounts department knows from the stores requisition the quantity of materials issued to production and knows from the invoice the price per unit charged by the supplier. This allows the cost of direct materials to be recorded as the materials are used. Each job will have a job number and that number will be entered on all stores requisitions so that the materials can be traced to the job cost record.

Direct labour costs will be calculated using hours worked and the hourly rate for each employee. The hours worked will be collected from employee time sheets which show each job under its own job number. Hourly rates for the employee will be available from personnel records.

Other direct costs will be charged to jobs by entering on the expense invoice the appropriate job number. The invoices will be used as the primary source from which information is transferred to the job cost record.

● Production overhead costs will be shared among the jobs to which they relate, as explained in Chapter 4

Activity 6.1

You have been employed as the management accountant at a car repair garage. Write down a list of the types of costs you would expect to find on a job cost record for a car service and repair. (You don't need to put any money amounts into the list.)

Exhibit 6.1 shows sufficient details of direct materials, direct labour and other direct costs to give the prime cost of production. Addition of indirect costs (production overhead) gives the **total product cost** of a job.

Definitions

Prime cost of production is equal to the total of direct materials, direct labour and other direct costs.

Production overhead cost comprises indirect materials, indirect labour and other indirect costs of production.

Total product cost comprises prime cost plus production overhead cost.

6.2 Job cost records: an illustration

Job costing is illustrated in the example of Specialprint, a company which prints novelty stationery to be sold in a chain of retail stores. The company has only one customer. Exhibit 6.2 contains relevant information for the month of June in respect of three separate jobs, 601, 602 and 603. Symbols are attached to each transaction so that the information may be traced through the job cost records.

6.2.1 Information for the job cost record

The job cost record requires information on direct materials, direct labour and production overhead. This information must be selected from the list of transactions for the month of June. Care must be taken to extract only that information which is relevant to each job.

Activity 6.2

From Exhibit 6.2 note the transactions which you think are directly relevant to the cost of jobs 601, 602 and 603. Then read the rest of this section and compare your answer with the text. (Use Exhibit 6.1 to remind yourself of the information needed for a job cost record.)

Exhibit 6.2
Specialprint: transactions for the month of June

Date	Symbol	Transaction
1 June	♪	Bought 60 rolls of paper on credit from supplier, invoiced price being £180,000. The rolls of paper acquired consisted of two different grades. 40 rolls were of medium-grade paper at a total cost of £100,000 and 20 rolls were of high grade at a total cost of £80,000.
1 June	♣	Bought inks, glues and dyes at a cost of £25,000 paid in cash. The inks cost £9,000 while the glue cost £12,000 and the dyes £4,000.
2 June	⊗	Returned to supplier one roll of paper damaged in transit, cost £2,500. The roll of paper returned was of medium grade.
3 June	†	Rolls of paper issued to printing department, cost £120,000. 20 high-grade rolls were issued, together with 16 medium-grade rolls. There were three separate jobs: references 601, 602 and 603. The high-grade rolls were all for job 601 (notepaper); 12 medium-grade rolls were for job 602 (envelopes) and the remaining 4 medium-grade rolls were for job 603 (menu cards).
4 June	ø	Issued half of inks, glues and dyes to printing department, £12,500. Exactly half of each item of inks, glue and dyes was issued, for use across all three jobs.
14 June	ψ	Paid printing employees' wages £8,000. Wages were paid to 10 printing employees, each earning the same amount.
14 June	λ	Paid maintenance wages £250. Maintenance wages were paid to one part-time maintenance officer.
16 June	‡	Paid rent, rates and electricity in respect of printing, £14,000 in cash. Payment for rent was £8,000, rates £4,000 and electricity £2,000.
28 June	ϖ	Paid printing employees' wages £8,000. Wages were paid to the same 10 employees as on 14 June.
28 June	φ	Paid maintenance wages £250. Maintenance wages were paid to the same maintenance officer as on 14 June.
30 June	♥	Employee records show that: 5 printing employees worked all month on job 601; 3 printing employees worked on job 602; and 2 printing employees worked on job 603.
30 June	ξ	It is company policy to absorb production overheads in proportion to labour costs of each job.
30 June	#	Transferred printed stationery to finished goods stock at a total amount of £160,000, in respect of jobs 601 and 602, which were completed, together with the major part of job 603. There remained some unfinished work-in-progress on one section of job 603, valued at £3,000. Separate finished goods records are maintained for notepaper, envelopes and menu cards.
30 June	≈	Sold stationery to customer on credit, cost of goods sold being £152,000. The customer took delivery of all notepaper and all envelopes, but took only £7,600 of menu cards, leaving the rest to await completion of the further items still in progress.

Direct material

Materials are purchased on 1 June and taken into store but that is of no relevance to determining the cost of a job. For job cost purposes what matters is the issue of paper on 3 June. That is entered on each of the job cost records using the detail given for the event on 3 June.

Direct labour

Employees are paid during the month and there are records (time sheets) of the jobs on which they work. It is only at the end of the month that the employee records are checked to find where the work was carried out. At that point the relevant direct labour costs are entered on each job cost record.

Production overhead

Production overhead comprises indirect materials (ink, glue and dyes), indirect labour (maintenance wages), rent, rates and electricity, all used in the production process.

		£
Indirect materials	ø	12,500
Indirect labour	λ φ	500
Rent	‡	8,000
Rates	‡	4,000
Electricity	‡	2,000
Total production overhead	ξ	27,000

An overhead cost rate is required to determine how much production overhead should be absorbed into each job. We are told in Exhibit 6.2 that it is company policy to absorb production overheads in proportion to the direct labour costs of each job. The total direct labour cost for the period is £16,000 and so the overhead cost rate must be calculated as:

$$\text{overhead cost rate (in £ per £ of direct labour)} = \frac{27,000}{16,000}$$

$$= £1.6875 \text{ per £}$$

This rate is then applied to the amounts of direct labour cost already charged to each job (which was £8,000 for job 601, £4,800 for job 602 and £3,200 for job 603). The resulting amounts are recorded in the relevant job records.

Job number	Calculation	Production overhead
		£
Job 601	8,000 × £1.6875	13,500 ζ
Job 602	4,800 × £1.6875	8,100 ζ
Job 603	3,200 × £1.6875	5,400 ζ
		27,000 ζ

6.2.2 Presentation of the job cost records

The job cost records are set out in Exhibit 6.3. Jobs 601 and 602 are finished in the period and this is shown on the job cost record by a transfer to finished goods of the full cost of the job. Job 603 has a problem with unfinished work-in-progress but the rest of that job is completed and transferred to finished goods. That information is recorded on the job cost record card as shown in Exhibit 6.3.

The total work-in-progress record is useful as a check on the separate job costs and is also useful for accounting purposes in providing a total record of work-in-progress at any point in time. It is created by using the totals of the direct materials issued to production, the total direct labour used on jobs and the total production overhead incurred during the month. Exhibit 6.4 shows the total work-in-progress record.

Exhibit 6.3

Job cost records for jobs 601, 602 and 603

	Job cost record: Job 601	
3 June	Direct materials	80,000 †
30 June	Direct labour	8,000 ♥
	Prime cost	88,000
30 June	Production overhead:	13,500 ξ
	Total production cost	101,500
	To finished goods	(101,500)
	Work-in-progress	nil
	Job cost record: Job 602	
3 June	Direct materials	30,000 †
30 June	Direct labour	4,800 ♥
	Prime cost	34,800
30 June	Production overhead:	8,100 ξ
	Total production cost	42,900
	Finished goods	(42,900)
	Work-in-progress	nil
	Job cost record: Job 603	
3 June	Direct materials	10,000 †
30 June	Direct labour	3,200 ♥
	Prime cost	13,200
30 June	Production overhead:	5,400 ξ
	Total production cost	18,600
	Finished goods	(15,600)
1 July	Work-in-progress	3,000

Exhibit 6.4

Record of total work-in-progress for month of June

	Total work-in-progress	
3 June	Direct materials	120,000 †
30 June	Direct labour	16,000 ♥
30 June	Production overhead	27,000 ξ
		163,000
30 June	Finished goods	(160,000)
1 July	Work-in-progress	3,000

Real world case 6.2

*The following advice is offered on the website of a
company designing and making wedding cakes to order.*

Costs involved in making a wedding cake:
Wedding cakes come in all shapes, sizes and price ranges.
Cost is calculated per slice depending on ingredients and
labor involved in creating your design. Average prices
fall between $1.50 and $5.00 a slice, but an elaborate
creation can run three to four times higher! That means a
five-tier cake that feeds 200 guests will cost at least $300
and could run up to $4,000 for a 'couture' creation like
those modeled in the bridal magazines. You are primarily
paying for the designer's time, but the ingredients you
choose can also influence the price. Check out Ways to
Save for ideas on taming this budget buster. Be prepared
to leave a substantial (and usually non-refundable!) deposit
to reserve your date. Many bakeries are booked up to two
years in advance. Fortunately, you won't have
to make your design selections this early. You are simply
reserving the date. Final payment is usually expected two
weeks or more prior to the wedding. Ask your designer
about delivery and set-up fees. Those costs are often – but not always – covered by the per-slice
cost. Make sure you get a written breakdown of all services and fees!

Ways to save:

- Decide on a particular style and size of cake before asking for quotes. You can always decide
  on a different design later, but you want to be sure that you are comparing the same costs.
- Ask about slice size. You can't compare per-slice costs unless the pieces are the same size.
  You may get more for your money with a 2-inch rather than a 1-inch slice of cake.
- Be realistic. The magnificent cakes you see in the magazines are usually in the $10- to $15-per-
  slice range. Ask about modifying designs or substituting ingredients. For example, buttercream
  icing is very tasty and quite a bit more affordable than the fondant style.
- Substitute fresh arrangements for expensive sugar flowers. Ask your baker to coordinate designs
  and duties with your florist.
- Be aware of hidden costs when making price comparisons. You may have to pay a fee to your
  reception site if you hire an outside designer. Or, you may get a great deal on the cake only to find
  out later that you'll be paying almost as much again to cover the serving fee.
- Order a smaller display cake and then serve your guest slices of sheet cake or a 'side cake.'
  You can do the traditional slicing of the cake in front of your guests and then have the side cakes
  served from a back room.
- If you want to impress, consider ordering a smaller cake that will sit on top of fake tiers.
- Order a wedding cake that will feed at least half of your guests and then offer several more-
  affordable desserts.
- You pay for excessive variety in additional ingredient expenses, design costs and service fees.
  Many couples are opting for sleeker, less-expensive creations.

Source: Shane Co., wedding cake designers, www.shaneco.com/weddings/cake_designers.asp

Discussion points

1 Why is job costing particularly suitable for a business making wedding cakes?

2 What information would you expect to find in a job cost record for a wedding cake contract?

6.3 Job costing: applying the accounting equation to transactions

The job cost record cards used only a part of the information contained in Exhibit 6.2. All the transactions must be recorded for purposes of preparing financial statements. This section analyses the transactions of Exhibit 6.2 using the accounting equation and concludes with a spreadsheet record of the transactions for the month. The symbols contained in Exhibit 6.2 are used throughout to help follow the cost trail.

In management accounting there is strong emphasis on the flow of costs. This flow starts when materials, labour and other resources are either acquired on credit terms or paid for immediately in cash (line A in Exhibit 6.5). The management accounting records trace these credit transactions and cash payments through to separate records for materials, labour, production overhead and the administration and selling costs (line B). The separate records are then considered in more detail.

The materials record includes both direct and indirect materials. When the direct materials are issued for use in production, a stores requisition note is produced and this is the basis for transferring that amount of direct materials cost from the materials record to the work-in-progress record (line C). When the indirect materials are issued for use in production a further stores requisition note is produced. This is the basis for transferring that amount of indirect materials cost from the materials record to the production overhead record.

The labour cost record (line B) will include both direct and indirect labour. Direct labour hours are recorded on a time sheet and calculation of the cost of these hours is the basis for transferring that amount of direct labour cost from the labour cost record to the work-in-progress record. Calculation of indirect labour cost is the basis for transferring that amount of indirect labour cost from the labour cost record to the production overhead record.

Some items of indirect cost, not involving either materials or labour, will be transferred from the bank payment record (such as payment of rent, electricity or gas). At the end of the accounting period, probably each month, all the production overhead of the period is transferred to the work-in-progress record.

Finally, on line B there is the record of administration and selling costs. These are not part of the cost of work-in-progress because they are not costs of production. At the end of the accounting period the total of these costs is transferred to the work-in-progress record.

When the work-in-progress is completed there is a transfer of cost to the record for finished goods stock (line D). When the finished goods are sold there is a transfer of the cost of those items to the profit and loss account as cost of goods sold.

The profit and loss account (line E) brings together the sales, cost of goods sold and administration and selling costs in a calculation of profit.

6.3.1 Acquisition of inventory: direct and indirect materials

In purchasing the rolls of paper, the business acquires an asset. In taking credit from the supplier it incurs a liability.

Asset ↑ − **Liability** ↑ = Ownership interest

Exhibit 6.5

Flow of costs in a management accounting information system

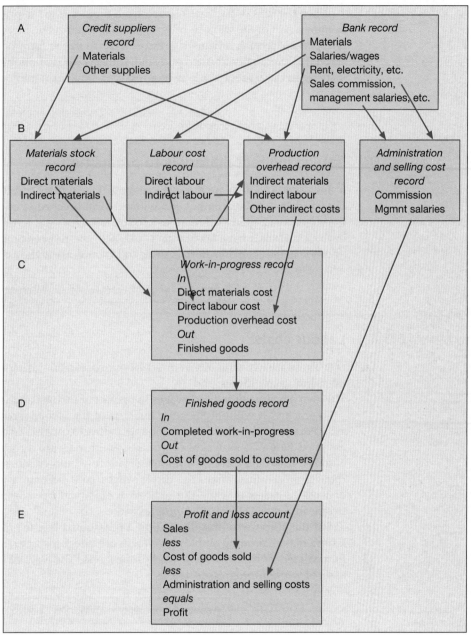

♣ In purchasing the inks, glue and dyes, the business acquires a further asset. In paying cash, the asset of cash is diminished.

> **Asset** ↑↓ − Liability = Ownership interest

⊗ Returning the damaged roll of paper reduces the asset of materials stock and reduces the liability to the trade creditor.

> **Asset** ↓ − **Liability** ↓ = Ownership interest

† 6.3.2 Converting raw materials into work-in-progress: direct materials

† When the rolls of paper are issued from the stores to the printing department, they become a part of the work-in-progress of that department. Since this work-in-progress is expected to bring a benefit to the enterprise in the form of cash flows from sales when it is eventually finished and sold, it meets the definition of an asset. There is an increase in the asset of work-in-progress and a decrease in the stock of materials.

> **Asset** ↑↓ – Liability = Ownership interest

ø 6.3.3 Issuing indirect materials to production

ø Inks, glue and dyes are indirect materials. The indirect cost is part of the production overhead cost, to be accumulated with other indirect costs and later added to work-in-progress as a global amount for production overhead. In this case, only half of the indirect materials have been issued (£12,500), the rest remaining in stock. There is a decrease in the asset of materials stock and an increase in the asset of work-in-progress.

> **Asset** ↑↓ – Liability = Ownership interest

ψ λ ϖ φ 6.3.4 Labour costs

ψ ϖ There are two amounts of direct labour costs paid during the period in respect of the printing employees; and
λ φ two amounts of indirect wages in respect of maintenance.

In practice, it will only be after analysis of the labour records for the period that an accurate subdivision into direct and indirect costs may be made. Although it is assumed here that all wages of printing employees are direct costs, it could be that enforced idle time through equipment failure would create an indirect cost. Taking the simplified illustration, the direct wages paid become a part of the prime cost of work-in-progress while the indirect wages paid become part of the production overhead cost within work-in-progress.

For the purposes of this illustration it is assumed that the manager of the business knows that all printing employees' wages are direct costs (♥) and so may be recorded immediately as direct costs of work-in-progress. The asset of cash decreases and the asset of work-in-progress increases.

> **Asset** ↑↓ – Liability = Ownership interest

It is further assumed that the manager of the business knows that all indirect labour costs will become production overheads (ξ) and hence added to the value of work-in-progress.

> **Asset** ↑↓ – Liability = Ownership interest

‡ξ 6.3.5 Production overhead costs

‡ ξ Rent, rates and electricity costs (‡) paid from cash in respect of printing are production overhead costs (ξ). For management accounting purposes they are regarded as part of the cost of the asset of work-in-progress.

$$\boxed{\textbf{Asset} \uparrow\downarrow - \text{Liability} = \text{Ownership interest}}$$

For financial reporting purposes the overhead costs paid are regarded immediately as reducing the ownership claim because they are part of the expense of production overhead. Exhibit 6.5 shows that in both financial reporting and management accounting the production overhead costs eventually emerge as a component of the expense of cost of goods sold.

6.3.6 Transferring work-in-progress to finished goods

When the asset of work-in-progress is completed, it changes into another asset, the stock of finished goods. In the accounting records the asset is removed from work-in-progress and enjoys a new description as the asset of finished goods.

$$\boxed{\textbf{Asset} \uparrow\downarrow - \text{Liability} = \text{Ownership interest}}$$

≈ 6.3.7 Sale of goods

≈ When a sale is made to a customer, that part of the asset of finished goods stock is transformed into the expense of cost of goods sold. Any finished goods remaining unsold continue to be reported as an asset.

$$\boxed{\textbf{Asset} \downarrow - \text{Liability} = \textbf{Ownership interest} \downarrow \textbf{(expense)}}$$

Activity 6.3

Go back to the start of section 6.3 and check that you understand the effect of each transaction on the accounting equation. When you are happy that you understand them all, work through the next section which records the transactions on a spreadsheet.

6.3.8 Spreadsheet analysis

The transactions are brought together in spreadsheet form in Exhibit 6.6. The entries on each line correspond to the detailed analyses provided in this section. The totals at the foot of each column represent the amounts of the various assets, liabilities and ownership interest resulting from the transactions of the month. Cash has decreased overall by £55,500. The asset of stock of materials (paper, inks, glues and dyes) has increased by £70,000 and the asset of work-in-progress has increased by £3,000. The asset of finished goods has increased by £8,000. The liability to the creditor stands at £177,500. Overall the transactions of the month, as recorded here, have decreased the ownership interest by £152,000, the amount which is recorded as the cost of goods sold.

	£
Overall increase in assets	25,500
Overall increase in liabilities	177,500
Difference	(152,000)
Decrease in ownership interest	(152,000)

Exhibit 6.6

Spreadsheet to show analysis of transactions for the month of June, using the accounting equation

Date	Transaction	Symbol	Assets				Liability	Ownership interest
			Cash	Stock of materials	Work-in-progress	Finished goods	Creditor	Cost of goods sold
			£	£	£	£	£	£
June 1	Bought 60 rolls of paper on credit from supplier, invoiced price being £180,000.	☞		180,000			180,000	
June 1	Bought inks, glue and dyes, cost £25,000 paid in cash.	♣	(25,000)	25,000				
June 2	Returned to supplier one roll, damaged in transit, £2,500.	⊗		(2,500)			(2,500)	
June 3	Rolls of paper issued to printing department, cost £120,000.	†		(120,000)	120,000			
June 4	Issued half of inks, glues and dyes to printing department, £12,500.	ø		(12,500)	12,500			
June 14	Paid printing employees' wages £8,000.	ψ	(8,000)		8,000			
June 14	Paid maintenance wages £250.	λ	(250)		250			
June 16	Paid rent, rates and electricity in respect of printing, £14,000, in cash.	‡	(14,000)		14,000			
June 28	Paid printing employees' wages £8,000.	ϖ	(8,000)		8,000			
June 28	Paid maintenance wages £250.	φ	(250)		250			
June 30	Transferred printed stationery to finished goods stock, valued at cost of £160,000.	#			(160,000)	160,000		
June 30	Sold stationery to customer on credit, cost of goods sold being £152,000.	≈				(152,000)		(152,000)
	Totals		(55,500)	70,000	3,000	8,000	177,500	(152,000)

6.4 Moving forward

Fiona McTaggart has participated in a number of consultancy projects where the traditional job costing approach has been modified to reflect changing circumstances. Here she talks about three of them.

FIONA: *I recall learning job costing at college and thinking that there must be more to life than this. Since then I have found much more excitement in management accounting but I still have to return to some of the basic principles – seeking where possible to identify costs with products and making sensible allocations where such identification is not possible.*

One of my clients was a production engineering business. I was working with the plant controller, a qualified engineer with a good head for figures. The controller was looking for a new management system which escaped from the traditional role of a financial system. What was wanted was management in terms of the activities of the unit, but with one eye on the consequences in dollars. The controller wanted the production and engineering personnel to feel that they were in ownership of the management system. So I found myself working in a team which drew on several specialisms, including engineering and human resource management. We had to ask the financial accounting department, very politely, to keep away while we developed our ideas because they kept quoting financial accounting guidelines which were cramping our style. At the end of the day we did work out the cost of a job undertaken by the business, but it was a cost which the engineers understood and could relate to.

Another client was a telecommunications division of a major conglomerate. Their problem was again related to engineers but with a different slant. The engineers were not sufficiently aware of how their choice of operating methods could significantly alter total costs. Traditional overhead costs were too blunt an instrument so we identified the actions which drove costs and effectively turned indirect costs into direct costs. Every time an engineer initiated a process, there was a cost reported. They soon began to concentrate on cost-effective solutions. The end result was to identify the cost of a job but the engineers knew how their choices had affected that cost.

My third client was a major hospital. In the area of health care, relations between medical specialists and the accountants are always somewhat strained and have to be dealt with carefully. The project in this case was to measure the cost of a treatment which involved balancing length of stay, costs and patient welfare. There is a widely held belief that the accountants merely calculate the cost of one overnight stay and then suggest reducing overnight stays for all patients. In reality we worked closely with the clinical specialists so that an element of mutual respect was built up. We helped them to understand our approach to determining the cost of a 'job' (not really the best term for treating a patient – the experts prefer a 'treatment protocol'). The treatment protocol is the standard method for treating a specific condition. That method is developed by the medical experts. The actual treatment does not necessarily follow the standard – if the patient needs extra care then it is given. However, knowing the cost of the standard protocol allows comparative evaluation of the actual treatment. Management accountants develop the cost systems which are used as information by the case managers. The relationship is a partnership – the accountants don't dictate the medical treatment, but it remains necessary for the medical experts to know what each treatment of each patient has cost.

The common feature of all these cases which I have described is that the management accounting system produced a report which included a cost for each 'job'. However, it was by no means a mechanical process carried out in isolation. It involved the management accountant becoming part of the operational team. The days of a separate management accounting department in some remote part of an administrative office are gone. The management accountant has to be alongside those who are delivering the product.

Real world case 6.3

This is an extract from a case study provided by Best Software, a company in the Sage group. It provides an example of a job cost system in a service business.

Auto Media is an internal advertising group supporting more than 20 automotive dealerships throughout Arizona, Texas, Georgia and California. Its project load is enormous – at least 1,000 different jobs every month, from mammoth tent sales for multiple dealerships to single-spot newspaper placements.

To obtain pricing discounts, Auto Media purchases newspaper, television, radio and special promotional ads in volume, allocating costs to individual dealerships. Sales managers submit monthly advertising requests to Auto Media on Excel spreadsheets. Internal graphic artists also use Excel to track accrued expenses. Each ad is treated as a separate project and identified by a unique job number, against which costs are accumulated and billed back to the correct dealership.

The years of accounting and MAS 90 expertise that Auto Media's BSAN Advisor brought to the table resulted in speedy insights. 'Our Advisor saw right away that reimplementing Job Cost would be better than tweaking what we had,' Sneden explains. 'As a result of her recommendations, we developed a system that would bring us into alignment with standard accepted accounting practices, and at the same time improve revenue recognition and cost tracking.' The new system includes additional fields for accounting, plus spreadsheets that pull data directly from the designers' budgets. The Visual Integrator module was deployed to automate information transfer from the spreadsheets to both the AR and Job Cost modules. Multiple layers were necessary to accommodate Auto Media's complicated data import requirements.

The savings have been dramatic. 'We used to spend 40 hours a month on data entry for Job Cost,' says Sneden. 'Those tasks have been eliminated by the new accounting and system changes. Now we just spend one day a month doing manual verification of balances. This has freed up staff time for other important tasks.'

Source: www.bestsoftware.com, 2003.

Discussion points

1 What kinds of jobs are carried out in this business?

2 Why is it important to have accurate job costs?

6.5 What the researchers have found

6.5.1 Job costing: book production

Walker and Wu (2000) described a method of breaking down the tasks required in planning a job for production in the book manufacturing industry. They analysed the work of the book engineering department of a US book publisher by collecting data over a six-month period for more than 500 planning jobs. Production planning is a major overhead cost of any book. A typical planning sequence for any one book contained 29 jobs. Some were repetitive, such as 'pick up a job from the backlog shelf' or 'determine the page count' while others were non-repetitive and varied from one book to the next, such as 'go through covering materials for the book' or 'enter any items still to come from the customer into the items-to-come screen'. The researchers showed that activity-based costing (ABC) gave the benefit of accurate costing of the overheads contained in the book planning function.

Finally the authors compared their ABC-based system with the previous method of estimating the job cost for planning by adding 2% to production cost. Under the previous system the proportion of planning overhead carried was related to the size of the book. Under the ABC system the planning overhead cost reflected the complexity of the work done on the book and the time taken to deal with the customer.

6.5.2 European perspective

Brierley *et al* (2001) surveyed product costing practice in Europe. They reviewed a range of literature that had asked about the accounting systems used, the types of overhead costing used, the bases for calculating overhead cost rates, the use of product costs in pricing and the use of activity-based costing. Predictably, a wide range of methods was found with no clear pattern. One of the problems of relying on other literature is that the survey collects mainly works that have been written in English. It would be desirable to follow up such a literature review with a wide-ranging survey.

6.6 Summary

This chapter has drawn on the information and definitions contained in Chapters 4 and 5 to show the method of preparing job cost statements. Job costing will be found in service businesses as well as in manufacturing. The essential condition is that there is an identifiable job (item of output) for which costs may be collected with a view to determining the cost of the job.

Key themes in this chapter are:

- A **job-costing system** is a system of cost accumulation where there is an identifiable activity for which costs may be collected. The activity is usually specified in terms of a job of work or a group of tasks contributing to a stage in the production or service process.
- A **job cost record** shows the costs of materials, labour and overhead incurred on a particular job.
- The **prime cost of production** is equal to the total of direct materials, direct labour and other direct costs.
- The **production overhead cost** comprises indirect materials, indirect labour and other indirect costs of production.
- The **total product cost** comprises prime cost plus production overhead cost.

References and further reading

Brierley, J.A., Cowton, C. and Drury, C. (2001) 'Research into product costing practice: a European perspective', *The European Accounting Review*, 10(2): 215–256.

Walker, C. and Wu, N.L'a (2000) 'Systematic approach to activity based costing of the production planning activity in the book manufacturing industry', *International Journal of Operations and Production Management*, 20(1): 103–114.

QUESTIONS

The Questions section of each chapter has three types of question. 'Test your understanding' questions to help you review your reading are in the 'A' series of questions. You will find the answer to these by reading and thinking about the material in the text book. 'Application' questions to test your ability to apply technical skills are in the 'B' series of questions. Questions requiring you to show skills in problem solving and evaluation are in the 'C' series of questions. The symbol [S] indicates that a solution is available at the end of the book.

A   Test your understanding

A6.1   What is a job-costing system (section 6.1)?

A6.2   What is a job cost record (section 6.1)?

A6.3   Define prime cost, production overhead cost and total product cost (section 6.1).

A6.4   List the items you would expect to find in a job cost record (section 6.1).

A6.5   What is the effect on the accounting equation of purchasing direct and indirect materials (section 6.3.1)?

A6.6   How does the accounting equation represent the conversion of raw materials into work-in-progress (section 6.3.2)?

A6.7   How does the accounting equation represent the issue of indirect materials to production (section 6.3.3)?

A6.8   How does the accounting equation represent the transfer of labour costs to work-in-progress (section 6.3.4)?

A6.9   How does the accounting equation represent the transfer of production overhead costs to work-in-progress (section 6.3.5)?

A6.10 How does the accounting equation represent the transfer of work-in-progress to finished goods (section 6.3.6)?

A6.11 How does the accounting equation represent the sale of goods (section 6.3.7)?

A6.12 [S] Explain how each of the following transactions is dealt with in a job-costing system:
    (a) The production department orders 16 components from store at a cost of £3 each, to be used on job 59.
    (b) An employee (A. Jones) receives a weekly wage of £600. In week 29 this employee's time has been spent two-thirds on job 61 and one-third on job 62.
    (c) On 16 June, job 94 is finished at a total cost of £3,500. The job consisted of printing brochures for a supermarket advertising campaign.

A6.13 What have researchers found about the use of job costing to record the cost of hand-producing a bound book (section 6.5)?

B   Application

B6.1 [S]
The following transactions relate to a dairy, converting milk to cheese, for the month of May:

1 May	Bought 600 drums of milk from supplier, invoiced price being £90,000.
1 May	Bought cartons, cost £6,000 paid in cash.
2 May	Returned to supplier one drum damaged in transit, £150.
3 May	500 drums of milk issued to cheesemaking department, cost £75,000.
4 May	Issued two-thirds of cartons to cheesemaking department, £4,000.

14 May	Paid cheesemakers' wages, £3,000.
14 May	Paid wages for cleaning and hygiene, £600.
16 May	Paid rent, rates and electricity in respect of dairy, £8,000, in cash.
28 May	Paid cheesemakers' wages, £3,000.
28 May	Paid wages for cleaning and hygiene, £600.
30 May	Transferred all production of cheese in cartons to finished goods stock. No work-in-progress at end of month.

Required

Prepare a calculation of the cost of production transferred to finished goods at the end of May.

B6.2 [S]

Restoration Ltd buys basic furniture units and creates period layouts in clients' homes. The following transactions relate to jobs 801, 802 and 803 in the month of May. Prepare job cost records for each job.

1 May	⅃	Bought 70 furniture units on credit from supplier, invoiced price being £204,000. The furniture units acquired consisted of two different grades. 50 units were of standard size at a total cost of £140,000 and 20 units were of king size at a total cost of £64,000.
1 May	♣	Bought stain, varnish and paint at a cost of £30,000 paid in cash. The stain cost £12,000 while the varnish cost £14,000 and the paint £4,000.
2 May	⊗	Returned to supplier one furniture unit damaged in transit, £2,800. The furniture unit returned was of standard size.
3 May	†	Furniture units issued to Finishing department. 40 standard-size units were issued, together with 14 king-size units. There were three separate jobs: references 801, 802 and 803. The standard-size units were all for job 801 (Riverside Hotel); 10 king-size units were for job 802 (Mountain Lodge); and the remaining 4 king-size units were for job 803 (Hydeaway House).
4 May	Ø	Issued stain, varnish and paint to Finishing department, £22,500.
14 May	ψ	Paid Finishing department employees' wages £10,000. Wages were paid to 8 printing employees, each earning the same amount.
14 May	λ	Paid security wages £350. Security wages were paid to one part-time security officer.
16 May	‡	Paid rent, rates and electricity in respect of Finishing department, £18,000 in cash. Payment for rent was £9,000, rates £5,000 and electricity £4,000.
28 May	ϖ	Paid Finishing department employees' wages £10,000. Wages were paid to the same 8 employees as on 14 May.
28 May	φ	Paid security wages £350. Security wages were paid to the same security officer as on 14 May.
30 May	♥	Employee records show that: 4 Finishing department employees worked all month on job 801; 2 Finishing department employees worked on job 802; and 2 Finishing department employees worked on job 803.
30 May	ξ	It is company policy to allocate production overheads in proportion to labour costs of each job.
30 May	#	Transferred all finished goods to finished goods stock. There remained no unfinished work-in-progress.
30 May	≈	Riverside Hotel and Mountain Lodge took delivery of their goods. Hydeaway House will take delivery on 10 June.

B6.3

Resistor Ltd manufactures electrical units. All units are identical. The following information relates to June and July Year 5.

(a) Budgeted costs and selling prices were:

	June £	July £
Variable manufacturing cost per unit	2.00	2.20
Total fixed manufacturing costs (based on budgeted output of 25,000 units per month)	40,000	44,000
Total fixed marketing cost (based on budgeted sales of 25,000 units per month)	14,000	15,400
Selling price per unit	5.00	5.50

(b) Actual production and sales recorded were:

	Units	Units
Production	24,000	24,000
Sales	21,000	26,500

(c) There was no stock of finished goods at the start of June Year 5. There was no wastage or loss of finished goods during either June or July Year 5.

(d) Actual costs incurred corresponded to those budgeted for each month.

Required

Calculate the relative effects on the monthly operating profits of applying the undernoted techniques:

(a) absorption costing;
(b) variable costing.

C   Problem solving and evaluation

C6.1 [S]

Frames Ltd produces wooden window frames to order for the building industry. The size of frame depends on the specification in the contract. For the purposes of providing job cost estimates the size of frame is ignored and the job cost estimate is based on the type of frame produced, being either single-glazing or double-glazing.

The standard specification is as follows:

	Single-glazing £	Double-glazing £
Direct materials per unit	90.00	130.00
Direct labour per unit		
6.5 hours at £5.00 per hour	32.50	
8.0 hours at £5.00 per hour		40.00
Variable production overhead charged at £6 per hour	39.00	48.00

Fixed overhead is estimated at £160,000 per month for single-glazing and £100,000 per month for double-glazing. Estimated production per month for single-glazing is 4,000 units and for double-glazing is 2,000 units per month.

Required

Prepare a job cost estimate for a customer who intends to order 500 single-glazing and 200 double-glazing units.

C6.2 [S]

Insulation Ltd has been established to manufacture insulation material for use in houses. At present, one machine is installed for production of insulation material. A further similar machine can be purchased if required.

The first customer is willing to place orders in three different sizes at the following selling prices:

Order size	Selling price per package £
430 packages per day	25.20
880 packages per day	25.00
1,350 packages per day	24.80

The customer will enter into an initial contract of 30 days' duration and will uplift completed packages on a daily basis from the premises of Insulation Ltd.

The following assumptions have been made in respect of Insulation Ltd:

(a) In view of the competitive market the selling prices are not negotiable.
(b) Direct materials will cost £23.75 per package irrespective of the order size.
(c) The output of one machine will be 350 packages per shift.
(d) A maximum of three shifts will be available on a machine within one day. The depreciation charge for a machine will be £100 per day, irrespective of the number of shifts worked.
(e) Labour costs to operate a machine will be £100 for the first shift, £120 for the second shift and £160 for the third shift of the day. If labour is required for a shift, then the full shift must be paid for regardless of the number of packages produced.
(f) The total cost of supervising the employees for each of the first two shifts in any day will be £20 per machine. The supervision cost of the third shift will be £40 per machine.
(g) Other fixed overhead costs will be £280 per day if one machine is used. Buying and using an additional machine would result in a further £100 of fixed costs per day.
(h) Production and sales volume will be equal regardless of order size.
(i) The company does not expect to obtain other work during the term of the initial contract.

Required

Prepare a report for the production director of Insulation Ltd giving:

(1) For each order size, details of the overall profitability per day and net profit per package.
(2) An explanation of the differing amounts of profit per package.

Case studies

Real world cases

Prepare short answers to case studies 6.1, 6.2 and 6.3.

Case 6.4 (group case study)

As a group, you are planning to establish a partnership supplying examination advice and tuition to school pupils in their homes. Each course of lessons will be regarded as a single 'job'. Courses may vary in length and in target ability level, depending on the requirements of the pupil to be tutored. Divide the group to take on three different roles. One role is that of a tutor who is also a member of the partnership, sharing equally the profits of the business. The second role is that of the accountancy adviser to the partnership. The third role is that of a parent making enquiries about the price charged and the justification for that price.

Each member of the group should take on one of the three roles and separately make a note of:

(a) The expected costs of a job (in terms of types of cost).
(b) How you would justify the costs (if supplying the service).
(c) How you would question the costs (if receiving the service).

Then all members of the group should come together, compare answers and finally prepare a joint report on the problems of job costing in a service business.

Case 6.5 (group case study)

As a group you are planning a garden renovation service to take advantage of the current popularity of television programmes dealing with garden design. Within the group, allocate the following roles:

- Design skills
- Labouring and building skills
- Business planning skills
- Marketing skills.

As a team discuss the approach you would take to estimating the cost of a job for quoting to an intending customer. Discuss also the proposal in a gardening advice magazine that those starting out in a new business should seek only to recover variable costs until the reputation is established. Report back to the rest of the class on:

- The costs to be recorded
- The extent to which team members agree or disagree on costs to be included
- Your views on the suggestion that only variable costs should be recovered initially.

Chapter 7

Recording transactions in a job costing system

This case study shows a typical situation in which management accounting can be helpful. Read the case study now but only attempt the discussion points after you have finished studying the chapter.

This extract is taken from a case study of a company making windows and side shutters. The company has started using a product from Best Software, a company in the Sage group.

'Our office is so much more relaxed these days,' smiles Pam. 'Now when a salesperson brings in a contract, I record the information in Order Entry and Job Cost. Order Entry gives me a sales order number, which I then enter as a job in Job Cost. The order information is prepared for the person who maintains material lists, and that's used to order all the supplies and materials we'll need for each job.' When Pam receives invoices from material suppliers, she compares them against figures quoted in Job Cost before entering them into Accounts Payable. 'As customers pay us, I update Accounts Receivable and deposit funds.' But nothing is easier for Pam than Payroll. 'Payroll is linked to sales orders and job numbers. I simply apply the information from the installer pay sheets into the Payroll module,' explained Pam. 'I just punch a couple of keys and all the deductions and tax calculations are performed and are automatically sent to Job Cost. I now finish Payroll in 45 minutes. I don't have to worry about keeping up with paperwork anymore. BusinessWorks Gold takes care of that for me.' Now, the aspirin bottle is absent from Pam's desk. 'On Fridays, I can go home in a good mood, because it's just another day. I'd highly recommend BusinessWorks Gold to anybody.' At Cook Siding and Window, BusinessWorks Gold makes a clear difference.

Source: www.bestsoftware.com, 2004.

Discussion points

1 What are the records that are important for the job cost system in this business?

2 Why does the owner feel happier about using a computerised system?

Contents

Learning outcomes	After reading this chapter you should be able to:

- Prepare ledger accounts to record transactions contributing to work-in-progress and finished goods for a job-costing system.
- Understand and prepare control accounts and supporting records.
- Explain the main features of calculating and reporting periodic profit on contracts, and prepare a contract ledger account.
- Describe and discuss an example of research into applications of job costing.

7.1 Introduction

Chapter 6 explained the elements of a job-costing system (direct materials, direct labour and production overheads). This chapter shows how the bookkeeping system may be used to record transactions in respect of direct materials, direct labour and production overheads and to show how these contribute to the recording of work-in-progress, finished goods and cost of goods sold.

If you have learned bookkeeping in **financial accounting** you will be aware of the bookkeeping rules as shown in Exhibit 7.1. These are the only rules you need for recording management accounting costs.

Exhibit 7.1
Bookkeeping rules for expenses and revenues

Type of account	Debit entries	Credit entries
Expense (cost) account	Increase in expense	Decrease in expense
Revenue account	Decrease in revenue	Increase in revenue

In management accounting the term 'cost' is used more frequently than 'expense'. Costs tend to move from one ledger account to another in a manner which reflects the physical activity of the enterprise. Changing the name from 'expense' to 'cost', and allowing for the flow of costs around the ledger, Exhibit 7.2 provides a useful summary of the basic approach to recording cost transactions.

Exhibit 7.2
Debit and credit entries for transactions in a ledger account for costs.

Type of account	Debit entries	Credit entries
Cost account	Increase in cost	Decrease in cost
	Transfer of cost from another cost account	Transfer of cost to another cost account

Exhibit 7.2 contains the basic requirements to build up a minimum set of ledger accounts for a job-costing system, sufficient for management accounting purposes but not over-elaborate. The application of this simple system is illustrated in a practical example in section 7.4. The need for control accounts and subsidiary records is then explained and a further practical example is presented in section 7.5 which elaborates on the first example, showing the use of control accounts and integration with the

financial accounting records. Finally a contract account, as a very specific form of job costing, is explained in section 7.6 and illustrated in section 7.7.

7.2 Types and titles of cost ledger accounts

In management accounting there is a need for detailed analysis of transactions and so there is a need for similar detail in the number and type of ledger accounts used.

There is an important question in how to keep track of both the financial accounting and the management accounting information in the ledger system. Some small businesses may prefer to keep their financial accounting ledger separately from the cost accounting records and have two separate sets of ledger accounts for the purpose. However, most larger businesses, especially where a computer is in use, will integrate the cost accounting ledger accounts with the financial accounting records. This chapter will concentrate on the **integrated system** approach.

The choice of headings used in ledger accounts for financial accounting purposes is to some extent constrained by the legislative regulations applied to external financial reporting. Those constraints are not present in management accounting so there are opportunities to choose the number and type of ledger accounts which best serve the management needs.

7.3 The flow of entries in a job-costing system

This description follows transactions through Exhibit 7.3 by reference to the letters used to label each ledger account. The diagram is based on a situation where materials are acquired on credit whilst wages are paid in cash. It also assumes that all overheads are paid for in cash. For completeness, it also shows the recording of revenue in the profit and loss account.

Activity 7.1

Look at Exhibit 7.3 and follow the flow of transactions down the diagram. Then use the diagram to explain how costs are collected in the profit and loss account

7.3.1 Materials inventory

When inventory is acquired an asset is created, shown by a debit entry in the inventory account (a). In this instance the inventory has been purchased on credit terms, shown by a credit entry in the account for trade creditors (a).

When direct materials are issued to production, they cease to be part of the asset of inventory and are transferred to the asset of work-in-progress (d). Some of the materials acquired may be indirect materials (e), which are transferred to the production overhead account (e). All production overhead costs are collected together before being transferred to work-in-progress using a suitable overhead cost rate.

7.3.2 Labour costs

In the situation where the wages are paid immediately from the bank account, an expense is incurred, so there is a debit entry in the wages account (b). The asset of cash is reduced, recorded as a credit entry (b).

Exhibit 7.3

Diagrammatic representation of the flow of costs and revenue in a job costing system

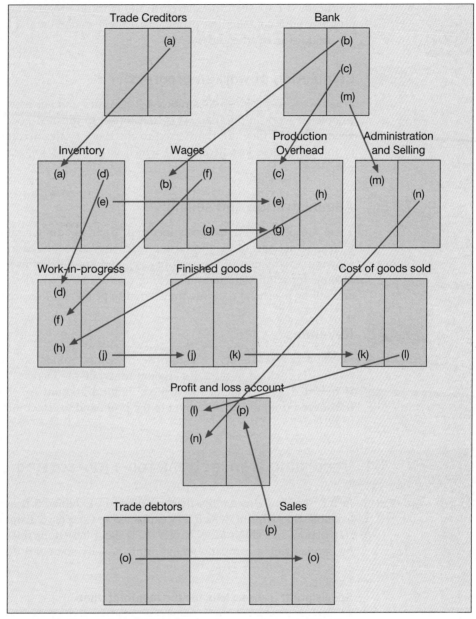

The wages are then subdivided for cost accounting purposes into direct labour and indirect labour. The direct labour (f) is transferred to the work-in-progress account while the indirect labour (g) is transferred to the production overhead account.

Detailed job cost records show the amount of direct labour time spent on each job.

7.3.3   Production overhead costs

Production overhead costs incurred as a result of cash payments are debited as costs in the production overhead account (c). There they join the production overhead costs transferred from other ledger accounts (e) and (g). Detailed job cost records will show the amount of time that employees have worked on the job, causing overhead costs to be incurred. This information will be sufficient to authorise transfers from the production overhead account to the work-in-progress account (h). All production overheads (h) are then transferred to the work-in-progress account so that work-in progress now contains the prime cost (direct materials and direct labour) and all the production overhead costs.

7.3.4 Completion of work-in-progress

When work-in-progress is completed it becomes another asset, finished goods. The completed work-in-progress (j) is transferred to finished goods. When the finished goods are sold they are transferred to the cost of sales account (k) and from there to the profit and loss account (l) which is produced for management accounting purposes.

7.3.5 Administration and selling

There are other overhead costs incurred, such as administration and selling costs, which are not part of the production cost. They are credited in the cash account (m), showing a reduction in the asset of cash, and are debited as expenses in a separate account for administration and selling overheads. From there these administration and selling overhead costs are transferred to profit and loss account (n).

7.3.6 Revenues

Revenue is created for the enterprise by selling goods on credit. The increase in revenue is credited in the sales account (o) while the increase in the asset of debtors is recorded as a debit in the debtors' control account (o). Finally the revenue is transferred from the sales account to the profit and loss account (p).

7.4 Recording transactions for a job-costing system

In this section the general scheme outlined in Exhibit 7.3 is applied to the practical example, Specialprint, which was explained in Chapter 6. Exhibit 7.4 summarises the transactions of Exhibit 6.2 (Chapter 6). These transactions relate to work undertaken by Specialprint, a company which prints novelty stationery to be sold to a chain of

Exhibit 7.4
Specialprint: transactions for the month of June

1 June	Bought 60 rolls of paper on credit from supplier, invoiced price being £180,000
1 June	Bought inks, glue and dyes, cost £25,000 paid in cash
2 June	Returned to supplier one roll, damaged in transit, £2,500
3 June	Rolls of paper issued to printing department, cost £120,000
4 June	Issued half of inks, glues and dyes to printing department, £12,500
14 June	Paid printing employees' wages £8,000
14 June	Paid maintenance wages £250
16 June	Paid rent, rates and electricity in respect of printing, £14,000, in cash
28 June	Paid printing employees' wages £8,000
28 June	Paid maintenance wages £250
30 June	Transferred printed stationery to finished goods inventory, valued at cost of £160,000
30 June	Sold stationery to customer on credit, cost of goods sold being £152,000

retail stores. The company has only one customer for this novelty stationery. Each transaction is now analysed to determine the relevant journal entry. A brief explanation is provided for each entry. The resulting ledger accounts are presented in Exhibit 7.5 (on p. 156). After reading the explanation of each transaction, you should follow it through into Exhibit 7.5 to see how the ledger entries are built up.

7.4.1 Acquisition of inventory: direct materials

In purchasing the rolls of paper, the business acquires an asset, shown by a debit entry in the ledger account for materials inventory. In taking credit from the supplier it incurs a liability, shown by a credit entry in the ledger account for a trade creditor.

| 1 June | Materials inventory | Dr | 180,000 | | |
| | Trade creditor | | | Cr | 180,000 |

7.4.2 Acquisition of inventory: indirect materials

In purchasing the inks, glue and dyes, the business acquires a further asset, shown by a debit entry in the ledger account for materials inventory. In exchange, the asset of cash has diminished, shown by a credit entry in the cash account.

| 1 June | Materials inventory | Dr | 25,000 | | |
| | Cash | | | Cr | 25,000 |

7.4.3 Return of inventory to a supplier

Returning the damaged roll of paper reduces the asset of materials inventory, shown by a credit entry, and reduces the liability to the trade creditor, shown by a debit entry.

| 2 June | Trade creditor | Dr | 2,500 | | |
| | Materials inventory | | | Cr | 2,500 |

7.4.4 Converting raw materials into work-in-progress: direct materials

When the rolls of paper are issued from the stores to the printing department, they become a part of the work-in-progress of that department. Since this work-in-progress is expected to bring a benefit to the enterprise in the form of cash flows from sales when it is eventually finished and sold, it meets the definition of an asset. The increase in the asset of work-in-progress is shown by a debit entry, while the decrease in the inventory of materials is shown by a credit entry.

| 3 June | Work-in-progress | Dr | 120,000 | | |
| | Materials inventory | | | Cr | 120,000 |

7.4.5 Treatment of indirect materials

Inks, glue and dyes are indirect materials. The ledger recording for indirect materials differs from that used for direct materials. The indirect cost is transferred to the production overhead account, to be accumulated with other indirect costs and later transferred to work-in-progress as a global figure for production overhead. In this case only half of the indirect materials have been issued (£12,500), the rest remaining in inventory.

4 June	Production overhead	Dr	12,500		
	Materials inventory			Cr	12,500

7.4.6 Paying the wages

There are two amounts of direct labour costs paid during the period in respect of the printing employees, and two amounts of indirect wages in respect of maintenance. For each amount the wages account is debited (because an expense has occurred) and the cash account is credited because the asset of cash has decreased. At this point no distinction is made between direct and indirect labour because they all form part of the total labour cost. That information is required for other purposes (such as the external financial reporting).

It will only be after analysis of the labour records for the period that an accurate subdivision into direct and indirect costs may be made. Although it is assumed here that all wages of printing employees are direct costs, it could be that enforced idle time through equipment failure would create an indirect cost. (For simplification in this example, income taxes and employer's costs in relation to employees are omitted.)

14 June	Wages	Dr	8,000		
	Cash			Cr	8,000
28 June	Wages	Dr	8,000		
	Cash			Cr	8,000
14 June	Wages	Dr	250		
	Cash			Cr	250
28 June	Wages	Dr	250		
	Cash			Cr	250

7.4.7 Payment for production overhead costs

Rent, rates and electricity costs paid from cash in respect of printing are production overhead costs. They are debited to the cost of production overhead. There is a credit entry in the cash account in this case. (In practice overhead costs are also incurred on credit terms.)

16 June	Production overhead	Dr	14,000		
	Cash			Cr	14,000

7.4.8 Recording indirect labour as a production overhead cost

The indirect labour cost is treated similarly to the indirect materials. At the end of the month the cost is transferred from wages to production overhead so that all overhead costs are accumulated together.

30 June	Production overhead	Dr	500		
	Wages			Cr	500

7.4.9 Completing the work-in-progress account: direct labour

The direct labour cost amounts to £16,000 and forms part of the prime cost of work-in-progress. At the end of the month a debit entry is made in the work-in-progress account because the direct labour cost is adding to the value of the asset of work-in-progress. A credit entry is made in the wages account because the cost previously recorded there is now being transferred elsewhere.

| 30 June | Work-in-progress | Dr | 16,000 | | |
| | Labour cost | | | Cr | 16,000 |

In a computerised accounting system the transfer to the work-in-progress account would follow immediately on the payment of wages, so that there would be a debit entry in the wages account recording the cost, and a credit entry transferring it to work-in-progress, both on the same date. In a manual system, more of the transfer entries may be left until the end of the month, when management reports are being prepared.

7.4.10 Taking production overheads to the work-in-progress account

It may be seen from Exhibit 7.5 that there is now a total of £27,000 debited to the production overhead ledger account. At the end of the month it is all transferred to the work-in-progress account by a credit entry in the production overhead account (reducing the expense recorded there) and debiting the work-in-progress account (adding to the value of the asset).

| 30 June | Work-in-progress | Dr | 27,000 | | |
| | Production overhead | | | Cr | 27,000 |

This transfer will enable the value of work-in-progress to be shown at full cost at the end of the month.

7.4.11 Transferring work-in-progress to finished goods

As the asset of work-in-progress is completed, it changes into another asset, the inventory of finished goods. A credit entry removes the asset from work-in-progress and a debit entry records its new existence as the asset of finished goods.

| 30 June | Finished goods inventory | Dr | 160,000 | | |
| | Work-in-progress | | | Cr | 160,000 |

7.4.12 Sale of goods

When a sale is made to a customer, the asset of finished goods inventory is transformed into the expense of cost of goods sold. The expense is recorded by making a debit entry in the cost of goods sold account. The reduction in the asset is shown by a credit entry in the finished goods inventory account. Any balance remaining on the finished goods inventory account represents unsold goods.

| 30 June | Cost of goods sold | Dr | 152,000 | | |
| | Finished goods inventory | | | Cr | 152,000 |

Activity 7.2

Check over each of the transactions described in sections 7.4.1 to 7.4.12. Make sure you understand each one. Using a pencil, tick each entry in Exhibit 7.5 to check that you have understood the entry for each transaction.

Exhibit 7.5
Specialprint – Ledger account entries

	£			£
		Cash account		
		1 June	Materials	25,000
		14 June	Wages	8,000
		14 June	Wages	250
		16 June	Rent, Rates, etc	14,000
		28 June	Wages	8,000
30 June	Balance c/d 55,500	28 June	Wages	250
	55,500			55,500
		1 July	Balance b/d	55,500
		Trade creditor		
2 June	Materials returned 2,500	1 June	Materials	180,000
30 June	Balance c/d 177,500			
	180,000			180,000
		1 July	Balance b/d	177,500
		Materials inventory		
1 June	Trade creditor, (paper rolls) 180,000	2 June	Returned to supplier	2,500
1 June	Cash (inks, glue, dyes) 25,000	3 June	Work-in-progress	120,000
		4 June	Production overhead	12,500
		30 June	Balance c/d	70,000
	205,000			205,000
1 July	Balance b/d 70,000			
		Wages		
14 June	Cash 8,000	30 June	Production overhead	500
14 June	Cash 250	30 June	Work-in-progress	16,000
28 June	Cash 8,000			
28 June	Cash 250			
	16,500			16.500
		Production overhead		
4 June	Materials inventory 12,500	30 June	Work-in-progress	27,000
16 June	Cash 14,000			
30 June	Wages 500			
	27,000			27,000
		Work-in-progress		
3 June	Direct materials 120,000	30 June	Finished goods	160,000
30 June	Direct labour 16,000	30 June	Balance c/d	3,000
30 June	Production overhead 27,000			
	163,000			163,000
1 July	Balance b/d 3,000			
		Finished goods inventory		
30 June	Work-in-progress 160,000	30 June	Cost of goods sold	152,000
		30 June	Balance c/d	8,000
	160,000			160,000
1 July	Balance b/d 8,000			
		Cost of goods sold		
30 June	Finished goods 152,000			

Real world case 7.2

This case study is taken from the Sage website. Sage is one of the major providers of accounting software to small and medium-sized businesses

Bell Microsystems Limited

Established in 1997, Bell Microsystems is an IT infrastructure solution provider, based in Portsmouth. Bell Microsystems use several Sage products including Sage Line 50, Forecasting, Personnel and Job Costing. Amy said: 'We chose Sage products because they are a well known name in supplying accounting products.'

Sage Job Costing is one of the products that Bell Microsystems finds most useful. Job Costing software is a powerful tool that helps prepare quick and accurate estimates for future jobs. Amy said: 'As all calculations are based on hard facts not guesswork, this allows our costs to be controlled more tightly. As a result of this the computerised Job Costing package provides an instant and accurate picture of job value to businesses, highlights which elements are under or over budget and gives a precise breakdown on the status of every job. The package also allows us to simplify billing with invoice totals being automatically calculated according to our preferred billing method. We can also track costs against budgets and projections, in a wide range of categories such as timesheets, stock, distribution costs, material and labour.' Amy is extremely impressed with her Sage software: 'I feel I cannot fault any feature in the Sage products I have. I love the reports I can produce as they are a crafty tool for briefing the managing director at Bell Microsystems. They make everyday tasks so simple and quick to do.'

Source: www.sage.com

Subsequently, Bell's business has grown and changed quite significantly and they have moved on from job costing to a system more suited to the larger needs of the business. This illustrates that costing systems are adapted to meet the changing needs of business.

Discussion points

1 Why is job costing important to this business?

2 What benefits does the owner see in the job-costing system?

7.5 The use of control accounts and integration with the financial accounts

Exhibit 7.4 has shown the recording of a set of transactions in ledger accounts which follow the diagram outlined in Exhibit 7.3, but although it shows the basic rules of bookkeeping applied to a set of transactions it is not sufficiently detailed to be of practical use in management accounting. The company will need to have separate information about the different types of novelty stationery produced, the different types of materials used in manufacture, the various labour resources used and the range of production overhead costs applied.

Where a business is complex and has large numbers of transactions, those transactions are collected together in what are called **cost control accounts** (also called total accounts because they control the total transactions of the type being recorded). Separate records for each job (also called secondary records) are available to show the detailed analysis of those control accounts.

Exhibit 7.6
Practical example of the use of control accounts (total accounts)

The following information for Specialprint is reproduced from Exhibit 6.2 of Chapter 6.

In this Exhibit, various symbols appear in the second column. These symbols are used in the ledger accounts of Exhibits 7.7 to 7.10 as an aid to identifying how the subsidiary records match up to the items in the control accounts.

Date	Symbol	Transaction
1 June	♪	Bought 60 rolls of paper on credit from supplier, invoiced price being £180,000. The rolls of paper acquired consisted of two different grades. 40 rolls were of medium-grade paper at a total cost of £100,000 and 20 rolls were of high grade at a total cost of £80,000.
1 June	♣	Bought inks, glues and dyes at a cost of £25,000 paid in cash. The inks cost £9,000 while the glue cost £12,000 and the dyes £4,000.
2 June	⊗	Returned to supplier one roll of paper damaged in transit, cost £2,500. The roll of paper returned was of medium grade.
3 June	†	Rolls of paper issued to printing department, cost £120,000. 20 high-grade rolls were issued, together with 16 medium-grade rolls. There were three separate jobs: references 601, 602 and 603. The high-grade rolls were all for job 601 (notepaper); 12 medium-grade rolls were for job 602 (envelopes) and the remaining 4 medium-grade rolls were for job 603 (menu cards).
4 June	ø	Issued half of inks, glues and dyes to printing department, £12,500. Exactly half of each item of inks, glue and dyes was issued, for use across all three jobs.
14 June	ψ	Paid printing employees' wages £8,000. Wages were paid to 10 printing employees, each earning the same amount.
14 June	λ	Paid maintenance wages £250. Maintenance wages were paid to one part-time maintenance officer.
16 June	‡	Paid rent, rates and electricity in respect of printing, £14,000 in cash. Payment for rent was £8,000, rates £4,000 and electricity £2,000.
28 June	ϖ	Paid printing employees' wages £8,000. Wages were paid to the same 10 employees as on 14 June.
28 June	φ	Paid maintenance wages £250. Maintenance wages were paid to the same maintenance officer as on 14 June.
30 June	♥	Employee records show that: 5 printing employees worked all month on job 601; 3 printing employees worked on job 602; and 2 printing employees worked on job 603.
30 June	ξ	It is company policy to absorb production overheads in proportion to labour costs of each job.
30 June	#	Transferred printed stationery to finished goods stock at a total amount of £160,000, in respect of jobs 601 and 602, which were completed, together with the major part of job 603. There remained some unfinished work-in-progress on one section of job 603, valued at £3,000. Separate finished goods records are maintained for notepaper, envelopes and menu cards.
30 June	≈	Sold stationery to customer on credit, cost of goods sold being £152,000. The customer took delivery of all notepaper and all envelopes, but took only £7,600 of menu cards, leaving the rest to await completion of the further items still in progress.

> A **cost control account** is a record of the total transactions relating to the costs being recorded. A control account is also called a **total account**. The control account is supported by secondary records showing detailed costs for each job separately.

The use of control accounts allows the management accounting records to be integrated with the financial accounting records. The main ledger contains the control accounts, while the detailed information is recorded outside the main ledger. The control accounts are sufficiently aggregated to be of use for financial accounting purposes where only the total costs of each main category are required.

This section explains the progress of costs through the control accounts in the main ledger until they reach the profit and loss account. It illustrates the use of control accounts and secondary records by expanding on the example contained in Exhibit 7.5.

You will find that the accounts shown in diagram form in Exhibit 7.3 and in the practical example of Exhibit 7.5 will become the control accounts and that new, more detailed, secondary records will be provided to support these control accounts.

The use of control accounts and subsidiary records may be illustrated by returning to the transactions of Exhibit 7.4 and the ledger accounts of Exhibit 7.5. Those ledger accounts are *all* control accounts (total accounts) because the total amount of each transaction was entered without any analysis into more detailed elements. Consider now the additional information contained in Exhibit 7.6, which will be used to prepare the subsidiary records supporting the control accounts.

7.5.1 Acquisition of inventory: direct and indirect materials costs (Exhibit 7.7)

For accurate control of stores it would be necessary to maintain a separate stores ledger record for each type of material held. Five different types of material are mentioned in Exhibit 7.6 and so five separate ledger accounts are shown in Exhibit 7.7. The separate debits and credits in each ledger account may be seen to equal the total entries in the main ledger account for materials inventory, reproduced here from Exhibit 7.5, and now renamed as the *materials inventory control account* (or total account). Symbols to the right of each monetary amount show the items which, added together, are equal to the corresponding total in the control account.

Activity 7.3

Compare the control account of Exhibit 7.7 with the materials inventory account of Exhibit 7.5 to satisfy yourself that they are the same. Then satisfy yourself that the separate job accounts in Exhibit 7.8 add up to the totals in the control account.

7.5.2 Wages: direct and indirect labour costs (Exhibit 7.8)

The wages account shown in Exhibit 7.5 becomes the wages control account which will be supported by records for 10 individual employees, each debited with £800 on 14 June and £800 on 28 June. There will be a separate employee record for the maintenance officer, debited with £250 on 14 June and £250 on 28 June. Transfers from the employee records will be to the various jobs on which each employee has worked.

There will be ten separate employee records. Employees 1 to 5 work on job 601 so the direct cost of their labour (£8,000) is transferred to job 601 at the end of the month. Employees 6 to 8 work on job 602 so the direct cost of their labour (£4,800) is transferred to job 602 at the end of the month. Employees 9 and 10 work on job 603 and the direct cost of their labour (£3,200) is transferred to job 603 at the end of the month.

Exhibit 7.7
Inventory accounts for each inventory item and inventory control account

		High grade paper				
1 June	Trade creditor (20 rolls)	80,000♪	3 June	Job 601		80,000†
		plus				
		Medium grade paper				
1 June	Trade creditor (40 rolls)	100,000♪	1 June	Returned (1 roll)		2,500⊗
			3 June	Job 602 (12 rolls)		30,000†
			3 June	Job 603 (4 rolls)		10,000†
			30 June	Balance c/d (23 rolls)		57,500*
		100,000				100,000
1 July	Balance b/d	57,500*				
		plus				
		Inks				
1 June	Cash	9,000♣	4 June	Production overhead		4,500ø
			30 June	Balance c/d		4,500*
		9,000				9,000
1 May	Balance b/d	4,500*				
		plus				
		Glue				
1 June	Cash	12,000♣	4 June	Production overhead		6,000ø
			30 June	Balance c/d		6,000*
		12,000				12,000
1 July	Balance b/d	6,000*				
		plus				
		Dyes				
1 June	Cash	4,000♣	4 June	Production overhead		2,000ø
			30 June	Balance c/d		2,000*
		4,000				4,000
1 July	Balance b/d	2,000*				
		equals				
		Materials inventory control account				
1 June	Trade creditor, (paper rolls)	180,000♪	2 June	Returned to supplier		2,500⊗
1 June	Cash (inks, glue, dyes)	25,000♣	3 June	Work-in-progress		120,000†
			4 June	Production overhead		12,500ø
			30 June	Balance c/d		70,000*
		205,000				205,000
1 July	Balance b/d	70,000*				

The transfer from the maintenance officer's record will be to a record which collects all indirect labour costs (which might include printing employee costs if they had unproductive time on their time-sheets). That indirect labour record is one of the subsidiary records supporting the production overhead control account.

The total of all the entries in each of the individual employee records equals the total shown in the wages account of Exhibit 7.5, now renamed as the *wages control account*.

Exhibit 7.8
Wages accounts for each employee and wages control account

Printing employee number 1						
14 June	Cash	800ψ	30 June	Job 601		1,600♥
28 June	Cash	800ϖ				
		1,600				1,600
Printing employee number 2						
14 June	Cash	800ψ	30 June	Job 601		1,600♥
28 June	Cash	800ϖ				
		1,600				1,600
Printing employee number 3						
14 June	Cash	800ψ	30 June	Job 601		1,600♥
28 June	Cash	800ϖ				
		1,600				1,600
Printing employee number 4						
14 June	Cash	800ψ	30 June	Job 601		1,600♥
28 June	Cash	800ϖ				
		1,600				1,600
Printing employee number 5						
14 June	Cash	800ψ	30 June	Job 601		1,600♥
28 June	Cash	800ϖ				
		1,600				1,600
Printing employee number 6						
14 June	Cash	800ψ	30 June	Job 602		1,600♥
28 June	Cash	800ϖ				
		1,600				1,600
Printing employee number 7						
14 June	Cash	800ψ	30 June	Job 602		1,600♥
28 June	Cash	800ϖ				
		1,600				1,600
Printing employee number 8						
14 June	Cash	800ψ	30 June	Job 602		1,600♥
28 June	Cash	800ϖ				
		1,600				1,600
Printing employee number 9						
14 June	Cash	800ψ	30 June	Job 603		1,600♥
28 June	Cash	800ϖ				
		1,600				1,600
Printing employee number 10						
14 June	Cash	800ψ	30 June	Job 603		1,600♥
28 June	Cash	800ϖ				
		1,600				1,600
Maintenance officer						
14 June	Cash	250λ	30 June	Indirect labour		500♦
28 June	Cash	250φ				
		500				500
Wages control account						
14 June	Cash	8,000ψ	30 June	Work-in-progress		16,000♥
14 June	Cash	250λ	30 June	Production overhead		500♦
28 June	Cash	8,000ϖ				
28 June	Cash	250φ				
		16,500				16,500

Activity 7.4

Compare the control account of Exhibit 7.8 with the wages account of Exhibit 7.5 to satisfy yourself that they are the same. Then satisfy yourself that the separate job accounts in Exhibit 7.8 add up to the totals in the control account.

7.5.3 Production overhead costs (Exhibit 7.9)

The *production overhead control account* will be supported by one subsidiary record for each type of overhead cost. The payments on 16 June relate to rent, rates and electricity,

Exhibit 7.9
Production overhead accounts for each cost item, and production overhead control account

Production overhead: Rent					
Overhead cost rate = 25p per £ of direct labour					
16 June	Cash	8,000‡	30 June	Job 601	4,000ξ
				Job 602	2,400ξ
				Job 603	1,600ξ
		8,000			8,000
Production overhead: Rates					
Overhead cost rate = 50p per £ of direct labour					
16 June	Cash	4,000‡	30 June	Job 601	2,000ξ
				Job 602	1,200ξ
				Job 603	800ξ
		4,000			4,000
Production overhead: Electricity					
Overhead cost rate = 12.5p per £ of direct labour					
16 June	Cash	2,000‡	30 June	Job 601	1,000ξ
				Job 602	600ξ
				Job 603	400ξ
		2,000			2,000
Production overhead: Indirect material					
Overhead cost rate = 78.125p per £ of direct labour					
4 June	Ink	4,500ø		Job 601	6,250ξ
	Glue	6,000ø		Job 602	3,750ξ
	Dyes	2,000ø		Job 603	2,500ξ
		12,500			12,500
Production overhead: Indirect labour					
Overhead cost rate = 3.125p per £ of direct labour					
30 June	Maintenance officer	500♦		Job 601	250ξ
				Job 602	150ξ
				Job 603	100ξ
		500			500
Production overhead control account					
4 June	Materials inventory	12,500ø	30 June	Work-in-progress	27,000ξ
16 June	Cash	14,000‡			
30 June	Wages	500♦			
		27,000			27,000

each of which will require a separate record. Additionally there are overheads of indirect materials and indirect labour created by transfers from other records.

We are told in Exhibit 7.6 that production overheads are allocated in proportion to the direct labour costs of each job. The total direct labour cost for the period is £16,000 and so for each item of production overhead the overhead cost rate must be calculated as:

$$\text{overhead cost rate (in £ per £ of direct labour)} = \frac{\text{overhead cost}}{£16,000}$$

For indirect material the calculations are slightly more complex. The total indirect material cost transferred to production overhead is £12,500. The overhead cost rate is therefore calculated as:

$$\frac{£12,500}{£16,000} = 78.125 \text{ pence per £ of direct labour}$$

This rate is then applied to the amounts of direct labour already charged to each job (which was £8,000 for job 601, £4,800 for job 602 and £3,200 for job 603). The resulting amounts are transferred from the indirect materials account to the relevant job records.

For indirect labour the only item is the cost of the maintenance officer.

Adding together all these subsidiary records gives amounts equal to the totals in the production overhead control account. In the ledger accounts different symbols are shown to the right-hand side of each monetary amount as an indication of the items which add to give the respective totals.

Activity 7.5   *Compare the control account of Exhibit 7.9 with the production overhead account of Exhibit 7.5 to satisfy yourself that they are the same. Then satisfy yourself that the separate wages accounts in Exhibit 7.8 add up to the totals in the control account.*

7.5.4   Work-in-progress (Exhibit 7.10)

Work-in-progress records are maintained for each job. The total of the separate job records will equal the total of the work-in-progress control account. The separate job records now follow, with symbols indicating those individual amounts which correspond to the totals in the *work-in-progress control account*.

7.5.5   Finished goods inventory (Exhibit 7.11)

There must be a separate record for each line of finished goods, the total of which is represented by the control account for finished goods. In this example there are three categories of finished goods, namely note paper (produced by job 601), envelopes (produced by job 602) and menu cards (produced by job 603).

There will be three different records for finished goods, which may be note paper, envelopes or menu cards. The total of the three separate records is £160,000 which equals the amount shown by the *finished goods control account*.

Finally, the sale of goods to the customer is recognised by a transfer from the finished goods inventory to the cost of goods sold account. In order to analyse each product line separately, there will be separate cost of goods sold accounts for each item (note paper, envelopes and menu cards) and a cost of goods control account to record the total amount.

Exhibit 7.10

Work-in-progress subsidiary records and control account

Work-in-progress: Job 601

3 June	Direct materials	80,000†	30 June	Finished goods	101,500#
30 June	Direct labour	8,000♥			
30 June	Production overhead:				
	Rent	4,000ξ			
	Rates	2,000ξ			
	Electricity	1,000ξ			
	Indirect materials	6,250ξ			
	Indirect labour	250ξ			
		101,500			101,500

Work-in-progress: Job 602

3 June	Direct materials	30,000†	30 June	Finished goods	42,900#
30 June	Direct labour	4,800♥			
30 June	Production overhead:				
	Rent	2,400ξ			
	Rates	1,200ξ			
	Electricity	600ξ			
	Indirect materials	3,750ξ			
	Indirect labour	150ξ			
		42,900			42,900

Work-in-progress: Job 603

3 June	Direct materials	10,000†	30 June	Finished goods	15,600#
30 June	Direct labour	3,200♥	30 June	Balance c/d	3,000*
30 June	Production overhead:				
	Rent	1,600ξ			
	Rates	800ξ			
	Electricity	400ξ			
	Indirect materials	2,500ξ			
	Indirect labour	100ξ			
		18,600			18,600
1 July	Balance b/d	3,000*			

Work-in-progress control account

3 June	Direct materials	120,000†	30 June	Finished goods	160,000#
30 June	Direct labour	16,000♥	30 June	Balance c/d	3,000*
30 June	Production overhead	27,500ξ			
		163,000			163,000
1 July	Balance b/d	3,000*			

Activity 7.6

Compare the control account of Exhibit 7.10 with the work-in-progress account of Exhibit 7.5 to satisfy yourself that they are the same. Then satisfy yourself that the separate job accounts in Exhibit 7.10 add up to the totals in the control account.

Exhibit 7.11
Finished goods subsidiary records and control account

Finished goods inventory: Note paper					
30 June	Job 601	101,500#	30 June	Cost of goods sold	101,500≈
Finished goods inventory: Envelopes					
30 June	Job 602	42,900#	30 June	Cost of goods sold	42,900≈
Finished goods inventory: Menu cards					
30 June	Job 603	15,600#	30 June	Cost of goods sold	7,600≈
Finished goods inventory control account					
30 June	Work-in-progress	160,000#	30 June	Cost of goods sold	152,000≈

Activity 7.7

Compare the control account of Exhibit 7.11 with the finished goods account of Exhibit 7.5 to satisfy yourself that they are the same. Then satisfy yourself that the separate job accounts in Exhibit 7.11 add up to the totals in the control account.

7.6 Contract accounts

One specific application of job costing is in recording contracts which are relatively large in relation to the magnitude of the organisation's activity as a whole, and usually require more than one accounting period for completion. Such large 'jobs' are normally carried out under a legal contract which sets out the conditions of performance required of the enterprise and the conditions of payment to be imposed on the customer.

Because of the size and significance of such a contract, it is common practice to open a separate job cost record in which to collect all costs and revenues of the project so that the document eventually records also the profit on the contract.

7.6.1 Main features of a contract

Before moving on to the accounting aspects, it is necessary to set out some of the main features of most contracts. The contract is usually for some substantial work based on building or engineering applications, but could be a contract for services such as cleaning a building or providing security cover. Because the contract is agreed in very specific terms, most costs will be directly related to the project. Materials, labour and direct expenses will be identifiable with the project. Labour requirements may be provided by employees of the organisation or may be subcontracted to other businesses. Special equipment may be required for the project. The head office of the organisation will seek to charge overhead costs to the project.

Incomplete contract

If the contract is incomplete at the year-end a portion of profit may nevertheless be recognised, on the basis that the work has been done and the profit on that work is earned. If there was no report on profit as the contract progressed, that would give a very distorted picture of the activity of the business. If a contract to build a bridge lasted three years then reporting profit only on completion would give an impression of no activity in the first two years and then high activity in the third year.

In order to achieve a measure of objectivity in assessing the amount of profit earned on a partly completed project, it is normal to seek the opinion of an expert (architect, surveyor or engineer, for example) on the *value of work completed* to date. Any work not certified as being completed at the balance sheet date is carried forward as work-in-progress.

Taking profit as the work progresses is attractive as an application of the accruals concept but is felt to be risky in the context of the prudence concept. In the case of contracts this has led to a wide range of practice across and within the various industries. However, it would be safe to assume that most companies would seek to make some provision against being over-optimistic on a long-term contract.

Payments by the customer

Where the contract lasts over a longer period of time, it is quite usual for the enterprise to ask the customer to make *payments on account of progress*. Invoices for these progress payments are made as soon as the technical expert has certified as complete a stage of the project. When the customer makes a progress payment in advance, the sum is effectively a liability from the point of view of the company receiving the payment. If for any reason the contract were not to be completed, the payment would have to be refunded to the customer.

Activity 7.8

Look at a major development contract under way somewhere near you. Write down some items of costs that relate to the project. Then think about the time scale to complete the project and how the costs will be spread over the contract life.

7.6.2 Recording transactions for a contract

Because a contract is usually a significant activity for the business, the job cost record is used to show every aspect of the contract, including all costs incurred, whether for the current or a later period, and the periodic profit. An example of a Job Cost Record is shown in Exhibit 7.12.

Exhibit 7.12
Job cost record

Contract Job Cost Record Year 1		
Year 1		*£000s*
date	Materials purchased	xx
date	Wages paid	xx
date	Direct costs paid	xx
date	Subcontractors paid	xx
date	Equipment at cost purchased	xx
date	Architect's fee paid	xx
date	Head office charges	xx
date	Due to subcontractor	xx
date	Direct costs due to suppliers	xx
	Total costs charged Year 1	xxx
	Carry to next period:	
End year	Materials on site	(xx)
End year	Equipment on site	(xx)
End year	Cost of work certified for Year 1	xxx

Costs incurred during the accounting period

The materials, labour, direct and indirect costs of a contract job are recorded on the job card when paid for or when acquired from a supplier who becomes a creditor of the business. One unusual feature is that any equipment purchased for the contract is recorded in full as soon as it is acquired. The entries for costs are highlighted in Exhibit 7.13.

Exhibit 7.13
Job cost record: entering all costs of the period

Contract Job Cost Record Year 1		
Year 1		£000s
date	Materials purchased	xx
date	Wages paid	xx
date	Direct costs paid	xx
date	Subcontractors paid	xx
date	Equipment at cost purchased	xx
date	Architect's fee paid	xx
date	Head office charges	xx
date	Due to subcontractor	xx
date	Direct costs due to suppliers	xx
	Total costs charged Year 1	xxx
	Carry to next period:	
End year	Materials on site	(xx)
End year	Equipment on site	(xx)
End year	Cost of work certified for Year 1	xxx

Items remaining at the end of an accounting period

At the end of each accounting period the value of equipment and materials remaining on site is estimated. The difference between the original cost and the valuation equals the amount of material and equipment consumed by the contract. Items remaining on site are regarded as assets for the next period. The cost of work certified for the period is the difference between the total costs recorded and the amount carried forward to the next period. These entries are highlighted in Exhibit 7.14.

Exhibit 7.14
Job cost record: items remaining at the end of the period

Contract Job Cost Record Year 1		
Year 1		£
date	Materials purchased	xx
date	Wages paid	xx
date	Direct costs paid	xx
date	Subcontractors paid	xx
date	Equipment at cost purchased	xx
date	Architect's fee paid	xx
date	Head office charges	xx
date	Due to subcontractor	xx
date	Direct costs due to suppliers	xx
	Total costs charged Year 1	xxx
	Carry to next period:	
End year	Materials on site	(xx)
End year	Equipment on site	(xx)
End year	Cost of work certified for Year 1	xxx

Matching costs with revenues of the accounting period

Exhibit 7.15
Statement of contract profit

		£
Revenue	Value of work certified	xx
Cost	Cost of work certified	xx
Profit calculated	Profit of the period	xx
Deduction for uncertainty	Less portion not reported this period (around one third of calculated profit)	xx
Profit reported	Profit to be reported for Year 1	xx

In the statement of contract profit, Exhibit 7.15, an entry will be made for the sales value of work certified by an expert as being complete. Deducting costs of the project from the estimated sales value of work certified will give a profit figure for the period. There are no firm rules as to how much of this profit should be reported for the period, but many companies would report less than the full amount, as a prudent measure. Various formulae are used to decide how much profit to report, but a useful rule of thumb at this stage might be to suggest reporting around two-thirds of the profit calculated.

7.6.3 Contract ledger accounts

When a contract commences, a new ledger account is opened. All direct costs are debited to the contract account and all assets acquired for the contract are also debited.

Direct labour and direct overhead costs should present no problem in being identified and charged to the contract account There may also be an indirect cost charged in the form of a head office overhead allocation.

At the end of the accounting period the value of equipment and materials remaining on site is estimated. The difference between the original cost and the valuation equals the amount of material and equipment consumed by the contract. Items remaining on site are carried forward as assets to the next period.

On the revenue side of the contract, an entry will be made for the sales value of work certified by an expert as being complete. Deducting costs of the project from the estimated sales value of work certified will give a profit figure for the period.

Finally, the balances taken forward at the end of the accounting period become the opening balances for the next period.

7.7 Illustration of contract accounting

The following sections set out the method of recording the transactions on a contract which lasts fifteen months in total and straddles two accounting periods. Office Builders Ltd undertook a contract to build the Western Office Complex for a fixed price of £390,000 during the period from May Year 1 to July Year 2. Exhibit 7.16 gives information for Year 1 which is presented as a job cost record in Exhibit 7.17, leading to a statement of contract profit in Exhibit 7.18. Exhibit 7.19 gives information for Year 2 which is presented as a job cost record in Exhibit 7.20 and a statement of contract profit

Exhibit 7.16

Office Builders Ltd: Contract for Western Office Complex

Office Builders Ltd undertook a contract to build the Western Office Complex for a fixed price of £390,000 during the period from May Year 1 to July Year 2. This table sets out transactions up to the company's year end in December, Year 1.

Transactions during Year 1:		£000s
May	Materials purchased and delivered to site	87
May	Equipment delivered to site	11
July	Architect's fee	6
June–Dec	Materials issued from store	51
May–Dec	Wages paid on site	65
Sept	Payment to subcontractors	8
May–Dec	Direct costs	25
Dec	Head office charges	7
At the end of Year 1		
Dec	Value of equipment remaining on site	7
Dec	Value of material remaining on site	32
Dec	Sales value of work certified	240
Dec	Amount due to subcontractors	5
Dec	Direct costs incurred but not yet paid	8

in Exhibit 7.21. The overall profit on the contract is presented in Exhibit 7.22 and explained in terms of the profit reported in the two separate reporting periods.

7.7.1   Recording the transactions

In respect of materials, £87,000 was purchased and £51,000 recorded as being issued. It might be expected that this would leave £36,000 to be carried forward in store. But only £32,000 of materials were found at the end of the year, implying that £4000-worth of materials has either been scrapped, because of some defect, or been removed without authority. In practice this would probably lead to an investigation of the control system to discover why some materials have apparently disappeared. The ledger account entries do not show the detail of materials issued, but instead assume that any material not contained in the physical check at the end of the year must have been used on the contract.

The equipment delivered to the site had a cost of £11,000 and an estimated value of £7,000 remaining at the end of the year. Depreciation is therefore £4,000.

The cost of work certified is the total of the costs incurred to date on that portion of the work approved by the architect. In this case the work has been certified at the end of the accounting year so there is no problem in deciding which costs to treat as cost of goods sold and which to carry forward. If the work had been certified before the end of the financial year, any subsequent costs would also need to be carried forward to be matched against future estimated sales value of work done.

An architect's fee would be quite common on contract work of this type. Provided the fee is specific to the project, it forms a direct cost which must be included in the contract account.

All further expenditure of the period, such as wages, other direct costs and payments to subcontractors, are debited to the contract because they are, or will become, costs of the contract. At the end of the accounting period a count is taken of everything remaining unused on the site and this count forms the basis for determining how much of the 'expense' should be carried forward as an asset for the next period.

Any costs not carried to the next period will become part of the cost of goods sold, to be compared with the value of work certified in determining the profit for the period. Those managing an enterprise prudently might decide to hold in suspense some of the profit calculated in the early stages of a project, as a precaution against unforeseen problems later. Various formulae are in use for calculating this 'prudent amount' but this example will take a 'rule of thumb' approach in suggesting that taking credit for two-thirds of the profit calculated might be a reasonably prudent approach.

Exhibit 7.17
Office Builders Ltd: Job cost record of Western Office Complex for Year 1

Contract Job Cost Record Year 1		
Year 1		£000s
May	Materials purchased	87
May	Equipment at cost	11
May	Architect's fee	6
May–Dec	Wages paid	65
Sept	Subcontractors	8
May–Dec	Direct costs	25
Dec	Head office charges	7
Dec	Due to subcontractor	5
Dec	Direct costs incurred	8
	Total costs charged Year 1	222
	Carry to next period:	
Dec	Materials on site	(32)
	Equipment on site	(7)
Dec	Cost of work certified for Year 1	183

The costs for Year 1 include all recorded payments plus costs incurred but not paid at the end of the period. These include liabilities to the subcontractor £5,000 and direct costs £8,000, which must be settled early in Year 2. Equipment on site and material on site have been paid in Year 1 but will not be used in earning revenue until Year 2. The overall cost of the work certified as completed during Year 1 is therefore £183,000 (as shown in Exhibit 7.17).

7.7.2   Reporting the profit of the period

In the profit and loss statement for Year 1 (see Exhibit 7.18), Office Builders Ltd has shown the total profit of £57,000 in two components. Two-thirds of this amount, £38,000, will be reported in the profit and loss account for Year 1. One-third will be held back until Year 2 as a precaution against unforeseen problems causing additional costs that might reduce the overall contract profit.

Exhibit 7.18
Statement of contract profit to be reported in Year 1

	£000s
Value of work certified	240
Cost of work certified	183
Profit of the period	57
Less portion not reported this period (one-third of calculated profit)	(19)
Profit to be reported for Year 1	38

Transactions for the following period

To show the complete picture on the contract it is necessary to consider Year 2 also. Exhibit 7.19 sets out the transactions undertaken during Year 2.

Exhibit 7.19
Office Builders Ltd: Transactions of Western Office Complex for Year 2

Transactions during Year 2:		
Jan	Paid subcontractor amount due	5
Jan	Paid direct costs due at end of Year 1	8
Feb	Materials purchased and delivered to site	24
June–Dec	Materials issued from store	56
May–Dec	Wages paid on site	31
Sept	Payment to subcontractors	17
May–Dec	Direct costs	15
Dec	Head office charges	7
At the end of Year 2		
Dec	Value of equipment remaining on site	nil
Dec	Value of material remaining on site	nil
Dec	Sales value of work certified	150
Dec	Direct costs incurred but not yet paid	8

Exhibit 7.20 sets out the statement of costs for the second year, showing that the cost of work certified for Year 2 is £141,000.

Exhibit 7.20
Office Builders Ltd: Job cost record of Western Office Complex for Year 2

Contract Job Cost Record Year 2		
Year 2		*£000s*
Jan	Material on site b/d	32
Jan	Equipment on site b/d	7
Jan–July	Materials purchased	24
Jan–July	Wages paid	31
Mar	Subcontractors	17
Jan–July	Direct costs paid	15
July	Head office charges	7
July	Direct costs incurred	8
	Cost of work certified	141

The statement of contract profit for Year 2 is set out in Exhibit 7.21. It shows that the calculated profit for Year 2 is equal to £9,000 (£150,000 value of work certified minus £141,000 costs incurred for the period). The profit 'held back', £19,000, is added to the profit and loss section of the contract account to give an overall profit of £28,000 reported in Year 2. With the benefit of hindsight it probably was a wise precaution to hold some of the Year 1 profit back from the reported profit and it would appear possible that some of the costs incurred in Year 1 were providing a benefit to the work of Year 2.

At the end of Year 2 all of the remaining profit can be reported since the outcome is certain. In practice, there will be a further period during which the builder has responsibility to put right any defects. It would therefore be prudent to make provision again for possible losses on repairs needed before the hand-over date, but that has not been done in this illustration.

Exhibit 7.21
Statement of contract profit to be reported in Year 2

	£000s
Value of work certified	150
Cost of work certified	141
Profit of the period	9
Add portion not reported in previous period	19
Profit to be reported for Year 1	28

7.7.4 Total contract profit

Exhibit 7.22 shows an overall statement of profit. It reports the full contract price, against which are matched all the costs of the contract. The total contract profit is shown to be £66,000, reported as £38,000 in Year 1 and £28,000 in Year 2.

Exhibit 7.22
Statement of total contract profit

	£000s	£000s
Contract price		390
Direct costs		
Materials (87 + 24)	111	
Labour (65 + 31)	96	
Direct costs (25 + 8 + 15 + 8)	56	
Payments to subcontractors (8 + 5 + 17)	30	
Depreciation of equipment	11	
Architect's fee	6	
	310	
Indirect costs		
Head office charges (7 + 7)	14	
		324
Total contract profit (reported as £38,000 in Year 1 and £28,000 in Year 2)		66

7.7.5 Ledger account records

The transactions of Exhibit 7.16 are recorded in the ledger accounts of Exhibit 7.23, showing how the debit and credit entries appear in the contract account. There will, naturally be other ledger accounts, such as cash, creditors and the profit and loss account, where the other half of the journal entry may be found.

In the profit and loss section for Year 1, Office Builders Ltd has shown the total profit of £57,000 in two components. Two-thirds of this amount, £38,000, will be reported in the profit and loss account for Year 1. One-third will be held in suspense to be carried forward to Year 2 in the ledger account and await recognition there.

In the 'balances brought forward' section, two assets and two liabilities are also brought forward. Equipment on site and material on site represent the items remaining in a good state for use in Year 2. There are liabilities to the subcontractor (£5,000) and to pay for direct costs (£8,000), which must be settled early in Year 2.

To show the complete picture on the contract it is necessary to consider Year 2 also. The transactions undertaken during Year 2, as set out in Exhibit 7.19, are set out in

Exhibit 7.23

Office Builders Ltd: Ledger accounts for Western Office Complex for Year 1

Contract account					
Current transactions section					
Year 1			*Year 1*		
May	Materials purchased	87			
May	Equipment at cost	11	Dec	Materials on site c/d	32
May	Architect's fee	6		Equipment on site c/d	7
May–Dec	Wages paid	65			
Sept	Subcontractors	8	Dec	Cost of work certified	183
May–Dec	Direct costs	25			
Dec	Head office charges	7			
Dec	Due to subcontractor c/d	5			
Dec	Direct costs incurred c/d	8			
		222			222
Profit and loss section					
Year 1			*Year 1*		
Dec	Cost of work certified b/d	183	Dec	Value of work certified	240
Dec	Profit and loss account	38			
Dec	Contract profit suspense c/d	19			
2		240			240
Balances brought forward section					
Year 2			*Year 2*		
Jan	Equipment on site b/d	7	Jan	Due to subcontractor b/d	5
	Material on site b/d	32	Jan	Due for direct costs b/d	8
			Jan	Contract profit suspense b/d	19

ledger accounts in Exhibit 7.24. The liabilities to pay for subcontractors and for direct costs are met by payment in January.

The profit in suspense (£19,000) which was brought down with other balances at the start of Year 2 is taken to the profit and loss section of the contract account. The profit for Year 2 is equal to £9,000 (£150,000 value of work certified minus £141,000 costs incurred for the period), but adding on the profit in suspense gives an overall profit of £28,000 reported in Year 2. With the benefit of hindsight it probably was a wise precaution to hold some of the Year 1 profit back from the reported profit and it would appear possible that some of the costs incurred in Year 1 were providing a benefit to the work of Year 2.

At the end of Year 2 all profit can be reported since the outcome is certain. In practice there will be a further period during which the builder has responsibility to put right any defects. It would therefore be prudent to make provision again for possible losses on repairs needed before the hand-over date, but that has not been done in this illustration.

Although the profit is completed, the ledger account is kept open because there is still a payment due to a subcontractor, recorded in the 'balances brought forward' section. Once that payment is made, the bookkeeping records for this contract may be terminated.

If ledger accounts are not required, this procedure may be regarded as a somewhat tedious process and it may be more convenient to move directly to an overall statement of contract profit, as seen in Exhibit 7.22.

Exhibit 7.24
Office Builders Ltd: Ledger accounts for Western Office Complex for Year 2

Contract account					
Current transactions section					
Year 2		£000s	Year 2		£000s
Jan	Equipment on site b/d	7	Jan	Due to subcontractor b/d	5
Jan	Material on site b/d	32	Jan	Due for direct costs b/d	8
Dec	Contract profit suspense c/d	19	Jan	Contract profit suspense b/d	19
Jan	Paid subcontractor	5			
Jan	Paid direct costs	8	July	Cost of work certified c/d	141
Jan–July	Materials purchased	24			
Jan–July	Wages paid	31			
Mar	Subcontractors	17			
Jan–July	Direct costs paid	15			
July	Head office charges	7			
July	Direct costs incurred c/d	8			
		173			173
Profit and loss section					
Year 2		£000s	Year 2		£000s
Dec	Cost of work certified b/d	141	Jan	Contract profit suspense b/d	19
Dec	Profit and loss account	28	July	Sales value of work certified	150
Dec		169			169
Balances brought forward section					
Year 3		£000s	Year 3		£000s
			Jan	Due to subcontractors b/d	8

7.8 What the researchers have found

As an example of a high-profile contract, Hayward (2003) reported progress on the new Wembley Stadium in London. The old football stadium, which was a well-known London landmark, was demolished in 2003 to make way for a new stadium with a target completion date of 2006. At the time of the report by Hayward, the project was scheduled to cost £757 million. The article explains the process of setting up a contract for such a large project where there are so many parties interested in the outcome.

Real world case 7.3

The following features are advertised by SAGE as being available within its 'job costing' software module:

- Define and track all cost elements of every job. With up to 10 analysis codes you can accurately track and analyse your costs.
- Split costs by their constitution component, e.g. labour, materials, etc. enabling you to analyse and report on these categories.
- Track the status of jobs easily, including milestones, summarise costs and revenue and budgets.
- Track how much of each employee's time has been used and on which jobs.
- Invoices can be automatically calculated according to your choice of billing methods, e.g. cost plus, fixed price or combination of charges based upon time, material and other costs.
- Post invoices against jobs as and when you like, improving cash flow.
- Offers a range of management analysis reports, including profitability reports that show costs, revenue and profit made against each job. This ensures that the you know exactly how much profit has been made on each job.
- True multi-user capability, enabling several employees to use the software simultaneously.
- Raise purchase orders against specific jobs, enabling you to analyse costs and increase control over what you buy for specific projects.
- Budget for costs that you have committed to, but haven't yet been invoiced for.
- Save time by processing all your timesheets in a single batch rather than entering all the details on an individual basis.

Source: www.sage.co.uk/

Discussion point

1 What are the advantages of a computerised package compared to manual recording?

7.9 Summary

Key themes in this chapter are:

- A detailed explanation of the use of debit and credit bookkeeping for recording the transactions of a business in a **job-costing system**.
- An explanation and illustration of how an **integrated system** may serve the needs of both financial accounting and management accounting.
- An explanation and illustration of the use and importance of **control accounts**.
- An explanation of the method of calculating and recording costs and profits of long-term contracts.

References and further reading

Hayward, C. (2003), 'They thought it was all over', *Financial Management (UK)*, November: 18–20.

QUESTIONS

The Questions section of each chapter has three types of question. 'Test your understanding' questions to help you review your reading are in the 'A' series of questions. You will find the answer to these by reading and thinking about the material in the text book. 'Application' questions to test your ability to apply technical skills are in the 'B' series of questions. Questions requiring you to show skills in problem solving and evaluation are in the 'C' series of questions. The symbol [S] indicates that a solution is available at the end of the book.

A   Test your understanding

A7.1 How does a cost account in management accounting relate to an expense account in financial accounting (section 7.1)?

A7.2 What types of transactions are recorded as debit entries in ledger accounts for costs (section 7.1)?

A7.3 What types of transactions are recorded as credit entries in ledger accounts for costs (section 7.1)?

A7.4 Why is there no definitive list of ledger account headings for management accounting purposes (section 7.2)?

A7.5 State the debit and credit entries for each of the following types of transaction:
(a) Acquisition of inventory of materials (section 7.4.1);
(b) Return of inventory to a supplier (section 7.4.3);
(c) Payment of wages (section 7.4.6);
(d) Payment for production overhead costs (section 7.4.7).

A7.6 State the debit and credit entries for each of the following types of transaction:
(a) transfer of inventory of materials to be used as part of work-in-progress (section 7.4.4);
(b) recognition that labour cost has been incurred in creating work-in-progress (section 7.4.9);
(c) transfer of production overhead costs to work-in-progress (section 7.4.10).

A7.7 State the debit and credit entries for each of the following types of transaction:
(a) transfer of completed work-in-progress to finished goods inventory (section 7.4.11);
(b) recognition that finished goods inventory has become part of cost of goods sold when a sale takes place (section 7.4.12).

A7.8 What is the purpose of the work-in-progress account and what types of entries would you expect to see there (section 7.5.4)?

A7.9 Why is the use of control accounts essential in both management accounting and financial accounting (section 7.5)?

A7.10 Why is profit calculated on incomplete contracts, rather than waiting until the contract is completed (section 7.6.1)?

A7.11 How is the profit on an incomplete contract calculated (section 7.6.1)?

A7.12 How are payments in advance from the customer recorded (section 7.6.1)?

A7.13 How are costs of a contract recorded during an accounting period (section 7.6.2)?

A7.14 How are costs remaining at the end of the accounting period carried forward (section 7.6.2)?

A7.15 What information is provided in a statement of contract profit (section 7.6.2)?

A7.16 What is the purpose of a contract ledger account and what types of entry would you expect to see there (section 7.6.3)?

A7.17 [S] In a job-costing system, the following list of transactions for a month is to be entered in the relevant ledger accounts. In which ledger accounts would each of these figures be located?

	£
Purchases of raw materials	45,000
Wages paid to production employees	16,000
Salary of personnel manager	2,000
Sales	65,000
Heat and light expense paid	6,500

A7.18 [S] In a job-costing system, the production department orders 20 components from store at a cost of £4 each, to be used on job 36. Explain how this transaction will be recorded in a debit and credit system where control accounts are in operation.

A7.19 [S] In a job-costing system, an employee (A Jones) receives a weekly wage of £600. In week 29 this employee's time has been spent two-thirds on job 61 and one-third on job 62. Explain how this transaction will be recorded in a debit and credit system where control accounts are in operation.

A7.20 [S] On 16 June, job 94 is finished at a total cost of £3,500. The job consisted of printing brochures for a supermarket advertising campaign. Explain how this transaction will be recorded in a debit and credit system where control accounts are in operation and the printing of brochures is one of three production activities in the business, all of which contribute to the inventory of finished goods.

B   Application

B7.1 [S]
The following transactions relate to a dairy, converting milk to cheese, for the month of May. Prepare ledger accounts which record the transactions.

1 May	Bought 600 drums of milk from supplier on credit, invoiced price being £90,000
1 May	Bought cartons, cost £6,000 paid in cash
2 May	Returned to supplier one drum damaged in transit, £150
3 May	500 drums of milk issued to cheesemaking department, cost £75,000
4 May	Issued two-thirds of cartons to cheesemaking department, £4,000
14 May	Paid cheesemakers' wages £3,000
14 May	Paid wages for cleaning and hygiene £600
16 May	Paid rent, rates and electricity in respect of printing, £8,000, in cash
28 May	Paid cheesemakers' wages £3,000
28 May	Paid wages for cleaning and hygiene £600
31 May	Transferred all production of cheese in cartons to finished goods inventory.
31 May	No work-in-progress at end of month.
31 May	Finished goods stock value at £6,000

B7.2 [S]
Write journal entries for the following transactions:

Transfer production overhead cost of £27,000 to work-in-progress account.
Transfer work-in-progress of £12,000 to finished goods inventory account.
Pay £1,500 cash for production overhead costs.
Return to a supplier items of inventory having a cost of £900.
Transfer finished goods inventory of £31,000 to cost of goods sold.
Transfer cleaner's wages of £500 from wages ledger account to production overhead cost ledger account.
Purchase inventory of raw materials on credit, cost of £14,000.
Transfer raw materials inventory of £980 to work-in-progress
Pay direct labour wages in cash £1,000.
Transfer direct labour wages £1,000 to work-in-progress.

B7.3

Set out below are three job cost records. Prepare the work-in-progress control account in the general ledger which represents the total of these three separate records.

Month of April	Job 1 £	Job 2 £	Job 3 £
Direct materials used	2,700	3,000	1,200
Direct labour worked	1,900	2,800	800
Allocation of production overheads:			
Rent	200	350	200
Rates	140	250	180
Electricity	160	170	140
Indirect materials	700	550	490
Indirect labour	660	400	320
Total cost incurred	6,460	7,520	3,330
Completed during period	5,000	7,100	2,800
Work not yet completed	1,460	420	530
	6,460	7,520	3,330

B7.4

The following statement shows a note of information relating to materials inventory during the month of May. Prepare the materials inventory control account in the general ledger.

	£
1 May	Purchased direct materials on credit, for various jobs:	
	Job 901	1,300
	Job 902	1,100
	Job 903	900
2 May	Returned materials which failed quality inspection	
	Job 901	200
	Job 902	300
5 May	Paid cash for indirect materials to be used during May and June	4,200
31 May	Job records for May showed the following information:	
	Job 901 All materials transferred to work-in-progress (1,300 – 200)	1,100
	Job 902 Start of work delayed. 75% of materials transferred to work-in-progress 75% of (1,100 – 300)	600
	Job 903 Start of work delayed. 50% of materials transferred to work-in-progress 50% of 900	450
31 May	Records show two-thirds of indirect materials used in production	2,800
31 May	Inventory at end of month:	
	For Job 901	nil
	For Job 902	200
	For Job 903	450
	Indirect materials	1,400

C   Problem solving and evaluation

C7.1 [S]

Bridge Builders Ltd undertook a contract to build a pedestrian footbridge for a fixed price of £400,000 during the period from May Year 1 to July Year 2. This table sets out transactions up to the company's year end in December, Year 1.

Transactions during Year 1:		£000s
May	Materials purchased and delivered to site	91
May	Equipment delivered to site	14
July	Architect's fee	7
June–Dec	Materials issued from store	76
May–Dec	Wages paid on site	71
Sept	Payment to subcontractors	10
May–Dec	Direct costs	22
Dec	Head office charges	6
At the end of Year 1		
Dec	Value of equipment remaining on site	9
Dec	Value of material remaining on site	15
Dec	Sales value of work certified	280
Dec	Amount due to subcontractors	3
Dec	Direct costs incurred but not yet paid	3

Required:

(a) Prepare relevant ledger account records.

(b) Prepare a statement of contract profit for Year 1.

C7.2

Builders Ltd has undertaken to refurbish the Black Swan Hotel. The contract price was agreed at £480,000 based on estimated total costs of £440,000. The contract work began on 1 January Year 8. The accounting year of Builders Ltd ended on 31 August Year 8 at which date the contract was not completed. The following information provides the full contract estimate and the payments up to 31 August:

	Original estimate for full contract	Actual cash paid up to 31 August
	£	£
Subcontractors' costs:		
Substructure	21,910	20,050
Superstructure	140,660	135,200
External works	111,256	95,000
Main contractors' costs:		
Materials –		
Internal finishing	22,800	23,370
Fittings and furnishings	9,300	10,000
Utilities	42,400	31,800
Direct labour and overheads –		
Internal finishing	23,100	17,325
Fittings and furnishings	9,100	6,916
Utilities	39,100	30,107
Administration overhead	20,374	15,402
	440,000	385,170

Further information:

1 The substructure was completed on 31 July but a subcontractor's invoice for £2,500 in respect of the final work done was not paid until 4 September.
2 The superstructure was also completed on 31 July and subcontractors were paid in full during August.
3 External works were 80% completed at 31 August. There was a delay in March due to adverse weather affecting the pebble-dashing, which cost £3,500 to remove and restore.
4 Cash paid for materials for internal finishing covered the cost of all paint and wallpaper necessary to complete the contract. The actual paint and wallpaper unused at 31 August was valued at £4,000.
5 All fittings and furnishings required for the contract had been bought and paid for before 31 August. Only 70% by value had been installed by 31 August.
6 Materials costs of utilities were 80% complete in respect to estimates.
7 Labour hours worked up to 31 August on internal finishing, fittings and furnishings and services were 70% of the estimated total.
8 Administration overhead is allocated as a percentage of total sales value.
9 It is company policy to credit to management profit and loss account not more than 75% of the profit earned in any period.
10 It is estimated that the main contractor's material and labour costs for the remainder of the contract will be incurred at the same rate as was experienced up to 31 August.
11 An independent surveyor estimated the contract value of work done up to 31 August at £400,000.
12 On 31 August the customer paid £380,000 on account of work completed.

Required

Prepare a report for the directors of Builders Ltd containing:

1 The profit on the contract for the accounting year ended 31 August Year 8 in a form which highlights variances from the initial estimate.
2 An estimate of the actual profit to be achieved on the contract as a whole.
3 Brief comments on the contract outcome.

Case studies

Real world cases

Prepare short answers to Case studies 7.1, 7.2 and 7.3.

Chapter 8

Process costing

This case study shows a typical situation in which management accounting can be helpful. Read the case study now but only attempt the discussion points after you have finished studying the chapter.

Sugar beet processing
British Sugar, part of Associated British Foods, provides sugar for the top brand names in sugar confectionery, chocolate confectionery, soft drinks and preserves, etc. The company has six factories in the UK, with each one split between a 'beet end' and a 'sugar end'. Typically, a factory processes beet between September and March, termed the 'Campaign'. The 'beet end' employs various processes to create 'thick juice', a liquid which has 65% sugar content. The 'sugar end' boils the 'thick juice' and seeds it with tiny sugar crystals, providing the nucleus for larger crystals to form and grow to create sugar. The business of processing beet gives rise to several challenges which directly affect process efficiency, sugar yields from the beet, and ultimately factory profitability.

Source: *Process and Control*, March 2003 'Maximising sugar beet processing', p. 22 www.connectingindustry.com

Discussion points

1 Why is a specific kind of costing needed for a process of this kind?
2 Why might the quantity of material output be less than the quantity input?

Contents

Learning outcomes

After reading this chapter you should be able to:

● Explain how process costing differs from job costing.

● Carry out calculations to allocate costs to products in a process industry.

● Explain and calculate joint product costs and by-product costs.

● Explain how decisions are made about joint products based on cost information.

● Describe and discuss examples of research into process costing and joint product costs.

8.1 Introduction

Special **process costing** techniques are required where there is a continuous flow of production of similar units of output. This situation of a continuous process arises in the chemical industry and in other industries such as textiles, paint, food, steel, glass, mining, cement and oil.

As an example of a company where processes are important, Exhibit 8.1 contains an extract from the annual report of a chemicals company describing the group's products. The products of this company which derive from these chemical processes are many and varied. Viscose rayon, the first cellulose fibre, is a chemical name most readily related to womenswear and furnishing fabrics, but it is also found in clutch linings, insulating material within railway signalling cables and tea bags. The rayon process is also used to make film for sweet wrappings, baked goods and soft cheeses. In the area of coatings, the company produces marine paint which keeps the hulls of ships and yachts free of barnacles. Another type of paint for the superstructure of ships transforms rust stains into colourless deposits. Other products involving a flow process include the manufacture of specialist film which makes glass shatter-resistant, toothpaste tubes and rigid packaging products such as special housings for asthma inhalers.

Exhibit 8.1
The products of a chemicals company

> We are a chemical materials company. Our products are made by chemical processes. But with a few exceptions they are not themselves pure chemicals: they are products made from chemicals. These products are based on two related technical disciplines. The first of these is polymer technology linked with surface science – used to coat, seal or protect a diverse range of surfaces. The second is fibre technology, with particular emphasis on cellulose chemistry.

This is the type of business where individual products are indistinguishable in nature and there are no special needs of customers in relation to individual items of product. What is of interest to management is the cost and performance of the continuous process as a whole.

Definition
> **Process costing** is appropriate to a business or operation where there is a continuous flow of a relatively high volume of similar products during a reporting period.

Management's purposes in a continuous process business are no different from those in any other organisation. There is an overall requirement on the part of management for decision making and judgement. In this context, accounting information is required for management purposes of planning, decision making and control.

Management accounting contributes by:

- directing attention
- keeping the score
- solving problems.

In particular, management accounting must be able to show, in relation to a flow process, how much cost has flowed through with the product into finished goods and how much remains with the work-in-progress. That is part of the score-keeping aspect of management accounting. If the process splits, taking different directions for different output, the management accountant will be expected to contribute information relevant to decision making about the various products. That is an example of the problem-solving aspects of management accounting.

This description of the management accountant's role is not substantially different from a description which could apply in any job-costing situation; however, there are some specific problems in the process industries which require specially designed management accounting techniques. This chapter deals with two of these problems, as follows:

1 Individual products cannot be distinguished for costing purposes. Costs cannot be assigned directly to products but must be allocated (spread) using some averaging basis.

2 Joint products and by-products are produced as an unavoidable result of the process of creating the main products. Total costs must therefore be shared across main products and by-products. Joint products each have a significant sales value. By-products usually have relatively low sales value.

8.2 Allocation of costs to products in a process industry

In process costing, items in production flow from one process to the next until they are completed. Each process contributes to the total operation and then passes its output to the next process until the goods are finished and can be stored to await sale. Recording of costs follows the physical flow as closely as possible. Because it is not possible to identify each unit of output on its way through the various processes, the concept of an **equivalent unit** is applied. Each completed item is equivalent to one unit of output, but each incomplete item is equivalent to only a fraction of a unit of output. This concept is particularly important at the end of the reporting period for dealing with items in process which are incomplete.

Definition

An **equivalent unit of output** is the amount of output, expressed in terms of whole units, which is equivalent to the actual amount of partly or fully completed production.

Process costing requires several stages of analysis of the costs. These are:

(a) collect the data for the period;
(b) prepare a statement of physical flows and equivalent units of output for the period;
(c) ascertain the total costs to be accounted for this period;
(d) calculate the cost per equivalent unit;
(e) apportion the cost between finished output and work-in-progress; and
(f) check that all costs are accounted for.

Collecting data requires information on the quantities of materials, labour and other resources put into the process and the quantities of products emerging from the process in any period of time. Because of the continuous nature of any process, it is likely that some products will be partly completed at the beginning and end of the period. Such partly completed work is referred to as *work-in-progress*. Information is also required on the costs of the period, separated into material, labour and production overheads. Sometimes the labour and overhead costs are referred to collectively as *conversion costs* because they convert the input materials into products.

Physical flows into and out of the process have to be identified. There will be *opening work-in-progress* at the beginning of the period which is completed during the period. Some products will be started and finished in the period. Some will be started but will be incomplete at the end and will be described as *closing work-in-progress*. Materials may be introduced at the beginning of the period, while further materials may be introduced part-way through the period.

Identifying the total costs to be accounted for requires some care. There will be costs incurred during the period, but there will also be costs brought forward from the previous period, included in the opening work-in-progress. All these costs must be shared between the products completed during the period and the work-in-progress remaining at the end of the period.

The *cost per equivalent unit* is a particular feature of process costing which takes into account the problem of partly completed units at the beginning and end of the period. If an item is 40 per cent completed, then it represents the equivalent of 40 per cent (or 0.4 as a fraction) of one completed unit. So if there are 3,000 units held, each of which is 40 per cent complete, they can be said to represent the equivalent of 1,200 completed units and would be described as 1,200 equivalent units.

Apportioning costs between finished output and work-in-progress is relatively straightforward. Once the cost per equivalent unit has been calculated, it is multiplied by the number of equivalent units of finished items to give the cost of finished output and by the number of equivalent units of closing work-in-progress to give the cost of closing work-in-progress.

Finally, it is essential to check that nothing has been gained or lost in the arithmetic process by comparing the total costs of input to the process with the total costs of output in the period. If the totals are the same, then the worst problem that can have occurred is a misallocation between finished goods and work-in-progress. If the totals are not the same, a careful search for errors is required.

These steps in the process-costing approach are conveniently illustrated and explained by working through an example and commenting on the main features of interest.

8.2.1   Process costing where there is no opening work-in-progress

Process costing can be a complicated exercise. However, to learn the approach it is best to start with a simplified example and work up to the various complications one at a time. Exhibit 8.2 illustrates process costing for the first month of a reporting period where there is no work-in-progress at the start of the month but there is some by the end. Five steps are shown, corresponding to the first five stages of the process described earlier in this section.

Exhibit 8.2
Process costing illustration: No opening work-in-progress

Step 1: Collect data for the period

The following information relates to the assembly department in a company manufacturing shower units for bathrooms. A pack of materials is introduced at the start of the process. The pack contains a plastic shower head, flexible hose and various plumbing items. These are assembled by employees and then passed from the assembly department to the electrical department for connection to the electric power unit. At the end of the month there will be some shower units only partly completed. The supervisor of the assembly department has estimated that these units are 40 per cent completed at that date.

Data in respect of month 1
No work-in-progress at start of month.
60,000 units of raw materials introduced for conversion.
40,000 units of output completed during the month.
20,000 units of work-in-progress, 40 per cent completed at end of month.
Costs incurred on material, labour and overheads: £120,000.

Exhibit 8.2 **continued**

Step 2: Prepare a statement of physical flows and equivalent units of output for the month

The physical flow involves 60,000 units entering the process for assembly. Of these, 40,000 are fully assembled and 20,000 partly assembled at the end of the period. This physical flow is shown in the left-hand column as a check that all items are kept under control. For accounting purposes the concept of an equivalent unit, as explained earlier, is more important. So the final column contains the equivalent units. For the goods which are finished during the month, the equivalent units are 100 per cent of the physical units. For the goods which are still in progress, the equivalent units of 8,000 are calculated as 40 per cent of the physical amount of 20,000 units of work-in-progress.

	Physical flow (units)	Equivalent units of output
Input:		
Materials introduced	60,000	
	60,000	
Output:		
Goods finished this month	40,000	40,000
Work-in-progress at end (40 per cent completed)	20,000	8,000
Total equivalent units	60,000	48,000

Step 3: Ascertain total costs to be accounted for this period

As there is no work-in-progress at the beginning of the period, the only costs to be accounted for are the costs of £120,000 incurred during the period.

	£
Opening work-in-progress	none
Incurred this month	120,000
Total to account for	120,000

Step 4: Calculate cost per equivalent unit

Continuing the emphasis on equivalent units (rather than physical units), a unit cost is calculated by dividing the costs of the period, £120,000 as shown in step 3, by the number of equivalent units, 48,000, as shown in step 2. The benefit of having a cost per equivalent unit is that it gives a fair allocation to completed and partly completed units, as shown in step 5.

$$\text{Cost per equivalent unit} = \frac{£120,000}{48,000} = £2.50$$

Step 5: Apportion cost between finished output and work-in-progress

The cost per equivalent unit, which is £2.50, is now applied to the finished output and to the work-in-progress, measuring the quantity of each in equivalent units.

	£
Value of finished output 40,000 × £2.50	100,000
Work-in-progress 8,000 × £2.50	20,000
Total costs accounted for	120,000

Fiona McTaggart has the following comment.

FIONA: *From step 5 of Exhibit 8.2 you will see that the total costs accounted for are the same as the costs in step 3 which required allocation. It is always important to check back to the starting data to make sure that nothing has been lost or created inadvertently in the calculation process. There could still be an error within the allocations if the wrong approach has been taken, so a separate check of all calculations is generally useful.*

It is also good practice to explain in words what each calculation is intended to achieve. If you cannot explain it in words, that is an indication that you do not fully understand the calculation and neither will anyone else reading your work. If you can explain with confidence, then it is more likely that you are correct or, if you are incorrect, that the cause of any error will be seen readily by another person.

Activity 8.1

Starting again with the data of Exhibit 8.2, close the book and check that you are able to produce the process cost information ending with the value of finished output and the value of work-in-progress. You must understand and be confident about Exhibit 8.2 before you read further.

8.2.2 Process costing where there is work-in-progress at the start of the period

The first complication to be introduced is the presence of work-in-progress at the start of the period. Opening work-in-progress introduces a complication because it carries costs from the end of one period to the beginning of the next. The problem faced by the management accountant is to decide between two possible courses of action. The first is to take those costs as being added to (*accumulated*) with the costs incurred in the current period and spread over all equivalent units of output. The second is to regard them as remaining firmly attached to the partly completed products with which they arrived. The first of these possibilities is called the *weighted average method* and the second is called the *first-in-first-out method*. It will be sufficient for the purposes of this textbook to illustrate the weighted average method, which is the more commonly used in practice.

Exhibit 8.3 takes on to month 2 the story which began in Exhibit 8.2. Work-in-progress is carried from the end of month 1 to the start of month 2. The weighted average method follows the same five steps as were used in Exhibit 8.2. The cost figure calculated at step 3 is the total of the costs brought forward with the opening work-in-progress and the costs incurred in the month. At step 4 the cost per equivalent unit is calculated by dividing all costs by total equivalent output.

Here is Fiona McTaggart to comment.

FIONA: *This method is called the weighted average approach because it averages all costs over all equivalent output and ignores the fact that some of the production started in the previous period.*

I usually like the weighted average method because it is not too fiddly and allows me to divide all costs of the period by the equivalent units of output without having to worry about what started where. However, some of my clients do not like this approach because, they say, it is mixing some of last month's costs with other costs incurred this month. Instead of spreading all costs over all production, their suggestion is to allocate this month's cost to the items started and finished in the month and to allow opening work-in-progress to carry the costs with which it arrived.

My answer is that it's a good idea, but more time consuming. I also mention, tactfully, that the approach has already been thought of and is called the first-in-first-out method of process costing. It requires more work by the accountant but generally gives results that are only marginally different from the weighted average method.

Exhibit 8.3
Process costing illustration: opening work-in-progress

Step 1: Collect data for the period

Step 1 starts by bringing forward the work-in-progress of month 1. If you look back to step 1 of Exhibit 8.2 you will see that the closing work-in-progress was 20,000 units, each 40 per cent complete. To this is added 30,000 shower head packs for assembly. We are then told that 35,000 units are completed and 15,000 are one-third completed at the end of month 2.

> *Data in respect of month 2*
> 20,000 units work-in-progress at start, 40 per cent complete.
> 30,000 units of raw materials introduced for conversion.
> 35,000 units of output completed during the month.
> 15,000 units of work-in-progress, one-third completed at end of month.
>
> Costs incurred on material, labour and overheads: £120,000.

Step 2: Prepare a statement of physical flows and equivalent units of output for the month

In step 2 the left-hand column is used to keep track of the physical flow of units and the right-hand column shows the equivalent units of output for month 2. For the finished goods the equivalent units are 100 per cent of the finished physical units but for the work-in-progress the equivalent units are one-third of the physical units, as specified in step 1.

	Physical flow (units)	Equivalent units of output
Input:		
Work-in-progress at start	20,000	
Material introduced	30,000	
	50,000	
Output:		
Goods finished this month	35,000	35,000
Work-in-progress at end (33.3 per cent completed)	15,000	5,000
Total equivalent units	50,000	40,000

Step 3: Ascertain total costs to be accounted for during this period

There are two separate elements of cost which together must be allocated to the total equivalent units of output for the period. The first element is the value of work-in-progress at the start of the period. This is a portion of the costs incurred in the first month that has been brought forward to the second month in order to match it with the units completed during the period. The second element is the new cost incurred during the second month.

	£
Opening work-in-progress brought forward	20,000
Incurred this month	120,000
Total to account for	140,000

Exhibit 8.3 continued

Step 4: Calculate cost per equivalent unit

Continuing the emphasis on equivalent units, the cost of £140,000 calculated in step 3 is divided by the total number of equivalent units calculated as 40,000 in step 2. The result is a cost of £3.50 per equivalent unit, calculated as follows:

$$\text{Cost per equivalent unit} = \frac{£140,000}{40,000} = £3.50$$

Step 5: Apportion cost between finished output and work-in-progress

The cost of £3.50 per equivalent unit is applied to the equivalent units of finished output and to the equivalent units of work-in-progress. This gives a fair allocation of the total cost of £140,000 between the finished and unfinished goods as follows:

	£
Value of finished output 35,000 × £3.50	122,500
Work-in-progress 5,000 × £3.50	17,500
Total costs accounted for	140,000

Activity 8.2

Pause here to test your confidence of Exhibit 8.3. Take a note of the data provided at the start of the example, close the book and write out the steps of the process cost calculations. Write down a brief explanation of each step which you could give to a fellow student who has not read this chapter but would like an idea of what it contains.

8.2.3 Separate material and conversion costs

The illustrations provided so far have assumed that all materials are introduced at the start of the process. In practice, materials may be added at intervals during the process, so that conversion work can be carried out in stages.

Exhibit 8.4 shows the separate analysis of materials and conversion costs. It relates to a company which introduces materials into the process in two batches, so that work-in-progress might have all its materials added or might contain only half of the total, depending on the stage of production reached at any particular month-end. The conversion work is continuous throughout the month.

Exhibit 8.4
Separate materials and conversion costs

Step 1: Collect data for the period

The business assembles plant propagation boxes. At the start of the process a set of plastic components is introduced, assembled and coated with a weather-proof protective coating. The glass plates are then added and a decorative finish given to the assembled unit. Because there are two points at which materials are introduced (plastic components and then glass plates), some items may be only 50 per cent complete in respect of materials at the end of the reporting period.

Exhibit 8.4 **continued**

Data in respect of the month of April
4,000 units work-in-progress at start, 100 per cent complete in respect of materials,
  25 per cent complete in respect of conversion.
6,000 units of raw materials introduced for conversion.
8,000 units of output completed during the month.
2,000 units of work-in-progress, 50 per cent complete in respect of materials, 10 per
  cent complete in respect of conversion.

Cost of opening work-in-progress, £60,000, consisting of £30,000 for materials and
  £30,000 for conversion costs.
Costs incurred in the month on materials are £150,000 and on conversion costs
  £216,000.

**Step 2: *Prepare a statement of physical flows and equivalent units of output for
the month***

As in Exhibits 8.2 and 8.3 the physical flow is recorded in the left-hand column. However,
there are now two columns to the right of this, each showing one component of the equivalent
units of output. Using two columns allows different percentages to be applied to work-in-
progress for materials and conversion costs as follows:

	Physical flow (units)	Equivalent units of output			
			Material		Conversion
Input:					
Work-in-progress at start	4,000				
Material introduced	6,000				
	10,000				
Output:					
Goods finished this month	8,000		8,000		8,000
Work-in-progress at end	2,000	50%	1,000	10%	200
Total equivalent units	10,000		9,000		8,200

Step 3: *Identify total costs to be accounted for this period*

In step 1 there is information about costs brought forward and costs incurred in the month.
In each case the costs of the components of materials and conversion are shown separately.
This separate classification allows the calculation of a separate unit cost for each component.
The total costs to be accounted for under each heading are as follows:

	Material £	Conversion £	Total £
Opening work-in-progress brought forward	30,000	30,000	60,000
Incurred this month	150,000	216,000	366,000
Total costs to be accounted for	180,000	246,000	426,000

Exhibit 8.4 **continued**

Step 4: Calculate cost per equivalent unit

Two costs per equivalent unit can now be calculated, one relating to materials and one to conversion. The total costs from step 3 are divided by the equivalent units from step 2. Materials have been used in 9,000 equivalent units of output but conversion costs have been applied to only 8,200 equivalent units of output. The calculations are as follows:

	Material	Conversion
Total costs to be accounted for	£180,000	£246,000
Number of equivalent units	9,000	8,200
Cost per equivalent unit	£20	£30

The total cost of an item of completed output is therefore £50 per equivalent unit. Work-in-progress at the end of the period is calculated in two separate components, using the figures of £20 per equivalent unit of materials and £30 per equivalent unit of conversion work.

Step 5: Apportion cost between finished output and work-in-progress

The unit costs calculated in step 4 may now be applied to the finished goods and work-in-progress. The finished goods are 100 per cent complete in respect of materials and conversion costs, so it saves calculation time to use the total unit cost of £50 and multiply it by the 8,000 finished units.

For work-in-progress some care is needed. For the materials component, the work-in-progress is equivalent to 1,000 units, but for conversion costs it is equivalent to only 200 units, as shown in step 2. Separate calculations are shown in the table below for each component. The total costs accounted for are £426,000 which is equal to the total costs shown in step 3 above.

	£	£
Value of finished output 8,000 × £50		400,000
Work-in-progress:		
Materials 1,000 × £20	20,000	
Labour 200 × £30	6,000	
		26,000
Total costs accounted for		426,000

Activity 8.3

Go back to the start of Exhibit 8.4. Take a note of the data provided and then close the book. Write out all the steps of cost allocation for the process and make sure that you understand each stage. Imagine that you are a manager instructing an employee who will prepare the monthly process cost statements. How would you explain the steps of cost allocation in such a way that the employee could produce reliable data? How would you check the work of such an employee?

Real world case 8.2

Decaffeination of coffee beans

SWISS WATER® Process 101
Lesson 3: The Art of Chemical-Free Decaffeination

Flavor-charged water is integral to the SWISS WATER® Process, which starts with top quality green beans and works as follows.

First, the beans are cleaned and soaked in water partially saturated with coffee flavor solids, in preparation for caffeine extraction.

Next, the beans are immersed in the flavor-charged water. Initially the water is caffeine-free, and as a result the caffeine diffuses from the beans into the water. Since the concentration of flavor components in the bean and in the water are equal, only the caffeine is removed, leaving the flavor intact. The water then passes through a carbon filter that traps the caffeine. The now caffeine-free, flavor-charged water flows back to the beans to remove more caffeine. This process continues for approximately 8 hours, until the beans are 99.9% caffeine-free.

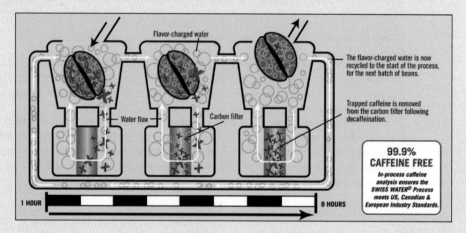

Following decaffeination, the trapped caffeine is removed from the carbon filter. The flavor-charged water is then recycled to the start of the process for the next batch of beans.
A typical green bean, after decaffeination, is composed of:

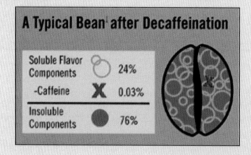

Source: www.swisswater.com/decaf/process/lesson3. Swiss Water Decaffeinated Coffee Company, located at 3131 Lake City Way, Burnaby, B.C., Canada V5A 3A3. SWISS WATER® Process coffees are available through Caffè Nero.

Discussion points

1 Why might a 'chemical-free' process of decaffeination be attractive to consumers?

2 What kinds of costs might you expect to find in a process cost statement for this decaffeination?

8.3 Joint product costs and by-products

A manufacturing process may result in more than one product. If the second item is produced as an unavoidable result of producing the first, but has a significant sales value in comparison with the first, then it is called a **joint product**. If the second item is produced as an unavoidable result of producing the first, but is of negligible sales value, then it is called a **by-product**. In the case of joint products, it is desirable to know the separate cost of each item. Product costs may be required for valuing stocks and work-in-progress, calculating product profitability, setting selling prices which cover costs and deciding whether to vary the mix of products.

The accounting treatment of a by-product is somewhat different. Any proceeds of sale of the by-product are used to offset the cost of the main product, which includes the cost of manufacturing the by-product. In the case of by-products it is not necessary to have a valuation for stock purposes because the item is relatively insignificant. It is more important for management purposes to know that the proceeds of sale of the by-product reduce the effective cost of the main product.

Definitions

> **Joint products** are two or more products arising from a process, each of which has a significant sales value.
>
> A **by-product** is a product arising from a process where the sales value is insignificant by comparison with that of the main product or products.

This section looks firstly at joint costs and then at by-products. There are several methods of allocating cost to joint products, two of which will be explored here. These are: by physical measures and by relative sales value. The example contained in Exhibit 8.5 will be used to compare both approaches.

Exhibit 8.5
Data for use in allocation of joint costs

> A chemical process requires input of materials costing £900 per batch. From each batch there are two products, being 1,000 litres of perfume oil base which sells for £2 per litre and 500 litres of oil for artists' paint which sells at £1 per litre.

8.3.1 Joint costs allocated on the basis of physical measures

As stated in Exhibit 8.5, the proportions of physical measures are 1,000 : 500, which reduces to 2 : 1. Allocating the joint costs of £900 on the basis 2 : 1 gives £600 as the cost of perfume oil and £300 as the cost of artists' paint oil.

A statement of product profit is shown in Exhibit 8.6. The calculation of profit on each product is based on subtracting the allocated joint costs from the separate sales figures. In the final line of the exhibit the profit as a percentage of sales is shown.

This is not a particularly good method of allocating costs because it shows one product as being much more profitable, in relation to sales, than the other. That profitability is very much dependent on the allocation method used for the joint costs. Taken out of context, such an allocation might lead the managers of the business into an over-hasty decision to raise the price of the perfume oil base. It would, however, be a mistake to base such a decision on an allocation of costs that could change when a

Exhibit 8.6
Statement of product profit for joint products: physical measures

	Perfume oil base	Oil for artists' paint
	£	£
Sales	2,000	500
Joint costs allocated	600	300
Profit	1,400	200
Profit as % of sales	70%	40%

different method is used. Now look at what happens when the joint costs are allocated by reference to the sales value at the point of separation.

8.3.2 Joint costs allocated by relative sales value at the point of separation

A method which is generally thought to be an improvement on allocation by physical measures is that of allocating the joint cost of £900 in relation to the sales value at the point of separation. The sales value proportions are 2,000 : 500 so that the allocation is as follows:

		£
Perfume oil base	2,000/2,500 × £900	720
Oil for artists' paint	500/2,500 × £900	180
		900

A statement of product profit, based on this allocation, would appear as in Exhibit 8.7.

Exhibit 8.7
Statement of product profit for joint products: relative sales value

	Perfume oil base	Oil for artists' paint
	£	£
Sales	2,000	500
Joint costs allocated	720	180
Profit	1,280	320
Profit as % of sales	64%	64%

This approach leads to a profit which is 64 per cent of sales for each product. Allocating joint costs in proportion to sales value means that the performance measure, taken as the profit margin on sales, is not distorted by the cost allocation process. The calculation would leave the managers of a business satisfied that they had no problems with either product and would avoid bringing on an ill-considered decision to cease production of one product item.

8.3.3 Further processing costs

Now consider a variation on the previous story. Suppose there are further costs incurred after the separation of the joint products. The information used earlier is now amended somewhat in Exhibit 8.8, to introduce and illustrate this variation. The amendments are shown in bold print.

Exhibit 8.8
Joint cost allocation where there are further processing costs

A chemical process requires input of materials costing £900 per batch. From each batch there are two products, being 1,000 litres of perfume oil base which sells for £2 per litre and 500 litres of oil for artists' paint which sells at £1 per litre. **After the two products have been separated, further processing costs are incurred, amounting to £600 per batch in the case of perfume oil base and £100 per batch in the case of oil for artists' paint.**

The recommended approach in this situation is to calculate a notional sales value at the point of separation. That is not as fearsome as it sounds. It requires taking the final sales price of the item and deducting the processing costs incurred after separation. That leaves the notional sales value at the point of separation. Calculations are shown in Exhibit 8.9, and from these calculations it may be seen that the profit as a percentage of sales is no longer the same for each product. That is to be expected, however, because the costs after separation have a relatively different impact on each product.

Exhibit 8.9
Cost allocation based on notional sales value at the point of separation

(a) Calculation of notional sales value at the point of separation

	£	£
Selling price per batch	2,000	500
Costs incurred after separation	600	100
Notional selling price before separation	1,400	400

(b) Allocation of joint cost based on notional selling price before separation

		£
Perfume oil base	1,400/1,800 × £900	700
Oil for artists' paint	400/1,800 × £900	200
		900

(c) Calculation of profit for each joint product

	Perfume oil base		Oil for artists' paint	
	£	£	£	£
Sales		2,000		500
Joint costs allocated	700		200	
Costs after separation	600		100	
		1,300		300
Profit		700		200
Profit as % of sales		35		40

8.3.4 Treatment of by-products

By-products are items of output from a process which have a relatively minor sales value compared with that of the main product.

The accounting treatment of by-products is similar to the accounting treatment of scrap. The proceeds of sale are offset against the cost of the main product. An example of a process which leads to a by-product is set out in Exhibit 8.10.

The calculation of the cost of the main product, perfume oil base, and the resulting profit is shown in Exhibit 8.11. The joint cost of £900 is reduced by the sales proceeds from the by-product, which are £50. The net cost of £850 becomes the cost of sales of the perfume oil, which is the main product. There would be no useful purpose in allocating cost to the by-product and then calculating a separate figure of profit, because the amounts are insignificant.

Exhibit 8.10
Process which creates a by-product

A chemical process requires input of materials costing £900 per batch. From each batch there are two products, being 1,000 litres of perfume oil base which sells for £2 per litre and 500 litres of waste oil which sells at 10 pence per litre.

Exhibit 8.11
Joint cost allocation and profit calculation

	£	£
Sales of perfume oil base, per batch		2,000
Joint costs	900	
Less: sales proceeds of waste oil by-product	(50)	
Net cost per batch		850
Profit per batch		1,150

8.3.5 Relevance of allocating joint costs

Is the allocation of joint costs useful? In this chapter we have shown that this type of cost allocation is an exercise where there is a variety of possible outcomes. Sometimes this variety of outcomes is described as an *arbitrary allocation process* because it depends so much on the choice made by the individual manager.

Throughout this management accounting text there is an emphasis on the management purposes of planning, decision making and control. If the purpose of the joint cost exercise is to allocate all costs in the fairest possible manner for purposes of planning and control, then using notional sales value at the point of separation will give a fair allocation in many circumstances. The allocation of full cost may be required for purposes of stock valuation or it may be required for control purposes to make senior managers aware that ultimately they have a responsibility for all costs.

If, however, a decision has to be made, such as processing further or changing a selling price, then that decision must be based on **relevant costs** rather than on a full allocation of joint costs.

Definition

Relevant costs are those future costs which will be affected by a decision to be taken. Non-relevant costs will not be affected by the decision. The decision-making process therefore requires careful attention to those costs which are relevant to the decision.

This chapter concludes by setting out a decision where joint costs are present, but the allocation of those costs is not relevant to the decision.

Activity 8.4

Explain to a production manager the joint cost problems raised by the following description of a process producing glass bottles.

A typical mixture might be sand 60%; limestone 8%; soda ash 18%; mineral additives 5%. Up to 25% of the mix can comprise cullet (recycled glass). From one mixture the molten glass would be run off into moulds for narrow bottles (such as wine bottles) and wide-mouth containers (such as jam jars). Bottles which have flaws or chips are broken up and recycled.

Real world case 8.3

The Seaweed site

Seaweeds are used in many maritime countries as a source of food, for industrial applications and as a fertiliser. The major utilisation of these plants as food is in Asia, where seaweed cultivation has become a major industry . . . Industrial utilisation is at present largely confined to extraction for phycocolloids and, to a much lesser extent, certain fine biochemicals. Fermentation and pyrolysis are not being carried out on an industrial scale at present, but are possible options for the 21st century.

The present uses of seaweeds are as human foods, fertilisers, and for the extraction of industrial gums and chemicals. They have the potential to be used as a source of long- and short-chain chemicals with medicinal and industrial uses. Marine algae may also be used as energy-collectors and potentially useful substances may be extracted by fermentation and pyrolysis.

The Irish seaweed industry employs nearly 500 people (full-time and part-time), exports 85–90% of its produce, and had a turnover of over IEP5 million in 1996. This somewhat unusual industry has a very high employment : export ratio, activity is mostly concentrated on the western seaboard, and most collection takes place in areas that are – by European Union standards – severely disadvantaged.

A 1996 consultative process on the marine sector carried out by the Irish Marine Institute identified the following problems in the industry:

- High failure rate of seaweed-based industries
- In harvesting, a lack of mechanisation
- Increasing affluence
- High fuel costs for drying
- Fluctuations in demand for certain seaweed products
- Lack of research and development
- Poor marketing and packaging
- A shortage of entrepreneurs.

Source: NUI Galway, www.seaweed.ie/defaultfriday.html
For seaweed products see www.arramara.ie/arramara/Main/Home.htm

Discussion points

1 What are the aspects of the seaweed industry that make process costing useful?

2 What are the problems that will not be solved by methods of costing?

8.4 Decisions on joint products: sell or process further

Where there are joint products there may be a decision required at the point where they separate. The decision usually involves the prospect of incurring further costs with the hope of improving revenue thereby. Is it worthwhile to incur the extra cost of adding perfume? The decision should be based on **incremental costs** and **incremental revenues,** as illustrated in the example shown in Exhibit 8.12, which is analysed in Exhibit 8.13.

Definition | **Incremental costs** are the additional costs that arise from an activity of the organisation. To justify incurring incremental costs it is necessary to show they are exceeded by **incremental revenue.**

Exhibit 8.12
Situation requiring a decision

In a company manufacturing personal care products, a process requires the input of ingredients costing £400 per batch. Separation of the output from each batch yields 200 litres of hand cream which sells at a price of £1.60 per litre and 200 litres of soap solution which sells at a price of 80 pence per litre. The soap solution in that form is suitable for industrial use, but at a further cost of £50 per batch of 200 litres it could be perfumed and sold for domestic use at £1.20 per litre.

Activity 8.5

Write down, with reasons, the action you would recommend for the situation described in Exhibit 8.12. Then read the commentary by Fiona McTaggart and check your answer against Exhibit 8.13. Did you arrive at the same answer? If not, what was the cause of the difference?

Fiona McTaggart has given some thought to this problem.

FIONA: *The decision question contained in Exhibit 8.12 is, 'Do we make soap for industrial use or do we make it suitable for domestic use?' What is not in question is the production of hand cream and the production of soap solution. This means that the information about hand cream is not relevant to the decision and neither is the information about the costs of ingredients. I have rewritten the information in Exhibit 8.12 and highlighted the information relevant to this decision problem, as follows:*

In a company manufacturing personal care products, a process requires the input of ingredients costing £400 per batch. Separation of the output from each batch yields 200 litres of hand cream which sells at a price of £1.60 per litre and **200 litres of soap solution which sells at a price of 80 pence per litre**. The soap solution in that form is suitable for industrial use, but at a **further cost of £50 per batch of 200 litres it could be perfumed and sold for domestic use at £1.20 per litre**.

My calculation of the incremental revenue and costs is shown in Exhibit 8.13. It shows that there is an extra profit of £30 per batch if the soap solution is perfumed for domestic use. So the decision should be to go ahead.

In relation to the decision, allocation of the joint cost of £400 is *not* relevant because it is a cost which is incurred regardless of whether the perfume is added. In a similar vein, pricing decisions should have regard to the need to cover total costs but should not be based on arbitrary allocations of costs across products.

Exhibit 8.13
Statement of incremental costs and revenues

	£	
	£	
Incremental revenue	200 litres × (£1.20 − 0.80)	80
Incremental cost		50
Incremental profit per batch		30

8.5 What the researchers have found

8.5.1 Process costs, standard costs and ABC

Sharman and Vikas (2004) are enthusiastic supporters of German cost accounting. Sharman in particular is concerned that there has been too much emphasis in the US on financial reporting and auditing. He sees management accounting as a part of the processes inside an organisation that help to create good governance. Their paper includes a description of process-based costing as applied by Deutsche Telekom. This process-based costing is described as 'a more disciplined form of activity based costing' where standard costs are linked to ABC in providing cost information about the processes in a terrestrial telephone system. Understanding the business process is an essential condition of designing a useful and relevant costing analysis.

The paper is interesting for its description of the system used by Deutsche Telekom, but it also illustrates how a major company can design its own management accounting by taking aspects of a range of text-book models. In this case it links ABC and standard costs to produce a company-wide costing of the processes of the business.

8.5.2 Joint costs

Trenchard and Dixon (2003) explain a real-life joint cost problem found in the not-for-profit manufacture of blood products in the UK. There is a legal requirement for cost-based transfer pricing. However, the cost of the blood products is not clear. Transfusion services provide a joint platelet product and a more costly, but better quality, non-joint alternative. For accounting convenience all the joint costs are allocated to red cells and none to platelets. So the platelets have a zero cost at the point of splitting them off from the red blood cells. The paper is a research note in which the authors describe the problem, rather than solving it. They suggest that one method of allocating the joint costs would be to relate these to a measure of the relative 'usefulness' of each product. Then they discuss the ways of measuring usefulness in a clinical sense. This proposal to evaluate usefulness gives a not-for-profit alternative to the sales-based method normally suggested for allocating joint costs.

8.6 Summary

Key themes in this chapter are:

● **Process costing** is a technique which can be applied to a business or operation where there is a continuous flow of a relatively high volume of similar products during a reporting period. It is a contrast to job costing (see Chapter 6) where separate jobs or products may be identified for cost allocation and apportionment.

- In a process some units are complete but others are part-complete. The idea of an **equivalent unit** of output allows whole units and part units to be added so that costs can be shared across them.

- The weighted average approach averages all costs over all the equivalent output of the period and ignores the fact that some of the production started in the previous period.

- **Joint products** arise when a manufacturing process leads to two or more products, each having a significant sales value.

- A **by-product** is a product arising from a process where the sales value is insignificant by comparison with that of the main product or products.

- When a decision is required on whether to process joint products further rather than sell them at the point of separation, **relevant costs** must be compared. The relevant costs are the **incremental costs**, which are justified if they produce a higher **incremental revenue**.

References and further reading

Sharman, P. and Vikas, K. (2004) 'Lessons from German cost accounting', *Strategic Finance*, December: 28–35.

Trenchard, P.M. and Dixon, R. (2003) 'The clinical allocation of joint blood product costs: research note', *Management Accounting Research*, 14: 165–176.

QUESTIONS

The Questions section of each chapter has three types of question. 'Test your understanding' questions to help you review your reading are in the 'A' series of questions. You will find the answer to these by reading and thinking about the material in the text book. 'Application' questions to test your ability to apply technical skills are in the 'B' series of questions. Questions requiring you to show skills in problem solving and evaluation are in the 'C' series of questions. The symbol [S] indicates that a solution is available at the end of the book.

A   Test your understanding

A8.1   Which industries might need to use the techniques of process costing (section 8.1)?

A8.2   What is meant by the term *equivalent unit* (section 8.2)?

A8.3   What are the steps to follow in calculating the cost of finished goods and the value of closing work-in-progress in respect of a reporting period (section 8.2.1)?

A8.4   Where there is work-in-progress at the start of any reporting period, how is this accounted for using the weighted average approach (section 8.2.2)?

A8.5   Why may it be necessary to account for materials and conversion costs separately (section 8.2.3)?

A8.6   What is the difference between a joint product and a by-product (section 8.3)?

A8.7   How may joint costs be allocated to joint products using a basis of physical measures (section 8.3.1)?

A8.8   How may joint costs be allocated to joint products using a basis of relative sales value (section 8.3.2)?

A8.9 How is relative sales value at the point of separation determined when there are further processing costs of each joint product after the separation point (section 8.3.3)?

A8.10 What is the accounting treatment of cash collected from the sale of a by-product (section 8.3.4)?

A8.11 Why should care be taken when using process costing information for decision making in respect of joint products (section 8.4)?

A8.12 Why is it necessary to use incremental revenues and costs in making a decision on whether to sell or to process further in the case of joint products (section 8.4)?

A8.13 What have researchers found about the potential for linking process costs, standard costs and activity-based costs (section 8.5.1)?

A8.14 What have researchers found about the impact of joint cost problems in a not-for-profit situation (section 8.5.2)?

A8.15 [S] Work-in-progress at the end of the month amounts to 2,000 physical units. They are all 40 per cent complete. What are the equivalent units of production? The cost of production is £3 per equivalent unit. What is the value of work-in-progress?

A8.16 [S] In process X there are 12,000 units completely finished during the month and 3,000 units of work-in-progress. The work-in-progress is 60 per cent complete for materials and 20 per cent complete for conversion costs (labour and overhead). What are the equivalent units of production for the work-in-progress?

A8.17 [S] XYZ Ltd processes and purifies a basic chemical which is then broken down by reaction to give three separate products. Explain the approaches to joint cost allocation using the following information:

Product	Units produced	Final market value per unit (£)	Costs beyond split-off point (£)
A	3,000	5.00	4,000
B	1,000	4.00	1,800
C	2,000	3.00	2,400

Joint costs incurred up to the split-off point are £2,000.

B Application

B8.1 [S]

In a continuous flow process, the following information was collected in relation to production during the month of May:

	Units
Work-in-progress at start of month (60% complete)	50,000
New units introduced for processing	80,000
Completed units transferred to store	100,000
Work-in-progress at end of month (20% complete)	30,000

Opening work-in-progress was valued at cost of £42,000. Costs incurred during the month were £140,000.

Required

Calculate the value of finished output and work-in-progress using the weighted average method.

B8.2 [S]

Clay Products Ltd produces handmade decorative vases. A process costing system is used. All materials are introduced at the start of the process. Labour costs are incurred uniformly throughout the production process.

The following information is available for the month of July:

Work-in-progress at 1 July (60% complete)	2,000 units
Work-in-progress at 31 July (30% complete)	1,200 units

The value of work-in-progress at 1 July is as follows:

	£
Direct materials cost	1,700
Direct labour costs	1,900
	3,600

During the month of July, 7,000 vases were transferred to finished goods stock. Materials introduced cost £14,700. Labour costs incurred were £12,820.

Required

Using the method of weighted averages, prepare a process cost statement for the month of July showing unit costs, the value of finished goods and the value of work-in-progress at the end of the month.

B8.3 [S]

Refinery Ltd buys crude oil which is refined, producing liquefied gas, oil and grease. The cost of crude oil refined in the past year was £105,000 and the refining department incurred processing costs of £45,000. The output and sales for the three products during that year were as follows:

Product	Units of output	Sales value	Additional processing costs
		£	£
Liquefied gas	10,000	20,000	12,000
Refined oil	500,000	230,000	60,000
Grease	5,000	8,000	–

The company could have sold the products at the split-off point directly to other processors at a unit selling price of 50p, 35p and £1.60 respectively.

Required

(1) Compute the net profit earned for each product using two suitable methods of joint cost allocation.

(2) Determine whether it would have been more or less profitable for the company to have sold certain products at split-off without further processing.

C   Problem solving and evaluation

C8.1 [S]

A product is manufactured in a continuous process carried on successively in two departments, Assembly and Finishing. In the production process, materials are added to the product in each department without increasing the number of units produced.

For July Year 2 the production records contain the following information for each department:

	Assembly	Finishing
Units in process at 1 July	0	0
Units commenced in Assembly	80,000	–
Units completed and transferred out	60,000	50,000
Units in process at 31 July	20,000	10,000
Cost of materials (£)	240,000	88,500
Cost of labour (£)	140,000	141,500
Cost of production overhead (£)	65,000	56,600
Percentage completion of units in process:		
Materials	100%	100%
Labour and overhead	50%	70%

Required

Determine the cost per equivalent unit for each department.

C8.2

Chemicals Ltd owns a supply of North Sea gas liquids, and is developing its downstream activities. It is producing two main products, propane and butane, and there is a by-product, arcone. There are four manufacturing processes involved where the gas passes through Modules 1, 2, 3 and 4.

Production information for April Year 2 is as follows:

1,000 tonnes of liquid A and 600 tonnes of liquid B were issued to Module 1.

Liquid C is issued to Module 2 at the rate of 1 tonne per 4 tonnes of production from Module 1.

Liquid D is added to Module 4 at the rate of 1 tonne per 3 tonnes of output from Module 2.

Arcone arises in Module 1 and represents 25% of the good output of that process. The remaining output of Module 1 passes to Module 2. Of the Module 2 output 75% passes to Module 3 and 25% passes to Module 4. The output of Module 3 is propane and the output of Module 4 is butane.

Materials costs are:

	£
Liquid A	60 per tonne
Liquid B	40 per tonne
Liquid C	75 per tonne
Liquid D	120 per tonne

The labour and overhead costs during the month were:

	£
Module 1	22,400
Module 2	38,750
Module 3	12,000
Module 4	10,000

The company is considering selling the products at the undernoted prices:

	£
Propane	130 per tonne
Butane	150 per tonne
Arcone	100 per tonne

Required

(1) Draw a diagram of the various processes described.

(2) Ascertain the percentage profit on selling price per tonne of each of these products.

Case studies

Real world cases

Prepare short answers to Case studies 8.1, 8.2 and 8.3.

Case 8.4 (group case study)

You are the management team of a tree-growing business. Your team consists of the financial adviser, the plant grower and the sales representative. The business has been growing small hedging conifers from seedlings to three years of age and then selling the plants through mail order in bundles of 25 small bare-rooted plants. A garden centre has offered to buy plants in pots for sale in its retail outlets provided the plants are between five and six years old and are symmetrical in shape. If the plants are grown to five years of age they will be too old to be sold as bare-rooted plants, but could be sold for use as shelter belts in parkland or country estates.

Your team has arranged a meeting to discuss the cost implications of the alternative courses of action. Each person should come to the meeting with a list of costs and benefits. The purpose of the meeting is to set out a list of factors to be investigated further for precise costing. Take five minutes for individual preparation, 10 minutes for a group discussion and then give feed-back from your meeting to the rest of the class.

Case 8.5 (group case study)

Divide your group into two teams. One team is the business advisory service of the local enterprise council which offers start-up funding for new ventures. The other team is a group of textile science researchers from the local university. The scientists have developed a new form of medical dressing for burns. The dressing is produced by a continuous flow process and can be cut to lengths specified by the customer. The main customers are hospitals. The health trusts which operate the hospitals will pay a price based on cost plus a percentage for profit. The scientists do not know how to work out the cost in a continuous flow process.

For five minutes the team acting as the business advisers should prepare a short list of key rules in process costing. At the same time, the team acting as the scientists should prepare a list of key questions to ask about process costing. Both teams should then meet and discuss their prepared lists and questions (10 minutes). Finally, one person should report to the rest of the class on the problems of explaining and understanding process costing.

DECISION MAKING

Managers need relevant information to help them make decisions and manage the decision-making process. For any particular decision there will be some costs that are relevant and others that are not relevant. The management accountant separates the relevant from the non-relevant and presents the information in a way that helps the manager see the expected consequences of a decision. Part 2 explains how management accounting helps answer questions of the following type:

- Can we make a profit from this new business proposal?
- What is the lowest price that we should charge for the service provided by our business?
- Should we close down an activity that appears to be making losses?
- What are the costs and benefits of investing in a new production process?
- Will the proposed investment in fixed assets earn a return that is higher than the cost of capital?
- If finance is scarce, which investment proposal will be our first choice?

Chapter 9 introduces the basic methods of breakeven analysis for short-term decision making. This allows you to calculate the contribution to fixed cost and profit, find the breakeven point and apply these techniques to examples of short-term decisions. Chapter 10 explains relevant costs in more detail, describes how pricing decisions are related to costs and explains how uncertainty is introduced into calculations for decision making. Chapter 11 moves into long-term decisions by explaining the basic methods of investment appraisal for capital budgeting. Chapter 12 applies these methods in illustrating applications of capital budgeting.

Part 2 DECISION MAKING		
LEVEL 1	**Chapter 9** Short-term decision making	**Chapter 11** Capital investment appraisal
LEVEL 2	**Chapter 10** Relevant costs, pricing and decisions under uncertainty	**Chapter 12** Capital budgeting applications

Short-term decision making

Real world case 9.1

This case study shows a typical situation in which management accounting can be helpful. Read the case study now but only attempt the discussion points after you have finished studying the chapter.

Flying Brands is a company which delivers goods to customers. The business began some years ago by flying flowers from the Channel Islands to the UK mainland.

The Group has continued to drive profits forward with profit before tax up by 24%, and profit before tax and before all exceptional items up by 10%. The business is focused on profitable growth, and although sales in 2003 showed a fall on 2002 of 3%, the temptation to chase marginal customers was resisted, and a greater emphasis was placed on increasing customer spend and improving operational efficiency. This is reflected in the contribution margin for the two main brands improving to 35% compared to 32% in 2002 . . . Overheads increased during the year by 5%, slightly above inflation, as the marketing team was considerably strengthened. Corporate overheads comprise the costs of the chief executive, the finance director, the non-executive directors and the legal, professional and other fees connected with the running of a public company . . . By driving increasing volumes of orders through our existing operations, we will see economies of scale and substantially improved recovery of fixed overheads.

Source: Flying Brands Limited, Annual report 2004, pp. 10 and 11. www.fbgl.co.uk, www.flyingflowers.com/

Discussion points

1 How did the company improve its contribution to fixed overheads and profit?

2 What was the alternative strategy for improving contribution which the company rejected?

Contents

Learning outcomes

After reading this chapter you should be able to:

- Explain how the accountant's view of cost behaviour differs from that of the economist.
- Define and calculate contribution and breakeven point, and prepare a breakeven chart and a profit–volume chart.
- Use breakeven analysis to explore the effect of changing unit selling price, unit variable cost or fixed cost.
- Explain the limitations of breakeven analysis.
- Explain applications of cost–volume–profit analysis.
- Show how calculation of contribution can be applied in short-term decision making.
- Describe and discuss examples of research into the use of information about contribution.

9.1 Introduction

In Chapter 1 the role of management accounting was explained in terms of directing attention, keeping the score and solving problems. This chapter turns to the problem-solving aspect of the management accountant's work and in particular to the use of management accounting information to help with decisions in the short term (where the short term is typically a period of weeks or months, extending to 12 months at the most, in which some costs are fixed and others are variable, depending on the level of activity). Chapters 11 and 12 explain the use of management accounting in making decisions about the longer term.

Activity 9.1

The classification of costs was explained at length in Chapter 2. If you have any doubts about that chapter, go back and work through it again. It is essential that you understand Chapter 2 before you attempt this chapter.

This chapter will first explain how costs and revenues behave in the short term as the volume of activity changes. This is called cost–volume–profit analysis. It makes use of graphs which will help you understand and present to others the analysis of costs, revenues and profits. The chapter explains the calculation of contribution and shows how it is used to identify the breakeven point of neither profit nor loss.

The chapter will then show how the distinction between variable cost and fixed cost may be used in short-term decision making in situations of special orders, abandonment of a product line, and the existence of limiting factors. Finally, in a set of short case studies, you will see that each problem, while using the same principles of cost–volume–profit analysis, requires some adaptability in using the analysis in the specific circumstances.

9.2 Cost behaviour: fixed and variable costs

Chapter 2 explained that cost classification systems are as varied as the businesses they serve. Types of cost classification system were identified in that chapter by reference to questions which needed answers. Chapter 2 also provided definitions of variable cost and fixed cost, while Exhibits 2.2, 2.5 and 2.7 showed different types of cost behaviour as activity increased.

Definitions

A **variable cost** is one which varies directly with changes in the level of activity, over a defined period of time.

A **fixed cost** is one which is not affected by changes in the level of activity, over a defined period of time.

This chapter now moves on from that starting point outlined in Chapter 2 to ask more questions about the relationships between cost, volume of output and profit.

There are two ways of viewing the behaviour of cost in relation to activity level. One is referred to as *the economist's view* and the other is referred to as *the accountant's view*. Each is discussed here, and the use of the accountant's view is then justified as a reasonable short-term approximation.

9.2.1   The economist's view

Exhibit 9.1 shows total cost related to activity level over a wide range of activity within a business. Starting at zero activity, there is a total cost of £200,000 shown representing the fixed cost of the operations, including items such as rent of premises, business rates, administration salaries and any similar costs incurred to allow operations to commence. Initially, the slope of the graph rises relatively steeply because high levels of costs are incurred as activity begins. Then the slope becomes less steep as the business begins to enjoy the economies of scale, sharing fixed costs over a wider range of activity so that the marginal cost of producing an extra item becomes progressively less. At the extreme right-hand side of the graph the slope begins to rise more steeply again as further fixed costs are incurred. Perhaps high rental has to be paid for new premises at this point to allow expansion, or labour resources become more scarce and higher labour rates have to be paid to employ staff.

Exhibit 9.1
Total cost varying with activity

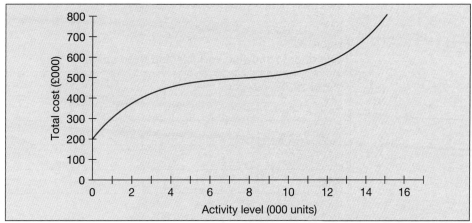

To calculate profit, a business must compare its cost with its revenue. The economist's portrayal of revenue is superimposed on the cost line in Exhibit 9.2. The total revenue starts at zero when there is zero activity. It rises rapidly when supply begins and customers are willing to pay relatively high prices for the goods. Then,

Exhibit 9.2
Revenue and costs: the economist's view

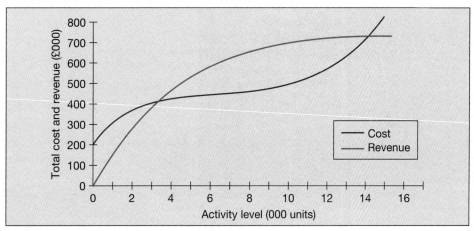

as supply increases, the marginal selling price of each item decreases progressively as it becomes more difficult to sell larger volumes of output. Where the total revenue line is below the total cost line the business is making a loss, and where the total revenue line is above the total cost line the business is making a profit. The business represented by the graph in Exhibit 9.2 shows losses at the left-hand and right-hand sides of the diagram and a profit in the centre. Successful businesses aim to stay in the profit-making region.

9.2.2   The accountant's view

The economist's view of costs covers a very wide range of output. In any particular period, especially in the short term, the actual range of output will be relatively narrow. Looking at Exhibit 9.2, the lines close to the breakeven point are close to being straight lines over a narrow range either side. Accounting assumes that at any point in time this relatively narrow range is available in practice and so the cost and revenue curves are approximately straight lines.

The data in Exhibit 9.3 is used in this section to illustrate the accountant's view of how costs change with levels of activity.

Exhibit 9.3
Table of data showing variable and fixed costs

Activity level	0 units	100 units	200 units	300 units
	£	£	£	£
Variable cost	0	10	20	30
Fixed cost	20	20	20	20
Total cost	20	30	40	50

The graph in Exhibit 9.2 represents activity level changes which could take some time to achieve as the business grows. The accountant takes a much shorter time perspective and looks at a relatively limited range of activity that might be achieved within that time period. In those circumstances, it may be reasonable to use straight-line graphs rather than curves, although great care is needed before assuming it is safe to use straight lines.

Using the data of Exhibit 9.3, a graph of variable cost is shown in Exhibit 9.4 and a graph of fixed cost is shown in Exhibit 9.5.

Exhibit 9.4
Variable cost

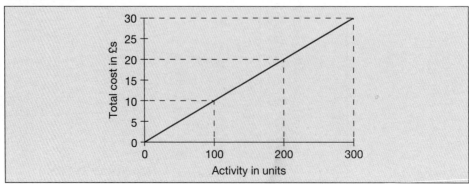

Exhibit 9.5
Fixed cost

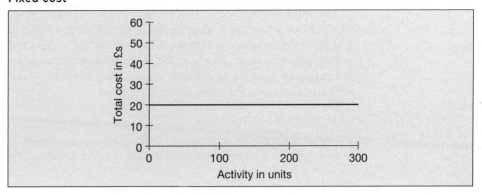

In Exhibit 9.6, these two graphs are added together to give a graph of total cost. The total cost starts at £20 and increases by £10 for every 100 units of activity. The total cost line meets the vertical axis at the fixed cost amount of £20. The slope of the total cost line gives a picture of how fast the variable costs are rising as activity level increases.

Exhibit 9.6
Total cost

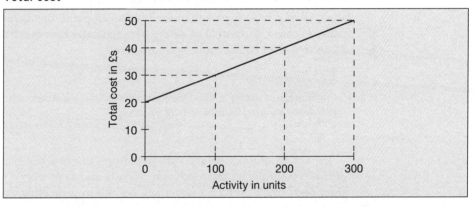

The profit of the business is measured by comparing costs with revenues. Here again, the accountant takes the view that it may be reasonable, over a short time-scale and relatively limited range of activity, to use a straight line. In Exhibit 9.7, a sales line

Exhibit 9.7
Total cost and total sales

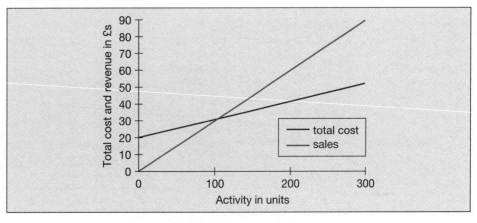

is added based on a selling price of 30 pence per unit, so that total sales are £30 for 100 units, £60 for 200 units and £90 for 300 units.

The sales line is below the cost line at the left-hand side of the graph, crossing the cost line when the activity is 100 units. This shows that for activity levels below 100 units the business will make a loss. At 100 units of activity the business makes neither profit nor loss. This is called the **breakeven point**. Beyond 100 units of activity the business makes a profit and the amount of profit is measured by the vertical difference between the sales and cost lines.

Definition

> The **breakeven point** is that point of activity (measured as sales volume) where total sales and total cost are equal, so that there is neither profit nor loss.

The graph shown in Exhibit 9.7 is more commonly called a **breakeven chart**. It shows the activity level at which total costs equal total sales and at which the business makes neither a profit nor a loss. It also shows what happens to costs and revenues on either side of this breakeven point. If activity falls below the breakeven level, then the amount of loss will be measured by the vertical distance between the cost and sales line.

If activity rises above the breakeven level, then the amount of profit will be measured by the vertical distance between the sales and cost line. If the business is operating at an activity level higher than the breakeven point, the distance between these two points is called the **margin of safety**. This indicates how much activity has to fall from its present level before profit becomes zero.

Definition

> The **margin of safety** is the difference between the breakeven sales and the normal level of sales (measured in units or in £s of sales).

Exhibit 9.8 summarises the various features of a breakeven chart. The use of a chart of this type to depict the behaviour of costs and sales over a range of activity in the short term has been found extremely helpful in presenting management accounting information to non-financial managers who are involved in making decisions which have financial consequences.

Exhibit 9.8
The features of a breakeven chart

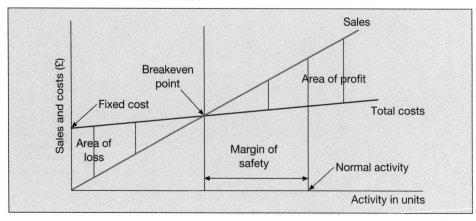

9.2.3 Contribution analysis

Contribution analysis is based on the idea that in the short term it is possible to survive in business providing sales revenue covers variable cost. The **contribution per unit** from a product is the amount by which its selling price exceeds its variable cost. The excess of selling price over variable cost makes a contribution to covering fixed costs and then making a profit. In the short term it may be worth continuing in business if the selling price is greater than variable cost, so that there is a contribution to fixed costs, even where some part of the fixed costs is not covered. In the long term, it is essential to earn sufficient sales revenue to cover *all* costs.

Definition

> **Contribution per unit** is the selling price per unit minus the variable cost per unit. It measures the contribution made by each item of output to the fixed costs and profit of the organisation.

9.3 Breakeven analysis

Breakeven analysis is a technique of management accounting which is based on calculating the breakeven point and analysing the consequences of changes in various factors calculating the breakeven point. The idea of contribution is central to breakeven analysis in evaluating the effects of various short-term decisions.

This section explains ways of finding the breakeven point. It uses the information in Exhibit 9.9 to compare different approaches.

Exhibit 9.9
Ilustration: market trader

> A market trader rents a stall at a fixed price of £200 for a day and sells souvenirs. These cost the trader 50 pence each to buy and have a selling price of 90 pence each. How many souvenirs must be sold to break even?

Activity 9.2

> *Hopefully, you will find the case study so easy to solve that you will already have computed the answer. If so, then analyse how you arrived at the answer before you read the next paragraphs and compare your method with the descriptions given there. It is always better to work out a method for yourself, if it is a good one, than to try remembering something from a book.*

9.3.1 Calculating the break-even point

Calculating contribution

The contribution from a product is the amount by which its selling price exceeds its variable cost. The idea of contribution is central to breakeven analysis in evaluating the effects of various decisions.

Once the contribution per unit is known it can be compared with the fixed costs. The business does not begin to make a profit until the fixed costs are covered, so the formula is applied as:

Breakeven point	equals	$\dfrac{\text{Fixed costs}}{\text{Contribution per unit}}$

Taking the data from the illustration in Exhibit 9.9, the contribution is 40 pence per souvenir (selling price 90 pence minus variable cost 50 pence) and the fixed costs are £200:

$$\text{Breakeven point} = \frac{200}{0.40} = 500 \text{ units}$$

Algebraic method

It is possible to use simple algebra to calculate the breakeven point, but only if you prefer mathematical methods of solving a problem.

The equation for the breakeven point is:

Sales	equals	Fixed costs + Variable costs

If the number of souvenirs sold at the breakeven point is n, then the total sales revenue is $0.9n$ and the total variable cost is $0.5n$:

$$0.9n = 200 + 0.5n$$
$$0.4n = 200$$

Solving the equation, $n = 500$ souvenirs to be sold to break even.

9.3.2　Breakeven chart

The general appearance of a breakeven chart has already been shown in Exhibit 9.8. To plot the graph some points on each line are necessary. Because they are all straight lines only two points are needed, together with a ruler and pencil to join them. Points on a graph may be defined by specifying two co-ordinates in the form (x, y). A point defined as (10, 100) means that it lies at the intersection of a line up from 10 on the horizontal (x) axis and a line across from 100 on the vertical (y) axis. In Exhibit 9.10, two points are plotted, namely, (10, 100) and (30, 300). These may then be joined by a straight line.

Exhibit 9.10
Plotting points for a graph

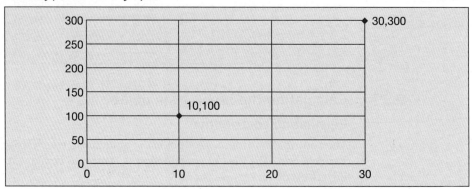

The graph needs to cover an activity scale wide enough to show both sides of the breakeven point, so it is a useful idea to work round the breakeven point by choosing one point which is loss making and one point which is profit making. The point of zero activity will usually be loss making because there is nil revenue but there are fixed costs. So the start of the sales line can be plotted at (0, 0) and the start of the cost line at (0, £200). For a position of profit, the sales and total cost must be calculated for a higher activity level, which in this case might be 900 souvenirs:

Sales of 900 souvenirs at 90 pence each = £810

The sales line will therefore join the points (0, £0) and (900, £810):

		£
Variable cost of 900 souvenirs at 50 pence each	=	450
Fixed cost	=	200
Total cost		650

The total cost line joins (0, £200) and (900, £650). Exhibit 9.11 shows the breakeven chart with a breakeven point at 500 units sold. Gridlines are added to show the points plotted.

Exhibit 9.11
Breakeven chart

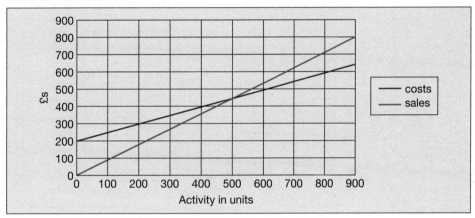

9.3.3 Profit-volume chart

Defining the profit-volume ratio

Profit is an important aspect of most management accounting reports. However, the breakeven chart does not show directly the amount of profit. It has to be estimated by measuring the vertical distance between the sales and total cost lines. There is another form of graph used in management accounting called a **profit–volume chart**. The horizontal axis plots the volume, measured by activity level in £s of sales, and the vertical axis plots the profit at that activity level.

The activity level is measured in £s of sales in order that the slope of the graph matches the profit/volume ratio, a slightly confusing name for the ratio which calculates contribution as a percentage of sales value:

Profit/volume ratio	equals	$\dfrac{\text{Contribution per unit}}{\text{Selling price per unit}} \times 100$

Exhibit 9.12 sets out a diagram showing the main features of a profit–volume chart.

Illustration of a profit-volume chart

Taking the data used in preparing Exhibit 9.11, the preparation of a profit–volume chart requires only the profit line to be drawn. When sales are zero, there will be a loss equal to the fixed cost, which gives the first point to plot at (£0, £–200). When 900 units

Exhibit 9.12
Profit–volume chart

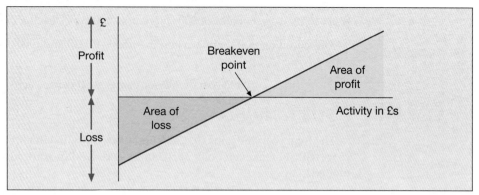

Exhibit 9.13
Profit–volume chart using data from the 'market trader' case study

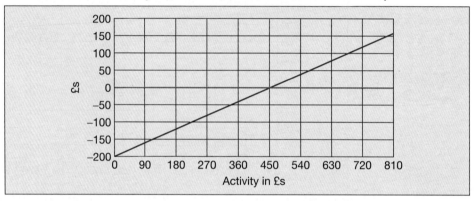

are sold the sales are £810 and the profit is £160, giving the second point to plot at (£810, £160). The result is shown in Exhibit 9.13.

The gridlines are included to show where the profit line has been plotted. The breakeven point of zero profit or loss is at a sales level of £450. The graph rises by £40 of profit for every £90 increase in sales activity, giving a slope of 44.4 per cent.

The profit–volume ratio is calculated by formula as:

$$\frac{\text{Contribution per unit}}{\text{Sales price per unit}} = \frac{40 \text{ pence}}{90 \text{ pence}} = 44.4\%$$

9.4 Using breakeven analysis

Breakeven analysis is a very useful tool. It may be used to answer questions of the following type:

- What level of sales is necessary to cover fixed costs and make a specified profit?
- What is the effect of contribution per unit beyond the breakeven point?
- What happens to the breakeven point when the selling price of one unit changes?
- What happens to the breakeven point when the variable cost per unit changes?
- What happens to the breakeven point when the fixed costs change?

Each of these questions is now dealt with in this section by an illustration and an explanation following the illustration.

9.4.1 Covering fixed costs and making a profit

To find the level of sales necessary to cover fixed costs and make a specified profit requires a knowledge of selling price per unit, variable cost per unit, and the fixed costs together with the desired profit. These are set out in the data table.

Data	
Selling price per unit	80 pence
Variable cost per unit	30 pence
Fixed cost	£300
Desired level of profit	£400

The contribution per unit is 50 pence (80 pence − 30 pence). To find the break-even point, the fixed costs of £300 are divided by the contribution per unit to obtain a breakeven point of 600 units.

To meet fixed costs of £300 and desired profit of £400 requires the contribution to cover £700 in all. This is achieved by selling 1,400 units.

$$\text{Volume of sales required} = \frac{700}{0.5} = 1,400 \text{ units}$$

Activity 9.3 *Check that 1,400 units at a contribution of 50 pence each gives a total contribution of £700. It is always a useful precaution to check the arithmetic of a calculation as a safeguard against carelessness.*

9.4.2 Beyond the breakeven point

Beyond the breakeven point the fixed costs are covered and the sales of further units are making a contribution to profit. The higher the contribution per unit, the greater the profit from any particular level of activity. The data table sets out some information on selling prices, variable costs and fixed costs of two products.

Data
A dry-cleaning shop takes two types of clothing. Jackets cost £6 to clean and the customer is charged £9 per garment. Coats cost £10 to clean and the customer is charged £12 per garment. The monthly fixed costs are £600 for each type of garment (representing the rental costs of two different types of machine). The shop expects to clean 500 jackets and 500 coats each month.

Activity 9.4 *Before reading the analysis of Exhibit 9.14, calculate the contribution made by each product, work out the breakeven point of each, and then explore the effect on the breakeven point of:*

(a) changes in the price charged to customers;
(b) changes in the variable costs; and
(c) changes in the fixed costs.

If you have access to a spreadsheet package this is the kind of problem for which spreadsheets are highly suitable.

The calculations set out in Exhibit 9.14 show that, although both products have the same fixed costs, the jackets have a lower breakeven point because they make a higher

Exhibit 9.14
Calculation of breakeven point and of sales beyond the breakeven point

	Jackets £	Coats £
Selling price	9	12
Variable cost	6	10
Contribution per item	3	2
Fixed costs	£600	£600
Breakeven point	200 units	300 units
Profit for sales of 500 units	900	400

contribution per unit. Beyond the breakeven point they continue to contribute more per unit. The profits at any given level of activity are therefore higher for jackets.

9.4.3   Margin of safety

The **margin of safety** has been defined as the difference between the sales level at the breakeven point and the normal level of sales (actual or forecast), measured in units or in dollars of sales. In the case of the dry-cleaning shop, the margin of safety for jackets is 300 jackets (500 − 200) when 500 jackets are cleaned each month. The margin of safety for coats is 200 coats (500 − 300) when 500 coats are cleaned each month. The margin of safety is interpreted by saying that cleaning of jackets may fall by 300 per month before the breakeven point is reached but cleaning of coats will reach the breakeven point after a reduction of only 200 in coats cleaned. Cleaning coats is therefore riskier than cleaning jackets, if expected output is compared to breakeven volume.

The margin of safety can also be expressed as a percentage using the formula:

$$\frac{\text{Normal output} - \text{breakeven volume}}{\text{Normal output}} \times 100\%$$

The *margin of safety percentage* is 300 × 100/500 = 60% for jackets and 200 × 100/500 = 40% for coats. The interpretation is that output has to fall by 60% from present levels for jackets before the breakeven point is reached, but only by 40% for coats.

9.4.4   Change in selling price

If the selling price per unit increases and costs remain constant, then the contribution per unit will increase and the breakeven volume will be lower. Take as an example the dry-cleaning business of the previous illustration. If the selling price of cleaning a coat rises to £15, then the contribution per unit will rise to £5. That will require cleaning only 120 coats to break even. The risk of raising the price is that customers may move elsewhere, so that while it may not be difficult to exceed the breakeven point at a selling price of £12, it may be extremely difficult at a selling price of £15.

9.4.5   Change in variable cost

The effect of a change in variable cost is very similar to the effect of a change in selling price. If the variable cost per unit increases, then the contribution per unit will decrease, with the result that more items will have to be sold in order to reach the breakeven point. If it is possible to reduce variable costs, then the contribution per unit will increase. The enterprise will reach the breakeven point at a lower level of activity and will then be earning profits at a faster rate.

9.4.6 Change in fixed costs

If fixed costs increase, then more units have to be sold in order to reach the breakeven point. Where the fixed costs of an operation are relatively high, there is a perception of greater risk because a cutback in activity for any reason is more likely to lead to a loss. Where an organisation has relatively low fixed costs, there may be less concern about margins of safety because the breakeven point is correspondingly lower.

9.4.7 More than one product

Breakeven analysis and breakeven charts can only represent one type of product. If a business is producing and selling more than one item, then separate charts and analyses will be needed. However, if there is a fixed proportion of sales of different items, breakeven analysis may be applied to a batch of goods in the specific proportion. A combined contribution is calculated for the batch of goods and then a combined breakeven point is calculated.

Suppose a sweet manufacturer produces chocolate bars, boiled sweets and walnut whirls. Experience shows that orders from retailers are always in the proportions: 5 chocolate bars, 1 bag of boiled sweets and 2 walnut whirls. The contribution from a chocolate bar is 3 pence, the contribution from a bag of boiled sweets is 2 pence and the contribution from a walnut whirl is 4 pence. Fixed costs for one month are £1,000. What is the breakeven point?

Calculation
Take a batch of goods in the fixed proportions 5 : 1 : 2.

The contribution of one batch is $(5 \times 3 \text{ pence}) + (1 \times 2 \text{ pence}) + (2 \times 4 \text{ pence}) = 25 \text{ pence}$.

The breakeven point is calculated as fixed overhead/contribution per unit. This equals £1,000/25 pence = 4,000 batches.

To find the actual volume of production multiply the number of batches by the contents of each. So 4,000 batches contain 20,000 chocolate bars, 4,000 bags of boiled sweets and 8,000 walnut whips. These are the activity levels required in combination for breakeven.

9.5 Limitations of breakeven analysis

Breakeven analysis is a useful tool for problem solving and decision making, but some of the limitations should be noted:

1 The breakeven analysis assumes that cost and revenue behaviour patterns are known and that the change in activity levels can be represented by a straight line.
2 It may not always be feasible to split costs neatly into variable and fixed categories. Some costs show mixed behaviour.
3 The breakeven analysis assumes that fixed costs remain constant over the volume range under consideration. If that is not the case, then the graph of total costs will have a step in it where the fixed costs are expected to increase.
4 Breakeven analysis, as described so far in this book, assumes input and output volumes are the same, so that there is no build-up of stocks and work-in-progress.
5 Breakeven charts and simple analyses can only deal with one product at a time.
6 It is assumed that cost behaviour depends entirely on volume.

These limitations may be overcome by modifying the breakeven analysis. However, that would involve considerably more computation work and is beyond the scope of this textbook.

9.6 Applications of cost–volume–profit analysis

Breakeven analysis is a particular example of the more general technique of **cost–volume–profit analysis**. This analysis emphasises the relationship between sales revenue, costs and profit in the short term. In this context the short term is a period of time over which some costs are fixed, whatever the level of output, within a range limited by the existing capacity of the business. In the longer term, all costs become variable because the capacity of a business can be altered by acquiring new premises, hiring more employees or investing in more equipment.

Definition

> **cost–volume–profit analysis** evaluates the effects of forecast changes in sales, variable costs and fixed costs, to assist in decision making.

In using cost–volume–profit analysis, management accounting is meeting the needs of directing attention and solving problems. In the short term, decisions have to be made within the existing constraints of the capacity of the business and the aim of that decision making will be to maximise short-term profit. Typical decision-making situations requiring cost–volume–profit analysis would be:

- accepting a special order to use up spare capacity
- abandoning a line of business
- the existence of a limiting factor
- carrying out an activity in-house rather than buying in a service under contract.

Each of these situations is now considered in turn.

Activity 9.5

Those who comment on the applications of cost–volume–profit analysis always emphasise that it is a short-run decision-making tool. Write a 200-word note explaining this view.

9.6.1 Special order to use up spare capacity

In the short term, a business must ensure that the revenue from each item of activity at least covers variable costs and makes a contribution to fixed costs. Once the fixed costs are covered by contribution, the greater the level of activity, the higher the profit. When the business reaches full capacity there will be a new element of fixed cost to consider should the business decide to increase its capacity. If there is no increase in capacity, then the business should concentrate on those activities producing the highest contribution per unit or per item.

But supposing the business is *not* operating at full capacity. Should it lower its sales price in an attempt to increase the volume of activity? The question may arise in the form of a request from a customer for a special price for a particular order. (Customers may well know that the business is not operating at full capacity and may therefore try to use their bargaining power to force a lower sales price.) Should the business accept the special order? cost–volume–profit analysis gives the answer that the special order is acceptable provided the sales price per item covers the variable costs per item and provided there is no alternative use for the spare capacity which could result in a higher contribution per item.

9.6.2 Abandonment of a line of business

The management of a business may be concerned because one line of business appears not to be covering all its costs. This situation may arise particularly where costs are being used for score-keeping purposes and all fixed costs have been allocated to products.

As was shown in Chapter 4, the allocation of fixed costs to products is a process which allows a range of choices, which may lead to confusion. However, the allocation of fixed costs is not relevant to decision making because the fixed costs are incurred irrespective of whether any business activity takes place.

When a line of business comes under scrutiny for its profitability, cost–volume–profit analysis shows that in the short term it is worth continuing with the line if it makes a contribution to fixed costs. If the line of business is abandoned and nothing better takes its place, then a worse situation results because that contribution is lost but the fixed costs run on regardless.

9.6.3 Existence of a limiting factor

In the short term, it may be that one of the inputs to a business activity is restricted in its availability. There may be a shortage of raw materials or a limited supply of skilled labour. There may be a delivery delay on machinery or a planning restriction which prevents the extension of a building on the business premises. There may then be a need to choose from a range of possible activities so as to maximise short-term profit. The item which is restricted in availability is called the **limiting factor**. In order to apply cost–volume–profit analysis the shortage must be short-term, with the expectation of a return to unrestricted activity.

Cost–volume–profit analysis shows that maximisation of profit will occur if the activity is chosen which gives the highest **contribution per unit of limiting factor**.

9.6.4 In-house activity versus bought-in contract

For a manufacturing business, there may be a decision between making a component in-house as compared with buying the item ready-made. For a service business there

---

Real world case 9.2

Royal Dutch/Shell Group discusses here its profit margins in the Chemical unit.

. . . earnings in 2003 were $185 million lower. Sales volumes, including traded products, increased by 19% from a year ago benefiting from capacity additions and volumes from new units. However, there was a decline in overall Chemicals unit margins (defined as proceeds less cost of feedstock energy and distribution per tonne of product sold). This was due to high and volatile feedstock and energy costs and surplus capacity, particularly in the USA. Fixed

costs were higher, reflecting planned increases in capacity and higher than normal asset maintenance activity, project expenses, increased costs for benefits including pensions, as well as the adverse impact of the weaker US dollar.

Source: Royal Dutch Shell, Annual Report 2003, p. 31. www.shell.com

Discussion points

1 What was the main cause of the fall in contribution margin?
2 What are the variable costs and the fixed costs described in the extract?

may be a decision between employing staff in-house and using the services of an agency which supplies staff as and when required. Cost–volume–profit analysis shows that the decision should be based on comparison of variable costs per unit, relating this to the difference in fixed costs between the options.

9.7 Cases in short-term decision making

Cost–volume–profit analysis is particularly well suited to management needs in short-term decision making. Fiona McTaggart now discusses four cases she has come across where cost–volume–profit analysis has been relevant. The first relates to a decision about taking on a special order to fill a gap where the business was not running at full capacity. The second relates to a potential abandonment of a line of business, the third deals with a limiting factor causing scarcity of an input to the production process, and the fourth relates to buying in services.

9.7.1 Decisions on special orders

FIONA: *My first story is about a car hire business in a holiday resort which was experiencing a temporary fall in activity in the run-up to the start of the tourist season. Their normal charge was £3.00 per mile, to cover all costs including the driver's wages. A telephone installation company offered a three-month contract to run engineers between two towns on a return journey of 100 miles, at a fixed price of £180 per journey. The car hire company asked my advice about accepting this offer of £1.80 per mile.*

I asked the company what the drivers and cars would be doing each day if the contract was not taken up and the answer was that they would not be doing anything other than waiting at the depot and cleaning their cars. My advice was that, on that basis, the contract would be worth undertaking if it covered the variable costs of each journey and made a contribution to fixed costs and profit.

We sat down to look at the fixed costs and produced the statement shown in Exhibit 9.15. Quite deliberately I did not write any amounts against the separate items of fixed costs because I wanted to emphasise that these are the unavoidable elements that will arise whether or not the contract is taken up.

From the data provided, I calculated the variable cost per mile as 20 pence for petrol and 8 pence for tyres, giving 28 pence in all. The normal charge of £3.00 per mile is intended to cover this 28 pence per mile plus the fixed cost per mile, amounting to £2.10 per mile using the average annual mileage per car. That total cost of £2.38 per mile leaves a profit of 62 pence per mile or £24,800 per annum if the average mileage is achieved.

It is clear that to cover all costs the charge of £3.00 is probably about right, but if the drivers and cars are otherwise unoccupied, extra journeys on the special contract contribute £1.52 per mile (£1.80 – £0.28) to fixed costs and profit. I advised them to take up the contract on two conditions:

(a) *they must be as sure as they could be that there will not be an upturn in business during the hire period which would mean they were turning down the possibility of carrying passengers who would pay £3.00 per mile; and*

(b) *if the journeys involve extra payments to drivers for overtime or late-night work, those extra payments should be regarded as part of the variable cost of the contract and the costings recalculated on that basis.*

They took my advice and carried out the contract. It fitted perfectly into the quiet period of business and the company realised later that the contract had made a useful contribution to profit at a time when drivers and cars would otherwise have been inactive.

Exhibit 9.15
Analysis of variable and fixed costs of car hire firm

Variable costs:	
Petrol	£1.20 per litre
Fuel consumption	6 miles per litre
Tyre costs	£1,600 per set of four tyres
Tyre replacement	every 20,000 miles
Fixed costs:	£84,000
These covered:	
Driver's wages	
Insurance	
Licence fee for airport waiting	
Licence fee to town council	
Depreciation of vehicle	
Annual testing	
Radio control membership	
Average annual mileage per car:	40,000 miles

In Fiona's example, the company made use of the idea that, in the short term, any contract is worth taking on if it covers variable costs and makes some contribution to fixed costs and profit. Care needs to be taken that the special order does not create a precedent for future work, particularly if existing customers find that special treatment is being given which appears to undercut the price they are paying. The company may find it difficult in future to return to the price which covers all costs. In the long term, the company must charge a price which covers fixed costs as well as variable costs if it is to survive.

Fiona's second illustration relates to a decision on abandoning a line of activity.

9.7.2 Abandonment decisions

FIONA: *A private tuition college was providing two types of secretarial training course. The first was teaching wordprocessing and the second was teaching office skills. The college had produced the profit and loss statement shown in Exhibit 9.16.*

Exhibit 9.16
Information for abandonment decision

	Wordprocessing £000s	Office skills £000s	Total £000s
Tuition fee income	485	500	985
Variable costs	200	330	530
Fixed overhead	120	220	340
Total costs	320	550	870
Profit/(loss)	165	(50)	115

On the basis of this profit and loss statement the owners of the business were on the point of cancelling all further courses in office skills. I asked them how they had decided on the allocation of fixed overheads and they explained that these comprised primarily administrative staff costs and permanent teaching staff, plus items such as rent and business rates as well as depreciation of wordprocessors and of the equipment used in the cabin which had been set up to simulate the most up-to-date office conditions. The cabin itself was depreciated over twenty years. Fixed overhead which could be allocated directly to the relevant courses, such as depreciation of equipment, was allocated in its entirety to the relevant course type. This approach was also used for teaching costs where these were specific to one course type. Fixed overhead which could apply to each type of course, such as administrative staff salaries, was spread in proportion to the number of courses given.

I pointed out to the owners that their profit and loss statement would be more informative if it were set out in the format shown in Exhibit 9.17.

Exhibit 9.17
Revised data for abandonment decision

	Wordprocessing £000s	Office skills £000s	Total £000s
Tuition fee income	485	500	985
Variable costs	200	330	530
Contribution	285	170	455
Fixed overhead			340
Profit			115

From Exhibit 9.17 it is relatively straightforward to see that the office skills programme is making a contribution of £170,000 to fixed costs and profit, after covering its own variable costs. If the programme were not offered, then the business would have only the contribution of £285,000 from wordprocessing which would not cover the fixed overhead of £340,000. Far from abandoning the office skills programme, it was essential to retain it. The allocation of fixed overheads was, for short-term analysis purposes, irrelevant. The cabin and office equipment had already been purchased and would continue to depreciate whether used or not. If put up for sale, these assets would have a negligible value. Administrative and permanent staff were also in place and could not instantly be disengaged.

I advised them that while it was preferable in the short term to keep both programmes running, there were some questions they should ask themselves for longer-term planning:

1 To what extent do clients take up the wordprocessing courses because the office skills course may be studied at the same time and in the same place?
2 How much fixed cost could be avoided in the longer term if either course ceased to exist?
3 Would it be a more effective use of resources to concentrate only on one type of course so that the fixed costs are restricted to one type of equipment and perhaps relatively fewer administrative staff?

The answers might lead to reorganisation towards one type of course only. On the other hand, it might be found that the two programmes are so interrelated that each needs the other and the fixed costs are effectively essential to both, whatever the accounting allocation process.

Fiona's third story concerns a business where there was a restriction in the amount of a factor of input to the production process.

9.7.3 Existence of limiting factors

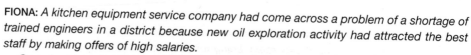

FIONA: A kitchen equipment service company had come across a problem of a shortage of trained engineers in a district because new oil exploration activity had attracted the best staff by making offers of high salaries.

On a short-term basis the company felt it could not continue to service washing machines, dishwashers and built-in ovens in that area and would prefer to concentrate on the most profitable use of its labour resource. Exhibit 9.18 shows the most recent annual data available, based on the situation before the employee shortage crisis arose. However, the total labour force now available was estimated in cost terms at £40,000.

Exhibit 9.18
Data for limiting factor problem

	Washing machines £000s	Dishwashers £000s	Built-in ovens £000s
Sales	80	120	180
Direct materials	10	20	18
Direct labour	30	30	60
Variable overhead	10	30	30
Total variable cost	50	80	108
Contribution	30	40	72

I advised them that, in these circumstances, the limiting factor of labour should be used so as to maximise the contribution from every £ of labour used. First, I calculated the contribution per £ of scarce resource for each of the three types of service contract (see Exhibit 9.19).

Exhibit 9.19
Calculation of contribution per £ of limiting factor

	Washing machines £000s	Dishwashers £000s	Built-in ovens £000s
Contribution	30	40	72
Direct labour	30	30	60
Contribution per £ of labour	£1.00	£1.33	£1.20

The highest contribution per £ of labour is therefore provided by dishwashers, followed by built-in ovens. So I explained that it would be best to use the scarce labour resource first of all to service dishwashers. At the existing level of sales that would take up £30,000 worth of labour, leaving the balance of £10,000 worth of labour to service built-in ovens on a restricted basis. If more dishwasher work became available, that would be the preferred choice for profit generation.

This would be a short-term solution, but in the longer term it would be essential to consider whether the market could stand higher charges for servicing equipment, which would allow higher wage rates to be paid and thus permit all three types of work to continue.

Fiona has used in this example a particular case of a general principle that where limiting factors apply, profit is made as high as possible where the greatest contribution is obtained each time the scarce resource is used.

9.7.4 Make or buy

The management of a manufacturing business may have to decide whether to make a component in-house or buy the item ready-made.

Fiona McTaggart explains the problem:

FIONA: A car manufacturer has a problem regarding one quite small component used on a production line. The component may be purchased from an external supplier at £100 per item. It is currently being manufactured in-house at a cost of £110 per item, comprising fixed cost £30 per item and variable cost £80 per item. Annual output is currently 50,000 components and the trend of output is expected to be rising.

The external price looks attractive at first glance but, before I can advise the car manufacturer, I need to know more about the fixed cost. It is currently £1,500,000 per annum (£30 times 50,000 components). If the company can avoid the fixed cost by purchasing from the outside supplier, then I will compare the additional variable cost of £20 (£100 – £80) with the saving of £1,500,000. The company breaks even at 75,000 components (calculated as fixed cost saving of £1,500,000 divided by additional variable cost of £20). If demand is less than 75,000, then it is more cost effective to buy from the external supplier. If demand is more than 75,000, then it is more cost effective to manufacture in-house (provided fixed costs do not change at a higher level of output).

If the fixed cost of £1,500,000 cannot be avoided (perhaps it represents rent and property costs which would be incurred even if there were no production), then there is no advantage in buying from the external supplier. The relevant comparison in such a situation is between the variable cost of £80 and the external price of £100.

I would also advise the company that non-financial matters such as quality control and reliability of supply should be taken into consideration when deciding on external purchase rather than internal production.

9.7.5 In-house activity compared with bought-in services

In her final example, Fiona describes a situation where a company was considering buying in services rather than employing its own staff. Cost–volume–profit analysis implies that the decision should be based on the costs saved by not undertaking the activity in-house (the variable costs and any fixed costs that are avoidable) together with the costs incurred in buying the product or service from an external supplier (price multiplied by quantity purchased).

Real world case 9.3

Delta Air Lines is an airline carrier based in Atlanta, USA.

Delta's hopes of survival rest on a series of initiatives: a new pilot contract; the simplification of its fares; and 'Operation Clockwork', an attempt to reduce the costs of running a 'hub and spoke' operation to get close to the

economies of low-cost carriers. Hubs have been central to the business of traditional airlines, in collecting customers from small cities that are too uneconomic to serve with direct air services. Hub schedules used to be organised around maximising revenues from marginal passengers – those willing to pay high fares for efficient connections. The director of operations strategy and planning said 'Historically we had to trade off the inefficiencies of the traditional hub for high fares from connecting passengers. Today, people pay low fares.' The overall aim of Operation Clockwork is to improve productivity: there will be a 22% reduction in the time aircraft spend on the ground as a result of increasing the number of departures per day from nine to 10.5. Employees will handle six to seven flights per day, up from four to five, incentivised by performance bonuses of up to $100 per month. Turnaround times will be reduced by asking passengers to board while the plane is being cleaned, closing the doors earlier and not waiting for late connecting flights, asking more staff to stay with the aircraft throughout the day, and reduce the number of gate changes, previously used to make customer connections more convenient.

Based on *Financial Times*, 2 February 2005, p. 12, 'Delta flies in the face of tradition'.
Source: Company website: www.delta.com

Discussion points

1 How will the company improve the contribution from selling flights to passengers?

2 What are the business risks the company faces in its plans to cut costs?

FIONA: *A company had been employing its own legal department, comprising a qualified solicitor and two assistants. The solicitor was about to retire and the company had to decide whether to advertise for a replacement or to use a commercial law service as and when required. There would be no redundancy costs in respect of the two assistants because the younger one could be redeployed to a vacancy elsewhere in the organisation and the other would continue to be required as the internal contact with the commercial law service.*

I showed the management that, because the commercial law service would charge on an hourly basis, the costs to be compared were the variable costs per hour charged by the commercial service and the fixed costs per annum of the in-house solicitor's salary. We compared the hourly charge rate of £400 with the solicitor's salary of £60,000 and the assistant's salary of £36,000 and worked out that the breakeven point would be 240 hours of the commercial law service each year. If more than 240 hours are requested next year, it would be worth continuing the in-house service.

9.8 What the researchers have found

9.8.1 Contribution in practice

Ring and Tigert (2001) used contribution analysis to explain why internet grocery retailing did not succeed in the United States. They compared the costs of store-based retailing and internet retailing. The variable costs of internet retailing are higher because there are the additional costs of selecting the goods in the warehouse to make up the order and delivering the order to the home. This additional variable cost reduces the contribution compared with that available with store-based retailing. Research showed that customers were expecting the same prices for the groceries purchased and were not prepare to pay a higher price for the convenience of home delivery. Traders were competing with each other by not charging for packing and delivery. The fixed costs of operating an internet-based system were not greatly different from the fixed costs of operating conventional stores. So the authors described the packing and delivery costs as 'killer costs' for the internet selling operation. The article described the different approaches taken in different countries, such as delivering to central 'pickup points' rather than to the home, or requiring customers to come to the store to select and pack their own goods. The authors concluded that online grocery shopping had not achieved large-scale success, partly because customers still want to visit stores for perishable food and partly because the additional costs did not leave sufficient margin.

9.8.2 Economics and accounting: views of contribution analysis

Groth and Byers (1996) compare views of economics and accounting on a range of issues in management accounting. They focus on the crucial importance of economic contribution margin in decision making and management. They list a range of situations in which contribution margin is a crucial factor in economic analysis. The list includes: pricing and marketing strategy in markets having elasticity of price-demand, the evaluation of incremental sales, bidding for incremental business, and risk management with respect to the behaviour of competitors.

9.9 Summary

Key themes in this chapter are:

- The accountant's view of cost behaviour differs from that of the economist. The accountant assumes that total cost and total revenue vary on a straight-line basis as the volume of output and sales increases. The economist sees total cost varying in a non-linear manner due to economies of scale and sees total revenue gradually levelling off as customers reach the point where they do not wish to buy more of the item.

- **Contribution** is defined as sales minus variable cost. **Contribution per unit** is compared with fixed overhead cost to calculate breakeven point. A breakeven chart and a profit–volume chart are useful ways of showing how contribution and profit change as the volume of output and sales increases.

- **Breakeven analysis** can be used to explore the effect of changing unit selling price, unit variable cost or fixed cost.

- **Breakeven analysis** has limitations because it is only suitable for *short-term decision making* and can only focus on one product at a time.

- A **breakeven chart** is a graph that shows sales and costs over a range of activity, including the activity level at which total costs equal total sales and at which the business makes neither a profit nor a loss.

- **Cost–volume–profit analysis** means comparing sales revenue with variable cost and fixed cost to calculate profit or loss over a range of activity, to help with short-term decision making.

- A **profit–volume chart** is a graph on which the horizontal axis shows the volume, measured by activity level in £s of sales, and the vertical axis shows the profit at that activity level.

- The **profit/volume ratio** is calculated as contribution as a percentage of sales value:

- The calculation of contribution can be applied in the short-term for decisions such as:
  - *Decisions on special orders* (does a lower price leave a positive contribution?)
  - *Abandonment decisions* (is the product or service making a positive contribution?)
  - *Limiting factors* (which product or service gives the highest contribution per unit of limiting factor?
  - *Make or buy* (how does the price of the external product or service compare with the internal variable cost and the fixed overheads that will be saved?)

References and further reading

Groth, J.C. and Byers, S.S. (1996) 'Creating value: economics and accounting – perspectives for managers', *Management Decision*, 34(10): 56–64.

Ring, L.J. and Tigert, D.J. (2001) 'Viewpoint: the decline and fall of Internet grocery retailers', *International Journal of Retail and Distribution Management*, 29(6): 264–271.

QUESTIONS

The Questions section of each chapter has three types of question. 'Test your understanding' questions which help you review your reading are in the 'A' series of questions. You will find the answer to these by reading and thinking about the material in the text book. 'Application' questions to test your ability to apply technical skills are in the 'B' series of questions. Questions requiring you to show skills in problem solving and evaluation are in the 'C' series of questions. A letter [S] indicates that there is a solution at the end of the book.

A   Test your understanding

A9.1   Define *variable cost* and *fixed cost* (section 9.2).

A9.2   Contrast the economist's view of costs and revenues with that taken in management accounting (sections 9.2.1 and 9.2.2).

A9.3   Sketch, and explain the main features of, a breakeven chart (section 9.3).

A9.4   Explain the algebraic method for determining the breakeven point (section 9.3.1).

A9.5   Explain the formula method for determining the breakeven point (section 9.3.1).

A9.6   Sketch, and explain the main features of, a profit–volume chart (section 9.3.2).

A9.7   What happens to the breakeven point when the sales price per unit falls (section 9.4.4)?

A9.8   What happens to the breakeven point when the variable cost per unit falls (section 9.4.5)?

A9.9   What happens to the breakeven point when fixed overheads increase (section 9.4.6)?

A9.10 State the limitations of breakeven analysis (section 9.5).

A9.11 Give three examples of applications of cost–volume–profit analysis (section 9.6).

A9.12 Explain how cost–volume–profit analysis may help in:
(a) decisions on special orders (section 9.7.1);
(b) abandonment decisions (section 9.7.2);
(c) situations of limiting factors (section 9.7.3); and
(d) a decision on buying in services (sections 9.7.4, 9.7.5).

B   Application

B9.1 [S]
Fixed costs are £5,000. Variable cost per unit is £3 and the unit selling price is £5.50. What is the breakeven volume of sales?

B9.2 [S]
Plot a breakeven chart based on the following data and label the features of interest on the chart:

Number of units	Fixed cost £	Variable cost £	Total cost £	Sales £
10	200	100	300	150
20	200	200	400	300
30	200	300	500	450
40	200	400	600	600
50	200	500	700	750

B9.3 [S]

Montrose Glass Products Ltd manufactures three ranges of high-quality paper-weights – Basic, Standard and Deluxe. Its accountant has prepared a draft budget for Year 7:

	Basic £000s	Standard £000s	Deluxe £000s	Total £000s
Revenue	45	35	40	120
Material	15	10	10	35
Labour	20	15	5	40
Variable overhead	5	12	5	22
Fixed overhead	9	5	6	20
	49	42	26	117
Profit/(loss)	(4)	(7)	14	3

Fixed overheads are allocated to each product line on the basis of direct labour hours.

The directors are concerned about the viability of the company and are currently considering the cessation of both Basic and Standard ranges, since both are apparently making losses.

Required

(a) If the directors close down only the manufacture of Basic paperweights, what is the effect on total profit?

(b) If the directors close down only the manufacture of Standard paperweights, what is the effect on total profit?

(c) What is the best decision with regard to keeping profit as high as possible?

B9.4 [S]

Chris Gibson Kitchenware Limited sells kitchen appliances to department stores. Product costs are ascertained using an absorption costing system from which the following statement has been prepared in respect of the business's three product lines.

	Dishwashers £000s	Fridges £000s	Ovens £000s	Total £000s
Sales	180	330	270	780
Less total costs	(200)	(250)	(220)	(670)
Profit/(loss)	(20)	8	50	110

It has been estimated that costs are 60 per cent variable and 40 per cent fixed.

Required

(a) Restate the table distinguishing variable and fixed costs.

(b) Advise whether dishwashers should be dropped from the product range in order to improve profitability.

B9.5 [S]

Capital Tours Limited sells weekend tours of London for £200 per person. Last month 1,000 tours were sold and costs were £180,000 (representing a total cost per tour of £180). These costs included £60,000 which were fixed costs.

A local college wishing to send 200 students on an educational trip has offered Capital Tours £140 per tour.

Required

(a) Explain, with reasons, whether Capital Tours should accept the offer.

(b) Explain the danger, in the long term, of Capital Tours using prices based on variable (marginal) costing.

C   Problem solving and evaluation

C9.1 [S]

Dairyproducts Ltd has recently developed sales of cream in aerosol dispensers which are sold alongside the company's traditional products of cartons of cream and packets of cheese. The company is now considering the sale of cream cheese in aerosol dispensers.

It is company policy that any new product must be capable of generating sufficient profit to cover all costs, including estimated initial marketing and advertising expenditure of £1,000,000.

Current weekly production, with unit costs and selling prices, is as follows:

	Units of output	Variable cost (£)	Fixed cost (£)	Selling price (£)
Cartons of cream	400,000	0.45	0.15	0.75
Aerosol cans of cream	96,000	0.50	0.25	1.05
Packets of cheese	280,000	1.00	0.20	1.30

Sales volume is equal to production volume. A 50-week trading year is assumed. Rates of absorption of fixed costs are based on current levels of output.

In order to produce cream cheese in aerosol dispensers, the aerosol machine would require modification at a cost of £400,000 which is to be recovered through sales within one year. Additional annual fixed costs of £500,000 would be incurred in manufacturing the new product. Variable cost of production would be 50 pence per can. Initial research has estimated demand as follows:

Price per can (£)	Maximum weekly demand (cans)
1.50	60,000
1.40	80,000
1.15	100,000

There is adequate capacity on the aerosol machine, but the factory is operating near capacity in other areas. The new product would have to be produced by reducing production elsewhere and two alternatives have been identified:

(a) reduce production of cream cartons by 20 per cent per annum; or
(b) reduce production of packet cheese by 25 per cent per annum.

The directors consider that the new product must cover any loss of profit caused by this reduction in volume. They are also aware that market research has shown growing customer dissatisfaction because of wastage with cream sold in cartons.

Required

Prepare a memorandum to the board of directors of Dairyproducts Ltd showing the outcome of the alternative courses of action open to the company and make a recommendation on the most profitable.

C9.2

A company is able to sell four products and is planning its production mix for the next period. Estimated costs, sales and production data are:

Product	L £	M £	N £	O £
Selling price per unit	60	90	120	108
Less Variable costs				
Labour (at £6 per hour)	18	12	42	30
Material (at £3 per kg)	18	54	30	36
= Contribution per unit	24	24	48	42
Resources per unit				
Labour (hours)	3	2	7	5
Material (kg)	6	18	10	12
Maximum demand (units)	5,000	5,000	5,000	5,000

Required

(a) Based on the foregoing information, show the most profitable production mix under each of the following mutually exclusive assumptions:

    (i) if labour hours are limited to 50,000 in a period; or

    (ii) if material is limited to 110,000 kg in a period.

(b) Write a short explanation, suitable for sending to the production director, explaining your recommendation in each case.

C9.3

You are employed as the accountant for Cars Ltd, a local garage which has a bodyshop. The bodyshop manager, Mr George, has contacted you saying that one of the company's present customers has offered the company a one-year contract for additional work. The customer requires a discount of 10% to be allowed on the total invoice value. Mr George provides you with the following information:

1 Additional capital expenditure will be:

	£
Video conferencing facility	10,000
Additional storage trolleys	5,000
Computerised estimated system	10,000

The customer insists on installation of the video conferencing facility which will not be usable for any other contract. The storage trolleys and estimating system may be used on other work after the end of this particular contract.

2 Additional staff will be required. Three full-time skilled technicians earning £8.00 per hour will each work 39 hours per week on the new contract. They are each allowed 6 weeks per year paid holidays and 2 weeks paid training. Labour efficiency is 95% measured as the ratio of sold hours/hours attended. Training time and holiday time are charged to direct costs of the department. For each technician the new contract will leave some unsold hours available for any other jobs coming into the bodyshop. One full-time car cleaner will be required earning £10,500 per annum.

3 The customer has said that the potential increase in sales due to chargeable hours from this contract could be 4,500 hours at a rate of £20.00 per hour before discount. In addition the increase in sales of car parts is calculated on the basis of £40.00 per hour with an average gross profit of 15% before discount. The increase in paint sales is calculated on the basis of £3.50 per hour with an average gross profit of 40% before discount.

4 Additional annual overheads will be as follows:

	£
Variable costs	5,500
Fixed costs	6,500

5 Depreciation is calculated on a straight line basis as follows:

	%
Storage trolleys	20
Computers	25

Mr George has asked your opinion on the acceptability of the customer's proposal.

Required

Write a memo to Mr George:

(a) assessing the financial aspects of the proposal; and

(b) commenting briefly on other considerations relevant to the decision-making process.

Case studies

Real life case studies

Prepare short answers to Case studies 9.1, 9.2 and 9.3.

Case study 9.4

Cans plc is developing a new form of 'crinkly can' for soft drinks. The crinkly can has grooves in the side which match the size of the fingers of a hand. The company's research and development department employs 50 people full-time and accounts for 2% of the company's costs. The design manager thinks that it may be important in future to develop special designs for particular commercial customers, even if this involves relatively small production runs and a higher price to the customer for each can. He said 'Our profit margins are not yet satisfactory. I would like to maintain our existing level of sales of the standard can at the standard price, but also take advantage of our design skills and sell additional cans of the new style cans in smaller batches but at a higher price.'

Explain the further information you would need in order to report on the benefits and problems for creating higher contribution margins and higher profit margins on the basis of the design manager's proposals.

Case study 9.5

Greetings Ltd operates a chain of shops selling birthday cards and related products. Each shop has a contribution target and a profit target. The monthly contribution target is calculated by deducting total variable cost of cards and related products from the total sales of the month. The profit target is calculated by deducting the shop's fixed costs (staff salaries, rent, business rates, insurance, heat and light) from contribution. The managers of each shop will earn a bonus if they exceed the contribution target or the profit target of the month. What actions can a shop manager take to exceed the targets set?

Chapter 10

Relevant costs, pricing and decisions under uncertainty

Real world case 10.1

This case study shows a typical situation in which management accounting can be helpful. Read the case study now but only attempt the discussion points after you have finished studying the chapter.

From April 2005 the Office of Gas and Electricity Markets (Ofgem) in the UK has put in place its British Electricity Trading and Transmission Arrangements (BETTA). The following article was written during the consultation period leading up to the implementation of BETTA.

It is an immutable physical fact of transmitting power by wire over long distances that costs rise and heat losses increase the further away you are from your customers. With 56% of existing UK generating capacity lying above a line between the Wash and the Severn, but 53% of the demand sitting below that line, Ofgem wants a pricing regime that encourages new generating plant to be built closer to where the main demand is.

But that ambition – in itself a thoroughly green approach to shaping future investment intentions – risks conflict with the government's determination to dramatically accelerate the share of UK electricity generation accounted for by renewable sources like wind and wave power.

The so-called locational pricing principle means generators furthest away from the main markets pay the biggest user charges, while those closest to the main centres of demand will, in some cases, attract a subsidy. So some of the generators paying the highest transmission charges will be the wind farms in the north of Scotland.

Ofgem [the price regulator] points out that a whole series of other charges – covering access to the transmission system, line losses and access to the interconnector – are all being abolished when BETTA comes into effect. Ofgem insists the net effect of even the current, unapproved, NGC pricing proposals on Scottish generators will be broadly neutral.

Source: *The Herald* (Glasgow), 20 January 2005, p. 24, 'Time for regime change if things can only get BETTA' Alf Young.

Discussion points

1 What are the cost-based arguments to support charging a higher price for carrying electricity longer distances?

2 What are the non-cost consequences of the decision to apply the 'locational pricing' principle?

Contents

Learning outcomes

After reading this chapter you should be able to:

- Explain the meaning of 'relevant costs' and show how relevant costs are used for analysis in decision making.

- Explain how pricing decisions may be related to cost considerations.

- Explain how uncertainty and risk can be incorporated in decision-making techniques.

- Describe and discuss examples of research.

10.1 Introduction

Chapter 9 showed how the distinction between fixed costs and variable costs allowed the use of relevant costs to help with decision making. The variable costs were relevant to a short-term decision, but the fixed costs were generally not relevant because they would continue regardless of what decision was taken. This chapter continues the explanation of the need to concentrate on relevant costs. This chapter also explains how pricing policies may be linked to cost considerations. Finally this chapter also explains how management accounting can help in organising the analysis where several options exist under conditions of uncertainty.

10.2 Relevant costs and revenues

When decisions are made, they relate to the future. Decisions will affect future costs and revenues of an organisation. Future costs and revenues will be **relevant costs** and **relevant revenues** in making a decision. Decisions can never change what has already happened. We may learn useful lessons from historical events but we can never change the costs and revenues of the past. To emphasise the non-relevance of the past, the term **sunk costs** is used to describe costs that have already been incurred.

Many decisions involve change. The costs and revenues will increase or decrease compared with the present position. This is called an 'incremental' change and so the decision requires analysis of incremental costs and revenues, or **incremental analysis**.

Making a decision about one course of action will often involve making another decision about *not* taking another course of action. The action not taken represents a lost opportunity. The benefit sacrificed with that lost opportunity is called an **opportunity cost**.

10.2.1 Definitions

Definitions

Relevant costs are the costs appropriate to a specific management decision. They are those future costs which will be affected by a decision to be taken. Non-relevant costs will not be affected by the decision.

Relevant revenues are the revenues appropriate to a specific management decision. They are those future revenues which will be affected by a decision to be taken. Non-relevant revenues will not be affected by the decision.

Sunk costs are costs that have been incurred or committed prior to a decision point. They are not relevant to subsequent decisions.

Incremental analysis means analysing the changes in costs and revenues caused by a change in activity.

Opportunity cost is a measure of the benefit sacrificed when one course of action is chosen in preference to another. The measure of sacrifice is related to the best rejected course of action.

10.2.2 Case study

Fiona McTaggart now explains how she advised on a decision where relevant costs and revenues were important considerations.

FIONA: *I have been working in a team advising an entrepreneur who wants to bring 'capsule' hotels to the business centres in our big cities. These capsule hotels provide sleeping pods which are prefabricated as self-contained units and then slotted together inside the shell of a hotel building. Each pod has a sofa that converts into a bed, a desk that swings out from the wall, and an ensuite mini-bathroom. The entrepreneur tells us that guests don't care about the amount of space when they are only staying for one night. He says people keep coming because of the quality of service. This idea has worked in Japan and with the right level of quality it ought to work here. The alternative is to use the hotel building shell to build a conventional budget hotel, so the opportunity cost is the lost revenue from renting rooms in a comparable budget hotel. The benefit of the capsule hotel is that it will give 20% higher occupancy rates for the same building space, so the decision is based partly on the incremental revenue available. The cost of the hotel building itself is a sunk cost because the entrepreneur already owns that. Relevant costs include the additional design costs in matching the sleeping pod to the requirements of business travellers in this country. The entrepreneur tells us there will be overall cost savings because the cost of constructing the pods will be less in total than the cost of refurbishing the existing hotel building to present-day standards. These are all relevant costs for the decision.*

The decision involves more than costs, of course. What appeals to business people in one country may not appeal to those in another. If it does succeed, then other operators may set up in competition, forcing down prices and squeezing profit margins. However, at this early stage it is important to reassure potential investors that the decision will bring incremental revenues that exceed the incremental costs sufficiently to reward the investment adequately.

10.2.3   Example

A ferry company knows that many of its customers are taking their cars to the continent by ferry but are returning by train through the Channel Tunnel. The company is considering whether or not to make a special offer of 'return journey for the price of a single journey' for a period of one month. It is predicted that this will attract 200 additional customers in the month but will lose the return fare portion of journeys by 50 existing customers. The net gain in fare revenue in the month is estimated as £3,750. Additional staff will be required to manage car flow at the port, but these staff can be transferred from other work to cover the additional activity during the month. It is estimated that the time they spend on this exercise will be worth £800 of their salary bill. The additional customers will spend money in the bar and restaurants during the ferry crossing. It is estimated that the additional gross profit will be £4,000 in the month. One additional catering employee will be hired from an agency at a cost of £600 for the month. Fixed overhead costs of £8,000 for the month will not be affected by the special offer. For the purposes of cost recording the fixed overhead will be apportioned over all journeys to give a cost per journey of £60.

The relevant benefits and costs are:

	£
Relevant benefits	
Incremental revenue from fares	3,750
Incremental revenue from catering	4,000
Relevant costs	
Incremental wages	(600)
Net incremental benefit	7,150

Note that time spent on this activity by car parking staff is not relevant because their salaries would be paid in any event. Also the allocation of fixed overheads is not relevant because these do not change as a result of the proposed course of action.

10.2.4   ## Method of analysis

In analysing the example for relevant and non-relevant costs and benefits ask yourself:

- Is this a future cost or benefit?
- Will the future cash flow change because of the decision?

The answer has to be 'yes' to both if the cost or benefit to be classed as 'relevant'.

The text of section 10.2.3 is set out in Exhibit 10.1 and marked up to show how you would highlight and analyse each cost and benefit in the narrative.

Exhibit 10.1
Analysis of text for relevant and non-relevant costs and benefits

A ferry company knows that many of its customers are taking their cars to the continent by ferry but are returning by train through the Channel Tunnel. The company is considering whether or not to make a special offer of 'return journey for the price of a single journey' for a period of one month. It is predicted that this will attract 200 <u>additional</u> customers in the month but will lose the return fare portion of journeys by 50 existing customers. The <u>net gain</u> in fare revenue in the month is estimated as **£3,750**. [YES] Additional staff will be required to manage car flow at the port, but these staff can be <u>transferred from other work</u> to cover the additional activity during the month. It is estimated that the time they spend on this exercise will be worth **£800** [NO] of their salary bill. The <u>additional customers</u> will spend money in the bar and restaurants during the ferry crossing. It is estimated that the <u>additional gross profit</u> will be **£4,000** [YES] in the month. One <u>additional</u> catering employee will be hired from an agency at a cost of **£600** [YES] for the month. Fixed overhead costs of **£8,000** [NO] for the month will <u>not be affected</u> by the special offer. For the purposes of the cost recording the fixed overhead will be apportioned over all journeys to give a cost per journey of **£60**. [NO]

It may be useful to use a table to compare two decisions using a table of the type set out in Exhibit 10.2:

Exhibit 10.2
Comparison table for two decisions

	Decision 1 *Make special offer*	Decision 2 *Do not make offer*	**Difference (relevant cost)**
Cost item 1: wages	+£800	+£800	0
Cost item 2: additional catering employee	+£600	–	+£600
Cost item 3: fixed overheads	+£8,000	+£8,000	0
Total relevant costs			+£600
Benefit 1: additional fare revenue	+£3,750	–	+£3,750
Benefit 2: additional bar gross profit	+£4,000	–	+£4,000
Total relevant benefits			+£7,750
Net gain/loss			+£7,150

10.2.5 Limitations of decision-relevant approach

An evaluation of relevant costs may involve considering the costs of alternatives that are not taken up. This information may be difficult to find. The manager making the decision must be careful to think about the time scale involved. In a short-term

---

Real world case 10.2

This extract discusses the costs that are relevant to an organisation that is already benefiting from relatively low labour costs.

In a vast sprawl of inter-linked factory buildings in southern China, 25,000 people are toiling to turn out tiny electric motors that are used in a variety of consumer and industrial products worldwide. Their labour underlines how the trend towards outsourcing in production – seized on by western manufacturers in recent years – makes very little sense for China's fast expanding economy.

The depth of manufacturing activity within the plant network in Shajing – run by Johnson Electric, the Hong Kong company – is so extensive that its workers even make small washers, in volumes running at 2bn a year, rather than follow the accepted route of buying such cheap and standardised components from outside groups . . .

. . . Johnson's 'do-it-yourself' approach is driven largely by two factors. First, China has relatively few small, technically advanced suppliers that are in a position to make components to the company's exacting requirements. Second, low labour costs at Shajing provide little incentive for Johnson to look for cheaper or more efficient subcontractors . . .

. . . Since the cost of employing the factory workers is very low – wages plus related costs come to roughly Rnb1,000 (£83) per month per person – these expenses account for only 5% of production costs at Shajing. Materials expenses comprise the rest.

The Hong Kong company routinely casts around for suppliers that can provide raw materials at a lower cost. However, there is a limit to which it can beat down prices of items that are largely sold as commodities. The skewed nature of the plant's cost structure provided little reason for Johnson to look closely at ways to reduce production costs by measures that are not linked to the wages of employees, such as by new assembly techniques or automating tasks.

Even so, the head of strategic marketing says, Johnson goes to some lengths to buy modern, highly accurate machines from well-known Japanese or European machine tool makers to cut costs of various in-house production steps. But the plant investment bill is, as is the case of factor labour costs, again much smaller than that for factory materials. 'I don't want to tell you the actual figure but [investment] costs are a lot lower than you might think,' says the head of strategic marketing.

Source: *Financial Times*, 28 September 2004, 'Motor maker that reversed expectations'.

Discussion points

1 What are the relevant costs that are used by Johnson Electric to justify continuing production in-house?

2 What are the non-cost factors that are relevant to Johnson's decision?

decision some costs may be non-relevant because they are fixed, but for a longer-term decision those costs would become relevant. Labour costs, for example, might not be relevant to a decision for a six-month project because the staff having the appropriate skills are already hired and must be paid. However, labour costs would become relevant to a decision for a six-year project because staff may have to be hired or replaced and will require training.

Non-financial factors may be important to a decision and may be relevant in the broader sense of maintaining good employee relations or maintaining a good reputation with customers.

Activity 10.1   *Think of a decision you have made recently, such as going on holiday or renting a new flat. What were the relevant costs and benefits that you considered in making the decision?*

10.3 Pricing decisions

One of the most important decisions taken by a business is that of pricing its product. If the price is too high, there will be no demand. If the price is too low, the organisation will be making a lower profit than could be achieved.

10.3.1 Economic factors affecting pricing

The method of arriving at a price depends on economic factors. If the business has a monopoly position (where one supplier has control of the market), it will be able to dictate its own price. However, the higher the price, the greater the attraction to incomers to break down the monopoly powers in seeking to share the benefits enjoyed by the monopolist.

Where the business is a market leader, it may be able to set its price by reference to covering its full costs and making a satisfactory profit. If there are only a few large sellers, each with a significant share of the market, the situation is described as an oligopoly. These few large sellers may compete with each other on price or they may prefer to set their prices at a level which covers all costs and to keep the price reasonably constant while competing on non-price factors such as quality of the product.

In a perfectly competitive market, no one supplier is in a position to dictate prices. Economic theory shows that the optimal price will be achieved where marginal cost equals marginal revenue. In other words, the additional cost of producing one more item of output equals the additional revenue obtained by selling that item. While the additional revenue exceeds the additional cost, the economist argues that it is worth producing more. When the additional revenue is less than the additional cost, production will not take place in the perfectly competitive market.

Pricing policy depends primarily on the circumstances of the business. In many situations there is strong competition and the organisation must accept the market price and try to maximise its profit by controlling cost. In that situation, the most efficient organisation will achieve the highest profit as a percentage of sales. Sometimes the organisation may be faced with pressure from customers to reduce selling price. The decision to do so will require an evaluation of the lower price against costs. In other cases, the organisation may have some ability to control price and therefore has to decide on a price related to what the market will bear and related to covering its costs.

There are therefore some situations in which a full cost pricing formula may be appropriate. These are now considered.

10.3.2 Full cost pricing

Full cost pricing is also called **cost-plus pricing**. The manager who is setting the price for goods or services calculates the total cost per unit of output and adds a percentage to that cost called the **percentage mark-up on cost**.

Calculation of total cost requires allocation of overhead costs. It was shown in Chapter 4 that there is more than one method of allocating production overhead costs. The same variety of method may be found in allocation of non-production overhead. Different organisations will have different ideas on which costs they want to cover in a full cost pricing approach. What really matters is that the organisation understands its cost structure and ensures that all overhead costs are covered in some way by revenue in the longer term.

When the company is a price taker and is asked to take a lower price, or not to raise its existing price, then full cost pricing is still important, but it is also important for the organisation to ensure that it makes a decision using relevant costs. If the pricing decision is based on a short-term perspective, then the organisation may decide to accept any price provided that the additional revenue covers the variable costs. That is the accountant's version of the economist's rule that marginal cost should equal marginal revenue. In management accounting terms, the item should make a contribution to fixed costs but does not necessarily need to cover all fixed costs. In the longer term, the business must cover all costs, whether fixed or variable, but it is possible that some fixed costs may be avoidable. If, for example, a reduced price is forced upon the business, it may accept this in the short term, but may also take a long-term decision to cut back on permanent staff and rental of premises. Such a decision may be unpleasant to take, in terms of human consequences for staff, but may allow the business to survive in a harsher economic situation.

10.3.3 Sales margin pricing

Section 10.3.2 explains how a percentage mark-up is applied to cost. Some business managers express the desired profit percentage in a different way. They might say 'we aim to achieve a 20 per cent margin on sales'. That means they want a profit that is 20 per cent of the *selling price*. So what percentage must be added to *cost price*? The answer is 25 per cent of the cost. Check the following calculation:

	£	
Selling price	100	
Cost	80	
Profit	20	which is 25% of £80

If you are given a sales margin percentage and asked for the percentage on cost, use the following pattern:

What is the percentage on cost equivalent to a sales margin of 30%?

	£	
Imagine a selling price of £100	100	(A)
Calculate the profit based on the sales margin, 30%	30	(B)
Deduct to give the cost	70	(C)

Divide (B) by (C) and express as a percentage $\dfrac{30}{70} \times 100 = 42.8\%$ of cost

A sales margin of 30% is equivalent to 42.8% on cost.

The answer can also be calculated as:

$$\frac{\text{sales margin}}{100 - \text{sales margin}} \times 100 = \frac{30}{100 - 30} \times 100 = 42.8\%$$

10.3.4   Mark-up percentages

The full cost approach to pricing requires a percentage to be added to cost. Where does this percentage come from? The answer is that it depends very much on the type of business and the type of product. Where the market is competitive, mark-up percentages will be low and the organisation relies for its success on a high volume of sales activity. This may be seen in the operation of supermarkets, which charge lower prices than the small shops and therefore have lower margins on the items sold, but customers take away their purchases by the car load rather than in small parcels. In the case of supermarket chains there is another aspect to pricing in that they themselves buy from suppliers. The supermarkets may use the strength of their position to dictate price terms to the suppliers, so that the margins are not as low as they would seem from the prices charged to the customers.

In some industries, or for some products, there appears to be a 'normal' mark-up which all companies apply fairly closely. This 'normal' mark-up may be so characteristic that it is used by the auditor as a check on how reasonable the gross profit amount appears and is also used by the tax authorities as a check on whether all sales and profit are being declared for taxation purposes.

For those businesses which are in a position to apply full cost pricing, it may encourage stability in the pricing structure because other businesses in the same industry may be in a position to predict the behaviour of competitors. Companies in an industry will know the mix of variable and fixed costs in the industry and will therefore have a good idea of how competitors' profits will be affected by a change of price.

10.3.5   Limitations of full cost pricing

Full cost pricing, used without sufficient care, may not take into account the demand for the product. A business may charge a profit margin of 20 per cent on sales when market research could have shown that the potential customers would have accepted up to 25 per cent as a profit margin and still bought the goods or services.

Apportionment of fixed costs is an arbitrary process, with more than one approach being available. The profit estimated using the cost-plus basis will depend on the apportionment of fixed costs. If the price is distorted by the costing process, an optimal level of sales may not be achieved.

There may be a lack of benefit to customers where businesses are able to set prices on a cost-plus basis and, as a consequence, a group of companies works together to 'agree' a price. Such a situation is described in economics as a 'cartel', and in some situations a government will legislate against price fixing by cartels because it creates a monopoly position in a situation which appears at first sight to be competitive.

10.3.6   Marginal cost pricing

Chapter 9 showed that, in the short term, a business may decide to accept a price that is lower than full cost providing the price offered is greater than the variable cost, so that there is a contribution to fixed overhead costs. This reflects the economist's position that a business will continue to sell providing the marginal revenue exceeds the marginal cost. It is therefore called marginal cost pricing. The most likely situation is that a customer, knowing that the business has spare capacity, will offer a contract at a reduced price to take up some of the spare capacity. The manager will accept the offer provided there is a contribution to fixed costs and profits and providing no additional fixed costs are incurred because of the extra contract.

10.3.7   A range of prices

Full cost pricing and marginal cost pricing are two extremes of a range of potential prices. If the business is a market leader, even where there is competition from other suppliers, the business may be able to charge a higher price (a premium) for its reputation or quality. Customers will pay more for a Coca-Cola than for a supermarket's 'own brand' cola drink. This is called **product differentiation**.

A business may lower its prices below those of competitors for a short period to gain market share and hopefully retain customer loyalty when prices start to increase again. This is seen when two bus companies are competing for business on a well-populated route.

The **product life cycle** will also have an influence on the price that can be obtained. When a product is relatively new there will be a period when customers are learning about it. The price will be low relative to the market and costs will be high because of development and marketing costs. As the product becomes better known, the volume of sales will increase but profits will still be relatively low because of continued marketing costs. As the market matures the rate of increase in sales will slow down to a steady state. Profits will increase because the heavy start-up costs have been recovered and the business begins to benefit from the economies of scale. Eventually the market becomes saturated, perhaps because competitors start to produce similar products. The price becomes closer to marginal cost. Finally the product declines in popularity and sales volumes decrease even when prices are reduced, because customers no longer want the product. This product life cycle is particularly visible in the pharmaceuticals industry when new medicines are developed, or in the motor industry when a new car comes to the market.

Real world case 10.3

The National Farmers' Union (NFU) has a long-standing concern about obtaining a fair price for dairy farmers who sell milk to the major supermarket chains and similar outlets.

NFU Scotland is continuing its campaign for higher milk prices by writing to all the major supermarkets, processors and co-operatives pointing out producers have been hit by higher costs in recent months. Verbal commitments have now been secured from the major multiples and processors that the farm gate price must more fairly reflect production costs.

John Kinnaird, the president of NFUS, said: 'This is a justifiable cost recovery from the producer's perspective. We are acutely aware of the difficulties in ensuring price increases actually happen across all milk and dairy products.'

Source: *The Scotsman*, 19 January 2005, 'NFUS backs call for price hike'.

Discussion points

1 Why is the NFU (National Farmers' Union) arguing for full cost pricing?

2 What view would you take of price negotiations if you were advising the milk buyer of a major supermarket chain?

Activity 10.2

Write down two products or services where the pricing might be based on cost plus a percentage to cover profits. Write down two products or services where the prices are determined in a highly competitive market. Write a short explanation (100 words) for an employee newsletter in a soap manufacturing business explaining why your product price is always a few pence higher in the shops than that of other leading brands.

10.4 Decision making under risk and uncertainty

All the quantitative examples studied so far have assumed that forecasts of future cash flows can be made with certainty. In the real world that is rarely the case. When we talk about 'uncertainty' relating to making a decision we are thinking of more than one possible outcome from that decision but with little or no evidence on which to predict the actual outcome. When the experts talk about 'risk' relating to making a decision, it usually means that they can attach probabilities to the possible outcomes, based on statistical analysis of previous events. So when the weather forecaster says there is a five per cent risk of rain, it may well be based on analysis of records showing that the predicted pressures, temperatures and wind direction have previously been associated with rain in five cases out of 100.

Most forecasting in business is based on a mix of the evidence needed for statistical prediction of risk and the intuition that is often applied to decisions in the face of uncertainty. Rather than spend too much time debating the meanings of 'risk' and 'uncertainty' it is more important to be aware of the extent of the estimation involved and to ask questions about the basis on which probabilities are quantified.

It is also important to be aware of managers' attitudes to risk. Some will seek the safest options because they are **risk averse**. A person who is risk averse will choose the less risky of two choices that have equal money value. Others will seek the most likely outcome because they are **risk neutral**. A person who is risk neutral is prepared to accept the level of risk which accompanies the most likely outcome. Some may feel that they can balance taking risk with the potential for greater rewards and so are described as **risk seekers**. A person who is a risk seeker enjoys the thrill of higher risk because it is associated with higher rewards if successful (despite facing greater losses if not successful).

10.4.1 Best, worst and most likely outcome

One way of indicating the risk and uncertainty relating to a proposed decision is to estimate a range of outcomes. Managers are asked 'what is the best outcome, what is the worst outcome, and what is the most likely outcome?' This is sometimes called three-level analysis.

Suppose that the manager of a town council's refuse collection and disposal department has been asked to make a decision on the allocation of the departmental budget for the year ahead. There are three possible states of demand, depending on factors beyond the control of the manager:

1 There is a possibility that the government will put in place a national campaign to encourage recycling.
2 There is a possibility that the government will do nothing about recycling and the number of households in the town remains the same.
3 There is a possibility that the government will do nothing about recycling and a new housing development will be completed faster than expected.

The manager estimates demand under each of these three possible states, in terms of wheelie bins per week for emptying as shown in Exhibit 10.3.

Exhibit 10.3
Estimates of demand for refuse collection

Outcome	Condition	Predicted bins per week for emptying
Worst possible	No government campaign for recycling, plus higher than expected increase in house completion	100,000
Most likely	Normal conditions, based on no government campaign and no change in housing completion	80,000
Best possible	Government's national campaign to encourage recycling	70,000

There is another factor beyond the control of the manager. There is a labour dispute in progress, so the manager has to make a range of estimates of the labour cost of collecting and emptying one wheelie bin. The council finance committee has threatened to impose a pay freeze and then make the local award for the final six months only. If the opposition councillors win the debate in the finance committee the local pay award will be made at the start of the year. A more expensive possibility is that the major unions will force a relatively higher national pay increase taking effect at the start of the year under budget. The estimates are shown in Exhibit 10.4.

Exhibit 10.4
Estimates of cost per collection based on varying wage settlements

Outcome	Condition	Predicted labour cost per bin collected
Worst possible	National pay increase agreed at start of year	£0.50
Most likely	Normal conditions, local pay award at start of year	£0.35
Best possible	Pay freeze for 6 months, local award for next 6 months	£0.25

Combining the effects of government policy, house completions and labour negotiations, the best, worst and most likely outcomes are calculated in Exhibit 10.5.

The departmental manager who seeks to be cautious in budgeting might focus on the worst possible outcome and budget £50,000 per week. The finance department, in scrutinising the budget, would almost certainly say that they expect senior management to persist with the pay freeze and local award, so that the budget should include only £17,500, representing the best possible cost outcome. The employee representatives, taking part in the pay negotiations, would seek inclusion of £50,000 per week in the budget as an indication of management support for the national pay award rather than a locally determined, lower, award.

The three-way analysis provides a basis for discussing a range of outcomes but does not cover all combinations of demand and labour cost. Also it gives no feeling for the probability of the best, worst or most likely outcome occurring. The next section takes the analysis a stage further by adding probability estimates.

Exhibit 10.5
Best, worst and most likely outcomes

	Condition	Predicted cost per week
Worst possible	No campaign for recycling, plus higher than expected increase in house completion + National pay increase agreed at start of year	100,000 × £0.50 = £50,000
Most likely	Normal conditions, based on no government campaign, no change in housing completion, and local pay award at start of year	80,000 × £0.35 = £28,000
Best possible	Government campaign to encourage recycling + Pay freeze for 6 months, local award for next 6 months	70,000 × £0.25 = £17,500

10.4.2   Probability analysis

The manager is now asked to estimate probabilities of each of the possible outcomes occurring. The probabilities will reflect the manager's best view of the quantifiable risks and the potential effects of uncertainties. If there is strong evidence on which to base the estimates these will be **objective probabilities**. If there is a strong element of the manager's intuition these will be **subjective probabilities**. Although subjective opinions are based on judgment and lack strong supportive evidence, they may nevertheless be based on skilled judgment which is relevant and useful to a decision.

Definitions

> **Objective probabilities** are based on verifiable evidence.
>
> **Subjective probabilities** are based on opinions.

The probabilities are used to calculate expected inflow and expected outflow. The word 'expected' has a meaning from statistics as the weighted average of the predicted cash flow and the probability of each. The expected flow is calculated by multiplying each predicted flow by its respective probability and adding all the results. The probabilities must add up to 1.0 (indicating certainty) because it is certain that one of the three outcomes will happen.

The rules of probabilities allow Exhibit 10.6 and Exhibit 10.7 to be combined. It is important that the two sets of events are independent – the eventual wages settlement will not affect the number of wheelie bins emptied. Provided that condition is satisfied we can apply the rule of joint probabilities.

Definitions

> **Joint probabilities:** The probability of BOTH condition 1 AND condition 2 is calculated by MULTIPYING the two separate probabilities.

Exhibit 10.6
Estimates of demand for refuse collection

	Condition	Predicted bins per week for emptying	Probability
Worst possible	No government campaign for recycling, plus higher than expected increase in house completion	100,000	0.2
Most likely	Normal conditions, based on no government campaign and no change in housing completion	80,000	0.7
Best possible	Government campaign to encourage recycling	70,000	0.1

Exhibit 10.7
Estimates of cost per collection based on varying wage settlements

	Condition	Predicted labour cost per bin collected	Probability
Worst possible	National pay increase agreed at start of year	£0.50	0.4
Most likely	Normal conditions, local pay award at start of year	£0.35	0.4
Best possible	Pay freeze for 6 months, local award for next 6 months	£0.25	0.2

So the joint probability of BOTH (No campaign for recycling, plus higher than expected increase in house completion) AND (National pay increase agreed at start of year) is equal to 0.2 multiplied by 0.4, which equals 0.08.

In Exhibit 10.8, columns 1 and 2 are taken from Exhibit 10.6 and Exhibit 10.7 respectively. Column 3 is calculated by multiplying columns 1 and 2. The joint probabilities in column 4 are calculated by multiplying the separate probabilities from Exhibit 10.6 and Exhibit 10.7. The expected cost in column 5 is calculated by multiplying columns 3 and 4. The expected costs of each outcome are then added to give the total expected cost for the project.

The final line of Exhibit 10.8 gives the weighted average of all possibilities, which is called the 'expected cost'. It is not easy to interpret the weighted average because it is not a cost that will appear as a payment in the cash book. It is a combination of all the costs that might arise. If the manager uses £32,370 as the budgeted cost, it will represent all possible outcomes forecast. Intuitively it is a compromise value between the best and worst outcomes of section 10.4.2, taking account of relative probabilities of occurrence.

10.4.3   Decision trees

Suppose now the council says: 'We need to make a decision. Do we continue to operate our own refuse collection service or do we close down this operation and offer it to private tender?' The departmental manager is asked to present a decision analysis involving two choices – continue or close down.

Exhibit 10.8
Table of combined probabilities

Condition	Predicted bins per week for emptying (1)	Predicted labour cost (2)	Predicted cost (3)	Joint probability (4)	Expected cost (5)
No campaign for recycling, plus higher than expected increase in house completion	100,000	£0.50	50,000	.2 × .4 = .08	4,000
		£0.35	35,000	.2 × .4 = .08	2,800
		£0.25	25,000	.2 × .2 = .04	1,000
Normal conditions	80,000	£0.50	40,000	.7 × .4 = .28	11,200
		£0.35	28,000	.7 × .4 = .28	7,840
		£0.25	20,000	.7 × .2 = .14	2,800
Government campaign to encourage recycling	70,000	£0.50	35,000	.1 × .4 = .04	1,400
		£0.35	24,500	.1 × .4 = .04	980
		£0.25	17,500	.1 × .2 = .02	350
Total expected cost					32,370

Exhibit 10.9
Symbols for a decision tree

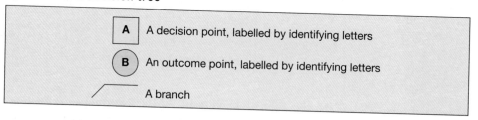

A decision tree is a map of all the possible outcomes. The symbols used in a decision tree are shown in Exhibit 10.9; Exhibit 10.10 shows the decision tree.

The 'close down' option shows a probability of 1 that the cost is zero. The 'continue' option shows three outcomes for demand, each combined with three outcomes for labour costs. There are nine branches coming out of the 'continue' option. For each branch an expected outcome is calculated. The calculations are shown in Exhibit 10.11. They are the same as the calculations in Exhibit 10.8.

The decision tree does not give any more information than the table in Exhibit 10.8, but it is helpful as a diagrammatic representation of the decisions and their effect. A decision tree is useful where there are two or three decisions to depict but, if there are more than that, there may be practical problems in setting them out on one sheet of paper.

Activity 10.3   *Think of a decision you have taken recently where there was some uncertainty at various stages of the process. How did you deal with the uncertainty? Could you represent the decision as a decision tree? What problems would you face in representing the decision as a decision tree?*

Exhibit 10.10
Decision tree for refuse collection decision

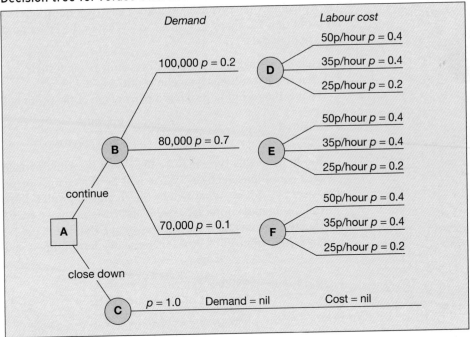

Exhibit 10.11
Expected outcomes for decision tree

Demand	Labour cost	Predicted cost (3)	Joint probability (4)	Expected cost (5)
100,000 p = 0.2 → D	50p/hour p = 0.4	50,000	.2 × .4 = .08	4,000
	35p/hour p = 0.4	35,000	.2 × .4 = .08	2,800
	25p/hour p = 0.2	25,000	.2 × .2 = .04	1,000
80,000 p = 0.7 → E	50p/hour p = 0.4	40,000	.7 × .4 = .28	11,200
	35p/hour p = 0.4	28,000	.7 × .4 = .28	7,840
	25p/hour p = 0.2	20,000	.7 × .2 = .14	2,800
70,000 p = 0.1 → F	50p/hour p = 0.4	35,000	.1 × .4 = .04	1,400
	35p/hour p = 0.4	24,500	.1 × .4 = .04	980
	25p/hour p = 0.2	17,500	.1 × .2 = .02	350
		Expected cost		32,370
p = 1.0 Demand = nil	Cost = nil	Nil	1.00	Nil

10.4.4   Sensitivity analysis

The availability of spreadsheets allows us to ask questions such as 'What is the effect on profit of a 1% change in sales?' or 'What is the effect on profit of a 1% change in costs of materials?'

1 What is the change in the cost or revenue being tested?
2 What is the resulting change in profit?
3 What is the resulting profit as a percentage of the profit before change?

4 Sensitivity factor $= \dfrac{\text{\% change in profit}}{\text{\% change in element being tested}}$

Questions of this type may be answered by using **sensitivity analysis**. This asks 'what if' questions such as: 'What will be the change in profit if the selling price decreases by 1%?' or 'What will be the change in profit if the cost increases by 1%?'

Assume an initial forecast of sales and costs as shown in Exhibit 10.12. The effect of a 1% increase in a variable cost is shown in Exhibit 10.13. A 1% increase in a fixed cost is shown in Exhibit 10.14. A 1% increase in contribution is shown in Exhibit 10.15.

Exhibit 10.12
Forecast of sales and costs

Transport service business: monthly forecast	
	£
Forecast sales	40,000
Forecast variable fuel costs	(15,000)
Forecast variable labour costs	(10,000)
Fixed costs	(5,000)
Profit	10,000

Exhibit 10.13
Effect of a 1% increase in variable cost

	£		£
Forecast sales	40,000		40,000
Forecast variable fuel costs	(15,000)		(15,000)
Forecast variable labour costs	(10,000)	+1%	**(10,100)**
Fixed costs	(5,000)		(5,000)
Profit	10,000		**9,900**

Percentage decrease in profit = 100/10,000 = 1%

So a 1% *increase* in a variable cost causes a 1% *decrease* in profit.

The sensitivity factor is −1

Exhibit 10.14
Effect of a 1% increase in fixed cost

	£		£
Forecast sales	40,000		40,000
Forecast variable fuel costs	(15,000)		(15,000)
Forecast variable labour costs	(10,000)		(10,000)
Fixed costs	(5,000)	+1%	**(5,050)**
Profit	10,000		**9,950**

Percentage decrease in profit = 50/10,000 = 0.5%

So a 1% *increase* in a fixed cost causes a 0.5% *decrease* in profit.

The sensitivity factor is –0.5.

Exhibit 10.15
Effect of a 1% increase in sales revenue and 1% increases in variable costs
(i.e. 1% increase in contribution)

	£		£
Forecast sales	40,000	+1%	40,400
Forecast variable fuel costs	(15,000)	+1%	(15,150)
Forecast variable labour costs	(10,000)	+1%	(10,100)
Fixed costs	(5,000)		**(5,000)**
Profit	10,000		**10,150**

Percentage increase in profit = 150/10,000 = 1.5%

So a 1% *increase* in forecast sales causes a 1.5% *increase* in profit.

The sensitivity factor is +1.5.

10.5 What the researchers have found

10.5.1 An economist's view of pricing decisions

Lucas (2003) compares the economist's view, which recommends a decision-relevant cost approach to pricing, with the business practice view, which is dominated by a full-cost approach to pricing. He argues that neither the economist's view nor the business practice view is strongly supported because the empirical evidence is conflicting. The evidence he cites is taken from previous papers, dating back to the 1970s and 80s.

He points out that leading management accounting text books have discussed the importance of using relevant costs for pricing decisions, but the same books have also referred to surveys showing the widespread use of full cost pricing. Econometric studies have, in some cases, shown support for full cost but, in other cases, support for marginal cost pricing. He reviews other forms of research, such as case studies, from various dates over a long time period, concluding that the empirical case is not clear.

10.5.2 Full cost pricing

Guilding *et al* (2005) reported a mailed survey of UK and Australian companies which asked about the importance of cost-plus pricing (full cost pricing). They found that companies attached importance to the idea of full cost pricing but actually applied it to a relatively small subset of their product and service lines. They found that the intensity of competition was positively related to the importance of full cost pricing. The authors discussed the heightened awareness of costs in a competitive situation and the need to ensure that those setting prices are aware of costs, whether or not this involves covering variable costs or full costs. The manufacturing sector attached relatively low importance to full cost pricing. The authors suggested that in manufacturing business it is relatively difficult to trace costs to products because of joint manufacturing costs and relatively high overheads.

10.5.3 Establishing relevant costs

Lowson (2003) explained the problems of determining the true cost of obtaining clothing from countries which have low labour costs. The hidden costs include delays in supply, the use of airfreight, administrative and quality costs. The inflexibility costs involve issues such as longer lead times and a general inflexibility in responding to changes in customer demand. Lowson then modelled the costs, checking the model through interviews with a retailer who was purchasing clothing from overseas suppliers. The fundamental quantities described were the lead time for supply, the inventory in the pipeline at any stage, the customer service level and the supplier performance. Lowson's research was reported as a stage of continuing development in modelling the costs relevant to the situation, but was limited to the one industry of clothing supply.

10.5.4 Challenging the predictive ability of accounting techniques

Cooper *et al* (2001) consider the ways in which accounting is used as a technology for planning and control and the problems involved in using accounting information for planning organisational decision making. They suggest that the use of accounting techniques resembles the use of a ritual to maintain social cohesiveness. Accounting creates an image of the organisation and helps to create a culture for the organisation. When accounting techniques are used to make predictions or look forward in decision making, they are doing so in the face of uncertainties that put limitations on the predictions or decisions. The authors say that the real purpose of using predictive accounting techniques is to bind the organisation as a whole to focusing on the future.

10.6 Summary

Key themes in this chapter are:

- **Relevant costs** and **revenues** are those that make a difference in respect of a decision. **Sunk costs** are not relevant because future actions cannot change the fact that such costs have been incurred. **Incremental costs** and **incremental revenues** allow calculation of the additional profit available from a new venture. **Opportunity cost** reflects what might have taken place.

- In decision making it requires those who understand the operations of a business to decide on cost structure.

- Pricing decisions may be related to cost if the market accepts **full cost pricing** (e.g. with a professional business where customers or clients seek out the personal service.

- Pricing decisions may be related to **marginal cost** if there is heavy competition and manufacturers take whatever price they can get in the market.

- Decision making under uncertainty requires the estimation of a range of outcomes each with its own probability. One simple approach is the three-level analysis which asks 'what is the best outcome, what is the worst outcome, and what is the most likely outcome?'

- Probabilities can be attached to predicted outcomes using either **objective probabilities** based on verifiable evidence or **subjective probabilities** based on opinions.

- Where an outcome takes the form 'both . . . and', the probabilities are multiplied.

- Uncertainty and risk can be incorporated in decision making by **sensitivity analysis**.

References and further reading

Cooper, S., Crowther, D. and Carter, C. (2001), 'Challenging the predictive ability of accounting techniques in modelling organizational futures', *Management Decision*, 39(2): 137–146.

Guilding, C., Drury, C, and Tayles, M. (2005) 'An empirical investigation of the importance of cost-plus pricing', *Managerial Auditing Journal*, 20(2): 125–137.

Lowson, R.H. (2003) 'Apparel sourcing: assessing the true operational cost', *International Journal of Clothing Science and Technology*, 15(5): 335–345.

Lucas, M. (2003) 'Pricing decisions and the neoclassical theory of the firm', *Management Accounting Research*, 14: 201–217.

QUESTIONS

The Questions section of each chapter has three types of question. 'Test your understanding' questions to help you review your reading are in the 'A' series of questions. You will find the answer to these by reading and thinking about the material in the text book. 'Application' questions to test your ability to apply technical skills are in the 'B' series of questions. Questions requiring you to show skills in problem solving and evaluation are in the 'C' series of questions. The symbol [S] indicates that a solution is available at the end of the book.

A Test your understanding

A10.1 What is a relevant cost? Give an example (section 10.2).

A10.2 What is a relevant revenue? Give an example (section 10.2).

A10.3 What is a sunk cost? Give an example (section 10.2).

A10.4 What is incremental analysis (section 10.2)?

A10.5 What is an opportunity cost? Give an example (section 10.2).

A10.6 What is the method used in analysing relevant and non-relevant costs (sections 10.2.2 to 10.2.4)?

A10.7 What are the limitations of the decision-relevant approach (section 10.2.5)?

A10.8 Explain how economic factors usually dictate prices of goods and services (section 10.3.1).

A10.9 Explain the situations where full cost pricing may be appropriate (section 10.3.2).

A10.10 Show that a sales margin of 10% is equal to 11% on sales (section 10.3.3).

A10.11 When may mark-up percentages be applied in pricing (section 10.3.4)?

A10.12 What are the limitations of full cost pricing (section 10.3.5)?

A10.13 Explain marginal cost pricing (section 10.3.6).

A10.14 What is the 'three-way analysis' method of decision making under risk and uncertainty (section 10.4.1)?

A10.15 What is an objective probability (section 10.4.2)?

A10.16 What is a subjective probability (section 10.4.2)?

A10.17 What is the rule for joint probabilities 'both . . . and' (section 10.4.2)?

A10.18 What is a decision tree (section 10.4.3)?

A10.19 What is sensitivity analysis (section 10.4.4)?

A10.20 What is a sensitivity factor (section 10.4.4)?

B   Application

B10.1 [S]

A hardware store is considering purchasing the shop next door to expand capacity. The shop next door will cost £140,000 to buy. The cost of the existing shop was £80,000 but it would now sell for £120,000. Fittings in the existing shop will be sold for £5,000 and a new refit for both shops together will cost £20,000. The cost of the refit will be depreciated at a rate of £4,000 per annum. The new shop will be depreciated by £7,000 per annum.

The employment cost of the manager of the existing shop is £30,000 per annum. She will spend half her time on the new part of the expanded shop. An additional part-time assistant will be employed at a cost of £12,000 per annum. Heating and lighting for the new shop space will cost £6,000 per annum but there will be a saving of £1,000 on the fixed costs of the heating and lighting contracts for the existing shop.

Required
(1) Explain the meaning of 'relevant costs'.
(2) Explain the use of relevant costs in making the decision on whether to expand the hardware shop.

B10.2 [S]

An outdoor pursuits centre is planning for the year ahead. There is a possibility that the government will give additional funds to the education budget under an 'active and healthy' policy. There is also a possibility that this money will be diverted for other use and as a result the local councils will cut back on funds for outside activities. Normal conditions will mean that neither of these extremes occurs.

	Condition	Predicted demand (pupil days)	Probability
Worst possible	Councils cuts back funds for activities	5,000	.4
Most likely	Normal	6,000	.3
Best possible	Schools 'active and healthy' programme	8,000	.3

The outdoor pursuits centre is facing three possible levels of surplus (fees minus costs) per pupil day. If new safety regulations are implemented from the start of the year more staff will be required, reducing the estimated surplus per day. If the long-term weather forecast is poor, bookings will be lower.

	Condition	Predicted surplus per pupil day	Probability
Worst possible	New safety regulations and poor weather forecast	£1.00	.2
Most likely	New safety regulations and reasonable weather	£1.50	.2
Best possible	Safety regulations delayed and reasonable weather	£2.50	.6

Required
(1) Evaluate the cost of all options, based on combining probabilities.
(2) Draw a decision tree for the choice: 'keeping open the outdoor centre versus closing down'.

B10.3 [S]
A souvenir shop makes the following forecast for one year's sales and costs.

Forecast	£
sales	80,000
variable costs of souvenirs purchased	(26,000)
fixed labour costs	(30,000)
other fixed costs	(5,000)
Profit	19,000

Required
Prepare tables showing the sensitivity of the profit forecast to each of the following:

(a) a 1% change in sales and variable costs,
(b) a 1% change only in the materials cost of souvenirs purchased,
(c) a 1% change only the labour costs, and
(d) a 1% change only in the other fixed costs.

C Problem solving and evaluation

C10.1
The directors of Hightown United Football Club Ltd are preparing for a meeting with their bank manager to discuss the availability of funds to be used to buy new players.

The following information is available:

1 The Hightown United stadium is divided into three separate spectator areas:

	Spectator entry fee per person £	Attendance norm
Ground	3.00	70% of crowd
Enclosure	4.00	20% of crowd
Stand	5.00	10% of crowd

2 Other income:
   Sponsorship: £100,000 fixed fee plus 5% of gross takings for each match.
   Advertising: £150,000 per year.
   Programmes and refreshments: 70 pence per spectator.
3 Cost of holding a match:
   Manning turnstiles: 15 pence per spectator.
   Police presence: £200 per 1,000 spectators.
   Advertising and crowd entertainment: £1,000 per match.

If a match is cancelled, turnstile manning and police costs are not incurred but the cost of advertising and crowd entertainments will be paid in advance and will not be recoverable.

4 Other annual running costs:

	£
Staff salaries	900,000
Rates and ground costs	200,000
Travel	150,000
Other	300,000

5 Expected attendances:

	Home games	Spectators per game
League	20	16,000
Cup	4	12,000
European trophy	2	25,000

The number of games predicted for the Cup and European Trophy matches is based on average past performance. At worst the team might play only one home game in each competition.

The bank manager has asked that the following information be provided for the meeting:

1 A statement showing the budgeted surplus expected to be generated during the forthcoming season.
2 A calculation of the percentage fall in average attendances which could be tolerated before reaching a break-even point.
3 A calculation of the percentage increase which would have to be applied to spectator charges to maintain the budgeted surplus if all expenses were 10% higher than budget but advertising revenue and the fixed sponsorship fee did not increase.

Required
Prepare a report for the directors, containing the information requested by the bank manager and identifying any limitations of the analysis carried out.

C10.2

Cleancloths Ltd has two production lines. One line produces Supersnake, an absorbent double strength cloth which soaks up spillage of industrial liquids. Supersnake cannot be sold for domestic use. The other production line manufacture rolls of absorbent cloth for domestic use.

The directors recently considered the following budget for the Supersnake production line for the year ending 31 March Year 5:

		£
Sales (600,000 units at £5 per unit)		3,000,000
	£	
Material (6,000,000 metres)	1,800,000	
Labour	420,000	
Packaging material	180,000	
Variable overhead	540,000	
Fixed overhead	480,000	
		3,420,000
Loss		(420,000)

The budgeted loss has caused the directors a great deal of concern. They are aware that future demand for Supersnake is uncertain because of new competition in the industrial cleaning market.

The directors have asked you, as the newly appointed management accountant, to investigate two alternative plans:

Plan A: Avoid the budgeted loss by closing the Supersnake production line on 31 March Year 4.
Plan B: Continue production for a further year and close the Supersnake production line on 31 March Year 5.

You have discovered the following information during your investigation:

1 Each unit of Supersnake contains 10 metres of material. It is estimated that at 31 March Year 4 Cleancloths Ltd will have in stock 1,000,000 metres of Supersnake material which would be unsuitable for domestic use. It could be sold for waste at a price of 5 pence per metre.

2 Packaging material for 200,000 units will be in stock at 31 March Year 4. As it is already printed it would have to be scrapped if production ceased on that date. Disposal costs would be negligible.

3 The machine used on the Supersnake production line is five years old. It originally cost £700,000 and is being depreciated on a straight line basis over a ten-year life with no scrap value expected at the end of that time. Depreciation is included in the variable overhead costs in the budget. It is estimated that the machine could be sold for £200,000 on 31 March Year 4. Continued use during the year to 31 March Year 5 would reduce the selling price by £7,000 for every 200,000 units of Supersnake produced.

4 The production manager of the Supersnake line has given notice of his intention to leave on 31 March Year 4. His salary cost of £35,000 per annum is included in the fixed overhead costs. If production were to continue to 31 March Year 5 a temporary supervisor would have to be hired at an estimated cost of £31,000 per annum.

5 Other fixed overhead costs comprise items which could not be avoided by closure of the Supersnake line.

6 Production and sales volumes will be equal throughout the year.

7 If production is to take place during the year to 31 March Year 5 it must be at one of three levels of output. The marketing manager has estimated the unit selling price which may be obtained for each of these alternative levels of output:

Production units to be sold	Selling price per unit (price for all units sold) £
200,000	5.20
400,000	5.10
600,000	5.00

8 Labour costs vary in proportion to output. Employees no longer required for production of Supersnake could be redeployed within the company at no extra cost.

Required

Prepare a report to the directors of Cleancloths Ltd on the relative costs and benefits of *Plan A* compared with *Plan B*.

Case studies

Real world cases

Prepare short answers to Case studies 10.1, 10.2 and 10.3.

Case 10.4

Leisure Furniture Ltd produces furniture for hotels and public houses using specific designs prepared by firms of interior design consultants. Business is brisk and the market is highly competitive with a number of rival companies tendering for work. The company's pricing policy, based on marginal costing (variable costing) techniques, is generating high sales.

The main activity of Home Furniture Ltd is the production of a limited range of standard lounge suites for household use. The company also offers a service constructing furniture to customers' designs. This work is undertaken to utilise any spare capacity. The main customers of the company are the major chains of furniture retailers. Due to recession, consumer spending on household durables has decreased recently and, as a result, the company is experiencing a significant reduction in orders for its standard lounge suites. The market is unlikely to improve within the next year. The company's pricing policy is to add a percentage mark-up to total cost.

Required

Explain why different pricing policies may be appropriate in different circumstances, illustrating your answer by reference to Leisure Furniture Ltd and Home Furniture Ltd.

Case 10.5 (group case study)

In groups of three, take the role of finance director, production director and sales director in a company manufacturing pressure die castings, gravity die castings and sand castings. The three types of casting are manufactured in different locations but each is no more than 20 miles from either of the other locations. All castings are brought to central premises for finishing treatment. The costs of materials are around 56 per cent of final sales price and the costs of labour are around 30 per cent of sales price.

The finance director has been asked to explain to the production director and the sales director the effect of measuring profit using variable costing rather than absorption costing. It is important to keep separate the profit on each of the three product types. The finance director should provide a short explanation and the production director and sales director should ask questions about anything which is unclear or omitted from the explanation. After the discussion is completed (say, 30 minutes in all), the group should make a presentation to the class outlining the nature of their discussion and the conclusion reached as to how profit for each product should be measured.

Case 10.6 (group case study)

Your company manufactures furniture units to customers' specifications. In groups of three, take the role of sales director, production director and finance director. You have met to decide on the price to be charged for each contract. The sales director aims to maximise revenue, the finance director seeks to maximise profit and the production director wishes to continue operating at full capacity. Discuss the approach you will take to deciding the company's pricing policy for the year ahead. Present to the rest of the class the arguments you will present to the entire board of directors.

Chapter 11

Capital investment appraisal

This case study shows a typical situation in which management accounting can be helpful. Read the case study now but only attempt the discussion points after you have finished studying the chapter.

John Armitt, chief executive of Network Rail, the 'not for dividend' successor to Railtrack as owner of the UK rail infrastructure, does not expect an ongoing review of the industry's performance payment system to produce any significant changes.

'The first half of 2004/5 marked the start of the new five-year regulatory period, which has put the company on a sound financial footing. Our new investment appraisal procedures are ensuring greater efficiency and maximising the effectiveness of every pound in the ground.' said Armitt.

Source: Network Rail's Armitt sees no change to performance payment system AFX Europe (Focus); 26 November 2004.

Discussion point

What questions would you ask in appraising investment in a railway track or a railway station?

Contents

Learning outcomes

After reading this chapter you should be able to:

- Explain the purpose of capital appraisal and the role of the management accountant.

- Explain the payback method and calculate the payback period.

- Explain and calculate the accounting rate of return.

- Explain and calculate the net present value of a project.

- Explain and calculate the internal rate of return of a project.

- Describe and discuss examples of research into the use of different forms of investment appraisal.

11.1 Capital project planning and decisions

The word 'capital' can have more than one meaning in accounting. In financial reporting in particular it is used to denote the finance provided to the business by owners and long-term lenders. Economists use the term 'capital' to refer to the fixed assets and working capital of a business which are purchased with the money provided by the owners and lenders. This chapter uses the term 'capital' in a manner similar to that used by the economists.

When the managers of a business make plans for the long term they have to decide whether, and how much, to invest in fixed assets and working capital to maintain or increase the productive capacity of the business. They will usually be faced with choices of projects available, each requiring a different type of investment, and with only a limited amount of finance available. They have to ask themselves a number of questions, including:

1 How many of the proposed projects are worth undertaking?
2 How much finance, in total, should we commit to new projects?
3 Where should the finance be obtained?
4 After the event, was the investment in the proposed project successful?

These questions cross an academic spectrum of study which begins in management accounting and ends in finance. The first and fourth of these questions are normally dealt with in management accounting textbooks, while the second and third form the focus of finance textbooks. Some books in either discipline will attempt to deal with all the questions. This chapter focuses on the first and fourth questions. It explains techniques that can be applied to evaluate ('appraise') an investment project in order to decide whether it is worthwhile to start the project.

Definition

> **Capital investment appraisal** is the application of a set of methods of quantitative analysis which give guidance to managers in making decisions as to how best to invest long-term funds.

11.1.1 The role of the management accountant in capital investment appraisal

The management accountant's role was set out in Chapter 1 as directing attention, keeping the score and solving problems. In **capital investment appraisal** it is the role of directing attention which is important. Information about proposed capital projects must be presented in a way which will direct management's attention towards the significant information for decision-making purposes. There will most probably be problems to solve in terms of gathering and presenting the information. After the project is implemented there will be a score-keeping aspect in terms of comparing the actual outcome with the plans and expectations.

This chapter concentrates on the techniques of presenting information so as to direct attention to the significant aspects of the capital project for decision-making purposes. It concludes with an explanation of how a project may be evaluated after it is completed (called a post-completion audit).

11.1.2 The assumptions adopted

Certainty of cash flows

This chapter makes the assumption that all future cash inflows and outflows of a long-term project may be predicted with certainty. Making an assumption of certainty may seem a rather unrealistic starting point, but it is necessary to do so in order to analyse the principles of capital investment appraisal without having too many real-world complications crowding in.

No taxes, no inflation

This chapter also assumes that there are no taxes and no inflation to cause prices to increase over the life of the project.

Timing of cash flows

For the calculations described in this chapter, simplifying assumptions are made about the timing of cash flows. In the payback method and the accounting rate of return the cash flows are assumed to be spread evenly throughout the accounting period. In the net present value method the cash flows are assumed to arise at one point in time, on the final day of the accounting period. These simplifying assumptions are necessary to allow simple models to be created for calculation. The unevenness of cash flows in practice is another real-world complication.

11.1.3 Making a decision on a capital investment

Chapter 1 contains a description of the processes of planning and control which are necessary for a systematic approach to making an investment decision in locating a new retail outlet. In general terms, that process is as shown in Exhibit 11.1.

To be successful the business must first of all discover projects which have the potential for success. All the management accounting in the world will not create a successful project. The successful entrepreneur is the person who has the flair and

Exhibit 11.1
Planning and control for a capital investment decision

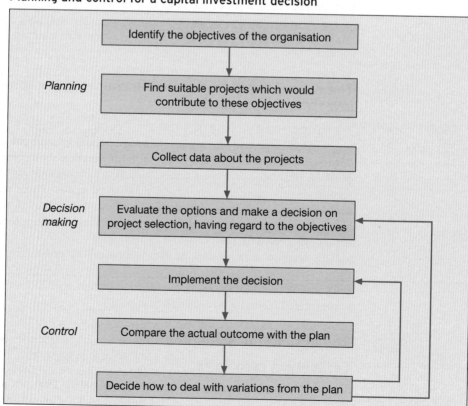

imagination to identify projects and to see how they might successfully operate. The role of management accounting, through the capital investment appraisal process, is to ensure that the excitement of creating new investment opportunities does not cause management to lose sight of the need to meet the organisation's objectives.

11.1.4 Selecting acceptable projects

Suppose there has been a meeting of the board of directors of a company at which the managing director has said: *'We want to ensure that any cash we invest in a project comes back as soon as possible in the form of cash flows which give us a profit overall and provide the cash to reinvest in the next project.'*

A second director has replied by saying: *'It's fine for you to talk about cash flows but the outside world judges our success by our profit record. I would like to see us choosing projects which maximise the return on assets invested in the project.'*

A third member of the board has joined in with: *'I agree with the cash flow perspective, but I want to be sure that, at the minimum, we cover the interest charges we have to pay on the money we borrow to finance the project. Ideally, there should be cash flows generated which exceed the cost of borrowing, so that we have surplus funds to use for investment in further projects or for increasing dividends to our shareholders.'*

Reading carefully what each has said, it is apparent that there are similarities and differences in the targets they would like to set. They are all looking to the cash flows that will be generated from the project, but the first director is emphasising the speed of collecting cash flows, while the second director wants to convert cash flows to profit by deducting depreciation, and the third director is more concerned about the amount of cash flows in total and whether they provide a surplus after covering all costs.

Management accounting can provide information for capital investment appraisal purposes which would satisfy the criteria set by any one of the three directors, but there would remain the question as to which of the three directors is using the best approach so far as the business is concerned. Four methods of capital investment appraisal will now be explained. These are: the payback method, the accounting rate of return, the net present value method and the internal rate of return method. Each management accounting technique will be described in turn and the advantages and disadvantages of each will be discussed.

Activity 11.1

Decide now which of the three directors you think has the most desirable approach and why you think that way. Then monitor the development of your views as you read the chapter.

11.2 Payback method

11.2.1 Method of calculation

The first director wanted cash invested in a project to come back as quickly as possible in the form of cash flows. To test whether this objective has been met by a capital project, the payback method of project appraisal is used. It provides a calculation of the length of time required for the stream of cash inflows from a project to equal the original cash outlay. The most desirable project, under the payback method, is the one which pays back the cash outlay in the shortest time. Data are set out in Exhibit 11.2 which will be used to illustrate all the capital investment appraisal methods explained in this chapter. An illustration of the payback calculation is provided in Exhibit 11.3, and from this table of calculations it may be seen that project A offers the *shortest* **payback period**. Thus, if the most important measure of success in investment is the recovery of the cash investment, then Project A is the preferred choice. Project C is next in rank and Project B is the least attractive.

Definitions

> The **payback method** of project appraisal calculates the length of time required for the stream of cash inflows from a project to equal the original cash outlay.
>
> The **payback period** is the length of time required for a stream of net cash inflows from a project to equal the original cash outlay.

Exhibit 11.2

Data for illustration of methods of capital investment appraisal

Data

A haulage company has three potential projects planned. Each will require investment in two refrigerated vehicles at a total cost of £120,000. Each vehicle has a three-year life. The three projects are:

A Lease the vehicles to a meat-processing factory which will take the risks of finding loads to transport and will bear all driver costs for a three-year period. Expected net cash inflows, after deducting all expected cash outflows, are £60,000 per annum.

B Enter into a fixed-price contract for three years to carry frozen foods from processing plants in the UK to markets in Continental Europe, returning with empty vehicles. This will require employing drivers on permanent contracts. Expected cash inflows, after deducting all expected cash outflows, are £45,000 per annum.

C Employ a contracts manager to find loads for outward and return journeys but avoid any contract for longer than a six-month period so as to have the freedom to take up opportunities as they arise. Drivers will be hired on short-term contracts of three months. Expected cash inflows, after deducting all expected cash outflows, are £40,000 in Year 1, £70,000 in Year 2 and £80,000 in Year 3.

Exhibit 11.3

Calculations for payback method

Cash flows	Project A	Project B	Project C
	£	£	£
Outlay	120,000	120,000	120,000
Cash inflows, after deducting all outflows of the year			
Year 1	60,000	45,000	40,000
Year 2	60,000	45,000	70,000
Year 3	60,000	45,000	80,000
Payback period	2 years	2.67 years	2.125 years
Workings	$60 + 60 = 120$	$45 + 45 + \dfrac{30}{45}$	$40 + 70 + \dfrac{10}{80}$

11.2.2 Impact of uncertainty in real life

This calculation assumes certainty about the cash flows predicted for each project. It also assumes that cash flows are spread evenly throughout the accounting period. Hopefully, as you were reading the conditions of the three different contracts set out in Exhibit 11.2, you had some thoughts about the relative commercial risk of each project and the risks attached to the cash flows. In this chapter we do not make allowance for the relative risks of each project, because we make an assumption of certainty of predicted cash flows but, in real life, Project C would be regarded commercially as the high-risk option, while projects A and B provide greater certainty through having contracts in place for the three-year period. Of these two, project B looks the less attractive but leaves opportunities for casual earnings if loads can be found for the return journey.

11.2.3 Usefulness and limitations of the payback approach

The payback method of capital investment appraisal is widely used in practice, possibly because it is relatively painless in its arithmetic. Furthermore, there is a reflection of commercial realism in concentrating on projects which give early returns of cash flow. That may be important to organisations which face cash flow constraints. It may also be seen as a cautious approach to take where product markets are uncertain and it is difficult to predict the longer-term cash flows expected from a product.

One major limitation of using the payback method of capital investment appraisal as described here is that it ignores the fact that investing funds in a long-term project has a cost in terms of the interest charged on borrowed funds (or interest forgone when money is tied up in fixed assets). Economists refer to this interest cost as the **time value of money**. This is the name given to the idea that £1 invested today will grow with interest rates over time (e.g. £1 becomes £1.10 in one year's time at a rate of 10%).

Definition

> The **time value of money** is the name given to the idea that £1 invested today will grow with interest rates over time (e.g. £1 becomes £1.10 in one year's time at a rate of 10%).

The cash flows earned from a project should repay the capital sum invested, but they should also be sufficient to provide a reward to investors which equals the interest cost of capital.

A second major limitation is that, in concentrating on the speed of recovery of cash flows, the method ignores any cash flows arising after the payback date. A project which would make a long-term contribution to the overall cash flows of the business could be sacrificed for short-term benefits in a project with a limited time horizon.

Activity 11.2

Check that you understand fully the calculation of the payback period and its interpretation. Check also that you can explain the meaning and usefulness of the payback period as a means of evaluating the suitability of a project.

11.3 Accounting rate of return

11.3.1 Method of calculation

The **accounting rate of return** differs from the payback method in using *accounting profits* rather than cash flows. The calculation of profits includes depreciation, which is an accounting allocation but has no cash flow effect. The attraction of using profit in a method of capital investment appraisal is that it links long-term decision making to profit as the conventional measure of success in business.

Definitions

> The **accounting rate of return** is calculated by taking the average annual profits expected from a project as a percentage of the capital invested.
>
> **Average annual profit** is calculated as average annual cash flow minus annual depreciation.

Some textbooks recommend as denominator the initial amount of capital invested while others suggest the use of the average capital invested. Calculation of the average involves making some arbitrary assumptions about the way capital is used up over the project. A simple pattern is to assume it is used up evenly. Suppose a project requires £1,000 invested at the start, there will be nothing left at the end and the capital is used up equally each year. Then the average investment is £500 (which is the average of £1,000 at the start and £nil at the end). This textbook will use the initial investment for illustrative purposes, but you should be aware that different definitions will be used in practice and it is important to know how any return on capital has been defined.

The data in Exhibit 11.2 may be used to illustrate the accounting rate of return as a method of capital investment appraisal. A straight-line method of depreciation is applied, assuming a zero residual value, so that depreciation of £40,000 per annum (calculated as £120,000/3) is deducted from cash flows. The resulting profits and accounting rate of return are shown in Exhibit 11.4.

Exhibit 11.4 shows that Project C has the highest rate of return, Project A is next in rank and Project B has the lowest rate of return. The accounting rate of return gives a ranking of the three projects different from that given by the payback method. Project B remains the least attractive but the positions of Projects A and C are reversed. C creates more cash flow in total, but the cash flows of A arise earlier than those of C.

Exhibit 11.4
Calculations for the accounting rate of return

Cash flows	Project A	Project B	Project C
	£	£	£
Outlay (a)	120,000	120,000	120,000
Profits, after deducting depreciation from cash flows			
Year 1	20,000	5,000	nil
Year 2	20,000	5,000	30,000
Year 3	20,000	5,000	40,000
Average annual profit (b)	20,000	5,000	23,000
Accounting rate of return (b × 100/a)	16.7%	4.2%	19.2%

11.3.2 Usefulness and limitations of accounting rate of return

The accounting rate of return is regarded as a useful measure of the likely success of a project because it is based on the familiar accounting measure of profit. It is also regarded as useful because it takes into the calculation all the profits expected over the project life (in contrast to the payback method which ignores all cash flows beyond the payback date). It assumes an even spread of cash flows throughout the accounting period.

A major defect of the accounting rate of return is that it ignores the time value of money. The time value of money means that there is greater value in a cash flow of £1 promised next year than in a cash flow of £1 promised in a later year. The accounting rate of return makes no distinction between two projects of the same average profit, one of which gives most of its profits at an early stage and the other of which gives most of its profits at a later stage.

A less serious defect, but nevertheless a limitation, is that the accounting rate of return depends on profit which, in turn, includes a subjective accounting estimate of depreciation. That may not matter too much in an example of the type illustrated in Exhibit 11.4, where average profits are used and straight-line depreciation is applied across all projects, but there could be situations where different depreciation policies could distort a decision based on the accounting rate of return.

Activity 11.3

Before proceeding further, make sure that you understand fully the calculation and usefulness of the accounting rate of return. Check also that you understand the limitations of relying on the accounting rate of return when evaluating a project.

Real world case 11.2

This extract from the annual report of Punch Taverns refers to 'return on investment' (ROI) as an alternative description of the accounting rate of return.

A further £48.7m was invested in the acquisition of 80 individual pubs during the year, together with investment of £46.2m on existing pubs within the estate and £5.0m on infrastructure. We continue to see excellent returns on our pub investments and good opportunities to develop our estate further. Of the £46.2m investment, £34.9m was spent on 580 profit enhancing projects (including 74 from the Pubmaster estate), generating a first-year pre-tax ROI of 29%.

Source: Punch Taverns plc, Annual report 2004, p. 16. www.punchtaverns.com

Discussion points

1 How will investors form a view on the accounting rate of return (ROI)?

2 How does the company reassure investors about the value of the investments in a non-quantified way?

11.4 Net present value method

The **net present value (NPV)** method of capital investment appraisal is a technique which seeks to remedy some of the defects of payback and the accounting rate of return. In particular it takes into account all cash flows over the life of the project and makes allowance for the time value of money. Before the net present value method can be explained further, it is necessary to say more about the time value of money.

11.4.1   Time value of money

If £100 is invested at 10 per cent per annum, then it will grow to £110 by the end of the year. If the £100 is spent on an item of business machinery, then the interest is lost. So the act of investing leads to a lost opportunity of earning investment. The idea of applying calculations of the time value of money is a way of recognising the reward needed from a project to compensate for the lost opportunity.

Suppose now that you have been given a written promise of £100 to be received in one year's time. Interest rates are 10 per cent. You do not want to wait one year to receive cash and would like the money now. What is the price for which you could sell that promise? Most students see the answer as £90.91 intuitively, but they do not all see immediately how they arrived at that answer. (It might be useful for you to think out your own approach before you read the next few paragraphs. It is much easier to work something out for yourself than to try remembering formulae which you will forget in a crisis.)

The intuitive answer is that £90.91 is the amount which, invested now at 10 per cent, would grow to £100 in one year's time. Provided the promise is a good one, there would be no problem in selling the £100 promise for £90.91 now. Both the buyer and the seller would be equally satisfied that the price reflected the time value of money.

Now make it a little harder. Suppose the promise of £100 was for payment in *two* years' time. What is the price for which you could sell that promise now? The answer is £82.64 because that would grow at 10 per cent to £90.91 at the end of one year and to £100 at the end of two years.

The calculation of the value of the promise today can be conveniently represented in mathematical notation as follows:

Definition

> The **present value** of a sum of £1 receivable at the end of n years equals:
>
> $$\frac{1}{(1 + r)^n}$$
>
> where r represents the annual rate of interest, expressed in decimal form, and n represents the time period when the cash flow will be received.
>
> The process of calculating present value is called *discounting*. The interest rate used is called the *discount rate*.

Using this **discounting** calculation to illustrate the two calculations already carried out intuitively, the present value of a sum of £100, due one year hence, when the **discount** rate (interest rate) is 10 per cent, is calculated as:

$$\frac{£100}{(1 + 0.1)^1} = £90.91$$

The **present value** of a sum of £100, due two years' hence, when the interest rate is 10 per cent, is calculated as:

$$\frac{£100}{(1 + 0.1)^2} = £82.64$$

The calculation using this formula is no problem if a financial calculator or a spreadsheet package is available, but can be tedious if resources are limited to a basic pocket calculator. In such circumstances, some people prefer to use tables of discount factors which give the present value of £1 for every possible rate of interest and every possible time period ahead. A full table of discount factors is set out in the appendix at the end of this chapter (p. 282). As an example from that supplement, the column for the discount rate of 10 per cent has the following discount factors:

At end of period	Present value of £1
1	0.909
2	0.826
3	0.751

Using the tables, for the discount rate of 10 per cent, it may be calculated that the present value of £100 receivable at the end of Year 1 is £100 × 0.909 = £90.90, while the present value of £100 receivable at the end of Year 2 is £100 × 0.826 = £82.60. (There is a difference in the second place of decimals when this answer is compared with the result of using the formula. The difference is due to rounding in the discount tables.)

In these calculations it is assumed that cash flows all arise on the final day of the relevant accounting period.

Now that you are familiar with the calculation of the present value of a promised future cash flow, the explanation of the net present value method of capital investment appraisal may be given.

Activity 11.4

Use your calculator to check the discount factors for the present value of £1 at the end of one year, two years and three years for a discount rate of 10%. Write a parallel table for 8% and 12%. Show that the discount factor decreases as the discount rate increases.

11.4.2 The net present value decision rule

The net present value (NPV) method of capital investment appraisal is based on the view that a project will be regarded as successful if the present value of all expected inward cash flows is greater than, or equal to, the capital invested at the outset. It is called *net* present value because, in calculation, the capital invested is deducted from the present value of the future cash flows. (Use of the word 'net' always means that one item is being deducted from another.) If the present value of the expected cash flows is greater than the capital invested, then the net present value will be positive. If the present value of the expected cash flows is less than the capital invested, then the net present value will be negative. A positive net present value indicates that the project should be accepted, while a negative net present value indicates that it should be rejected.

Definitions

The **net present value (NPV)** of a project is equal to the present value of the cash inflows minus the present value of the cash outflows, all discounted at the cost of capital.

Cash flows are calculated as profit before deducting depreciation and amortisation.

The NPV decision rule is as follows:

Definitions

Decision rule: NPV
- Where the net present value of the project is *positive*, accept the project.
- Where the net present value of the project is *negative*, reject the project.
- Where the net present value of the project is zero, the project is acceptable in meeting the cost of capital, but gives no surplus to its owners.

If an organisation seeks to maximise the wealth of its owners, then it should accept any project which has a positive net present value. If finance markets are working efficiently, funds will always be available to finance projects which meet or exceed their cost of capital.

11.4.3 The cost of capital

The rate of interest used in the calculation of net present value is called the discount rate. It is based on the cost to the business of raising new finance. This is called the **cost of capital**. If the project is to be financed only by borrowing from banks then the cost of capital is the rate of interest that a bank would charge for a new loan. If the project is to be financed only by issuing new share capital, then the cost of capital is the dividend yield required by investors. If the project is to be financed by cash that has been saved within the business, then the shareholders have allowed this saving rather than take a dividend, so the cost of capital is the opportunity cost reflected in the dividend yield.

When the business finances projects by a mixture of sources of finance, the cost of capital is a mixture of the related costs. It is calculated by a weighted average of the interest rate on loans and the dividend yield on share capital. The weights used are based on the relative amounts of loan finance and equity finance used by the company. If you study corporate finance you will learn more about estimating the weighted average cost of capital. Investors may expect a higher rate of return on their investment for a project of higher risk. The cost of capital may therefore depend on the risks associated with a project. For any exercise in this textbook you will be informed of the discount rate to be used.

11.4.4 Residual value

At the end of a project's life there may be cash flows that can be collected from sale of equipment or recovery of cash invested in inventories and debtors. Any cash flows from **residual value** should be included in the projected cash flows and discounted from the end of the project.

11.4.5 Illustration

The illustration in Exhibit 11.5 sets out the data for Project A taken from Exhibit 11.2. Exhibit 11.6 sets out the net present value calculation, assuming a discount rate of 10 per cent. Based on the net present value rule Project A will be accepted as it gives a positive net present value.

Exhibit 11.5
Data for net present value illustration

Cash flows	Project A £
Outlay	120,000
Cash inflows, after deducting all outflows of the year:	
Year 1	60,000
Year 2	60,000
Year 3	60,000

Exhibit 11.6
Calculation of net present value: Project A

Using the formula approach the net present value is calculated as:

$$\frac{£60,000}{(1.10)} + \frac{£60,000}{(1.10)^2} + \frac{£60,000}{(1.10)^3} - £120,000$$

$$= £54,550 + £49,590 + £45,080 - £120,000 = £29,220$$

Using the discount tables the net present value is calculated as:

End of year	Cash flow £	Discount factor	Present value £
0 Initial outlay	(120,000)	1.000	(120,000)
1	60,000	0.909	54,540
2	60,000	0.826	49,560
3	60,000	0.751	45,060
Present value of cash flows			149,160
Less initial outlay			(120,000)
Net present value			29,160

Rounding errors

The answer obtained from the discount tables (£29,160) differs marginally from that obtained from the formula (£29,220), because the discount factors are rounded to three decimal places. In many cases, such differences are marginal to the overall calculation and you should not worry about them. If, in any particular case, the rounding errors are likely to have an impact, then the formula should be used rather than the tables of discount factors. In real life it is questionable whether any decision should be based on fine-tuning of rounding errors. The conclusion should be clear from the overall magnitudes being calculated and should not be dependent on differences of very small magnitude.

Activity 11.5

If you have access to a spreadsheet package, find out whether it has a net present value (NPV) function. If so, use the data in Exhibit 11.5 to satisfy yourself that the spreadsheet produces answers similar to those derived here.

Cash flow patterns assumed by the net present value calculation

It is worth pausing to analyse the cash flow patterns which are assumed by the net present value calculation. This analysis helps in understanding when it is safe to use the net present value approach to capital investment appraisal and when it should be applied with caution.

Assume the investor who has provided the capital of £120,000 requires 10 per cent interest at the end of each year, to be paid out of the cash flows. Assume that any surplus cash flows are retained in the business and reinvested at 10 per cent. The accumulation of cash generated by the project is shown in Exhibit 11.7. The cash balance at the end of Year 3 is £159,000, out of which the original capital of £120,000 is repaid, leaving an actual surplus of £39,000. That surplus arising at the end of Year 3 has a present value of £29,000 (£39,000 × 0.751) which is the answer derived earlier by the net present value calculation (allowing for rounding differences).

Exhibit 11.7 is provided here to illustrate one of the assumptions of the net present value calculation which requires some thought. It assumes that surplus cash generated during the project can be invested at the cost of capital. Whether or not that is the case for a particular project is more an issue for study in the area of finance, but in real

Exhibit 11.7
Accumulation of cash during a project

Year	Balance of cash at start of year (1) £000s		Interest earned on balance invested (2) £000s		Cash flow (3) £000s		Interest paid (4) £000s		Balance of cash at end of year (1 + 2 + 3 − 4) £000s
1	nil	+	–	+	60	–	12	=	48
2	48	+	5	+	60	–	12	=	101
3	101	+	10	+	60	–	12	=	159

life it is rare that the interest earned on deposited funds is as high as that paid on borrowings. What is possible in many situations is that the surplus cash is used to start further projects in the business and those new projects are also successful in creating positive net present values of cash flows at the organisation's cost of capital.

Projects B and C

Now consider Projects B and C. The net present value of each project is calculated in Exhibit 11.8 and Exhibit 11.9.

Exhibit 11.8
Calculation of net present value: Project B

Using the discount tables the net present value is calculated as follows:

End of year	Cash flow £	Discount factor	Present value £
1	45,000	0.909	40,905
2	45,000	0.826	37,170
3	45,000	0.751	33,795
			111,870
Less initial outlay			(120,000)
Net present value			(8,130)

Exhibit 11.9
Calculation of net present value: Project C

Using the discount tables the net present value is calculated as follows:

End of year	Cash flow £	Discount factor	Present value £
1	40,000	0.909	36,360
2	70,000	0.826	57,820
3	80,000	0.751	60,080
			154,260
Less initial outlay			(120,000)
Net present value			34,260

Project C has the highest net present value, followed by Project A. Both would be acceptable because both have a positive net present value. Project B would be rejected because it gives a negative net present value.

In real life, obtaining finance may be difficult because of temporary imbalance in the capital markets or because the supply of capital within the organisation is constrained. If the organisation is in the public sector it may be subject to a cash limit of capital expenditure. If it is in the private sector and is a subsidiary or a division within a group, it may be restricted by the group's plans for total fund-raising by the group. Such practical problems are sometimes referred to as **capital rationing** and will lead to organisations devising decision rules for ranking projects. These ranking decisions will not be explored in detail here but it is important to note that any project which is rejected, when it has a positive net present value, will be a loss to the potential wealth of the owners of the business.

11.4.6 Impact of uncertainty

In real life it is unlikely that cash flows for each accounting period can be predicted with certainty. It is also unlikely that the cost of capital can be estimated precisely. One method of dealing with this kind of uncertainty is to carry out net present value calculations for a range of scenarios, using the 'best, worst, most likely' approach shown in Chapter 10.

11.5 Internal rate of return

Net present value is only one method in capital investment appraisal which takes into account the time value of money. The decision rule is based on the absolute amount of the net present value of the surplus generated by the project. There is some evidence from research into the practical use of capital investment appraisal techniques that decision makers feel more comfortable with a percentage rather than an absolute amount. (The reason is not so clear, but could be linked to the historical reliance on the accounting rate of return as a percentage.)

The **internal rate of return (IRR)** is another method in capital investment appraisal which uses the time value of money but results in an answer expressed in percentage form. It is a discount rate which leads to a net present value of zero, where the present value of the cash inflows exactly equals the cash outflows.

Definition

> The **internal rate of return (IRR)** is the discount rate at which the present value of the cash flows generated by the project is equal to the present value of the capital invested, so that the net present value of the project is zero.

11.5.1 Method of calculation

The calculation of the internal rate of return involves a process of repeated guessing at the **discount rate** until the present value of the cash flows generated is equal to the capital investment. That guessing may be carried out by computer, asking the computer to try values of the discount factor in the formula. Most spreadsheet computer packages have the facility to perform a calculation of internal rate of return once the initial investment and cash flows have been entered on the spreadsheet.

$$\text{Initial investment} = \frac{C_1}{(1+d)} + \frac{C_2}{(1+d)^2} + \frac{C_3}{(1+d)^3} + \cdots + \frac{C_n}{(1+d)^n}$$

That process of repeated guessing is extremely time-consuming if a computer is not used. Even where a computer is used, it needs to be provided with a first guess which is reasonably close. For a manual process of estimation it may be easier to use discount tables, with an aim of arriving at a reasonably close answer, rather than worrying too much about figures beyond the decimal point.

Take, as an illustration, the data on Project A of Exhibit 11.2, repeated in Exhibit 11.5. The starting point for calculating IRR is to find two values of NPV using discount rates lying either side of the IRR. Exhibit 11.10 sets out two such calculations. A first guess of 20 per cent produces a net present value which is positive. The aim is to find the discount rate which gives a zero net present value, so the first guess must have been too low and a higher discount rate of 24 per cent is used for the second guess.

Exhibit 11.10
Calculation of net present value at 20 per cent and at 24 per cent

	Cash flows £	Discount rate 20%	£	Discount rate 24%	£
End of Year 1	60,000	0.833	49,980	0.806	48,360
End of Year 2	60,000	0.694	41,640	0.650	39,000
End of Year 3	60,000	0.579	34,740	0.524	31,440
			126,360		118,800
Outlay			(120,000)		(120,000)
Net present value			6,360		(1,200)

The second guess was a fortunate one because the net present value changed from being positive at 20 per cent to being negative at 24 per cent. That means that the net present value of zero must be found at a discount rate between these two rates. If the second guess had failed to give a negative net present value, a further guess would have been required.

The actual discount rate which gives a zero net present value may now be found by assuming a linear interval between 20 per cent and 24 per cent. (The interval is not exactly linear but may be taken as approximately so over a narrow difference in rates.)

The difference between the two net present values is £6,360 − (−£1,200), that is £7,560. The difference between the two discount rates is four per cent and therefore, using simple proportion calculations, the net present value of zero lies at:

$$20\% + \left(\frac{6,360}{7,560} \times 4 \right) = 23.365\%$$

Exhibit 11.11 sets out the linear relationship which is assumed in the calculation. The process of estimation shown there is called *interpolation*. In words, the formula used in this calculation is:

$$\text{Lower of the pair of discount rates} + \left(\frac{\text{NPV at lower rate}}{\text{Difference between the NPVs}} \times \text{Difference in rates} \right)$$

Exhibit 11.11
Locating the internal rate of return between two discount rates of known net present value

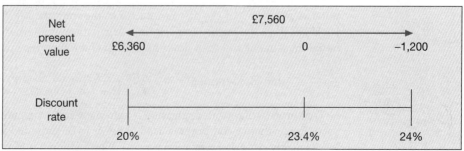

The internal rate of return answer, as produced by a computer package, is 23.375 per cent. The use of a simple proportion calculation appears to provide a good approximation.

If you have access to a computer spreadsheet package which has an internal rate of return function, test the data used in the chapter. It will ask you for a first guess and will then proceed to repeat the calculation of IRR until it arrives at a net present value of zero.

It is also possible to plot a graph of net present value against discount rate, as shown in Exhibit 11.12. The IRR is the discount rate at which the graph crosses the horizontal line representing zero net present value. That point is designated with a letter P in the graph and is shown to be around 23.4 per cent by a vertical dotted line from P to the horizontal axis.

Exhibit 11.12

Graph of net present value against discount rate showing internal rate of return

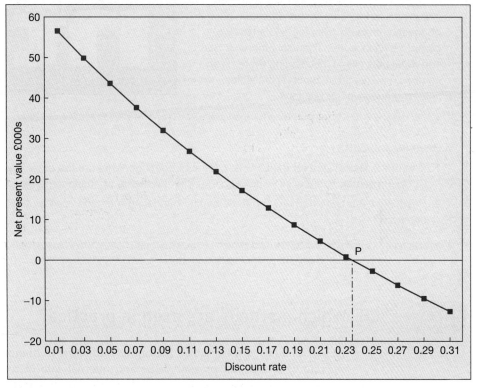

11.5.2 The internal rate of return decision rule

The decision rule is that a project is acceptable where the internal rate of return (IRR) is greater than the cost of capital. Under those conditions the net present value of the project will be positive. A project is not acceptable where the IRR is less than the cost of capital. Under those conditions the net present value of the project will be negative.

Definition

Decision rule: IRR
- Where the IRR of the project is greater than the cost of capital, accept the project.
- Where the IRR of the project is less than the cost of capital, reject the project.
- Where the IRR of the project equals the cost of capital, the project is acceptable in meeting the required rate of return of those investing in the business, but gives no surplus to its owners.

When the net present value and the internal rate of return criteria are applied to an isolated project, they will lead to the same accept/reject decision because they both use the discounting method of calculation applied to the same cash flows. For an isolated project the use of either technique is a matter of personal preference. Where a choice of competing projects has to be made, the practice may be more complicated. Chapter 12 explains the evaluation of projects that are competing for scarce resources.

Real world case 11.3

Senior Management Appointment

ntl Incorporated has appointed Jacques Kerrest as its Chief Financial Officer. As CFO, Jacques is responsible for all of ntl's financial activities including cash and credit management, capital budgeting, financial planning and analysis, corporate finance, tax, financial reporting, SEC and regulatory filings, accounting systems and controls, internal audit, bank relationships, financing and investor relations.

Source: *Business Wire*, 3 November, 2004 'ntl Incorporated's Third Quarter Results Led by Continued Growth in ntl: Home'.

Discussion points

1 One of the tasks listed for the CFO is 'capital budgeting'. What are the other ways in which the CFO is expected to show skills developed under the theme of 'management accounting'?

2 How could you find out more about the capital budgeting methods used by the CFO in this company?

11.6 Which methods are used in practice?

This chapter has now explained the capital budgeting techniques of payback, accounting rate of return, net present value and internal rate of return. The benefits and limitations of each have been discussed in the respective sections. It could be argued that the proof of the value of each technique lies in the extent to which it is used in practice. There exists a considerable volume of survey research seeking an answer to the question of which methods are most commonly used in practice. The conclusions from each project are not totally unanimous because they depend on the time period covered by the research, the nature of the sample chosen, the country in which the questions are asked and the questions asked. There are themes which may be discerned in the research results, the first of which is that the payback method appears to be the most frequently used technique in the UK but discounted cash flow methods are found more commonly in the US. It is also found that organisations will use more than one method of capital budgeting. Where discounting methods are used, internal rate of return appears more popular than net present value.

One benefit of using internal rate of return is that large companies with operations in different countries may set different hurdle levels of IRR to reflect the risk inherent in the different countries.

Research investigations are able to collect information of this type. Once the patterns are known, it is interesting to speculate on the motives behind these patterns of choice. Perhaps the payback method is most frequently used because there are many small businesses undertaking lots of small projects. It might not matter that discounting methods are used less frequently provided they are used on the larger projects in larger organisations. This issue has also been tested in research and it has been shown that larger companies do make relatively more use of discounting techniques. Perhaps the payback method, in many cases, shows so clearly that a project is acceptable that it would be a waste of time to carry out lengthy discounting calculations to arrive at the same conclusion. Perhaps those using payback realise that, in some instances, its emphasis on early cash flows is not so different from that of the net present value approach in situations where the later cash flows are relatively low.

11.7 What the researchers have found

11.7.1 Which methods of investment appraisal are used?

Brounen *et al* (2004) reported a survey of corporate finance in Europe. They asked 313 European Chief Finance Officers (CFOs) about their methods of investment appraisal. The survey was carried out in 2002. Most European respondents selected the payback period as their most frequently used investment appraisal technique. The use of payback was: UK (69.2% of respondents) the Netherlands (64.7%), Germany (50%) and France (50.9%). The use of IRR was strongest in Germany at 56% but NPV was even stronger in Germany at 70%. In the other three countries IRR was more commonly used than NPV.

The researchers expressed some surprise in their conclusions that firms in the UK and the Netherlands were consciously striving to maximise shareholder wealth while firms in France and Germany attached low priority to that corporate goal. It would not surprise someone who knows the relative strength of capital markets in the UK and the Netherlands and the societal focus of French and German companies. Their findings confirmed many previous studies in observing that net present value criteria are more likely to be seen in larger companies.

11.7.2 Caution over using NPV in public sector evaluation

Cooper and Taylor (2005) reported on an investigation of proposals to the Scottish Parliament which, if implemented, would lead to a considerable expansion of prison privatisation. Both the Scottish Prison Service and the Scottish Executive used what they claimed to be an independently verified cost saving of £700 million as the major justification for these proposals. The Executive minister who presented the report to the Parliament said 'In order to compare the costs of the options, they have been assessed on the standard Treasury-approved net present value – or NPV – basis over 25 years. Using NPV, an option that would involve expenditure being incurred over a long time can be compared objectively with one in which a greater proportion of the expenditure is incurred up front.' The researchers challenged the assumptions behind the cost projections used in the net present value calculation, showing that some cost items had not been treated on a comparable basis in the relative NPV evaluations. Additionally they showed that NPV is unable to accommodate broader social costs, such as programmes of prisoner reform and rehabilitation, which are difficult to quantify.

The paper shows that questions have to be asked about the amount and timing of cash flows used in NPV calculations. Questions also have to be asked about the wider social costs and benefits that cannot be incorporated in an NPV calculation.

Is there some merit in the accounting rate of return?

It can be shown that there are close links between the accounting rate of return and the internal rate of return when 'economic' depreciation is applied (Stark, 2004). The economic depreciation uses present value calculations that are quite complex so it is unlikely that these would be found in practice. Nevertheless, even where accounting rate of return is different from the internal rate of return because of the depreciation method used, there may be links in terms of relative ranking of projects. The accounting rate of return may be regarded as an estimate which has some relationship with the internal rate of return, providing the effect of depreciation is understood. Comparisons within industries might have some meaning, where depreciation policies are similar.

11.8 Summary

Key themes in this chapter are:

- **Capital investment appraisal** is the application of a set of methods of quantitative analysis which give guidance to managers in making decisions as to how best to invest long-term funds. Four methods of quantitative analysis are explained in the chapter:

- The **payback period** is the length of time required for a stream of net cash inflows from a project to equal the original cash outlay.

- The **accounting rate of return** is calculated by taking the average annual profits expected from a project as a percentage of the capital invested.

- The process of calculating present value is called **discounting**. The interest rate used is called the **discount rate**. The net present value method of investment appraisal and the internal rate of return method are both based on discounting.

- The **net present value** of a project is equal to the present value of the cash inflows minus the present value of the cash outflows, all discounted at the cost of capital. The decision rules are:
  - Where the net present value of the project is *positive*, accept the project.
  - Where the net present value of the project is *negative*, reject the project.
  - Where the net present value of the project is zero, the project is acceptable in meeting the cost of capital but gives no surplus to its owners.

- The **internal rate of return** (IRR) is the discount rate at which the present value of the cash flows generated by the project is equal to the present value of the capital invested, so that the net present value of the project is zero. The decision rules are:
  - Where the IRR of the project is greater than the cost of capital, accept the project.
  - Where the IRR of the project is less than the cost of capital, reject the project.
  - Where the IRR of the project equals the cost of capital, the project is acceptable in meeting the required rate of return of those investing in the business but gives no surplus to its owners.

References and further reading

Brounen, D., de Jong, A. and Koedijk, K. (2004) 'Corporate finance in Europe: confronting theory with practice', *Financial Management*, Tampa USA, 33(4): 71–101.

Cooper, C. and Taylor, P. (2005) 'Independently verified reductionism: prison privatisation in Scotland', *Human Relations*, April, 58: 497–522.

Stark, A. (2004) 'Estimating economic performance from accounting data: a review and synthesis', *The British Accounting Review*, 36: 321–43.

QUESTIONS

The Questions section of each chapter has three types of question. 'Test your understanding' questions to help you review your reading are in the 'A' series of questions. You will find the answer to these by reading and thinking about the material in the text book. 'Application' questions to test your ability to apply technical skills are in the 'B' series of questions. Questions requiring you to show skills in problem solving and evaluation are in the 'C' series of questions. The symbol [S] indicates that a solution is available at the end of the book.

A   Test your understanding

A11.1   What is the purpose of capital investment appraisal (section 11.1)?

A11.2   What is meant by the assumption of certainty of cash flows (section 11.1.2)?

A11.3   What are the main steps in making a decision about a capital investment (section 11.1.3)?

A11.4   What is the payback method of evaluating a project (section 11.2)?

A11.5   What are the advantages and limitations of the payback method (section 11.2.3)?

A11.6   What is the accounting rate of return (section 11.3)?

A11.7   What are the advantages and limitations of the accounting rate of return as a technique for use in capital investment appraisal (section 11.3.2)?

A11.8   What is meant by the time value of money (section 11.4.1)?

A11.9   What is meant by the present value of a cash flow (section 11.4.1)?

A11.10 What is meant by the term 'discounting' (section 11.4.1)?

A11.11 Define net present value and explain how it is calculated (section 11.4.2).

A11.12 State the net present value decision rule to be used in capital investment appraisal (section 11.4.2).

A11.13 How is the cost of capital decided upon (section 11.4.3)?

A11.14 Define internal rate of return and explain how it is calculated (section 11.5).

A11.15 State the internal rate of return decision rule to be used in capital investment appraisal (section 11.5.2).

A11.16 [S] Calculate the present value of £100 receivable at the end of (a) one year, (b) two years and (c) three years, using a discount rate of 8% per annum.

A11.17 [S] Calculate the present value of £100 receivable at the end of five years using a discount rate of (a) 4%, (b) 6% and (c) 8% per annum.

B   Application

B11.1 [S]
Projects Ltd intends to acquire a new machine costing £50,000 which is expected to have a life of five years, with a scrap value of £10,000 at the end of that time.

Cash flows arising from operation of the machine are expected to arise on the last day of each year as follows:

End of year	£
1	10,000
2	15,000
3	20,000
4	25,000
5	25,000

Calculate the payback period, the accounting rate of return and the net present value, explaining the meaning of each answer you produce. (Assume a discount rate of 10% per annum.)

B11.2 [S]
In a calculation of the internal rate of return of a project it is found that the net present value is +£122m at 22% discount rate and –£58m at 24% discount rate. What is the Internal Rate of Return?

B11.3 [S]
XYZ Ltd is considering purchasing a new machine, and the relevant facts concerning two possible choices are as follows:

	Machine A	Machine B
Capital expenditure required	£65,000	£60,000
Estimated life in years	4	4
Residual value	nil	nil
Cash flow after taxation each year	£25,000	£24,000

The company's cost of capital is 10%.

Required
Calculate, for each machine, the payback period, the net present value and the profitability index. State, with reasons, which machine you would recommend.

B11.4
In a calculation of the internal rate of return of a project it is found that the net present value is +£60m at 24% discount rate and –£20m at 26% discount rate. What is the Internal Rate of Return?

C Problem solving and evaluation

C11.1 [S]
Marsh Limited has investigated the possibility of investing in a new machine. The following data have been extracted from the report relating to the project:

Cost of machine on 1 January Year 6: £500,000.
Estimated scrap value at end of Year 5: Nil

Year	Net cash flows £000
1	50
2	200
3	225
4	225
5	100

The company's cost of capital is 8%.

Required

Evaluate the acceptability of the project using the net present value method of investment appraisal.

C11.2

BY Ltd is considering carrying out a major programme of staff training. The training scheme will cost £100,000 and will be paid for immediately. It is expected to produce additional cash flows as follows:

	Additional cash inflow
One year from today	£50,000
Two years from today	£40,000
Three years from today	£30,000
Four years from today	£30,000
Five years from today	£20,000

The cost of capital to the company is 6%.

Required

(a) Evaluate the expenditure on the staff training scheme.

(b) Comment on other factors to be considered before taking up the training scheme.

C11.3

HOP Ltd forecasts cash flows of £30,000 per annum for four years. It will invest £80,000 in fixed assets having a four-year life and no residual value.

Calculate: (a) the accounting rate of return (b) the internal rate of return.

Case studies

Real world cases

Prepare short answers to Case studies 11.1, 11.2 and 11.3.

Case 11.4

Using a suitable computer spreadsheet package, set up a spreadsheet which will calculate net present values and internal rates of return for projects having cash flows for a ten-year period. Test the spreadsheet with sample data and then write a brief instruction sheet. Save the spreadsheet to a disk and exchange disks and instruction sheets with another group in the class.

Case 11.5

Now exchange your spreadsheet with that of another student and write an evaluation of the spreadsheet you have received from the other person. Consider the following:

(a) Does it deal with all possible types of cash flows (e.g. a negative flow at some point)?

(b) Does it provide a recommendation on accept/reject (e.g. using a conditional function)?

(c) Does it allow for relatively easy variation of the discount rate?

(e) Does the instruction sheet explain how to produce graphs of net present value plotted against discount rate?

List any other features of the spreadsheet which you would use in evaluating its effectiveness and user-friendliness.

Appendix: Table of discount factors

Present value of £1 to be received after *n* years when the rate of interest is *r*% per annum equals $1/(1 + r)^n$.

Number of years	1%	2%	3%	4%	5%	6%	7%	8%	9%	10%	11%	12%	13%	14%	15%
1	0.990	0.980	0.971	0.962	0.952	0.943	0.935	0.926	0.917	0.909	0.901	0.893	0.885	0.877	0.870
2	0.980	0.961	0.943	0.925	0.907	0.890	0.873	0.857	0.842	0.826	0.812	0.797	0.783	0.769	0.756
3	0.971	0.942	0.915	0.889	0.864	0.840	0.816	0.794	0.772	0.751	0.731	0.712	0.693	0.675	0.658
4	0.961	0.924	0.888	0.855	0.823	0.792	0.763	0.735	0.708	0.683	0.659	0.636	0.613	0.592	0.572
5	0.951	0.906	0.863	0.822	0.784	0.747	0.713	0.681	0.650	0.621	0.593	0.567	0.543	0.519	0.497
6	0.942	0.888	0.837	0.790	0.746	0.705	0.666	0.630	0.596	0.564	0.535	0.507	0.480	0.456	0.432
7	0.933	0.871	0.813	0.760	0.711	0.665	0.623	0.583	0.547	0.513	0.482	0.452	0.425	0.400	0.376
8	0.923	0.853	0.789	0.731	0.677	0.627	0.582	0.540	0.502	0.467	0.434	0.404	0.376	0.351	0.327
9	0.914	0.837	0.766	0.703	0.645	0.592	0.544	0.500	0.460	0.424	0.391	0.361	0.333	0.308	0.284
10	0.905	0.820	0.744	0.676	0.614	0.558	0.508	0.463	0.422	0.386	0.352	0.322	0.295	0.270	0.247
11	0.896	0.804	0.722	0.650	0.585	0.527	0.475	0.429	0.388	0.350	0.317	0.287	0.261	0.237	0.215
12	0.887	0.788	0.701	0.625	0.557	0.497	0.444	0.397	0.356	0.319	0.286	0.257	0.231	0.208	0.187
13	0.879	0.773	0.681	0.601	0.530	0.469	0.415	0.368	0.326	0.290	0.258	0.229	0.204	0.182	0.163
14	0.870	0.758	0.661	0.577	0.505	0.442	0.388	0.340	0.299	0.263	0.232	0.205	0.181	0.160	0.141
15	0.861	0.743	0.642	0.555	0.481	0.417	0.362	0.315	0.275	0.239	0.209	0.183	0.160	0.140	0.123
16	0.853	0.728	0.623	0.534	0.458	0.394	0.339	0.292	0.252	0.218	0.188	0.163	0.141	0.123	0.107
17	0.844	0.714	0.605	0.513	0.436	0.371	0.317	0.270	0.231	0.198	0.170	0.146	0.125	0.108	0.093
18	0.836	0.700	0.587	0.494	0.416	0.350	0.296	0.250	0.212	0.180	0.153	0.130	0.111	0.095	0.081
19	0.828	0.686	0.570	0.475	0.396	0.331	0.277	0.232	0.194	0.164	0.138	0.116	0.098	0.083	0.070
20	0.820	0.673	0.554	0.456	0.377	0.312	0.258	0.215	0.178	0.149	0.124	0.104	0.087	0.073	0.061
21	0.811	0.660	0.538	0.439	0.359	0.294	0.242	0.199	0.164	0.135	0.112	0.093	0.077	0.064	0.053
22	0.803	0.647	0.522	0.422	0.342	0.278	0.226	0.184	0.150	0.123	0.101	0.083	0.068	0.056	0.046
23	0.795	0.634	0.507	0.406	0.326	0.262	0.211	0.170	0.138	0.112	0.091	0.074	0.060	0.049	0.040
24	0.788	0.622	0.492	0.390	0.310	0.247	0.197	0.158	0.126	0.102	0.082	0.066	0.053	0.043	0.035
25	0.780	0.610	0.478	0.375	0.295	0.233	0.184	0.146	0.116	0.092	0.074	0.059	0.047	0.038	0.030
26	0.772	0.598	0.464	0.361	0.281	0.220	0.172	0.135	0.106	0.084	0.066	0.053	0.042	0.033	0.026
27	0.764	0.586	0.450	0.347	0.268	0.207	0.161	0.125	0.098	0.076	0.060	0.047	0.037	0.029	0.023
28	0.757	0.574	0.437	0.333	0.255	0.196	0.150	0.116	0.090	0.069	0.054	0.042	0.033	0.026	0.020
29	0.749	0.563	0.424	0.321	0.243	0.185	0.141	0.107	0.082	0.063	0.048	0.037	0.029	0.022	0.017
30	0.742	0.552	0.412	0.308	0.231	0.174	0.131	0.099	0.075	0.057	0.044	0.033	0.026	0.020	0.015

Number of years	16%	17%	18%	19%	20%	21%	22%	23%	24%	25%	26%	27%	28%	29%	30%
1	0.862	0.855	0.847	0.840	0.833	0.826	0.820	0.813	0.806	0.800	0.794	0.787	0.781	0.775	0.769
2	0.743	0.731	0.718	0.706	0.694	0.683	0.672	0.661	0.650	0.640	0.630	0.620	0.610	0.601	0.592
3	0.641	0.624	0.609	0.593	0.579	0.564	0.551	0.537	0.524	0.512	0.500	0.488	0.477	0.466	0.455
4	0.552	0.534	0.516	0.499	0.482	0.467	0.451	0.437	0.423	0.410	0.397	0.384	0.373	0.361	0.350
5	0.476	0.456	0.437	0.419	0.402	0.386	0.370	0.355	0.341	0.328	0.315	0.303	0.291	0.280	0.269
6	0.410	0.390	0.370	0.352	0.335	0.319	0.303	0.289	0.275	0.262	0.250	0.238	0.227	0.217	0.207
7	0.354	0.333	0.314	0.296	0.279	0.263	0.249	0.235	0.222	0.210	0.198	0.188	0.178	0.168	0.159
8	0.305	0.285	0.266	0.249	0.233	0.218	0.204	0.191	0.179	0.168	0.157	0.148	0.139	0.130	0.123
9	0.263	0.243	0.225	0.209	0.194	0.180	0.167	0.155	0.144	0.134	0.125	0.116	0.108	0.101	0.094
10	0.227	0.208	0.191	0.176	0.162	0.149	0.137	0.126	0.116	0.107	0.099	0.092	0.085	0.078	0.073
11	0.195	0.178	0.162	0.148	0.135	0.123	0.112	0.103	0.094	0.086	0.079	0.072	0.066	0.061	0.056
12	0.168	0.152	0.137	0.124	0.112	0.102	0.092	0.083	0.076	0.069	0.062	0.057	0.052	0.047	0.043
13	0.145	0.130	0.116	0.104	0.093	0.084	0.075	0.068	0.061	0.055	0.050	0.045	0.040	0.037	0.033
14	0.125	0.111	0.099	0.088	0.078	0.069	0.062	0.055	0.049	0.044	0.039	0.035	0.032	0.028	0.025
15	0.108	0.095	0.084	0.074	0.065	0.057	0.051	0.045	0.040	0.035	0.031	0.028	0.025	0.022	0.020
16	0.093	0.081	0.071	0.062	0.054	0.047	0.042	0.036	0.032	0.028	0.025	0.022	0.019	0.017	0.015
17	0.080	0.069	0.060	0.052	0.045	0.039	0.034	0.030	0.026	0.023	0.020	0.017	0.015	0.013	0.012
18	0.069	0.059	0.051	0.044	0.038	0.032	0.028	0.024	0.021	0.018	0.016	0.014	0.012	0.010	0.009
19	0.060	0.051	0.043	0.037	0.031	0.027	0.023	0.020	0.017	0.014	0.012	0.011	0.009	0.008	0.007
20	0.051	0.043	0.037	0.031	0.026	0.022	0.019	0.016	0.014	0.012	0.010	0.008	0.007	0.006	0.005
21	0.044	0.037	0.031	0.026	0.022	0.018	0.015	0.013	0.011	0.009	0.008	0.007	0.006	0.005	0.004
22	0.038	0.032	0.026	0.022	0.018	0.015	0.013	0.011	0.009	0.007	0.006	0.005	0.004	0.004	0.003
23	0.033	0.027	0.022	0.018	0.015	0.012	0.010	0.009	0.007	0.006	0.005	0.004	0.003	0.003	0.002
24	0.028	0.023	0.019	0.015	0.013	0.010	0.008	0.007	0.006	0.005	0.004	0.003	0.003	0.002	0.002
25	0.024	0.020	0.016	0.013	0.010	0.009	0.007	0.006	0.005	0.004	0.003	0.003	0.002	0.002	0.001
26	0.021	0.017	0.014	0.011	0.009	0.007	0.006	0.005	0.004	0.003	0.002	0.002	0.002	0.001	0.001
27	0.018	0.014	0.011	0.009	0.007	0.006	0.005	0.004	0.003	0.002	0.002	0.002	0.001	0.001	0.001
28	0.016	0.012	0.010	0.008	0.006	0.005	0.004	0.003	0.002	0.002	0.002	0.001	0.001	0.001	0.001
29	0.014	0.001	0.008	0.006	0.005	0.004	0.003	0.002	0.002	0.002	0.001	0.001	0.001	0.001	0.000
30	0.012	0.009	0.007	0.005	0.004	0.003	0.003	0.002	0.002	0.001	0.001	0.001	0.001	0.000	0.000

Capital budgeting applications

This case study shows a typical situation in which management accounting can be helpful. Read the case study now but only attempt the discussion points after you have finished studying the chapter.

The transition towards common systems across the chain is the key element of our infrastructure development. During the year, investment in Woolworths' IT [Information Technology] systems totalled £14.7 million.

Investment in systems for buying and replenishing is nearing completion, with a majority of the purchase orders and store deliveries now controlled by the new systems. This contributed to a 1.7 per cent improvement in single sku (stock keeping unit) in-store availability over the year.

The rollout of the Kingstore till system continues and is now installed in 320 stores, accounting for 63 per cent of Woolworths' retail space. Faster transaction times reduce store costs and improve customer service and the item specific information provided by Kingstore supports improvements to on-shelf availability and shrinkage rates. As a result, we have decided to accelerate the rollout of Kingstore to all remaining Woolworths' stores by Christmas 2004. This will require a capital investment of £19 million, advancing £9 million planned for 2005/06.

Source: Woolworths Group, Annual Report and Accounts 2004, www.woolworthsgroupplc.com

Discussion points

1 What are the benefits expected from the capital expenditure on new IT and new cash registers?

2 What items of cash flow would you include in a capital investment appraisal of the expenditure on IT and cash registers?

Contents

Learning outcomes

After reading this chapter you should be able to:

- Explain how discounted cash flow methods are used to evaluate situations of capital rationing and mutually exclusive projects.
- Explain how cash flows are budgeted for discounting cash flows, including the treatment of working capital, taxation, inflation, depreciation and interest charges.
- Explain why a range of methods of capital budgeting and investment appraisal may be observed in practice.
- Explain the control procedures available for authorisation and review of investment projects.
- Explain how advanced manufacturing technologies lead to a demand for new ways of evaluating investment projects.
- Describe and discuss examples of research into the application of capital budgeting.

12.1 Introduction

Chapter 11 has explained the basic methods used for investment appraisal. In particular it has described net present value and internal rate of return as two methods of evaluating a stream of future cash flows by taking into account the time value of money. Arithmetically these two methods are equivalent and will lead to the same decision on whether to invest. In practice some care may be needed in identifying the future cash flows for planned projects. It is also important to review the project after it has started, in order to be satisfied that the conditions expected at the initial investment appraisal are being met in the outcome. The process of estimating, evaluating and monitoring the cash flows expected from an investment project is called **capital budgeting**.

Definition   **Capital budgeting** is a process of management accounting which assists management decision making by providing information on the investment in a project and the benefits to be obtained from that project, and by monitoring the performance of the project subsequent to its implementation.

12.2 Capital rationing

Capital rationing means that there is not sufficient finance (capital) available to support all the projects proposed in an organisation. In an ideal world any project which can earn a positive net present value or earn an internal rate of return greater than the cost of capital should be able to find a source of finance because there are rewards to the providers of capital.

12.2.1 Types of capital rationing

However, the world is not ideal and there may be restrictions on capital for any of the following reasons:

1 There may be temporary uncertainty in the economy (perhaps over rates of interest or rates of foreign currency exchange) and lenders are limiting the amount that they will provide as long-term finance until the uncertainty is resolved. This is called 'external' capital rationing because it is beyond the control of the management of the organisation.
2 The managers of the organisation may want to impose some overall limits to the extent of expansion or development in the organisation as a whole, perhaps to control the risk profile of the organisation as a whole. This is called 'internal' capital rationing because it is imposed from within the organisation.
3 In the public sector the government may wish to control the overall amount of borrowing by the public sector as a whole and accordingly it sets limits for financing new investment projects in each activity of the public sector.

There are two questions to ask at the outset:

1 What type of capital rationing exists?
2 Are the proposed projects divisible?

Type of capital rationing - single period or multiple period?

- Is the capital rationing only imposed at the start of the project? This means there is a shortage of funds at one point in time only. It is described as **single-period capital rationing**.
- Is the capital rationing imposed continuously over time? This is described as multiple period capital rationing.

In practice, for internal capital rationing, the second is more likely but is also more complex to solve mathematically. This section will explain methods of appraising single-period capital rationing. This is capital rationing which occurs in one period only during the life of a project (usually in the first period).

Divisible or non-divisible projects?

Is it essential to carry out the entire project that is planned? Could part of the project be started now and the rest deferred until capital is available? If the project is a **divisible project** then the separate parts may be evaluated separately. If the proposed project is a **non-divisible** project then it must be evaluated in total.

12.2.2 Decisions under capital rationing

The aim of evaluating projects under capital rationing is to obtain the highest possible net present value for the capital available. It may not be possible to obtain as much net present value as would be available in the absence of capital rationing. The managers of the organisation must therefore ask 'what is the greatest benefit obtainable for the capital that we have available?'

Profitability index

If the business has the aim of maximising net present value, then managers will find it helpful to calculate a ratio which compares the present value of the expected cash inflow with the intended amount of investment. This ratio is called the **profitability index**. Any project having a profitability index of 1.0 or higher is acceptable.

Definition

> The **profitability index** is the present value of cash flows (discounted at the cost of capital) divided by the present value of the investment intended to produce those cash flows.

The decision rule is that the projects should be ranked in order of profitability index, with the highest being the most attractive, and accepted in that sequence until the capital available is used up.

Definition

> **Decision rule: capital rationing**
> In situations of capital rationing, rank projects in order from highest to lowest profitability index and accept projects in that sequence until the capital available is used up, provided the profitability index is greater than or equal to 1.0.

12.2.3 Mutually exclusive projects

An organisation may need to make a choice between two projects which are mutually exclusive. This means that choosing one eliminates another, perhaps because there is only sufficient demand in the market for the output of one of the projects, or because there is a limited physical capacity which will not allow both. Some care is then required in using the net present value and the internal rate of return as decision criteria. In many cases they give the same answer on relative ranking, but occasionally they may give different answers, as shown in the following case example.

Case study: whisky distillery

A distillery is planning to invest in a new still. There are two plans, one of which involves continuing to produce the traditional mix of output blends and the second of which involves experimentation with new blends. The second plan will produce lower cash flows in the earlier years of the life of the still, but it is planned that these cash flows will overtake the traditional pattern within a short space of time. Only one plan may be implemented. The project is to be appraised on the basis of cash flows over three years. The cash flows expected are shown in Exhibit 12.1. The cost of capital is 12% per annum. At this discount rate the net present values are shown in the lower part of Exhibit 12.1. The internal rates of return are also shown in that part of the table.

Exhibit 12.1
Cash flows, NPV and IRR for two mutually exclusive projects

| Project | Initial investment £ | Cash flows | | |
		Year 1 £	Year 2 £	Year 3 £
A	120,000	96,000	48,000	12,000
B	120,000	12,000	60,000	108,000

Project	NPV at 12% £	IRR
A	12,521	20.2%
B	15,419	17.6%

It may be seen from Exhibit 12.1 that, looking at the net present value at the cost of capital, project B appears the more attractive with the higher net present value. Looking at the internal rate of return, project A appears most attractive. Both are acceptable because they give a positive net present value and the ideal answer would be to find the resources to undertake both projects. In this example, the two are mutually exclusive (which means that taking on one project excludes the possibility of the other).

The project with the highest profitability index will give the highest net present value for the amount of investment funding available. Taking the data in Exhibit 12.1, the profitability index calculations are:

$$\text{Project A: Profitability index} = \frac{132,521}{120,000} = 1.10$$

$$\text{Project B: Profitability index} = \frac{135,419}{120,000} = 1.13$$

This confirms that, of the two, project B is preferable at a cost of capital of 12 per cent. Where the investment in both projects is of the same amount, as in this case, the profitability index confirms what is already obvious, but where there are competing projects of differing initial investment, it is a useful device for ranking projects to maximise net present value.

Activity 12.1   *Explain how a project having a positive net present value will also have a profitability index greater than 1.0.*

12.2.4 Sensitivity to changes in the discount rate

To understand the apparently different conclusions from the NPV and IRR approaches, it is helpful to plot a graph of the net present value of each project against a range of discount rates. The graph is shown in Exhibit 12.2.

Exhibit 12.2
Net present value of competing projects using a range of discount rates

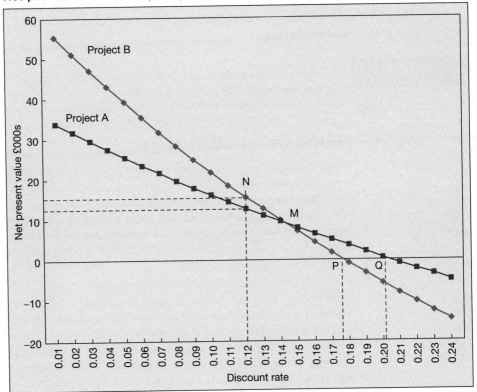

From Exhibit 12.2, it will be seen that, for both projects, the net present value decreases as the discount rate increases, but that the net present value of project B decreases more rapidly. Starting at the left-hand side of the graph, the net present value of project B is higher than that of project A at all discount rates above the point, M, at which they intersect (around 14.2 per cent). In particular project B has a higher net present value than project A at the cost of capital 12 per cent (point N on the graph). For discount rates above 14.2 per cent, the net present value of project B is always higher than that of project A. The internal rate of return of each project is the discount rate at which they cross the line of zero net present value (i.e. at point P for project B and point Q for project A).

How does this help the decision maker? If it is absolutely certain that the cost of capital will remain at 12 per cent throughout the life of the project, then the net present value method correctly leads to a choice of project B in preference to project A. On the other hand, 12 per cent is quite close to the point of intersection at 14.2 per cent, where project A takes over. If there is a chance that the cost of capital will in reality be higher than the 12 per cent expected, then it might be safer to choose project A. The line of the graph for project A is less steep and this project is said to be less sensitive to changes in the discount rate. There is therefore no clear-cut answer to the problem and the final decision will be based on an assessment of sensitivity. Looking at Exhibit 12.2, the different ranking by net present value and by internal rate of return was a useful clue to the need to consider the relative sensitivities as shown in the graph.

12.3 Cash flows for discounting calculations

This section describes some of the questions that may arise when estimating cash flows for discounting calculations. It describes the inclusion of amounts to cover working capital requirements, the effect of taxation on cash flow projections, the effect of inflation on capital budgeting calculations, and the exclusion of depreciation and interest charges.

Activity 12.2   *Consider a project to start a business selling shoes from a chain of shops. Explain how the business would plan its working capital requirements.*

12.3.1 Working capital requirements

When managers are forecasting the cash flows for a project, they will consider the expected revenues and costs, but they must also include an estimate for working capital requirements. The working capital will be required in period 1 to allow the business to acquire inventories and build up debtors (receivables) to the extent that these are not matched by trade. The working capital will be recovered at the end of the project when the inventories are sold, cash is collected from customers, and final payments are made to suppliers.

Example

A project is planned to last for three years. Net cash inflows are forecast as £12,000 per year for three years, assumed to arise on the final day of the relevant year. Working capital of £3,000 will be required on the first day of business. The cost of capital is 6% per year. In the calculation shown in Exhibit 12.3 the working capital has to be available at the start of Year 1 (i.e. end of Year 0) but is returned at the end of the project (i.e. end of Year 3).

Exhibit 12.3
Cash flows including working capital requirements

End of year	Year 0	Year 1	Year 2	Year 3
Cash inflows (£)		12,000	12,000	12,000
Working capital (£)	**(3,000)**			**3,000**
Net flows (£)	(3,000)	12,000	12,000	15,000
Discount factor 5%	1.000	$(1 + 0.05)$	$(1 + 0.05)^2$	$(1 + 0.05)^3$
Net flows (£)	(3,000)	12,000	12,000	15,000
Discount factor	1.000	(1.05)	(1.1025)	(1.1576)
Net flows (£)	(3,000)	12,000	12,000	15,000
Discount factor	1.000	(1.05)	(1.1025)	(1.1576)
Discounted net flows (£)	(3,000)	11,429	10,884	12,958
Present value	£32,271			

The effect of taxation on cash flows

Taxation has an effect on capital budgeting for two reasons. Tax payments are a cash outflow of the business, so it is important to know when they are payable. The government's tax policy may also try to encourage investment by reducing tax payable (also called tax incentives).

Timing of tax payments

If the company pays tax then the flows in respect of tax payments have to be included. The cash flows must then be discounted at the after-tax cost of capital. UK companies that are *not* classed as 'small' for tax purposes pay their annual corporation tax in four instalments spread across the year, so they have a cash outflow for tax every three months. For such companies the usual assumption in cash flow planning is that the tax outflow takes place in the year in which the profit is earned.

The test of being 'small' is based on the amount of taxable profit. The small UK companies pay their corporation tax in one amount, nine months after the end of the accounting year. Discounted cash flows are usually calculated on an annual basis so these payment dates do not fit easily with an annual cash flow model. Examination questions usually make simplifying assumptions such as assuming the tax payment is made after 12 months rather than nine months.

In the real world, an assumption has to be made about the timing of cash flows. In examination questions you will be given information about the assumption to be made.

Tax incentives: capital allowances

The government may try to encourage investment by making depreciation allowances (called **capital allowances**). The capital allowance will be used to reduce the taxable profit and hence to reduce the tax bill payable. Suppose a business has a taxable profit of £100,000 and the tax rate is 20 per cent. The tax payable is £20,000. However, if a capital allowance of £10,000 is available the taxable profit is reduced to £90,000 and the tax payable becomes £18,000, which is a tax saving of £2,000. As a short cut calculation, the tax saving of £2,000 can be calculated as 20 per cent of the capital allowance. If the tax authorities find later, when the asset is sold, that the tax allowance has been too generous they may apply a balancing charge to recover some of the tax benefit. Different countries have different rules about the timing and amount of the allowances and charges relating to fixed assets so in a real life case it is important to know the tax rules. Examination questions in management accounting usually explain the tax procedures to be applied.

Example

John James is operating a business located in an enterprise zone. This allows him to claim a tax deduction up to 100 per cent of expenditure on workshop buildings. His rental incomes net of cash expenses are expected to be £70,000 per year for three years. The workshop buildings will cost £5,000 at the start of year 1. They will be depreciated for accounting purposes over 10 years. The after-tax cost of capital is 5 per cent per annum. It is expected that the workshop buildings could be sold for £3,500 at the end of three years. Tax at 20 per cent is paid 12 months after the relevant income is earned. A balancing charge is applied when an asset is sold. The cash flows are shown in Exhibit 12.4 with a key below the table to explain each line.

Comment

It can be seen from Exhibit 12.4 that the timing of cash flows is important for investment planning. There is a strong cash flow benefit in the capital allowance for the investment at the start because it arises at the end of year 1. Eventually part of this

Exhibit 12.4
Discounting cash flows with taxation included

		Year 0 £	Year 1 £	Year 2 £	Year 3 £	Year 4 £
				End of year		
Forecast cash flows	a		70,000	70,000	70,000	
Workshop building cost	b	(5,000)				
Tax payable at 20%	c			(14,000)	(14,000)	(14,000)
Tax benefit of allowance	d		1,000			
Sale of workshop building	e				3,500	
Balancing charge	f					(700)
Net cash flow		(5,000)	71,000	56,000	59,500	(14,700)
Discount factor at 5% (from tables)		1.000	0.952	0.907	0.864	0.823
Present value		(5,000)	67,592	50,792	51,408	(12,098)
Net present value		152,694				

Key:
(a) This line shows the forecast cash flows expected each year for 3 years. It assumes that the cash flow of each year all occurs on the final day of the year.
(b) This line shows the immediate outlay required to pay for the workshop building.
(c) This line shows the tax payable on the forecast cash flows, one year after each cash flow has been earned.
(d) This line shows the tax saving at 20% of the allowed expenditure of £5,000, amounting to £1,000. It is shown one year after the date of the payment because the tax flows are one year later than the relevant cash inflows or outflows. Line (d) assumes that the £1,000 saving will either be used to reduce a tax bill elsewhere in the organisation or it will be refunded in cash by the tax authorities.
(e) At the end of three years the workshop building will be sold for £3,500. Originally a capital allowance of £5,000 was given, leaving a written-down asset value of nil. The tax authorities now want to reverse part of that allowance by making a 'balancing charge' equal to the tax rate multiplied by the difference between the proceeds of sale and the tax written-down value. The calculation is 20% of (£3,500 – £0) = 20% of £3,500 = £700. The overall effect is that the organisation has only enjoyed a tax benefit for the part of the asset cost that was used up during the project.

benefit has to be repaid through the balancing charge but that only arises at the end of year 4 and so has a much lower discounted present value.

12.3.3 The effect of inflation

Where inflation is expected during the forecast period, the question arises: do we have to adjust the forecast cash flows to take account of the expected rate of inflation? This section shows how the cash flows and discount rate can be adjusted for inflation, and also shows that it is equally valid to forecast cash flows at constant prices discounted at the inflation-free rate (the 'real' rate) of discount.

Example

Office Cleaners Co earns cash flows from contract cleaning. The directors have forecast cash flows of £10,000 per year at today's prices. The required cost of capital is 4%. Assume cash flows arise on the final day of each year. The calculation of the present value is shown in Exhibit 12.5.

Exhibit 12.5
Calculation of present value, discounting at today's prices

Present value		Year 1		Year 2		Year 3
=		$\dfrac{10,000}{(1+r)}$	+	$\dfrac{10,000}{(1+r)^2}$	+	$\dfrac{10,000}{(1+r)^3}$
=		$\dfrac{10,000}{(1+0.04)}$	+	$\dfrac{10,000}{(1+0.04)^2}$	+	$\dfrac{10,000}{(1+0.04)^3}$
=		$\dfrac{10,000}{(1.040)}$	+	$\dfrac{10,000}{(1.0816)}$	+	$\dfrac{10,000}{(1.1249)}$
=		9,615	+	9,245	+	8,890
=		£27,750				

Now assume there is a forecast of 5 per cent inflation each year for the next three years. If the cash flows are adjusted for the effect of inflation then the discount rate must also be adjusted.

The discount rate is adjusted using the formula $(1 + i)(1 + r)$ where i = the rate of inflation and r = the inflation-free cost of capital.

In this examples the calculation is $(1 + i)(1 + r) = (1.05)(1.04) = 1.092$

(This calculation can be thought of as consisting of 4% return for the cost of capital, plus 5% return for inflation, equalling 9%, plus {5% of 4%} equalling 0.2% for the effect of inflation on the cost of capital itself.)

The discounting of the inflation-adjusted cash flows is shown in Exhibit 12.6.

Exhibit 12.6
Calculation of present value, with adjustment for inflation

Present value		Year 1		Year 2		Year 3
=		$\dfrac{10,500}{(1+r)}$	+	$\dfrac{11,025}{(1+r)^2}$	+	$\dfrac{11,576}{(1+r)^3}$
=		$\dfrac{10,500}{(1+0.092)}$	+	$\dfrac{11,025}{(1+0.092)^2}$	+	$\dfrac{11,576}{(1+0.092)^3}$
=		$\dfrac{10,500}{(1.092)}$	+	$\dfrac{11,025}{(1.1925)}$	+	$\dfrac{11,576}{(1.3022)}$
=		9,615	+	9,245	+	8,890
=		£27,750				

Definition

Discounting under conditions of inflation
The discounting calculation will give a correct answer if cash flows are forecast at constant prices (today's prices) and the discount rate is equal to the real (inflation-free) cost of capital.

Where the forecast cash flows are adjusted for inflation then the discount rate must also be adjusted for inflation.

12.3.4 Depreciation and interest charges

Depreciation

Depreciation does not appear in the cash flows to be discounted because it is an accounting expense that does not involve any flow of cash. When a fixed asset is purchased there is a cash outflow at the time of payment and there may be a cash inflow when the asset is eventually sold or scrapped. Those are the only cash flows. In the period of the asset's use within the business an expense of depreciation is reported in the profit and loss account as an accounting estimate of the use of the asset in earning revenues of the period. Depreciation is sometimes called an allocation of cost. It does not cause any cash flow.

Interest charges

Interest charges do not appear in the cash flows to be discounted because the interest cost is included in the cost of capital. The discounting calculation asks 'will the forecast cash flows from operations provide sufficient return to satisfy the cost of capital and make a surplus for the owners?'. If the net present value is positive there will be sufficient cash to pay interest charges equal to the cost of capital. If you are not convinced, look back to Chapter 11, where Exhibit 11.7 shows that the project can repay interest and earn a surplus net present value.

Real world case 12.2

This extract from the annual report of Tate and Lyle describes its investment in a new sweetener called Sucralose.

TATE & LYLE

CONSISTENTLY FIRST IN RENEWABLE INGREDIENTS

Growing the contribution from value added and consumer branded products is a key element of our strategy and the sucralose ingredients business will be a major contributor. Sucralose is an exciting growth opportunity, ideally placed to meet consumer demands for reduced calorie options in many categories including soft drinks, dairy and confectionery.

The total cash cost including capitalised expenses on the sucralose realignment of US$137 million (£75 million) remains subject to working capital adjustments. Payment occurred after the March 2004 year-end. The pro forma profit before tax for the year to December 2003 was US$33 million (£17 million) but we expect, as previously announced, significant one-off costs in the first year of operation. Even after these costs, we expect the return on this investment to exceed the Group's cost of capital in the year to March 2005.

Source: Tate and Lyle Annual Report 2004, p. 6, www.tate&lyle.com

Discussion points

1 Why is a cost adjustment required for working capital?

2 What is the company's measure of success of the project in its first year?

12.4 Control of investment projects: authorisation and review

The capital investment projects of an organisation represent major commitments of resources. It would be a mistake to be overenthusiastic about decision-making techniques without considering also how management accounting may help in the subsequent implementation of the project.

The organisation should have in place a procedure by which new project suggestions are investigated and evaluated using the techniques described in this chapter, or suitable alternatives. There should then be a decision-making group, perhaps called the capital budgeting committee or the management review committee, which makes decisions on the projects to be selected. Once the decision has been made and the capital budgeting committee has authorised the project to proceed, the management accountant is again needed in implementing a system for reviewing and controlling the project.

The two important aspects of control and review are:

(a) controlling the amount of the expenditure needed to make the project operational;
(b) post-completion audit of cash inflows and outflows.

12.4.1 Controlling capital expenditure

The specification of the project will have included an estimate of the initial outlay required and the timing of that outlay. For simplification, the illustrations used in this chapter assumed a single amount being paid out at the start of the project, but in real life the capital expenditure will be spread over a period of time on an agreed schedule. If the capital expenditure involves constructing a building, there will be a contract for the building work which sets out the dates for completion of each stage and the amount of cash to be paid at that point. The payment will only be made when an expert (such as the architect supervising the project) has confirmed that the work has been carried out according to the specification. If a contract has been drawn up with care, it will contain safeguards to ensure that the work is completed on time and within the original cost estimates. There may be a penalty clause, so that a part of the cash payment may be withheld if the contract is not performed as promised.

Activity 12.3

Write a list of key points to be made in a recommendation to the board of directors on the implementation of an expenditure control process for capital investment plans.

12.4.2 Post-completion audit

A **post-completion audit** involves a review of the actual results of a project in order to compare these with the expectations contained in the project proposals. It is called an audit because it requires an independent assessment and involves a more flexible approach than would be found in management accounting evaluations of short-term plans (as covered in Chapters 9 and 10). The post-completion audit might require a view of the wider implications of the project rather than concentrating too much on annual cash flows item by item. A project might take a different turn from that envisaged at the outset and a longer-term view would be required of the likely outcome of that different turn. In real life, uncertainty is a factor which cannot easily be built into the project plans and the audit may have to take account of factors which could not have been foreseen at the outset.

There could be dangers in such an audit process if managers of projects see themselves as being held to blame for a subsequent failure to meet expectations. They might be motivated to put forward only those projects which they saw as safe but unadventurous. The review process has to be flexible to allow for the unknown, but also to discourage unrealistic or overenthusiastic plans.

Questions that might be asked in a post-completion audit:

- What methods were used to collect a sufficiently wide range of project proposals?
- What methods were applied in evaluating the proposed project?
- How was sensitivity analysis applied to cash flow projections and cost of capital estimates?
- How was the project authorised for implementation?
- Was there an adequate amount of supervision by senior management?
- How did the annual performance compare to the projected costs and cash inflows?
- What lessons may be learned for the next project?

The value of post-completion audit lies in the lessons learned for the future. Each new project will be different from any previous project but the analysis will help identify those managers who can plan a project and then achieve what was planned. The risk of imposing an audit process is that managers may be more conservative in their initial proposals because they do not want to show an adverse performance in the post-completion audit.

12.5 Advanced manufacturing technologies

Advanced manufacturing technologies (AMTs) have been developed by engineers as a means of competing more effectively. To compete, organisations need to manufacture innovative products of high quality at low cost. The product life-cycle may be short, demand may be changing more rapidly and international competition creates a further element of uncertainty. As with any business activity, these changes represent new approaches to the management of the business, and management accounting must keep pace with the change in management approach.

12.5.1 Types of new technology

Engineers have produced new technology of four main types:

(a) design innovations;
(b) planning and control techniques;
(c) execution; and
(d) overarching technologies.

Each of these new technologies is considered in turn.

The *design innovations* have covered computer-aided design (CAD), computer-aided engineering (CAE), computer-aided process planning (CAPP) and design for manufacture and assembly. CAD uses computers to evaluate various designs of the product, while CAE includes design but also encompasses evaluation and testing so that the initial design becomes a working product. CAPP uses computers to plan the detailed processes required to manufacture the design proposed. Finally, the computer can also be used to design a system which makes the manufacture and assembly process meet the demand for the output.

Planning and control techniques have covered materials requirements planning (MRP), manufacturing resource planning (MRP II), enterprise resource planning (ERP) and statistical process control (SPC). MRP involves matching stock levels to the production process and controlling incoming customer orders to match the availability of materials. MRP II applies similar controls to all resources used in the manufacturing process. They both use computers to break down a customer's order into various stages which can be matched against resource availability. ERP is a system of software modules that are integrated to support the business processes of the organisation. It supports production, purchasing, inventory control, customers orders, human resource planning and finance functions. SPC uses statistical analysis to identify the most likely causes of bottlenecks in the manufacturing process, which can then be corrected before a crisis arises.

Execution means converting raw materials and components into finished goods. The technologies have included robotics, automated guided vehicles (AGVs), flexible manufacturing systems (FMS) and automated storage and retrieval systems (ASRS). These titles are self-descriptive of the activities involved.

The *overarching technologies* are those which take a total perspective of the organisation. They include just-in-time (JIT), total quality management (TQM), focused factory and computer-integrated manufacturing (CIM). JIT is described in Chapter 18, TQM in Chapter 19.

12.5.2 Capital investment appraisal of AMT projects

The conventional methods of investment appraisal have been presented as payback, accounting rate of return, net present value and internal rate of return. These techniques have considerable benefit for many situations where a fixed investment is made and the outcome may be projected forward. However, they are not capable of taking into account the flexibility which management may have in some situations. As flexible technology takes over from fixed inflexible capital equipment, there are options facing the business manager which must be considered in project evaluation.

In particular there are options to make modifications to projects or add on new aspects. Abandonment may be less difficult where technology is flexible. Companies may feel that they can afford to wait and learn before investing. A project can be scaled down if there are changes in demand for a product. These options make project development quite exciting but they also offer a challenge to the management accountant in making sure the options are evaluated.

Fiona McTaggart describes an example of capital investment in an AMT situation:

FIONA: *One case I encountered was that of a flexible manufacturing system being used to machine metal into engineering components. There was hardly a person in sight on the production line. Computer controlled machines were each performing one part of the treatment of the metal. Cutting tools were making metal shapes, transport systems were moving components around and then, depending on where the shapes were delivered, there were more machines to turn, mill, polish and shape. The whole process was controlled by a host computer and was sufficiently flexible that if the transport system was revised, then the activities performed on the metal changed as well.*

The company adapted its investment appraisal methods by involving the engineers and the management accountants as a team. Essentially they evaluated reduced labour costs, increased effectiveness in utilisation of machines, cost saving through just-in-time control of materials and the reduction in indirect costs. Discounted cash flows were included in order to take account of the longer term but the emphasis was more strongly on the short term and the flexibility for change if conditions changed.

The debate on the role of capital budgeting techniques in relation to advanced manufacturing technologies is a useful example of the wider point that management accounting must continually be changing to adapt to changed circumstances. A textbook can present basic ideas, but those ideas will only work effectively in a practical situation if moulded to meet the needs of the situation.

Real world case 12.3

The Renewables Obligation (RO) is a programme of the UK government that requires electricity suppliers to create more of their sales from renewable sources. Businesses who do this receive a Renewables Obligation Certificate (ROC), which they can sell. This extract describes a way of evaluating the projects.

The figures show the evolution of IRRs through time for two expensive technologies (offshore wind and energy crops) and two cheap technologies (onshore wind and landfill gas), along with the expected cost of capital used for each technology. Two cost assumptions have been used – high and low – covering a range of assumptions about the initial level and the subsequent possible evolution of capital and operating costs. The figures suggest that there will be some tendency for the cost of capital required for the most risky technologies to decline over time. This is a reflection of an assumed reduction in risk as the market becomes more comfortable with investments of this kind. In all cases, the estimated IRR tends to fall through time: build costs fall over time and ROC prices also decline from their highest levels during the early years of the RO. Under the high electricity price scenario, new offshore wind and energy crop plant would cease to be built from 2013/14 or so, whereas onshore wind and landfill would cease to be built from 2018/19. Under the low electricity price scenario, there would be no offshore wind or energy crop build, and onshore wind and landfill plant construction would cease a year or so earlier. It might be thought that declining build costs would lead to an increase in rates of return over time, but the merit of the RO is that, as generation costs fall, and with a static target, the ROC price falls below the buy-out price. Thus, the scheme manages to extract these gains for the consumer.

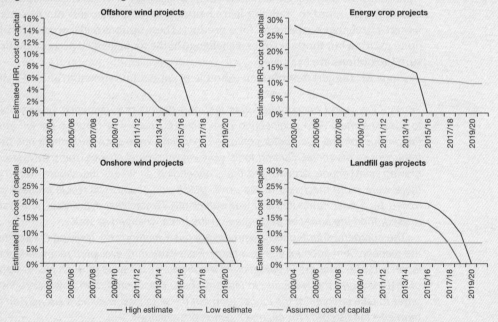

Source: Economic analysis of the design, cost and performance of the UK Renewables Obligation and the capital grants scheme, www.nao.org.uk/publications/ © National Audit Office

Discussion points

1 Why has IRR been used to compare the projects?

2 How does the calculation of IRR allow for sensitivity to a range of economic conditions?

12.6   What the researchers have found

12.6.1   Capital budgeting where owner and manager are separate

Guilding (2003) reported a study of a range of hotels located in Australia's Gold Coast. The owner of each hotel held legal ownership of the building and its contents but a separate operator managed the day-to-day activities by providing a general manager and financial controller to run the hotel. Hotel staff were employed by the owner. This separation of ownership and operation provided an interesting situation for capital budgeting plans. The general manager was required to put a proposal to the owner for investment in an improvement to the hotel or its fixtures and fittings. The owner would want to be sure that there would be sufficient return on the investment. In this situation, formal procedures for capital budgeting were commonly found. Guilding explained the need for such formal procedures as a mechanism of the principal-agency relationship where the owner (as principal) wanted to control the manager (as agent). The managers tended to bias their cash flow projections upwards to encourage the owners to invest in new projects. There was relatively little use of ex-post monitoring so the managers knew that it was unlikely that the owners would match the actual outcome against the cash flow projections.

12.6.2   Enterprise resource planning

Newman and Westrup (2003) describe a survey of CIMA members to collect their experiences of enterprise resource planning (ERP). Respondents described the change to an ERP system which integrates all aspects of the operations of a business. It was an initial shock for some to find that purchasing, production, inventory and finance were all linked for the first time. There were practical problems where different parts of an organisation worked in different ways, such as where the inventory controller kept records in kilogrammes while the production units measured in tonnes. Data entry originated in more than one location so the management accounting function had to learn to cope with having less control over the information used for accounting purposes. The accounting records were more up-to-date than they had previously been, but contained a greater number of small inaccuracies.

The change to ERP was a major investment project for those involved. Baker (2003) asked whether companies had gained maximum value from their investments in ERP systems. He noted that the average cost of one system was around £10 million. Despite the size of the investment very few companies produced a business case and even where this was done, a post-completion audit was rare. Baker described a case study undertaken by the chief executive of a UK subsidiary of a major US manufacturing company, in investigating the potential for introducing an ERP system. The tangible benefits identified were reductions in administrative staff and overhead savings. Intangible benefits were increased revenue and improved cash flow from smarter working. External consultancy was reduced. Costs and benefits were quantified and discounted at the cost of capital to give an estimated net present value and a payback period. Further consideration suggested that the cost–benefit analysis had underestimated training costs. Based on the evaluation the company decided not to proceed with ERP because it would not have sufficient resources to implement the change and maintain activity in its operations.

12.6.3   The Private Finance initiative in the NHS

Broadbent *et al* (2004) reported on the nature, emergence and role of management accounting in decision making and post-decision project evaluation in PFI projects.

These projects were joint arrangements between a public-sector National Health Service Trust and a private developer. They found that value for money was assessed by a discounted cost comparison of the PFI option relative to procuring the same service through a traditional public sector financed route. The authors felt that the accurate calculation and allocation of cost and quantitative transferred risks had to be matched with qualitative shared risks and benefits in order to make decisions. They found that at the time of their study the quantitative matters were more persuasive than the non-financial.

12.7 Summary

Key themes in this chapter are:

- **Capital rationing** means that there is not sufficient funding available to take up all projects that have a positive NPV.
- **Mutually exclusive** projects are found wherever a choice is needed because of limited resources of capital, labour, materials, or any other constraint.
- The **profitability index** may be used to rank projects in situations of capital rationing or mutually exclusive projects.
- **Capital budgeting** depends on careful forecasting of cash flows. In particular:
  - Cash will be needed for **working capital** at the start but will be recovered at the end of the project.
  - *Taxation* will cause outflows of cash; fiscal incentives may provide cash flow savings. In both cases the timing is important, as well as the amount. The discount rate must represent the after-tax cost of capital.
  - *Inflation* may be allowed for by discounting the inflation-adjusted cash flows at the inflation-adjusted cost of capital, or by discounting the real cash flows (measured at current prices) at the inflation-free cost of capital.
  - *Depreciation* does not appear in capital budgeting calculations because it does not represent a flow of cash.
  - *Interest charges* do not appear in capital budgeting because they are represented in the cost of capital.
  - The methods of capital budgeting used in practice will depend on the size of the project, the importance of early recovery of cash invested, and the benefits of accurate evaluation compared to the cost of the exercise.
- Effective **capital budgeting** requires control procedures to be in place for establishing the suitability of a project and for post-completion audit to evaluate the success of the project.
- **Advanced manufacturing technologies** have led to a demand for new ways of evaluating investment projects because new projects may require continuous investment of resources rather than a single outlay at the outset.

Further reading and references

Baker, M. (2003) 'Benefit gigs', *Financial Management*, July/August: 28–9.

Broadbent, J., Gill, J. and Laughlin, R. (2004) *The Private Finance Initiative in the National Health Service*, CIMA Research Report, CIMA Publishing.

Guilding, C. (2003) 'Hotel owner/operator structures: implications for capital budgeting process', *Management Accounting Research*, 14: 179–99.

Newman, M. and Westrup, C. (2003) 'Perpetrators', *Financial Management*, February: 32–3.

QUESTIONS

The Questions section of each chapter has three types of question. 'Test your understanding' questions to help you review your reading are in the 'A' series of questions. You will find the answer to these by reading and thinking about the material in the text book. 'Application' questions to test your ability to apply technical skills are in the 'B' series of questions. Questions requiring you to show skills in problem solving and evaluation are in the 'C' series of questions. The symbol [S] indicates that a solution is available at the end of the book.

A   Test your understanding

A12.1   What is 'capital budgeting' (section 12.1)?

A12.2   What is 'external capital rationing' (section 12.2.1)?

A12.3   What is 'internal capital rationing' (section 12.2.1)?

A12.4   What is 'single period' capital rationing (section 12.2.1)?

A12.5   What is 'multiple period' capital rationing (section 12.2.1)?

A12.6   What is the profitability index (section 12.2.2)?

A12.7   What is the decision rule based on the profitability index (section 12.2.2)?

A12.8   What is meant by 'mutually exclusive projects' (section 12.2.3)?

A12.9   Why might the NPV method of appraisal give an apparently different decision from the IRR method when evaluating mutually exclusive projects (section 12.2.4)?

A12.10   How is the working capital requirement included in cash flows for capital budgeting (section 12.3.1)?

A12.12   How may taxation rules affect cash flow projections in capital budgeting (section 12.3.2)?

A12.13   How may the effect of inflation be included in capital budgeting (section 12.3.3)?

A12.14   Why are (a) depreciation and (b) interest charges not found in the cash flow projections for capital budgeting (section 12.3.4)?

A12.15   Explain the processes necessary for authorisation and review of capital projects (section 12.5).

A12.16   Explain what is meant by post-completion audit (section 12.5.2).

A12.17   Explain what is meant by Advanced Manufacturing Technologies (section 12.6.1).

A12.18   Explain why present value techniques may not be suitable for project evaluation where a business uses Advanced Manufacturing Technologies (section 12.6.2).

B   Application

Note: In answering these questions you may need to use the discount tables in the Appendix to Chapter 11, p. 282.

B12.1 [S]
Peter Green is planning a new business operation. It will produce net cash flows of £80,000 per year for four years. The initial investment in fixed assets will cost £90,000. The business is located in an enterprise zone and so is entitled to claim a tax deduction up to 100% of the cost of the fixed assets. It is expected that the fixed assets will sell for £10,000 at the end of four years. The corporation tax rate is 20%. Corporation tax is payable 12 months after the relevant cash flows arise. The after-tax cost of capital is 6% per annum.

Required

Calculate the net present value of the project.

B12.2 [S]

Foresight Ltd plans an investment in fixed assets costing £120m. The project will have a three-year life, with the predicted cash flows as:

Year 1	£55m
Year 2	£71m
Year 3	£45m

Finance for inventories and debtors amounting to £75m will be required at the start of the project. Trade credit will provide £45m of this amount. All working capital will be recovered at the end of year 3. The expected scrap value of fixed assets at the end of year 3 is £15m. The cost of capital is 10%. Taxation is to be ignored.

Required

(a) Calculate the net present value of the project.
(b) Show that the project can pay interest at 10% per annum on the capital invested and return a surplus equivalent to the net present value calculated in (a).

C Problem solving and evaluation

Note: In answering these questions you may need to refer to the discount tables in the Appendix to Chapter 11, p. 282.

C12.1 [S]

Offshore Services Ltd is an oil-related company providing specialist firefighting and rescue services to oil rigs. The board of directors is considering a number of investment projects to improve the cash flow situation in the face of strong competition from international companies in the same field.

The proposed projects are:

Project	Description
ALPHA	Commission an additional firefighting vessel.
BRAVO	Replace two existing standby boats.
CHARLIE	Establish a new survival training course for the staff of client companies.
DELTA	Install latest communications equipment on all vessels.

Each project is expected to produce a reduction in cash outflows over the next five years. The outlays and cash benefits are set out below:

	End of year	ALPHA £000s	BRAVO £000s	CHARLIE £000s	DELTA £000s
Outlay	–	(600)	(300)	(120)	(210)
Cash flow benefits:					
	1	435	–	48	81
	2	435	–	48	81
	3	–	219	48	81
	4	–	219	48	81
	5	–	219	48	81
Internal rate of return		28.8%	22.0%	28.6%	26.8%

Any project may be postponed indefinitely. Investment capital is limited to £1,000,000. The board wishes to maximise net present value of projects undertaken and requires a return of 10% per annum.

Required

Prepare a report to the board of directors containing:

(a) calculations of net present value for each project; and

(b) a reasoned recommendation on maximisation of net present value within the £1,000,000 investment limit.

C12.2 [S]

The directors of Advanced plc are currently considering an investment in new production machinery to replace existing machinery. The new machinery would produce goods more efficiently, leading to increased sales volume. The investment required will be £1,150,000 payable at the start of the project. The alternative course of action would be to continue using the existing machinery for a further five years, at the end of which time it would have to be replaced.

The following forecasts of sales and production volumes have been made:

Sales (in units)

Year	Using existing machinery	Using new machinery
1	400,000	560,000
2	450,000	630,000
3	500,000	700,000
4	600,000	840,000
5	750,000	1,050,000

Production (in units)

Year	Using existing machinery	Using new machinery
1	420,000	564,000
2	435,000	637,000
3	505,000	695,000
4	610,000	840,000
5	730,000	1,044,000

Further information

(a) The new machinery will reduce production costs from their present level of £7.50 per unit to £6.20 per unit. These production costs exclude depreciation.

(b) The increased sales volume will be achieved by reducing unit selling prices from their present level of £10.00 per unit to £8.50 per unit.

(c) The new machinery will have a scrap value of £150,000 after five years.

(d) The existing machinery will have a scrap value of £30,000 at the start of Year 1. Its scrap value will be £20,000 at the end of Year 5.

(e) The cost of capital to the company, in money terms, is presently 12% per annum.

Required

(1) Prepare a report to the directors of Advanced plc on the proposed investment decision.

(2) List any further matters which the directors should consider before making their decision.

C12.3

The board of directors of Kirkside Glassware Ltd is considering the following proposed investment projects:

Project	Nature
A	Establishment of a staff training scheme.
B	Major improvements to the electrical system.
C	Installation of a computer.
D	Development of a new product.
E	Purchase of a warehouse space, presently leased.

It is estimated that each product will provide benefits in terms of reduced cash outflows, measured over the coming five years. The outlays and cash flow benefits, net of taxation, are set out below:

	End of year	Project A £	Project B £	Project C £	Project D £	Project E £
Outlay	–	(40,000)	(70,000)	(180,000)	(100,000)	(200,000)
Cash flow benefits:						
	1	16,000	27,000	66,000	–	145,000
	2	16,000	27,000	66,000	–	145,000
	3	16,000	27,000	66,000	73,000	–
	4	16,000	27,000	66,000	73,000	–
	5	16,000	27,000	66,000	73,000	–
Internal rate of return		28.65%	26.82%	24.32%	22.05%	28.79%

Each project has two separate phases of equal cost and providing equal cash flow benefits. The board is willing to consider adopting the first phase of any project without the second, if this appears necessary. Any project or phase not undertaken immediately may be postponed indefinitely. Capital available for investment is limited to £300,000. The board aims, as far as possible, to maximise the net present value of projects undertaken.

The company requires a return of 10 per cent per annum based on the net cash flows of any project.

Required

Prepare a report to the board of directors:

(a) setting out a decision rule which could be applied in ranking the investment projects; and
(b) listing other factors which the board of directors might wish to consider when selecting projects for implementation.

C12.4

You are employed as the accountant for Cars Ltd, a local garage which has a bodyshop. The bodyshop manager, Mr George, has contacted you saying that one of the company's present customers has offered the company a one year contract for additional work. The customer requires a discount of 10% to be allowed on the total invoice value. Mr George provides you with the following information.

1 Additional capital expenditure will be:

	£
Video conferencing facility	10,000
Additional storage trolleys	5,000
Computerised estimated system	10,000

The customer insists on installation of the video conferencing facility which will not be usable for any other contract. The storage trolleys and estimating system may be used on other work after the end of this particular contract.

2 Additional staff will be required. Three full-time skilled technicians earning £8.00 per hour will each work 39 hours per week on the new contract. They are each allowed 6 weeks paid holidays per year and 2 weeks paid training. Labour efficiency is 95% measured as the ratio of sold hours/hours attended. Training time and holiday time are charged to direct costs of the department. For each technician the new contract will leave some unsold hours available for any other jobs coming into the bodyshop. One full-time car cleaner will be required earning £10,500 per annum.

3 The customer has said that the potential increase in sales due to chargeable hours from this contract could be 4,500 hours at a rate of £20.00 per hour before discount. In addition the increase in sales of car parts is calculated on the basis of £40.00 per hour with an average gross profit of 15% before discount. The increase in paint sales is calculated on the basis of £3.50 per hour with an average gross profit of 40% before discount.

4 Additional annual overheads will be as follows:

	£
Variable costs	5,500
Fixed costs	6,500

5 Depreciation is calculated on a straight line basis as follows:

	%
Storage trolleys	20
Computers	25

Mr George has asked your opinion on the acceptability of the customer's proposal.

Required
Write a memo to Mr George:

(a) assessing the financial aspects of the proposal; and
(b) commenting briefly on other considerations relevant to the decision-making process.

Case studies

Real world cases

Prepare short answers to Case studies 12.1, 12.2 and 12.3.

PERFORMANCE MEASUREMENT AND CONTROL

Managers need information to help them measure relative successes and failures in performance. They also need information to help control operations. Evaluation of performance and control of activity requires a forward-looking plan, followed by a system that monitors achievements against that plan.

Part 3 explains how management accounting helps answer questions of the following type:

- What is our budget for all activities for the next 12 months, analysed into components for each part of the organisation?
- How can we use budgets for performance measurement and control?
- What are the limitations of budgets as a tool of management planning and control?
- How should information be presented to various levels of management and to employees within the organisation, to give information on performance and feedback for improvement?
- How is the performance of a division within an organisation measured?
- How do standard costs help in setting performance targets and monitoring achievements?
- What special methods are required to deal with continuous processes?

Chapters 13 and 14 explain the use of budgets and some of the challenges faced in budgeting. In particular, Chapter 14 explains how to compare budgets with actual outcomes by calculating variances. Chapter 15 extends the analysis of variances by describing standard costing. Chapter 16 describes methods of evaluating and reporting on performance within departments of an organisation, while Chapter 17 extends this analysis to divisional performance.

Part 3 PERFORMANCE MEASUREMENT AND CONTROL			
LEVEL 1	**Chapter 13** Preparing a budget		**Chapter 16** Performance evaluation and feedback reporting
LEVEL 2	**Chapter 14** Control through budgeting	**Chapter 15** Standard costs	**Chapter 17** Divisional performance

Preparing a budget

This case study shows a typical situation in which management accounting can be helpful. Read the case study now but only attempt the discussion points after you have finished studying the chapter.

Transport for London produced the budget shown below for Walking, Cycling and Accessibility. The budget description follows the table:

	2003/04 Total costs £m	2004/05 Operating budget £m	2004/05 Capital budget £m	2004/05 Total budget £m
Walking	7.1	0.9	6.7	7.6
Cycling	13.6	0.6	11.6	12.2
Accessibility	6.1		6.9	6.9

Walking
This activity consists of a programme of measures that aim to create and promote a connected, safe, convenient and attractive environment that increases the levels of walking in London in accordance with the Mayor's Transport Strategy objectives. Proposals have been developed in partnership with TfL, the London boroughs and interest groups (London cycling campaign & Living Streets).

Deliverables in 2004/05
- New and upgraded pedestrian crossings (21 crossings under development)
- Removal of footbridges and closures of subways and replacement with surface level facilities (4 junctions under development)
- Provision of new or improved facilities at signalised junctions and footway upgrading existing strategic routes (numerous locations)
- Providing new footbridges across railways and upgrading existing facilities (4 sites)
- Improved interchanges between bus and rail services (5 sites)
- Pedestrian signing, security improvements, refuges, pavement widening at crossings, removal of clutter and installation of dropped kerbs (numerous locations)
- Co-ordination of the annual Car Free Day.

Indicators of success
- 90 pedestrian schemes to be delivered by March 2005.

Source: Transport for London website www.tfl.gov.uk/tfl/

Discussion points

1 How does this budget provide useful information for managing transport activity?

2 If you were a member of the Council being asked to approve this budget, what further information would you need?

Learning outcomes

After reading this chapter you should be able to:

- Explain the purpose and nature of a budget system.
- Describe the administration of the budgetary process.
- Explain the benefits of budgeting.
- Prepare the separate budgets that lead to a master budget.
- Prepare quarterly budgets.
- Describe and discuss examples of research into the budget process.

13.1 Introduction

This chapter considers the purpose and nature of the budgetary process and explains the method of preparation of budgets, with particular emphasis on the planning process. The use of budgets for control is touched upon in this chapter but is discussed in more detail in Chapter 14. No two businesses will have an identical approach to budget preparation. Some involve all employees in the process, while others deliver the budget as handed down from senior management with little or no consultation. This chapter discusses systems where there is a relatively high degree of participation and negotiation in setting budgets. It should be recognised that in some businesses the senior managers will take decisions without such extensive consultation. A discussion of the relative merits of consultation are well beyond the scope of this book, but in learning about the budgetary process it may help the student to think about the ways in which each person having responsibility for administering a budget might also have a part to play in its construction.

13.2 Purpose and nature of a budget system

The purpose of a **budget system** is to serve the needs of management in respect of the judgements and decisions it is required to make and to provide a basis for the management functions of planning and control, described in Chapter 1. That chapter also refers to the importance of communication and motivation as an aspect of management to which management accounting should contribute.

In Exhibit 1.2 there is an illustration of the interrelationships of these management functions in respect of the process by which a business such as a chain of shops supplying motor cycles might go about planning to open a new shop in the suburbs of a city. Where this type of planning is taking place, management accounting assists through a budget system by providing quantification of each stage of the planning process. That example of the motor cycle shop illustrates a simple type of long-range planning but a more complex example would show the way in which the long-range planning leads on to successively more detailed developments, finishing with a collection of short-term operational budgets covering a period such as a year, six months or perhaps no more than one month ahead.

13.2.1 Long-range planning

In **long-range planning**, the senior managers of a business will begin by specifying a vision statement which sets out in the broadest terms their vision of the future direction of the organisation. Based on this, the senior managers will then prepare a list of objectives which will specify the intended future growth and development of the business. For example, a company might state its vision and its long-range corporate objectives, for a five-year period ahead, in the terms shown in Exhibit 13.1.

The corporate objectives shown in Exhibit 13.1 relate to the business as a whole. They will then be taken down to another level of detail to create objectives for each division of the business. Within divisions, they will be translated into departmental objectives.

13.2.2 Strategy

Having a vision statement and corporate objectives is an essential first step, but the organisation must then decide exactly how it will achieve those objectives. The term **strategy** is used to describe the courses of action to be taken in achieving the objectives set.

Exhibit 13.1

Company's vision statement and long-range corporate objectives

Vision

The company intends to maintain its position as the market leader in the electrical goods repair industry, having regard to providing investors with an adequate rate of growth of their investment in the business.

Corporate objectives

- The company intends to increase the value of the investment by its shareholders at a minimum rate of 4% per annum, in real terms.
- The company intends to remain in the electrical goods repair business and to concentrate on this as the core business.
- The company will provide service in the customer's home and at its main repair centres.
- The company will continue to maintain its geographical focus on the high-earning sub-urban areas around the three largest cities.
- The company seeks to enlarge its market share in those geographical areas to 20% of the total market.
- The company has a profit objective of 30% gross profit on turnover.

Developing the strategy will involve senior management from the various functions such as marketing, customer service, production, personnel and finance. These functions are separate, but must work together in the interests of the company as a whole. Each functional manager has to understand how the plans made by that function will affect other functions and the company as a whole. This requires communication and co-ordination with the assistance of a management accountant.

For the purposes of quantifying the strategy of the business, management accounting has developed specialist techniques under the global heading of **budgetary planning and control**. The rest of this chapter explains the processes involved.

13.2.3 Budgets

Definition

A **budget** is a detailed plan which sets out, in money terms, the plans for income and expenditure in respect of a future period of time. It is prepared in advance of that time period and is based on the agreed objectives for that period of time, together with the strategy planned to achieve those objectives.

Each separate function of the organisation will have its own **budget**. Exhibit 13.2 shows a typical scheme of budget structure within an organisation. It shows how the organisation moves from setting objectives, through the strategy stage and into the preparation of budgets. The long-term objectives are set first. It is important to note at that stage any key assumptions which might have a critical effect on future implementation of those objectives. The implementation of those long-term objectives is then formed into a strategy which results in some intermediate objectives for the short term. Again it is important to note any key assumptions which might later cause the organisation to question the objectives. In many businesses the critical factor determining all other budgets is the sales forecast. The business exists primarily to make sales and hence generate profit, so each separate function will be working towards that major target. Each function of the business then prepares its own budget as a statement of its operational plan for achieving the targets that have been set.

In practice these budgets would be prepared at the same time with a great deal of interaction among the managers of the various functions. That is difficult to show in a diagram. Exhibit 13.2 shows only the main budget relationships, moving from the sales forecast to the production plan and the resulting working capital needs (stock, debtors and trade creditors) and capital investment in fixed assets. The various detailed budgets are brought together within a finance plan and then formed into conventional accounting statements such as budgeted profit and loss account, cash flow statement and balance sheet. This package is sometimes referred to as the master budget. The process leading to the preparation of the master budget, as outlined in Exhibit 13.2, will be used in the next section of this chapter as a basis for explaining the administration of the budgeting process.

Exhibit 13.2
Budget planning and relationships

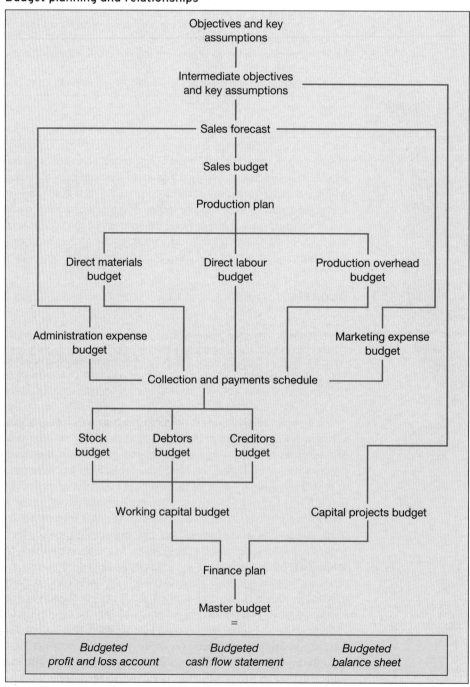

Imagine you are the managing director of a large company about to embark on budget preparation for the following year. How would you manage the various people you would need to meet in order to make operational the budget relationships shown in Exhibit 13.2? Would you meet them all together or have separate meetings? Would you take sole charge or would you establish teams? Write down your thoughts on this before you read the next section and then check it against your ideas.

13.2.4 Forecasts

Forecasts involve making predictions. The prediction could be a description such as 'we forecast that sales prices next year will rise by more than cost inflation.' Or the prediction could be quantified, for example 'we forecast a five per cent increase in demand for our product.' For planning purposes, a forecast is more useful if it contains some quantification.

Definition   A **forecast** is a prediction of future events and their quantification for planning purposes.

So what is the difference between a budget and a forecast? Both are looking forward and both involve quantification. However, the forecast generally comes at an early stage in the planning process when managers are looking to the future to make plans and anticipate problems. Once the plans are made the budget is prepared as a quantification of the planning. The sequence is:

13.3 Administration of the budgetary process

The budgetary process has to be administered effectively in terms of initial planning, final approval and subsequent monitoring of implementation. A budget committee is usually formed to manage each stage of the budgetary process. The accounting staff will have a close involvement. The budget preparation procedures will need to be set out in a manual which is available to all participants. A continuing cycle evolves in which initial budgets are prepared, negotiations take place with line managers, the initial budgets are revised, the final budget is accepted and, later on, there is a review of actual and budgeted performance. The cycle then starts over again.

13.3.1 The budget committee

To implement the strategy decisions, a **budget committee** will be formed, comprising the senior managers who are responsible for designing the strategy. The budget committee receives the initial budgets from each functional manager. If the initial budget is based on unrealistic targets, then the functional manager will be asked to modify the budget within the organisation's overall targets. There is a motivational aspect of budget preparation, so it is important that the functional manager understands the need for revising the budget within the organisation's strategy. Budget negotiation can be quite a delicate process.

Fiona McTaggart describes her experiences of the initial budget formation in a conglomerate company having a stock exchange listing:

FIONA: *There are four divisions whose activities are quite dissimilar but the linking theme is their ability to generate cash for the group which, in turn, is translated into dividends for the shareholders and capital investment for the divisions. The budget committee is formed from the board of directors of the holding company. Budget negotiations start each year when each divisional manager sets targets in six critical areas: capital expenditure, turnover, gross and net profit margins, cash flow and working capital requirements.*

The budget committee knows over the years that the transport division manager is always too enthusiastic for capital expenditure and has to be persuaded to be more cautious in replacing and expanding the fleet.

The musical instrument division is on a steady-state pattern without much growth, but is regarded as a steady source of cash flow, so is not encouraged to be more ambitious.

The knitwear division has some problems associated with fashion goods and tends to be too conservative in its planning. A measure of risk taking is encouraged and almost every year that division has to be asked to revise its initial turnover targets upwards.

The fourth division is stationery supplies and their problem is profit targets in a competitive sector. Little can be done about gross profit, but there is plenty of scope for cost efficiencies to improve the contribution of net profit to cash flow.

13.3.2 The accounting department

The staff of the accounting department will work with operations managers to initiate the preparation of budgets and will advise and assist in the practical aspects of budget preparation. They should have the knowledge and experience to provide advice to line managers on the preparation of budgets. The accounting department will have the computer facilities to prepare and co-ordinate the budget preparation process. The accounting staff must involve themselves with the operations team in the budget exercise and must understand the commercial issues. They may have to offer challenges to the operations managers, but such challenges will be aimed at ensuring improved budgets for the benefit of the whole organisation as well as for the operational unit.

13.3.3 Sequence of the budgetary process

Exhibit 13.2 shows the relationships among the various budgets but does not portray the time sequence of the budgeting process. The principal stages of this sequence are:

(a) communicate the details of objectives and strategy to those responsible for preparation of budgets and co-ordinate the overall linkage of objectives and strategy;
(b) communicate the details of budget preparation procedures to those responsible for preparation of budgets and respond to concerns or questions;
(c) determine the limiting factor which restricts overall budget flexibility and forms the focus of the budget cascade and evaluate the impact of the limiting factor;
(d) prepare an initial set of budgets;
(e) negotiate budgets with line managers;
(f) co-ordinate and review budgets;
(g) accept budgets in final form;
(h) carry out ongoing review of budgets as they are implemented.

Communicate objectives and strategy

The long-range plan should be contained in a strategy document which is circulated within the organisation at intervals throughout the year. Regular circulation, with invitations to comment and a visible process of revision to accommodate changing circumstances, means that those responsible for the preparation of budgets have the fullest understanding of the basis for the budget process. The strategy document should contain clear narrative descriptions of the objectives of the organisation, supplemented by quantified illustrations of the impact on the organisation as a whole and on major divisions. The objectives may initially be expressed in non-financial terms such as production or sales targets by volume, or workforce targets by quantity and quality. Ultimately, all these non-financial targets will have a financial implication.

Communicate procedures

For communication of budget preparation procedures within the organisation there must be a **budget manual**. This will set out the timetable for budget preparation, formats to be used, circulation lists for drafts and arbitration procedures where conflicts begin to show themselves.

Determine the critical factor

The critical factor sets the starting point of the budgeting process. For many organisations, sales are the critical factor. There is no point in producing goods and services which do not sell. There may be occasions when the demand is not a problem but the supply of materials or labour resources is restricted. (Such restrictions on production factors should be temporary in a competitive market because materials will eventually be found at a higher price, while labour will move from one geographical area to another or will train to develop new skills within the area.) For this chapter it will be assumed that sales are the critical factor. That assumption is the basis of the chart of budget relationships shown in Exhibit 13.2 where the cascade flows down from the top to the foot of the page.

Preparing an initial set of budgets

The **sales budget** is a representation of the volume of sales planned for the budget period, multiplied by the expected selling price of each item. For most organisations, sales volume is the major unknown item because it depends on customers whose choices may be difficult to predict. In practice an organisation will carry out some form of market research, ranging from very sophisticated market research surveys to some simple but effective techniques such as contacting past customers and asking them about their intentions for the period ahead. Sales representatives will, as part of their work, form continuous estimates of demand in their region of responsibility. Past performance in sales may usefully be analysed to identify trends which may be an indicator of future success in sales.

From the sales plan flow the **operational budgets**. Exhibit 13.2 shows the subsequent pattern of budget development once the sales budget has been determined. The **production plan**, setting out quantities of resource inputs required, leads into operational budgets for direct labour, direct materials and manufacturing overhead which combine resource quantities with expected price per unit. At the same time, budgets for administration and marketing are being prepared based on quantities and prices of resources needed for production and sales.

That information provides the basis for a profit and loss account matching sales and expenses. A cash flow estimate is also required based upon working capital needs and fixed asset needs. Working capital depends on the mix of stock, debtors and creditors planned to support the sales and production levels expected. Fixed asset needs derive from the capital projects budgeted as a result of the objectives of the organisation.

This all feeds into a finance plan from which the **master budget** emerges containing the budgeted profit and loss account, the budgeted cash flow statement and the budgeted balance sheet.

Negotiate budgets with line managers

The success of the budgetary process is widely held to depend on the extent to which all participants are involved in the budget preparation process. A **bottom-up budget** process starts by asking those who will ultimately implement the budget to make proposals, and have an involvement in, the budget process. That does not mean that they take over control of the budget but it does give them a greater sense of ownership of the resulting budget.

Definition

> A **bottom-up budget** is initiated by inviting those who will implement the budget to participate in the process of setting the budget. It is also called a **participative budget**.

A **top-down budget** process starts with the senior management sending down budgets and targets based on the organisational goals and strategies. The budget is imposed on those who will implement it, without inviting them to share in its preparation.

Definition

> A **top-down budget** is set by management without inviting those who will implement the budget to participate in the process of setting the budget. It is also called an **imposed budget**.

A negotiated budget combines these two approaches so that the budget allowances are set as the result of negotiation between budget holders and the management to whom they are responsible.

In a negotiated process, the budgets will be initiated in each of the departments or areas responsible but each budget may have an impact on other line managers. There may be a problem of restricted resources which requires all budgets to be cut back from initial expectations. There may be a programme of expansion which has not sufficiently been taken into account by those preparing the budgets. Whatever the particular circumstances, a negotiation stage will be required which will usually involve the budget committee in discussions with various line managers. At the very least this will be a communications exercise so that each participant understands the overall position. More often it will be an opportunity for fine-tuning the plans so that the benefit to the organisation as a whole is maximised.

Although Exhibit 13.2 is presented as a downward-flowing cascade because of the increasing level of detail involved, it does not adequately represent the negotiation processes involved. Exhibit 13.3 is a different way of showing the budgetary process outlined in Exhibit 13.2. It emphasises people rather than the documentation resulting from the process, and also shows the combination of the 'bottom-up' preparation of budgets with the 'top-down' approval by senior management.

In Exhibit 13.3, the mauve lines show some of the interactions which might take place in the negotiation stage, distinguishing negotiations among the line managers and negotiations between the line managers and the budget committee. Quite deliberately, the lines are shown without directional arrows because the negotiation process is two-way. Even then a two-dimensional diagram cannot do justice to the time span and the sequence of negotiations over a relatively short space of time.

Co-ordinate and review budgets

The mauve lines of Exhibit 13.3 depict one-to-one links in the negotiation process. Participants in each separate negotiation will reach a point where they are satisfied with the discussion, or else they understand where and why their opinions differ. However, the budget committee has an obligation to serve the interests of the organisation as a whole. The separate budgets resulting from the negotiation process are brought together in a meeting of the budget committee. At this meeting the separate budgets are co-ordinated. If the sales manager has budgeted for a 10 per cent

Exhibit 13.3
The negotiating aspects of budget planning

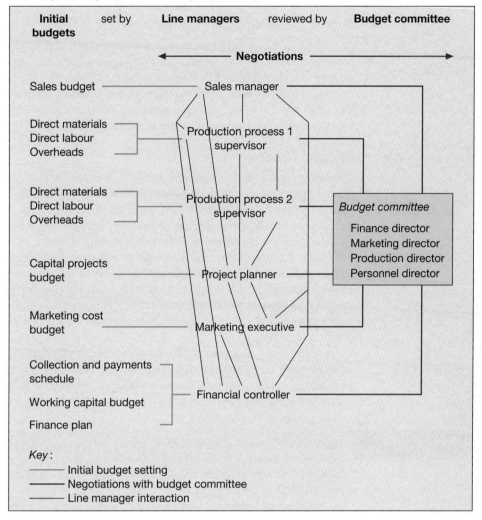

Key:
——— Initial budget setting
——— Negotiations with budget committee
——— Line manager interaction

expansion in the volume of sales in the coming year, while the production director has budgeted for steady-state levels of production, then this co-ordination exercise will show a potential reduction in stock levels. This may be acceptable in the circumstances, but the risks of inadequate stock levels must be added to the planning considerations. If the production director has budgeted for a change in employee grade which will increase the wages cost, but the finance director has planned for a 'freeze' on payroll costs, the co-ordination exercise may result in one or the other budget giving way.

Co-ordination will involve examining all the separate budgets in terms of how well they serve the objectives and strategy defined at the outset.

Review could take a variety of forms. The budget committee might review the budgets for reasonableness by comparing them with the budgets for the previous year and the outcome of that year. The review might concentrate on the effective use of cash. It might link the budget requests to indicators of performance. For example, there might be a view that departments that have performed well should receive even greater budgets to support this high performance. On the other hand, there might be a view that a department that has failed to perform to expectations needs greater budgets to support a catching-up exercise.

Co-ordination and review may lead to a further round of negotiation in order to arrive at the best position for the entity as a whole.

Accept the budgets in final form

At the end of the negotiation period it will be necessary for the budget committee to approve and accept a definitive set of budgets which will set out the organisation's plan for the period ahead. It is possible that, as a result of the negotiation stage, some managers will feel more satisfied than others. A good system of budget setting will by this stage have ensured that all managers, whether disappointed or not, understand the reasoning and understand what is expected in their area of responsibility.

Ongoing review

The budget process is not an end in itself. It is a formal process of planning which guides subsequent action. Monitoring that subsequent action against the budget plan is therefore an essential follow-up to the budget process. An organisation might decide that monthly monitoring of progress against budget is adequate for control purposes and for contributing to future planning.

Within the control function, monthly monitoring of the actual outcome against the budget will allow corrective action to be taken at the earliest opportunity, although care is required in this respect. It could be that conditions have changed since the budget was set and the actual outcome is a better representation than the budget. In such a case it might even be appropriate to revise the budget in line with the changed conditions.

Budgeting is a continuous process which requires adaptation of existing budgets where a need for change is indicated, and the consideration of performance against past budgets when the next round of budget preparation begins. The budget committee is therefore active the whole year around.

Activity 13.2

Write down five ways in which budgets appear to benefit an organisation. Then read the next section. How does your list compare with the text? Have you identified benefits additional to those described? Have you used different words to describe a benefit which is in the text?

13.4 The benefits of budgeting

The budgetary process contributes to effective management in the following areas: planning, control, communication and co-ordination, and performance evaluation. Each of these areas is now considered in turn.

13.4.1 Planning

The preparation of budgets forces management to carry out a formal planning exercise which identifies every part of the organisation and brings the separate parts together on a quantified basis. Major planning decisions are made as part of the long-term planning process, and these are then refined into progressively greater detail as management turn them into short-term operational plans. A formal planning process encourages all parts of the organisation to contribute on a regular basis to the formation of the overall plan and to identify potential difficulties at an early stage. Here is Fiona McTaggart to describe the budget planning process in a major multi-national company.

FIONA: *I once participated in the planning process within a major international oil company. The financial year ran from January to December. The company's head office was in Brussels, with operational centres around the world. I was working in one of the UK operational centres, seeing the process from part-way along the chain. A company strategy group, comprising the senior management from head office and the operational centres, would form a rolling five-year statement of objectives. Having a rolling plan means that the company always looks to the next five years, but each January the rolling plan is reviewed, the current year is deleted and the fifth year ahead is added.*

The effect is that the rolling five-year plan is updated every January in respect of the five-year period starting the following January. That means the company has 12 months in which to prepare its operational budgets for the one year starting in the following January. Preparation of the five-year plan is described as Stage A. Each operational centre around the world then has two months to come back to head office with the results of its one-year budgeting, described as Stage B.

Stage B involves each operational centre specifying how the implementation of the five-year plan will be carried out for one year ahead within the operational centre, bringing out a master budget of quarterly cash flows and profit. At that stage they don't produce the detailed operational budgets within the operational centre, but each centre will have consulted with its various managers as to the way in which their departmental objectives for one year ahead will mesh with the five-year plan from head office and from the operational centre.

Stage C lasts one month and allows some fine-tuning of the five-year plan, by the head office, in the light of the reaction from the operational centres. That takes matters up to the end of June, and after that point there is little further opportunity for change in the five-year plan, or in the one-year targets of each operational centre, short of a major change in circumstances in the company or in the industry.

Stage D lasts four months and involves detailed budget planning within each operational centre. That will be an iterative process, where each manager of an operational unit produces a draft budget covering a 12-month period, the draft budgets are collected together, an overall view is taken and the draft budgets go back to the managers for revision.

Everything is tidied up by the end of October and then there are two months left to put the documentation together so that budgets are ready for implementation from the start of the next year in January.

Meanwhile, in October the senior managers in Brussels will have started their deliberations with a view to revising the rolling five-year plan in the following January. Then the whole process starts over again!

13.4.2 Control

Once the budget is in place, implementation of the organisation's plans takes place and the actual outcome may be compared against the budget. Some revenues and costs will behave according to expectations, but some will not. Attention needs to be given to the items which are not meeting expectations. Having a budget as a basis for comparison allows management to identify the exceptions which require attention. Identifying such matters at an early stage allows corrective action to be taken to remedy the problem.

Differences between the actual outcomes and budget expectations may signal the need for urgent action by the managers or the need for revisions to the budget. If the budget differences arise from factors under the control of the line managers, then urgent action may be required to rectify the causes of those differences. However, if the budget differences are the result of unforeseen or uncontrollable factors, then the need is for modification of the budget.

Here is Fiona to continue her story.

FIONA: *I've told you how the oil company produces its budgets for the year ahead. From January of each year the actual out-turn of the operations has to be compared against the budget. That is where the problems really start, because the oil industry is at the high end of the uncertainty spectrum. The price of oil is controlled in world markets and influenced by world events well beyond the power of any company. A threat of war in some far-away country which borders on the main shipping lanes will send the price of oil up, but threaten supplies for individual production companies seeking to take advantage of the price rise. Recession in developed countries will lower the demand and hence lower the price, so that companies have oil in the ground but may as well leave it there if demand has disappeared. These major changes occur on a short-term basis and may cause the short-term plans to require urgent change.*

It would not be feasible to return to the five-year plan every month because of a crisis, so the operational centres have to adapt to change. A few years ago, the operational centres did nothing to amend the budgets after they had been finalised. The consequence was that the budgets grew increasingly irrelevant to reality as the year progressed. As a result, the operational managers largely ignored the budgets and set their own unofficial targets in operational terms without having regard to the precise financial implications.

Senior management realised that this by-passing of the management accounting budgets was linked to a lack of awareness of cost control – vital to a business which has little control over its selling prices. So a quarterly revision process was devised whereby the operational centre is allowed to revise the budgets to keep them relevant to changing circumstances. This may lead to a deviation from the five-year plan set at the start of the year, but the view is that the increased relevance to operational practice is more important than the deviation from the plan. Of course, information about the revision is fed back to head office as input to the next round of five-year planning.

It seems to be working, and the managers at the operational level, such as platform supervisors and supply service managers, now use their quarterly budgets as a basis for explaining how they control costs for which they are responsible. There is also a benefit to the five-year planning exercise, because indications of change are fed in during the year and the long-term exercise itself is becoming smoother.

13.4.3 Communication and co-ordination

In Chapter 1 there is an organisation chart (Exhibit 1.1) which shows line relationships and horizontal relationships where effective communications are essential. Lines of communication ensure that all parts of the organisation are kept fully informed of the plans and of the policies and constraints within which those plans are formed.

Fiona continues with her experiences in an oil company.

FIONA: *One of the major problems of any large organisation is to encourage communication and co-ordination within the separate parts of the entity. The oil company is organised into divisions based on the six different exploration fields. Sometimes those different fields appear to regard themselves as self-contained units with no other relationships. It is important to overcome this insularity by skilful use of communication and co-ordination. The process of communication and co-ordination starts with the early stages of the budget planning process when each divisional head is required to review the plans for the division in the context of the other five divisions. Targets set within the budget are comparable across the divisions, but there is an allowance for the relative exploration difficulty. That first stage of review may encourage a self-centred attitude of protecting the division's interests, but it does at least encourage a wider awareness of global targets.*

The communication process continues when detailed budget plans are prepared. Divisional heads attend monthly meetings when the budget planning team sets out the main features of the budgets. That allows one-to-one communication and creates an awareness of the possibilities of mutual savings by co-ordination. As one small example, a helicopter might be leaving the airport to take supplies out to a rig. The return trip could usefully be turned into a full payload by calling at a rig on a nearby field on the way back. That requires some co-ordination, but could halve the overall flight cost for each field.

The control stage encourages further awareness of the need for co-ordination when the actual costs are compared with the budget. Each divisional head receives an exception report showing costs which are running over budget, and there is a system of marking cost headings where co-ordination could reduce overall costs. A commentary section attached to the exception report gives the divisional head guidance as to where co-ordination might usefully be applied.

13.4.4 Basis for performance evaluation

Performance evaluation within organisations must sooner or later be taken to the stage of detail which requires evaluation of the performance of individuals working within the organisation. In some situations there will be a monetary reward for high performance standards, in terms of bonus payments and possible promotion. There may be penalties for underperforming, the most drastic of which is to be dismissed from the post. Apart from the organisation's needs to evaluate the performance of those working within the organisation, there is also an individual's need for self-assessment. Whatever the type of performance evaluation of the individual or group of individuals, targets must be set in advance which are known to, and understood by, all participants. The budgetary process forms a systematic basis for setting performance targets in financial terms.

The financial targets may then have to be translated into non-financial targets (such as number of items produced per week, or frequency of corrective work, or number of administrative tasks undertaken) because the person concerned will identify more readily with the non-financial performance measure. The subject of non-financial performance measures is explored further in Chapter 16.

> **Activity 13.3**
>
> *Write down your personal budget for (a) the week ahead, and (b) the month ahead. Show money coming in and money going out. How difficult is it to prepare a budget? What problems did you encounter? To what extent is uncertainty about the future a problem? In the example which follows there is no uncertainty – it assumes the future may be forecast precisely. Work through the example and then consider how much such an exercise would be affected by uncertainty in the real world.*

13.5 Practical example – development of a budget

This practical example is based on the operational budgeting in the company called BestGear Partnership. There are two working partners who have built up, over ten years, a small but successful business which makes a range of women's fashion clothing sold through boutiques and selected regional department stores. The image of an exclusive label is maintained by not selling through national department stores. The example sets out the vision statement and objectives of the company in Exhibit 13.4. It then sets out the budget details for Year 5, as agreed by line managers after negotiations in the later months of Year 4, together with the balance sheet expected at 31 December, Year 4 as a starting point to the budget preparation for Year 5.

To help the reader follow the trail through the practical example, each table of information has a reference of the type **(T 1)** at the top left-hand corner. This reference is used in later tables to give a cross-reference to the source of data used in calculation. It is always good practice, in working practical examples, to give plenty of cross-referencing and to show full workings so that the reader can follow the sequence.

13.5.1   Vision statement and objectives

A vision statement and objectives can be quite short. The vision statement in Exhibit 13.4 tells the reader about the business of the BestGear Partnership and the strong personal involvement of the working partners. The objectives focus on the quality of staff, which is an essential component of a business offering personal service to customers. They also focus on supporting the confidence of customers with a 'money-back' guarantee. The final objective reminds us that this is a business that intends to make profits for its owners.

Exhibit 13.4
Example of vision statement and objectives

> **BestGear Partnership Ltd**
>
> *Vision statement*
> The company intends to maintain its position in a niche market in supplying fashionable designer clothing at affordable prices for the discerning buyer. The relatively small scale of the operation will be maintained as part of the attraction of the product.
>
> The two working partners, who together own the business, are committed to maintaining a close relationship with customers and staff so that quality of service remains uppermost at all times.
>
> *Objectives*
> - The company intends to recruit high-quality staff.
> - The company will continue its no-quibble money-back-within-30-days policy.
> - The company has a target gross profit of at least 35 per cent on total sales.

13.5.2   Budget details for Year 5 as agreed by line managers after negotiations

The information presented in Tables T 1 to T 5 has been agreed by the line managers as a basis for preparation of the master budget and its component parts for Year 5.

Sales and production volumes and direct costs

(T 1)

	Evening	Smart casual	Holiday wear
Unit sales for year	900	1,200	1,500
	£	£	£
Unit selling price	510	210	150
Unit variable cost:			
Direct material	100	80	70
Direct labour	80	70	65

Direct labour costs are based on an average cost of £16,000 per person per year.

Other costs

(T 2)

Production heat and light	£7,000 for the year
Production business rates	£5,000 for the year
Partners' salaries	£60,000 for the year
Rent of premises	£10,000 for the year
Office staff salaries	£56,250 for the year
Marketing and distribution	20 per cent of sales

Working capital targets

(T 3)

Debtors at end of year	One-and-a-half months' sales.
Trade creditors for material	One month's purchases.
Stock of raw materials	Enough for 80 per cent of next month's production.
Stock of finished goods	No stock held, as goods are made to order and delivered to the customer when completed.

Sales and purchases are planned to be spread evenly over the year.

Capital budget plans

(T 4)

Purchase one new cutting and sewing machine at £80,000, at the start of the year.
Depreciate all machinery for full year at 15 per cent per annum on a straight-line basis.

Balance sheet at 31 December Year 4

(T 5)

	£	£
Equipment at cost		100,000
Accumulated depreciation		30,000
Net book value		70,000
Stock of raw materials:		
For 56 evening @ £100 each	5,600	
For 85 smart casual @ £80 each	6,800	
For 80 holiday wear @ £70 each	5,600	
Trade debtors	83,000	
Cash	3,000	
	104,000	
Trade creditors	23,000	
Net current assets		81,000
Total assets *less* current liabilities		151,000
Partners' ownership interest		151,000

13.5.3 Preparation of individual budgets

From the information presented in Tables T 1 to T 5 the various detailed budgets are prepared as shown in Tables T 6 to T 18. These lead to the master budget set out in Tables T 19 to T 21.

Sales budget: sales and debtors

The sales budget sets out the volume of sales expected for each product, multiplied by the expected selling price, to obtain the total sales by value expected for each product. The total sales for the year ahead may then be calculated, shown in bold print in the sales budget.

(T 6)

Sales budget	Ref	Evening	Smart casual	Holiday wear	Total for year
Unit sales for year	T 1	900	1,200	1,500	
		£	£	£	£
Unit selling price	T 1	510	210	150	
Total sales		459,000	252,000	225,000	**936,000**

The year-end debtors are calculated as one and a half months' sales (one-eighth of the total year's sales if these are spread evenly throughout the year).

(T 7)

Debtors budget	Ref	Evening £	Smart casual £	Holiday wear £	Total for year £
Total sales	T 6	459,000	252,000	225,000	936,000
		divide by 8	divide by 8	divide by 8	
Debtors at year-end		57,375	31,500	28,125	**117,000**

Production plan

The production plan starts with the volume of output, calculated by taking the planned sales volume and adjusting this for planned levels of opening and closing stock of finished goods. If it is planned to have a level of closing stock, then this will require additional production. To the extent that there exists stock at the start of the period, that will reduce the need for current production. From T 3 it may be noted that the business plans have no opening or closing stock because all units are made to specific order. That is a simplification introduced to keep the length of this exercise reasonable, but it is somewhat unusual because most businesses will hold stock of finished goods ready for unexpected demand. As a reminder that stock plans should be taken into account, the production plans in T 8 are shown with lines for opening and closing stock of finished goods.

(T 8)

Production plan in units	Ref	Evening	Smart casual	Holiday wear
Planned sales volume	T 1	900	1,200	1,500
add: Planned closing stock of finished goods*	T 3	–	–	–
less: Opening stock of finished goods*	T 3	–	–	–
Planned unit production for year		900	1,200	1,500

*For a continuing business it is likely that there will be stock figures to be included here.

Direct materials budget: purchases, stock and trade creditors

Once the production plan has been decided, the costs of the various inputs to production may be calculated. Direct materials must be purchased to satisfy the production plans, but the purchases budget must also take into account the need to hold stock of raw materials. After the purchases budget has been quantified in terms of cost, the impact on trade creditors may also be established.

The *purchases budget* (calculated in T 9) is based on the units of raw material required for production in the period, making allowance for the opening and closing stock of raw materials. The plan is to hold sufficient stock at the end of the period to meet 80 per cent of the following month's production (*see* T 3). The number of units to be purchased will equal the number of units expected to be used in the period, plus the planned stock of raw materials at the end of the period minus the planned stock of raw materials at the start of the period (calculated in T 9).

(T 9)

Purchases budget in units	Ref	Evening	Smart casual	Holiday wear
Production volume	T 8	900	1,200	1,500
add: Raw materials stock planned for end of period	T 3	60 (80% of 900/12)	80 (80% of 1,200/12)	100 (80% of 1,500/12)
less: Raw materials stock held at start of period	T 5	56	85	80
Purchases of raw materials planned		904	1,195	1,520

(T 10)

Purchases budget in £s	Ref	Evening	Smart casual	Holiday wear	Total for year
Volume of purchases (units)	T 9	904	1,195	1,520	
		£	£	£	£
Cost per unit	T 1	100	80	70	
Total purchase cost		90,400	95,600	106,400	**292,400**

Trade creditors are calculated as one month's purchases (*see* T 3), a relatively uncomplicated procedure in this instance because the purchases remain constant from month to month. The purchases made during December will be paid for after the end of the accounting period.

(T 11)

One month's purchases 292,400/12	**£24,367**

The direct materials to be included in the cost of goods sold must also be calculated at this point, for use in the budgeted profit and loss statement. The direct materials to be included in the cost of goods sold are based on the materials used in production of the period (which in this example is all sold during the period).

(T 12)

Direct materials cost of goods sold	Ref	Evening	Smart casual	Holiday wear	Total for year
Production (units)	T 8	900	1,200	1,500	
		£	£	£	£
Materials cost per unit	T 1	100	80	70	
Total cost of goods to be sold		90,000	96,000	105,000	**291,000**

Direct labour budget

The direct labour budget takes the volume of production in units and multiplies that by the expected labour cost per unit to give a labour cost for each separate item of product and a total for the year, shown in bold print.

(T 13)

Direct labour budget	Ref	Evening	Smart casual	Holiday wear	Total for year
Production (units)	T 8	900	1,200	1,500	
		£	£	£	£
Labour cost per unit	T 1	80	70	65	
Total cost		72,000	84,000	97,500	**253,500**

It is also useful to check on the total resource requirement which corresponds to this total labour cost, since it takes time to plan increases or decreases in labour resources. The average direct labour cost was given in T 1 as £16,000 per person per year. The following calculation assumes that the employees can work equally efficiently on any of the three product lines.

(T 14)

Resource requirement:
Based on an average cost of £16,000 per person per year, the total labour cost of £253,500 would require 15.8 employees. All employees are part-time workers.

Production overhead budget

Production overheads include all those overhead items which relate to the production activity. In this example it includes heat and light, business rates and depreciation. Depreciation is calculated at a rate of 15 per cent on the total cost of equipment held during the year (£100,000 at the start, as shown in T 5, plus an additional £80,000 noted in T 4).

(T 15)

Production overhead budget	Ref	£
Heat and light	T 2	7,000
Business rates	T 2	5,000
Depreciation	T 4	27,000
Total		**39,000**

Total production cost budget

Total production cost comprises the cost of direct materials, direct labour and production overhead.

(T 16)

Production cost budget	Ref	£
Direct materials	T 12	291,000
Direct labour	T 13	253,500
Production overhead	T 15	39,000
Total		**583,500**

Administration expense budget

The administration expense budget includes the partners' salaries because they are working partners and their labour cost represents a management cost of the operations. The fact that the managerial role is carried out by the partners, who are also the owners of the business, is not relevant to the purposes of management accounting. What is important is to record a realistic cost of managing the business. Other administration costs in this example are rent of premises and the salaries of office staff (as shown in T 2).

(T 17)

Administration budget	Ref	£
Partners' salaries (drawn monthly in cash)	T 2	60,000
Rent of premises	T 2	10,000
Office staff	T 2	56,250
Total		**126,250**

Marketing expense budget

The marketing expense budget relates to all aspects of the costs of advertising and selling the product. The information in T 2 specifies a marketing cost which is dependent on sales, being estimated as 20 per cent of sales value.

(T 18)

Marketing expense budget	Ref	£
20 per cent of £936,000	T 2 & T 6	187,200

13.5.4 Master budget

The master budget has three components: the budgeted profit and loss account for the year, the budgeted cash flow statement and the budgeted balance sheet. These are now set out using the foregoing separate budgets. Where the derivation of figures in the master budget should be evident from the earlier budgets, no explanation is given, but where further calculations have been performed these are shown as working notes.

Budgeted profit and loss account

(T 19) Budgeted profit and loss account for the year ended 31 December Year 5

	Ref	Evening £	Smart casual £	Holiday wear £	Total for year £
Total sales	T 6	459,000	252,000	225,000	936,000
Materials cost	T 12	90,000	96,000	105,000	291,000
Labour cost	T 13	72,000	84,000	97,500	253,500
Total variable cost		162,000	180,000	202,500	544,500
Contribution		297,000	72,000	22,500	391,500
% on sales		64.7%	28.6%	10.0%	41.8%
Production overhead	T 15				39,000
Gross profit					352,500
Administration cost	T 17				126,250
Marketing cost	T 18				187,200
Net profit					39,050

Budgeted cash flow statement

Where expenses are paid for as soon as they are incurred, the cash outflow equals the expense as shown in the budgeted profit and loss account. In the case of cash collected from customers, debtors at the start and end of the period must be taken into the calculation. In the case of cash paid to suppliers the creditors at the start and end of the period must be taken into account. The cash flow statement contains references to working notes which follow the statement and set out the necessary detail.

(T 20) Budgeted cash flow statement for the year ended 31 December Year 5

	Note	£	£
Cash to be collected from customers	1		902,000
Cash to be paid to suppliers	2	291,033	
Direct labour	3	253,500	
Heat and light	3	7,000	
Business rates	3	5,000	
Partners' salaries	3	60,000	
Rent of premises	3	10,000	
Office staff costs	3	56,250	
Marketing costs	3	187,200	
			869,983
Net cash inflow from operations			32,017
New equipment to be purchased			80,000
Net cash outflow			(47,983)
Cash balance at beginning			3,000
Cash balance at end			(44,983)

Note 1: Cash to be collected from customers	Ref	£
Sales during the period	T 6	936,000
less: Credit sales which remain as debtors at the end of the year	T 7	117,000
		819,000
add: Cash collected from debtors at the start of the year	T 5	83,000
Cash to be collected from customers		902,000

Note 2: Cash to be paid to suppliers	Ref	£
Purchases during the period	T 10	292,400
less: Credit purchases which remain as creditors at the end of the year	T 11	24,367
		268,033
add: Cash paid to creditors at the start of the year	T 5	23,000
Cash to be paid to suppliers		291,033

Note 3: Other cash payments
It has been assumed, for the convenience of this illustration, that all other expense items are paid for as they are incurred. In reality, this would be unlikely and there would be further calculations of the type shown in Note 2, making allowance for creditors at the start and end of the period.

Budgeted balance sheet

(T 21) Budgeted balance sheet at 31 December Year 5

	Note	£	£
Equipment at cost	1		180,000
Accumulated depreciation	2		57,000
Net book value			123,000
Stock of raw materials	3	19,400	
Trade debtors (T 7)		117,000	
		136,400	
Bank borrowing (T 20)		44,983	
Trade creditors (T 11)		24,367	
		69,350	
Net current assets			67,050
Total assets less current liabilities			190,050
Partners' ownership interest	4		190,050

			£
Note 1			
Equipment at cost = £100,000 + £80,000		=	180,000
Note 2			
Accumulated depreciation = £30,000 + £27,000		=	57,000
Note 3			
Stock of raw materials:			
For 60 evening @ £100 each			6,000
For 80 smart casual @ £80 each			6,400
For 100 holiday wear @ £70 each			7,000
			19,400
Note 4			
Partners' ownership interest = £151,000 + £39,050		=	190,050

13.5.5 Interpretation of the practical example

Fiona McTaggart has reviewed the budget illustrated here and now offers some comments.

FIONA: *This illustration shows how much detail has to go into even the simplest of budgeting exercises. Comparing the budget with the statement of objectives, I was a little surprised to find no provision in the budgeted profit and loss account in relation to the money-back promise. If I were involved in this exercise I would include a provision based on past experience of the level of returns. That wouldn't affect the cash flow of course, because provisions are accounting allocations with no cash flow implications.*

The target gross profit percentage will be achieved overall (gross profit shown in the master budget is 41.8 per cent of total sales) but this is heavily dependent on the high margin on evening wear. I hope there is plenty of market research to back up those sales projections. The overall net profit budgeted is 4.2 per cent of total sales, which means there is little scope for error before the budgeted profit turns to a budgeted loss.

The budgeted cash flow statement shows an overall surplus on operations of the year, turning to a cash deficit when the effect of buying the new equipment is brought into the calculation, but that does not tell the whole story. The £80,000 cash outlay for the new equipment is needed at the start of the year whereas the cash inflows will be spread over the year, so the company will need to borrow early in the year to pay for the equipment. There will have to be a monthly statement of cash flows to show the bank how the cash will flow out and in over the year as a whole. The borrowing could perhaps be short-term borrowing in view of the overall surplus, but there are other potential cash flows which are not dealt with here. The partners are working partners and are taking salaries in cash, but they may also need to draw out more cash to pay their tax bills.

It is interesting to compare these management accounts with the way in which external reporting for financial purposes might appear. The textbooks always suggest that partners' salaries are an appropriation of profit for financial reporting purposes and should appear as such in the partners' capital accounts with a matching entry for drawings.

That's all far too elaborate for management accounting purposes. What matters here is that these are working partners and if they did not do the work, someone else would have to. Provided the salary is a reasonable representation of a reward for the work done, it is far more sensible to show the expense in the profit and loss account.

Real world case 13.2

This commentary relates to the results announced by British Coal, a mining company. It also indicates the approach taken by an incoming chief executive.

Production cost: 130p per gigajoule. Sale price: 118p per gigajoule. Result, to paraphrase Mr Micawber: misery. For UK Coal's shareholders, reeling at the 80% cut in the final dividend, the consolation is that unlike Dickens' eternal optimist, they do not have to wait for 'something to turn up'. It already has, in the shape of Gerry Spindler.

The new chief executive's results commentary savaged almost every aspect of the group's operational performance, from industrial relations to budgeting and marketing. And there was plenty to criticise: total sales fell to 14.3m tonnes from 18.9m, leaving the field clear for an 18% rise in imports. Costs in the deep mines rose 14%, while the contracted sale price was some way short of international spot prices. Mr Spindler is promising big changes, although he is already describing 2005 as a year of transition.

Source: *Investors Chronicle – United Kingdom*, 11 March 2005, 'UK COAL (UKC)'.

Discussion points

1 Why might the new chief executive be critical of the budget?
2 What changes might the chief executive be considering in relation to budget preparation?

13.6 Shorter budget periods

The illustration in section 13.5 is based on a 12-month period for relative ease of illustration. In reality, management accounting information is demanded more frequently than this. The following example of Newtrend shows the budget preparation on a quarterly basis. Most businesses budget monthly, with some producing figures more frequently than that.

13.6.1 Worked example: data

Newtrend Ltd is a new business which has been formed to buy standard DVD units and modify them to the specific needs of customers.

The business will acquire fixed assets costing £200,000 and a stock of 1,000 standard DVD units on the first day of business. The fixed assets are expected to have a five-year life with no residual value at the end of that time.

Sales are forecast as follows:

	Year 1				Year 2
	Quarter 1	Quarter 2	Quarter 3	Quarter 4	Quarter 1
Modified DVD units	8,100	8,400	8,700	7,800	8,100

The selling price of each unit will be £90.

The cost of production of each unit is specified as follows:

	£
Cost of standard unit purchased	30
Direct labour	33
Fixed overhead	12
	75

The fixed overhead per unit includes an allocation of depreciation. The annual depreciation is calculated on a straight-line basis and is allocated on the basis of a cost per unit to be produced during the year.

Suppliers of standard DVD units will allow one month's credit. Customers are expected to take two months' credit.

Wages will be paid as they are incurred in production. Fixed overhead costs will be paid as they are incurred.

The stock of finished goods at the end of each quarter will be sufficient to satisfy 20 per cent of the planned sales of the following quarter. The stock of standard DVD units will be held constant at 1,000 units.

It may be assumed that the year is divided into quarters of equal length and that sales, production and purchases are spread evenly throughout any quarter.

Required

Produce, for each quarter of the first year of trading:

1 the sales budget;
2 the production budget; and
3 the cash budget.

13.6.2 Quarterly budgets

This section sets out a solution in the form of quarterly budgets. Note that in cases of this type there will often be more than one way of interpreting the information given. That is not a problem provided the total column is used to check for arithmetic consistency.

Sales budget

Selling price £90 per unit:

	Year 1				Total
	Quarter 1	Quarter 2	Quarter 3	Quarter 4	
Modified DVD units	8,100	8,400	8,700	7,800	33,000
	£	£	£	£	£
Sales	729,000	756,000	783,000	702,000	2,970,000

Production budget for each quarter

By units, production must meet the sales of this quarter and 20 per cent of the planned sales of the next quarter:

	Year 1				Total
	Quarter 1	Quarter 2	Quarter 3	Quarter 4	
Modified DVD units	8,100	8,400	8,700	7,800	33,000
For sales of quarter	8,100	8,400	8,700	7,800	33,000
Add 20% of next quarter sales	1,680	1,740	1,560	1,620	1,620
	9,780	10,140	10,260	9,420	
Less stock of previous quarter	–	1,680	1,740	1,560	
Production required	9,780	8,460	8,520	7,860	34,620

Converting from units of production to costs of production

	Year 1				Total
	Quarter 1	Quarter 2	Quarter 3	Quarter 4	
Units to be produced	9,780	8,460	8,520	7,860	34,620
	£	£	£	£	£
Direct materials	293,400	253,800	255,600	235,800	1,038,600
Direct labour	322,740	279,180	281,160	259,380	1,142,460
Fixed overhead*	117,360	101,520	102,240	94,320	415,440
	733,500	634,500	639,000	589,500	2,596,500
*Includes depreciation of	11,300	9,776	9,844	9,080	40,000

Note that fixed overhead includes depreciation of £40,000 per annum, allocated on the basis of a cost per unit produced. Total production is 34,620 units, so depreciation is £1.155 per unit.

Cash budget for each quarter

	Year 1				Total
	Quarter 1	Quarter 2	Quarter 3	Quarter 4	
	£	£	£	£	
Cash from customers					
⅓ current quarter	243,000	252,000	261,000	234,000	
⅔ previous quarter	–	486,000	504,000	522,000	
Total cash received	243,000	738,000	765,000	756,000	2,502,000
Purchase of fixed assets	200,000				200,000
Payment to suppliers**	225,600	267,000	255,000	242,400	990,000
Wages	322,740	279,180	281,160	259,380	1,142,460
Fixed overhead (excl. depn.)	106,060	91,744	92,396	85,240	375,440
Total cash payments	854,400	637,924	628,556	587,020	2,707,900
Receipts less payments	(611,400)	100,076	136,444	168,980	(205,900)

**Schedule of payments to suppliers.

	Quarter 1	Quarter 2	Quarter 3	Quarter 4	Total
	£	£	£	£	£
Direct materials purchased	293,400	253,800	255,600	235,800	1,038,600
Payment for initial stock	30,000				30,000
Two months' purchases	195,600	169,200	170,400	157,200	
One month from previous qtr	–	97,800	84,600	85,200	78,600
Total payment	225,600	267,000	255,000	242,400	990,000

There are three months in each quarter so some care is required in working out what amounts are paid to suppliers in each quarter. The schedule of payments to suppliers shows, in quarter 1, the payment for initial stock of 1,000 units (which occurs at the beginning of month 2). It also shows in quarter 1 the payment for purchases that took place in the first two months of that quarter. The purchases of the final month of quarter 1 are paid for in quarter 2, along with the purchases of the first two months of that quarter. Stock remains constant at 1,000 units and so the pattern of payments continues to the end of the year where there is a trade creditor for the one month's unpaid purchases of quarter 4. Exhibit 13.5 shows the pattern of purchases and payment.

Real world case 13.3

Councils sometimes provide garden space, called allotments, which can be rented by people who want to grow flowers and vegetables but do not have sufficient garden space at home. Taking care of the allotments is an important part of the allotment-holders' activities.

A facelift is on the cards for Barnstaple's allotment sites. The town council, which runs Bryant's Field, Sunny Bank, Fair View and Higher Raleigh allotments, is looking to carry out a three-year improvement plan. It follows an inspection carried out in the summer which highlighted five main themes.

Security was a major issue at Fairview allotments while weeds and overgrown plots were the most significant problem at Bryant's Field. The distribution of water, caused by low pressure and a lack of taps, was a big concern on all sites. And other issues which came to the fore were health and safety and allotment management.

The information gleaned will be taken on board by the council's new allotment sub-committee when drawing up its recommendations for improvements. It is intended that the work will be carried out over the next three financial years, dealing with the worst faults first as funding allows.

One of the recommendations is likely to suggest the appointment of an allotments warden. For the first time there would be a link between the council and those working the sites. The person appointed would also be expected to carry out some of the remedial work to improve the allotments. The rest of the improvements would be done by outside contractors or the council's own work force.

The recommendations will be discussed as part of budget planning for the Cemetery and Grounds Maintenance Committee next year.

Cllr Jeremy Phillips, chairman of the committee responsible for allotments, said: 'The three-year improvement plan for town council allotments should offer enormous benefits to our tenants. We want to provide a really good service for our allotment holders and I hope they will contact the town council if they have any problems and work with us to bring about these much needed improvements.'

Source: North Devon Journal, 16 December 2004, p. 8, 'Improvement plan for town allotments'.

Discussion points

1 What are the cost headings that need to be included in the budget statement?

2 What are the costs which will appear in the budget for the first time?

Exhibit 13.5
Purchases and payment where suppliers allow one month's credit

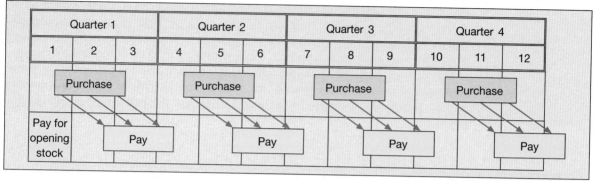

13.6.3 Comment on cash budget

A cash budget is the type of statement which would be required by someone being asked to lend money to the business. The start-up situation requires cash but there is a positive cash flow from operations. The lender would want to add to the cash budget a schedule of loan repayments and interest payments to see whether the operational cash flows could meet the financing needs of the business.

13.7 What the reseachers have found

13.7.1 The budget process

Evans (2001) described the process of budget preparation in a library. He suggested that those individuals who succeed in obtaining funds for their library are those who understand that budgeting is a complex year-round process. They also recognise that the process is political and competitive. He describes a bottom-up process where the supervisors pass their estimates to higher level management. These in turn are passed to top management which forms the general budget for the library. The planning cycle helps all those involved to learn about the planning and development of the organisation. Although programme budgets based on output would be more useful, time constraints meant that line item budgets based on inputs were more common. He also explained the importance of maintaining good relations with those in charge of budget allocation, and the need to be aware of the political nature of the process.

13.7.2 Frequency of budgeting

Barrett (2005) commented on a survey by the firm Ernst & Young noting the increase in profits warnings during 2004. Listed companies issue a profits warning in the UK when managers know that their expected profit is unlikely to meet the expectations indicated in market forecasts. Companies blamed economic turbulence in 2004. Ernst & Young pointed out that 12-month budgets are too long. They can take several weeks to prepare and the assumptions behind them are already out-of-date when they are finalised. Investors are looking for companies that can meet quarterly forecasts and so the companies in turn need to review their budgets more frequently. Previous surveys had indicated that the barrier to frequent forecasting lay in the finance department, which was too slow. In this survey the barrier was now seen as the line manager, who found quarterly budgeting was too short an interval. The survey indicated that quarterly reforecasting was the most common interval but monthly was the most frequently stated as a desired frequency.

13.8 Summary

This chapter has presented the definition of a budget as a detailed plan that sets out, in money terms, the plans for income and expenditure in respect of a future period of time. It is prepared in advance of that time period and is based on the agreed objectives for that period of time, together with the strategy planned to achieve those objectives.

The short-term budgetary process plays its part in long-range planning. Preparing a master budget has been set out in diagrammatic form in Exhibit 13.2. The administration of the budgeting process has been described and the benefits of budgeting have been put forward in terms of planning and control. The chapter has developed in detail a practical example of the preparation of a master budget.

Key themes in this chapter are:

- A **budgetary system** serves the needs of management in making judgments and decisions, exercising planning and control and achieving effective communication and motivation.

- **Long-range planning** begins with a vision statement setting out a vision for the future direction of the organisation. From this vision the **long-range objectives** are set covering a period of perhaps three to five years.

- A **strategy** describes the courses of action to be taken in achieving the long-range objectives. The different functions of the organisation will work together in developing the strategy.

- **Budgetary planning and control** provides a method of quantifying the strategy of the business.

- A **budget** is a detailed plan which sets out, in money terms, the plans for income and expenditure in respect of a future period of time. It is prepared in advance of that time period and is based on the agreed objectives for that period of time, together with the strategy planned to achieve those objectives.

- Administration of a budget requires a **budget committee** which will design the strategy, co-ordinate the inputs and communicate the objectives and strategy.

- Budget preparation usually starts with the **sales budget** because sales are the critical factor. From this the operational budgets are formed, leading to a finance plan and then the **master budget**, which consists of a budgeted profit and loss account, a budgeted balance sheet and a budgeted cash flow statement.

- Budgets may be participative through a **bottom-up** process, or imposed through a **top-down** process. A **negotiated budget** is based on a mixture of both approaches.

- Co-ordination and review by the budget committee may lead to a further round of negotiation in order to arrive at the best position for the entity as a whole, before final acceptance by the budget committee.

- The benefits of budgeting are seen in planning, control, communication and co-ordination. They also provide a basis for performance evaluation.

- The detailed case study in the chapter shows the sequence of preparation of all budgets leading to the master budget.

References and further reading

Barrett, R. (2005) 'Budgeting and reforecasting', *Financial Management* (UK), March: 12.

Evans, G.E. (2001) 'The ins and outs of library budget preparation', *Managing Library Finances*, 14(1): 19–23.

QUESTIONS

The Questions section of each chapter has three types of question. 'Test your understanding' questions to help you review your reading are in the 'A' series of questions. You will find the answer to these by reading and thinking about the material in the text book. 'Application' questions to test your ability to apply technical skills are in the 'B' series of questions. Questions requiring you to show skills in problem solving and evaluation are in the 'C' series of questions. The symbol [S] indicates that a solution is available at the end of the book.

A Test your understanding

A13.1 Explain the purpose of long-range planning (section 13.2.1).

A13.2 Explain the purpose of setting a strategy (section 13.2.2).

A13.3 Define the term 'budget' (section 13.2.3).

A13.4 Explain the budget planning process and the main relationships within that process (section 13.2.3).

A13.5 What is the role of the budget committee (section 13.3.1)?

A13.6 What is the sequence of the budgeting process (section 13.3.3)?

A13.7 How does budgeting help the management function of planning (section 13.4.1)?

A13.8 How does budgeting help the management function of control (section 13.4.2)?

A13.9 How does budgeting help the management function of communication and co-ordination (section 13.4.3)?

A13.10 How does budgeting provide a basis for performance evaluation (section 13.4.4)?

A13.11 [S] A company has 1,000 units of finished goods held in store at the start of the month. It produces a further 4,000 units during the month and sells 4,200. How many units are in store at the end of the month?

A13.12 [S] The sales budget for the BeeSee Company for the first six months of the year is:

	£
January	12,000
February	13,000
March	14,000
April	13,500
May	12,600
June	11,100

There are no debtors at the start of January. One month's credit is allowed to customers. What is the budgeted cash received in each month?

A13.13 [S] Trade creditors at the start of January are £12,500. They are all paid during January. During the month, goods costing £18,000 are purchased, and at the end of January there is an amount of £13,600 owing to trade creditors. State the amount of cash paid to trade creditors during January.

A13.14 [S] The cost of indirect materials in any month is 40% variable (varying with direct labour hours) and 60% fixed. The total cost of indirect materials during the month of March was budgeted at £500. During the month of April it is expected that the direct labour hours will be 20% higher than during March. What should be budgeted for the cost of indirect materials in April?

B Application

B13.1 [S]
The Garden Ornament Company manufactures two types of garden ornament: a duck and a heron. The information presented in Tables T 1 to T 5 has been prepared, as a result of discussions by line managers, for the purposes of preparing a master budget for Year 6.

Sales and production volumes and direct costs
(T 1)

	Ducks	Herons
Unit sales for the year	8,000	15,000
	£	£
Unit selling price	30	45
Unit variable cost:		
Direct material	14	16
Direct labour	12	13

Direct labour costs are based on an average cost of £15,000 per person per year.

Other costs
(T 2)

Production heat and light	£8,000 for the year
Production fixed overheads	£4,000 for the year
Partners' salaries	£55,000 for the year
Rent of premises	£11,000 for the year
Office staff salaries	£48,450 for the year
Marketing and distribution	18 per cent of sales

Working capital targets
(T 3)

Debtors at end of year	Half of one month's sales.
Trade creditors for materials	One month's purchases.
Stock of raw materials	Enough for 60 per cent of next month's production.
Stock of finished goods	No stock held, as goods are made to order and delivered to the customer on completion.

Sales and purchases are planned to be spread evenly over the year.

Capital budget plans
(T 4)

Purchase one new moulding machine at £70,000, at the start of the year. Depreciate all machinery for a full year at 20% per annum on a straight-line basis.

**Balance sheet at 31 December Year 5
(T 5)**

	£	£
Equipment at cost		190,000
Accumulated depreciation		40,000
Net book value		150,000
Stock of raw materials:		
For 400 ducks @ £14 each	5,600	
For 750 herons @ £16 each	12,000	
Trade debtors	32,000	
Cash	2,500	
	52,100	
Trade creditors	30,000	
		22,100
		172,100
Partners' capital		172,100

Required

Prepare a master budget and all supporting budgets.

B13.2 [S]

Tools Ltd is a new business which has been formed to buy standard machine tool units and adapt them to the specific needs of customers.

The business will acquire fixed assets costing £100,000 and a stock of 500 standard tool units on the first day of business. The fixed assets are expected to have a five-year life with no residual value at the end of that time.

Sales are forecast as follows:

	Year 1				Year 2
	Quarter 1	Quarter 2	Quarter 3	Quarter 4	Quarter 1
Modified tool units	4,050	4,200	4,350	3,900	4,050

The selling price of each unit will be £90.

The cost of production of each unit is specified as follows:

	£
Cost of standard unit purchased	24
Direct labour	30
Fixed overhead	10
	64

The fixed overhead per unit includes an allocation of depreciation. The annual depreciation is calculated on a straight-line basis and is allocated on the basis of a cost per unit to be produced during the year.

Suppliers of standard tool units will allow one month's credit. Customers are expected to take two months' credit.

Wages will be paid as they are incurred in production. Fixed overhead costs will be paid as they are incurred.

The stock of finished goods at the end of each quarter will be sufficient to satisfy 10% of the planned sales of the following quarter. The stock of standard tool units will be held constant at 500 units.

It may be assumed that the year is divided into quarters of equal length and that sales, production and purchases are spread evenly throughout any quarter.

Required

Produce, for each quarter of the first year of trading:

(a) the sales budget;
(b) the production budget; and
(c) the cash budget.

B13.3 [S]

Bright Papers Ltd has established a new subsidiary company to produce extra-large rolls of wall covering. Management forecasts for the first four years of trading are as follows:

	Year 1	Year 2	Year 3	Year 4
Sales (in units)	800,000	950,000	1,200,000	1,500,000
Production (in units)	850,000	1,000,000	1,300,000	1,600,000
	£	£	£	£
Selling price per unit	10.20	10.56	11.04	12.00
Costs per unit:				
Direct materials	2.04	2.28	2.64	3.00
Direct labour	0.60	0.75	0.90	0.90
Variable overhead	0.40	0.50	0.60	0.60
Fixed overhead	£5,000,000	£5,100,000	£5,200,000	£5,300,000
Average credit period given to customers	1 month	1 month	1.5 months	2 months
Average credit period taken from suppliers of materials	2 months	1.5 months	1.5 months	1 month

Further information

(a) Estimates for the average credit period given and taken are based on balances at the end of each year.
(b) Costs other than direct materials are to be paid for in the month they are incurred.
(c) The company will adopt the FIFO assumption in relation to cost of goods sold.
(d) No increases in production capacity will be required during the first four years of business.
(e) Fixed overhead costs include depreciation of £1,500,000 per annum.
(f) No stock of direct materials will be held. The supplier will deliver goods daily, as required. No work-in-progress will exist at the end of any year.

Required

Prepare annual cash budgets for the new subsidiary for each of the first four years of trading.

C Problem solving and evaluation

C13.1 [S]

The following budgeted accounting statements were submitted to the board of directors of Alpha Ltd on 1 October Year 4:

Budgeted profit and loss account for the year to 30 September Year 5

	£	£
Sales		15,600,000
Cost of sales		10,452,000
Gross profit		5,148,000
Fixed overheads:		
Selling and advertising	1,500,000	
General administration	1,094,500	
		2,594,500
Operating profit		2,553,500
Interest payable on medium-term loan	135,000	
Royalties payable on sales	780,000	
		915,000
Net profit		1,638,500

**Budgeted balance sheet at 30 September Year 5,
with comparative figures at 1 October Year 4**

	30 September Year 5 £	1 October Year 4 £
Fixed assets at cost	2,300,000	1,800,000
less: Accumulated depreciation	585,000	450,000
	1,715,000	1,350,000
Trading stock	3,200,000	4,000,000
Trade debtors	2,600,000	2,200,000
Cash in bank	1,854,750	–
Total assets	9,369,750	7,550,000
Share capital	4,400,000	4,400,000
Retained earnings	3,313,500	1,675,000
	7,713,500	6,075,000
Medium-term loan	1,000,000	1,000,000
Trade creditors	656,250	475,000
	9,369,750	7,550,000

At 31 March Year 5 the following information was available in respect of the first six months of the trading year:

(a) Sales were 20% below the budgeted level, assuming an even spread of sales throughout the year.
(b) The gross profit percentage was two percentage points below the budgeted percentage.
(c) Actual advertising expenditure of £100,000 was 50% below the budgeted amount. All other selling expenses were in line with the budget.
(d) General administration costs were 10% below the budgeted level.
(e) Trading stock at 31 March was £200,000 higher than the budgeted level. It was assumed in the budget that stock would decrease at a uniform rate throughout the year.
(f) Trade debtors at 31 March were equivalent to two months' actual sales, assuming sales were spread evenly throughout the six months.
(g) Trade creditors at 31 March were equivalent to one month's actual cost of goods sold, assuming costs were spread evenly throughout the six months.
(h) On 1 January Year 5 the rate of interest charged on the medium-term loan was increased to 16% per annum.

The budget for the second six months was revised to take account of the following predictions:

(a) Revenue during the second six months would continue at the level achieved during the first six months.
(b) Cost control measures would be implemented to restore the gross profit percentage to the budgeted level.
(c) Advertising, selling and general administration costs would be maintained at the levels achieved in the first six months.
(d) Trading stocks would be reduced to the level originally budgeted at 30 September.
(e) Trade debtors would be reduced to the equivalent of one month's sales.
(f) Trade creditors would be maintained at the equivalent of one month's cost of goods sold.
(g) Interest on the medium-term loan would remain at 16% per annum.

The directors of the company wish to know what change in the cash in bank will arise when the revised budget for the second six months is compared with the consequences of continuing the pattern in the first six months.

Taxation has been ignored.

Required
(1) Prepare an accounting statement for the six months to 31 March Year 5 comparing the actual results with the original budget.
(2) Prepare a revised budget for the second six months and compare this with the actual results which would have been achieved if the pattern of the first six months had continued.

C13.2

Holyrood Products Ltd makes DVD recorders. The management accountant has produced the following summary of the company's trading in the year ended 30 June Year 3:

	£	£
Sales: 30,000 recorders		375,000
Add: Increase in finished goods stock		16,000
		391,000
Deduct:		
Direct materials	128,000	
Direct labour	96,000	
Works and administration overhead	50,000	
Selling overhead	20,000	
		294,000
Trading profit		97,000

The following additional information is available:

(a) Works and administration overhead was 64% variable and 36% fixed, the latter including £2,500 for depreciation of plant surplus to current requirements.
(b) Selling overhead was 75% variable and 25% fixed.
(c) For management accounting purposes, finished goods stock is valued at variable cost excluding selling overhead.
(d) There was an increase of 2,000 units in finished goods stock over the year.

The production manager has made the following estimates for the year to 30 June Year 4 which show that:

(a) The excess plant will be utilised for the production of calculators and digital watches in quantities of 5,000 and 10,000 respectively. The variable costs are:

	Calculators £	Watches £
Direct materials	15,000	10,000
Direct labour	10,000	25,000
Works and administration overhead	2,500	15,000
Selling overhead	4,500	2,250

(b) Finished goods stock of DVD recorders will remain unchanged and stocks of calculators and watches will be built up to 10% of production.
(c) Production of DVD recorders will be at the same level as that achieved in the year to 30 June Year 3.
(d) Fixed overhead:

	DVD recorders	Calculators £	Watches £
Works and administration	No change	8,000*	13,500*
Selling	60% increase	2,250	6,750

Note: excluding depreciation.

(e) Materials costs for DVD recorders will be increased by £1 per unit. Other variable costs will be held at the level attained in the year ended 30 June Year 3.

The marketing director has advised that each product should be priced so as to achieve a 25% profit on total cost.

Required

Prepare a statement of budgeted profit for the year ended 30 June Year 4.

Case studies

Real world cases

Prepare short answers to Case studies 13.1, 13.2 and 13.3.

Case 13.4

Today's task is to review the first stage of budget preparation in a major hospital dealing with a wide range of medical conditions, including accident and emergency services. (There are indications within the case study of how to allocate the time on the presumption that one hour is available in total, but the times may be adjusted proportionately for a different overall length.)

Before the activity starts, obtain and look through the annual report and accounts of a hospital trust and a regional health authority, looking for discussion of the budgetary process and the way in which budgets are presented in the annual report.

Half of the group should form the budget committee, deciding among themselves the role of each individual within the hospital but having regard to the need to keep a balance between medical services, medical support staff and administration. The other half of the group should take the role of speciality team leaders presenting their budgets (speciality being the term used to describe one particular specialist aspect of hospital treatment, e.g. children's specialisms (paediatrics) women's health (obstetrics and gynaecology), or dealing with older persons (geriatrics)).

Initially the group should work together for 20 minutes to write a vision statement and a set of corporate objectives. The budget committee should then hold a separate meeting lasting 10 minutes to decide: (a) what questions they will ask of the speciality team leaders when they present their budget plans, and (b) where the sources of conflict are most likely to be found. In the meantime, each speciality team leader should set out a brief statement of objectives for that speciality team and a note of the main line items which would appear in the budget, indicating where conflict with other teams within the hospital is most likely to arise as a result of the budgeting process.

The budget committee should then interview each speciality manager (5 minutes each), with the other speciality managers attending as observers. After all interviews have been held, the budget committee should prepare a brief report dealing with the effectiveness and limitations of the budgetary process as experienced in the exercise. The speciality managers should work together to produce a report on their perceptions of the effectiveness and limitations of the budgetary process (15 minutes).

Case 13.5

As a group you are planning to launch a monthly student newsletter on the university's website. The roles to be allocated are: editor, reporters, webmaster, university accountant, student association representatives. Work together as a team to prepare a list of budget headings for the year ahead and suggest how you would gain access to realistic figures for inclusion in the budget. Include in your budget plan a note of the key risks and uncertainties.

Chapter 14

Control through budgeting

This case study is arguing a case for replacing a budget model with something new. It is an enthusiastic statement from a group promoting its own new ideas. Read the case study now but only attempt the discussion points after you have finished studying the chapter.

'Budgeting has few admirers'

Gaming the numbers is pervasive. One large survey of U.S. companies concluded that managers either did not accept the budgetary targets and opted to beat the system, or they felt pressured to achieve the targets at any cost. This pressure is squeezing the life and spirit out of many organizations and their people. It's the mentality that says, 'Do what I say or your future is at risk.'

Beyond Budgeting, a more adaptive and devolved alternative

Replacing the budgeting model with a more adaptive and devolved alternative is the solution that organizations need to achieve their goals of becoming devolved networks. Criticizing budgets is not new. But defining a set of principles that guides leaders toward a new lean, adaptive and ethical management model is a new idea – perhaps the first great new idea of the twenty-first century.

Source: Website of the Beyond Budgeting Round Table www.bbrt.org (2005).

Discussion points

1 How can budgets be used for planning and control if managers are 'gaming the numbers' as described above?

2 How would a devolved approach reduce the 'gaming' by managers?

Contents

Learning outcomes

After reading this chapter you should be able to:

- Explain and discuss the behavioural aspects of budgeting.

- Explain the application of flexible budgets in variance analysis.

- Explain methods of budgeting used in a range of organisations.

- Explain and discuss the views that have questioned the need for budgets.

- Describe and discuss examples of research results in the use of budgets and their effects.

14.1 Introduction

Chapter 13 has explained the budgetary process and illustrated in detail a method of preparing budgets for planning purposes. The use of budgets for control purposes was explained in that chapter in terms of comparing the actual outcome with the expected results as shown by the budget.

The use of budgets within an organisation may affect relationships and behaviour inside the organisation. This chapter discusses some of the potential problems and ways of avoiding or minimising them.

When actual costs are compared with budgeted costs, the comparison is of the total cost for the line item under consideration (e.g. cost of various types of material, cost of various categories of labour or cost of a range of categories of overheads). Where there is a significant difference between the budget and the actual outcome, that difference may be investigated. (It has to be remembered, however, that the investigation will itself have a cost.)

Budgets are particularly important for planning and control in the public sector (such as national and local government services, health services and education). This chapter explains some of the features of public sector budgets.

Finally the chapter explains why some writers have questioned the need for budgets.

Activity 14.1

Real world case 14.1 starts with the heading 'Budgeting has few admirers'. This reflects the position taken by the Beyond Budgeting Round Table. What arguments could you present to support the usefulness of budgeting?

14.2 Behavioural aspects of budgeting

Chapter 13 describes the technical process of setting a budget. It emphasises the need for involvement at all stages of the process. In an ideal world that would produce the best solution. However, the world is not ideal and not everyone can be allowed to do exactly as he or she would wish at the first instance. So potential conflicts arise and those involved in the budgetary process need to be aware of the behavioural aspects in order to maximise the good points and minimise the problems.

The behavioural aspects may conveniently be summarised as relating to motivation, participation, feedback, group effects, budget slack and the politics of the organisation. In each of these areas there has been research into the effects, sometimes with inconclusive results. This chapter does not seek to give detailed reference to the research work, but rather to bring out some of the findings as points to consider in relation to the technical process.

14.2.1 Motivation

Chapter 13 suggests that budgets should help in performance evaluation because they provide formal targets against which to measure performance. If the targets are set with care, there should be motivation for the individual to achieve those targets. The question then arises as to what type of targets should be set. Relatively easy targets will be achieved by all, but they will know the targets were easy and will not feel fully motivated by that level of evaluation of performance. If the targets are moderately difficult there will be a stronger motivation for some individuals to achieve those targets, with a sense of personal satisfaction in doing so. Others will fail and will become despondent. They may decide not to put any further effort in because the targets are too difficult.

The literature on goal setting suggests that it is important that the budget targets are accepted by the individuals involved. In that context, budget targets should be at the 'difficult' end of the range, by way of creating a challenge, but should be seen as being attainable. If budget targets are unrealistic there may be a negative reaction where the individual does not even attempt a reasonable level of performance. Communication between levels in the organisation is also important, so that the individual knows that achievement of targets is reported at a higher level and recognised in some form. Within all these considerations of positive factors of motivation, there may be personality problems which invalidate approaches which would otherwise be successful.

14.2.2 Participation

A full understanding of the behavioural aspects of the budgetary process requires an understanding of psychology. Research into behavioural aspects of budgeting has therefore included psychological studies of the individuals participating in the budgetary process. It is argued that individuals have needs for a sense of belonging, a sense of self-esteem and a sense of personal fulfilment. These needs do not necessarily have to be provided through remunerated employment or self-employment. They could be achieved through charitable work or dedication to a particular way of life. To the extent that people do spend a considerable part of their lives in paid employment, these needs may most readily be satisfied by that work.

Participation is one way of meeting those needs, and therefore participation in the budgetary process is a significant aspect of meeting human needs. Those individuals who participate in the budgetary process will gain a sense of ownership of the process, or belonging to the process. They will experience an increase in self-esteem through having a defined role in the process and will achieve a sense of personal fulfilment through successful implementation of the budget plans.

14.2.3 Feedback

Feedback on actual performance, as compared with the budget, is an essential part of the control process which follows from the setting of the budgets. Feedback is only effective if it is provided in a short time-frame. Good news is preferred to bad news; individuals may thus concentrate on the positive feedback and hope that the negative feedback will disappear. The information on negative feedback may have to be presented in a constructive manner if it is to result in action. For example, 'Sales this month were 10 per cent down' may be seen as a negative aspect about which little can be done after the event, but a statement such as 'Next month's sales effort must take account of the cause of last month's 10 per cent decrease' requires positive action in identifying and seeking to remedy the cause of the decrease.

Feedback must relate closely to the responsibility level of the individual if it is to encourage remedial action. There may be a personality problem here, as elsewhere, if individuals see the feedback as criticism of their work. That adverse reaction to criticism could be a function of age or insecurity. Negative aspects of feedback may need a different form of communication from that needed for positive aspects.

14.2.4 Group effects

The impact of the budgetary process on a group of persons may be quite different from the impact on the individual within the group. Participation by individuals will lead to greater group interaction, which will be a good thing if the individuals value their membership of the group and see the goals of the group as being collective targets that they all regard as desirable. Such a group will show cohesion, which will be increased by participation in the budget process.

Where a group does not have such cohesion, or the majority pressure is towards lower targets, the performance of the individual may be reduced by participation within the group. It may therefore be important for senior management, wishing to make effective use of the budgetary process, to have careful regard for the composition of groups within the organisation.

14.2.5 Budget slack

Where budgets are used to measure performance, the managers who set those budgets may be tempted to build in some element of spare resources that allows a lapse from actual high levels of performance without deviating from budget targets. The element of spare resources could involve overestimating the time required for any particular task, or using the highest price of input materials available in the price list, or asking for more equipment than is strictly necessary. Quite apart from such deliberate creation of slack there could also be unintentional errors such as planning activity for 52 weeks in the year when the premises are only open for 50 weeks.

Real world case 14.2

Lyne and Dugdale (2002) carried out a survey of the opinions of financial and non-financial managers of companies in the South-West of England. They asked the managers about the importance of a range of business uses. This table sets out the perceptions of the managers. Financial and non-financial managers gave similar answers.

Purpose of budgeting	Not very important, or almost irrelevant %	Fairly important %	Very important, or extremely important %
Overall	5.1	23.1	71.8
Planning	2.5	25.0	72.5
Control	5.0	20.0	75.0
Co-ordination	17.5	37.5	45.0
Communication	17.5	35.0	47.5
Authorisation	10.0	40.0	50.0
Motivation	37.5	30.0	32.5
Performance evaluation	12.5	22.5	65.0

Source: CIMA/ICAEW (June, 2004), p. 11, Presentation 3: 'Beyond budgeting or better budgeting', downloaded from www.cimaglobal.com/main/resources/knowledge/

Discussion points

1 What conclusions may be drawn here about the relative importance of planning and control as reasons for preparing budgets?

2 What conclusions may be drawn here about the relative importance of communication and motivation as reasons for preparing budgets?

The use of such bias at a lower level of budget preparation may be countered by a correspondingly strict attitude at a higher level to compensate for the built-in slack. That could be unfortunate for the lower-level manager who does not build in slack but is penalised along with the rest. The answer to this problem is that the process of budget setting should be specific as to input information so that built-in slack is identified at the earliest possible stage. Flexibility in budgeting is also important to ensure that where slack does become evident it is dealt with by budget revision.

14.2.6   Politics of the organisation

Irrespective of the type of entity, it is almost inevitable that there will be a political aspect to its management structure. The word 'politics' here refers to the power struggle within the organisation. It might be a power struggle in which labour unions seek to impose their will on management. It might be a power struggle within the board of directors or between divisions of the enterprise. Whatever its nature, such a power struggle is evidenced in the budget process where various units of the enterprise are engaged in rivalry over the formulation of the budget. Thus the budgetary process may be more important as a manifestation of the political struggle than as an item of financial planning.

There may be two aspects to budgeting: the public image of resource allocation, and the private image of resolving conflict. The first of these aspects involves a focus on the technicalities of providing information for resource allocation, to be studied as a starting-point in exploring the use of budgets for planning and control. The second aspect forms a significant element of more advanced study in management accounting.

14.3   Flexible budgets and variance analysis

When the budget is set at the beginning of a reporting period, it will be presented on the basis of activity levels expected at that point. Suppose that activity levels subsequently fall because of a downturn in demand. Is it preferable to base the variance analysis on the budget set for the original level of output, or to introduce some flexibility and compare actual outcome with the budget adjusted for the new lower level of activity? Putting the question in that form leads to an almost inescapable conclusion that flexibility is required, but it is surprising how that obvious need for flexibility may be overlooked when a table of figures appears on a page. A case study is used in Section 14.3.1 to show the application of a **flexible budget**.

The case study shows that there must be adjustment for the flexibility of variable costs as volume of output changes. Fixed costs do not vary because they are not affected by volume of output.

Definition

> A **flexible budget** is designed to change when the volume of activity changes. The budget should be adjusted to match the actual volume of activity, for purposes of comparability.

When the actual outcome is known, the actual costs are compared with the budget. The difference between actual cost and budgeted cost is called a **variance**. If the actual cost is greater than the budgeted cost, the variance is called an adverse variance and written (A) in tables. If the actual cost is less than the budgeted cost, the variance is called a favourable variance and written (F) in tables.

Definition   **Variance** is the difference between actual cost and budgeted cost. If actual cost is greater than budgeted cost the variance is *adverse*. If actual cost is less than budgeted cost the variance is *favourable*.

14.3.1   Case study: Brackendale Ltd

Case study description
When the budget for the year ahead was set, it was expected that monthly output of units manufactured would be 10,000 units. By the time July was reached, output had fallen to 8,000 units per month because of a fall in market share of sales. Exhibit 14.1 reports the original budget and the actual outcome for the month of July.

Data relevant to the month of July are set out in Exhibit 14.1, as follows:

Exhibit 14.1
Original budget and actual costs for July

	Original budget	*Actual for July*
Units manufactured	10,000	8,000
	£	£
Direct material	20,000	16,720
Direct labour	10,000	11,000
Variable overhead	6,000	5,600
Fixed overhead	7,000	7,500
Total product costs	43,000	40,820

Fiona McTaggart now talks through the problem.

FIONA: *It is quite tempting to compare these two columns of figures directly and call the difference the cost variance. But that would be totally misleading because the budget is based on 10,000 units of output and the actual output was down to 8,000 units. Direct materials, direct labour and variable overhead are all variable costs which depend on the level of output. I would introduce a new column headed 'flexible budget' which shows the expected cost of all variable costs for the new output level. Finally, I would write a brief report setting out some guide to the figures so that the production supervisor can give some thought to possible causes.*

The summary statement of variances (*see* Exhibit 14.2) takes the information for original budget and actual costs contained in the case study description. The flexible budget is created by taking 8/10ths of the original budget costs (because the units manufactured are 8/10ths of the volume originally budgeted). The variances are then calculated by deducting the actual costs from the flexible budget figures. Italics are used to show the flexible budget figures which have been calculated as 8/10ths of the original budget. The only exception is fixed overhead cost, where it would not be expected that the cost was variable. Accordingly there is no flexibility with regard to fixed overhead.

A summary report on the variances is shown in Exhibit 14.3.

14.3.2   Linking to the original budget

In Exhibit 14.2 the variance is calculated by comparing the actual cost with the flexible budget. However, there is also a volume effect because the level of manufacture is less

Exhibit 14.2
Using a flexible budget: summary statement of variances

	Original budget (1)	Flexible budget (2)	Actual for July (3)	Variance (2) – (3)
Units manufactured	10,000	8,000	8,000	
	£	£	£	£
Direct materials	20,000	16,000	16,720	720 (A)
Direct labour	10,000	8,000	11,000	3,000 (A)
Variable overhead	6,000	4,800	5,600	800 (A)
Fixed overhead	7,000	7,000	7,500	500 (A)
Total product costs	43,000	35,800	40,820	5,020 (A)

Exhibit 14.3
Budget variance report

To: Production manager
From: Management accountant
Subject: **Variance report for July**

During the month of July there were 8,000 units manufactured, as compared with 10,000 expected when the budget was set. Allowing flexibility for the lower level of output, there was nevertheless an adverse variance of £5,020 for the month, of which £720 related to direct material, £3,000 related to direct labour, £800 related to variable overhead and £500 related to fixed overhead. The most serious of these is the labour cost variance, which may be due to rates of pay rising above expectations or it may be due to inefficient working. Further investigation is required, by enquiring into rates of pay authorised for staff, possible overtime payments and records of work carried out.

than expected. A further column could be inserted between columns (1) and (2) to show a volume variance. In some organisations there may be problems elsewhere because of the reduced level of output; this department has not met its targets and its cost savings may be offset by wastage or inefficiency elsewhere. So an evaluation of the effect of the change in volumes may be relevant to a larger discussion of the impact of a change in volume.

14.4 Methods of budgeting

Chapter 13 describes in detail the preparation of a master budget from its component parts. The preparation of each separate part of the master budget required information about the management's view of what activities would be carried out and what these activities would cost. Managers have to decide how they intend to describe the activities of the organisation and how they make projections of costs.

In designing the presentation of the budget, some organisations produce **line item budgets** where each line in the budget relates to functions in the organisation. This approach emphasises the *inputs* to the work of the enterprise.

In predicting the new levels of costs in the budget some organisations budget for the year ahead by an **incremental budget** adjustment to the current year's budget to allow for inflation and for changes in resource inputs. Others start each year with a blank paper and forecast each cost without regard to the current year's position. This is called a **zero-based budget**.

Rather than look at *inputs*, some organisations focus on planned *output* activities, each of which will use more than one of the organisational functions and present the budget in the form of a planning programming budget system. An output-based approach may be particularly appropriate in a public benefit organisation.

This section explores each approach.

14.4.1   Input-based budget systems

The budgetary process described in this chapter has focused on the separate items which contribute to the overall budget. There will be a line for each item, such as direct materials, direct labour, various kinds of production overhead, various kinds of administration and selling and distribution costs. That type of budget is called a line item budget. The line item budget concentrates on the inputs to the process.

As an example, in the National Health Service the hospital services and support facilities are provided by NHS Trusts, each covering a geographical area. The Trusts must plan their budgets with regard for the objectives set by the government. As an example, Exhibit 14.4 sets out the financial objectives for one Trust.

Exhibit 14.4
Financial objectives for an NHS Trust

> **1** Taking one financial year with another, to ensure that a balance is maintained between income available to the Trust and expenditure properly chargeable against that income.
>
> **2** To achieve a surplus before interest of 6% on average net assets.

The budget shown in Exhibit 14.5 fails by £2m to meet the required surplus. Since there is another target of maintaining a balance, taking one year with another, we would now ask whether the previous year also fell below the required standard. If a trend of continuing deficits developed there would be some concern.

Exhibit 14.5
Budget for next year

Sources of income	£m
For patient services	
Health Board	144
Other Boards	16
Education and training grants	23
Total income from activities	183
Operating expenses	
Clinical services	120
Hotel services	6
Other support services	22
Transport and travel	2
Depreciation and amortisation	20
Research and development	4
	174
Budgeted surplus	9
Required surplus to meet 6 per cent target	11

14.4.2   Incremental budgets

One commonly used approach to estimating the budgeted costs is to start with the previous year's expenditure budget, adding a percentage to cover inflation and making adjustment for any unusual factors or incremental changes. The success of the **incremental budget** approach depended critically on the suitability of the previous year's figures. Any errors in estimation would continue indefinitely. If there was inefficient use of resources in previous periods, that inefficiency will be built into the budgets. No challenges are made to separate departments to review their use of resources in a more fundamental manner. If a new activity has been developed it may be difficult for those involved to bid for support because there will be no previous budget on which to build.

The advantages of incremental budgeting are:

- It is relatively straightforward and low cost to implement.
- It will give a reasonable estimate where activities do continue relatively unchanged from period to period.
- It gives a continuing benchmark over a longer period of time.

The disadvantages of incremental budgeting are:

- It assumes activities continue at the current levels.
- It does not leave space for new developments.
- It is backward-looking and does not encourage innovation.
- It builds in inefficiency and discourages cost saving initiatives.
- It is seen as being driven by the accounting processes rather than by those who deliver the products and services of the organisation.

14.4.3 Zero-based budgeting (ZBB)

Zero-based budgeting was devised as a reaction to the traditional incremental approach to budgeting. Zero-based budgeting requires a completely clean sheet of paper every year. Each part of the organisation has to justify over again the budget it requires. Some thought-provoking questions may need to be answered, such as:

- What is the need for this activity?
- How much of it is needed?
- Is there a more cost-effective way of carrying it out?
- What is the optimal cost?

The approach is particularly useful for the output-driven approach to budgeting (see section 14.4.4) because it forces questions to be asked about the programmes planned and the cost–benefit aspects of the plans. On the negative side, it is a time-consuming activity and is perhaps most usefully applied on a selective basis where the questioning approach is most useful. Some activities of an organisation carry an element of discretion and it is worthwhile reappraising them on occasions. Others form an essential core, so that it might be less appropriate to take a zero-based approach.

The advantages of zero-based budgeting are:

- It encourages management to focus on the goals and objectives of the organisation.
- It forces management to consider whether activities continue to be necessary.
- It leaves space for new initiatives.
- It allows management to set priorities over the activities of the business.
- It gives an up-to-date benchmark to be used in evaluating actual outcomes.

The disadvantages of zero-based budgeting are:

- It is a time-consuming exercise.
- It requires management to apply higher skills in planning.
- It diverts managers' attention from their primary areas of responsibility.
- It could lose the benefit of longer-term comparisons of trends in efficiency and control.

14.4.4 Output-based budget systems

Rather than quantify *inputs*, it would be equally valid to approach the budgetary process from a totally different direction and concentrate on *outputs* from the process. An output-based approach could be taken by any organisation, but the greatest extent of its practical application has been observed in the non-profit-making organisations, where their activity output is the most important focus of their work.

An output-based approach to budgeting requires starting with an estimate of the quantity and quality of service to be provided. For the non-profit-making organisation the service output takes the place of sales for the profit-seeking organisation. Having defined the desired output the organisation then budgets to determine what will be required to achieve that output. If the organisation is a charity, it will then set about fund-raising. If it is central or local government, it will levy taxes. If the charitable funds available, or the tax revenues to be generated, do not meet all the requirements, then the output activities may be curtailed.

Such an output-based approach focuses on programmes of action. Various budgeting techniques have been suggested for dealing with output-based budgets. One such technique is planning, programming budgeting systems.

A **planning, programming budgeting system (PPBS)** is an approach that seeks to separate the policy planning aspects of budgeting from the short-term financial planning process. From the overall objectives, the organisation moves on to identify the programmes that will achieve those objectives. The costs and benefits of each programme are then identified so that they may be given relative priorities. Subjective judgement is required to select the most suitable programmes for implementation and the resources required are then allocated to those programmes.

The techniques of PPBS were advocated with enthusiasm in the US for government budgeting in the 1970s, but by the 1980s had disappeared from favour. The reason was that, although the system sounds ideal, it is very difficult to administer because government departments are not organised by outcomes. They are organised on an input basis. In the late 1990s the state of Florida began new attempts to use programme budgets, with a focus on performance. As an example, the Department of Children and Family Services proposed programmes around specific groups such as persons with mental health problems. The agency then focused on achievement targets such as improving mental health, rather than on input targets such as providing specific hours of consultation. It was difficult to plan budgets forward on a programme basis because of the lack of adequately robust unit cost information. The budgets were mainly used as quantified confirmation that targets had remained within funding limits.

A programme to integrate into the community patients who have suffered mental illness may be taken as an example of PPBS. Such a programme will require the establishment of houses where the former patients may enjoy a degree of independence but will have access to help should it be required. That will involve a social welfare aspect and will increase the burden on the budget of the social services. The hospitals will have fewer long-stay mental patients and so will be able to close psychiatric wards. The health service will regard the corresponding funding as being released for other health service purposes such as acute medical care. Thus a programme which might be seen as having a positive social outcome may not result in a mutually amicable budgetary process where the two input departments are not under any constraint to work in harmony on achieving the overall objective.

The fact that PPBS has not always worked effectively in a government budgeting context may be due more to the organisation of government departments than to any intrinsic weakness in the concept. If the organisation's objectives are set in terms of programmes, then the organisational structure needs to reflect those programmes or it risks being ineffective if employees relate more closely to their input function than to the defined outputs. Real world case 14.3 shows how the National Health Service in the UK is now using 'Programme Budgeting' as a retrospective appraisal of the cost of programmes that cross a range of input services.

Activity 14.2

Suggest one activity (or a collection of activities) for which PPBS would be particularly useful.

Real world case 14.3

In the National Health Service (NHS) in England, Primary Care Trusts (PCTs) are allocated funds by the Department of Health. The PCTs are responsible for the first line of patient care (e.g. when patients see their general practitioner). If the patient then needs hospital treatment (acute care), the PCTs then purchase ('commission') health care from the Acute Healthcare Trusts (which operate the major hospitals). (The system in other parts of the United Kingdom operates differently.) This extract describes the use of Programme budgets within the NHS in England.

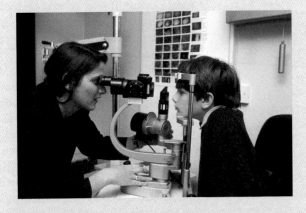

11.7 Programme Budgeting is a retrospective appraisal of resource allocation, broken down into meaningful programmes, with a view to tracking future resource allocation in those same programmes.

11.8 Programme Budgeting had its roots in the Rand Corporation in the USA in the 1950s. Its first major application was not in healthcare, but for the US Department of Defence in the 1960s where it was used as part of a cost accounting tool that could display, over time, the deployment of resources towards specific military objectives. Such objectives were looked at in terms of wars overseas, the support of NATO or the defence of the homeland, instead of the conventional 'inputs based' budgetary headings of tanks, missiles or diesel fuel. Allocation of new resources, or shifts between budgets, could be judged on their relative contribution to these specific objectives.

11.9 Such an approach can equally be applied to healthcare. Instead of seeing investment on the level of a hospital or drug budget, the focus switches to specific health objectives or medical conditions. The aim is to maximise health gain through deploying available resources to best effect. Clearly, this aim complements the commissioning role of Primary Care Trusts.

Examples of programmes are:

 8 Eye/Vision problems
 9 Hearing problems
22 Social care needs

Source: Department of Health (December, 2004) Programme Budgeting Guidance Manual, downloaded from www.dh.gov.uk/PublicationsAndStatistics

Discussion points

1 What kind of health objectives might be evaluated in the area of 'eye/vision problems'?

2 Can the term 'budget' be applied to a retrospective (backward-looking) appraisal?

14.4.5   Public benefit organisations

In using budgets as part of their planning, organisations providing a public service must have regard to the conditions under which they operate. Such organisations could be public sector bodies (town councils, government departments) or private sector bodies (charities, educational establishments). Public benefit organisations are not normally seeking to make a profit in the way that a private business might. However, they will wish to avoid a deficit where cash paid out exceeds cash received. Very often they start the budget with a level of income that depends on government funding plans or on the decision of an external donor. The non-profit-making organisation, such as a local government organisation, an educational body or a charity, has to concentrate on managing its expenditure so as to match income and expenditure where both are measured using the accruals concept. Some of the examples provided in this section are from the public sector because public sector bodies make more information available in public. Private sector bodies regard budgets as commercially sensitive and usually do not disclose them to anyone outside the organisation.

14.5   Questioning the need for budgets

The 'Beyond Budgeting' Round Table (BBRT)[1] is a discussion group with members from several countries, whose aim is to help organisations achieve continuous improvement (see Real world case 14.1 for an extract from the BBRT website). Budgets are seen as a relic from the past that can no longer be improved. The complaints against budgeting are:

- It is too time-consuming.
- It is too expensive.
- It is out of touch with the needs of managers.
- It contains fixed targets and financial incentives which drive people to behave in ways that are not in the best interests of the organisation as a whole.
- It focuses on central command and control.

The organisations who have rejected budgets have moved to a system of performance contracts with rewards being based on relative performance measures rather than fixed budget targets. Forecasts are created on a 'rolling' basis with updating every few months so that there is never a 'year-end' budget. A forecast shows what will happen if specific assumptions are made. The forecast is compared with targets and goals to allow any gaps to be managed. The management philosophy is described as 'adaptive performance management'. The principles of adaptive performance management are:

- Set aspirational goals.
- Reward success based on performance.
- Plan continuously, not annually.
- Base controls on key performance indicators, not on variances from budget.
- Make resources available as required.
- Co-ordinate interaction dynamically, not through annual planning cycles.

In this approach, a customer focus is essential, and teams need freedom to act. Information should be open and shared across the organisation.

Activity 14.3   *Read over this section again and think about the complaints against budgeting that are made by the BBRT. Decide whether you would support these complaints in a discussion*

14.6 What the researchers have found

This section summarises some of the research published on budgeting. Section 14.6.1 describes the 'better budgeting' initiatives. These are based on the view that 'better budgeting' is preferable to the abandonment of budgeting proposed in 'beyond budgeting'. Section 14.6.2 describes practical research into reasons for budgeting. Section 14.6.3 describes support for traditional budgeting. Section 14.6.4 discusses the links between budget participation and job satisfaction.

14.6.1 Better budgeting

A round table discussion was held in 2004 (CIMA/ICAEW 2004), organised by the ICAEW and CIMA. Those present debated possible ways of improving the budgeting process and highlighted areas for further research. The participants felt that formal budgeting was still a useful activity, despite all that has been written in the 'beyond budget' literature. They knew about the problems of budgeting but felt that the formal budgeting system and its related processes were indispensable. They felt that the budget provides a framework of control and a focus for co-ordinating activities within the business. Large companies would struggle to plan, co-ordinate and control without a budget, but even small companies need a road map showing their destination and how to get there. Budgets were seen as forward-looking and linked to strategic planning, with a relationship to forecasts. Forecasts were seen as high-level plans, with budgets showing more detail. The discussion forum concluded that budgeting was evolving, rather than becoming obsolete. Although the participants did not agree with abandoning budgets, they did feel that the criticisms of budgets had helped expose the problems and would lead to improvements.

14.6.2 Reasons for budgeting

Hansen and van der Stede (2004) investigated four potential reasons for budgeting to be used in organisations. The reasons they specified were: operational planning, performance evaluation, communication of goals and strategy formation. They sent questionnaires to 309 managers in US organisations. The managers were all members of the Consortium for Advanced Management International (CAM-I). The researchers received 57 usable replies. They found that these four reasons for budgeting are affected by different environments. Operational planning is a more prominent reason in a job-based environment than in a flow-based business process. Performance evaluation is the prominent reason where resources can be traced to products or outputs and there is a stronger element of competition for selling these products or outputs. Communication is the prominent reason where there is a job-based environment of products or services, strong interdependence between units of the organisation, and a stronger element of competition for selling the products or outputs. Organisations use the budget for strategy formation where they are divisionalised, pursue a strategy of differentiating their product or service, and operate in a job-based system with stronger competition for selling the products or output. The researchers also asked whether managers thought the budget approach performed well. Not surprisingly, the agreement was greatest where managers were satisfied with the budget process and their units had performed well against the budget set.

14.6.3 Support for traditional budgets

Ekholm and Wallin (2000) used a postal questionnaire to survey 650 companies in Finland. They found that 25 per cent of respondents had no plans to abandon annual budgets but 61 per cent said that they were constantly trying to develop the annual budget to meet new demands. Only six per cent had abandoned the annual budget altogether. Another two per cent were in the process of abandoning it altogether and six per cent had considered abandoning it. The first two groups were classed as 'conservative' and the final three groups as 'radical'. The most common system in use appeared to be a hybrid system consisting of the budget, rolling forecasts and, in some cases, a balanced scorecard.

14.6.4 Budgets and job satisfaction

Chong, Eggleton and Leong (2005) examined the impact of market competition and budgetary participation on performance and job satisfaction. They received responses from 77 senior managers across the financial sector in Australia. They found that higher levels of market competition were related to the more positive relationships between budgetary participation and job satisfaction. They concluded that it seemed likely that the presence of market competition encourages more active monitoring and gives more opportunities for those involved to participate in setting budgets that are likely to help improve their performance. Where there is less competition the outcomes are more predictable and budgetary processes have less impact.

14.7 Summary

Key themes in this chapter are:

- **Budgeting** may encourage co-ordination and communication. It may also have a positive or a negative impact on motivation, participation, feedback and group effects. The amount of budget slack may affect the behaviour of those implementing budgets. The politics of the organisation may have an influence on the nature of the budget and on its practical operation.

- The evaluation of outcomes against budget requires careful consideration of whether the comparison is valid. If the level of activity has changed since the budget was prepared, the budget must be revised so as to reflect the new level of activity.

- In public sector organisations, cost control and value for money are important. Generally, profit is not important. The targets are economy, efficiency and effectiveness. Some public sector organisations prepare **line item budgets** but these have the weakness of focusing on inputs. Programme budgeting focuses on programmes of outputs, where costs may be contributed from different departments and different line items.

- Some commentators have suggested that budgets hold back progress because what really matters is continuous improvement rather than waiting for periodic budgets and the cycle of activities related to preparing and implementing budgets. They call this 'beyond budgets'.

- Those who support continued use of budgets argue for 'better budgets' rather than 'beyond budgets'. The reasons for preparing budgets are linked to the nature of tbe business: different reasons are given for different types of budget. The link between job satisfaction and budget participation has been found to be stronger in situations of higher competition.

References and further reading

CIMA/ICAEW (2004) *Better Budgeting: A Report on the Better Budgeting Forum from CIMA and ICAEW*, July 2004, available on website www.cimaglobal.com

Chong, V.K., Eggleton, I.R.C. and Leong, M.K.C. (2005), 'The impact of market competition and budgetary participation on performance and job satisfaction: a research note.' *The British Accounting Review*, 37: 115–33.

Department of Health (2004) Chapter 11 'Programme Budgeting Guidance', in *Manual for Accounts*, NHS Finance Manual.

Ekholm, B.-G. and Wallin, J. (2000) 'Is the annual budget really dead?' *The European Accounting Review*, 9(4): 519–39.

Hansen, S.C. and Van der Stede W.A. (2004) 'Multiple facets of budgeting: an exploratory analysis' *Management Accounting Research*, 15: 415–39.

Hope, J. and Fraser, R. (2003) 'Who needs budgets?' *Harvard Business Review*, February.

QUESTIONS

The Questions section of each chapter has three types of question. 'Test your understanding' questions to help you review your reading are in the 'A' series of questions. You will find the answer to these by reading and thinking about the material in the text book. 'Application' questions to test your ability to apply technical skills are in the 'B' series of questions. Questions requiring you to show skills in problem solving and evaluation are in the 'C' series of questions. The symbol [S] indicates that a solution is available at the end of the book.

A Test your understanding

A14.1 How do budgets help with motivation? How might budgets discourage motivation (section 14.2.1)?

A14.2 Why is it considered important to have employees participate in preparation of budgets section (14.2.2)?

A14.3 What kind of feedback is needed on performance against budget (section 14.3.3)?

A14.4 How does negative feedback differ from positive feedback (section 14.2.3)?

A14.5 What are the problems for management in creating budgets that affect groups of employees (section 14.2.4)?

A14.6 What is budget slack? What are the problems of having (a) too much and (b) too little budget slack (section 14.2.5)?

A14.7 How may the use of budgets be affected by the 'politics' of an organisation (section 14.2.6)?

A14.8 What is meant by a flexible budget (section 14.3)?

A14.9 How are (a) variable costs and (b) fixed costs treated in a flexible budget (section 14.3)?

A14.10 What is a variance (section 14.3)?

A14.11 How are adverse and favourable variances calculated (section 14.3)?

A14.12 What is a line item budget (section 14.4.1)?

A14.13 What is an incremental budget (section 14.4.2)?

A14.14 What is zero-based budgeting (section 14.4.3)?

A14.15 What is an output-based budget (programme budget) (section 14.4.4)?

A14.16 What are the arguments against periodic preparation of budgets (section 14.5)?

A14.17 What have researchers found in surveying opinions on the usefulness of budgeting (section 14.6.1)?

A14.18 What have researchers found about the reasons for budget preparation (section 14.6.2)?

A14.19 What have researchers found about the support for traditional budgets (section 14.6.3)?

A14.20 What have researchers found about the links between budgets and job satisfaction (section 14.6.4)?

B Application

B14.1 [S]

When the financial controller of Bakers Company set the budget for the year ahead, it was expected that monthly output of cake packages would be 12,000 units. In March the output was increased to 14,000 per month following negotiation with a chain of corner shops. The following table reports the original budget and the actual outcome for the month of March.

	Original budget	Actual for March
Cake packages output	12,000	14,000
	£	£
Direct materials	48,000	53,000
Direct labour	24,000	29,000
Variable overhead	6,000	7,200
Fixed overhead	4,000	4,500
Total production costs	82,000	93,700

Required
(1) Prepare a statement showing a flexible budget and variances.
(2) Make a recommendation on the most significant variance for investigation, and suggest *two* possible causes to investigate.

B14.2

The financial controller of the local town council set a budget for street cleaning in one estate as shown in the first column below. In the month of April the cleaning supervisor cut back on 20 miles of cleaning to save costs. The actual costs for April are shown in the second column below.

	Original budget	Actual for April
Miles of streets cleaned per week	400	380
	£	£
Cleaning materials (variable)	1,600	1,550
Fuel for vehicle (variable)	6,000	5,800
Direct labour (fixed)	1,500	1,550
Fixed overhead	1,000	1,000
Total production costs	10,100	10,100

Required
(1) Prepare a statement showing a flexible budget and variances.
(2) Write a short comment to the financial controller on the effectiveness of the cleaning supervisor's attempt to reduce costs.

B14.3

Write a short essay (250–300 words) on the following subject: 'What are the arguments for and against using budgets for planning and control?'

B14.4

Write a short essay (250–300 words) on the following subject: 'Budgeting is a technical accounting exercise with no behavioural aspects.'

C Problem solving and evaluation

C14.1

Seats Ltd ('Seats') manufactures seats for installation in buses. It obtains its raw materials from Comfort Ltd ('Comfort'), a wholly owned subsidiary which sells only to Seats. The raw materials of foam and covering are cut to shape by Comfort and sold to Seats in packages ready for assembly. Seats could obtain raw materials from suppliers other than Comfort but would pay a price 10% higher than that charged by Comfort.

One-third of the output of Seats is bought by Buses Ltd ('Buses'), a company which produces buses. Buses has at present significant unutilised production capacity and could produce and sell more buses if the price of buses could be reduced. To achieve this, Buses would require Seats to reduce its selling prices and has asked Seats to quote a lower price.

Buses has indicated its willingness to increase its total purchases from Seats to one of the following options:

	If the price charged by Seats is:	Then Buses will buy a total of:
Option I	£24 per seat	35,000 seats
Option II	£23 per seat	45,000 seats
Option III	£22 per seat	60,000 seats

The total volume includes in each case the number of seats currently being purchased by Buses from Seats.

The directors of Seats are prepared to offer a lower price to Buses subject to the following restrictions:

1 Other existing customers must be guaranteed to receive their present level of supplies at present-day prices.
2 There can be no expansion of the productive capacity of either Seats or Comfort.

Sales and production volumes are always equal.

The following budgets for the year to 30 June Year 9 were prepared before Buses made the request for a price reduction:

	Comfort	Seats
Sales in units	50,000	75,000
Unutilised productive capacity	20%	25%
	£	£
Unit selling price	8.00	25.00
Unit cost of production		
Materials	2.00	8.00
Labour	1.50	7.00
Variable overhead	1.00	5.00
Fixed overhead per annum	60,000	110,000

Required

Write a report to the directors of Seats Ltd:

(a) advising on the effect of each of the options proposed by Buses; and
(b) containing a statement comparing the original budgeted profits of Comfort and Seats with the profits which would arise if Seats group were to adopt the most advantageous option.

C14.2

You have been appointed financial controller of Constructabus plc, a coach building company, which specialises in two types of bus, a standard double-deck vehicle and a luxury coach model. The chassis and engine are bought in and the framework of each bus is built on the assembly floor. All the fixtures and fittings are added in the finishing shed to meet customers' specifications.

The head of the accounts department has provided you with the following information for the year ended 31 August Year 8:

	Standard bus	Luxury coach
Sales in units	100	120
Total sales value	£3,075,000	£4,020,000
Production in units	90	80
Stock of finished units at 31 August Year 8	20	30
Labour hours per unit:		
Assembly floor	2,000	1,000
Finishing shed	1,000	1,500
Direct materials cost per unit	£4,000	£4,000
Total variable selling costs	£150,000	£144,000

Departmental Costs:	Assembly floor £	Finishing shed £
Labour	1,300,000	1,260,000
Variable overhead	520,000	210,000
Fixed overhead	200,000	180,000

Further information:

1 Stocks are valued at variable cost of production for management accounting purposes. Work in progress may be ignored. At 1 September Year 7, stock values were £25,000 per standard bus and £21,500 per luxury coach.

2 The assembly floor has achieved full working capacity during the year but the finishing shed was 25% under-utilised.

The head of the accounts department has prepared the following budget for the year ending 31 August Year 9:

	Standard Bus	Luxury coach
Sales in units	60	150
Total sales value	£1,845,000	£5,475,000
Production in units	60	145
Direct materials costs	£240,000	£725,000
Total variable selling costs	£105,000	£180,000

Departmental Costs:	Assembly floor £	Finishing shed £
Labour	1,590,000	1,665,000
Variable overhead	795,000	277,500
Fixed overhead	200,000	220,000

Further information:

1 Labour hours per unit are assumed to be the same as for the year ended 31 August Year 8.

2 Due to changing patterns in public transport, the budget has recognised that demand for standard buses has fallen by 40% but that sales of the luxury coaches will expand by 25%.

Required:

Prepare a report for the board which provides:

(a) a statement of budgeted profit for each product for the year ending 31 August Year 9;

(b) a comparison of this budget with the actual results for each product for the year ended 31 August Year 9; and

(c) comments on your analysis.

Case studies

Real world cases

Prepare short answers to Case studies 14.1, 14.2 and 14.3.

Case study 14.4

You have been approached by James Johnstone for advice on budgeting techniques. Mr Johnstone has recently inherited a majority shareholding in, and been appointed managing director of, Nicholas Knitwear Ltd ('NK'). NK is a small, long-established family firm which manufactures knitwear for sale to several department stores. It also owns and operates three retail outlets in tourist areas which sell NK products and other gift items.

NK is profitable, but Mr Johnstone is concerned that no one seems to know exactly how profitable it could be or should be. The quarterly management accounts report this year's actual figures compared with last year's actual figures, with no comment on the differences. Mr Johnstone realises that NK should have budgets against which annual performance can be measured, but has no idea as to how to proceed.

Write a report to Mr Johnstone advising him on appropriate budgeting techniques for NK.

Note

1. Bunce, P. 'The "beyond budgeting" journey towards adaptive management', in CIMA/ICAEW (2004). See also the BBRT website: www.bbrt.org

Chapter 15

Standard costs

This extract describes the evaluation of a project to explore and develop the production of the precious metal platinum in South Africa.

Anooraq Resources Corporation announces the results of a preliminary economic assessment of the Drenthe and adjacent Overysel North platinum group metals ('PGM') deposits. The Drenthe and Overysel North deposits are being explored and developed under the Boikgantsho Platinum Mine Joint Venture agreement ('Boikgantsho JV') between Anooraq and Anglo American Platinum Corporation Limited ('Anglo Platinum'). Anooraq is the operator of the joint venture. The Boikgantsho JV property is located on the northern limb of the Bushveld Complex, about 250 kilometres north of Johannesburg, South Africa.

....

As operator, Anooraq is responsible for exploration and engineering activities. This Preliminary Assessment has been conducted by in-house and external independent qualified persons employed by Anooraq. Anglo Platinum has not been involved in the preparation of the Preliminary Assessment nor in the evaluation of the results thereof. The study uses industry standard costs for all phases of the proposed development including the smelting and refining, and makes assumptions about the concentrate to be produced. Industry standard costs are also used in estimates of the cost for socio-economic activities, i.e. community involvement, relocation and other related issues. However, until there are final agreements on these and related matters there is no assurance that these costs will not change.

Source: *Business Wire*, 9 March 2005, 'Anooraq Resources Corporation: Preliminary Assessment Indicates Strong Returns for Development of Drenthe & Overysel North Platinum Group Metals Deposits'.

Discussion point

1 How will the use of standard costs help to reassure potential investors in this project?

2 Why will the standards need to be specific to the industry?

Contents

Learning outcomes

After reading this chapter you should be able to:

- Define the terms 'standard cost' and 'variance'.
- Explain the purpose of using standard costs.
- Describe the problems of choosing the level of output for standards.
- Explain how the control process uses standard costs and variances.
- Calculate and interpret variances for product costs and sales margins.
- Combine calculation of all variances in a case study.
- Explain how variances may be investigated.
- Use flexible budgeting to calculate variances in a case study.
- Discuss the usefulness of variance analysis.
- Understand the broader views that exist regarding variance analysis.
- Describe and discuss research into the use of standard costing.

15.1 Introduction

Chapter 13 explains the budgetary process and illustrates in detail a method of preparing budgets for planning purposes. The use of budgets for control purposes is explained in Chapter 14 in terms of comparing the actual outcome with the expected results as shown by the flexible budget.

When actual costs are compared with budgeted costs, the comparison is made of the total cost for the line item under consideration (e.g. cost of various types of materials, cost of various categories of labour or cost of a range of categories of overheads). Where there is a significant variance between the budget and the actual outcome, that variance may be investigated. (It has to be remembered, however, that the investigation will itself have a cost and that cost may be minimised by first trying to narrow down the causes of the difference.)

To analyse the difference between what was expected and what actually happened, it is useful to make comparisons in terms of *cost per unit* rather than total cost of a line item in the budget. Such costs per unit may be estimated in advance and used as a standard against which to compare the actual costs incurred. The cost per unit, measured in advance of the operations to be undertaken, is called a **standard cost**.

Definition

> **Standard cost** is the planned unit cost of the products, components or services produced in a period.[1]

Once the standard cost has been decided, the actual cost may be compared with the standard. If it equals the standard then the actual outcome has matched expectations. If the actual cost is greater than, or less than, the standard cost allowed, then there will be a variance to be investigated. This chapter explains how the standard costs may be determined and how the variances may be quantified. In the definition of a variance the use of a standard cost is now added.

Definition

> A **variance** is the difference between a planned, budgeted or standard cost and the actual cost incurred.[2]

15.2 Purpose of using standard costs

Chapter 2 has already shown that calculation of the cost of an item of input or output may be analysed in terms of two measurements:

1 A physical quantity measurement
multiplied by
2 A price measurement.

Real world case 15.2

The US government has strict accounting rules for those involved in defence contracts. This extract outlines the process and then sets out the rules for applying Standard Costing.

Administratively a function located within OFPP is the Cost Accounting Standards Board (CASB), an independent legislatively established board consisting of five members, including the OFPP Administrator, who serves as chairman, and four members with experience in Government contract cost accounting, two from the Federal government,

one from industry, and one from the accounting profession. The Board has the exclusive authority to make, promulgate, and amend cost accounting standards and interpretations designed to achieve uniformity and consistency in the cost accounting practices governing the measurement, assignment, and allocation of costs to contracts with the United States.

One of the standards set by this body is for the use of standard costs:
CAS 407 Use of Standard Costs for Direct Material and Direct Labor

Purpose
To improve cost measurement and cost assignment for contractors that choose to use a 'standard' type accounting system.

Requirement
Standard costs may be used for estimating, accumulating, and reporting costs of direct material and direct labor when:

● Standard costs are entered into the books of the account;

● Standard costs and related variances are appropriately accounted for at the level of the production unit; and

● Practices regarding the setting and revising of standards, use of standard costs, and disposition of variances are stated in writing and are consistently followed.

Source: www.whitehouse.gov/omb/procurement/casb.html

Discussion points

1 Why are standard costs particularly important for use in defence contracts?

2 What does the standard indicate about (a) the nature of the standard costs and (b) the recording of the standard costs?

Actual costs are measured after the event by reference to the quantity of the resource used and its price. When the actual cost is measured there is no doubt as to the quantity and price.

Standard costs are measured in advance of the period of time to which they relate, so that estimation is necessary. This requires estimation of physical inputs and outputs, and monetary estimates of prices of inputs and outputs. In order to determine useful standards it is necessary first of all to consider the purpose for which the standards will be used. The purpose could cover any or all of the following:

(a) to provide product costs for stock valuation;
(b) to increase control within a budgeting system;
(c) to gauge performance of a business unit by use of variance analysis;
(d) to integrate costs in the planning and pricing structure of a business;
(e) to reduce record-keeping costs when transactions take place at different prices.

This chapter will concentrate on items (b), (c) and (d) of the foregoing list, showing how variance analysis may be used for purposes of control, performance evaluation and planning. First, the standard cost is explained. The control process is then outlined by means of a flow diagram. Most of the chapter deals with the calculation and interpretation of variances in the cost of direct materials, direct labour and production overhead. That provides information to management for use in making judgements and carrying out performance evaluations. The final section discusses the usefulness of variance analysis based on standard costing in planning the efficient operation of the business.

15.3 The level of output to be used in setting standards

Calculation of the standard cost requires a view to be taken on the most appropriate physical measurement to incorporate in the cost calculation. Three approaches are instanced here. The first uses a basic level of output, the second looks to an ideal level of output and the third uses a currently attainable level of output.

The **basic standard** is one which never changes and consequently remains a permanent basis for comparison. This gives a base line against which to make long-term comparisons. It has the disadvantage of becoming increasingly unrealistic as circumstances change.

The **ideal standard** is one which applies in dream conditions where nothing ever goes wrong. It represents the cost to be incurred under the most efficient operating conditions. It is an almost unattainable target towards which an organisation may constantly aim, but it may also cause a lowering of morale in the organisation if staff can never reach the target.

Currently attainable standards lie between these two extremes, defined as standards which should normally equal expectations under 'normally efficient operating conditions'. They may represent quite stiff targets to reach, but they are not beyond possibility. Currently attainable standards are the most frequently used because they give a fair base for comparisons, they set a standard which ought to be achieved and they give staff a sense of achievement when the attainable target is reached. Thus they contribute to all the management functions of planning and control which were explained in Chapter 1.

Setting standards also relates to performance. A standard may be set by estimating in advance the expected performance of a work unit. This sometimes is called an *ex ante* standard (where 'ex ante' means 'before the event takes place'). Alternatively a standard may be set by observing performance and estimating what is realistically attainable. Because this method learns from the past performance it is sometimes called an *ex post* standard (where 'ex post' means 'after the event has taken place').

Although the standard cost may be quantified as a single figure, it may in practice represent a whole range of possible figures because it is an estimate from a range of possible outcomes. This chapter will apply a single-figure standard in illustrative case studies, without questioning further the basis on which the standard was created.

Activity 15.1

These first three sections of the chapter have explained the meaning of a standard and the various different approaches to the creation of a standard. Read the sections again and satisfy yourself that you are aware of the differences. That awareness will help you in thinking about the interpretation of variances.

We now turn to an explanation of how standards are used in the control process.

15.4 The control process

Exhibit 15.1 shows the process of calculating and using standard costs for control purposes. The calculation of standards involves asking technical specialists, who are probably not management accountants, to specify the standard inputs of resources. The management accountant takes this information and prepares a standard cost

Exhibit 15.1
Use of standards in the control process

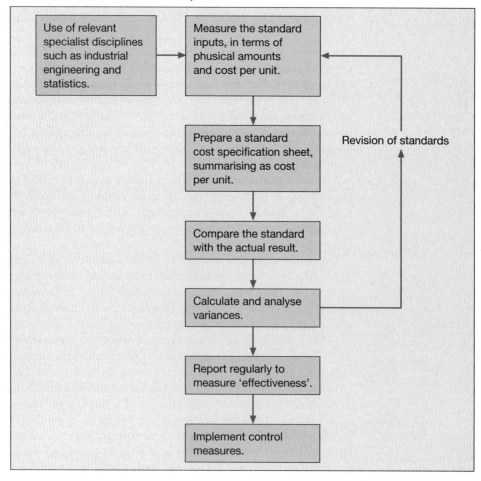

specification, usually converting that to a cost per unit of
costs are then measured and compared with the standard. \
are quantified, analysed and reported. This may lead to contr\
eliminating variances. It may also lead to revision of the standa.
longer relevant.

The presence of a standard cost provides a benchmark against w
actual cost. The technical term for this process is variance analysis. (\
be described as adverse or favourable, depending on how the standa   _y
costs compare. If the actual cost is greater than the standard expected, then the variance is said to be 'adverse'. If the actual cost is less than the standard expected, then
the variance is said to be 'favourable'. The existence of either type of variance could
lead to investigation of the cause. The component costs must be investigated separately
so that they may be separately analysed and interpreted. We now move on to give
more detail on the process of calculating and analysing variances for direct materials
cost and direct labour cost.

Definitions	An **adverse variance** arises when the actual cost is greater than the standard cost. A **favourable variance** arises when the actual cost is less than the standard cost.

Activity 15.2

Suggest three situations in which a business organisation might decide to revise standards, as indicated in Exhibit 15.1, following calculation and analysis of variances. Is revision equally likely for adverse and for favourable variances? Make sure that you know the definitions of adverse and favourable variances. They will appear frequently in the following sections.

15.5 Calculating and interpreting variances

This section explains the method of calculating variances and the interpretation
of variances based on subdivisions of calculations. The subdivisions of cost variances
are summarised in Exhibit 15.2 and explained in sections 15.5.1 to 15.5.4. Sales
margin variances are explained in section 15.5.5. The variances are brought together
in section 15.5.6 in a comparison of budgeted profit to actual profit using a reconcila-
tion statement.

Exhibit 15.2
Summary of cost variances

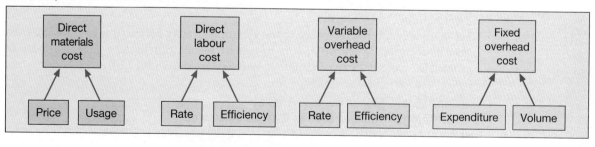

15.5.1 Direct materials variances

Take as a starting point one of the ingredients of prime cost: direct materials. If the actual
cost differs from the standard cost, then the cause may lie in the materials usage, or

in the price of the materials, or in a mixture of both. An adverse cost variance could indicate that the price paid was higher than expected when the standard was set, or it could indicate that the amount of materials used was greater than that expected.

In diagrammatic form:

Direct materials cost variance	
equals	
Direct materials price variance	Direct materials usage variance

Exhibit 15.3 sets out in words the calculation of variances. Alongside there are abbreviated symbols for readers who are comfortable with an algebraic representation.

Exhibit 15.3
Calculation and formulae for direct materials variances

Variance	Calculation	Formula
Total cost variance	Standard cost of materials (SC) minus actual cost of materials (AC)	SC – AC
	This may be shown in more detail as:	
	Standard cost (SC) = standard price per unit (SP) multiplied by standard quantity allowed (SQ)	SC = (SP × SQ)
	minus	minus
	Actual cost (AC) = actual price per unit (AP) multiplied by actual quantity used (AQ)	AC = (AP × AQ)
Direct material price variance	Actual quantity used (AQ), multiplied by the difference between the standard price per unit (SP) and the actual price per unit (AP)	AQ (SP – AP)
Direct material usage variance	Standard price per unit of materials (SP) multiplied by the difference between the standard quantity (SQ) allowed and the actual quantity used (AQ)	SP (SQ – AQ)

At this point in learning about variance analysis, some students will ask: 'Why are the formulae in this form? I can see other combinations of symbols which could break the cost variance down into two components.' The answer is that there are other combinations, but one of the aims of management accounting is to present relevant information. In the form given in the exhibit, these variances produce relevant information.

To understand the relevance of the variances, it may help to think of the standard cost as a rectangle whose area is measured by multiplying the standard price of materials by the standard quantity of materials used (Exhibit 15.4).

Exhibit 15.4
Representing standard cost as a rectangular area

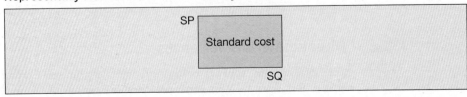

Now imagine that the actual cost is greater than standard cost so that a rectangle representing actual cost will fit around the outside of the standard cost rectangle. Exhibit 15.5 shows the two rectangles together. The total cost variance is represented by the shaded area in the shape of an 'inverted L' to the top and right-hand side of the diagram. The top part of the shaded area represents variance caused by actual price being greater than standard price. The right-hand side represents variance caused by the actual quantity used being greater than the standard quantity allowed. In terms of management responsibility, the price variance will be in the hands of the purchasing department, while the usage variance will be in the hands of the production department. But who should be held accountable for the top right-hand corner where a question mark appears? This is a mixture of price variation and usage variation. The production manager will disclaim any responsibility for the price aspect and the buying department will say it has no control over quantity.

Exhibit 15.5
Representing actual cost and standard cost as two areas superimposed

AP	Price variance	?	
SP	Standard cost	Usage variance	
		SQ	AQ

Management accounting is full of hard decisions and as far as possible tries to be fair. For the top right-hand corner of the diagram, that is almost impossible; however, there is a view that usage is within the organisation's control to a greater extent than the price of inputs taken from an external supplier. Management accounting therefore takes the view that the production manager's responsibility for usage should be limited in order to leave out the area containing the question mark. By default, therefore, that area at the top right-hand corner is allowed to fall entirely into the price variance.

Activity 15.3

Read this section again to ensure that you understand fully the method of calculating direct materials cost variance. Compare the formulae in Exhibit 15.3 and the diagram in Exhibit 15.5. If there is any step which you do not understand, seek help at this stage from your tutor or a fellow student.

15.5.2 Direct labour variances

The starting point in analysis of direct labour cost variances resembles closely that used for direct materials, except that the price variance changes its name to labour rate variance and the usage variance changes to labour efficiency variance.

Direct labour cost variance	
equals	
Direct labour rate variance	Direct labour efficiency variance

The formulae for calculating direct labour variances are similar to those used for direct materials. They are shown in Exhibit 15.6.

Exhibit 15.6

Calculation and formulae for direct labour variances

Variance	Calculation	Formula
Total cost variance	Standard cost of labour (SC) minus actual cost of labour (AC)	SC − AC
	This may be shown in more detail as:	
	Standard cost (SC) = standard labour rate (SR) multiplied by standard hours allowed (SH)	SC = (SR × SH)
	minus	minus
	Actual cost (AC) = actual labour rate (AR) multiplied by actual hours worked (AH)	AC = (AR × AH)
Direct labour rate variance	Actual hours worked (AH), multiplied by the difference between the standard labour rate (SR) and the actual labour rate (AR)	AH (SR − AR)
Direct labour efficiency variance	Standard labour rate (SR) multiplied by the difference between the standard hours allowed (SH) and the actual hours worked (AH)	SR (SH − AH)

At this point you meet a new idea, that of the standard hour. A **standard hour** is defined as the amount of work achievable, at standard efficiency levels, in one hour.[3] Suppose that a study has been carried out of work patterns at standard efficiency. It has been estimated that one employee can assemble 10 computer boxes in one hour. That defines the standard hour for that particular work. If 100 computer boxes are produced then the standard hours allowed are 10 hours. If the employee takes 11 hours to produce the 100 boxes, that is more than the standard allowed. Investigation will be required to find the cause. It could be the case that the employee worked too slowly. On the other hand, it could be the case that the employee worked at normal efficiency, but the components supplied were not of the usual specification and there were difficulties with the assembly process.

Definition

A **standard hour** is defined as the amount of work achievable, at standard efficiency levels, in one hour.

If you try to draw a diagram for direct labour variances, superimposing the actual cost on the standard cost as shown for direct materials in Exhibit 15.5, you will find that the area labelled with a question mark in Exhibit 15.5 has all been allocated to the rate variance. It is argued in management accounting that the organisation is more likely to have control over efficiency than it is over the labour rate, which may well be determined by the labour market in general. The efficiency variance should therefore not include any element of variation in labour rate, and the top right-hand corner of the diagram is all taken into the rate variance.

Activity 15.4

Read this section again to make sure that you understand fully the formulae in Exhibit 15.6. Try to produce a diagram for direct labour similar to that drawn in Exhibit 15.5 for direct materials. Note down the similarities and the differences between the formulae for direct materials variances and the formulae for direct labour variances.

15.5.3 Variable overhead variances

Chapter 2 explains that the most effective method of calculating an overhead cost rate is to calculate the overhead cost per direct labour hour. This is because labour working usually causes most of the overhead costs to be incurred (unless the business is highly machine-intensive). It will be assumed throughout this chapter that a standard cost of variable overheads can be expressed as a cost per direct labour hour. As well as being the preferred choice from Chapter 2, it also makes the calculation of variable overhead variances look very similar to the calculation of direct labour variances.

Variable overhead cost variance	
equals	
Variable overhead rate variance	Variable overhead efficiency variance

The variances are expressed in words and formulae in Exhibit 15.7.

Exhibit 15.7
Calculations and formulae for variable overhead variances

Variance	Calculation	Formula
Total cost variance	Standard cost of variable overhead (SC) minus actual cost of variable overhead (AC)	SC – AC
	This may be shown in more detail as:	
	Standard cost (SC) = standard variable overhead rate (SR) multiplied by standard hours allowed (SH)	SC = (SR × SH)
	minus	minus
	Actual cost (AC) = actual variable overhead rate (AR) multiplied by actual hours worked (AH)	AC = (AR × AH)
Variable overhead rate variance	Actual hours worked (AH), multiplied by the difference between the standard variable overhead cost rate (SR) and the actual variable overhead cost rate (AR)	AH (SR – AR)
Variable overhead efficiency variance	Standard variable overhead cost rate (SR) multiplied by the difference between the standard hours allowed (SH) and the actual hours worked (AH)	SR (SH – AH)

Activity 15.5

Read this section again and make sure that you understand fully the formulae for calculating variable overhead cost variances. Compare these formulae with those used for direct labour cost variances. What are the points of similarity? What are the points of difference? Can you see consistent patterns in the variances for direct materials costs, direct labour costs and variable overhead costs?

15.5.4 Fixed overhead cost variances

There are two questions to ask in relation to fixed overheads:

● Has the activity level recovered more or less overhead cost than expected (a volume question)?
● Have we spent more or less than expected (an expenditure question)?

These are combined in a total cost variance which asks: Is the actual overhead cost more or less than the actual output valued at the standard overhead cost rate (a comparative cost question)?

Total fixed overhead cost variance	
equals	
Fixed overhead volume variance	Fixed overhead expenditure variance

Chapters 4 and 5 explain that overhead recovery in any period is calculated by applying a predetermined fixed overhead cost rate to the actual level of output to calculate the overhead recovered in a period. You have also seen in these chapters that the over-recovery or under-recovery was calculated by comparing the fixed overhead recovered with the actual fixed overhead cost of the period. In standard costing this is described as the total fixed overhead cost variance (Exhibit 15.8).

- If the *actual* fixed overhead incurred is *greater than* the fixed overhead recovered, then the variance is adverse.
- If the *actual* fixed overhead incurred is *less than* the fixed overhead recovered, then the variance is favourable.

Exhibit 15.8
Calculation and formula for total fixed overhead variance

> **Total fixed overhead cost variance** = Fixed overhead recovered ('applied') (calculated as standard FO rate × AO) minus actual fixed overhead (AFO)
>
> Standard FO rate = Budgeted fixed overhead cost divided by budgeted output
> AO = actual output
> AFO = actual fixed overhead cost

The total fixed overhead cost variance is adverse if the actual fixed overhead cost is *greater than* the actual overhead multiplied by the fixed overhead cost rate. Why is it adverse? Because the actual cost is greater than would be expected based on actual output and the budgeted cost of fixed overhead per unit.

The calculation of total fixed overhead variance shows over- or under-recovery of fixed overhead cost but does not explain the reason. There are two possible explanations. One is that the *actual* fixed overhead expenditure is different from the *budgeted* level of fixed overhead expenditure. The other is that the *actual* volume of output is different from the *budgeted* level of output.

The fixed overhead expenditure variance is calculated by subtracting the actual fixed overhead incurred from the amount of fixed overhead budgeted (*see* Exhibit 15.9).

- If the *actual* fixed overhead is *greater than* the *budget*, there is an adverse variance.
- If the *actual* fixed overhead is *less than* the *budget*, there is a favourable variance.

Exhibit 15.9
Calculation and formula for fixed overhead expenditure variance

> **Fixed overhead expenditure variance** = Budgeted fixed overhead (BFO) minus actual fixed overhead (AFO)

The fixed overhead volume variance is calculated as the budgeted fixed overhead cost rate multiplied by the difference between the actual volume of output and the budgeted volume of output (Exhibit 15.10).

Exhibit 15.10

Calculation and formula for fixed overhead volume variance

> **Fixed overhead volume variance** = Standard FO rate × (actual output AO minus budgeted output BO)

- If the *actual* volume of output is *greater than* the *budgeted* volume of output there is an over-recovery. The volume variance is said to be favourable.
- If the *actual* volume of output is *less than* the *budgeted* volume of output there is an under-recovery. The volume variance is said to be adverse.

The fixed overhead volume variance is favourable if the actual volume of output is *greater than* the actual overhead multiplied by the fixed overhead cost rate. Why is it favourable? Because the additional volume recovers more cost than was expected when the budgeted volume was set.

Summarising these variances:

Total fixed overhead cost variance	
(standard FO rate × AO) – (AFO)	
equals	
Fixed overhead volume variance	Fixed overhead expenditure variance
Standard FO rate × (AO – BO)	(BFO) – (AFO)

15.5.5 Sales variances

A variance in sales has two possible causes. One is that the *sales price* is different from the budgeted price. The other is that the *sales volume* is different from the budgeted volume. Two variances are defined in this section – the sales price variance and the sales margin volume variance.

The *sales margin* is the profit earned on sales. Profit margins are seen as an important measure of management success and so it is useful in variance analysis to highlight the extent to which actual profit departs from budgeted profit because of changes in sales volumes from those expected when the budget was set.

When the budget is set, it is based on an expected level of sales. If the actual volume of sales is greater than the budget, then the sales will generate greater profit margin than was expected for the reporting period. If the actual volume of sales is less than budget, then there will be a corresponding loss of profit margin.

When the budget is set, it is also based on an expected selling price per unit. If the actual selling price is higher than expected, it will cause a higher profit margin than expected. If the actual selling price is lower than expected, it will cause a lower profit margin than expected.

Exhibit 15.11

Formula for sales variances

Variance	Calculation	Formula
Sales price variance	= Actual sales volume × (actual selling price per unit – standard selling price per unit)	AV (ASP – SSP)
Sales margin volume variance	= Standard profit per unit × (actual sales volume – budgeted sales volume)	SP (AV – BV)

The sales price variance asks the question: What is the effect of the change in selling price on the profit margin for the actual sales, assuming that all costs remain at standard costs? If the selling price is higher than expected, then the variance is favourable. If the selling price is less than expected, then the variance is adverse.

The sales margin volume variance asks the question: How does the change in sales volume affect the standard profit expected? If the actual sales volume is greater than budget then the variance is favourable. If the actual sales volume is less than budget, then the variance is adverse.

15.5.6 Reconciling budgeted profit and actual profit

When all variances have been calculated it is useful to summarise them all in a statement comparing the budgeted profit of the period with the actual profit of the period. A typical layout for absorption costing is shown in Exhibit 15.12.

Exhibit 15.12
Reconciliation of budgeted and actual profit

Budgeted net profit		XXX
Sales price variance	XX	
Sales margin volume variance	XX	
Direct materials price variance	XX	
Direct materials usage variance	XX	
Direct labour rate variance	XX	
Direct labour efficiency variance	XX	
Variable overhead rate variance	XX	
Variable overhead efficiency variance	XX	
Fixed overhead expenditure variance	XX	
Fixed overhead volume variance	XX	
Actual profit		XX

If a variable costing system is in use, then the sales margin volume variance is based on contribution rather than total profit and the fixed overhead volume variance is not required. The illustrations in this chapter all apply absorption costing.

Activity 15.6

As a final check, go back to the start of the chapter and satisfy yourself that you understand everything presented up to this point. The rest of the chapter introduces no new technical material, but it applies the formulae to a full example.

15.6 Case study: Allerdale Ltd

The chapter now moves into a case study as a means of providing an illustration of the calculation and interpretation of variances. Allerdale Ltd uses a manufacturing process which involves fastening laminated surfaces on to workbenches. The material for the laminated plastic surface is purchased in large sheets and cut to size at the start of the process. The sheets of laminated plastic represent the direct materials cost of the process. Employees work on cutting and fastening the laminated surfaces and trimming them to fit. This work is classed as direct labour cost. Overhead costs are incurred in using indirect materials such as glues and staples, indirect labour such as cleaners for the production area, and the costs of heating, lighting and maintaining the factory premises. The overheads are partly variable (such as the indirect materials and power) and partly fixed (such as insurance, rent and business rates).

The variances in respect of direct materials, direct labour, variable overhead and fixed overhead are now explained in turn, using data provided by the accounting records.

15.6.1 Direct materials variances

Data for direct materials

The standard amount of laminated material allowed is two square metres per workbench. The standard price of the material is £1.80 per square metre. During the month of June, 2,500 workbenches were laminated. The amount of material used was 5,375 square metres and the price paid was £1.90 per square metre.

Calculations of direct materials variances are shown in Exhibit 15.13 and Exhibit 15.14, using the formulae set out in Exhibit 15.3.

Exhibit 15.13
Calculation of direct materials total variance

The standard allowance is 2 square metres each for 2,500 workbenches, which is 5,000 square metres standard quantity (SQ) in total. Standard price per unit (SP) is £1.80 per square metre. Actual quantity used (AQ) is 5,375 square metres and actual price per unit (AP) is £1.90 per square metre.

$$\text{Total cost variance} = \text{standard cost minus actual cost (SC} - \text{AC)}$$
$$= (\text{SP} \times \text{SQ}) \text{ minus } (\text{AP} \times \text{AQ})$$
$$= (£1.80 \times 5{,}000 \text{ sq metres}) \text{ minus } (£1.90 \times 5{,}375 \text{ sq metres})$$
$$= £9{,}000 \text{ minus } £10{,}212.50$$
$$= £1{,}212.50 \text{ adverse variance}$$

In Exhibit 15.13, the variance is adverse because the actual cost is greater than the standard cost set for the direct materials to be used. The total variance may be subdivided into direct materials price and usage variances, using the formulae from Exhibit 15.3 to give the analysis shown in Exhibit 15.14. The data for this calculation have already been set out in words and in symbols at the start of Exhibit 15.13. The same symbols and figures are used in Exhibit 15.14.

Exhibit 15.14
Calculation of direct materials price and usage variances

Price variance	Usage variance
= AQ (SP − AP)	= SP (SQ − AQ)
= 5,375 sq metres (£1.80 − £1.90)	= £1.80 (5,000 − 5,375)
= £537.50 adverse variance	= £675 adverse variance

You will see that the actual price per unit of materials is £1.90, which is greater than the £1.80 per unit set as a standard cost. The price variance of £537.50 is therefore adverse. The actual amount of direct materials used is 5,375 square metres, which is greater than the 5,000 square metres set as a standard. The usage variance is therefore also adverse. The two variances, added together, equal the total adverse variance of £1,212.50 calculated in Exhibit 15.13. We now know that the overall variance is caused by both price and usage effects but that the usage problem is the greater of the two.

15.6.2 Adverse or favourable variances?

If you have followed these calculations yourself you will have obtained negative signs in each calculation. The negative sign corresponds to an adverse variance because in each case the actual outcome is worse than the predetermined standard. However, it is risky to rely on plus and minus signs, because it is easy to make careless errors in calculations and to turn the formula round accidentally. It is always safer to look at each calculation on a commonsense basis. The total cost variance will be adverse where the actual outcome is worse than the standard cost allowed. The price variance will be adverse where the actual unit price is greater than the standard price allowed. The usage variance will be adverse where the actual quantity used is greater than the standard quantity allowed.

15.6.3   What caused the variance?

It is often impossible to be definite about the cause of a particular variance but suggestions may be made as a basis for further investigation. A variance in the *price* of materials indicates that the actual price paid per unit differs from that expected when the standard was set. That could be because the price has changed, in which case the standard should be revised. The variance could be due to purchasing a more expensive quality of material, in which case there will need to be an investigation as to whether this was due to the production department requesting a higher quality than that permitted when the standard was set, or whether it was a procedural error in the buying department. Perhaps the higher quality was found to be necessary because the previous quality of materials was causing too much labour time to be wasted on substandard products. Variances may interact, which means it is important to look at the cost control picture as a whole.

A variance in the *usage* of materials may be an indication that lack of quality in the materials is causing too much wastage. It may be that employees have not received sufficient training in the best way of using the material. Perhaps a new machine has been installed which operates much faster to meet expanding demand levels but has a naturally higher wastage rate.

Once the calculation of two variances has been mastered, the mathematically minded student soon realises that the subdivisions could be taken further. The usage variance may be split into a yield variance, comparing what goes in with what comes out of the process, and a mix variance, looking at the effect of having a different mix of input materials than was planned when the standard was set. That level of detailed analysis will not be taken further here, but you should be aware that there is a world of detail, to explore at another time, in relation to variance analysis.

Some of the foregoing causes of variance may lead to remedial action. Others may lead to a decision that it is in the interests of the organisation to accept the difference and revise the standard accordingly. Fiona McTaggart gives her views.

FIONA: *I see my job as reporting the variances accurately and in good time. The decisions on how to use those variances are for those who manage the operations of the business. If they tell me that a variance has become an accepted part of the operation, I will discuss with them whether the new data should be incorporated in a revised standard, or whether there is a continuing control aspect of identifying that variance to ensure that it stays within acceptable limits.*

The case study now continues to illustrate the calculation of direct labour cost variances.

15.6.4   Direct labour variances

Data for direct labour
Allerdale Ltd has set a standard labour rate of £8 per direct labour hour. Actual hours worked in June were 4,910 at an actual cost of £37,316. The standard allowance of direct labour hours, for the output achieved, was 5,000 hours.

Calculations of variances are shown in Exhibit 15.15 and Exhibit 15.16, using the formulae set out in Exhibit 15.6. In Exhibit 15.15, the variance is favourable because the actual cost is less than the standard cost set for the direct labour to be used. The total variance may be subdivided into direct labour rate and efficiency variances, using the formulae from Exhibit 15.6, to give the analysis shown in Exhibit 15.16. The symbols and the relevant figures needed for these variances are set out at the start of Exhibit 15.15.

The actual rate of pay per hour is less than the standard rate and the rate variance is therefore favourable. The actual hours worked are less than the standard hours allowed which means that the efficiency variance is also favourable. The total favourable variance of £2,684 has, therefore, two components of which the rate variance of £1,964 is the more significant.

Exhibit 15.15
Calculation of direct labour total variance

The standard allowance of direct labour time is 5,000 standard hours (SH). The standard labour rate set (SR) is £8 per hour. Actual hours worked (AH) are stated to be 4,910. The actual labour rate (AR) is not stated but can be calculated by dividing the actual cost (AC) of £37,316 by the actual hours of 4,910, to give £7.60 per hour.

$$\text{Total cost variance} = \text{standard cost minus actual cost (SC – AC)}$$
$$= (SR \times SH) \text{ minus } (AR \times AH)$$
$$= (£8 \times 5{,}000) \text{ minus } (£7.60 \times 4{,}910)$$
$$= £40{,}000 \text{ minus } £37{,}316$$
$$= £2{,}684 \text{ favourable variance}$$

Exhibit 15.16
Calculation of direct labour rate and efficiency variances

Rate variance	Efficiency variance
= AH (SR – AR)	= SR (SH – AH)
= 4,910 hours (£8.00 – £7.60)	= £8.00 (5,000 – 4,910)
= £1,964 favourable variance	= £720 favourable variance

15.6.5   What caused the variance?

With direct labour, as with direct materials, it is easier to apply conjecture than to find sure and certain explanations. A favourable variance in the *labour rate* is an indication that the actual wage rate per employee was lower than that which was expected when the standard was set. That could be due to an anticipated pay increase having failed to materialise. Alternatively, it could suggest that the mix of employees is different from that intended when the standard was set, so that the average wage paid is lower than planned. A variance in *labour efficiency* means that fewer hours were worked than were expected when the standard was set. This could be due to a new training scheme, or less than the expected amount of enforced idle time when machinery is not operating. Perhaps better quality material was purchased, giving a higher purchase price, but this caused less wastage and allowed employees to work more efficiently in producing the finished goods.

As with direct materials, there is no particular reason to stop with analysing only two variances. A change in the mix of employees could be a cause for variance within the overall efficiency variance. The number of subdivisions depends only on the ingenuity of those devising the variance analysis. This textbook will, however, be content with analysing only two causes of direct labour cost variance.

Fiona McTaggart has discovered that often there are interlocking effects in variances on direct materials and direct labour. She was recently in discussion with the plant manager:

FIONA: *It is the management accountant's job to produce the variance report and it is the plant manager's job to interpret the result, but naturally I am always interested in the explanation. Last month we had a favourable variance on direct materials price but unexpected adverse variances on direct materials usage and direct labour efficiency. On investigation, it was found that the buying department had seen a special offer on metal sheeting which dramatically cut the unit cost of material, so they bought six months' supply. What they didn't know was that the machinery on the factory floor can't deal with that particular type of metal sheeting because it slips intermittently in the rollers. The result was far more wastage of materials than expected, labour time lost through having to process materials twice, and some very irate operatives who lost bonuses because so much time was wasted. The problem was so bad that after one month the remaining unused material was sold for scrap and the correct specification was purchased. It was a very expensive lesson in the need for interdepartmental communication.*

15.6.6   Variable overhead cost variances

> **Data for variable overhead**
> Allerdale Ltd has set a standard variable overhead cost rate of £2 per direct labour hour. Actual hours worked in June were 4,910 and the actual variable overhead cost incurred was £11,293. The standard allowance of direct labour hours, for the output achieved, was 5,000 hours.

Calculations of variances are set out in Exhibit 15.17 and Exhibit 15.18, using the formulae set out in Exhibit 15.7. The standard allowance of direct labour time is 5,000 standard hours (SH). The standard variable overhead cost rate set is £2 per direct labour hour. The actual variable overhead cost rate (AR) is not stated but can be calculated by dividing the actual cost (AC) of £11,293 by the actual direct labour hours of 4,910, to give £2.30 per direct labour hour.

Exhibit 15.17
Calculation of variable overhead cost variance

Total cost variance = standard cost minus actual cost (SC – AC)
= (SR × SH) minus (AR × AH)
= (£2 × 5,000) minus (£2.30 × 4,910)
= £10,000 minus £11,293
= £1,293 adverse variance

Exhibit 15.18
Calculation of variable overhead rate and efficiency variances

Rate variance	Efficiency variance
= AH (SR – AR)	= SR (SH – AH)
= 4,910 hours (£2.00 – £2.30)	= £2.00 (5,000 – 4,910)
= £1,473 adverse variance	= £180 favourable variance

The symbols and the relevant figures needed in order to calculate the variable overhead rate and efficiency variances are set out at the start of Exhibit 15.17. The actual variable overhead cost rate of £2.30 per direct labour hour is greater than the standard rate of £2 and there is an adverse variance of £1,473. This is offset to some extent by a favourable efficiency variance due to the actual hours worked being less than the standard allowed, but this gives a favourable variance of only £180 so that the combination of the two explains the overall adverse variance of £1,293.

15.6.7 What caused the variance?

The adverse rate variance means that some item of variable overhead has cost more than expected. There is not sufficient detail available here for an answer to emerge but, in practice, the management accountant would now look at the unit cost of each item, such as glues, staples, paint, cleaning costs and any other variable cost items, to find which had risen above the standard set. The favourable efficiency variance is directly due to labour hours being less than expected when the standard was set. The explanation will be the same as that given for the favourable efficiency variance on direct labour.

15.6.8 Fixed overhead expenditure variance

Data for fixed overhead
Allerdale Ltd budgeted fixed overhead expenditure at £10,000 for the month of June. The actual amount of fixed overhead expenditure was £11,000.

The most important question to answer here is, 'Why did we spend more than expected?' This is quantified in the fixed overhead expenditure variance, calculated as budgeted fixed overhead minus actual fixed overhead. In this example, the result is an adverse variance of £1,000. Causes could include an increase in the cost of fixed overhead or an extra category of fixed overhead, neither of which was expected when the budget was set.

The fixed overhead cost variance could be subdivided into a volume variance and an expenditure variance (see section 15.5.4). However in this case there is no change in volume of output from the level set in the budget (2,500 workbenches). So the fixed overhead variance is entirely due to the expenditure variance.

15.6.9 Sales variances

Data for sales
Allerdale Ltd sold its output of 2,500 workbenches for £31 each. The budgeted selling price was £30.

The sales margin volume variance is zero because there is no change in volume from the budgeted level of sales.

The sales price variance is calculated as:

Actual sales volume × (actual selling price per unit – standard selling price per unit)
= 2,500 × (£31 – £30) = £2,500 favourable.

The sales price variance is favourable because the actual selling price is greater than the budgeted selling price.

15.6.10 Reconciling budgeted profit and actual profit

The budgeted profit of the period is calculated as shown in Exhibit 15.19.

Exhibit 15.19
Budgeted profit for output of 2,500 units

	£	£
Sales 2,500 at £30		75,000
Materials 2,500 × 2 sq metres × £1.80	9,000	
Labour 2,500 × 2 hours × £8	40,000	
Variable overhead 2,500 × 2 hours × £2	10,000	
Fixed overhead	10,000	
		69,000
Budgeted profit		6,000

The actual profit of the period is calculated as shown in Exhibit 15.20.

Exhibit 15.20
Actual profit for output of 2,500 units

	£	£
Sales 2,500 at £31		77,500.00
Materials	10,212.50	
Labour	37,316.00	
Variable overhead	11,293.00	
Fixed overhead	11,000.00	
		69,821.50
Actual profit		7,678.50

The reconciliation of budgeted profit to actual profit is shown in Exhibit 15.21.

Exhibit 15.21
Reconciliation statement incorporating variances

(*Note:* In this statement, adverse variances are presented in brackets)

	£	£
Budgeted net profit		6,000.00
Sales price variance	2,500.00	
Sales margin volume variance	–	
Direct materials price variance	(537.50)	
Direct materials usage variance	(675.00)	
Direct labour rate variance	1,964.00	
Direct labour efficiency variance	720.00	
Variable overhead rate variance	(1,473.00)	
Variable overhead efficiency variance	180.00	
Fixed overhead expenditure variance	(1,000.00)	
Fixed overhead volume variance	–	
Total variances		1,678.50
Actual profit		7,678.50

Activity 15.7

Copy out the data for the case study, then close the book and test yourself by producing the calculations and analyses. That exercise will establish your confidence in knowing the technical material of the chapter.

15.7 Investigating variances

Once the variances have been calculated, those who manage the business have to decide which variances should be investigated. Should every adverse variance be investigated? Such an investigation takes time and so itself involves a further cost in searching for a cause. Is it worth incurring this further cost to find out what happened to the costs under investigation? Such an investigation might unearth some unwelcome facts about the world beyond accounting. It has been suggested that the accountant feels 'safe' in a separate accountant's world. Perhaps no one, other than the management accountant, believes in the system in any event. These radical thoughts have been expressed in various parts of the academic literature. One extreme conclusion which might be drawn is that it is safer to avoid any type of investigation.

It is fairly obvious that a reasonable answer lies between the two extremes of investigating everything and investigating nothing. Nevertheless, it may be useful to think about the extreme cases in order to justify the middle ground. Many who take a traditional approach prefer to use judgement in deciding which variance to investigate. Such persons would run their eye down the variance report, item by item, using their knowledge and experience to identify variances for further investigation. That approach is called 'intuition' and is fine for the experienced manager, but risky when applied by a trainee or someone not familiar with the operational factors behind the variances. It is also difficult to write a computer program for the intuitive approach. If the accounting information is being processed by computer, it is often convenient to let the computer do the work of highlighting the variances for investigation. So some systematic approach is needed.

This may be achieved by setting a *filter rule* which filters out the unimportant but draws attention to the matters regarded as significant. This might be, 'Investigate all variances which are more than 10 per cent of the total standard cost of this cost centre'. It might be, 'Investigate all variances which are more than £10,000 in amount each month'. Establishing filters is a matter of experience and judgement in order to ensure that no significant difference by amount is overlooked.

Using filters may not always be the perfect approach. The choice of what is important may vary depending on the nature of the variance or the nature of the cost item. Using the filter does not take into account the costs and benefits of variance investigation. It does not incorporate the past history of performance in that item, where inefficiencies are persisting through lack of remedial action. The item may be one where the variance has suddenly worsened dramatically, but still falls within the filter limits. (For example, where a cost item has habitually shown a variance within two per cent of standard cost but then suddenly increases to 15 per cent, that could be highly significant even though the predetermined filter is set at 20 per cent.)

The selection of variances for investigation is therefore very much dependent on circumstances and on the person making the selection. Fiona McTaggart gives her description of the management accountant's role in deciding on which variances to investigate.

FIONA: *In my work I keep in close contact with each of the production supervisors. We have informal meetings once each month to look at the specifications for the standards. They give me their views on the type and level of variance which they regard as significant to their part of the business. From that list I create a set of filters which I apply to the monthly report on how actual costs measure up against standards. I also add some filters based on company policy as to what is material to the overall production operations. My choice of filters has regard to existing pricing policy and a need for management of working capital. These filters produce a variance exception report. The production supervisors are expected to make a comment to the production director on the action to be taken in respect of the*

variances highlighted by the filter process. Every six months I meet with the production director to review the effectiveness of the filters being applied.

We now move on to consider the practical problems of calculating variances when the level of output is different from that expected at the time the budget was set.

15.8 Flexible budgets: case study

One of the most commonly occurring problems in variance analysis is deciding which benchmark to use as a basis for comparison. When the standard costs are set at the beginning of a reporting period, they will be presented in the form of a budget based on activity levels expected at that point. Suppose activity levels subsequently fall because of a downturn in demand? Is it preferable to base the variance analysis on the standard set for the original level of output, or to introduce some flexibility and compare actual outcome with the standard expected for the new lower level of activity? Putting the question in that form leads to an almost inescapable conclusion that flexibility is required, but it is surprising how that obvious need for flexibility may be overlooked when a table of figures appears on a page. A case study is now used to show the application of a flexible budget.

In Chapter 14, section 14.3.1, flexible budgeting is illustrated using the case study of Brackendale. Exhibit 14.2 shows the calculation of variances by comparing the flexible budget with the actual outcome. This section shows how the analysis of variances may be take a stage further using the formulae of standard costing variances. For ease of reference the case study data are reproduced in Exhibit 15.22.

Exhibit 15.22
Case study description, Brackendale

When the standards for the year ahead were set, it was expected that monthly output of units manufactured would be 10,000 units. By the time July was reached, output had fallen to 8,000 units per month because of a fall in market share of sales. The table set out below reports the original budget and the actual outcome for the month of July.

The original budget is based on a standard direct material cost of £4 per kg of raw material, a standard direct labour cost of £10 per hour and a standard variable cost rate of £6 per direct labour hour. Each unit of output requires 0.5 kg of raw materials and 6 minutes of labour time. The actual cost of direct materials was found to be £4.40 per kg, the actual cost of direct labour was found to be £11.00 per hour and the actual variable overhead cost rate was £5.60 per direct labour hour. 3,800 kg of materials were used and the actual labour hours worked were 1,000.

Data relevant to the month of July are as follows:

	Original budget	Actual for July
Units manufactured	10,000	8,000
	£	£
Direct material	20,000	16,720
Direct labour	10,000	11,000
Variable overhead	6,000	5,600
Fixed overhead	7,000	7,500
Total product costs	43,000	40,820

The budgeted selling price is £6 per unit. The actual selling price is also £6.

In section 14.3.1 Fiona McTaggart explains the preparation of a flexible budget statement as shown in Exhibit 14.2. Fiona's working notes for more detailed analysis are now set out in detail. Italics are used in each exhibit to show where she has calculated a new figure using the data already provided. You should follow her workings through the exhibits and check that you understand how the figures in italics have been calculated.

15.8.1 Summary statement of variances

The summary statement of variances (*see* Exhibit 15.23) takes the information for original budget and actual costs contained in the case study description. The flexible budget is created by taking 8/10ths of the original budget costs (because the units manufactured are 8/10ths of the volume originally budgeted). The variances are then calculated by deducting the actual costs from the flexible budget figures. Italics are used to show the flexible budget figures which have been calculated as 8/10ths of the original budget. The only exception is fixed overhead cost, where it would not be expected that the cost was variable. Accordingly there is no flexibility with regard to fixed overhead.

Exhibit 15.23
Calculation of variances using a flexible budget: summary statement of variances

	Original budget (1)	Flexible budget (2)	Actual for July (3)	Variance (2) – (3)
Units manufactured	10,000	8,000	8,000	
	£	£	£	£
Direct materials	20,000	16,000	16,720	720 (A)
Direct labour	10,000	8,000	11,000	3,000 (A)
Variable overhead	6,000	4,800	5,600	800 (A)
Fixed overhead	7,000	7,000	7,500	500 (A)
Total product costs	43,000	35,800	40,820	5,020 (A)

15.8.2 Data analysis sheet

The data analysis sheet (*see* Exhibit 15.24) uses the information contained in the case study description Exhibit 15.22 or in Exhibit 15.23 and fills in the gaps by calculation. Italics show the calculated figures in Exhibit 15.24, and the workings are at the foot of Tables (a) and (b). Note that fixed overheads are not flexible and are therefore excluded from Tables (a) and (b). The output level for the period is 8,000 units.

Exhibit 15.24
Calculation of variances using a flexible budget: data analysis sheet

(a) Analysis of standard cost

Item	Standard cost of item	Standard amount of item per unit of output	Standard quantity for output level 8,000 units[1]	Standard cost for output level 8,000 units[2]
	£			£
Direct material	4.00 per kg	0.5 kg	4,000 kg	16,000
Direct labour	10.00 per hour	6 mins	800 hours	8,000
Variable overhead	6.00 per dlh[3]	6 mins dlh	800 dlh	4,800

Notes: [1] [8,000 × 0.5 kg = 4,000 kg] and [8,000 × 6 mins = 800 hours].
[2] [4,000 kg × £4 = £16,000]; [800 hours × £10 = £8,000]; [800 hours × £6 = £4,800].
[3] dlh = direct labour hours.

Exhibit 15.24 **continued**

(b) Analysis of actual cost				
Item	Actual cost of item £	Actual amount of item per unit of output[1]	Actual quantity for output level 8,000 units	Actual cost for output level 8,000 units £
Direct material	4.40 per kg	0.475 kg	3,800 kg	16,720
Direct labour	11.00 per hour	7.5 mins	1,000 hours	11,000
Variable overhead	5.60 per dlh	7.5 mins	1,000 hours	5,600

Note: [1] [3,800 kg/8,000 = 0.475 kg] and [1,000 hours/8,000 = 7.5 mins].

15.8.3 Direct materials variances

Total cost variance = standard cost minus actual cost (all based on the new output level)
= £16,000 minus £16,720
= £720 adverse variance

The variance is adverse because the actual cost is greater than the standard allowed by the flexible budget for the output of 8,000 units.

Price variance	Usage variance
= AQ (SP − AP)	= SP (SQ − AQ)
= 3,800 kg (£4.00 − £4.40)	= £4.00 (4,000 − 3,800)
= £1,520 adverse variance	= £800 favourable variance

The price variance is adverse because the actual price per kg is greater than the standard price per kg. The usage variance is favourable because the actual quantity used, 3,800 kg, is less than the standard allowed, 4,000 kg, for the actual level of output.

15.8.4 Direct labour variances

Total cost variance = standard cost minus actual cost
= £8,000 minus £11,000
= £3,000 adverse variance

The variance is adverse because the actual cost is greater than the standard allowed by the flexible budget for the output of 8,000 units.

Rate variance	Efficiency variance
= AH (SR − AR)	= SR (SH − AH)
= 1,000 hours (£10.00 − £11.00)	= £10.00 (800 − 1,000)
= £1,000 adverse variance	= £2,000 adverse variance

The direct labour rate variance is adverse because the actual rate is higher than the standard rate per hour. The direct labour efficiency variance is adverse because the actual hours worked (2,000) were greater than the standard allowed (1,600) for the output achieved.

15.8.5 Variable overhead variances

Total cost variance = standard cost minus actual cost
= £4,800 minus £5,600
= £800 adverse variance

The variance is adverse because the actual cost is greater than the standard allowed by the flexible budget for the output of 8,000 units.

Rate variance	Efficiency variance
= AH (SR − AR)	= SR (SH − AH)
= 1,000 hours (£6.00 − £5.60)	= £6.00 (800 − 1,000)
= £400 favourable variance	= £1,200 adverse variance

The variable overhead rate variance is favourable because the actual rate is less than the standard rate per hour. The variable overhead efficiency variance is adverse because the actual hours worked (2,000) were greater than the standard allowed (1,600) for the output achieved.

15.8.6 Fixed overhead variances

The fixed overhead expenditure variance is equal to the budgeted fixed overhead minus the actual fixed overhead. That has already been shown to be £500 adverse due to overspending compared with the budget. The fixed overhead rate is £0.70 (£7,000/10,000). The volume variance is 2,000 × £0.70 = £1,400. It is adverse because less overhead has been absorbed than is actually incurred.

The fixed overhead cost variance is equal to the actual output at the fixed overhead rate minus the actual overhead cost. The actual output is 8,000 units and the fixed overhead rate is £0.70 per unit giving £5,600 in total. The actual fixed overhead is £7,500. The variance is £1,900 adverse in total because the actual output has absorbed less than the budgeted output.

15.8.7 Sales margin variances

The actual sales price is the same as the budgeted sales price and therefore the sales price variance is nil. The standard profit is £4.30 per unit (£43,000/10,000).

The actual sales volume is 2,000 units less than the budgeted volume and therefore the sales margin volume variance is the standard profit of (£6 − £4.3) = £1.7 × 2,000 units = £3,400. It is an adverse variance because the lower level of activity has generated less profit.

15.8.8 Reconciliation statement

		£
Budgeted sales 10,000 at £6		60,000
Budgeted costs		(43,000)
Budgeted profit		17,000
		£
Actual sales 8,000 at £6		48,000
Actual costs		40,820
Actual profit		7,180
	£	£
Budgeted profit		17,000
Sales price variance	–	
Sales margin volume variance	(3,400)	
Direct materials price variance	(1,520)	
Direct materials usage variance	800	
Direct labour rate variance	(1,000)	
Direct labour efficiency variance	(2,000)	
Variable overhead rate variance	400	
Variable overhead efficiency variance	(1,200)	
Fixed overhead expenditure variance	(500)	
Fixed overhead volume variance	(1,400)	
Total variances		(9,820)
Actual profit		7,180

15.8.9 Variance report

From the foregoing calculations a variance report may be prepared. This brings to the attention of the production manager the main items highlighted by the process of variance analysis, as shown in Exhibit 15.25.

Exhibit 15.25
Brackendale Ltd: variance report

BRACKENDALE LTD
Variance report

To: Production manager
From: Management accountant
Subject: **Variance report for July**

During the month of July there were 8,000 units manufactured, as compared with 10,000 expected when the budget was set. Allowing flexibility for the lower level of output, there was nevertheless an adverse profit variance of £9,820 for the month. The most serious is the adverse sales margin volume variance of £3,400.

The most serious cost variance is the direct labour variance, where adverse changes in labour rate contributed £1,000 and less efficient working contributed £2,000 to the total £3,000. The direct materials cost variance of £720 looks worse when decomposed into an adverse price variance of £1,520 offset partially by a favourable usage variance of £800. The variable overhead cost variance of £800 adverse also looks worse when decomposed into an adverse efficiency variance of £1,200, partly offset by a favourable rate variance of £400. Overspending on fixed overheads was £500 for the month.

While the investigation of these problems is a matter for yourself, I might venture to suggest that from past experience we have noticed that a favourable materials usage variance may arise when employees are instructed to work more carefully and, as a consequence, take

Exhibit 15.25 **continued**

longer time, which leads to an adverse labour efficiency variance. If that is the case, then the more careful working has had an overall negative effect because the £800 favourable materials usage variance must be compared with the £2,000 adverse labour efficiency variance and the £1,200 adverse variable overhead efficiency variance.

The variance in materials price is almost certainly due to the recent increase in the price of goods supplied. That is not a matter we can control from within the company and the standard cost will be revised next month.

The variance in labour rate is due partly to a recent pay award not included in the original budget, but it is also due to employees being paid at overtime rates because of the extra time spent on working more carefully with materials. There may need to be a major review of how this part of the business is operating, with a view to minimising total variance rather than taking items piecemeal.

Although the variable overhead rate variance is favourable, the categories of variable overhead will be reviewed to see whether any of the standard costs are out of date. Overspending on fixed overhead was due to a change in the depreciation rate of equipment due to revised asset lives. The budget will be revised at the half-yearly review which is coming up next month.

Real world case 15.3

This extract describes the accounting support available from a commercial provider to help house builders with costing.

IDS Scheer North America, the leading provider of business process excellence services and tools, today announced that it is teaming closely with SAP and will unveil a new ARIS Reference Model specifically developed for the needs of the home building sector at the 2004 Big Builder Conference in Las Vegas, November 9–11, 2004 at the Mandalay Bay Convention Center. The ARIS Reference

Model for Home Building will be a part of the ARIS SmartPath for Home Building. IDS Scheer's ARIS SmartPath includes a process-oriented approach to the configuration, implementation, methodology and management of SAP(R) solutions.

- ARIS SmartPath for Home Building modules will include:
- Support for the National Association of Home Builders (NAHB) chart of accounts
- Configuration of the construction industry requirement of actual costs vs. standard costs for projects
- Management of the entire construction to cash cycle, including the scheduling and purchasing functions.
- Support purchasing and all aspects of sub-contracting management
- Warranty management specific to the construction industry

Source: *Business Wire*, 9 November 2004, 'IDS Scheer Announces ARIS(TM) Reference Model for Home Builders for Construction Industry'.

Discussion points

1 What is the role of standard costing in the process described here?

2 How might a standard costing system for housebuilding differ from a standard costing system for defence contracts (Real world case 15.2)?

Activity 15.8

Copy out the data for the foregoing case study, close the book and attempt the variance analysis yourself. This will test your understanding of the technical material. Make a note of any problems or difficulties and consult your tutor about these.

Activity 15.9

Look back to the example of Allerdale in section 15.6. The following information relates to the month of July which had the same budgeted profit as that of June but saw an unexpected increase in output and sales to 2,550 units. The following tables set out the budgeted and actual profit. Prepare a reconciliation of the budgeted profit and actual profit, based on variances.

Budgeted profit for output of 2,500 units

	£	£
Sales 2,500 at £30		75,000
Materials 2,500 × 2 sq metres × £1,80	9,000	
Labour 2,500 × 2 hours × £8	40,000	
Variable overhead 2,500 × 2 hours × £2	10,000	
Fixed overhead	10,000	
		69,000
Budgeted profit		6,000

Actual profit for output of 2,550 units

	£	£
Sales 2,550 at £31		79,050
Materials (5,483 sq metres)	10,417	
Labour (5,008 hours)	38,062	
Variable overhead	11,518	
Fixed overhead	11,000	
		70,997
Actual profit		8,053

15.9 Is variance analysis, based on standard costs, a useful exercise?

Academic opinion is divided on the usefulness of variance analysis. Solomons (1978) has claimed that standard costing probably represents the greatest advance in accounting since the development of bookkeeping. There is another view that perhaps this historical leap forward has given standard costing more importance than it deserves. In this chapter the standard has been portrayed as a single figure, but it is actually an estimate based on the best expectations of the future conditions envisaged in the organisation. If the organisation has a stable technology and works within safely attainable levels of productivity, then there is relatively little likelihood of finding that the expected cost is far away from the true cost. But if the organisation is much riskier in the nature of its operations, perhaps using a less stable technology and working at the upper limits of productivity, then the expected standard cost may be an average measure of a wide range of possible outcomes.

Anthony (1997) has questioned whether any scientific enquiry into variance analysis is in reality carried out and has questioned further whether such enquiry is worth doing in any event. He has identified, in practice, a strong intuitive approach to variance analysis.

It may be that accountants tend to overemphasise their own importance. The causes and control of variances lie with those managing and operating the technical aspects of the business. Management accountants only present the information which, if in a relevant and useful form, may help in identifying cause and establishing better control. Setting standards is first and foremost an industrial engineering problem. It might be safer to leave the variance analysis to the engineers and forget about the cost aspects.

Chapter 1 explains the management functions of planning and control, and the importance of communication and motivation. Well-planned variance reports, based on up-to-date and realistic standards, will provide information for the planning process, encourage control and communicate the effects of operational actions on the costs of the organisation. Motivation will be enhanced if the variance report is seen to be specific to the information needs of each level of management and if the standard costs are seen to be a fair measure of expected achievement. Motivation could be reduced by a badly designed or carelessly implemented variance report.

Chapter 1 lists three management accounting functions of directing attention, keeping the score and solving problems. Standard costs contribute to all three, when used in conjunction with variance analysis. The variance report, by using predetermined filters, may direct attention to areas of significance. The preparation of the report, on a regular basis, is a vital part of the score-keeping operation. Analysis of the variances, to which the management accountant will make a contribution in deciding on the level of detail, will be a problem-solving exercise requiring logical and systematic analysis of the problem represented by the accounting figures.

15.10 A broader view of applications of variance analysis

At the start of the chapter a list was set out of five ways in which standard costs may be used by an organisation:

(a) to provide product costs for stock valuation;
(b) to increase control within a budgeting system;
(c) to gauge performance of a business unit by use of variance analysis;
(d) to integrate costs in the planning and pricing structure of a business;
(e) to reduce record-keeping costs when transactions take place at different prices.

Are these purposes useful? Is it worthwhile to make the effort of developing standard costs? Some brief answers are now provided.

(a) The objective of providing product costs for purposes such as stock valuation falls within the general heading of 'What should it cost?', a question which in turn leads to more questions about the effective use of resources. It is as important to ask questions about the cost of goods not sold as it is to look at the variance in cost of the goods which have been sold. If stock is valued at actual cost, it will carry with it a share of the problems which led to a cost variance and will burden the next reporting period with those problems. If the stock is valued at standard cost, all variances in price are dealt with in the period when they arise.

(b) A budgeting system may be based on actual costs, but it will have greater usefulness if it is based on standard costs as a measure of the predetermined targets for a period. A budget relates to an activity or operation as a whole, while a standard cost is a cost per unit which gives a very precise focus to the budgetary planning process. Budgets do not necessarily need to be based on standard cost, but the standard costs bring additional benefits in allowing the organisation to examine more precisely how the budget compares with the actual outcome.

(c) Performance is gauged by comparing actual costs with standard costs and analysing the differences. The resulting variance may indicate where, in the control of the organisation, future action is required. Performance may be related to responsibility so that the management accounting information is matched to the management aims of the organisation.

(d) Planning and pricing are aspects of long-term decision making which require a strategic outlook on business problems. Pricing will usually be a forward-looking activity based on estimated costs and out-turns. Standard costs provide a benchmark against which to plan pricing and, in retrospect, to evaluate the success of a pricing policy in terms of recovering costs incurred.

(e) If all costs are recorded on a standard basis, then the variations in quantity may be separated analytically from the variations in price. In practice, the price variations are isolated as soon as the goods are purchased. Thereafter, the progress of costs, in moving through to finished goods and to output in the form of sales, is all monitored at standard cost so that the emphasis is on quantity and variations in quantity. That reflects the control process in that, once the goods have been purchased, or services paid for, there is no further opportunity to take action over price. Success in cost control thereafter depends entirely on control of usage, which is in the hands of those controlling and carrying out operations.

15.11 What the researchers have found

15.11.1 Use in manufacturing industry

Sulaiman *et al* (2005) asked whether standard costing is obsolete, based on evidence from Malaysia. This is a country with a significant base of manufacturing industry, seeking to compete globally by using advanced manufacturing technologies and shorter product life cycles. The researchers sent questionnaires to a range of Malaysian companies and received 66 replies. Some were local Malaysian companies, while others were Malaysian subsidiaries of Japanese parent companies. Across both groups there was strong evidence for continuing use of standard costing. The highest importance attached to standard costing in the Japanese companies related to costing inventories. The highest importance attached to standard costing in the native Malaysian companies related to cost control and performance evaluation. Other reasons given high importance were computing product cost for decision making, acting as an aid to budgeting, and for economies of data processing.

Companies were asked how they decided on the variances to be investigated. A specific monetary amount was mentioned in some cases. A percentage of standard was mentioned in a similar number of cases. In terms of importance of calculation, the direct cost variances (materials, labour) were relatively more popular than overhead variances. Sales volume and price were seen as important.

15.11.2 Use in the public sector

Northcott and Llewellyn (2002) discussed the National Reference Costing Exercise of the National Health Service in England. This represented a major exercise to standardise costs across the NHS in order to encourage benchmarking of best practice. Problems observed in the exercise related to the quality of the information, variations in allocations of indirect costs and different assumptions about matters such as length of stay by a patient. The researchers concluded that although there was merit in the efforts to improve comparability it did not at that time alleviate all concerns about comparability across the service.

15.12 Summary

Key themes in this chapter are:

- How control through the use of **standard costs** per unit leads to a more specific analysis than is available where control is through the use of budgets. Budgets give only the total cost of each line item. Standard costing allows decomposition into cost per unit and quantity of units.

- **Variances** have been defined and illustrated for:
  - direct materials (total cost variance, analysed into price and usage variances)
  - direct labour (total cost variance, analysed into rate and efficiency variances)
  - variable overhead (total cost variance, analysed into rate and efficiency variances)
  - fixed overhead (total cost variance, analysed into volume and expenditure variances)
  - sales price and sales volume.

- **Flexible budgeting** has been explained, showing that where the level of output is different from that expected when the budget was prepared, the standard costs should be used to prepare a new flexible budget for the new level of output. All variable costs should be recalculated to reflect the change in output. Fixed overhead costs are independent of activity level and therefore have no flexibility.

- The chapter has also given some flavour of the debate on the importance and usefulness of **standard costs**. They are widely used but, to be effective, must be chosen with care to meet the needs of the business and of the management purposes of planning and control.

References and further reading

Anthony, R. and Govindarajan, V. (1997) *Management Control Systems*, 9th edn, McGraw-Hill, New York.

Solomons, D. (1978) 'Flexible budgets and the analysis of overhead variances', in Antony, H.R., Firmin, P.A., and Grove, H.D. (eds), *Issues in Cost and Managerial Accounting: A Discipline in Transition*, Houghton Mifflin, Boston.

Sulaiman, M., Ahmad, N.N. and Alwi N.M. (2005) 'Is standard costing obsolete? Empirical evidence from Malaysia, *Managerial Auditing Journal*, 20(2): 109–24.

Northcott, D. and Llewellyn, S. (2002) 'Challenges in costing health care services: recent evidence from the UK', *The International Journal of Public Sector Management*, 15(3): 188–203.

QUESTIONS

The Questions section of each chapter has three types of question. 'Test your understanding' questions to help you review your reading are in the 'A' series of questions. You will find the answer to these by reading and thinking about the material in the text book. 'Application' questions to test your ability to apply technical skills are in the 'B' series of questions. Questions requiring you to show skills in problem solving and evaluation are in the 'C' series of questions. The symbol [S] indicates that a solution is available at the end of the book.

A   Test your understanding

A15.1   What is a standard cost (section 15.1)?

A15.2   Why are standard costs useful (section 15.2)?

A15.3 How are standard costs related to levels of output (section 15.3)?

A15.4 How are standard costs used in the control process (section 15.4)?

A15.5 How are direct materials price and usage variances calculated (section 15.5.1)?

A15.6 Give three possible causes of an adverse direct materials price variance (section 15.5.1).

A15.7 Give three possible causes of a favourable direct materials usage variance (section 15.5.1).

A15.8 How are direct labour rate and efficiency variances calculated (section 15.5.2).

A15.9 Give three possible causes of a favourable direct labour rate variance (section 15.5.2).

A15.10 Give three possible causes of an adverse direct labour efficiency variance (section 15.5.2).

A15.11 How are variable overhead cost variances calculated (section 15.5.3)?

A15.12 How are fixed overhead cost variances calculated? (Section 15.5.4)?

A15.13 How are sales margin variances calculated (section 15.5.5)?

A15.14 Explain how you would identify which variances to investigate (section 15.7).

A15.15 Explain the importance of using a flexible budget with variance analysis (section 15.9).

A15.16 Give three reasons for regarding variance reports as a useful tool of management (section 15.10).

A15.17 [S] It was budgeted that to produce 20,000 concrete building blocks in one month would require 100,000 kg of material. In the month of May, only 16,000 blocks were produced, using 80,080 kg of material. The standard cost of materials is £3 per kg. What is the materials usage variance?

A15.18 [S] The standard cost of direct labour in the month of August is £36,000. There is a direct labour rate variance of £6,000 adverse and a direct labour efficiency variance of £2,500 favourable. What is the actual cost of direct labour in the month?

A15.19 [S] Fixed overhead for the month of October has been budgeted at £16,000 with an expectation of 8,000 units of production. The actual fixed overhead cost is £17,500 and the actual production is 7,000 units. What is the variance?

B   Application

B15.1 [S]

The monthly budget of Plastics Ltd, manufacturers of specialist containers, was prepared on the following specification:

Production and sales	30,000 units
Selling price	£70 per unit
Direct materials input	5 kg per unit at a cost of £1.20 per kg
Direct labour input	2 hours per unit at a rate of £4 per hour
Variable overhead	£2 per direct labour hour
Fixed overhead	£90,000 per month

The following actual results were recorded for the month of May Year 8:

Stock of finished goods at start of month	8,000 units
Sales	40,000 units
Production	42,800 units
Stock of finished goods at end of month	10,800 units

Actual costs incurred were:

	£
Direct material	267,220 (213,776 kg at £1.25 per kg)
Direct labour	356,577
Variable overhead	165,243
Fixed overhead	95,000

Further information

(a) Throughout May the price paid for direct materials was £1.25 per kg. Direct material is used as soon as it arrives on site. No stocks of materials were held at the start or end of May.

(b) The labour rate paid throughout the month was £4.10 per hour.

(c) The selling price of finished goods was £70 per unit throughout the month.

(d) Stocks of finished goods are valued at standard cost of production.

Required

(a) Calculate the budgeted profit for May Year 8, based on the actual sales volume achieved.

(b) Calculate the cost variances for the month of May.

(c) Explain how cost variances may be used to identify responsibility for cost control within the company.

B15.2 [S]

The upholstery department of a furniture manufacturing business prepared the following statement of standard costs at the start of the calendar year:

Standard cost per unit

	£
Direct material	250
Direct labour	150
Fixed manufacturing overhead	100
	500

In preparing the statement, it was budgeted that 100 units would be completed each month.

During the month of May the following results were reported:

	£
Direct materials cost	31,200
Direct labour cost	16,800
Fixed manufacturing overhead	9,600
	57,600

The actual level of production achieved in May was 120 units.

The budget for direct materials was based on an allowance of 10 kg materials per unit produced. The budgeted cost of materials was £25 per kg. Actual materials used during May amounted to 1,300 kg.

The budget for direct labour was based on an allowance of 15 hours per unit, at a labour rate of £10 per hour. At the start of May, an agreed incentive scheme increased the labour rate to £12 per hour. All employees receive the same rate of pay.

Stocks of finished goods are valued at full standard cost of manufacture.

Required

(a) Prepare an accounting statement reconciling the budgeted costs for the month of May with the actual costs incurred, including in your answer relevant cost variances.

(b) Suggest possible causes for the variances you have calculated.

B15.3 [S]

Carrypack Ltd manufactures and sells plastic cases for portable computers. Production each month equals sales orders received.

The following monthly budget was prepared at the start of Year 6, to apply throughout the year:

	Units	£	£
Sales (@ £50 per unit):	12,000		600,000
Production:	12,000		
Production costs:			
Direct materials		132,000	
Direct labour		108,000	
Variable overheads		72,000	
Fixed overheads		48,000	
			360,000
Budgeted profit			240,000

Further information

(a) Budgeted direct materials used per month were set at 26,400 kg.

(b) Budgeted direct labour hours per month were set at 36,000 hours.

The following actual report was produced for the month of April Year 6:

	Units	£	£
Sales (@ £50 per unit):	12,300		615,000
Production:	12,300		
Production costs:			
Direct materials		136,220	
Direct labour		129,200	
Variable overheads		72,200	
Fixed overheads		49,400	
			387,020
Actual profit			227,980

Further information

(a) Actual direct materials used during April were 27,800 kg.

(b) Actual direct labour hours worked during April were 38,000 hours.

Required

(1) Prepare an explanation, using variances, of the difference between the budgeted profit and the actual profit for the month of April.

(2) Comment on possible causes for the variances you have calculated.

B15.4

DEF Products Ltd manufactures and assembles one type of furniture unit. The following information is available for the year ended 31 August Year 7.

The budgeted costs and the actual costs incurred during the year were as follows:

Cost	Budgeted production overhead cost £000s	Actual production overhead cost £000s	Nature of cost
Supervision	100	85	Fixed
Machine power	30	22	Varies with machine hours
Heat and light	30	27	Varies with direct labour hours
Rates and insurance	220	203	Fixed
Lubricants	60	45	Varies with machine hours
Indirect materials	50	38	Varies with units of output
Machine depreciation	180	180	Fixed
Maintenance and repairs	80	60	Varies with machine hours
	750	660	

The budgeted and actual activity for the year was as follows:

	Machine hours	Direct labour hours	Units of output
Budget	255,000	500,000	100,000
Actual	180,000	440,000	80,000

At the end of the year, the production director made the following report to his colleagues on the board of directors: 'We budgeted for £750,000 overhead cost based on 500,000 direct labour hours. We incurred £660,000 actual cost but only worked 440,000 hours. This appears to me to be a satisfactory proportionate reduction in costs and there are consequently no adverse variances from budget to be explained.'

The other directors felt this comment ignored the distinction between fixed overhead cost and variable overhead cost. They were also concerned that the production director referred only to the fall in direct labour hours worked, when it was known that some overheads depended on the number of machine hours worked. They asked for a more detailed analysis of the expected level of overhead costs in relation to the activity levels achieved.

Required

Prepare a memorandum to the production director:

(a) proposing, with reasons, a suitable method for calculating overhead cost rates;
(b) setting out a variance analysis which distinguishes fixed overheads from variable overheads.

C Problem solving and evaluation

C15.1 [S]

The following report has been prepared for the production department of Cabinets Ltd in respect of the month of May Year 4:

	Actual costs or quantities recorded	Variance £
Direct materials price	£2.80 per kg	2,240 favourable
Direct materials usage	11,200 kg	4,800 adverse
Direct labour rate	£9 per hour	5,600 adverse
Direct labour efficiency	3.5 hours per unit	6,400 adverse
Fixed overhead expenditure	£39,000	3,000 adverse

The department manufactures storage cabinets. When the budget was prepared, it was expected that 1,800 units would be produced in the month but, due to a machine breakdown, only 1,600 units were produced.

Required

(a) Reconstruct the original budget, giving as much information as may be derived from the data presented above.
(b) Provide an interpretation of the performance of the production department during the month of May Year 4.

C15.2 [S]

Fixit Ltd is a manufacturing company which produces a fixed budget for planning purposes. Set out below is the fixed monthly budget of production costs, together with the actual results observed for the month of July Year 7.

	Budget	Actual
Units produced	5,000	5,500
	£	£
Costs:		
Direct materials	20,000	22,764
Direct labour	60,000	75,900
Variable production overhead	14,000	14,950
Fixed production overhead	10,000	9,000
Depreciation	4,000	4,000

In preparing the fixed budget, the following standards were adopted:

Direct material	10 kg of materials per unit produced.
Direct labour	2 hours per unit produced.
Variable production overhead	A cost rate per direct labour hour was calculated.
Fixed production overhead	A cost rate per unit was calculated.
Depreciation	Straight-line method is used for all assets.

The following additional information is available concerning the actual output:

(a) the actual usage of materials in July was 54,200 kg; and
(b) the nationally agreed wage rate increased to £6.60 per hour at the start of July.

Required
(a) Prepare a flexible budget in respect of Fixit Ltd for the month of July Year 7.
(b) Analyse and comment on cost variances.

C15.3 [S]

Concrete Products Ltd manufactures heavy paving slabs for sale to local authorities and garden paving slabs for domestic use.

The board of directors meets early in each month to review the company's performance during the previous month. In advance of each meeting, the directors are presented with a computer print-out summarising the activity of the previous month. The computer print-out in respect of the month of December Year 8 is set out below:

	Heavy paving		Garden paving	
	Actual *tonnes*	*Budget* *tonnes*	*Actual* *tonnes*	*Budget* *tonnes*
Sales volume	29,000	27,500	10,500	8,500
Production volume	29,000	27,500	10,500	8,500
	£000s	*£000s*	*£000s*	*£000s*
Revenue	720	690	430	300
Variable cost of sales	280	270	170	127
Contribution	440	420	260	173

Further information
(a) The actual fixed costs incurred during the month equalled the budgeted fixed costs of £310,000.
(b) Stocks are valued at standard cost.

You have recently been appointed a director of Concrete Products Ltd. At an earlier meeting with the finance director you received an explanation of the basis for the company's monthly budget and you are satisfied that the budget has been prepared on a realistic basis.

Required
(1) Prepare, from the information contained in the computer print-out, your analysis and comments on the company's performance during the month of December Year 8, as background for the board meeting.
(2) List, with reasons, three questions you would ask at the meeting in order to give you a fuller understanding of the company's performance during the month.

C15.4

Nu-Line Ltd purchases manufactured machine tools for conversion to specialist use. The converted tools are sold to the textile industry. The following information relates to the month of July Year 3.

	Budget *(units)*	*Actual* *(units)*
Purchases of machine tools	180	180
Completed production	180	140
Sales	130	150
Stock of finished goods at 1 July Year 3	15	15
Stock of finished goods at 31 July Year 3	65	5

There was no stock of purchased machine tools or work-in-progress at either the start or the end of the month.

Finished goods are valued at full standard cost of production. The standard cost of one completed production unit is:

	£
Purchased machine tool	600
Direct labour	300
Fixed production overhead	200
Variable production overhead	100
	1,200

The fixed production overhead per unit was determined by reference to the budgeted volume of production per month.

A standard selling price of £2,000 per completed unit was specified in the budget and was achieved in practice.

Actual costs incurred during the month were as follows:

	£
Invoiced price of machine tools purchased	86,800
Direct wages paid	47,500
Fixed production overhead	35,000
Variable production overhead	13,000

Required

(1) Prepare a statement of the budgeted profit and the actual profit for the month of July.
(2) Using variances, reconcile the budgeted profit with the actual profit.

Case studies

Real world cases

Prepare short answers to Case studies 15.1, 15.2 and 15.3.

Case 15.4 (group case)

You are the Student Union management committee representative in charge of student transport affairs. Members have proposed that the Union should operate a campus bus service to operate between the campus and the nearby shopping precinct (five miles distant and 15 minutes by bus). Prepare a five-minute presentation to the rest of the management committee explaining how you would use standard costing to plan and control the activities of the proposed bus service.

Case 15.5 (group case)

You are the Student Union management committee representative in charge of academic affairs. Members have proposed that the Union should publish a study guide for sale to incoming students. It is expected that 2,000 new students will register at the start of the academic year. Prepare a five-minute presentation to the rest of the management committee explaining how you would use standard costing to plan and control the publication of the study guide.

Notes

1. CIMA (2000) *Management Accounting: Official Terminology*, CIMA Publishing.
2. *Ibid.*
3. *Ibid.*

Chapter 16

Performance evaluation and feedback reporting

Real world case 16.1

This case study shows a typical situation in which management accounting can be helpful. Read the case study now but only attempt the discussion points after you have finished studying the chapter.

As part of the annual Group business planning process, challenging financial, operational and sustainable development targets are set to form a Group Scorecard. Performance during the year is then measured against this Scorecard and annual bonus awards are made on this basis. The financial objectives relate to Total Shareholder Return (TSR)* relative to other major integrated oil companies (see the industry peer group table on page 115), and to Return on Average Capital Employed (ROACE). The operational objectives relate to portfolio value growth with key targets for each business. The sustainable development objectives focus on people, health, safety, environment and reputation. The 2003 Scorecard weightings are 60% for financial objectives, each factor equally weighted, 20% for operational objectives and 20% for sustainable development objectives. The same approach has been adopted for 2004.

*TSR is measured by the average weighted share price performance plus dividend of Royal Dutch and Shell Transport over the 10-day period at the beginning and end of the relevant financial year.

Source: Royal Dutch Petroleum, Annual Report, 2003, p. 113.

Discussion points

1 What is the mix of financial and non-financial performance measures mentioned in this extract?

2 How easy would it be to measure the performance of an individual against these targets?

Contents

Learning outcomes

After studying this chapter you should be able to:

- Distinguish feed forward control from feedback control.
- Explain the main features of performance reports.
- Explain how performance evaluation is carried out.
- Explain the use of benchmarking in performance evaluation.
- Explain and give examples of non-financial performance indicators.
- Explain the nature and use of the Balanced Scorecard.
- Understand how management may set standards of performance and reward achievement of standards.
- Describe and discuss examples of research into performance measurement.

16.1 Introduction

This management accounting text has been based throughout on the view that those who manage a business have a need and a desire to make informed judgements and decisions. In a continuing cycle of management action, there will be a judgement, from which a decision will be formed, followed by evaluation of that decision and a new judgement based on that evaluation. The stage at which the decision is evaluated requires management accounting to exercise its score-keeping function by devising quantitative measures of performance. It also calls on management accounting to direct attention to those areas most urgently requiring a judgement and a further decision. Management functions have been described in Chapter 1 in terms of planning, decision making and control.

Planning is sometimes referred to as **feed forward control**. This means making predictions of outputs expected at some future time and then quantifying those predictions, in management accounting terms. The budgetary process (Chapter 13) is an example of a management accounting approach which has a feed forward (or planning) aspect. Feed forward control systems are very effective, if carried out well, because they anticipate problems rather than wait for them to happen.

Chapter 14 explained budget variance analysis as a technique for control in comparing the actual outcome with the standard expected. This is sometimes referred to as **feedback control**. This is useful for looking back at what went wrong (or what went well) and for taking corrective action to ensure that a problem does not continue.

This chapter considers in more depth feedback control, which involves comparing outputs achieved against outputs desired and taking corrective action if necessary. To provide this type of control it is essential to identify the responsibility for the costs and for taking whatever action is required. The term **responsibility centre** is used to identify the unit to which a feedback report is to be made. A responsibility centre could be a cost centre where the individual manager has responsibility only for costs, a profit centre where the individual manager has responsibility for costs and revenues, or an investment centre where the individual manager has responsibility for costs, revenues and investment in assets.

Definitions

> **Feed forward control** means making predictions of outputs expected at some future time and then quantifying those predictions, in management accounting terms.
>
> **Feedback control** involves comparing outputs achieved against outputs desired and taking corrective action if necessary.
>
> A **responsibility centre** is an area of responsibility which is controlled by an individual. It might be a cost centre, a profit centre or an investment centre.

In any control process, whether feed forward or feedback, there are three essential elements:

1 There must be objectives which state the aim or purpose of the control.
2 There must be a model which can be used to predict an expected outcome.
3 There must be power to act in order to take corrective action.

In addition, for feedback control there must be the ability to measure the actual outcome on the same basis as the predicted outcome.

For a feedback control system to be effective, the following basic principles should be observed:

(a) the benefits from the system should exceed the costs of implementing it;
(b) the performance criteria being measured should be reported promptly so that rapid action may be taken;

(c) reports should be as simple as possible and readily understood;

(d) reports should highlight the significant factors requiring management attention;

(e) the reporting framework should be integrated with the organisational structure so that responsibility is identified correctly.

The operation of feedback control will be explored in this chapter in relation to short-term decision making. (Feedback on long-term decision making has been covered in Chapter 12 under the heading of 'Post-completion audit'.) First, in this chapter we discuss the nature of the report to be written for performance measurement purposes.

16.2 Preparing performance reports

There are three basic questions in relation to report preparation:

1 To whom should the report be addressed?

2 What should be reported?

3 How frequently should the report be presented?

16.2.1 To whom should the report be addressed?

In the context of the management of responsibility centres, the report should be addressed to the manager in charge of the responsibility centre. That could be a cost centre, a profit centre or an investment centre. If the report is to have meaning for the manager concerned, it must include only those costs which may be controlled by the manager of the responsibility centre.

The level of detail in the report will be influenced by the managerial position of the person to whom it is addressed. Reports to senior management will be condensed so that those managers can see the broader picture. They will of course also have access to the more detailed reports, should they so wish.

16.2.2 What should be reported?

The report should be designed to identify clearly those items that are controlled by the manager of the particular responsibility centre. If the responsibility centre controls the price and quantity of an item, then both should be reported and the combined effect quantified. If the responsibility centre controls quantity but not the price of an item, then the report should be designed to emphasise the quantity aspects of transactions in the reporting period.

It could be that, despite a lack of direct responsibility, it would be helpful for the manager of the responsibility centre to be aware of all the costs incurred as a result of the activity of the centre. If that information is felt to be useful, then it could be included in the report, but subheadings would be required to make clear the distinction between controllable and non-controllable costs.

The design of the report is extremely important because the manager of the cost centre, profit centre or investment centre will not use the report effectively if it does not provide useful information in a helpful manner. Managers should be consulted on design of reports, and there should be trial periods of experimentation with a new design of report before it comes into routine use. Graphs, bar charts and pie diagrams may be ways of communicating more effectively than through tables of figures alone.

16.2.3 How frequently should the report be presented?

The frequency of reporting should be related to management's information needs. There may be a need for information on a daily basis. Computers provide on-screen access to information so that the traditional concept of a reporting period, with a printed report at the end of each period, may no longer be appropriate in all circumstances. There is, however, a danger in reporting all items too frequently. Reports have to be read and acted upon, and reporting which occurs too frequently could result in too much time being spent on the review activities.

The question of frequency of reporting is perhaps best answered in terms of the frequency of the cycle of review and corrective action. If daily action is required in an operation, then daily provision of information about the activity will allow corrective action at the earliest possible opportunity. If a monthly review cycle is more appropriate, then the reporting system should be designed to provide monthly summaries. It is vitally important that, whatever the frequency chosen, the reports are produced in a timely manner.

If a computer is in use to record costs and quantities, then the program used should be such that the reports required are generated as part of the process so that there is no delay in transferring information for reporting purposes.

Activity 16.1

Look back to the variance report on Brackendale presented in Chapter 14. Comment on the good and weak points of that report, in the light of the first two sections of this chapter, and suggest ways in which the report could be improved.

16.3 Performance evaluation

Performance evaluation requires the management accountant to carry out the following process:

- Decide on what to measure.
- Plan how to report.
- Consider the behavioural aspects.

16.3.1 What to measure

In looking at what to measure, we will draw on the material of previous chapters, selecting aspects of management accounting which lead to a measure of performance. Because each management accounting technique serves a different purpose, the decision on what to measure will also depend on the intended purpose and will be discussed in the context of specific applications.

16.3.2 How to report

In planning how to report, the general principles applied will be those of responsibility and the separation of **controllable costs** and **non-controllable costs**. All costs are controllable at some level of management, but they may not be controllable at a lower level. Breaking down cost into the separate elements of quantity and price, the extent of control may vary for each element. There will be those in the organisation who have authority to acquire resources, thus controlling quantity and price. There will be others whose job it is to make use of the resources acquired, in which case they will control only the quantity element of cost. There will be others again whose job is to find the best price for resources. They will control only the price element of cost.

It is important to distinguish controllable from non-controllable costs when seeking to establish responsibility for costs. Frequently, the responsibility will be shared, and it is important that the sharing is correctly identified.

Definitions

> A **controllable cost** is a cost which is capable of being regulated by a manager within a defined boundary of responsibility.
>
> A **non-controllable cost** is one which is not capable of being regulated by a manager within a defined boundary of responsibility, although it may be a cost incurred so that the responsibility may be exercised.

Performance reporting is partly concerned with planning and control, so the idea of controllable and non-controllable costs is important. However, it is also applied in decision making, and further classifications into relevant/non-relevant and avoidable/unavoidable costs may therefore also be used within the same report.

When a decision is taken there is usually more than one option available. **Avoidable costs** are those costs that may be saved by not taking a particular option. **Unavoidable costs** will not be saved by such an action.

Definitions

> An **avoidable cost** is one which may be eliminated by not taking a particular option.
>
> An **unavoidable cost** will not be eliminated by taking a particular action.

16.3.3 Behavioural aspects

Performance evaluation has behavioural aspects because measurement of performance has a direct impact on the organisation's perceptions of how its staff are performing and on the individual staff member's perception of his or her relative performance. As a general guide, favourable reactions to performance reporting are likely to be maximised if staff are made aware in advance of how the performance measures will be calculated and how the responsibility for costs will be allocated. If the individual has control over quantities and prices, then that person should be regarded as having control over, and responsibility for, that item. If the individual has control over quantities but not prices, then it may be appropriate to report the cost to that individual but only regard responsibility as extending to the quantity aspects. If the individual has no control over quantity or price, then no responsibility for the cost of that item can be identified, although there may be a separate question of whether that item should be reported to the individual in order to heighten awareness of the impact of non-controllable costs.

Activity 16.2

> You are the team leader for a group of social workers who specialise in dealing with the needs of elderly persons in their homes. You have been told by your line manager that your team's budgeted spending limit will be exceeded by the end of the year if you continue with the present level of activity. The major items of cost are: team members' salaries, travel to clients' homes for visits and a charge from the local authority for the provision of office facilities. Salaries have increased because of a national pay award not allowed for in the budget. Travel costs have increased over budget because of fuel price increases. The local authority has kept the charge for office facilities within the budget. Your line manager has some discretion to make savings under one expense heading to match overspending under another. How will your team explain its performance in the end-of-year report?

Chapter 14 explained how budgets may be used for cost control by way of variance analysis. There also needs to be a concern with the human implications of variance analysis. It may be that the variance analysis approach is seen as a means of managerial review of subordinates, in which favourable variances receive praise and adverse variances are seen as a cause for corrective action to be taken. That approach may have undesirable consequences for a number of reasons:

1 Employees may reject standards because they were not adequately consulted in setting them.
2 Those under review may divert their efforts into minimising the adverse variances rather than making positive steps towards overall performance improvement.
3 Negative feedback may reduce motivation, leading to reduced effort and lower performance levels.

Those who are concerned at these negative aspects of variance analysis have suggested that there may be a need for accounting systems which are less evaluative in approach. The emphasis should perhaps move to learning and improvement rather than stressing personal responsibility, accountability and past achievement. Later in this chapter there are some ideas about performance measurement using non-financial measures which may be more relevant than financial measures at the individual manager level. First, however, a case study is used to illustrate the traditional variance analysis approach to performance evaluation and control.

Activity 16.3

You are the financial manager of a school where some teaching departments are spending more than their budget allowance on materials and others are being frugal and spending less. It is six months into the financial year and you would like to give a warning to the overspenders, but also find out why there are underspenders. Suggest two ways of dealing with this problem, of which one way would probably create friction between yourself and the teachers, while the other would encourage the teachers to work with you in controlling the overall budget for the school.

16.3.4 Case study: evaluating and reporting performance

Fiona McTaggart now explains a situation where she prepared performance reports using flexible budgets and also shows how the performance report appeared in each case.

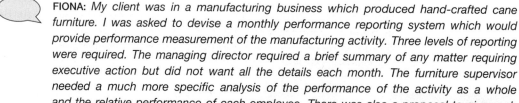

FIONA: *My client was in a manufacturing business which produced hand-crafted cane furniture. I was asked to devise a monthly performance reporting system which would provide performance measurement of the manufacturing activity. Three levels of reporting were required. The managing director required a brief summary of any matter requiring executive action but did not want all the details each month. The furniture supervisor needed a much more specific analysis of the performance of the activity as a whole and the relative performance of each employee. There was also a proposal to give each employee a personal performance statement that showed some indication of the average performance of the activity as a whole, without giving individuals access to information which was best kept personal to each employee.*

The budget was set at the start of the year based on average monthly output of 300 chairs and 80 tables. In practice the actual monthly output varied around this average. I recommended a three-column form of report which would show the original budget for one month's output, the flexible budget showing the costs expected for the actual level of output achieved and the actual costs incurred.

I made a list of all the costs incurred in making cane furniture. The main direct costs were materials and skilled labour. Although the employees were employed on full-time contracts, it was useful to identify separately the time they spent in productive activity making the furniture, which I classed as a direct cost, and the time they spent in non-productive activity, which I classed as an indirect cost.

I then listed all the indirect costs and subdivided them according to various levels of responsibility. Each employee was responsible for a portion of indirect materials used in fastening the cane together and was also responsible for a portion of equipment maintenance and depreciation. This indirect cost was allocated in proportion to the output produced. It might sound rather hard that the employee's responsibility for cost increased as the output increased, but it was decided in discussion that staff needed to be aware of the costs incurred when productive output takes place. Individual employees would not be regarded as being responsible for unproductive time unless they directly caused it as a result of their individual actions.

The furniture supervisor was responsible for control of the total costs allocated to the individual operative staff, plus the cost of non-productive time (to the extent that this was in the control of the supervisor), and the overhead costs of heating and lighting the workshop area.

The managing director had ultimate responsibility for all costs, including the cost of administration, providing adequate working conditions, the employer's share of employment costs and any non-productive work due to causes beyond the control of the furniture supervisor.

Exhibit 16.1 shows how the performance report was designed. There were three separate parts to the report. The first was for individual members of staff. The second was for the

Exhibit 16.1
Monthly performance report: (a) employee report; (b) supervisor's report; (c) managing director's report

Part A: Employee report	Name...............*Employee X*...............			
Date of statement	....			
	Budget	Flexible budget	Actual	Variance
Output: target/actual	100 chairs 20 tables	110 chairs 18 tables	110 chairs 18 tables	
Direct materials	...	...	...	...
Direct labour	...	...	...	...
Controllable indirect costs	...	...	...	...
Indirect materials	...	...	...	...
Total controllable costs for employee X	...	...	...	...
Cumulative controllable costs for year to date	...	...	...	...
Maintenance	...	...	...	...
Depreciation	...	...	...	...
Total for exployee X	...	...	...	...
Cumulative for year to date	...	...	...	...
Matters for attention				
Action planned				

Exhibit 16.1 **continued**

Part B: Supervisor's report	Name..			
Date of statement	....			
	Budget	Flexible budget	Actual	Variance
Output: target/actual	300 chairs 80 tables	320 chairs 76 tables	320 chairs 76 tables	
From Part A Controllable costs for each employee				
Costs of employee X	...	...	...	...
Costs of employee Y	...	...	...	...
Costs of employee Z	...	...	...	...
Total controllable costs				
Overheads				
Controllable indirect costs	...	...	...	...
Non-productive time	...	...	...	...
Heating & lighting	...	...	...	...
Matters for attention				
Action planned				
(In practice this report would also include cumulative totals for the year to date, as shown on Part A, but they are omitted here so that the main features are more readily seen.)				

furniture supervisor, who also had access to the individual staff reports, and the third was for the managing director, who had access to the more detailed reports if these were required.

Each report set out the variances from flexible budget for each element of cost. At the foot of the report was a section for highlighting matters for attention and a space below for the person receiving the report to write a comment. In the case of individual employees, a comment was expected on any action planned in response to matters noted. This action plan would be discussed and agreed with the supervisor. In the case of the report to the supervisor, the comment was expected to show the action planned for the production activity as a whole, or for individual employees where there was a particular problem. In the case of the report to the managing director, the comment was expected to confirm discussions with the supervisor but also to note any action on indirect costs regarded as the managing director's responsibility.

We had a trial run of this reporting format for three months, to iron out any wrinkles, and during that time there were some difficulties in getting the overhead responsibility allocation right. Everyone denies responsibility for indirect costs but, at the end of the day, they have to be incurred and are an unavoidable consequence of business activity. It was eventually agreed that the direct cost allocation would remain, but that, for employees

Exhibit 16.1 **continued**

Part C: Managing director's report	Subject: *Cane furniture production*			
Date of statement	....			
	Budget	Flexible budget	Actual	Variance
Output: target/actual	300 chairs 80 tables	320 chairs 76 tables	320 chairs 76 tables	
From Part B				
Total employee controllable costs	...	...	...	...
Total indirect costs for which supervisor is responsible	...	...	...	...
Other overheads				
Administration	...	...	...	...
Employment costs	...	...	...	...
Abnormal non-productive time	...	...	...	...
Total				
Matters for attention				
Action discussed with supervisor				
(In practice this report would also include cumulative totals for the year to date, as shown on Part A, but they are omitted here so that the main features are more readily seen.)				

and the supervisor, the emphasis would be on responsibility for the volume aspects of the allocation, with any external price increases being regarded as non-controllable or else a matter for discussion with the purchasing section.

Fiona's description has concentrated very much on the two questions of what to measure and how to report. Since she is describing the early stages of designing and implementing a new system, there is no information on the behavioural aspects of how the reporting system operated in practice. There is a description of the trial run and the extent to which the views of participants were taken into account in the design of the final report. The case study would need to be followed up after a period of, say, three months of operation, to find out how effectively the new system was achieving satisfactory control.

Activity 16.4

Read the case study again and identify the points at which Fiona McTaggart's actions match the principles of reporting set out in this chapter.

The bonuses for 2004 have been paid in the basis of the level of satisfaction of the performance targets. The table below shows the principal performance targets used for 2004.

Chief Executive Officer	Finance Director	Chief Operating Officer
EBITDA	EBITDA	EBITDA
Internal Financial Measures	Internal Financial Measures	Internal Financial Measures
Pubmaster Integration	Pubmaster Integration	Pubmaster Integration
EPS Growth	Debt Management	Operational Targets
Investor Relations	Investor Relations	Divisional Targets

(Note: EBITDA – Earnings Before deducting Interest, Taxation, Depreciation and Amortisation)

Source: Punch Taverns, Annual Report 2004, p. 30.

Discussion points

1 Why are there some targets that are similar and some that are different for each post-holder?

2 The detailed results of these ratios do not appear in the annual report. What are the possible reasons for confidentiality?

16.4 Benchmarking

Benchmarking is the name given to the process of measuring the organisation's operations, products and services against those of competitors recognised as market leaders, in order to establish targets which will provide a competitive advantage.

The stages of benchmarking are:

1 Decide what area of activity to benchmark (e.g. customer services, business processes in particular departments, quality of employees, standard of training).

2 Select a competitor who is reputedly the best in the area of activity to be benchmarked. Major companies in one country may target an international competitor rather than a domestic company. In some benchmarking situations the competitor may agree to an exchange of information because both parties believe they can benefit from the exchange.

3 Decide on the appropriate measurements to be used in defining performance levels.
4 Determine the competitor's strengths and compare these with the company's own record.
5 Use the information collected as the basis for an action plan. To be effective, this action plan must involve all grades of employee working in the area of activity.

The management accountant has a role throughout this process because the emphasis is on improving profit and measuring performance. The management accounting role starts with directing attention, by producing the performance measures and showing the relationship with profit improvement. It moves into problem solving as the information on comparative performance measures is collected and has to be transformed into an action plan for the organisation. It then takes on the scorekeeping aspect as the achievement of total quality is monitored.

16.5 Non-financial performance measures

Within an organisation, people are employed to carry out specific activities. The only aspect of their work over which they have direct control may well be the volume and the quality of tasks they undertake. Applying revenues and costs to these activities may be important for the organisation as a whole, but will have little meaning for the individual employee who does not sell the goods or services directly and does not purchase the input materials.

To ensure that the motivation of employees is consistent with the profit objectives of the organisation, it may be necessary to use **non-financial performance measures** to indicate what is required to achieve the overall financial targets. Using non-financial performance measures does not mean that the financial performance measures may be disregarded. They are ways of translating financial targets and measures into something that is more readily identifiable by a particular employee or group of employees.

The non-financial performance measures should cover both quantity and quality.

16.5.1 Quantity measures

It is necessary to convert the accounting numbers to some measure of quantity which relates more closely to individual members of an organisation. If the employees are involved in the entire productive process, then the financial target may be converted to units of product per period. That approach may be more difficult when a service activity is involved or a group of employees is involved in only part of a production process.

As an illustration of the problems of performance measurement in a service business, take an example of a school where activities are subdivided by subject area. The primary measure of activity will be the number of pupils taught, but the individual departments will have no control over that number. If teaching staff are appointed on permanent contracts, so that salary costs are largely fixed costs, then the cost per student will vary depending on the number of students taught in any period. A performance measure of cost per student may be attractive to the management accountant but will have little impact on the staff of the history department whose main aim is to ensure that their pupils achieve high grades in the end-of-year examinations. For them, examination success rates are the prime performance measure and they will be concerned to ensure that fluctuations in pupil numbers do not affect that success rate. A performance report on the history department would therefore emphasise first of all the non-financial performance, in terms of examination success, but would then additionally report the cost implications so that the consequences of achieving a high, or a low, success rate could be linked to the cost of that activity.

16.5.2 Quality measures

The ultimate measure of quality is customer satisfaction. Companies will invest time and effort in measuring customer satisfaction, perhaps by questionnaire survey or possibly by telephone interview. Indirect measures of customer satisfaction may be found in complaints records, frequency of repairs under warranty and level of goods being returned as unwanted.

Another important aspect of quality is the process undertaken by the organisation. This is so important that an external agency (often the auditors) may be employed to provide independent certification of the quality of the process and the controls within the process.

Finally, quality is measured also in terms of the inputs to the process, where inputs may be materials, labour and capital equipment. Quality of inputs may be controlled directly by imposing standards on suppliers, or may be monitored by reviewing the rate of return of unsatisfactory goods, the non-productive time incurred because of faulty equipment, or the reliability of delivery dates and quantities.

Some examples of non-financial performance measures are:

1 In respect of demand for products:
   (a) number of enquiries per advertisement placed; and
   (b) percentage of customers who remember the advertisement;
2 In respect of delivering the products:
   (a) error free deliveries as a percentage of total deliveries;
   (b) number of complaints as a percentage of units sold; and
   (c) time between receiving customer order and supplying the goods or service.

An electricity supply company provided the following information about non-financial performance over a one-year period:

Restore supply in 3 hours	Target	80%
	Performance	**83.8%**
Restore supply in 24 hours	Target	99%
	Performance	**99.9%**
Moving a meter inside 15 working days	Target	95%
	Performance	**96.7%**
Reply to telephone calls within 10 seconds	Target	90%
	Performance	**91.1%**

16.5.3 Key performance indicators

There has been increased interest from regulatory bodies in encouraging businesses to report externally the key performance indicators (KPIs) that are used internally. These are now found in some descriptions of reward schemes for directors and senior managers. The UK government planned for, but then rejected, compulsory reporting of KPIs. However, market pressure is likely to encourage companies to disclose more KPIs.

Activity 16.5

Write out five non-financial performance measures which could be reported by an organisation which delivers parcels to the general public and to businesses.

16.6 The Balanced Scorecard

Section 16.5 has illustrated some of the non-financial measures of performance that may be used alongside the financial measures. There is a danger of creating increasingly long lists of performance measures with no way of balancing the perspectives resulting from these different aspects of performance. Kaplan and Norton (1992) put forward an idea which they called the **Balanced Scorecard** as a way of linking performance measures. It focuses on the key goals of the organisation and the measurement of performance in achieving those goals.

They suggested that performance measurement can be viewed by asking four questions:

- How do our customers see us? (Customer perspective)
- How do our shareholders see us? (Financial perspective)
- How do we see ourselves? (Internal business perspective)
- Can we learn and grow to improve and create value? (Learning and growth perspective)

16.6.1 Presenting the scorecard

For each of these four questions the organisation should set major goals and define performance measures which demonstrate that the goals are being achieved. It might be reasonable to set three or four goals in each case. This would lead to a scorecard that would fit on a single sheet of paper. There is no specific form for the scorecard. Exhibit 16.2 shows an example. Here we see the management strategy

Exhibit 16.2
Creating a Balanced Scorecard

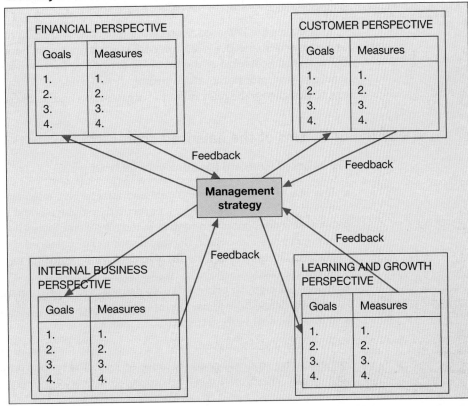

being applied to set the goals for each section of the scorecard, and the performance measures being used to give feedback to management on how well the goals have been achieved.

Fiona now gives an example of work she has carried out to create a balanced scorecard system in a service business.

FIONA: *I have recently worked on designing a Balanced Scorecard for a company which owns a chain of hotels in major towns and cities around the country and wanted to evaluate the relative performance of the separate hotels. The hotels are designed to a standard model of 'no-frills' value for money and comfort, with secure parking for cars. Customers are likely to stay for one or two nights, either as business customers looking for convenience and reasonable pricing, or as families and tourists on short-stay visits. As this was the first attempt at creating a scorecard we used only three goals for each aspect of the balanced scorecard. It was important to involve all staff in setting up the scorecard so we established focus groups in each city or town to give their input to the goals and measurements. Each focus groups included an operations manager, catering and cleaning staff and a regular customer. The result is set out in Exhibit 16.3.*

16.6.2 Scorecard in strategic management

Kaplan and Norton soon realised that the Balanced Scorecard was more than a performance report. It was a useful tool in the system of strategic management. They set out five principles for a strategy-focused organisation:

1 Translate the strategy into operational terms.
2 Align the organisation to the strategy.
3 Make strategy everyone's everyday job.
4 Make strategy a continual process.
5 Mobilise leadership for change.

This makes the Balanced Scorecard a tool of forward planning for change, as well as being a retrospective view of past performance. An important aspect of using the Balanced Scorecard is the involvement of employees in all stages of setting the scorecard and monitoring the outcome. It is flexible so that the Balanced Scorecard can be designed to be relevant to the organisation and its operations or procedures.

16.6.3 Criticisms of the balanced scorecard[1]

The balanced scorecard has attracted some criticisms.

- It is biased towards shareholders and fails to give adequate attention to the contribution of other stakeholders, particularly employees and suppliers.
- Because it does not give attention to the role of employees it fails to consider aspects of human relations within the organisation. The balanced scorecard cascades down the organisation with little involvement from senior managers. This may lead to employee dissatisfaction.
- It does not help the organisation to define specific performance measures and does not help define how to use performance targets.
- It does not deal with strategic uncertainties.

To avoid these problems it is suggested that the scorecard should be used for implementing strategic goals, because of its visibility, but only after the strategy is set in place. The project must be supported actively by senior management and the

Exhibit 16.3
Creating a Balanced Scorecard for a hotel chain

Financial perspective

Goal	Measure
1 To reduce unfilled room rate by 3% over the previous year, by offering discount for a third-day stay.	Marginal revenue from additional room occupancy, compared with marginal costs of creating that occupancy, with estimate of revenue lost on third-day discount.
2 To control fixed overhead costs within 3% overall increase on previous year.	Cost records – monthly update of fixed overhead actual cost against target.
3 To control variable costs per room per night at 50% of room charge.	Cost records – monthly report on variable room costs compared to room rents received.

Customer perspective

Goal	Measure
1 To increase market share by 5% over 12 months.	Market share surveys published in trade journals, plus reports commissioned from benchmarking organisations.
2 That 50% of customers return for a second visit.	Customer satisfaction questionnaire left in bedroom plus follow-up telephone enquiry.
3 That 90% of customers express general satisfaction with the service, especially cleanliness and staff courtesy.	Customer satisfaction questionnaire left in bedroom plus follow-up telephone enquiry.

Internal business perspective

Goal	Measure
1 To improve customer satisfaction by improving checkout times.	Number of checkouts completed between 7a.m. and 9a.m. each day.
2 To improve the cycle of laundry delivery and return from 4 days to 3 days, on average.	Records of laundry despatch and return.
3 To identify and implement one innovative practice.	Staff suggestion box – list of staff suggestions and note of actions taken to review and implement each.

Learning and growth perspective

Goal	Measure
1 To achieve 60% participation of relevant staff in a vocational training programme.	Staff records of attendance and achievement in vocational training programme.
2 To empower staff in setting personal goals that are consistent with organisational goals.	Record of annual appraisal reviews where appraising manager confirms that personal development plans are consistent with organisational goals.
3 To improve internal communication process by weekly bulletin to staff.	Record of bulletin issues and staff feedback on relevance and usefulness.

scorecard must be explained when it is introduced. It must be tailored to the needs of the organisation rather than using a more general package. It must not be over-complicated and there must be sufficient time and resources for communication and training.

Activity 16.6

Imagine that you are planning to start a business operating a taxi service. Write a Balanced Scorecard containing two goals and two measurements of achieving the goals for each of the four sections of the Balanced Scorecard (Customer perspective, Financial perspective, Internal business perspective and Learning and growth perspective).

16.7　Management use of performance measurement

This chapter has concentrated largely on how the management accountant may provide measures of performance. For such measures to have relevance in a managerial context, they should satisfy three criteria:

- There should be well-defined performance measures which represent a range of performance from bad to good.
- There should be defined standards of performance which indicate what is good and what is not good.
- There should be rewards attached to successful attainment of targets and penalties attached to non-attainment of targets.

Sections 16.7.1 to 16.7.3 present a case study bringing together the use of benchmarking and performance standards to achieve the objectives and strategy of the organisation. Section 16.7.4 explains a performance measurement method called 'Six Sigma' which is intended to improve results. Section 16.7.8 explains some of the particular features of performance measurement in public sector organisations.

16.7.1　Performance measures

Fiona McTaggart describes a recent experience in establishing performance measures through benchmarking:

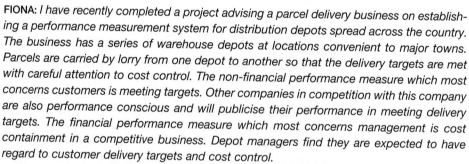

FIONA: *I have recently completed a project advising a parcel delivery business on establishing a performance measurement system for distribution depots spread across the country. The business has a series of warehouse depots at locations convenient to major towns. Parcels are carried by lorry from one depot to another so that the delivery targets are met with careful attention to cost control. The non-financial performance measure which most concerns customers is meeting targets. Other companies in competition with this company are also performance conscious and will publicise their performance in meeting delivery targets. The financial performance measure which most concerns management is cost containment in a competitive business. Depot managers find they are expected to have regard to customer delivery targets and cost control.*

My first task in advising the company was to contact a benchmarking expert in order to find out as much as possible about the competition. The expert had plenty of information on non-financial targets, including surveys undertaken by consumer organisations. The expert also had a broad outline of the cost structure of the leading operator in the field, which regards itself as a very well-controlled business.

Fiona emphasises here the importance of a **strategic management** approach, looking beyond the organisation, and of understanding the effective limits on targets where there is an established leader in the field. In the next section she explains how the targets were set at a level which would be acceptable to depot managers while meeting customers' expectations.

16.7.2   Standards of performance

Standards may be set by an inward-looking process which builds on the management perception of the performance required to achieve desired goals. Demonstrating that such targets are achievable may require reference to the performance of previous time periods and of similar units elsewhere in the organisation. The competitive position of the organisation requires that standards are set by reference to performance in other organisations. That may be relatively difficult or relatively easy to obtain, depending on the relative secrecy or openness of the sector.

Fiona McTaggart continues her description:

FIONA: *After collecting all the information available, senior management decided they wanted depot managers to concentrate on: (a) performance as a profit centre; (b) delivery targets; and (c) sales and customer care. The system is now in place.*

Performance as a profit centre requires targets for sales and costs. Each depot had initial targets set by reference to average performance over the past three years. The national reporting of target achievement is achieved by concentrating on percentages above and below target.

Delivery targets are reported according to the depot which last handled a parcel before it reached the customer. However, where a delivery target is not met, it is permissible for the depot manager to produce a summary of documentation showing where a previous depot in the chain caused a delay. These summaries are reviewed by head office and a supplementary report prepared showing bottleneck situations.

Customer care is monitored by customer feedback questionnaires. These are sent out by head office and collected there. The questions concentrate on delivery target time, condition of parcel, attitude of company personnel and perceived value for money. Depot summary reports are prepared.

Weekly reports are provided for depot managers which summarise the performance of the specific depot and show rankings against other depots. A narrative commentary by the managing director makes specific mention of the highest and lowest performers and explains how well the company is performing in relation to competitors.

Fiona has indicated that a mixture of financial and non-financial performance measures is used to create a part of the Balanced Scorecard. In the next section she comments on the rewards and penalties.

16.7.3   Rewards and penalties

If there are no rewards and no penalties it may be difficult to motivate employees in relation to performance targets. One view is that self-satisfaction in personal attainment is sufficient reward. Equally it could be argued that personal shame in not achieving a target would be sufficient penalty. However, more may be required.

Rewards and penalties are often difficult to administer because they involve human relations. The input of the individual must be seen in the context of the contribution of a team. Achieving a goal of the organisation may require team effort where it is difficult to identify the relative contributions of each member of the team. That may be overcome in relation to rewards by ensuring that no team member is deprived of a reward. Application of penalties, however, is more difficult because employment law generally seeks to protect employees against unjust treatment.

Rewards and penalties are linked to motivation. It has been suggested by experts in the theory of motivation that there are different needs at different levels of employment. Initially the employee is seeking the basic satisfaction of food and shelter which a paid job provides. A secure job provides safety in the longer term. Working in an organisation with clear goals provides the security of membership of a group.

Developing personal potential in meeting performance targets leads to rewards of respect and praise. Taking a lead in meeting the goals of the organisation is evidence of realising one's potential. Studies of motivation have at various times emphasised achievement, recognition, challenge and promotion as aspects of rewards which motivate. Fairness (equity) is also seen as important, as is meeting expectations.

Fiona McTaggart completes her description of performance measurement in a transport company:

FIONA: *As I have already mentioned, the managing director writes a weekly letter to all depot managers noting in particular the best and worst performers. That gives a sense of achievement to some managers and perhaps shames others into moving up from the bottom of the league tables. There is also a real reward of an all-expenses-paid weekend break holiday for the best-performing manager over the year. The difficulty with league-table-type performance is that someone necessarily has to be bottom of the league, so while this system is motivating in a competitive sense, it has some negative aspects in that the performance measures are relative to other depots rather than relative to achievable targets. I have pointed out to the managing director that there may be some demotivating aspects to this system, but he is very keen on competition and survival of the fittest.*

Fiona has indicated that using performance targets for motivation is not an easy matter and depends very much on the personalities involved.

16.7.4 Six Sigma

Six Sigma is an approach to performance measurement that was initially developed by Motorola but is now advertised more widely by consultants. In statistics the standard deviation from the mean of a normal distribution (the bell-shaped curve) is usually represented by the Greek letter sigma σ. We know that 99.9 per cent of the area under the bell-shaped curve lies within three standard deviations either side of the central mean value. So we can say with 99.9 per cent confidence that a value lies within a total of six standard deviations, or 'six sigma'. The easy way to summarise this is to say 'we want to get things right 99.9 per cent of the time'.

If managers want to improve a particular aspect of a business, they choose a goal, measure how well the business is achieving at present, and then define improvements that will achieve the Six Sigma standard. The aim is to eliminate waste without destroying value.

It could be thought that mysterious titles like 'Six Sigma' are a veneer over a very obvious way to make improvements, but it is felt to have value because it emphasises a basic idea of continuous improvement.

16.7.5 Performance management in the public sector

The public sector covers central government, local government and bodies funded from public funds, such as the National Health Service and the many Executive Agencies. In all cases there is keen attention paid to performance management.

A long-established approach to measuring value-for-money in the public sector is to examine economy, efficiency and effectiveness.

- An economy measure involves considering and controlling the costs of inputs.
- An efficiency measure relates the costs of inputs to the benefits of outputs.
- An effectiveness measure asks whether the outputs of a programme achieve the desired outcomes of a programme.

Many bodies providing a public service set and report their own performance measures. Examples are shown in Exhibit 16.4.

Real world case 16.3

The UK government provides some of its services through Executive Agencies which are managed like private businesses but have to meet targets set by the Secretary of State and Ministers of State. The Driving Standards Agency (DSA) is one of these agencies, responsible for setting and operating driving tests. The following information is extracted from the 2003–04 annual report and accounts.

DSA Key Ministerial Priorities 2003–04

Road safety
- Contribute to casualty reductions by delivering all tests fairly and consistently
- Deliver a national programme of Arrive Alive presentations for 16–19 year olds
- Active involvement in EU policy development
- Increase take up of Pass Plus Scheme
- Improve the quality of candidates by promoting a learning agenda
- Deliver improved theory and practical tests associated with the new European standards in 2003

Customer service
- Provide an internet booking service for practical tests
- Achieve 90% satisfaction with theory and practical test candidates
- Deliver an annual average practical car waiting time of 6 weeks
- Improve business customer satisfaction including ADIs above the baseline of 65%
- Increase the number of ADI check tests conducted from around 7,000 to 8,500

People
- Recruit and train adequate resources to ensure that customer service standards are delivered
- Progress towards achieving a fair reward for staff
- Continue a five year rolling programme of training and development for existing examiner and administrative staff

Business improvement
- Deliver value for money by keeping fee increases within the cumulative Retail Price Index target whilst improving customer service
- Prepare for contract renewal for IT and theory test services
- Reduce sick absence to below 2002–03 levels

The report provides quantified evidence of achievement of targets. Two targets not achieved in 2003/04 were:

	2001–02	2002–03	2003–04
National average practical car test waiting time	6.8 weeks	7.8 weeks	9.6 weeks
Business customer satisfaction	65%	64%	40%

The Finance section includes the following information:

Actual capital expenditure was £6.8 million compared with a plan of £11.7 million. The balance has been carried forward to 2004 and represents ADLI [Automatic Driving Licence Issue] project delays and certain test centre improvements.

The target return on capital employed was achieved with an outturn for 2003–04 of minus 2.6%, against a cumulative target of 6% annual return on capital employed over the period April 1997 to March 2007.

Source: Annual report and accounts 2003–04, DSA, pp. 5, 25, www.dsa.gov.uk.

Discussion points

1 What view might customers take of the achievements against the Ministerial targets?

2 What is the link between delay in capital projects and achieving a target return on capital employed?

Exhibit 16.4

Examples of performance measurement targets

An ambulance trust

During the year we were able to maintain response time performance above the national targets of reaching 75% of life threatening calls attended within eight minutes and 95% attended within 19 minutes. We also achieved financial balance. This is a great achievement and is entirely due to the professionalism and dedication of all our staff, and our community lay responders.

A service providing official documents in response to telephone and postal enquiries
- Answer 80% of our telephone calls in 10 seconds, 90% in 20 seconds and 95% in 30 seconds
- Achieve an abandon call rate of no more than 2% of call volumes answered
- Average time to answer of 6 seconds
- Process standard written post order requests within an average of 2 working days of receipt
- Deliver a service that achieves a benchmarked satisfaction score of 83.1%
- Achieve a fair outcome for customers when things go wrong and achieve less than 1% of complaints received against overall dispatches.

A train operating company

Punctuality: 90% of all trains Monday to Saturday in the published timetable to arrive within 10 minutes of their scheduled time at their final destination.

Reliability: 99% of all trains Monday to Saturday in the published timetable to run.

Activity 16.7

How useful are performance targets of the type set out in Exhibit 16.4? How easy or difficult would it be for the organisations involved to be selective in presenting actual results that fall within the target? Is the achievement of the performance target sufficient to ensure a good quality of customer service.

16.8 What the researchers have found

Section 16.8.1 reports investigation of the benefits of the Balanced Scorecard. Section 16.8.2 explains the French view that their *tableau de bord* pre-dates the US creation of the Balanced Scorecard. Section 16.8.3 indicates steps to be taken in developing measures of corporate performance. Section 16.8.4 notes criticisms of performance targets in the public service.

16.8.1 Benefits of the Balanced Scorecard

Davis and Albright (2004) investigated whether bank branches implementing the Balanced Scorecard outperformed branches in the same banking organisation. They found evidence of superior performance in branches operating the Balanced Scorecard. The bank researched was in the southeastern United States. The southern division contained seven branches. The president of the southern division of the branch decided to implement the balanced scorecard after learning about it in a graduate management course. The researchers selected four branches in the southern division and compared them with five branches in the northern division that had not implemented the balanced scorecard. Nine key financial measures identified by the group management as performance measures were used to make comparisons. The branches using the Balanced Scorecard outperformed the others. The researchers explained their reasons for believing that their findings could be attributed to the use of the Balanced Scorecard. However, it is possible that a division with a more enthusiastic managing director would achieve better results in any event. Perhaps the most persuasive evidence was the note that the managing director of the northern division later asked the managing director of the southern division to help set up a Balanced Scorecard.

16.8.2 American balanced scorecard vs French *tableau de bord*

Bourguignon *et al* (2004) explain that the Balanced Scorecard is received with less enthuasiasm in France than in some other countries, because French companies have used the *tableau de bord* for more than 50 years. The authors show that the main differences between the two systems may be explained by differences in ideology. The US approach is built on contracts where individuals choose to be committed and to have a general moral claim to fairness. US managers create hierarchies of management. In France social hierarchy, obedience, legitimacy and security are matters of education and honour, not of management devices. The *tableau de bord* is designed for each manager's view of strategy. It does not require the rigid classifications imposed by the US model. The French authors emphasise learning from the *tableau de bord*. The US system focuses on rewards from the balanced scorecard.

16.8.3 Trends in corporate performance management

A Technical Briefing published by CIMA (2002a) reviews a range of initiatives in performance measurement. It lists the factors required for a successful performance management system as:

- It must be integrated with the overall strategy of the business
- There must be a system of feedback and review
- The performance measurement system must be comprehensive
- The system must be owned and supported throughout the organisation
- Measures need to be fair and achievable
- The system needs to be simple, clear and understandable.

It also lists some common issues raised with performance measurement systems:

- Key drivers of success are not easily measured
- Behaviour is not in line with strategic objectives
- The system conflicts with the culture of the organisation
- The development process is too time-consuming or difficult

The Technical Briefing also summarises research into Value-based Management (as a broad-based heading which included Economic Value Added but also other methods of evaluating shareholder value); the Balanced Scorecard; Benchmarking; Strategic Enterprise Management and the Performance Prism (a three-dimensional view of performance devised at Cranfield School of Management, described on their website www.performanceprism.com).

16.8.4 Criticisms of performance targets in public service

Performance targets are now widely used in the public service arena as a means by which government relaxes direct control of an activity, but still retains indirect control. CIMA (2002b) Technical Briefing explains how the modernised government agenda has applied to the executive agencies. These are agencies that carry out government policy under delegated day-to-day management. Key themes in setting targets are economy, efficiency and effectiveness. However, the critics say that the targets create the kind of bureaucracy that the agencies were set up to eliminate. It is suggested that staff spend more time on meeting and recording targets than they spend on the main activity of the agency. Rigid measurement systems provide areas for inventiveness in meeting targets and also encourage neglect of areas that are not being measured. There is also a danger that the targets are short-term because they are set by politicians who have a short-term perspective.

16.9 Summary

Key themes in this chapter are:

- **Feed forward control** means making predictions of outputs expected at some future time and then quantifying those predictions, in management accounting terms.

- **Feedback control** involves comparing outputs achieved against outputs desired and taking corrective action if necessary.

- A **responsibility centre** is an area of responsibility which is controlled by an individual. It might be a cost centre, a profit centre or an investment centre.

- The key questions to ask in designing a performance report are:
  - To whom should the report be addressed?
  - What should be reported? and
  - How frequently should the report be presented?

- The key stages in performance evaluation are:
  - Decide on what to measure;
  - Plan how to report; and
  - Consider the behavioural aspects.

- It is important to distinguish **controllable costs** from **non-controllable costs** when seeking to establish responsibility for costs.

- **Benchmarking** is the name given to the process of measuring the organisation's operations, products and services against those of competitors recognised as market leaders, in order to establish targets which will provide a competitive advantage.

- A **Balanced Scorecard** has four perspectives: Customer perspective; Financial perspective; Internal business perspective; and Learning and growth perspective.

- **Non-financial performance measures** should cover both quantity and quality of performance. The measures should be related to the procedures under consideration. **Six Sigma** is explained as an example of a quantified performance target based on remaining within the 'tails' of the normal distribution. Performance management in the public sector focuses on economy, efficiency and effectiveness.

References and further reading

Bourguignon, A., Malleret, V. and Nørreklit, H. (2004) 'The American Balanced Scorecard versus the French Tableau de Bord: the ideological dimension', *Management Accounting Research*, 15: 107–34.

CIMA (2002a) *Latest Trends in Corporate Performance Measurement*, Technical Briefing, CIMA Publishing, download available on website www.cimaglobal.com

CIMA (2002b) *Performance Management in Executive Agencies*, Technical Briefing, CIMA Publishing, download available on website www.cimaglobal.com

Davis, S. and Albright, T. (2004) 'An investigation of the effect of Balanced Scorecard implementation on financial performance', *Management Accounting Research*, 15: 135–53.

Kaplan, R. S. and Norton, D. P. (1992) 'The Balanced Scorecard: measures that drive performance', *Harvard Business Review* (January–February): 71–9.

Kaplan, R. S. and Norton, D. P. (2001) 'Transforming the Balanced Scorecard from performance measurement to strategic management: part I', *Accounting Horizons*, 15(1): 87–104.

Kaplan, R. S. and Norton, D. P. (2001) 'Transforming the Balanced Scorecard from performance measurement to strategic management: part II', *Accounting Horizons*, 15(2): 147–60.

Merchant, K. and Van der Stede, W. (2003) *Management Control Systems: Performance Measurement, Evaluation and Incentives*, Pearson Education.

Simons, R. (1999) *Performance Measurement and Control Systems for Implementing Strategy: Text and Cases* (International edition), Prentice Hall.

Smith, M. 'The Balanced Scorecard', *Financial Management* (2005), Feb: 27–8.

QUESTIONS

The Questions section of each chapter has three types of question. 'Test your understanding' questions to help you review your reading are in the 'A' series of questions. You will find the answer to these by reading and thinking about the material in the text book. 'Application' questions to test your ability to apply technical skills are in the 'B' series of questions. Questions requiring you to show skills in problem solving and evaluation are in the 'C' series of questions. The symbol [S] indicates that a solution is available at the end of the book.

A Test your understanding

A16.1 Define 'feedback control' (section 16.1).

A16.2 Define 'feed forward control' (section 16.1).

A16.3 Define 'responsibility centre' (section 16.1).

A16.4 What are the three basic questions to be asked in relation to report preparation (section 16.2)?

A16.5 How does an organisation decide on the frequency of internal reporting (section 16.2.3)?

A16.6 What is required of the management accountant in carrying out performance evaluation (section 16.3)?

A16.7 Define a 'controllable cost' (section 16.3.2).

A16.8 Define a 'non-controllable cost' (section 16.3.2).

A16.9 Define an 'avoidable cost' (section 16.3.2).

A16.10 Define an 'unavoidable' cost (section 16.3.2).

A16.11 What are the behavioural aspects of performance evaluation (section 16.3.3)?

A16.12 Explain what is meant by 'benchmarking' (section 16.4).

A16.13 Explain the meaning of 'non-financial performance measures' (section 16.5).

A16.14 Give two examples of quantitative non-financial performance measures (section 16.5.1).

A16.15 Give two examples of qualitative non-financial performance measures (section 16.5.2).

A16.16 What are the four main aspects of a Balanced Scorecard (section 16.6)?

A16.17 Give one example of a goal and one example of a matching measurement for each of the four main aspects of a Balanced Scorecard (section 16.6).

A16.18 What are the benefits and problems of linking rewards and penalties to a performance measurement system in an organisation (section 16.7.3)?

A16.19 What is the 'six sigma' approach to performance measurement (section 16.7.4)?

A16.20 What have researchers found about the benefits of using a Balanced Scorecard (section 16.8.1)?

A16.21 What have researchers described as the factors required for a successful performance management system (section 16.8.2)?

B   Application

B16.1
Suggest six non-financial performance measures for a company which offers contract gardening services to companies which have landscaped sites surrounding their offices. Give reasons for your choice.

B16.2
Suggest three financial and three non-financial performance measures for a business which provides training in the workplace for updating wordprocessing and computing skills. Each training course lasts two weeks and there is a standard fee charged per trainee.

B16.3
Design a Balanced Scorecard for a restaurant business which owns three restaurants in the same town. Include three goals and three measurements of performance for each of the four aspects of the Balanced Scorecard, and write a short note justifying your choices.

C   Problem solving and evaluation

C16.1 [S]
Standard pine benches are assembled and packed in the bench assembly department of Furniture Manufacture Ltd. The department is treated as a cost centre. Control reports prepared every month consist of a statement comparing actual costs incurred in the department with the level of costs which was budgeted at the start of the month.

For the month of June Year 6 the following control report was produced, and received favourable comment from the directors of the company.

Bench Assembly Department Control Report for June Year 6

	Budgeted cost			Actual cost	Variance[1]	
	Fixed	Variable	Total			
	£	£	£	£	£	
Direct labour	–	36,000	36,000	30,000	6,000	(F)
Indirect labour	6,000	8,000	14,000	14,000	–	
Indirect materials	–	4,000	4,000	3,500	500	(F)
Power	3,000	12,000	15,000	9,000	6,000	(F)
Maintenance materials	–	5,000	5,000	3,000	2,000	(F)
Maintenance labour	5,000	4,000	9,000	15,000	6,000	(A)
Depreciation	85,000	–	85,000	75,000	10,000	(F)
Production overhead	–	20,000	20,000	15,000	5,000	(F)

Note: [1] (F) = favourable; (A) = adverse.

Due to a power failure, the level of production achieved was only 75% of that expected when the budget was prepared. No adjustment has been made to the original budget because the departmental manager claims that the power failure which caused the loss of production was beyond his control.

Required

Prepare a memorandum to the directors of the company:

(1) Explaining the weaknesses in the existing form of control report.
(2) Presenting the control report in such a way as to give a more meaningful analysis of the costs.
(3) Assessing the performance of the Bench Assembly Department during the month.

C16.2 [S]

Dairies Ltd operates a milk processing and delivery business. The retail distribution of milk is controlled by a regional head office which has overall responsibility for five geographical distribution areas. Each area is run by an area manager who has responsibility for ten depots. At each depot there is a depot manager in charge of 20 drivers and their milk floats. Milk is bottled at a central processing plant and sent to depots by lorry.

All information regarding the operation of each depot and each area office is sent to the divisional head office accounting department. This department produces weekly reports to be sent to each depot manager, each area manager and the manager of the distribution division.

A pyramidal system of reporting is in operation whereby each manager receives an appropriate weekly report containing the financial information on the operations for which he is responsible.

Required

(1) Explain what is meant by responsibility accounting.
(2) List, giving reasons, the information which should be contained in the weekly reports to each of the three levels of manager specified.

C16.3

You are the management accountant at the head office of a company which owns retail shoe shops throughout the country. The shops are grouped into areas, each having an area manager. Goods for sale are bought through a central purchasing scheme administered by head office. Shop managers have discretion to vary sales prices subject to the approval of the area manager. It is the responsibility of shop managers to record on a wastage sheet any shoes which are discarded because of damage in the shop. Shop managers have total control over the number of staff they employ and the mix of permanent and casual staff, subject to interview in the presence of the area manager. Shop managers also arrange for cleaning of the premises and are responsible for heat and light and other overhead costs.

The head office accounting system has produced the following information with regard to the Southern area:

	Shop A £	Shop B £	Shop C £	Area target %
Turnover	450,000	480,000	420,000	100
Costs:				
Cost of goods sold	355,000	356,000	278,000	69
Wastage	5,000	4,000	2,000	
	360,000	360,000	280,000	
Salaries and wages:				
Branch manager	15,000	16,000	16,000	
Bonus for manager	1,000	1,500	1,500	
Permanent assistants	9,000	7,000	7,000	
Bonus for assistants	450	480	420	
Casual workers	3,000	4,000	5,000	
	28,450	28,980	29,920	6
Heat, light, cleaning and other overheads	7,600	8,500	8,200	2
Operating profit before area office recharges	53,950	82,520	101,880	
Area office recharges	3,000	3,000	3,000	
	50,950	79,520	98,880	22

Further information

(a) The Southern area has an overall operating profit target of 20% of sales. The area office has a target allowance of 2% of sales to cover its expenses other than those recharged to shops.

(b) Details of area office expenses are:

	£
Area manager's salary	18,000
Area manager's bonus	3,000
Other office expenses	2,400
	23,400
Area office recharges	(9,000)
	14,400

(c) It is the policy of the company to disclose sufficient information to motivate and inform the appropriate level of management or staff, but to avoid reporting excessive detail, particularly where such detail would unnecessarily disclose information about wages or salaries of individual employees.

Required

Prepare three separate reports including comments on and interpretation of the quantitative performance data as follows:

(1) To the area manager on the overall performance of the area and the relative performance of each shop within the area.

(2) To the manager of shop A on the performance of that shop relative to the rest of the area and to the area target.

(3) To the employees of shop B showing them how their shop performed relative to the rest of the area.

Case studies

Real world cases

Prepare short answers to Case studies 16.1, 16.2 and 16.3.

Case 16.4

Lightwave Radio Ltd produces a range of products at its assembly plant. Due to recent rapid expansion the company's system of management control is now inadequate. The board has established a working party drawn from all disciplines of management to develop the structure for a new computer-based management control and reporting system.

As chief accountant, you represent the finance department on the working party and believe that the management reporting system should be based on the division of the production process into a series of cost centres.

Required

(a) Explain the essential features of a cost centre.
(b) Identify the main features you would expect to find in a cost control report prepared for use at individual cost centre level.
(c) List three objections or questions which you might anticipate receiving from other members of the working party, and explain how you would answer each.

Case 16.5

You are the managing director of Combine Ltd, a company engaged in the manufacture and sale of refrigerators and freezers. The board of directors has agreed to reorganise the company into two divisions – the domestic refrigerator division and the industrial freezer division. At the next board meeting the measures to be used to monitor management performance are to be discussed.

Prepare a five-minute presentation to your fellow directors which explains:

- the key factors to be considered in the design of financial performance measures for the divisional managers; and
- the use of non-accounting measures for appraising short-term divisional management performance.

Suggest three examples of non-accounting measures which could be used to monitor sales performance in the company.

Case 16.6

Obtain the annual report of a large listed company. Look throughout the report for mention of non-financial performance indicators. Having read the report, prepare a list of non-financial performance indicators which you think would be useful to readers in understanding more about the company. For each indicator suggested, you should give a reason. The aim should be to have a table of indicators covering no more than one side of A4 paper in printed form.

Note

1. Smith (2005).

Divisional performance

This case study shows a typical situation in which management accounting can be helpful. Read the case study now but only attempt the discussion points after you have finished studying the chapter.

This extract describes Kerry Foods, an Irish company producing a range of foodstuffs.

The best performance came from the food ingredients division, which made a profit of €257m, up 17.5%, with acquired businesses contributing €23m. The chilled convenience foods division raised profit 2% from €113.9m to €116m. However, the company, which for the first time disclosed operating margins for its divisions, said the consumer foods business, which includes the Wall's sausage brand and Cheestrings snacks, achieved margins of 7%, which it said would have been better but for adverse currency effects.

Source: *Financial Times*, 2 March 2005, p. 25, 'Kerry Foods hit by Quest charges'.

Discussion points

1 How does a company identify divisions for its business?

2 What are the measures used in the newspaper article to compare divisional performance?

Contents

Learning outcomes

After studying this chapter you should be able to:

- Explain what is meant by divisionalisation of a business.

- Define and explain return on investment as a measure of divisional performance.

- Define and explain residual income as a measure of divisional performance.

- Evaluate the relative merits of return on investment and residual income.

- Explain how transfer pricing between divisions can affect performance evaluation

- Explain the meaning and application of 'economic value added'.

- Describe and discuss examples of research into divisional performance and transfer pricing.

17.1 Introduction

Large organisations have a variety of activities which they carry out in different locations. In order to manage it effectively, such an organisation may be subdivided into separate units, each of which is responsible for planning and control of its own activities and for some aspects of decision-making. Each of the separate units is called a **division** of the company. This chapter explains ways in which divisional performance can be measured and compared.

17.2 Divisionalised companies

The benefit of creating a divisional structure is that those managing and working in each division have a sense of responsibility for their own area of operations, but the risk lies in the divisional management taking actions which may appear to be beneficial to the division but which are not good for the organisation as a whole.

Definition

> A **division** is a part of the organisation where the manager has responsibility for generating revenues, controlling costs and producing a satisfactory return on capital invested in the division.

It was explained in Chapter 1 that the management accounting approach to any situation will depend on the nature of the organisation. The size of a department may vary from one organisation to the next and the nature of a department will merge with that of a division as the department becomes larger. In some cases the words may be used interchangeably. For the purposes of this text, a division will have responsibility for its costs, profits and return on investment in assets, whereas a department would be responsible only for its costs, or possibly for costs and profits.

17.2.1 Advantages of divisionalisation

Where divisions exist and managers have decision-making power, their decisions about the business may be made more readily and with greater regard for the nature of the division. If all decisions are taken at a remote head office, the process may be delayed and may not have sufficient regard for any special circumstances of the division.

The freedom to make decisions also creates a challenge for those who manage the division and may make them feel more highly motivated towards achieving success for it. They will have responsibility for investment in assets and investment in employees, which gives a sense of controlling an entire business operation rather than being sandwiched between those who make the decisions and those who are required to implement them.

The existence of the division may also give employees a greater sense of identity with the operation of the division, particularly if it is in a separate geographical area or carries out a different operation from the rest of the organisation.

17.2.2 Disadvantages of divisionalisation

Managers of divisions may forget that they also have a responsibility towards the organisation as a whole and may make decisions which have adverse consequences elsewhere in the organisation. Take the case of a company where one division was producing flour in a flour mill and selling it to another division which was a bakery. The manager of the flour mill decided to attempt to increase profit by increasing the price charged for the flour, whereupon the manager of the bakery decided it was cheaper to buy flour from a rival organisation and did so. The result was that, although the bakery kept its costs under control, the flour mill went out of business and there was a substantial loss to the organisation as a whole. That loss could have been avoided if there had been a mechanism within the organisation to reconcile the separate objectives of the managers of the flour mill and the bakery.

Divisional organisation may also mean that some of the economies of central organisation are lost. Purchasing goods for all divisions from a central location may allow quantity discounts to be negotiated which would not be available to the separate divisions.

Placing too much emphasis on the divisional structure may cause those in each division to fail to identify with the organisation as a whole and may cause the senior management of the organisation as a whole to be remote from the day-to-day activities of the separate parts of the overall business. Communication and motivation may become more significant in achieving effective management in such circumstances.

Activity 17.1 *A road repair company has set up two divisions: one is motorway repairs and the other is town street repairs. Write down the advantages and disadvantages of establishing these divisions.*

17.2.3 Management accounting approach

Management accounting techniques required in dealing with a division need to cover the entire range of directing attention, keeping the score and solving problems. In relation to the classification of costs, the division may be regarded as an investment centre. In Chapter 2, an investment centre was defined as a unit of the organisation in respect of which a manager is responsible for capital investment decisions as well as revenue and costs. One very important aspect of management accounting is to measure the performance of the divisional manager in relation to capital investment, revenue and costs.

The statement of profit for a division will contain many of the management accounting features explained in earlier chapters. Exhibit 17.1 shows the main components of divisional profit and uses italics to highlight three possible measures of profit performance.

Exhibit 17.1
Statement of divisional profit

	£
Sales to external customers	xx
Transfers to other divisions	xx
Total revenue	xx
Variable costs of operations	xx
Contribution	xx
Fixed costs controllable by the division	xx
Profit controllable by the division	xx
Fixed costs not controllable by the division	xx
Total divisional profit	xx

Of the three profit measures highlighted, contribution may be useful to the management of the division in taking short-term decisions on production and pricing but is inappropriate as a measure of performance because it does not take into account the fixed costs which are controllable by the division. The management of the division may accept that performance is best measured by profit controllable by the division but the management of the organisation as a whole may be reluctant to accept this figure on the grounds that, at the end of the day all costs must be covered including the fixed costs incurred centrally which are beyond divisional control. (The term contribution is applied to the difference between revenue and variable cost of sales. It is a term which is dealt with in greater detail in Chapter 13.)

There may be some energetic debate as to which are controllable and which are non-controllable fixed costs so far as the division is concerned. Depreciation of fixed assets is a controllable cost for the division because the division has control of the investment in fixed assets. The division will take a share of head office service costs, such as personnel, accounting and legal services. To the extent that the divisional manager has a choice as to the extent to which such service costs are taken on, there should be a controllable fixed cost in respect of these items.

Because of the various conflicts that may arise in deciding on the best profit measure to use in performance measurement, the view is taken that divisional profit is not a satisfactory means of measuring the performance of management. It is also regarded as unsatisfactory because profit is an absolute measure and if managers think they are successful in making higher and higher profits, they may have no regard for the investment in fixed assets used in earning those profits. In a situation where it was discovered that stolen money had been used to finance the purchase and refurbishment of a hotel, the disgruntled manager of a rival hotel commented: *'It's not surprising that they could undercut our prices and take all our customers – they never had to worry about earning a return on their investment.'*

17.3 Return on investment

17.3.1 Method of calculation

A better measure of divisional performance is to relate the profit earned by a division to the investment in assets which produced that profit. This is referred to as the *profitability* of the division (where 'profitability' means the rate of profit per unit of investment).

Definition

> **Return on investment (ROI)** is calculated by taking profit controllable by the division as a percentage of the investment in assets which produces that profit.

Exhibit 17.2 compares the ROI for new projects with the existing ROI for each division.

Exhibit 17.2
Return on investment for each division

	Division A	Division B
Investment funding available for each project	£2m	£2m
Profit controllable by the division, to be generated by each project	£400,000	£260,000
ROI of each project	20%	13%
ROI of division at present	22%	12%

The calculation in Exhibit 17.2 shows that the **return on investment** is higher for division A. However, it is possible that the manager of division A will decide not to take up the new project because it has a lower ROI than the division's existing performance. The manager of division B will be pleased that the new project has a higher ROI than the existing average.

There may be technical problems in deciding on the division's investment in assets because the assets are owned by the organisation as a whole, rather than the division. It will usually require assets to be traced to a division, either on the basis that they are physically located there or on the basis that they are used by the division. It may be that use of assets is shared by more than one division, so that a portion of asset value is assigned to each division. The investment in assets may include an element of investment in working capital.

There may also be problems in deciding how to value the assets. Historical cost could be used, taking the net book value as applied for financial accounting purposes, but in times of rising prices that could allow the highest return on capital employed to arise in the division having the oldest assets, because these would have a low value. It could discourage a division from investing in new assets. If all divisions have to use the current value of the assets used, then the valuation base is comparable across all divisions.

There could be more than one view of which measure of profit to apply. There are no specific rules as to the choice to be made but there should be regard for the general principle that performance measurement should take account of relevant costs. If the focus of the ROI calculation is the motivation of divisional managers then allocation of non-controllable costs may have a negative effect. If the focus is economic performance of divisions within the organisation as a whole, then it may be important to include the impact of apportioned costs.

17.3.2 Advantages of ROI

ROI is the most widely used measure of divisional performance. Its first advantage, therefore, is its general acceptance. It is widely understood and it encourages managers to concentrate on projects which make best use of resources.

17.3.3 Disadvantages of ROI

There are practical difficulties in deciding on the data to be used in the formula. Both the numerator and denominator have more than one possible source. It could distort performance where a manager of one division avoids a project which lowers the average ROI for that division but would nevertheless be of benefit to the organisation as a whole. It is undesirable to have the entire performance of a division taken down to a single measure. It is always valuable to look at a situation from more than one angle.

17.4 Residual income

17.4.1 Method of calculation

Residual income is another method of measuring divisional performance. It is calculated by deducting from the operating profit an interest charge based on the assets used and controlled by the division. The view taken is that the assets are owned by the company and therefore are financed from the company's resources. If the division were an independent entity it would have to borrow money to acquire equivalent assets, so it is reasonable to charge the division with an amount representing interest on borrowed funds. There is no actual interest payment within the company, so the figure has to be created using interest rates which might apply to borrowed funds. This created figure is called *imputed* interest. ('Imputed' used in this sense means 'thought to belong to'.)

Definition	**Residual income (RI)** is defined as operating profit less an interest charge based on the assets used and controlled by the division.

Exhibit 17.3 continues with the new project proposed in Exhibit 17.2.

Exhibit 17.3
Residual income for each division

	Division A	Division B
Investment funding available for each project	£2m	£2m
Profit controllable by the division, to be generated by each project	£400,000	£260,000
Interest charge applied to projects:		
9% of investment	£180,000	£180,000
Residual income	£220,000	£80,000

The calculation in Exhibit 17.3 shows that the residual income of both divisions would increase if the investment of £2m was made. Division A has the higher residual income and might therefore be preferred if there were a limited amount of funding so that only one division could receive investment funding.

17.4.2 Advantages of residual income

The main advantage of using residual income is that managers will be more readily encouraged to act in the best interests of the organisation because this will match their own best interests in terms of performance measurement. If a new project is undertaken the residual income is affected only by the additional profit as compared with interest on the additional investment. It does not average out the new project with the existing projects as happens with the return on investment calculation.

A second advantage is that the interest charge may be varied according to the risk of the investment project. The return on investment calculation allows only one overall percentage to be calculated.

17.4.3 Disadvantage of residual income

A disadvantage of residual income is that it provides an absolute measure rather than a relative measure. A large division produces more residual income in total than does a small division. To avoid any problems of relative size, the target residual income for a division needs to match, in order of magnitude, the investment in assets.

Activity 17.2	*Look back at the calculations of ROI and RI and make sure that you understand and can explain each of them.*

Real world case 17.2

This extract describes changes in the UK company Bunzl, which announced at the start of 2005 that it would sell Filtrona, a business making cigarette filters, and concentrate on its outsourcing business.

The group generated almost £3bn in sales and £200m in pre-tax profits in 2004. Earnings per share increase year on year and its shares have risen three fold in the past 10 years. But getting there involved flexing some muscle and when he took up the reins Mr Habgood had to separate the wheat from the chaff. The only two businesses consistently growing were Filtrona and outsourcing. He set about simplifying the group's structure by selling the businesses with weaker returns and poor positions. The companies earmarked for disposal represented more than half of group sales and the proceeds were reinvested in the superior businesses . . . Mr Habgood said 'We have sold 60% of the businesses and more than quintupled the size of the remaining group.' Konrad Zomer, analyst at Chevreux, said 'Habgood has done a great job in moving away from capital intensive areas. The sale of the plastics business marked an important step in that respect.' The outsourcing business is now purely value-added – finished goods are bought from suppliers and sold on to customers. For example, Bunzl supplies supermarkets and caterers with disposable goods. This process does not require much capital.

Source: *Financial Times*, 1 March 2005, p. 24, 'Chief who turned a ragbag into a silk purse'.

Discussion points

1 What strategy was used by Mr Habgood in selecting divisions for development?

2 Compare the relative merits of Return on Investment and Residual Income as suitable measures of performance for deciding on which divisions to develop in this case.

17.5 Which to use – ROI or RI?

Both return on investment and residual income could be criticised as placing too much emphasis on the short term. They both emphasise profit when it may be that other factors of a more qualitative nature are important. They both have the problem of identifying the asset base used and controlled by the division. As a result, either of them could lead to inappropriate comparisons across divisions.

It has been suggested that residual income is more appropriate where the divisional manager has considerable freedom to determine the investment in assets. The return on investment may be more appropriate where the divisional manager has little or no control over the level of investment in the division. If return on investment is calculated, it is important that an imputed interest charge is *not* deducted from the operating profit, since to do so would involve double-counting. Between these two extremes it may be appropriate to use both techniques and compare the outcome.

Evidence from research shows that the dominant measure used in practice is return on investment, but it is also common to find return on investment and residual income used together. Residual income is rarely used alone, but this may be a reflection of the dominance of central control, rather than divisional control, of asset investment.

17.5.1 Case study: ROI and Residual income

Here is Fiona McTaggart to explain a situation where she compared the impact of return on investment with that of residual income as a measure of performance.

FIONA: *I was called in to discuss performance measurement with the washing powder division and the toothpaste division of a large chemical company. They provided the following data:*

	Washing powder £	Toothpaste £
Investment in assets	5,000,000	15,000,000
Profit controllable by the division	1,000,000	5,000,000
Return on investment	20%	33.3%

Their problem was that they had done what the text books recommend in calculating the return on investment but the management team in the washing powder division was now feeling aggrieved about being shown as underperforming in comparison with the toothpaste division. To improve the return on capital employed, the washing powder division proposed closing down an operation at a remote branch where there was an investment of £500,000 in assets, earning a return of 15% to yield a profit of £75,000. If that disappeared then they would have a divisional profit of £925,000 on assets of £4,500,000, improving the ROI to 23.1%. Although they could see the potential for improving ROI, they were of the view that closing down did not seem logical or sensible.

My reply was that of course it was not a logical action. The branch operation was yielding 15% at a time when the company's cost of capital was 13%. If the company pulled out of that area, a competitor would jump in with a replacement. Where the divisional managers have discretion over levels of investment, then residual income may be preferred as giving a relative measure of performance which will not lead to actions against the company's interest. I recalculated the performance measures using residual income as follows:

	Washing powder £	Toothpaste £
Investment in assets	5,000,000	15,000,000
Profit controllable by the division	1,000,000	5,000,000
Charge for cost of capital at 13%	650,000	1,950,000
Residual income	350,000	3,050,000

If the washing powder division were to dispose of its branch as tentatively suggested, then the residual income would fall:

Washing powder division	Before disposal £	After disposal £
Investment in assets	5,000,000	4,500,000
Profit controllable by the division	1,000,000	925,000
Charge for cost of capital at 13%	650,000	585,000
Residual income	350,000	340,000

On this comparison the performance measure would worsen because the division's total residual income would fall and it would be seen to be contributing less to the overall well-being of the company.

I explained that where the managers of a profit centre have discretion to acquire and dispose of substantial amounts of assets, the residual income is a preferable method of performance measurement. It is an absolute measure and leads to the conclusion that the higher the residual income, the better for the organisation as a whole. The only condition on expanding into new assets or retaining existing ones is that these should earn a profit which exceeds the cost of capital. If the profit earned is less than the cost of capital then the activity should cease.

I also pointed out the dangers of relying on one performance measure only. I recommended that in future the divisional performance should be assessed by reference to all the following criteria, as a starting point:

- Is the target cash flow being achieved?
- Is the target ROI being met?
- Is the actual profit within the budget?
- Is the residual income maximised, subject to any organisational constraints?

I explained that I was emphasising meeting targets rather than making comparisons between divisions. There could be good reasons for the different ROI in the two divisions, the most likely of which is relative competition in the industry. Targets should be set in advance having regard to the economic conditions so that the division is measured against its own statement of achievable performance rather than against a comparison which may not be valid.

Real world case 17.3

The following information is extracted from the annual report of Wolseley plc.

Finance objectives (extract)
To deliver an incremental return on gross capital employed at least 4% in excess of the pre-tax weighted average cost of capital. In 2005 the Group's return on capital was 19.1%, 7.2% ahead of our estimated pre-tax weighted average cost of capital of 11.9%.

Segmental analysis (extract)

By class of business	Turnover		Operating profit		Net assets	
	2005 **£m**	2004 £m	**2005** **£m**	2004 £m	**2005** **£m**	2004 £m
European Distribution	**4,638.4**	4,248.0	**270.4**	242.9	**1,429.9**	1,190.2
North American Plumbing and Heating Distribution	**4,370.4**	3,836.4	**283.9**	240.1	**1,419.0**	1,147.0
US Building Materials Distribution	**2,248.9**	2,043.7	**123.1**	97.2	**754.4**	591.3
Parent and others	**–**	–			**(52.5)**	6.3
	11,257.7	10,128.1	**677.4**	580.2	**3,550.8**	2,934.8

Source: Wolseley plc, Annual report and Accounts 2005, pages 27 and 67. www.wolseley.com

Discussion points

1 What is the relative performance of the three divisions, in profitability and return on capital employed?

2 Using the company's stated cost of capital, what is the relative performance based on residual income?

17.5.2 Comment

Return on investment and residual income are competing as alternative methods of performance evaluation for divisions of a business but the usefulness of each should be considered in the light of all the circumstances. It is more important to think carefully about the interpretation of results from calculations and to cross-check by more than one evaluation, as Fiona did for the washing powder division.

17.6 Transfer pricing between divisions

When goods and services are transferred between divisions of an organisation, a price is needed to reflect the value transferred. The price is called the **transfer price** and it is used to record a sale for one division and a cost for the other division. The transfer price affects the profit of each division but has no effect on the profit of the organisation as a whole because the internal sale and purchase have no effect on the total result.

The transfer price is important to each division because their profit is used to measure performance, as explained in section 17.5. If the price charged is too high, the buying department will reject the transaction and will want to look outside for a cheaper supplier. If the price charged is too low, the supplying department will reject the transaction and will look outside for a customer who will pay a better price.

The managers of the organisation as a whole need to find a transfer pricing system that will encourage divisions to trade with each other willingly. The important aim is to maximise the profit of the organisation as a whole. This is most likely to be achieved if divisions perceive a fair division of the total profit and a fair evaluation of divisional performance.

Transfer pricing becomes particularly problematic when the divisions are located in different countries. The transfer price will affect the taxable profit of each division. Governments are aware of ways in which a multinational company might try to use transfer prices to create profits in low-tax regimes and losses in high-tax regimes. Some countries (called 'tax havens') want to attract economic activity and so provide generous tax treatments. Other countries resent losing potential tax and impose rules to cancel out any attempt to reduce profits by a transfer pricing scheme.

There are three possible methods for setting transfer prices:

- Cost-based transfer price.
- Market-based transfer price.
- Negotiated transfer price.

Activity 17.3

Think again about the road repair company described in Activity 17.1 It has set up two divisions: one being motorway repairs and the other being town street repairs. The division carrying out town street repairs has started processing its own asphalt surfacing using specialist equipment. From time to time the motorway division buys asphalt surfacing from the town repairs division. Explain the potential problems faced in deciding on a transfer price for this service.

17.6.1 Cost-based transfer price

If cost is the basis of transfer pricing then the selling department will earn no profit and the buying department will have a cost that is lower than it would pay in an external market. In general a cost-based transfer price will not be effective because it will not give a fair evaluation of the performance of each division.

If, however, the selling department has spare capacity and cannot sell any more output externally then a cost-based transfer price would be justified. The internal

demand is keeping the division operating and there will eventually be a benefit to the
organisation when the finished output is sold.

17.6.2 Market-based transfer price

Ideally the market price of goods or services will make both the selling division and
the buying division indifferent between an internal transfer and external transactions.
However, in many cases there will not be a precisely comparable market price available. Perhaps the goods or services are only partly completed. In that case the external
market price of the finished product or service will have to be adjusted to calculate an
equivalent market price at the point of transfer.

17.6.3 Negotiated transfer price

A negotiation between managers could be based on the economic model where the
price is the point on the demand and supply curves where the marginal cost equals
the marginal benefit. If the managers involved cannot agree, then head office may
have to direct the negotiations or impose a solution. There is also danger that giving
managers the discretion to negotiate may take up too much of their time and also
cause problems in a power struggle between them.

17.6.4 Resolving differences

If there is an external market for the goods or services being transferred then it may be
relatively straightforward to persuade the buying and the selling division to accept a
market-based transfer price. If there is no internal market and negotiations between
the divisions fail then senior managers in the organisation may have to impose a
price that reflects cost but also provides an incentive to trade internally. If the selling
division is required to charge marginal cost only, there will be no internal profit and
no incentive. If the buying department is required to pay a price that covers marginal
cost and a profit there may be reluctance to pay the profit element. So the imposed
solution may be based on marginal cost with a fee added that provides some reward
to the selling division without discouraging the buying division. What matters is that
both divisions take decisions that are in the best interests of the organisation overall.

17.6.5 Case study

The IT Training Company provides training support to business for secretarial employees.
The publishing division of the IT Training Company supplies manuals to the training
division. The training division sells a support package which is based on the manual
plus internet communication. Exhibit 17.4 sets out an the estimate of how many
support packages could be sold each year at various levels of demand.

Exhibit 17.4
Estimates of selling prices for different levels of demand

Selling price per support package	Number of support packages sold per month
£	
12	150
11	300
10	450
9	600
8	750
7	900

The variable costs and fixed costs of each division are shown in Exhibit 17.5.

Exhibit 17.5
Variable costs and fixed costs of divisions

Variable cost
Publishing division: £3 per manual
Training division: Variable cost of internet communication is £2 per support package

Fixed cost
Fixed cost per month for publishing division is £600
Fixed cost per month for training division is £500

The manager of the publishing division has offered the training division a transfer price of £5 per manual to cover variable cost of £3 plus £2 for profit.

Profit calculations

The manager of the publishing division calculates profit or loss for each level of demand (Exhibit 17.6).

Exhibit 17.6
Estimate of profit for publishing division

Number of manuals	Revenue from transfer @ £5	Variable cost @ £3	Fixed cost	Profit/loss
	£	£	£	£
150	750	450	600	(300)
300	1500	900	600	0
450	2250	1350	600	300
600	3000	1800	600	600
750	3750	2250	600	900
900	**4500**	**2700**	**600**	**1200**

Based on Exhibit 17.6 the manager of the publishing division says 'I don't mind how many manuals I transfer to the training division. The more I transfer the better my divisional performance.'

The manager of the training division calculates profit using the transfer price offered by the manager of the publishing division (Exhibit 17.7).

Exhibit 17.7
Estimate of profit for training division

Number of support packages	Revenue from sale (Exhibit 17.4)	Variable cost @ £2	Transfer price of manuals @ £5	Fixed cost	Profit/loss
	£	£	£	£	£
150	1800	300	750	500	250
300	3300	600	1500	500	700
450	**4500**	**900**	**2250**	**500**	**850**
600	5400	1200	3000	500	700
750	6000	1500	3750	500	250
900	6300	1800	4500	500	(500)

Based on Exhibit 17.7 the manager of the training division says 'I will buy 450 manuals per month from publishing. If I take more or less than 450 my divisional performance will be worse.'

The finance director calculates the profit for the business as a whole (Exhibit 17.8).

Exhibit 17.8
Estimate of profit for training division

Number of support packages	Revenue from sale £	Variable cost @ £5 £	Fixed cost £	Profit/loss £
150	1800	750	1100	(50)
300	3300	1500	1100	700
450	4500	2250	1100	1150
600	**5400**	**3000**	**1100**	**1300**
750	6000	3750	1100	1150
900	6300	4500	1100	700

Based on Exhibit 17.8 the finance director says 'The best results for the business will be obtained by selling 600 support packages per month'.

At this stage there is no agreement on the level of output that pleases all parties. The manager of the training division is looking to make a decision that is not in the best interests of the company as a whole. The next section shows how the manager of the training division can be persuaded to make a decision that is in the best interests of the company as a whole.

Decision based on marginal cost of supplying division

This section shows that the manager of the training division will make the best decision for the company as a whole if the transfer price is set at the marginal cost (cost of one extra unit) of the publishing division. The marginal cost is the variable cost per unit which is £3 per manual. If the profit for each division is calculated using a transfer price of £3 per manual, the manager of the training division finds that a monthly purchase of 600 manuals gives the best divisional performance. This is the amount that also gives the best performance for the company as a whole (Exhibit 17.9).

Exhibit 17.9
Estimate of profit for training division

Number of support packages	Revenue from sale £	Variable cost @ £2 £	Transfer price of manuals @ £3 £	Fixed cost £	Profit/loss £
150	1800	300	450	500	550
300	3300	600	900	500	1300
450	4500	900	1350	500	1750
600	**5400**	**1200**	**1800**	**500**	**1900**
750	6000	1500	2250	500	1750
900	6300	1800	2700	500	1300

The manager of the publishing division is less happy because the selling price only covers variable cost. There is a loss equal to the amount of fixed cost (Exhibit 17.10).

Exhibit 17.10
Estimate of profit for publishing division

Number of manuals	Revenue from transfer £	Variable cost @ £3 £	Fixed cost £	Profit/loss £
150	450	450	600	(600)
300	900	900	600	(600)
450	1350	1350	600	(600)
600	1800	1800	600	(600)
750	2250	2250	600	(600)
900	2700	2700	600	(600)

If the marginal cost pricing policy is to be applied, the organisation as a whole must not judge the performance of the publishing division on the basis of profit. Alternatively the price charged to the training division could be based on publishing's variable cost of £5 plus a fixed fee of £600 per month. That would leave the publishing division with a zero profit and would still encourage the training division to choose 600 packages as the best level of output, although with £600 less of divisional profit.

17.7 Economic value added

Economic value added is the name given to an idea developed by the Stern Stewart consulting organisation, based in the USA. They have registered the abbreviation EVA™ as their trade mark. Economic value added is based on the idea of residual income. For each division the EVA™ is calculated by deducting from divisional profit a cost of capital charge based on the assets of the division. The Stern Stewart method makes accounting adjustments to divisional profit in order to arrive at a result that reflects economic profit, rather than relying on the financial accounting rules within historical cost accounting. As an example, if the company treats all development expenditure as an expense in the year in which it is incurred, for financial accounting purposes, then the EVA™ adjustment might treat it as an asset to be amortised over the period of its useful life, giving a smoother divisional profit.

Some companies mention in their annual reports that they are using EVA™ as a performance measure. Exhibit 17.11 is taken from the annual report of The Metro Group, an international trading and retailing company. It shows that EVA™ is used for assessing strategic and operational activities and also for calculating part of the remuneration of executives. The extract refers to 'delta EVA' which means the change in EVA from one period to the next.

Exhibit 17.11
Use of EVA™

EVA-instrument of corporate management: value-oriented corporate management is the cornerstone of sustainable profitable growth

The METRO Group is dedicated to a corporate management geared to boosting company value on a sustainable basis. The central benchmark by which to measure economic success is Economic Value Added (EVA). EVA is an internationally proven control and management system which enables all strategic and operating activities at the group to be analyzed and assessed on the basis of their contribution to the enhancement of the company value. That is why EVA is the touchstone for all strategic and capital allocation decisions at the METRO Group. Moreover, the development of EVA is the essential element in the variable remuneration

Exhibit 17.11 **continued**

system of METRO Group executives. All the way from the Management Board members of METRO AG through to the store managers of the sales divisions, the major portion of their variable income is linked to the delta EVA, i.e. the positive development of EVA, of their respective business units.

EVA established group-wide as the central benchmark for value growth
The ability of METRO Group to continuously increase the economic value of the company bears evidence to the performance potential of the group. It demonstrates that the METRO Group employs its capital successfully. The increase in company value is reflected in a positive EVA. It is achieved when the net operating profit exceeds the necessary cost of the capital to be used for financing the capital employed.

The net operating profit is defined as the operating profit before financing cost but after deduction of taxes on income (NOPAT). The capital cost is the compensation expected by investors for the capital they make available and for their investment risk. To determine the cost of capital, the capital employed is multiplied by the weighted average cost of capital (WACC) i.e. the weighted average of the cost of equity capital and borrowed capital, being calculated by applying the capital asset pricing model (CAPM). The WACC dropped in 2003 to 6.5% as against 7.3% a year earlier. This mainly reflects the improved risk profile of the METRO Group, for example thanks to the continued internationalization and the resulting restriction of dependency on individual markets as well as the lower level of interest at the capital markets. This calculation makes allowance for an equity capital cost rate of 10.0% (previous year 10.8%) and a borrowed-capital cost rate before taxes of 6.0% (previous year 6.3%). The capital employed is made up of the sum total of fixed assets tied up over the period under review of one year and the net current assets including all rent obligations. Hence the following formulae are applicable to calculate EVA:

$$EVA = NOPAT - \text{capital cost}$$

or

$$EVA = NOPAT - (\text{capital employed} \times \text{weighted average cost of capital rate})$$

EVA is calculated by deducting the cost of capital from the NOPAT of the group and of the sales divisions, respectively. The crucial value for the assessment of the entrepreneurial success is delta EVA, i.e. the difference between the current EVA and that of the previous year.

Consistently applied as a control instrument in corporate practice, EVA will always channel capital into those business units which promise to achieve the highest value added. EVA exercises a resource-allocating function.

EVA and delta EVA at METRO Group in fiscal 2003
In the 2003 fiscal year, the METRO Group achieved a positive EVA of 203.7 million for the first time since the introduction of this control and management tool. The total improvement of 213.2 compared to the prior-year mark results in an amount of 88.3 million from operational business developments and an amount of 124.9 million from structural effects. This means that METRO Group was in a position to employ its working capital so successfully that economic value was added. As in the previous year, the return on capital employed (RoCE) reached the mark of 7.5%. Consequently, it distinctly exceeded the capital cost rate of 6.5% in fiscal 2003. With this development, METRO Group again proved successful in its corporate strategy geared to profitable growth.

The NOPAT of the METRO Group climbed by 114.6 million to 1,541.1 million. At the same time, the capital employed rose by 405.4 million to 20.575.7 million. Aside from the expansive strategy of the METRO Group, the increase in capital is attributable to the lower borrowed-capital cost rate before taxes which causes a theoretical increase in cash values from rental obligations. The cost of capital only rose slightly by 26.4 million to 1,337.4 million due to the lower WACC compared to the previous year's mark. The return on sales referred to the capital employed rose slightly above the comparable prior-year value of 2.8%, at 2.9%. The capital turnover remained constant at 2.6%.

Source: Annual Report Metro (2003), p. 37.

17.8 What the researchers have found

17.8.1 Who uses EVA?

Lovata and Costigan (2002) identified 115 companies in the US that used EVA as a performance measure for determining management bonuses. They found the information by searching the proxy statements that are published by US companies ahead of the annual general meeting. The proxy statements provide detailed information on directors' remuneration. The researchers then compared these companies with similar companies, in matching industries, which did not use EVA. They found that companies with less insider ownership and a higher proportion of institutional investors tended to employ EVA. The use of EVA was also higher in companies with a lower ratio of research and development to sales. The researchers suggested that this is relevant because Stern–Stewart criticise the expensing of research and development expenditure and prefer to regard it as an asset. This adjustment to reported profit is therefore less important where the research and development expenditure is relatively low.

The researchers conclude that EVA is used in a manner that is consistent with agency theory because it is more evident in companies that need ways in which shareholders can monitor the performance of directors.

17.8.2 EVA bonus schemes

Riceman *et al* (2002) were given access to a company focused on EVA which had some managers on EVA-based bonus schemes and other managers on traditional bonus schemes. Their results indicated that, provided the managers understand the EVA concept, those on the EVA bonus schemes outperform those on traditional bonus schemes. They found a relatively low understanding of the EVA system, which did not surprise them in the light of the complexities of the EVA adjustment processes.

The measure of management performance was based on a commonly used self-rating performance measure containing nine items. The EVA measure itself focuses on use of capital employed, but it is important that managers also have the general skills to manage people which are measured in the self-rating performance score.

One explanation could be that the kind of managers who have good managerial skills are the kind of managers who will choose a new bonus incentive scheme rather than stick with the traditional version. The researchers defended their work against this potential limitation by focusing on the extent to which the managers understood the reward system, rather than the specific choice of a bonus scheme.

17.8.3 Transfer pricing

Perera *et al* (2003) reported a study of transfer pricing in a electricity supply company in Australia in the period 1991–2000. Initially transfer pricing was used within the organisation on a cost-plus basis to encourage changes in behaviour. It was abandoned after five years but reintroduced three years later. The authors found that they could not explain the abandonment and reintroduction in terms of models of transfer pricing. The explanation required an understanding of attitudes to innovation. The abandonment of transfer pricing in 1995 matched the departure of the chief executive officer. Its reintroduction in 1998 used a negotiated market basis to overcome the 'performance gap' perceived in the original 'cost plus' model. The use of a negotiated market price made transactions more transparent and more competitive with outside suppliers and customers.

Oyelere and Turner (2000) carried out a survey of transfer pricing practices in UK banks and building societies. They surveyed 25 large deposit-taking institutions. They received 16 usable replies, of which 14 explained their transfer pricing policies. Branch managers were encouraged to take responsibility for their branch activities by giving notional interest on cash surpluses held and charging notional interest on surplus lending by the branch. Market price was used in transfer pricing by eight respondents, a cost-based method by five and negotiation by one. The sample is relatively small but gives an indication of the range of answers that is possible within one industry.

17.9 Summary

Key themes in this chapter are:

- A **division** is a part of the organisation where the manager has responsibility for generating revenues, controlling costs and producing a satisfactory return on capital invested in the division.
- Performance of divisionalised companies may be measured either by the **return on investment (ROI)** or by the **residual income (RI)**.
- Return on investment is calculated by taking profit controllable by the division as a percentage of the investment in assets which produces that profit
- Residual income is defined as operating profit less an interest charge based on the assets used and controlled by the division.
- While ROI is more frequently encountered in practice, it may discourage investment projects which would be in the best interests of the organisation as a whole. In situations where the divisional manager has discretion to decide long-term investment in assets, RI may lead to a more useful and relevant measure of performance.
- **Transfer pricing** is used for transactions between departments or divisions within an organisation. Three possible methods of transfer pricing are: cost-based; market based; and negotiated prices.
- **Economic value added** is based on the idea of residual income. For each division the EVA™ is calculated by deducting from divisional profit a cost of capital charge based on the assets of the division.

References and further reading

Lovata, L. and Costigan, M.L. (2002), 'Empirical analysis of adopters of economic value added', *Management Accounting Research*, 13: 215–28.

Oyelere, P.B. and Turner, J.D. (2000) 'A survey of transfer pricing practices in UK banks and building societies', *European Business Review*, 12(2): 93–9.

Perera, S., McKinnon, J.L. and Harrison, G. (2003) 'Diffusion of transfer pricing innovation in the context of commercialisation: a longitudinal case study of a government trading enterprise', *Management Accounting Research*, 14: 140–64.

Riceman, S.S., Cahan, S.F. and Lal, M. (2002) 'Do managers perform better under EVA bonus schemes?', *The European Accounting Review*, 11(3): 537–72.

QUESTIONS

The Questions section of each chapter has three types of question. 'Test your understanding' questions to help you review your reading are in the 'A' series of questions. You will find the answer to these by reading and thinking about the material in the text book. 'Application' questions to test your ability to apply technical skills are in the 'B' series of questions. Questions requiring you to show skills in problem solving and evaluation are in the 'C' series of questions. The symbol [S] indicates that a solution is available at the end of the book.

A   Test your understanding

A17.1   What is a division (section 17.2)?

A17.2   What are the advantages of divisionalisation (section 17.2.1)?

A17.3   What are the disadvantages of divisionalisation (section 17.2.2)?

A17.4   Why is profit not a suitable measure of divisional performance (section 17.2.3)?

A17.5   Explain, in terms of divisional performance evaluation, the difference between using 'profit' and 'profitability' (section 17.3).

A17.6   Define, and explain the use of, return on investment as a measure of divisional performance (section 17.3).

A17.7   Define, and explain the use of, residual income, as a measure of divisional performance (section 17.4).

A17.8   Explain the circumstances in which return on investment is preferable as a measure of divisional performance (section 17.5).

A17.9   Explain the circumstances in which residual income is preferable as a measure of divisional performance (section 17.5).

A17.10 Explain what is meant by a 'transfer price' (section 17.6).

A17.11 Explain the methods of transfer pricing (section 17.6.1).

A17.12 Explain what is meant by 'economic value added' (section 17.7).

A17.13 Explain why companies regard economic value added as a useful tool for assessing managerial performance (section 17.7).

A17.14 What have researchers found about the use of EVA (section 17.8.1)?

A17.17 What have researchers found about the use of EVA bonus schemes (section 17.8.2)?

B   Application

B17.1 [S]
The following table sets out information in respect of Division X and Division Y.

	Division X	Division Y
Amount to be invested in new project	£4m	£4m
Sales	£2m	£2m
Net profit	£1.2m	£0.8m
ROI of existing investment	33%	4%

The cost of borrowing new finance is 10% per annum.

Required

Explain what view the managers of each division might take, depending on the method of performance evaluation applied.

B17.2 [S]

Comfy Chairs Co manufactures a standard office chair in Division A. The standard chair is improved in Division B with extra cushioning and easy-run castors. The manager of Division A has offered Division B a transfer price of £10 per chair to cover variable cost of £8 plus £2 for profit.

The estimated selling prices for a range of weekly output from Division B are as follows:

Estimates of selling prices for different levels of demand

Selling price per chair £	Weekly output of chairs
24	30
23	40
22	50
21	60
20	70
19	80

The variable costs and fixed costs of each division are as follows:

Variable cost
    Division A: £8 per chair
    Division B: £7 per chair for additional upholstery and castors
Fixed cost
    Division A: £200 per month
    Division B: £60 per month

Required

(a) Show that on the basis of a transfer price of £10 per chair the manager of Division B will prefer a level of activity that is not the best solution for the company as a whole.

(b) Show that if the transfer price is equal to the marginal cost (variable cost) of Division A then the manager of Division B will make a choice that is the best solution for the company as a whole.

(c) Discuss the view of the manager of Division A regarding a marginal cost transfer price.

B17.3

Write a short essay (250 words) on the similarities and differences between Economic Value Added and Residual Income.

B17.4

Department A is required to transfer 50% of its output to Department B at cost. Department B adds value to the product and then sells to outside customers. Manager A complains that the performance of Department B is overstated while that of Department A is understated. Manager B says that if a higher transfer price is charged, Department B will reject the output of Department A and seek an external supplier. As an independent expert, you have been asked to recommend a solution to the dispute. Write a short essay (250 words) recommending, with reasons, a fair system of transfer pricing.

C Problem solving and evaluation

C17.1 [S]

Musical Productions Ltd, a client of your firm, has two divisions. The Compact Disc division ('CD') assembles and markets portable compact disc players. The Portable Stereo division ('PS') assembles and markets portable tape players.

Budgets for the coming year have been prepared by the managers of each division and agreed by the head office, as follows:

	CD £000s	PS £000s
Investment in fixed assets	840	700
Revenue	420	210
Operating expenses	210	140
Profit	210	70

A new investment opportunity has arisen. It could be adopted by either division. The initial investment in fixed assets will be £140,000 and the expected annual operating profits from this investment are £28,000.

Musical Productions Ltd presently uses Return on Investment (ROI) as a criterion for evaluating divisional performance, but the finance director is aware that a close competitor applies the Residual Income (RI) method, using a required rate of return of 18% per annum.

Required

Write a report to the finance director explaining:

(a) the relative merits and limitations of ROI, as compared with RI, as a criterion for evaluation of divisional performance; and

(b) the acceptability of the new investment opportunity from the viewpoint of each divisional manager and of Musical Productions Ltd as an entity, using both ROI and RI methods.

C17.2

You are the accountant of Hill Ltd ('Hill'), an electrical retailer having a chain of shops. Hill has recently acquired two other similar businesses. The sales director has come to you with a problem regarding one particular street which now has three shops owned by Hill, each displaying and selling the same product range. The sales director has approached a local property agent who has given an indication of the likely rental income from each shop, should Hill decide to let any or all of them.

	Shop 1 10 West Street 1,000 sq ft £000s	Shop 2 25 West Street 2,500 sq ft £000s	Shop 3 54 West Street 1,500 sq ft £000s
Floor space			
Market value of property	150	500	200
Turnover	300	800	1,000
Variable costs	240	640	800
Property costs (fixed)	5	10	6
Net profit of shop	55	150	194
Expected annual rental income	30	75	45

Further information

1 The average level of working capital for a shop is expected to be 15% of turnover.
2 If all sales were concentrated on shop 2 then the turnover could be as high as £2.1m or as low as £1.6m. In either case the ratio of variable costs to sales and the amount of fixed property costs would be the same as they are for shop 2 alone.

The sales director has heard that calculating return on investment is the best way of deciding divisional performance but has accepted your offer to compare the return on investment with the residual income, calculated on the basis of an interest rate of 10% per annum. He has asked you to consider whether performance would improve if all sales were concentrated on shop 2 for continued retail use, leaving shops 1 and 3 available for rental.

Required

Prepare a memorandum to the sales director of Hill containing:

(1) Appropriate calculations of return on investment and residual income.

(2) Brief comments explaining the usefulness of the residual income approach in the context of the particular situation faced by Hill.

Case studies

Real world cases

Prepare short answers to Case studies 17.1, 17.2 and 17.3.

Case 17.4

Obtain the annual report of a large listed company. Look throughout the report for mention of divisions. Then look for any reference to relative performance of divisions, including non-financial performance indicators. Having read the report, prepare a list of financial and non-financial performance indicators which you think would be useful to readers in understanding more about the division within the company.

Part 4

FINANCIAL MANAGEMENT AND STRATEGIC PLANNING

It is increasingly recognised that the role of management accounting requires an understanding of financial management and strategic planning. Financial management, for many small businesses, means controlling costs to maximise profits and then converting those profits to cash as efficiently as possible. Working capital soaks up cash, so control of inventory and debtors (credit customers) is very important. A company should also take care of its liabilities to trade suppliers (accounts payable) in order to balance the outflow of cash with the need to maintain the confidence of suppliers in the company's ability to pay. Chapter 18 explains basic aspects of financial management of cash flow and working capital. It also sets out the main features of a business plan for a small or medium-sized enterprise. The importance of financial management as a strand of management accounting is evidenced in the change of title of the CIMA monthly magazine from *Management Accounting* to *Financial Management* and in the changing editorial content of the magazine which is targeted at practitioners.

Strategic management accounting means paying attention to the activities of competitors rather than focusing solely on the organisation itself. Chapter 19 provides an introduction to strategic management accounting and to other techniques by which management accounting can help managers plan and control the activities of an organisation.

Part 4 FINANCIAL MANAGEMENT AND STRATEGIC PLANNING	
Chapter 18 Financial management: working capital and business plans	**Chapter 19** Business strategy and management accounting

LEVEL 2

Financial management: working capital and business plans

This case study shows a typical situation in which management accounting can be helpful. Read the case study now but only attempt the discussion points after you have finished studying the chapter.

The Company is also making significant changes in manufacturing which will continue to increase margins through efficiency improvements, range changes and capital investment. Production activity is being better planned which enables more even utilisation of the factory at Thorntons over more of the year. This smoothing of the Christmas peak means we are carrying more stock [inventory] for longer periods but the reduction in unit cost of products more than outweighs the additional interest cost.

Source: Thorntons plc Annual report, 2004, p. 6
www.thorntons.co.uk

Discussion points

1 How does the company reduce the unit cost of products by smoothing out the production?

2 What are the other costs of holding stocks, apart from the interest cost mentioned in the extract?

Contents

Learning outcomes

After studying this chapter you should be able to:

● Define working capital.

● Explain the management of current assets.

● Explain the management of current liabilities.

● Explain and calculate the working capital cycle.

● Explain the planning and control of inventory.

● Explain the main contents of a business plan.

● Describe and discuss examples of research into management of working capital.

18.1 Introduction

Management accounting seeks to help planning and control. One area where planning and control are important, especially for small businesses, is the financial management of **working capital**. Working capital is the amount of finance which a business must provide to finance the **current assets** of a business, to the extent that these are not covered by **current liabilities**. It is calculated by deducting current liabilities from current assets. If the non-cash current assets (inventories and debtors) are allowed to rise to excessive levels, the business may find it has insufficient cash to meet its day-to-day needs. If the current liabilities (such as trade creditors and bank overdraft) are allowed to grow to excessive levels, the business may find itself unable to meet these obligations as they fall due.

The management of working capital involves **controlling** and **planning** levels of inventory, **debtors** and **creditors**, to allow an efficient flow of cash into and out of the entity. This chapter explains some of the main features of working capital management.

Definitions

> **Current assets** are assets held for conversion into cash in the normal course of trading, usually within one year. They include cash, debtors (credit customers) and inventory (stocks)
>
> **Current liabilities** are liabilities that fall due for payment within one year. They include bank overdrafts, trade creditors (suppliers) and unpaid expenses (accruals)
>
> **Working capital** is the amount of finance which a business must provide to finance the current assets of a business, to the extent that these are not covered by current liabilities. It is calculated by deducting current liabilities from current assets.

18.2 Current assets

This section defines and explains the main categories of current assets.

18.2.1 Inventories (stocks)

There are three main categories of inventory: finished goods, **work in progress** and raw materials.

Finished goods

The future economic benefit expected from finished goods is that they will be sold to customers for a price which exceeds the cost of purchase or manufacture, so making a profit. There is some risk attached to holding inventories of finished goods because they may become out of date, or may not sell for the expected selling price.

Work in progress

During the course of production the asset of finished goods is gradually being created. The expected future benefit of that activity is gradually building up as the work moves towards completion.

The risks attached to work in progress are often greater than those attached to finished goods because there is the risk of non-completion to add to all the risks faced when the goods are completed and awaiting sale.

Raw materials

Raw materials are expected to create a benefit by being used in the manufacture of goods for sale. There is a risk that the value of the raw materials may fall because commodity prices fluctuate in the markets. There is also a risk of the raw materials deteriorating or become unsuitable for use because production processes change.

Stockholding period

A simple calculation allows us to estimate the average period for which inventory (stock) is held. The stockholding period is calculated in days:

For raw materials

$$\frac{\text{Average inventory (stock) of raw materials}}{\text{Cost of raw materials used in production}} \times 365$$

For finished goods

$$\frac{\text{Average inventory (stock) of finished goods}}{\text{Cost of goods sold}} \times 365$$

The average inventory may be calculated as the average of the inventory levels at the start and end of the period.

Managing inventory (stock) levels

Section 18.5 contains a detailed discussion of the approach to planning and controlling inventory.

18.2.2 Debtors and prepayments

Debtors

Debtors are those customers or clients who owe money to a business. Usually the largest amount shown under this heading relates to customers buying goods on credit. These are the **trade debtors**. Additionally, the business may have lent money to another enterprise to help that enterprise in its activities. There may be loans to employees to cover removal and relocation expenses or advances on salaries. The business may be due to receive a refund of overpaid tax.

Trade debtors represent an expectation of benefit when the customer pays. There is a risk that the customer will not pay. The risk of non-payment is dealt with by reducing the reported value of the asset by an estimate for doubtful debts.

Debtors' (customers') collection period

The debtors' collection period is calculated in days

$$\frac{\text{Average trade debtors}}{\text{Credit sales}} \times 365$$

Managing trade debtors

A business which sells on credit has to manage its trade debtors. The business sells on credit in order to attract business but it must then ensure that the cash is collected as efficiently as possible. Key issues to watch are:

- Choose customers carefully and only allow credit after checking for creditworthiness.
- On the invoice sent to the customer, state the conditions for payment date and any penalties for late payment.
- Offer discounts for early payment (but balance the cost of discount against the benefit of early cash).

- Ensure that invoices are sent out as soon as the goods are despatched.
- Maintain an 'aged accounts receivable' analysis and send reminder letters as soon as key dates are reached.
- Cut off credit facilities if the customer exceeds a specified payment period.
- Arrange with a debt collection agency to have late debts pursued for collection.

Activity 18.1

Write down two types of business that sell goods on credit and two types of business that sell only for cash. What explanations might be given for these different strategies?

Prepayments

Prepayments are amounts of expenses paid in advance. Insurance premiums, rent of buildings, lease charges on a vehicle and road fund licences for the delivery vans and lorries are all examples of items which have to be paid for in advance. At the balance sheet date some part of the future benefit may remain. This is recognised as the prepayment. Take the example of an insurance premium of £240 paid on 1 October to cover a twelve-month period. At the company's year end of 31 December, three months' benefit has expired but nine months' benefit remains. The balance sheet therefore reports a prepayment of £180.

18.2.3 Cash

Cash may be used to buy fixed assets or to contribute to the working capital cycle so that the business earns a profit. In the meantime cash which is surplus to immediate requirements should be deposited in such a way that it is earning interest. Where a company has substantial cash balances there should be indications in the profit and loss account that investment income has been earned, to provide a benefit to the business.

Investments held as current assets are usually highly marketable and readily convertible into cash.

18.3 Current liabilities

The most significant current liabilities for most companies are bank borrowing and **trade creditors**. Both of these are essential sources of finance for small companies and are an important aspect, if not essential, for larger companies. In addition most companies have some unpaid expenses at the balance sheet date. These are recorded as expenses in the profit and loss account and as **accrued liabilities** in the balance sheet.

18.3.1 Bank borrowing

Banks provide short-term finance to companies in the form of an overdraft on a current account. The advantage of an overdraft is its flexibility. When the cash needs of the company increase with seasonal factors, the company can continue to write cheques and watch the overdraft increase. When the goods and services are sold and cash begins to flow in, the company should be able to watch the overdraft decrease again. The most obvious example of a company which operates in this pattern is farming. The farmer uses the overdraft to finance the acquisition of seed for arable farming or feeding through the winter for stock farming and to cover the period when the crops or animals are growing and maturing. The overdraft is reduced when the crops or the animals are sold.

The major disadvantage of an overdraft is that it is repayable on demand. The farmer whose crop fails because of bad weather knows the problem of being unable to repay the overdraft. Having overdraft financing increases the worries of the company. The other disadvantage is that the interest payable on overdrafts is variable. When interest rates increase, the cost of the overdraft increases. Furthermore, for small companies there are often complaints that the rate of interest charged is high compared with that available to larger companies. The banks answer that the rates charged reflect relative risk and it is their experience that small companies are more risky.

18.3.2 Trade creditors

It is a strong feature of many industries that one enterprise is willing to supply goods to another in advance of being paid. Most suppliers will state terms of payment (e.g. the invoice must be paid within 30 days) and some will offer a discount for prompt payment. In the UK, it has not been traditional to charge interest on overdue accounts but this practice is growing as companies realise there is a high cost to themselves of not collecting cash from their customers.

Trade creditors rarely have any security for payment of the amount due to them so that if their customer fails to pay they must wait in the queue with other suppliers and hope for a share of some distribution. They are described as **unsecured creditors**. Some suppliers will include in the contract a condition that the goods remain the property of the supplier should the customer fail to pay. This is called **retention of title** and will be noted in the balance sheet of a company which has bought goods on these terms. Retention of title may offer some protection to the unpaid supplier but requires very prompt action to recover identifiable goods in the event of difficulty.

Some suppliers send goods to a customer on a *sale-or-return* basis. If there are no conditions to prevent return then the goods will not appear as stock in the balance sheet of the customer and there will be no indication of a liability. This practice is particularly common in the motor industry where manufacturers send cars to showrooms for sale or return within a specified period of time.

Suppliers send **invoices** to the customer showing the amount due for payment. These invoices are used in the customer's accounts department as the source of information for liabilities. At the end of the month the suppliers send **statements** as a reminder of unpaid invoices. Statements are useful as additional evidence of liabilities to suppliers.

Creditors (suppliers) payment period

The creditors payment period is calculated in days

$$\frac{\text{Average trade creditors}}{\text{Credit purchases}} \times 365$$

Managing trade creditors

A business which buys on credit has to manage its trade creditors. The business buys on credit in order to finance its holding of inventory, but it must then ensure that payments are made in sufficient time to maintain a good reputation with the supplier and to avoid penalties for late payment. Key issues to watch are:

- Maintain an 'aged accounts payable' analysis and make payments in time to avoid any liabilities exceeding the period stated by the supplier (particularly where there may be penalties).
- Watch for discounts allowed for early payment and check whether the cost of losing the discount exceeds the benefit of interest saved on the bank overdraft.
- Plan ahead for major purchases and ensure the cash flow will be available.
- Plan ahead for seasonal fluctuations in cash outflows for expense items.

Write down two types of business that buy goods on credit and two types of business that buy only for cash. What explanations might be given for these different strategies?

18.3.3 Accrual of liabilities

At the balance sheet date there will be obligations of the enterprise to pay for goods or services received but which are not contained in the accounting records because no document has been received from the supplier of the goods or service. It is essential that all obligations are included at the balance sheet date because these obligations fall under the definition of liabilities even although the demand for payment has not been received. The process of including in the balance sheet all obligations at the end of the period is called the **accrual** of liabilities.

Write down two types of expense that might be unpaid at the accounting date and so recorded as accruals.

Real world case 18.2

Legislation to sweep away a culture of late payment in business has been a failure, according to research that shows it has triggered no improvement in the time it takes companies to pay their bills. Experian, the business information group, found that companies waited an average of 58 days, including agreed credit periods, to settle invoices. This compares with 57.5 days in 1998, when the government brought in laws to cover late payment. The study found the delay in the UK was greater than for any other large European Union country, averaging 27 days beyond agreed payment terms. This compares with 10 days for France, 17 for Germany and 21 for Italy.

. . .

In Britain, it is typically small companies, whose intermittent cash flows make them vulnerable to collapse, who are paid latest, with some reporting that up to six months' turnover is tied up in debts owed to them. According to Bank of Scotland, half of small businesses have to wait up to a year for at least one debt to be settled, with a quarter waiting for up to two years. The problem is fostered by company structures that discourage contact between buyers and finance departments eager to win a cash flow advantage by paying suppliers late.

Source: *Financial Times*, 18 February 2004, p. 3, 'Legislation "has failed to curb late payments" '.

Discussion points

1 Why might the government's disclosure regulation have failed to persuade companies to pay their suppliers more promptly?

2 What problems does the article identify within structures of companies?

18.4   The working capital cycle

A business needs current assets (inventory, debtors and cash) to enable it to carry out day-to-day operations smoothly. Some short-term finance for current assets is provided by suppliers who give credit by allowing time to pay, but that is not usually sufficient. Some short-term finance for current assets is provided by short-term bank loans but, in most cases, there still remains an excess of current assets over current liabilities. **Working capital** is the amount of long-term finance the business has to provide in order to keep current assets working for the business.

The working capital cycle of a business is the sequence of transactions and events, involving current assets and current liabilities, through which the business makes a profit.

18.4.1   Describing the working capital cycle

Exhibit 18.1 shows how the working capital cycle begins when suppliers allow the business to obtain goods on credit terms, but do not insist on immediate payment. While they are waiting for payment they are called creditors. The goods obtained by the business are used in production, held for resale or used in providing a service. While the goods acquired are held by the business they are called the inventory (stock) of the business. Any products manufactured from these goods and held for resale are also part of the stock of the business. The resulting product or service is sold to customers who may pay immediately in cash or may be allowed time to pay. If they are allowed time to pay they become debtors of the business. Debtors eventually pay and the business obtains cash. Cash is a general term which includes money held in notes and coins on the business premises and also money held in the bank. Cash held in the bank will be in an account such as a current account which allows immediate access. Finally the cash may be used to pay the suppliers who, as creditors, have been waiting patiently for payment. They in turn supply more goods to the business and the cycle begins again.

Exhibit 18.1
The working cycle for a manufacturing or service business

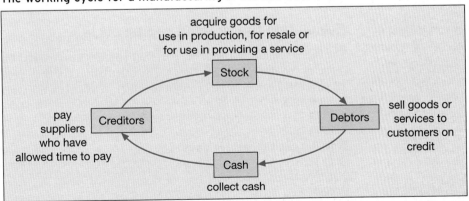

Working capital is calculated as *current assets minus current liabilities*. If the working capital is low, then the business has a close match between current asset and current liabilities but may risk not being able to pay its liabilities as they fall due. Not all the current assets are instantly available in cash (particularly the stocks of unsold goods) and an impatient supplier or bank manager may decide to cause difficulties if cash is not available when payment of a liability is due. On the other hand, if current assets are very much greater than current liabilities, then the business has a large amount of finance tied up in the current assets when perhaps that finance would be better employed in the acquisition of more fixed assets to expand the profit-making capacity of the operations.

18.4.2 Measuring working capital

There are two main ratios for measuring working capital.

Current ratio

$$\frac{\text{Current assets}}{\text{Current liabilities}}$$

The current ratio measures the relative level of current assets compared with current liabilities. It indicates the extent to which all current liabilities are covered by all current assets. If the ratio is greater than 1 : 1 then the entity can meet all of its current liabilities out of current assets. Many companies operate with this ratio in the region from 1 : 1 to 1.5 : 1. If the ratio is higher than this then the current liabilities are very safely covered. However, if the ratio is very much higher than 2 : 1 there could be questions about holding excessive levels of inventory and debtors, with a possible risk of outdated inventory and slow-paying customers.

Liquid ratio

$$\frac{\text{Current assets minus inventory}}{\text{Current liabilities}}$$

The liquid ratio is a measure of solvency. On the top line of the ratio the inventory is removed to leave the liquid assets of debtors and cash. These are available to pay current liabilities in an immediate crisis. Inventory will take longer to sell. It is fairly unlikely that all trade creditors will demand payment at the same time and so many companies operate with this ratio in the region from 0.75 : 1 to 0.9 : 1. If the ratio is higher than 1 : 1 then the current liabilities are safely covered, although there could be a concern that excessive levels of debtors and cash are held. If the ratio is lower than 0.75 : 1 then suppliers might become worried and demand payment, so forcing a crisis.

18.4.3 Calculating the working capital cycle

The ratios tell us how well the current liabilities are covered but they do not give any sense of the timing of cash flows. The calculations of time periods set out in sections 18.2 and 18.3 can now be brought together to calculate the working capital cycle as in Exhibit 18.2.

Exhibit 18.2
Working capital cycle in days

Number of days for which inventory is held (stockholding period)	xx
Plus	
Number of days taken by credit customers to pay (debtors collection period)	xx
Minus	
Number of days taken to pay suppliers (creditors payment period)	(xx)
Equals	
Number of days for which long term financing is needed from shareholders or lenders	xx

18.4.4 Overtrading

Overtrading is the name given to the situation where an entity is expanding its sales rapidly, but is not managing its cash flow. When a business is expanding and sales are increasing, there will be correspondingly higher levels of inventory and debtors. These need to be financed. If the business reaches its overdraft limit and has no access to other sources of funding, it may have insufficient cash to pay suppliers and pay wages. It is very frustrating for an enterprising business person, who has been focusing on

---

Real world case 18.3

The CFO Magazine in the USA publishes information to help chief finance officers (finance directors) in companies. The following information is extracted from its annual Working Capital Survey.

For those who rejoiced when the New York Yankees faltered at the start of this season or thought 2003 surely had to be Lance Armstrong's last Tour de France win, here's some exciting news: Dell Computer's working capital performance has slipped. Well, sort of. The undisputed champion saw its overall working capital grow by 2 days – putting it still at a mind-blowing negative 30 days in CFO's annual survey, conducted by Purchase, New York-based REL Consultancy Group, Which, of course, leaves even Dell's best competitors trailing behind like the Boston Red Sox. Indeed, despite a deterioration in receivables collection [days taken by credit customers to pay], Dell once again shaved its days inventory outstanding by 9% to three days (four by Dell's slightly different reckoning). That's so low that chief accounting officer Robert W. Davis says the company now thinks of inventory in dollars rather than days.

The CFO survey calculates the working capital in days for 67 industry sectors. Two examples are:

Auto parts and suppliers

Number of days for which inventory is held (stockholding period)	31
Number of days taken by credit customers to pay (debtors collection period)	55
Number of days taken to pay suppliers (creditors payment period)	(43)
Number of days for which long term financing is needed from shareholders or lenders	43

Home construction

Number of days for which inventory is held (stockholding period)	181
Number of days taken by credit customers to pay (debtors collection period)	19
Number of days taken to pay suppliers (creditors payment period)	(32)
Number of days for which long term financing is needed from shareholders or lenders	168

Source: *CFO Magazine*, The 2004 Working Capital Survey, www.cfo.com

Discussion points

1 What do these figures tell us about the autoparts industry compared with the home construction industry?

2 Dell Computers assembles computers to customers' orders received on the internet. How does the company's operation help it to keep down its inventory holding period?

expanding business in a time of strong demand for the product, to find that the business is on the verge of collapse. The message is that cash flow has to be managed, by preparing and monitoring monthly cash budgets as described in Chapter 13.

Brown (2001) describes the ways in which over-trading arises when there is too much focus on marketing, perhaps with low profit margins, leading to a lack of sufficient cash flow. He points out that marketing managers seek to maximise sales and foster total awareness of the brand. However, if this happens through low pricing or through investing in expensive promotions, the business may run out of cash. Margins are too low and investments are not earning an adequate return. On the other hand, excessive prudence may lead to short-term boosts to profits through keeping prices high and avoiding investment. At the same time the long-term prospects are neglected and the sales fall. Brown says that investors are looking at the long-term growth potential, sustainable margins and the amount of investment needed to maintain market performance.

18.5 Planning and controlling inventory (stock)

Many organisations hold inventory as part of their business operations. Some are manufacturing businesses and so need to buy in raw materials, convert the raw materials to work-in-progress and then hold inventories of finished goods awaiting sale to customers. Others are service businesses which hold inventories of materials to be used in providing a service. Retail stores buy goods to sell in their shops; restaurants buy food to cook in their kitchens; government departments buy stationery to use in their office activities. They are all holding inventory and in the process are incurring costs.

18.5.1 Describing the process

Costs of holding inventory can be divided into the costs of inventory levels that are too high ('overstocking') and the costs of inventory levels that are too low ('understocking'). These are summarised in Exhibit 18.3.

Exhibit 18.3
Costs of holding inventory

Inventory levels too high
If inventory levels are too high, there will be excessive costs of storage. These include:
- Interest charges on finance used to support the inventory levels until used or sold.
- Costs of space used for storage, including rent, heating, lighting.
- Equipment costs, such as storage racks, bins, temperature controlled cases.
- Personnel cost, such as storekeeping, security and cleaning.
- Insurance
- Risk of deterioration and obsolescence as inventory becomes out of date.

Inventory levels too low
If inventory levels are too low, the organisation may run out of supplies for its needs. This leads to:
- Wages being paid for idle time.
- Disruption of business activity.
- Loss of profit through lost sales.
- Cancelled customers' orders because of delayed delivery.
- Penalty payments claimed by customers due to delay.
- Increased costs of finding replacement supplies in an emergency.

The costs of holding inventory, and the risks of shortages from having inadequate inventory, might lead an organisation to decide on a policy of frequent regular orders of smaller amounts, calculated to match expected demand. Again there are costs to consider in the frequent number of orders required. **Costs of ordering inventory** are summarised in Exhibit 18.4.

Exhibit 18.4
Costs of ordering

The administrative costs related to buying and receiving materials will increase with the frequency of ordering. Such costs include:

- Increased costs of clerical staff for placing orders, checking deliveries and paying invoices.
- Increased administrative oversight and checking.
- Increased stationery, phone calls, faxes, emails.
- Increased inward transport costs.

Inventory control is based on planning for four levels of control:

- Maximum level.
- Minimum level.
- Re-order level.
- Re-order quantity.

The *maximum level* is the uppermost level that the buying department should not exceed. Above this point the holding costs become unacceptable, perhaps because more warehouse staff have to be recruited or more storage space has to be rented. The *minimum level* is the lowest level that allows the activity of the organisation to be maintained. It is also called the **buffer stock** and can be thought of as a kind of safety cushion. As soon as the inventory level touches this lower level it should bounce up again with another incoming order of materials.

The **re-order level** is the point at which the buying department places its order for replacement materials. This will be a level that is higher than the minimum level because time will be required for the new order to arrive, and during that time the levels of inventory will fall further. This delay between order date and delivery date is called the lead time. The re-order level will depend on:

- the rate of consumption
- and the lead time.

The re-order quantity is the quantity to be ordered when the re-order level is reached. If this quantity is specified in advance, the buying department knows how much to order as soon as the re-order level is reached. The re-order quantity should be set after considering:

- the rate of consumption of materials
- the cost of holding compared to the cost of purchasing
- the availability of bulk discounts
- transport costs
- risks of obsolescence and deterioration.

The average inventory (average stock) held in any period is the average of the starting and closing levels, if a uniform pattern of usage is assumed,

$$\frac{opening\ inventory + closing\ inventory}{2}$$

If the opening inventory is zero then the average is half of the closing inventory.

These ideas are summarised in Exhibit 18.5. At point A the organisation is holding the maximum inventory level. The materials are then used or sold in a straight-line pattern, down to the re-order point B. At this point an amount is ordered, calculated as the difference between the minimum and maximum levels. The order arrives at point C, when inventories are at the minimum level of inventory stock, and the inventory is replenished up to the level M. The pattern then repeats itself.

Exhibit 18.5
Controlling inventory levels

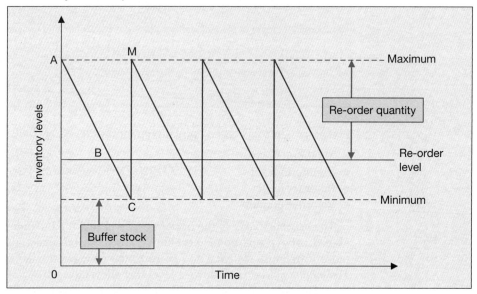

18.5.2 Economic order quantity

If inventory is maintained at relatively high levels, the costs of holding inventory are higher but the costs of re-ordering are lower. If inventory is maintained at relatively low levels, the costs of holding inventory are lower but the costs of re-ordering are higher. The aim of inventory planning is to find the most efficient middle ground to minimise the combined costs of holding inventory and re-ordering inventory. A model that minimises the combined cost is called the model to calculate the **economic order quantity (EOQ)**.

Exhibit 18.6
Information for illustration of economic order quantity

An organisation purchases materials from an external supplier at a cost of £10 per item. All items are identical. The total annual demand for this item is 30,000 units.

The organisation requires a 6% return on investment in assets, which means expecting a return of 60 pence on each item costing £10. Other holding costs are 12 pence per item. The cost of each purchase order is 80 pence.

What is the economic order quantity?

Spreadsheet solution

One way of solving this is to prepare a spreadsheet. The spreadsheet for Exhibit 18.6 is shown in panel A of Exhibit 18.7 in increments of order size. From this the minimum total cost appears to be at or near an order quantity of 250. The spreadsheet is then used in shorter increments (panel B) to narrow down the minimum total cost which appears to be at or near an order quantity of 260. This is very easy to do by trial-and-error once you have set up the spreadsheet.

Exhibit 18.7
Spreadsheet for holding cost and ordering cost as order quantity varies

Panel A Range of order sizes						
Order quantity	50	150	250	350	450	550
Average stock[1]	25	75	125	175	225	275
Number of purchase orders[2]	600	200	120	86	67	55
	£	£	£	£	£	£
Annual holding cost @ 72 pence	18	54	90	126	162	198
Annual ordering cost @ 80 pence	480	160	96	69	53	44
Total cost	498	214	186	195	215	242

[1] Average stock = order quantity/2. The order quantity is the maximum held. It falls to zero at the point of arrival of the next order so the average stock is half of the order quantity.
[2] Number of purchase orders = total demand divided by order quantity

Panel B Spread in order increments of 10, either side of minimum			
Order quantity	250	260	270
Average stock	125	130	135
Number of purchase orders	120	115	111
	£	£	£
Annual holding cost @ 72 pence	90	94	97
Annual ordering cost @ 80 pence	96	92	89
Total cost	186.0	185.9	186.1

Graphical solution

An alternative way of finding the minimum total cost is to draw a graph of the annual holding cost and the annual ordering cost and find the point where they intersect. This point represents the minimum total cost. You will see from Exhibit 18.8 that the point of intersection is at or near the order quantity 260.

Exhibit 18.8
Economic order quantity graph

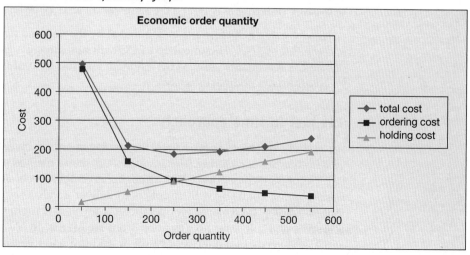

Algebraic solution

Equations may be written for the cost of holding and the cost of ordering inventory. Adding these gives the total cost. Using differential calculus gives the minimum point on the total cost curve. We need not worry about differential calculus here because the formula is reasonably intuitive.

$$\text{The cost of holding the average stock for a period} =$$
$$\text{cost of holding one item} \times \frac{\text{number of items}}{2}$$

Call this $C_h \times D/2$

$$\text{The cost of ordering for a period} = \text{cost per order} \times \frac{\text{total demand}}{\text{quantity in one order}}$$

Call this $C_o \times D/q$

Add them together to give total cost $= (C_h \times D/2) + (C_o \times D/q)$

It can be shown by calculus that the minimum total cost occurs where

$$EOQ = \sqrt{\frac{2\,D\,C_o}{C_h}}$$

Substitute in this equation the data from Exhibit 18.6

$$EOQ = \sqrt{\frac{2 \times 30,000 \times .80}{.72}}$$

$$EOQ = 258 \text{ units}$$

So the trial-and-error spreadsheet and the graphical solution were reasonably close with an estimate of 260 units.

Applicability of the EOQ formula

It is unlikely that any business would be able to use the EOQ formula precisely as shown here because it is based on assumptions that are unlikely to apply exactly in the real world.

- Average stock may not be exactly half the re-order quantity if the pattern of usage is uneven.
- Costs of holding inventory may not be constant across all levels of inventory.
- Costs of ordering may not be the same for all sizes of order.

However, the EOQ formula is dominated by the demand figure, D, on the top line, and the ratio C_o/C_h. The calculated EOQ will not change a great deal provided the demand is reasonably close to the estimate and the ratio of C_o/C_h does not change greatly from the original estimates.

18.5.3 The just-in-time approach

An entirely different approach to the management of inventory levels is seen in 'just-in-time' manufacturing. This is much more than a method of inventory control, but it has important consequences for managing inventory levels. **Just-in-time purchasing** is a system of contracts with suppliers to deliver goods as closely as possible to the time when they are required for operations. It involves accepting only perfect incoming resources and allowing no deviation from standards. Every activity occurs exactly at the time needed for effective execution, and the activity always happens exactly as planned. Just-in-time purchasing reduces stockholding costs, minimises idle time for production resources and creates a demand-driven business.

In this approach inventory levels become very low or non-existent because deliveries are timed to arrive as they are needed. Inventory planning is not treated as a separate exercise – it is one part of the streamlining of the whole process.

Fiona McTaggart describes her experience of a just-in-time management system.

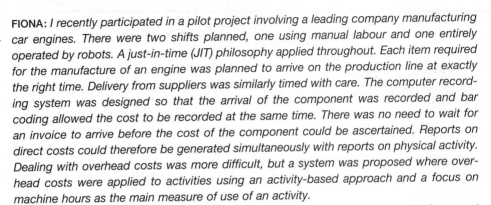

FIONA: *I recently participated in a pilot project involving a leading company manufacturing car engines. There were two shifts planned, one using manual labour and one entirely operated by robots. A just-in-time (JIT) philosophy applied throughout. Each item required for the manufacture of an engine was planned to arrive on the production line at exactly the right time. Delivery from suppliers was similarly timed with care. The computer recording system was designed so that the arrival of the component was recorded and bar coding allowed the cost to be recorded at the same time. There was no need to wait for an invoice to arrive before the cost of the component could be ascertained. Reports on direct costs could therefore be generated simultaneously with reports on physical activity. Dealing with overhead costs was more difficult, but a system was proposed where overhead costs were applied to activities using an activity-based approach and a focus on machine hours as the main measure of use of an activity.*

The JIT approach emphasises elimination of waste. The management accounting report for the two shifts had a waste exception report section which allowed rapid identification of departure from accepted waste levels on each shift. Linking the accounting records to the physical activity meant that each shift could be identified separately.

The pilot project was receiving a cautious welcome by the technical managers. They had regarded traditional management accounting as an unavoidable nuisance but they could see that the pilot scheme was bringing the accounting information closer to their perspective of the operation.

Activity 18.4
Write down two benefits and two risks of using just-in-time purchasing. Think of one type of business for which just-in-time purchasing would be useful and one type of business for which it would be unsiutable.

18.6 Business plans

When the owner of a small business wants to raise finance to develop or expand the business, those who provide finance will ask for a business plan. The business plan will set out at least the following items, some of which you have met in earlier chapters:

- Nature of the business.
- Key persons involved in managing the business.
- Business goals.
- Market for the product or service offered.
- Nature of the product or service offered.
- A description of the business plan for three to five years ahead.
- Financial statements (balance sheet and profit and loss account) at the present time.
- Master budget, comprising budgeted cash flows, budgeted balance sheet and budgeted profit and loss account with supporting schedules (see Chapter 13).
- Performance measures (financial and non-financial) used to monitor performance (see Chapter 16).

- Management accounting information such as breakeven analysis (see Chapter 9) and plans for capital expenditure (see Chapters 11 and 12).
- Risk analysis covering operating risk and financial risk.

Many of these items have been covered in this book. In particular, Chapter 13 explains the preparation of cash budgets within the master budget. A bank manager will ask for cash budgets to show the borrowings needed for each month or each quarter of a year. If a business has a strong management accounting system then the information needed for the business plan will be readily available because it will already be used to support management activities.

Activity 18.5

Look back to Chapter 13 and make sure that you understand how to present cash flows for planning purposes.

18.7 What the researchers have found

18.7.1 Small businesses

Working capital management is particularly important for small businesses which may have limited access to sources of external funding. Howorth and Westhead (2003) mailed a questionnaire to 1,900 companies and received 343 responses. That may seem low but is comparable to the success rate of similar studies. The questionnaire asked: How often do you review each of the following:

- Inventory (stock) turnover
- Inventory (stock) levels
- Inventory (stock) re-order levels
- Customer credit periods
- Customer discount policy
- Bad debts
- Doubtful debts
- Customer credit risk
- Payment period to creditors
- Finance of working capital
- Use of cash budgeting.

The researchers found that different businesses behaved in different ways, so it was not possible to form a general conclusion about small businesses. Firms that focused on cash management tended to be younger firms with more external finance and possibly with more cash flow problems. Firms that focused on inventory management routines tended also to be younger, but smaller and with less external finance. Firms that focused on credit management had lower profitability, more credit purchases and fewer customers paying on time. It seems that small businesses focus on areas that are key to their particular problems, but do not follow a comprehensive policy of paying attention to all aspects of working capital management.

18.7.2 Working capital cycle

Drickhamer (2004) reported the results of a survey in which respondents were asked to calculate the working capital cycle by adding the days supply of inventory plus outstanding debtors minus the average payment period for materials. Of the responses,

26 per cent had a cycle of less than 30 days, 36 per cent had a cycle of 30–60 days, 20 per cent had a cycle of 60–90 days and 18 per cent had a cycle over 90 days. So there is no clear picture of a 'normal' length of working capital cycle.

18.7.3   Types of business

McCosker (2000) describes and discusses the working capital position of three companies: a football club (Manchester United), a supermarket chain (Tesco) and a travel business (Airtours). He shows that the current ratio of Manchester United is close to 2 : 1 but the ratios for Tesco and Airtours are much lower than this. He explains that a business such as Tesco, with strong cash flows, can afford to have a much lower current ratio, even to the extent of having current liabilities higher than current assets. Airtours generally receives customers' cash ahead of the date of the holiday so cash flow is strong. The author concludes that the level of the current ratio is very much dependent on the nature of the business.

18.7.4   The banker's perspective

Strischek (2001) writes as a practising banker rather than a researcher. He explains that lenders have a particular interest in sound processes for collecting cash from customers, good inventory controls and discipline over trade credit. He explains some of the simple calculations carried out by bankers, such as calculating the working capital cycle in days and checking on the ration of net working capital to sales. He points out that efficient management of working capital ensures that bank borrowing is kept to a minimum and the cost of capital is controlled, for the benefit of investors.

18.7.5   Just-in-time production

Hoque (2000) surveyed companies in New Zealand by using a postal questionnaire. This sampled a set of companies using JIT operations in production and a matching set that did not use JIT operations. The researcher found that managers in organisations operating in a JIT production environment tended to rely relatively less upon a broader set of cost data for managerial activities. Use of an automated manufacturing process did not show significant differences in the use of cost data for managerial activities. The study claimed to provide evidence supporting the contingency theory of management accounting, suggesting that a changing manufacturing environment will influence the design and use of management accounting systems in organisations.

González-Benito (2002) surveyed the use of JIT purchasing over a sample of 152 Spanish auto component manufacturers. JIT purchasing practices were mainly applied to fragile and expensive products. Purchasing policies are also affected by the importance of ensuring continuity of supply and a co-operative relationship with suppliers. The JIT practices were not motivated by a desire to reduce the costs of holding inventory. They were determined more closely by the need for flexibility and the desire to avoid the risk of deterioration of fragile items. The availability of working capital also appeared to be important in using JIT purchasing for expensive items.

Schniederjans and Cao (2001) wrote a mathematical paper comparing the EOQ approach to inventory management with the JIT approach. They suggested that it was important to consider the saving on storage space which is achieved under JIT planning. This makes JIT more cost effective than EOQ in most cases. Although the mathematical formulae in this paper might make it appear a little daunting, the authors do include some numerical examples and also a table discussing the impact of JIT on a range of cost categories.

18.8 Summary

Key themes in this chapter are:

- **Current assets** are assets held for conversion into cash in the normal course of trading, usually within one year. They include cash, debtors (credit customers) and inventory (stocks).

- **Current liabilities** are liabilities that fall due for payment within one year. They include bank overdrafts, trade creditors (suppliers) and unpaid expenses (accruals).

- **Working capital** is the amount of finance which a business must provide to finance the current assets of a business, to the extent that these are not covered by current liabilities. It is calculated by deducting current liabilities from current assets.

- The stockholding period for raw materials is calculated as:

$$\frac{\text{Average inventory (stock) of raw materials}}{\text{Cost of raw materials used in production}} \times 365$$

- The stockholding period for finished goods is calculated as:

$$\frac{\text{Average inventory (stock) of finished goods}}{\text{Cost of goods sold}} \times 365$$

- The **debtors'** collection period is calculated in days:

$$\frac{\text{Average trade debtors}}{\text{Credit sales}} \times 365$$

- The **creditors'** payment period is calculated in days:

$$\frac{\text{Average trade creditors}}{\text{Credit purchases}} \times 365$$

- The current ratio is calculated as:

$$\frac{\text{Current assets}}{\text{Current liabilities}}$$

- The liquid ratio is calculated as:

$$\frac{\text{Current assets minus inventory}}{\text{Current liabilities}}$$

- The **working capital** cycle calculates the number of days for which long-term financing is needed from shareholders or lenders as being equal to the number of days for which inventory is held (stockholding period) *plus* the number of days taken by credit customers to pay (debtors collection period) *minus* the number of days taken to pay suppliers (creditors payment period).

- Planning and controlling inventory requires consideration of the stock levels to be held, the **costs of holding inventory** (stock), the **costs of ordering inventory** (stock) and the lead time between placing an order and receiving the goods. The calculation of the **economic order quantity** minimises the combined cost of holding and ordering stocks.

References and further reading

Brown, M. (2001) 'Over-trading and out', *Financial Management*, October: 18.

CIMA (2001) *Business Basics: Cash-flow Management*, CIMA Publishing, available on www.cimaglobal.com

CIMA (undated) *A Practical Guide to Preparing a Business Plan for Smaller and Medium-sized Enterprises*, CIMA Publishing/Finance Wales, available on www.cimaglobal.com

Drickhamer, D. (2004) 'Calculating capital costs: supply chain planning', *Industry Week*, January, 253 i1: 51.

González-Benito, J. (2002) 'Effect of the characteristics of the purchased products in JIT purchasing implementation', *International Journal of Operations and Production Management*, 22(8): 868–86.

Hoque, A. (2000) 'Just-in-Time production, automation, cost allocation practices and importance of cost information: an empirical investigation in New Zealand-based manufacturing organizations', *British Accounting Review*, 32: 133–59.

Howorth, C. and Westhead, P. (2003) 'The focus of working capital management in UK small firms', *Management Accounting Research*, Vol. 14, pp. 94–111.

McCosker, P. (2000) 'The importance of working capital', *Management Accounting* (UK) 78(4): 58. (Note that the journal *Management Accounting* is now called *Financial Management*)

Schniederjans, M.J. and Cao, Q. (2001) 'An alternative analysis of inventory costs of JIT and EOQ purchasing', *International Journal of Physical Distribution and Logistics Management*, 31(2): 109–23.

Strischek, D. (2001) 'A banker's perspective on working capital and cash flow management', *Strategic Finance*, October: 38–45.

QUESTIONS

The Questions section of each chapter has three types of question. 'Test your understanding' questions to help you review your reading are in the 'A' series of questions. You will find the answer to these by reading and thinking about the material in the text book. 'Application' questions to test your ability to apply technical skills are in the 'B' series of questions. Questions requiring you to show skills in problem solving and evaluation are in the 'C' series of questions. The symbol [S] indicates that a solution is available at the end of the book.

A   Test your understanding

A18.1   Define working capital (section 18.1).

A18.2   Define current assets and give three examples (section 18.2).

A18.3   Define current liabilities and give three examples (section 18.3).

A18.4   Explain how the stockholding period is calculated (section 18.2.1).

A18.5   Explain how the debtors' collection period is calculated (section 18.2.2).

A18.6   Explain how the creditors' payment period is calculated (section 18.3.2).

A18.7   Explain what is meant by the accrual of liabilities (section 18.3.3).

A18.8   Describe the working capital cycle (section 18.4.1).

A18.9   Explain how the current ratio is calculated (section 18.4.2).

A18.10   Explain how the liquid ratio is calculated (section 18.4.2).

A18.11   Explain how the working capital cycle is calculated (section 18.4.3).

A18.12   Explain the meaning of over trading (section 18.4.4).

A18.13   What are the costs of holding inventory (section 18.5.1)?

A18.14 What are the costs of ordering inventory (section 18.5.1)?

A18.15 How is the economic order quantity calculated (section 18.5.2)?

A18.16 What is the just-in-time approach to purchasing inventory (section 18.5.3)?

A18.17 Describe the main contents of a business plan for presenting to a bank providing finance for a small business (section 18.6).

A18.18 What have researchers found about the frequency of review of working capital in small businesses (section 18.7.1)?

A18.19 What have researchers found about the length of the working capital cycle in practice (section 18.7.2)?

A18.20 What have researchers found about the idea that different types of business have different types of working capital (section 18.7.3)?

A18.21 What are bankers looking for when they evaluate working capital (section 18.7.4)?

A18.22 What kinds of organisation are likely to use JIT production (section 18.7.5)?

B   Application

B18.1 [S]

Company A is a wholesaler selling grocery goods to retail stores on credit. Company B is a manufacturing company selling its products to other manufacturers for use in their products.

	A £m	B £m
During year		
Sales	200	200
Cost of sales*	150	150
Gross profit	50	50
At end of year		
Inventory (stock)	12	24
Trade debtors	3	13
Trade creditors	11	11

*Assume cost of sales is equal to purchases, based on constant levels of inventory.

Required
(1) Calculate the working capital cycle for companies A and B.
(2) Comment on each answer.

B18.2

The following statement was made in the finance director's report of a company making retail sales:

> The increase in cash has resulted from improved trading, the benefits of a working capital reduction of £8m and a reduced level of capital expenditure in the period.

The cash flow statement showed the following information:

	£m
Decrease in inventories	3.0
Decrease in debtors	0.1
Increase in creditors	4.9

Required
Explain how the management improved the cash position by managing the working capital.

C   Problem solving and evaluation

C18.1

Dallas (UK) Ltd is a wholly owned subsidiary of a US parent and has been set up as a new manufacturing facility in the UK. The projected capital costs and sources of funds are as follows:

Costs
   Buildings: £1,500,000 paid at the start of year 1.
   Land: leased for 100 years for a single payment of £120,000
   Machinery: £500,000 initial payment at the start of year 1 and £50,000 per annum subsequently on the first day of each year.

Financing
   Share capital: £600,000
   Special area cash grant £520,000 spread evenly over four years.
   Long-term loan: £1,000,000 for eight years at 5% with capital repayments of one-quarter in each of the last four years at the end of the year.
   Medium-term loan: £500,000 for five years at 8% with repayments in equal instalments at the end of each year. The loan is received at the start of year 1.
   Overdraft facility: £1,400,000 (interest assumed constant at 9% on actual usage).

The following details are available from the profit forecasts prepared to support the new factory:

1

	Year 1 £	Year 2 £	Year 3 £	Year 4 £	Year 5 £
Turnover	2,500,000	2,800,000	6,500,000	9,000,000	12,500,000
Profit (see note 2)	(200,000)	–	150,000	400,000	1,000,000
Inventory, debtors *less* creditors	500,000	700,000	1,800,000	2,200,000	3,000,000
Manpower levels	100	180	400	480	600

2   Profit is defined as being stated after including depreciation and overdraft interest but before including loan interest, royalties, grants and taxation.
3   The company is eligible for machinery grants at 20% on cost, receivable in the year following expenditure.
4   The company is due to pay the parent 10% of profit, as defined in 2 above, by way of royalties. Payment is made in the year following the profit being earned.
5   The company calculates depreciation on a straight-line basis as follows:
   land – over the length of the lease
   buildings – 50 years
   plant – 10 years.

Notes:
Ignore taxation. No dividend is payable in the first five years.

Required
Prepare calculations to show whether the overdraft facility is adequate to finance the business over its first five years.

C18.2

AB Ltd manufactures units for drills. All units are identical. The following working capital requirements are budgeted:

	At end of Sept Year 6 £	At end of Oct Year 6 £	At end of Nov Year 6 £
Inventory (stock) of raw materials	15,000	17,500	16,000
Inventory (stock) of finished goods	24,000	16,800	18,800
Trade debtors	76,800	87,600	83,400
Cash balances	1,800	2,300	1,900
	117,600	124,200	120,100
Trade creditors for raw materials	(14,500)	(16,500)	(15,500)
Creditors for other expenses	(4,950)	(5,730)	(6,945)
	98,150	101,970	97,655

Budgeted profit and loss accounts are as follows:

	£	£	£	£	£	£
Sales		70,000		80,000		76,000
Manufactured cost of finished goods						
Raw materials	15,000		17,000		19,500	
Labour	9,000		10,200		11,700	
Production overheads	9,000		10,600		13,400	
Depreciation	3,000		3,000		3,000	
	36,000		40,800		47,600	
Adjustment for inventory of finished goods	6,000		7,200		(2,000)	
Cost of goods sold		42,000		48,000		45,600
Gross profit		28,000		32,000		30,400
Administration overheads	6,200		6,000		6,000	
Discounts allowed	800		2,000		1,600	
		7,000		8,000		7,600
Net profit		21,000		24,000		22,800

Notes:
1 Each month is assumed to consist of four working weeks.
2 Wages are paid one week in arrears.
3 70% of production overheads and 100% of administration overheads are paid for as they are incurred. The remaining expense is paid in the following month.

Required
1 Prepare a detailed cash budget for each of the months of October and November Year 6.
2 Reconcile the projected net profit of the months of October and November respectively with the surplus or deficit shown in the cash budget for each month.

C18.3

The purchasing manager of a manufacturing business knows that its total production requirement for raw materials will be 7,200 units per month. Each unit has a price of £10. The cost of holding stocks of raw materials is £3 per unit per month. The cost of ordering is £9 per order. The purchasing manager has asked for your advice on two situations facing the business.

Situation 1
The supplier has offered 1% discount on the price of each unit of raw material provided at least 100 units are ordered each time an order is placed.

Situation 2

It is expected that when the next order is placed, lead-time may vary due to transport difficulties. To cover this uncertainty it is proposed to hold a buffer stock for one month.

The amount ordered will be 60 units. Demand is linear with respect to time. Assume there are 30 days in a month.

The range of possible lead-times and the likelihood of occurrence of each are as follows:

Lead-time (days)	0	1	2	3	4	5	6
Probability	.06	.12	.18	.28	.18	.12	.06

The costs of holding stock are expected to remain at £3 per unit per month. The cost of running short of stock is estimated at £20 per unit per day.

(a) Show that, before considering Situation 1 or Situation 2, the economic order quantity is 60 units and state the assumptions of your calculation.

(b) In Situation 1:
  (i) Advise the purchasing manager on whether to accept the supplier's offer.
  (ii) Calculate the discount rate which would make the purchasing manager indifferent between ordering 60 units and ordering 100 units.

(c) In Situation 2:
  Establish the total cost of holding stock and of running short of stock for buffer levels of 60 units, 40 units, 20 units and zero units respectively, in each case held for one month.

Case studies

Real world cases

Prepare short answers to Case studies 18.1, 18.2 and 18.3.

Chapter 19

Business strategy and management accounting

Real world case 19.1

This case study shows a typical situation in which management accounting can be helpful. Read the case study now but only attempt the discussion points after you have finished studying the chapter.

This news item shows how strategic management is helped by surveys that evaluate relative competition.

Research and Markets (http://www.researchandmarkets.com/reports/c11963) has announced the addition of Chocolate Confectionery Industry Insights: Future Profit Opportunities And Growth Indicators to their offering.

Companies that fail to innovate, look ahead or anticipate customers' needs will not be successful in the current, competitive and highly saturated chocolate marketplace.

In general, NPD [new product development] is viewed as holding the most exceptional importance out of the seven main issues addressed in the survey, with 71% of the vote.

Chocolate Confectionery Industry Insights: Future profit opportunities and growth indicators is a **strategic management report** that analyses the chocolate market by sub-categories of 'boxed', 'Moulded bars', 'Seasonal', 'Countlines', 'Straightlines' and 'other' chocolate in each of the following countries: Belgium, Spain, Germany, France, Italy, Hungary, Poland, Czech Republic, United Kingdom and the United States.

The report analyses the chocolate confectionery market between 1998 and 2003 and forecasts the next generation of chocolate confectionery products to 2008 as manufacturers increase innovation levels. The report will enable you to increase your market share and turnover by identifying the sectors and countries that provide the best profit opportunities for your specific chocolate confectionery product.

Source: *Business Wire*, 21 February 2005, Research and Markets: Opportunities for New Chocolate Confectionery Products Examined, Research and Markets (www.researchandmarkets.com/reports/c11963).

Discussion points

1 Why is market share so important in strategic management for this industry?

2 How could any one company within the industry improve its profit performance compared to the others?

Contents

Learning outcomes

After studying this chapter you should be able to:

- Explain how strategic management accounting is a feature of business strategy.

- Explain the methods of managing costs with an aim of gaining competitive advantage.

- Explain value chain analysis and the role of management accounting.

- Explain the nature of activity-based management.

- Explain total quality management and the cost of quality.

- Explain business process re-engineering.

- Explain e-business and e-commerce and outline ways in which management accounting may help in developing business strategies that use e-business methods in general and e-commerce in particular.

19.1 Introduction

This chapter provides an initial exploration of the theme of business strategy and the role of management accounting. It is very much an outline of each topic but it may give you ideas for projects where you use library resources for deeper exploration. It also gives you a taste of subjects covered in greater depth in more advanced courses in management accounting. The theme that has flowed through all the chapters of this book is that management accounting is essentially focused on reading the signs and creating a successful business strategy. Simple strategic decisions are shown in the cases of Chapter 1. This chapter takes you into some more complex situations and techniques.

A **strategy** may be defined as 'an integrated set of actions aimed at securing a sustainable competitive advantage'.[1] Using this definition a strategy is something more than a long-term plan. It is a statement of how the business intends to reach some preferred state in the future by changing its competitive position to meet changing circumstances.

This chapter explains and illustrates some of the approaches that have been proposed to developing business strategy, where management accounting has a contributory role to play. You have already encountered activity-based costing (Chapter 4), and investment appraisal for advanced manufacturing technologies (Chapter 12), benchmarking (Chapter 16) and the Balanced Scorecard (Chapter 16), all of which are techniques developed to support strategic change. They have become an established part of the management accountant's contribution to ensuring that a business stays vigilant to competitive forces.

19.2 Strategic management accounting

The successful management of a business depends on having a successful business strategy. It has been argued that if the business strategy gives the organisation its competitive edge, then the management accounting should reflect that strategy as closely as possible. The traditional emphasis on costs and revenues may not achieve this aim. What really matters is the influence of the external environment.

19.2.1 Competitive position

Strategy usually includes planning to achieve a better performance than competitors. It is argued that management accounting should show the extent to which the organisation is beating its competitors. Market share, market prospects and the impact of product mix would all be useful information to include in a management accounting report as factors contributing to sales, profits and cash flows.

Another way of looking at the influence of the external environment is to consider competitive advantage in costs. If the business has an influential position as a purchaser of goods and services, then its strategy may include an aggressive policy of negotiating contracts for those goods and services. The just-in-time strategy of ordering goods from suppliers to arrive exactly when they are needed may put strains on the suppliers and force up their costs, increasing the price of the goods. The concept of a value chain has been proposed to describe how the corporate strategy affects the entire chain of value-creating activities. **Strategic management accounting** might show that £1 saved at one point in the chain has been offset by an extra £2 incurred at another stage.

Advocates of strategic management accounting seek to provide financial and other related information on competitors' costs and cost structures so that the company's strategies may be monitored against those of its competitors over a period of time. Furthermore there is a need for new forms of internal analysis and accounting processes that will help management devise better strategies. There is strong support for this general direction of strategic management accounting but less agreement on how it may be achieved.

It is not necessary to abandon all that has been learned in the earlier chapters of this textbook. Advocates of strategic management accounting would relate the accounting technique to the strategic aims of the business. Take the example of two companies, one of which is aiming to achieve cost leadership (carrying out activities in a more cost-effective manner than competitors) while the other is focusing on product differentiation (persuading customers that there is a unique aspect of the company's products). The use of standard costing in assessing performance is very important to the cost leadership company but relatively unimportant to the product differentiation company. Analysis of marketing costs may not be so important in a cost leadership setting, but is absolutely essential to the product differentiation situation.

You have already seen the Balanced Scorecard approach which requires an organisation to translate its vision and strategy into four perspectives: financial focus, customer focus, internal business processes and learning and growth. Companies are encouraged to develop performance indicators under each of these headings which provide a complete view of the company's performance.

19.2.2 Case study

Fiona McTaggart describes her experience of a situation where a strategic approach helped a business to achieve improved performance.

FIONA: *One of my clients was a telephone utility company. It was in a competitive market where the customer base was growing fast. Costs had been reduced to the limit and competition focused on delivering a good quality of service to the customer.*

The first action taken by management was to change the attitude of employees, moving away from an organisation based on functions and towards an organisation based on process. As an example, the sales ledger department was disbanded. Some of the staff joined a customer enquiry unit which allowed one point of contact for matters ranging from sales orders through repairs to accounts enquiries. Others moved to the information technology unit which concentrated on providing information within the organisation. This move recognised internal 'customers' as well as external customers.

The next move was to invest in a training programme to encourage customer focus. Staff joining the customer enquiry unit were all trained in customer focus but were also made aware of the way in which their activities drive the costs of the organisation. Their training included a course provided by benchmarking experts who had information about the standards achieved by leading competitors. The company was quite surprised to find how much other companies will share through benchmarking.

You might be thinking that this does not sound much like management accounting, but the focus on activities driving costs led to a rearrangement of management accounting information to use cost drivers and activity-based costing. That approach was used to evaluate type of customer, geographical area of sales and types of product promotion.

The result was continued growth in sales and profit for the company and an expansion in employment opportunities for staff.

19.2.3 What the researchers have found

Roslender and Hart (2003) pointed out that after many years of discussion in the academic and professional literature there was still no real agreement on precisely what constitutes strategic management accounting. They traced the various strands of thought on strategic management accounting and, in particular, identified links with strategic marketing. They reported a field study of company practices based on 10 companies that could be regarded as leading edge companies in their respective industries. The companies were asked about the ways in which they linked management accounting and marketing functions.

In what was labelled as a 'traditional' approach the management accounting function was based on a budgetary control system. Marketing managers accepted such controls on their activities as being in the best interests of the business and part of responsibility accounting.

In a transitional approach the management accounting and marketing functions worked together to explore a wider range of management accounting practices within a framework of budgetary control and responsibility accounting. Activity-based costing, customer profitability analysis and direct product profitability were observed, along with attribute costing, strategic cost analysis and target costing. Each of the parties was bringing a wider range of techniques from their respective disciplines. The techniques described under the label of 'strategic management accounting' were observed.

The greatest extreme from the traditional approach was seen in what the authors described as synergistic relationships where the management accountants and the marketing managers abandoned the traditions of their respective disciplines to construct what could be described as strategic marketing management accounting. In particular brand management appeared to be important. The authors concluded that these synergistic relationships had moved beyond the techniques that were usually associated with strategic management accounting.

Activity 19.1

Use the specialist searches available through your college library or information service to find two recent articles or research papers covering 'strategic management accounting'. Write a 50-word summary of each, explaining the main purposes and findings.

19.3 Costing for competitive advantage

This section continues the theme of strategic management accounting by explaining some of the costing techniques that have been proposed for gaining a competitive advantage in cost control. Although the techniques are described separately, in practice they are interrelated as explained by Cooper and Slagmulder (2003). They explain how costs can be reduced by links between customer and supplier as well as cost initiatives within the organisation.

19.3.1 Target costing and product profitability

In a competitive market a business may have little influence on the selling price of a product. What the business can do is control its costs more effectively than its competitors, in order to achieve higher profits. The business decides on the profit it needs to achieve from the product, deducts this amount from the selling price, and arrives at a target cost. The target cost is the highest cost that can be incurred if the desired profit is to be achieved.

Target costs can be set at the design stage so that the product profitability can be evaluated before full production begins. The products of competitors may be analysed to work out how they keep costs under control.

Activity 19.2

Use the specialist searches available through your college library or information service to find two recent articles or research papers covering 'target costing'. From the papers write down one benefit and one potential criticism or question about target costing.

What the researchers have found

Everaert and Bruggeman (2002) investigated the impact of cost targets during new product development. They used a laboratory-based research method involving 64 undergraduate students in business administration. The students were asked to design an attractive carpet for a given interior. Some students were given a cost target, while others had no target. Some were given a tight time constraint, while others had more time. This gave four combinations of cost target and time constraint. Complexity of design and use of colours increased the cost, so that there was a trade off between design quality and cost. A team of judges decided the best designs. There was a modest financial reward for those completing the task within a specified time period and another modest reward for the lowest cost designers who satisfied the judges. The experiment showed that the cost target prevented designers from experimenting, while the time constraint took precedence over cost concerns. The conclusion was that target costing is only effective where designers have sufficient time to explore alternatives.

Such laboratory-based studies suffer from the lack of reality and the limitations of using students for the experiment, but they have value in being able to control the conditions and achieve comparability.

Lin *et al* (2005) reported on China's use of target costing integrated with an incentive compensation (salary) system. The case study describes the change to target costing in an iron and steel company in 1991, and the subsequent use of target costing in the 1990s. The company achieved significant cost reductions in the period 1991–95 and says that if this had not been achieved it would have been facing bankruptcy. The incentives took the form of a 'veto' system – if the subsidiary did not meet the cost targets then the bonus was denied and so were promotions. The authors concluded that the business focused on cost reduction more than on customer satisfaction but this reflected the economic situation of the time.

19.3.2 Customer profitability analysis

Customer profitability analysis focuses on the revenues and costs associated with particular customers or groups of customers. Chapter 4 showed how activity-based costing (ABC) can be used to identify cost drivers. Customers may be one of the cost drivers. Customer profitability analysis calculates the contribution from each customer category. The factors that might differ across customer groups will include:

- geographic location
- size of customer order
- purchasing patterns and preferences of customers
- outlets (retail, direct sales).

19.3.3 Life-cycle costing

A product starts to incur costs long before it comes to the market. The life cycle of a product consists of the entire story from the initial ideas about the product to the end of its life. The early stages are particularly important because a relatively large proportion of the total cost of a product is incurred in the development stage.

When a new product is planned a life-cycle budget should be prepared. The life-cycle costs that would be contained in this budget include:

- Development costs (research and testing)
- Design costs (making the product acceptable to the market)
- Manufacturing costs
- Marketing costs
- Distribution costs.

These costs become particularly important where the product life cycle is relatively short and all these costs have to be recovered within a short time period. Those managing the business need to be sure that the sales revenue earned over the projected life of the product will cover the start-up costs as well as the manufacturing or service costs.

What the researchers have found

Dunk (2004) noted that life-cycle costing attracts attention in the literature, because of the shorter life cycles of many products. However, relatively little evidence was available about the use of life-cycle costing in practice. He tested the hypothesis that customer profiling, competitive advantage and the quality of information systems information would all have a positive influence on the use of product life cycle analysis. Customer profiling means that a business gives careful attention to the needs of its customers and how these can be incorporated in product design. Competitive advantage means that a company is using techniques such as fast delivery, flexibility of manufacturing in responding to changes in volume, and control of inventory. The quality of the information system relates to the speed at which businesses can react to such information.

The results of surveying 119 managers in manufacturing companies in Australia was to find relatively little evidence of the use of life-cycle cost analysis. To the extent that it did exist, the positive relationships expected were observed. One possible barrier to life-cycle costing is that the bookkeeping system is not designed to bring out this information.

Moussatche and Languell (2001) used life-cycle costing to compare the costs of different types of flooring materials in schools. They found that the materials ranked as most economical by LCC analysis were not necessarily those with the lowest capital cost. So a policy which selected lower cost materials at the point of installation did not lead to the lowest life-cycle cost. Because of the low initial cost the education authorities chose to replace rather than maintain floor coverings. This appeared to give a cost saving year-on-year but it led to a higher life-cycle cost.

19.3.4 Kaizen costing

Kaizen costing is a technique taken from Japanese management practices. It means making improvements by frequent small amounts rather than having major changes at longer intervals. The aim in kaizen costing is to reduce variable costs below the cost level in the base period. It is based on the view that nothing is ever perfect so there will always be some way of making a small improvement. It is part of the culture of the organisation that all employees are encouraged to identify and implement small improvements that reduce costs.

Activity 19.3

Use the specialist searches available through your college library or information service to find two recent articles or research papers covering 'kaizen costing'. From the papers write down one benefit of kaizen costing and one reason for it not being used in all businesses.

What the researchers have found

Modarress *et al* (2005) reported a case study on the use of kaizen costing to develop measures of costing that were suited to lean production systems. They collected information from the Boeing aeroplane manufacturing company in relation to its Interiors Responsibility Center Division. The article describes the implementation of target costing based on a kaizen approach.

19.3.5   Lean accounting

Lean manufacturing involves slimming down and eliminating any unnecessary procedure or resource. The aim is to find the essential resources and essential procedures and use only these. Waste in production has to be identified and eliminated.

What the researchers have found

Nelson (2004) describes how the Delphi Corporation in the USA applied lean manufacturing to its Global Supply Management. Nine strategies were applied and these are presented in the paper by a diagram of cogs in a machine where all the cogs turn at the same time. The company was formed from the parts-making operations of General Motors, the US car manufacturer. It now supplies mobile electronics, transportation components and systems technology around the world. The Delphi manufacturing system aimed at eliminating waste and improving production by employee involvement, workplace organisation, focus on quality, minimising non-productive time, using just-in-time delivery of materials and responding rapidly to customer demand. The Global Supply initiative extended the ideas from the manufacturing system. The nine 'gears' could be summarised as covering strategic sourcing, cost management and supplier development engineering. Previously, Delphi had negotiated continuous price reductions with suppliers, but that only gave marginal savings. The new approach identified strategic suppliers who would work closely with Delphi in new methods of supplying high quality materials. The company helped the suppliers to become more competitive compared to other suppliers.

19.3.6   Value chain analysis

The idea of the value chain was popularised by Porter (1985) as a way of describing and analysing the sequence of activities that bring a product or service from its initial stage of production to the final stage of delivery to the customer.

In a competitive environment the business manager should ask: 'What is our competitive advantage; what do we do well?' That requires questions about competition – where are the threats? There could be new entrants seeking to join the sector; there could be substitute products or services. There may be strong rivalry within the industry or there may be little interest in competing. Suppliers may have a strong bargaining position; customers may have a strong bargaining position. The manager considers the kind of competition that exists and then plans to deal with that position. Perhaps this business can reduce costs below those of competitors; perhaps it can find a way of differentiating its product to make it attractive to consumers. Porter took the view that a business should choose either a cost focus or a differentiation focus, rather than try to do too much at the same time.

The value chain for any business is a description of the key processes, starting with inputs. Take the example of a plant nursery which grows plants from seedlings and sells them to customers in a garden centre. The managers have identified the competitive advantage as their reputation for growing plants that are hardy to the climate of this region. The value chain is shown in Exhibit 19.1.

Exhibit 19.1
Value chain for nursery and garden centre

Seed selection → Growing seedlings →
Transfer to retail outlet → Advice desk → Sale to customer

Each stage of the value chain adds value for the business. It is focused on product differentiation. The price may be marginally higher than the prices that would be charged by national chains selling plants as part of home improvement stores, but the customer is less likely to find the plant has wilted and died within weeks of planting. Advice is given to any enquirers coming into the garden centre, and the advice is based on local knowledge.

Fiona McTaggart has been advising the business on the steps required for value chain analysis. She explains here how she worked with management.

FIONA: *First we identified the value chain and assigned costs and assets to each stage. Seed selection involves labour cost and storage for seeds taken from the nursery's own plants. The nursery also buys in new varieties to strengthen the existing strains. Growing seedlings involves further labour cost, greenhouse maintenance, security and plant care materials. There is also a wastage rate to be built in. Transfer to the retail outlet involves transport costs and a risk of loss through inadequate handling. The advice desk is a heavy labour cost specific to this business. The retail sales outlet carries costs similar to those of any retail operation.*

Next we considered the cost drivers of each value activity and the interaction of cost drivers. Then we considered the value chains of competitors who can undercut the business on price, but compete less well on product durability. We worked out the relative costs and looked at ways for this business to cut its costs. For example, transferring plants to the garden centre on a just-in-time basis would reduce wastage but requires customer surveys to know when the peaks of demand will arise. We were able to identify some areas for cost control that would enable the business to remain competitive on price without eroding the product differentiation. The managers are pleased that they have this approach to focusing on how they add value at each stage of the chain.

Real world case 19.2

Supply chain analysis is part of value chain analysis. This news item indicates the types of businesses that feel they need to know more about their supply chains.

Six leading consumer products companies have joined forces to conduct an in-depth review of the supply chain best practices and metrics of the world's leading consumer products companies. Campbell Soup Company, Coca-Cola, Coors, Hallmark, Whirlpool, and Polo Ralph Lauren Corporation have formed the Advisory Board for the Consumer Products Supply Chain Best Practices Review.

Focused on **supply chain processes**, the Advisory Board will define the specific processes and metrics to be surveyed and will oversee the collection and analysis of responses from participating companies through a web-based interview tool. The data analyzed will be presented to participants in a series of reports and review meetings that will provide very specific insights into the current and best practices of consumer products companies within various industry sub-categories.

Source: *Business Wire*, 15 March 2005, 'Top Consumer Products Companies Form Board to Review Supply Chain Best Practices'.

Discussion points

1 What kinds of costs might be involved in the supply chains of each of these businesses?

2 How could businesses of this type 'add value' by improving the supply chain?

19.4 Activity-based management[2]

19.4.1 Meaning of ABM

Chapter 4 explains the use of activity-based costing (ABC) in establishing the cost of activities by identifying the factors driving the cost of each activity.

ABC is a technique for reporting costs but it does not of itself encourage management to make strategic plans and decisions. Activity-based management (ABM) makes the cost information useful to management by providing cost drivers and performance measures that initiate or support decision making, and supports business planning by providing information to help management in taking long-term strategic decisions. One example might be the decision to sell goods on mail order rather than deliver to shops in town centres. Another example might be the decision to use five different suppliers in different locations rather than one central supplier. These are decisions that require a wide range of considerations but the cost of the activity is one of those considerations. ABM could help with product design by analysing the costs of different approaches to the production process.

ABM encourages continuous improvement by allowing managers to consider the strategic impact of activities and to plan the incentives that will encourage operational teams to implement the desired strategy. A system of ABM would produce the following output in relation to any potential management decision:

- Information on the cost of activities and business processes
- The cost of activities that do not add value, such as wastage
- Performance measures based on activities, such as a scorecard
- Projected costs of products and services
- Cost drivers.

Definition

> **Activity-based management** is a system of management which uses activity-based cost information to support and improve decision making. Examples are: cost reduction, cost modelling and customer profitability analysis.[3]

19.4.2 A hierarchy of costs

Activity-based management can be used by managers in identifying the scope for cost reduction. One approach is to consider a 'hierarchy', which means thinking about the structure of costs at different levels, starting at the level of the units of output and moving up the organisation to the level of the entire service or production facility. For each level of costs the manager asks: 'What drives costs?' Then the manager asks 'How efficient is this activity and can we manage these costs more effectively?'

Take the example of a company which manufactures children's clothing. An illustration of a hierarchy of costs and an assessment of efficiency is set out in Exhibit 19.2.

The organisation migh have guidelines such as:

- A potential cost saving of 50% or more indicates an activity that should not continue in its present form – there is a highly likely opportunity for improving the activity.
- A potential cost saving of 25% to 50% is a major opportunity for improvement.
- A potential cost saving of 15% to 25% is a good opportunity for improvement.
- A potential cost saving of 5% to 15% is relatively modest with opportunities for marginal improvement.
- A potential cost saving of 5% or less indicates that the activity is already efficient.

Exhibit 19.2
Hierarchy of costs: drivers and assessment

Basis of cost	Drivers	Management assessment
Unit level	The costs of each unit are driven by the volume of output, e.g. variable costs of materials and labour.	Our materials are imported at the lowest prices available in the market. Any management of costs will lie in greater efficiency of labour but potential savings are probably 6% at most.
Batch level	We sell output in batches to major stores. Each batch carries costs of administration, packing and despatch.	We could reduce batch costs if we could concentrate on fewer customers with larger orders, but that would carry greater commercial risk for at most a 3% cost saving.
Process level	Our process costs consist of supervision and quality controls. At present these costs are largely driven by time and are relatively insensitive to volume of output.	One of the supervisors is reaching retirement age. If we did not replace that person we could save 30% on process costs. It would involve redefining the supervision process and an assessment of the potential risks.
Product level	We have forty product lines, each with its own costs of design, administration and sales negotiation. Costs are therefore driven by the number of product lines.	If we reduced the current forty product lines to thirty, we could save around 20% on product level costs.
Facility level	The production currently takes place in two locations, 20 miles apart. Each has costs of rent, business rates, maintenance and general management.	We could reduce facility operating costs by 40% if we moved all production to one site and enlarged that operation. The cash raised from selling the second site could be invested in upgrading the other facilities.

19.4.3 Customer-driven costs

Customers are essential to an entity because they provide sales revenue, but there are also costs associated with gaining and retaining customers. If the drivers of customer-related costs are understood then the costs can be managed more effectively. Drivers of customer costs are:

- *Location of customers*: The distance and geographical spread of customers drives the cost of making contact, communication and delivering to customers.
- *Supply and delivery costs*: If customers order small amounts of product frequently then there will be higher costs associated with taking orders, making up delivery packages and arranging delivery.
- *Sales and promotion costs (including discounts and other incentives)*: These will be higher if there are more potential customers or new potential markets for products. These costs will be lower if the business relies largely on established customers making repeat orders.

- *Quality costs*: Some customers may specify standards of quality that cause additonal costs to be incurred. If the quality is not sufficiently high the customers may be lost.
- *After-sales service or warranty costs*: Customers may have paid additional fees for after-sales service or repairs under warranty but it is still important to control costs within that amount in order to avoid losses while offering a competitive service.

If the managers of a business understand customer-driven costs they can make strategic decisions about the relative costs of different types of marketing initiatives. One strategy might be to find a small number of high-value customers and invest effort in customer retention and loyalty. An alternative strategy might be to target larger numbers of smaller-value customers and accept a higher rate of customer replacement. Each strategy drives customer-related costs in a different way.

19.4.4 What the researchers have found

A Technical Briefing published by the Chartered Institute of Management Accountants (CIMA 2001) summarises the activity-based management model as described by Miller (1996). It explains that ABM has grown out of the work of the Texas-based Consortium for Advanced Manufacturing-International (CAM-I). ABM thinking is not confined to manufacturing businesses because activity-based thinking can equally well apply to service businesses and not-for-profit organisations. The Technical Briefing provides a summary of the circumstances that make ABM useful. It explains that ABC becomes ABM when it is used to:

- Design products and services that meet or exceed customers' expectations, while making a profit.
- Indicate that improvements in quality, efficiency and speed are needed.
- Guide decisions on product mix or investment.
- Choose among alternative suppliers.
- Choose methods of targeting markets and customers, and of providing delivery or service to customers.
- Improving the value of the organisation's products or services.

Soin *et al* (2002)[4] reported a case study observing the implementation of ABC in a clearing bank at the same time that other organisational changes were taking place. They found that the ABC team were able to implement a form of ABC that revealed new links between costs and products, but they were not able to go so far as to transform the strategic thinking of the bank's senior management. The researchers analysed the reasons for this apparent failure to turn ABC into ABM. They found that the ABC system was not totally integrated with other management accounting systems and so there was no exploitation of the strategic potential of ABM. Managerial conservatism and a desire to maintain the previous level of managerial discretion led to behaviour which restricted institutional change. There was also a lack of understanding of the value of the additional ABC information. The researchers used the idea of 'regressive versus progressive change' as proposed by Burns and Scapens (2000). Progressive (forward-looking) change was seen in the implementation of ABC, but regressive change (backward-looking pressures) was seen in the failure of management to take strategic benefit from the ABC information.

Searcy (2004) described a case study of a company in the employment services industry. The company was acting as an agency supplying employees to a range of customers. Some customers made very frequent demands for temporary staff covering very short-term placements. Other customers made less frequent demands for staff to cover longer-term placements. ABC costing was used to identify the profitability of the different types of customer and also to assess the four largest customers. From the ABC analysis some management issues were identified for discussion with the customers to achieve more cost-effective ways of requesting temporary agency staff.

Major and Hopper (2005) reported a case study of implementing ABC in a Portuguese telecommunications company. It was problematic because employees provided inaccurate data, production personnel thought it might cause them to lose their jobs and production engineers were sceptical about the usefulness of ABC. Senior managers were enthusiastic. The authors proposed that studies of implementation of ABC should include issues relating to labour processes, consent and resistance.

19.5 Total quality management and cost of quality

The success of Japanese companies in recent years has caused intense interest in Japanese styles of management. One aspect of Japanese management is the approach of 'get it right first time'. In this spirit, **total quality management (TQM)** has the customer as its focal point.

Quality is defined as fully satisfying agreed customer requirements at the lowest internal price. TQM is therefore a management function which could be added to those explained in Chapter 1. It straddles the traditional management functions of planning and control. The use of the TQM approach is seen as the key to improving profitability because there is a cost associated with failing to meet quality standards in products and services. Such costs could arise through loss of customers, claims for refunds in respect of defective supplies, and the work of putting right mistakes. If costs can be controlled through TQM, then profits will increase.

Those who are enthusiastic for TQM believe that it is possible to obtain defect-free work first time on a consistent basis. That may be an idealistic target, but to have such a target in the first place encourages a culture where prevention of error is a key feature of the operations.

This activity of improving quality to improve profits will itself cause cost to be incurred. The term **cost of quality** is a collective name for all costs incurred in achieving a quality product or service.

Cost of quality may be defined by the 'prevention-appraisal-failure' model. *Prevention costs* are the costs of designing, implementing and maintaining the TQM system. They include: quality planning, quality assurance, training and determining specifications for incoming materials, for processes carried out in the operations of the business and for finished products. *Appraisal costs* are the costs of evaluating suppliers and obtaining an evaluation by customers. They include checking incoming materials and supplies, inspecting equipment and collecting information from customers on satisfaction with goods and services. *Failure costs* are of two main types: *internal failure costs* are the costs incurred when it is found, before delivery to customers, that the work does not reach the desired specification; *external failure costs* are the costs incurred when poor quality work is discovered after the supply to the customer has taken place. Examples of internal failure costs are: waste, scrap, rectification, re-inspection of rectified work and analysis of the causes of failure. External failure costs include: repairs, warranty claims, complaints, returns, product liability litigation and loss of customer goodwill.

The traditional picture of quality control is that in the absence of quality control, failures occur which create *failure costs*. Detection of failure relies on checking after the failure has occurred. The checking process involves further *checking costs*. With quality controls in place, as prevention work is undertaken, the costs of failure should begin to fall. At the outset, the prevention costs will be additional to the costs of checking for failures, but as confidence grows, and the frequency of failure decreases, the need for checking should diminish. The quality exercise will be successful in cost terms if there is a reduction in total cost over the three headings of prevention, appraisal and failure costs.

TQM ideas are widely practised and there are many non-financial performance measures being used in business organisations. Measuring the cost of quality is a relatively undeveloped area although a few businesses have a well-developed approach. The management accountant as scorekeeper is ideally placed to record and monitor cost of quality, but many of the initiatives emerging are in special units within an organisation which are separate from the 'traditional' management accounting functions. Management accountants may need to be proactive in seeking out new ways of applying their generic skills.

Real world case 19.3

ACT Doorland was founded in 1957 as a small concern whose core business was the supply and installation of garage doors. Since then it has diversified its interests and expanded to become Canberra's largest speciality door company.

ACT Doorland is currently involved with the supply, service and installation of: Domestic garage doors and operators; Commercial and industrial roller shutters, grilles and operators; Sliding and swing boom gates and operators; External and internal household doors; Automatic glass sliding doors; Door hardware; Carport conversions; Car park entry systems; and Operable, flexible and concertina doors.

Through a commitment to total quality management and first class performance, ACT Doorland has empowered its team members to take whatever steps are necessary to guarantee outstanding service and customer satisfaction.

Source: *Canberra Times*, 6 March 2005, 'Opening the doors to success'.

Discussion points

1 What would you expect to see in a system of total quality management for a company producing special types of door?

2 What kinds of cost might be found in the 'cost of quality' for this company?

19.6 Business process re-engineering

Business process re-engineering involves a dramatic re-design of business processes, organisation structures and use of technology to achieve breakthroughs in business competitiveness. The benefits claimed are that operations can be streamlined, and consequently costs can be cut, while creating process excellence in all key aspects of the organisation.

The phrase 'breaking the china' has been used by those who describe the technique. They are looking for a quantum leap into being a world leader. They draw the analogy of passing a treasured set of family china from one generation to the next. One day the entire collection falls to the floor in pieces. Putting it together again produces a totally different pattern in the china. In a similar way, if the whole business process is broken up and then restructured with the aim of being a world leader, an entirely new policy will emerge.

The advocates of business process re-engineering explain that, while concentrating on MRP, MRP II, TQM and JIT (*see* section 12.5), businesses were retaining the traditional ways of working in functional groups. Quality teams were given the task of creating new ways of working within their specific areas or functions. In contrast, business process re-engineering concentrates on the process rather than the function.

Take an example of a company manufacturing engines for heavy goods vehicles. The castings provided by the supplier did not align exactly with the machine which carried them to the assembly line. This had always been accepted as a function of the business operation despite the fact that it caused a pause in production at regular intervals to allow maintenance work necessitated by wear and tear. As a re-engineering of the business process, the supplier was asked to manufacture the castings to a different specification which would align with the machine. This allowed the process to speed up by 30 per cent on previous activity levels and quickly recovered the extra costs charged by the supplier due to the redesign of the castings.

Take as a second example the processing of customer orders. Using the traditional approach, a sales representative visited the customer and took an order. The sales representative initiated the order documentation, giving it an order number and setting up a file on the computer. The product manager received the order, checked that the resources were available for implementation and rewrote the order so that the customer's description of what was required could be specified in terms of the operations carried out by the business. The customer's credit rating was checked by the credit controller. This process all took a considerable amount of time because it was not well co-ordinated and there were gaps of time between the stages. As a re-engineering move, the business process was shortened by giving the sales representative a portable computer and a modem to be taken out on visits to clients. This allowed credit rating to be checked on-line, even while the job specification was being discussed with the customer. The computer also included a data sheet on which the sales representative could enter the customer's order in such a way as to match the specification required by the production department. The information passed directly to the manufacturing premises by way of the modem and the confirmed specification was returned by fax to the customer. The entire operation of specifying and confirming the order could be completed within one hour, while the sales representative was still on hand at the customer's premises.

The advocates of business process re-engineering emphasise three goals: customer satisfaction, market domination and increased profitability. To win the claim to be a world leader requires success in all three. The business therefore has to identify the core business processes which drive it and to think in terms of process enhancement. Identifying the core business process and 'reading the market' helps the company to find a 'break point' where a change in the business process can cause a significant positive reaction in the market and take the company into a leadership position.

For some business, re-engineering may be too drastic, especially when new products are being introduced. Continuous quality improvement may be a more achievable target, where analysis of strengths and weaknesses is used to identify short-term achievable improvements on an incremental basis.

19.7 E-business and e-commerce

This section gives a very brief summary of some aspects of **e-business** and shows how management accounting has a role to play. You can learn more about e-business by using the 'Further reading' listed at the end of the chapter.

Electronic business, usually described as '**e-business**', uses technology to automate and to change existing business practices. It affects product development, marketing, sales and the ways in which goods and services are delivered to customers.

Electronic commerce, usually described as '**e-commerce**', is one part of e-business. It relates to all transactions between the company and its customers or suppliers, where electronic media are involved. The customer may wish to inspect a catalogue advertising products. The supplier may wish to draw the company's attention to changes in prices or products. The acts of buying and selling may take place electronically. E-commerce involves aspects of sharing business information about products and services, together with carrying out business transactions.

The theme throughout this book has been that management accounting has a role in:

- planning
- decision making
- control.

Now we consider each aspect of the role of management accounting in e-business and e-commerce.

Activity 19.4   *Write down two benefits of e-business and two possible problems of applying accounting controls to e-business.*

19.7.1   Planning

The first question that might be asked is: 'Should we start an e-business venture?' The entrepreneur may have a vision of a new product or a new market but for any business the key accounting-related questions are: 'Can we make a profit?' and 'Will there be adequate cash flow?'

Revenue and cash inflow

There are examples of e-commerce where businesses sell existing products or services over the internet rather than through shops and offices or by postal mail. From the management accounting point of view there are new challenges in ensuring that the recording of revenue matches the delivery of goods and services. New control procedures must be devised, with particular attention to the security of electronic data and cash transmission. The accounting records for revenue earned and cash received will be broadly similar to those used in any business. Cash flow may speed up if customers make electronic payment ahead of delivery. Revenue may be lost if the internet-based system is difficult to use, or is not available throughout the day.

Greater challenges arise for management accounting where new forms of revenue are earned by a company through the nature of e-business. These may be described generally as 'digital services'. Examples include:

- selling banner advertising space on the company's website;
- earning commission on sales of goods by other business that have a hyperlink from the company's website;
- fees charged for allowing another business to have a 'shop-front' on the company's website.

These create accounting problems where two businesses 'swap' advertising space. 'I will let you advertise on my website if you will let me advertise on yours.' No cash changes hands but each business is gaining a benefit. This is called 'barter', a system of trading which starts in the school playground and extends around the world in places where cash is not readily available. Clearly there is no cash flow. Should each business estimate 'revenue' earned from the sale of advertising? There are costs in creating the advertisements so it seems a reasonable idea to estimate a figure for revenue. However, there is no transaction for the sale of advertising and it is far from clear that the advertiser would actually pay a fee if asked. If that is the case then the estimated value of revenue is zero. There are no easy answers on how to record the value gained from barter transactions.

Costs and cash outflow

For the business selling products and services electronically there remain the costs of producing the product or service. Beyond that, the e-business approach may reduce some costs and increase or create others. The costs that involve cash outflows may be subdivided into (a) set-up costs and (b) operating costs. The role of management accounting in planning is to estimate these costs for comparison with expected revenues.

Set-up costs include the costs of hardware and software, including internal networks and external links to suppliers and customers. The set-up costs also include the costs of managing the introduction of the project, developing and testing software, transferring data from the conventional business records to the new electronic system and training staff in using the new technology.

Operating costs include all staff costs relating to operating the new system, plus maintenance costs for the electronic system.

Cost savings may be set against these new operating costs. The business may be able to reduce the costs of staffing branch outlets, or having more staff time available to deal with problematic incoming telephone enquiries because the routine enquiries are dealt with through the website.

19.7.2 Decision making

Chapter 11 has explained various approaches to decision making related to long-term investments. Payback, accounting rate of return, discounted cash flow and internal rate of return have been explained and the calculations illustrated. At the end of Chapter 12 the problems of appraising advanced manufacturing technologies were discussed. They require a different approach to investment appraisal and decision making. E-business offers similar challenges to management accounting for investment appraisal.

Typical questions that might be asked in an e-business decision are:

- Should we make the proposed investment in hardware, software and staff training for information systems to support e-commerce?
- Which of our existing business operations will give the highest return if converted to e-commerce methods?

The difficult task for the management accountant is to identify the incremental cash flows. The questions to be asked are: How much additional revenue can be generated by this new way of working? How much additional cost will be incurred after taking into consideration any planned cost saving? The uncertainties relating to e-business and e-commerce are such that discounted cash flow techniques may be of limited relevance. Payback focuses on how quickly the original outlay can be recovered through cash flows generated.

19.7.3 Control

Management accounting helps managers in their control activities through comparing actual costs and revenues with budgeted estimates and through quantifying and highlighting variances. The management accountant is also involved in systems design and the processing controls necessary to protect the assets and the accuracy of accounting records. Non-financial performance measures are a significant element of controlling the e-business activity.

The business receiving cash from e-commerce transactions must have adequate security measures in place. Secure connections are necessary to set up secure links between supplier and customer. Encryption (a coded message) is used for information that is being transferred and for the records held at either end of the link. The customer must be given confidence in the security controls of the supplier. The supplier must be sure that the customer has a good reputation and that the transaction will be honoured.

Data migration is one important aspect of moving to e-commerce where the management accountant may have a particularly useful role. Data migration means transferring data from the existing system to the new system. Sometimes this activity is called *populating the database*. Whatever it is called, the activity requires careful control and testing to ensure that no data are lost or corrupted in the process.

Indicators of success that evaluate the relative effectiveness of an e-business activity must include a mixture of financial and non-financial measures (sometimes called *metrics*). Two questions to be asked about effectiveness might be:

1 Is the marketing effective?
2 Is the business outcome effective?

Effective marketing requires attracting the attention of the potential customer. *Visitor activity* on the site can be measured by *hits* or by *site visits*. A 'hit' is recorded every time a piece of information is downloaded, so one visit to the site might result in several hits. Intending customers may be asked to register an e-mail address or to give information about themselves. This is all part of the marketing information that will be analysed by the organisation to reflect activity.

Effective business outcomes are assessed using accounting information on revenues and costs. The business might set a target proportion of revenues to be achieved by internet selling. The management accountant will report on achievement of the target. Analysts often enquire about marketing costs because these are effectively an investment for the future. The ratio of marketing costs to revenues for internet business might be compared with the ratio for conventional business.

Non-financial indicators of effective business outcomes might include customer satisfaction surveys, delivery response times, complaints received or frequency of errors in delivery and invoicing.

19.7.4   Advising small businesses

Fiona has found that her work advising small and medium-sized enterprises (SMEs) is requiring her to develop an expertise in e-business and e-commerce.

FIONA: *I read a survey recently which found that most British SMEs prefer to maintain their own website and run their own e-business. That means they have to cover the cost of designing the website and they pay an in-house webperson to maintain it, involving a salary and other costs of employment. More than 80 per cent of UK businesses have a website. Some 500,000 companies are trading online but many more companies, including most of the 1.9m SMEs, use the internet as a shop window. Many UK companies are saying that the internet has transformed sales and marketing, delivery, operations and processing.*

However, it seems to me, as a management accountant, that cost planning and control do not appear to rank highly in the decision to move to e-business activity. There is perhaps too strong a focus on revenue and lack of attention to costs and cash flow. As a result we have seen the failure of some 'dot.com' businesses where the cash resources have become exhausted. Another survey that I came across found there was little emphasis on budgets or management in the development of e-commerce strategies.

Is e-commerce suited to all SMEs? A decision to move to e-commerce must be related to the overall business strategy and the sales strategy. The business should ask itself:

- Will e-commerce contribute to the competitive advantage of the business?
- Will it add value?
- Will the benefits outweigh the costs?

Take the example of a family business which has built its reputation for selling specialist hand tools to tradespersons and do-it-yourself enthusiasts. It has shops in several large towns but its reputation extends beyond those towns and customers will travel considerable distances to buy specialist tools. The business would be well placed to enter into e-commerce selling because its name is well known, its reputation is established in the retail outlets, which will continue to operate, and the internet can widen the market through direct customer order and delivery to the door.

Take another example of an antiquarian bookseller who buys and sells rare books. Again the bookseller has an established reputation in trade journals and has been using catalogue-based mail order sales for some years. The business would be well placed to enter into e-commerce by adding a website reference to existing advertising material. It may also improve the bookseller's ability to find sources of rare books well beyond the local sources traditionally used. Furthermore, since competitors have already established e-commerce outlets, the bookseller may lose market share if it does not move to internet buying and selling.

19.8 Summary

You might ask, having read this chapter, why it is necessary to pay any attention to the previous 18 chapters. The answer is that the ideas described in this chapter are exciting and forward-looking, but they are being used primarily by a selection of the market leaders and the innovators. There are a vast range of businesses which are still using traditional management accounting techniques. That will necessitate an understanding of the traditional approach for some time yet, in a spirit of evolution rather than revolution. So while you should read and think about the new ideas, you will also find it necessary to understand and apply the aspects of management accounting which have been taught traditionally. If you have a strong command of the approach to management accounting set out in the chapters of this book, then you will have the basis on which to build an understanding of the present practice in most business organisations. You will also be in a position to move on to an in-depth study of developments in management accounting in both the academic and the practical spheres.

References and further reading

Burns, J. and Scapens, R. (2000) 'Conceptualising management accounting change: an institutional framework', *Management Accounting Research*, 11: 3–25.

Chaffey, D. (2002) *E-Business and E-Commerce Management*, FT Prentice Hall.

CIMA (2001) *Activity-based Management: An Overview*, Technical Briefing, CIMA Publishing, available on www.cimaglobal.com

Cleveland, J. (2005) 'Benefits of lean in the accounting department', *Automotive Design & Production*, Feb, 117(2): 16.

Cooper, R. and Slagmulder, R. (2003) 'Interorganizational costing, part 2', *Cost Management* (Boston), 17(6): 12–24.

Dunk, A.S. (2004) 'Product life cycle cost analysis: the impact of customer profiling, competitive advantage, and quality of IS information', *Management Accounting Research*, 15: 401–14.

Everaert, P. and Bruggeman, W. (2002) 'Cost targets and time pressure during new product development', *International Journal of Operations and Production Management*, 22(12): 1339–53.

Lin, T.W., Merchant, K.A., Yang, Y. and Yu, Z. (2005) 'Target costing and incentive compensation', *Cost Management* (US), 19(2): 29–42.

Major, M. and Hopper, T. (2005) 'Managers divided: implementing ABC in a Portuguese telecommunications company', *Management Accounting Research*, 16: 205–29.

Miller, J.A. (1996) *Implementing Activity-Based Management in Daily Operations*. New York: Wiley.

Modarress, B., Ansari, A. and Lockwood, L. (2005) 'Kaizen costing for lean manufacturing: a case study', *International Journal of Production Research*, 43(9): 1729.

Moussatche, H. and Languell, J. (2001) 'Flooring materials: life-cycle costing for educational facilities', *Facilities*, 19(10): 333–43.

Nelson, D. (2004) 'How Delphi went lean', *Supply Chain Management Review*, Nov/Dec, 8(8): 32–7.

Pierce, B. (2002) 'Target cost management', *Accountancy Ireland*, April 34(2): 30–32.

Porter, M.E. (1985) *Competitive Advantage: Creating and Sustaining Superior Performance*, New York: Free Press.

Roslender, R. and Hart, S.J. (2003) 'In search of strategic management accounting: theoretical and field study perspectives', *Management Accounting Research*, 14: 255–79.

Searcy, De W.L. (2004) 'Using activity-based costing to assess channel/customer profitability', *Management Accounting Quarterly*, 5(2): 51.

Soin, K., Seal, W. and Cullen, J. (2002) 'ABC and organizational change: an institutional perspective', *Management Accounting Research*, 13: 249–71.

Teresko, J. (2005) 'It came from Japan: lean management', *Industry Week*, Feb, 254(2): 49–50.

QUESTIONS

The Questions section of each chapter has three types of question. 'Test your understanding' questions to help you review your reading are in the 'A' series of questions. You will find the answer to these by reading and thinking about the material in the text book. 'Application' questions to test your ability to apply technical skills are in the 'B' series of questions. Questions requiring you to show skills in problem solving and evaluation are in the 'C' series of questions.

A   Test your understanding

A19.1   Define 'business strategy' (section 19.1).

A19.2   How does strategic management accounting make use of information about competitors (section 19.2)?

A19.3   How do the managers of a business maintain its competitive position (section 19.2)?

A19.4   What have researchers found about the definition of what strategic management accounting means (section 19.2.3)?

A19.5   How does target costing help maintain competitive advantage (section 19.3.1)?

A19.6   What is customer profitability analysis (section 19.3.2)?

A19.7   How does life-cycle costing help maintain competitive advantage (section 19.3.3)?

A19.8   What is 'kaizen costing' (section 19.3.4)?

A19.9   How does lean accounting help maintain competitive advantage (section 19.3.5)?

A19.10   How does value chain analysis help maintain competitive advantage (section 19.3.6)?

A19.11   How does activity-based management develop out of activity-based costing (section 19.4)?

A19.12   What is the management philosophy represented by total quality management (section 19.5)?

A19.13   What are the main components of the cost of quality (section 19.5)?

A19.14   What is the stated purpose of 'business process re-engineering' (section 19.6)?

A19.15   What are the three goals of business process re-engineering (section 19.6)?

A19.16   What is e-business (section 19.7)?

A19.17   What is e-commerce (section 19.7)?

A19.18   How can management accounting contribute to planning, decision making and control in e-business and e-commerce (sections 19.7.1, 19.7.2 and 19.7.3)?

B   Application

B 19.1

The directors of Coatings plc have decided that specialist paints for use on buses and lorries should become the focus of a new e-business strategy. 'All we have at present is a call centre where our customers phone in orders,' said the sales manager. 'Our two main competitors are improving their business-to-business activities by linking to internet providers. Our strengths lie in customer loyalty and the reputation of our product for quality.'

Explain how value chain analysis can be combined with the development of an e-business strategy (300 words).

B19.2

A company manufacturing specialised medical equipment and supplies is currently having a debate internally about developing an e-business strategy. The sales manager wants to develop an e-commerce website. The managing director thinks that electronic methods are not necessary; what really matters is intensive marketing and offering good technical support for the products.

Explain how the management accountant could provide useful information to help this debate come to a conclusion (300 words).

B19.3

Explain how a low-cost airline can use strategic management accounting in developing a business strategy for competing with the traditional airlines (300 words).

C   Problem solving and evaluation

C19.1

A company is reviewing its total quality management programme, which does not appear to be making the progress expected. Problems have been identified in:

- Fear of exposing weaknesses in the organisation.
- Lack of commitment from senior executives.
- Seeing it as someone else's problem.

How could the management accountant help in addressing these problems (300 words)?

C19.2

How could planning of business strategy be useful to a public sector organisation such as a public library service? Does the idea of competition have any meaning? How can the management accountant help in planning a business strategy for a public library service (300 words)?

Case studies

Real world cases

Prepare short answers to Case studies 19.1, 19.2 and 19.3.

Case 19.4 (group case)

A manufacturer of toothpaste has estimated the price at which the product will sell, making use of market surveys and consumer analysis. A profit margin has been set. Finally a target cost has been established by subtracting the expected profit from the estimated selling price. The plant manager and the research and development unit have been asked to design the product in such a way that it can be produced within the target cost.

A rival manufacturer of toothpaste takes a different approach. Here the selling price is again estimated from market surveys and consumer analysis and a profit margin is set. However, the product design is then accepted on the recommendation of the research and development unit and the plant manager focuses on a programme of continuous improvement which will keep costs within acceptable limits.

Is there a role for management accounting in either of these situations?

Notes

1. Wilson, R.M.S. (1995) 'Strategic Management Accounting', in Ashton, D., Hopper, T. and Scapens, R.W. (eds) *Issues in Management Accounting*, FT Prentice Hall, ch. 8.

2. CIMA (2001).

3. CIMA Official Terminology (2000), Ch.3.

4. See also Chapter 4, section 4.5.2.

Quick checklist: A glossary of management accounting terms

The definition of one word or phrase may depend on understanding another word or phrase defined elsewhere in the glossary. Words in **bold** indicate that such a definition is available.

ABC See **activity-based costing**.

absorb, absorbed See **absorption**.

absorption The process by which overhead costs are absorbed into units of output, or 'jobs'.

absorption costing All production costs are absorbed into products and the unsold inventory is valued at total cost of production.

accounting The process of identifying, measuring and communicating financial information about an entity to permit informed judgements and decisions by users of the information.

accounting rate of return Calculated by taking the average annual profits expected from a project as a percentage of the capital invested.

accrual See **accrued expense**.

accrued expense (accrued liability) An expense which remains unpaid at the accounting date and is therefore recognised as a liability.

activity Any physical operation that takes place in an enterprise. For **ABC** see also **unit activity, product-sustaining activities, batch-related activities** and **cost drivers**.

activity-based costing (ABC) Traces **overhead costs** to products by focusing on the **activities** that drive costs (cause costs to occur).

activity cost pool See **cost pool**.

advanced manufacturing technologies New methods developed by engineers in order to compete more effectively.

allocate To assign a whole item of cost, or of revenue, to a simple cost centre, account or time period.

allocated, allocation See **allocate**.

AMTs See **advanced manufacturing technologies**.

annual report A document produced each year by limited liability companies containing the accounting information required by law. Larger companies also provide information and pictures of the activities of the company.

apportion To spread cost over two or more cost units, centres, accounts or time periods on some basis which is a fair representation of how the cost item is used by each cost centre.

apportioned, apportionment See **apportion**.

assets Rights or other access to future economic benefits controlled by an entity as a result of past transactions or events.

avoidable cost One which may be eliminated by taking a particular action.

balance sheet A statement of the financial position of an entity showing assets, liabilities and ownership claim.

balanced scorecard Links performance measures for key goals in customer perspective, financial perspective, internal business perspective and learning and growth perspective.

basic standard A **standard cost** that remains a permanent basis for comparison.

batch-related activities (in ABC) Product-sustaining activities that are fixed for a given batch of products.

benchmarking The process of measuring the organisation's operations, products and services against those of competitors recognised as market leaders, in order to establish targets which will provide a competitive advantage.

bottom-up budget Initiated by inviting those who will implement the budget to participate in the process of setting the budget. Also called a **participative budget**.

breakeven analysis A technique of management accounting which is based on calculating the breakeven point and analysing the consequences of changes in various factors calculating the breakeven point.

breakeven chart Graph that shows sales and costs over a range of activity, including the activity level at which total costs equal total sales and at which the business makes neither a profit nor a loss.

breakeven point That point of activity (measured as sales volume) where total sales and total costs are equal, so that there is neither profit nor loss.

budget A detailed plan which sets out, in money terms, the plans for income and expenditure in respect of a future period of time. It is prepared in advance of that time period and is based on the agreed objectives for that period of time, together with the strategy planned to achieve those objectives.

budget committee A group of people brought together to manage each stage of the budgetary process.

budget manual A document setting out procedures and instructions including the timetable for **budget** preparation, formats to be used, circulation lists for drafts and arbitration procedures where conflicts begin to show themselves.

budget system Serves the needs of management in making judgments and decisions, exercising planning and control and achieving effective communication and motivation.

budget planning and control Specialist techniques to quantify the strategy of the enterprise.

budgeted fixed overhead cost rate Fixed overhead cost rate per unit set in advance. See **predetermined fixed overhead cost rate**.

buffer stock Holding the minimum level of inventory that allows the activity of the organisation to be maintained.

business strategic planning Involves preparing, evaluating and selecting **strategy** to achieve objectives of a long-term plan of action within a defined business activity.

by-product A product arising from a process where the sales value is insignificant by comparison with that of the main product or products.

capital allowances Depreciation allowances allowed for tax purposes.

capital budgeting A process of management accounting which assists management decision making by providing information on the investment in a project and the benefits to be obtained from that project, and by monitoring the performance of the project subsequent to its implementation.

capital expenditure Spending on resources which bring a long-term benefit to an organisation, in generating cash flows or providing other benefits relating to the purpose of the organisation.

capital investment See **capital expenditure**.

capital investment appraisal The application of a set of methods of quantitative analysis which give guidance to managers in making decisions as to how best to invest long-term funds.

capital rationing There is not sufficient finance (capital) available to support all the projects proposed in an organisation.

cash flow projections Statements of cash expected to flow into the business and cash expected to flow out over a particular period.

contingency theory An explanation that management accounting methods have developed in a variety of ways depending on the judgements or decisions required.

contribution per unit The sales price minus the variable cost per unit. It measures the contribution made by each item of output to **fixed costs** and **profit**.

contribution per unit of limiting factor Used in ranking, choosing the highest value of this ratio to make the most profitable use of restricted resources.

control The power to govern the financial and operating policies of an entity so as to obtain benefits from its activities. One of three functions of management that are supported by management accounting. See also **decision making** and **planning**.

control account (for cost) A record of the total transactions relating to the costs being recorded. A control account is also called a **total account**. The control account is supported by secondary records showing detailed costs for each job separately.

controllable cost A cost which is capable of being regulated by a manager within a defined boundary of responsibility.

controlling See **control**.

corporate strategic planning Involves preparing, evaluating and selecting *strategies* to achieve objectives of a long-term plan of action for the corporate **entity** as a whole.

cost An amount of expenditure on a defined activity. The word 'cost' needs other words added to it, to give it a specific meaning.

cost centre A unit of the organisation in respect of which a manager is responsible for costs under her or his control.

cost code A system of letters and numbers designed to give a series of unique labels which help in classification and analysis of cost information.

cost coding Codes used for recording costs in an accounting system.

cost drivers The factors that most closely influence the cost of an activity.

cost driver rate Total costs in a **cost pool** divided by the number of times that the **activity** occurs.

cost of capital The cost to the business of raising new finance.

cost of holding inventory The costs related to storing inventory until it is sold.

cost of ordering inventory The administrative costs related to buying and receiving materials.

cost of quality All costs incurred in achieving a quality product or service.

cost-plus pricing Setting a price based on full cost of production plus desired profit. Also called **full cost pricing**.

cost pool The costs collected that relate to each **activity**.

cost–volume–profit analysis Emphasises the relationship between sales revenue, costs and profit in the short term.

creditors Persons or organisations that are owed money by the **entity**.

current asset An asset that is expected to be converted into cash within the trading cycle.

current liability A liability that is expected to be repaid within a short period of time, usually within one year.

currently attainable standard A **standard cost** based on expectations under normally efficient operating conditions.

debtors Persons or organisations who owe money to the **entity**.

decision making One of three functions of management which are supported by management accounting. See also **planning** and **control**.

depreciable amount The cost of an asset, or another amount such as replacement cost substituted for cost, less its **residual value**.

depreciation The systematic allocation of the **depreciable amount** of an asset over its useful life.

direct cost Cost that is directly traceable to an identifiable unit, such as a product or service or department of the business, for which costs are to be determined.

directing attention One of three functions of management accounting to support management actions of **planning**, **decision making** and **control**. See also **keeping the score** and **solving problems**.

discount rate Most suitable rate of interest to be applied in calculating **present value**. Could be based on one particular type of finance but more usually is the cost of mixed sources.

discounting The process of calculating **present value** of projected cash flows.

divisible project A long-term investment project having parts that may be evaluated separately. See also **non-divisible project**.

division A part of the organisation where the manager has responsibility for generating revenues, controlling costs and producing a satisfactory return on capital invested in the division.

e-business Electronic business: the use of technology to automate business practices.

e-commerce Electronic commerce: the use of electronic media for transactions between the company and its customers or suppliers; one aspect of **e-business**.

economic order quantity (EOQ) A model that minimises the combined cost of holding and ordering inventory.

economic value added Calculated by deducting from divisional profit a cost of capital charge based on the assets of the division.

entity A legal or economic unit which exists independently of its owners. An identifiable organisation for which accounting information is needed e.g. limited liability company, public sector body.

equivalent unit of output The amount of output, expressed in terms of whole units, which is equivalent to the actual amount of partly or fully completed production.

facility-sustaining activity (in ABC) **Activity** that is not driven by making products.

feed forward control Means making predictions of outputs expected at some future time and then quantifying those predictions, in management accounting terms.

feedback control Involves comparing outputs achieved against outputs desired and taking corrective action if necessary.

financial accounting A term usually applied to external reporting by a business where that reporting is presented in financial terms.

financial statements Documents containing accounting information presented to meet the needs of users.

fixed asset An asset that is held by an enterprise for use in the production or supply of goods or services, for rental to others, or for administrative purposes on a continuing basis in the reporting entity's activities.

fixed cost One which is not affected by changes in the level of output over a defined period of time.

flexible budget A **budget** that is designed to change when the volume of activity changes, to achieve comparability.

full cost of production Direct cost plus **indirect cost** of production. Also calculated as **prime cost** plus **production overhead cost**.

full cost pricing See **cost-plus pricing**.

functional strategic planning Also called **operational planning**. The detailed plans by which those working within an organisation are expected to meet the short-term objectives of their working group, based on the functions that are carried out by the group.

gross Before making deductions.

ideal standard A standard cost set under the most efficient operating conditions.

impairment An asset is impaired when the business cannot expect to recover the carrying value of the intangible asset (as shown in the balance sheet), either through using it or through selling it.

imposed budget See **top-down budget**.

incremental analysis Analysing the changes in costs and revenues caused by a change in **activity**.

incremental budget Prepared by adding a percentage to the **budget** of the previous year, usually to represent the effects of inflation.

incremental costs The additional costs that arise from an activity of the organisation. To justify incurring incremental costs it is necessary to show they are exceeded by **incremental revenue**.

incremental revenue The additional revenue that arises from an **activity** of the organisation. To justify accepting incremental revenue it is necessary to show it exceeds **incremental costs**.

indirect cost Cost that is spread over a number of identifiable units of the business, such as products or services or departments, for which costs are to be determined.

indirect labour Labour costs that cannot be allocated directly to an identifiable unit for which costs are to be determined.

indirect materials Materials costs that cannot be allocated directly to an identifiable unit for which costs are to be determined.

integrated system Accounting records that serve the needs of both financial accounting and management accounting.

internal rate of return The discount rate at which the present value of the cash flows generated by the product is equal to the present value of the capital invested, so that the net present value of the project is zero.

internal reporting Reporting financial information to those users inside a business, at various levels of management, at a level of detail appropriate to the recipient.

investment centre A unit of the organisation in respect of which a manager is responsible for capital investment decisions as well as revenue and costs.

Invoice A document sent by a supplier to a customer showing the quantity and price of goods or services supplied.

job cost The cost of a product or service provided to a customer, consisting of **direct** and **indirect** costs of production. See also **product cost**.

job cost record Shows the costs of materials, labour and overhead incurred on a particular job.

job-costing system A system of cost accumulation where there is an identifiable **activity** for which costs may be collected. The **activity** is usually specified in terms of a job of work or a group of tasks contributing to a stage in the production or service process.

joint products Two or more products arising from a process, each of which has a significant sales value.

just-in-time purchasing A system of contracts with suppliers to deliver goods as closely as possible to the time when they are required for operations.

keeping the score One of three functions of management accounting to support management actions of **planning**, **decision making** and **control**. See also **directing attention** and **solving problems**.

limiting factor An item which is temporarily restricted in availability.

line item budget Each line in the budget relates to a function in the organisation.

liquidity The extent to which a business has access to cash or items which can readily be exchanged for cash.

long-range planning Begins with a vision statement setting out a vision for the future direction of the organisation. From this vision the long-range objectives are set covering a period of perhaps three to five years.

management Collective term for those persons responsible for the day-to-day running of a business.

management accounting Reporting accounting information within a business, for **management** use only.

margin Frequently used as a short description of **profit**, particularly in the financial press. May be expressed as a percentage of **sales** or percentage of **revenue**.

margin of safety The difference between the **breakeven** sales and the normal level of sales (measured in units or in £s of sales).

marginal costing See **variable costing**.

master budget Combination of budgeted profit and loss account, cash flow statement and balance sheet, created from detailed budgets brought together within a finance plan.

mutually exclusive Investment projects that are competing for scarce resources, where choosing one eliminates another.

net After making deductions.

net present value (NPV) The net present value (of a project) is equal to the present value of the cash inflows minus the present value of the cash outflows, all discounted at the **cost of capital**.

non-controllable cost One which is not capable of being regulated by a manager within a defined boundary of responsibility, although it may be a cost incurred so that the responsibility may be exercised.

non-divisible project A long-term investment project which does not have parts that may be evaluated separately. See also **divisible project**.

non-financial performance measures Measurement of performance using targets that are not available in the financial reporting system.

normal level of activity Estimated by management, taking into account the budgeted level of activity in recent periods, the activity achieved in recent periods, and the expected output from normal working conditions.

objective probabilities Estimates supported by strong evidence. **See subjective probabilities.**

operational budgets Budgets representing the quantification of **operational planning**, including materials and labour budgets.

operational planning The detailed plans by which those working within an organisation are expected to meet the short-term objectives of their working group. See also **functional strategic planning**.

opportunity cost A measure of the benefit sacrificed when one course of action is chosen in preference to another. The measure of sacrifice is related to the best rejected course of action.

output The product or service provided by the enterprise or one of its operating units.

overhead cost Cost that cannot be identified directly with products or services. See also **indirect costs**.

overhead cost recovery Absorbing overhead cost into a unit of product so that the overhead cost will eventually be **recovered** in the sale of the product.

overhead recovery See **overhead cost recovery**.

over-recovered fixed overhead cost The overhead recovered (applied) using a **predetermined overhead cost rate** is greater than the actual overhead cost of the period.

ownership interest The residual amount found by deducting all of the entity's liabilities from all of the entity's assets.

participative budget See **bottom-up budget**.

payback period The length of time required for a stream of cash inflows from a project to equal the original cash outlay.

percentage mark-up on cost This adds a percentage to the total cost per unit to calculate a selling price.

performance evaluation Requires the management accountant to decide on what to measure, plan how to report and consider the behavioural aspects.

period costs Costs that are treated as expenses in the period in which they are incurred.

planning Involves setting objectives, then establishing, evaluating and selecting strategy, tactics and actions required to achieve those objectives. One of three functions of management which are supported by management accounting. See also **control** and **decision making**.

planning programming budget system (PPBS) An output-based approach to **budgets** that focuses on programmes of action in the enterprise.

post-completion audit A review of the actual results of a project in order to compare these with the expectations contained in the project proposals.

predetermined fixed overhead cost rate Estimated before the start of a reporting period.

prepayments Expenses paid in advance, such as rent or insurance, where a future benefit remains at the accounting date.

present value A sum of £1 receivable at the end of n years when the rate of interest is $r\%$ per annum equals

$$\frac{1}{(1 + r)^n}$$

where r represents the annual rate of interest, expressed in decimal form, and n represents the time period when the cash flow will be received.

primary records Provide the first evidence that a transaction or event has taken place.

prime cost of production Equal to the total of direct materials, direct labour and other **direct costs**.

process costing Appropriate to a business or operation where there is a continuous flow of a relatively high volume of similar products during a reporting period.

products See **output**.

product cost Cost associated with goods or services purchased, or produced, for sale to customers. See also **job cost**.

product differentiation The business may be able to charge a higher price (a premium) for the reputation or quality of its product.

product life cycle The sequence of development of a product from initial development through maturity of sales to eventual decline in sales.

product-sustaining activities (in ABC) Activities that are performed to enable output of products but are not closely dependent on how many units are produced.

production Creating output in a business process, by using materials, labour and other resources available within the business.

production cost centre Cost centre that produces output of goods or services.

production overhead cost Comprises **indirect** materials, **indirect** labour and other **indirect** costs of production.

production plan Sets out quantities of resource inputs required, for use in **operational budgets**.

profit The increase in the ownership interest in an entity over a specified period of time, due to the activities of the entity. The word 'profit' needs other words added to it, to give it a specific meaning.

profit centre A unit of the organisation in respect of which a manager is responsible for **revenue** as well as **costs**.

profit margin Profit as a percentage of **sales**.

profit-volume chart A graph showing on the horizontal axis the volume, measured by activity level in £s of sales, and on the vertical axis the profit at that activity level.

profit–volume ratio Contribution as a percentage of **sales** value.

profitability index The **present value** of cash flows (discounted at the **cost of capital**) divided by the present value of the investment intended to produce those cash flows.

recovered Costs are recovered by charging a selling price that covers **costs** and makes a **profit**.

relevant costs Those future costs which will be affected by a decision to be taken. Non-relevant costs will not be affected by the decision.

relevant revenues Those future revenues which will be affected by a decision to be taken. Non-relevant revenues will not be affected by the decision.

re-order level The point at which the buying department places its order for replacement materials.

repeated distribution method Continuous reapportionment of service department costs across **cost centres** until the amount remaining in any service department is so small that it can be ignored.

reporting period The period in respect of which the accounting information is prepared. In management accounting the period may be as frequent as the management chooses – weekly, monthly, quarterly and annual reporting are all used.

residual income (RI) Operating profit less an interest charge based on the **assets** used and controlled by the division.

residual value The estimated amount that an entity would currently obtain from disposal of an **asset**, after deducting the estimated costs of disposal, if the asset were already of the age and condition expected at the end of its useful life.

responsibility centre An area of responsibility which is controlled by an individual. It might be a cost centre, a profit centre or an investment centre.

retention of title A supplier provides goods to a customer but retains ownership (title), the right to claim the goods if they are not paid for.

return (in relation to investment) The reward earned for investing money in a business. Return may appear in the form of regular cash payments (dividends) to the investor, or in a growth in the value of the amount invested.

return on investment (ROI) Profit controllable by the division as a percentage of the investment in assets which produces that profit.

revenue Created by a transaction or event arising during the ordinary activities of the business which causes an increase in the **ownership interest**.

risk averse A person who chooses the less risky of two choices that have equal money value.

risk neutral A person who is is prepared to accept the level of risk which accompanies the most likely outcome.

risk seeker A person who enjoys the thrill of higher risk because it is associated with higher rewards if successful (despite facing greater losses if not successful).

sales Delivering goods or services to a customer, either for cash or on credit terms.

sales budget Budget of sales volumes and prices for a future period.

scrap Unwanted material sold for disposal, usually at a very low price in relation to its original cost.

semi-variable cost One which is partly fixed and partly varies with changes in the level of **activity**, over a defined period of time.

sensitivity analysis Asks 'what . . . if' questions such as 'What will be the change in profit if the selling price decreases by 1%?' or 'what will be the change in profit if the cost increases by 1%?'

service cost centre **Cost centre** that provides services to other **cost centres** within the organisation. See also **repeated distribution method**, **step method**.

short-term finance Money lent to a business for a short period of time, usually repayable on demand and also repayable at the choice of the business if surplus to requirements.

single period capital rationing Capital rationing in one period only during the life of a project (usually in the first period).

six sigma A measurable target for improvement schemes that say 'we want to get things right 99.9% of the time'.

solving problems One of three functions of management accounting to support management actions of **planning**, **decision making** and **control**. See also **directing attention** and **keeping the score**.

standard cost Target cost which should be attained under specified operating conditions. Expressed in cost per unit.

standard hour The amount of work achievable, at standard efficiency levels, in one hour.

statement (from supplier) A document sent by a supplier to a customer at the end of each month summarising all **invoices** awaiting payment by the customer.

step method Apportions the service department with the largest overhead cost across all other departments. The service department with the next largest overhead is then apportioned across all departments other than the one already dealt with.

step cost A fixed cost which increases in steps over a period of several years.

strategic management accounting The provision and analysis of financial information on the firm's product markets and competitors' costs and cost structures, and the monitoring of the enterprise's strategies and those of its competitors in these markets over a number of periods.

strategic planning Involves preparing, evaluating and selecting *strategies* to achieve objectives of a long-term plan of action.

strategy A plan setting out the actions and resources needed to achieve a stated objective of the long-term plan.

subjective probabilities Estimates based on skilled judgment but lacking strong supportive evidence. See **objective probabilities**.

sunk cost Cost that has been incurred or committed prior to a decision point. It is not relevant to subsequent decisions.

time value of money The name given to the idea that £1 invested today will grow with interest rates over time (e.g. £1 becomes £1.10 in one year's time at a rate of 10%).

top-down budget Set by management without inviting those who will implement the budget to participate in the process of setting the budget. Also called an **imposed budget**.

total account See **control account**.

total cost Calculated as **variable cost** plus **fixed cost**; or **direct cost** plus **indirect cost**; or **product cost** plus **period cost**.

total product cost Comprises **prime cost** plus **production overhead cost**.

total quality management Obtaining defect-free work first time on a consistent basis.

trade creditors Persons (suppliers) who supply goods or services to a business in the normal course of trade and allow a period of credit before payment must be made.

trade debtors Persons (customers) who buy goods or services from a business in the normal course of trade and take a period of credit before paying what they owe.

traditional approach to overhead costs **Allocate** and **apportion** to cost centres and then **absorb** into products which pass through those **cost centres**.

transfer price The price charged between two **divisions** of an organisation in transferring goods and services between each other.

turnover The **sales** of a business or other form of **revenue** from operations of the business.

unavoidable cost A cost that is *not* eliminated by taking a particular action.

under-recovered fixed overhead cost The overhead recovered (applied) using a **predetermined overhead cost rate** is less than the actual overhead cost of the period.

unit activity (in **ABC**) An **activity** performed each time a product is produced.

unit cost The **cost** of one unit of **output**.

unsecured creditors Persons who have lent money to an **entity** and have no secured claim on assets of the entity.

variable cost One which varies directly with changes in the level of **output**, over a defined period of time.

variable costing Only **variable costs** of production are absorbed into products and the unsold inventory is valued at variable cost of production. **Fixed costs of production** are treated as a cost of the period in which they are incurred.

variance The difference between a planned, **budgeted** or **standard cost** and the actual cost incurred. An adverse variance arises when the actual cost is greater than the standard cost. A favourable variance arises when the actual cost is less than the standard cost.

waste Any materials that have no value.

work-in-progress A product or service that is partly completed.

working capital Finance provided to support the short-term **assets** of the business (inventory and **debtors**) to the extent that these are not financed by short-term **creditors**. It is calculated as **current assets** minus **current liabilities**.

zero-based budget (ZBB) Budget preparation starts with a blank sheet of paper and justifies every item entered.

Solutions to numerical and technical questions

Note that solutions are provided only for numerical and technical material since other matters are covered either in the book or in the further reading indicated.

Chapters 1 and 19 have no solutions given in this Appendix because there are no numerical questions.

Chapter 2

Test your understanding

A2.3
(a) variable cost; parts for repairs
(b) fixed cost; rent of the garage
(c) semi-variable cost; telephone bill with fixed charge and call charges
(d) step cost; equipment hire on fixed charge with step reviews for level of usage
(e) direct cost; parts for repairs, payment to mechanic for hours worked on jobs
(f) indirect cost; insurance charge for the property and contents
(g) product cost; parts for repairs, payment for labour
(h) period cost; depreciation of tools.

A2.4
(a) Raw materials could be variable, direct and product cost.
(b) Sub-contracted labour could be fixed, direct and product cost.
(c) Rent of warehouse could be fixed, indirect and period cost.

Application

B2.5
(a) Cost X is a fixed cost because *total* cost does not vary with output.

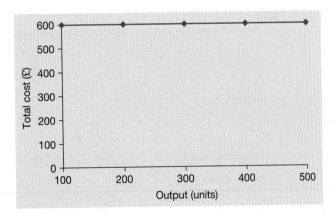

(b) Cost Y is a variable cost because total cost varies in direct proportion to output and is zero when output is zero.

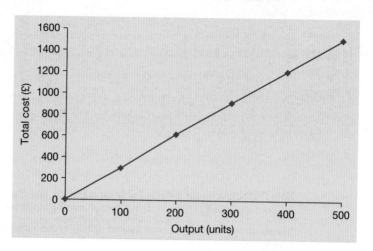

(c) Cost Z is a semi-variable cost because total cost varies in direct proportion to output but has a value of £600 when output is zero (seen by extending the graph until it meets the vertical axis). The fixed cost is £600.

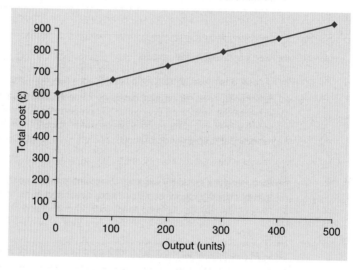

B2.6

(a) **Table of costs for one year based on variable mileage within the year**

Mileage per annum	5,000 £	10,000 £	15,000 £	20,000 £	30,000 £
Variable costs					
Spare parts	180	360	540	720	1,080
Fuel	700	1,400	2,100	2,800	4,200
Tyres (see (d))	400	800	1,200	1,600	2,400
Total variable cost	1,280	2,560	3,840	5,120	7,680
Fixed costs					
Service costs per year	900	900	900	900	900
Insurance	800	800	800	800	800
Depreciation	4,800	4,800	4,800	4,800	4,800
Total fixed cost	6,500	6,500	6,500	6,500	6,500

(b) Note that in drawing the graph it is necessary to insert a point for 25,000 miles (although no calculation is required because the straight line is formed from the data already calculated).

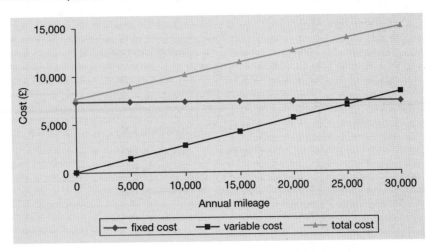

(c) Average cost per mile

Mileage per annum	5,000	10,000	15,000	20,000	30,000
Variable cost per mile (pence)	25.6	25.6	25.6	25.6	25.6
Fixed cost per mile (pence)	130.0	65.0	43.3	32.5	21.7
Average cost per mile (pence)	155.6	90.6	68.9	58.1	47.3

(d) All total costs follow a straight line. Total fixed costs do not depend on mileage. Total variable costs increase directly with mileage. Total fixed plus variable costs start at £6,500 for zero miles and increase in direct proportion to mileage. The average cost per mile for each year falls as the annual mileage increases. Note that for tyres a proportionate cost has been calculated where the mileage is not exactly 15,000 miles. Note also that depreciation has been included as a fixed cost because it does not depend on mileage covered.

B2.7

		£
Metal piping	Product	12,000
Wages to welders and painters	Product	9,000
Supplies for welding	Product	1,400
Advertising campaign	Period	2,000
Production manager's salary	Period	1,800
Accounts department computer costs for dealing with production records	Period	1,200

The costs incurred during May relate to 4,000 towel rails, so allocate costs on this basis. Product costs are £22,400 in total, or £5.60 per towel rail. There are 500 towel rails remaining in stock at the end of the month which would have a value of £(500 × 5.60) = £2,800.

Most businesses would use a value higher than £5.60 to take some of the period costs into account (e.g. a proportion of the production manager's salary). However, this is a matter of judgement where others would charge all period costs in the profit and loss account.

Chapter 3

Application **B3.1**

Basis	Date	Quantity and unit price	Issued to outlets	Held in inventory	Total
FIFO			£	£	£
	22 May	80 units at £30	2,400		
	30 May	40 units at £30 30 units at £34	1,200 1,020		
	31 May	30 units at £34		1,020	
Total			4,620	1,020	5,640

Basis	Date	Quantity and unit price	Issued to outlets	Held in inventory	Total
LIFO			£	£	£
	22 May	60 units at £34 20 units at £30	2,040 600		
	30 May	70 units at £30	2,100		
	31 May	30 units at £30		900	
Total			4,740	900	5,640

Basis	Date	Quantity and unit price	Issued to outlets	Held in inventory	Total
Average			£	£	£
	22 May	80 units at *£31.33	2,507		
	30 May	70 units at *£31.33	2,193		
	31 May	30 units at *£31.33		940	
Total			4,700	940	5,640

*Weighted average [(120 × 30) + (60 × 34)]/180 = £31.33

B3.2
(a) Purchases requisition.
(b) Purchase order.
(c) Delivery note.
(d) Materials received note (quantities) plus supplier's invoice (prices).
(e) Stores requisition.

B3.3
(a) Direct.
(b) Indirect.
(c) Indirect.
(d) Indirect.

Chapter 4

A4.4

The following are suggestions but there could be valid arguments for alternatives. Discuss the relative costs and benefits of greater precision in measuring what drives cost. Note that these are not necessarily precise measures of what drives the cost, but they are relatively readily accessible measures that give a reasonable approximation.

(a) Number of employees in each cost centre.
(b) Number of employees in each cost centre.
(c) Floor area of each cost centre.
(d) Number of employees supervised in each cost centre.
(e) Floor area of each cost centre.
(f) Number of workstations in each cost centre.
(g) Shared equally across all cost centres.
(h) Shared equally across all cost centres.

A4.5

The following are suggestions but there could be valid arguments for alternatives:

(a) Number of machines in each cost centre.
(b) Number of vans used by each cost centre, assuming all have similar mileage.
(c) Number of employees in each cost centre.
(d) Value of output from each cost centre.
(e) Value of contract for each activity.
(f) Value of output from each cost centre.

B4.1

Step 1: Allocate costs to departments using a suitable method for each department

	Total £	Assembly £	Joinery £	Canteen £
Indirect labour[1]	90,000	48,000	36,000	6,000
Indirect material[2]	81,000	54,000	27,000	–
Heating and lighting[3]	25,000	10,000	12,000	3,000
Rent and rates[4]	30,000	12,000	14,400	3,600
Depreciation[5]	56,000	30,000	24,000	2,000
Supervision[6]	45,000	24,000	18,000	3,000
Power[7]	36,000	18,000	16,000	2,000
	363,000	196,000	147,400	19,600

Notes
1 Allocate indirect labour on the basis of number of employees 80 : 60 : 10.
2 Allocate indirect materials in proportion to direct materials 100 : 50.
3 Allocate heating and lighting in proportion to floor space 20 : 24 : 6.
4 Allocate rent and rates in proportion to floor space 20 : 24 : 6.
5 Allocate depreciation by reference to the value of machinery used in each department 300 : 240 : 20.
6 Allocate supervision on the basis of number of employees 80 : 60 : 10.
7 Allocate power on the basis of kilowatt hours 9 : 8 : 1.

Step 2: Apportion service department costs to production departments.

	Total £	Assembly £	Joinery £	Canteen £
From previous table	363,000	196,000	147,400	19,600
Apportion canteen to assembly and joinery 80 : 60		11,200	8,400	(19,600)
	363,000	207,200	155,800	

Step 3: Absorb total overhead costs of each production department to units produced during the period.

Divide the total cost of each department by the number of direct labour hours.

Assembly: £207,200/12,640 = £16.39 per direct labour hour
Joinery: £155,800/8,400 = £18.55 per direct labour hour

Step 4: Find the overhead cost of a specific job.

		£
Assembly	£16.39 × 3 hours	49.17
Joinery	£18.55 × 4 hours	74.20
Total overhead cost		123.37

B4.2

Statement of cost of production of 5,000 golf bags:

	£	£
Direct materials 5,000 × £40	200,000	
Direct labour 5,000 × £25	125,000	
Prime cost		325,000
Variable production overhead 5,000 × £10	50,000	
Fixed production overhead	100,000	
Production overhead cost		150,000
Total product cost		475,000

B4.3

(a) The use of a machine hour rate is appropriate for Department 1, which is heavily dependent on machine hours, but not for Department 2, which is more dependent on labour hours. The production overhead should be allocated according to the factor which most closely causes it to be incurred. In Department 1 this is likely to be machine hours but in Department 2 it is more likely to be labour hours.

(b) Applying a rate of £5.60 to 48,000 machine hours, the overhead absorbed was £268,800. This was less than the amount of overhead incurred, £275,000, and so it is said that overheads are underabsorbed by £6,200. The use of estimated overhead absorption rates, based on budget, is necessary for an estimation of cost before the true costs are known. However, the full actual costs have to be accounted for at the end of the period and so a further £6,200 must be charged to the profit and loss account in addition to the costs charged as jobs proceeded.

B4.4

The refectory costs are apportioned first because it provides services to all three of the other departments. The proportions used are the staff numbers, 4 : 4 : 2. The sub-total gives a new amount of overhead for each department. The total of the library overhead is next apportioned in proportion to students numbers 4 : 3.

This leaves zero overhead cost in the staff refectory and library, with all costs now in the teaching departments where they can be used to calculate total cost per student and form a basis for deciding on levels of fees to be charged.

Note that the total costs (in the total column) never changes. This exercise is concerned with apportioning (sharing) costs but it cannot create or destroy costs.

Apportioning service cost centre overheads

	Languages	Science	Library	Refectory	
	£	£	£	£	£
Overhead costs allocated	20,000	15,000	12,000	10,000	
Apportion refectory costs to other departments 4 : 4 : 2	4,000	4,000	2,000	(10,000)	
Sub-total	24,000	19,000	14,000	–	57,000
Apportion library costs to other departments 4 : 3	8,000	6,000			
Total	32,000	25,000			57,000

Spreadsheet iteration: Five iterations give the same answer.

Chapter 5

B5.1

SITUATION A: Sales 4,700 units in March

Profit and loss statement, month of March, based on absorption costing

Cost per unit = variable cost £44 plus fixed cost £8 = £52

	£	£
Sales (4,700 at £60)		282,000
Opening inventory (200 at £52)	10,400	
Costs of production (5,000 at £52)	260,000	
Less closing inventory (500 at £52)	(26,000)	
Cost of goods sold		(244,400)
Profit		37,600

Profit and loss statement, month of March, based on marginal costing

	£	£
Sales (4,700 at £60)		282,000
Opening inventory (200 at £44)	8,800	
Costs of production (5,000 at £44)	220,000	
Less closing inventory (500 at £44)	(22,000)	
Variable cost of goods sold		(206,800)
Contribution to fixed overhead cost		75,200
Fixed overhead costs		(40,000)
		35,200

The difference in profit is £37,600 – £35,200 = £2,400. The profit based on absorption costing is higher in this example because the increase in inventory of 300 units carries £8 of fixed overhead per unit = £2,400, as a product cost, to the next accounting period.

SITUATION B: Sales 5,100 units in March

Profit and loss statement, month of March, based on absorption costing

Cost per unit = variable cost £44 plus fixed cost £8 = £52

	£	£
Sales (5,100 at £60)		306,000
Opening inventory (200 at £52)	10,400	
Costs of production (5,000 at £52)	260,000	
Less closing inventory (100 at £52)	(5,200)	
Cost of goods sold		(265,200)
Profit		40,800

Profit and loss statement, month of March, based on marginal costing

	£	£
Sales (5,100 at £60)		306,000
Opening inventory (200 at £44)	8,800	
Costs of production (5,000 at £44)	220,000	
Less closing inventory (100 at £44)	(4,400)	
Variable cost of goods sold		(224,400)
Contribution to fixed overhead cost		81,600
Fixed overhead costs		(40,000)
		41,600

The difference in profit is £41,600 – £40,800 = £800. The profit based on absorption costing is lower in this example because the decrease in inventory of 100 units carries £8 of fixed overhead per unit = £800, as a product cost, to the next accounting period.

B5.2

Selling price per unit is £20
Variable cost per unit is £10
Fixed production overhead costs of one period are £800
Normal level of production activity is 200 units

	Period 1 units	Period 2 units	Period 3 units
Produced	250	200	180
Sold	210	210	210
Held in stock at end of period	40	30	nil

Using normal level of activity, fixed production overhead cost per unit is £800/200 = £4 per unit.
  Value stock at £(10 + 4) = £14 per unit.

Calculations for absorption costing

	Period 1 units	Period 2 units	Period 3 units
Opening stock	nil	40	30
Produced (units)	250	200	180
	£	£	£
Opening stock at £14 each	nil	560	420
Variable cost of production	2,500	2,000	1,800
Fixed cost	800	800	800
(Closing stock)	(560)	(420)	nil
Cost of goods sold	2,740	2,940	3,020
Sales in units	210	210	210
Sales at £20 each	4,200	4,200	4,200
Profit	1,460	1,260	1,180

Calculations for marginal costing

	Period 1 units	Period 2 units	Period 3 units
Opening stock	nil	40	30
Produced (units)	250	200	180
	£	£	£
Opening stock at £10 each	nil	400	300
Variable cost of production	2,500	2,000	1,800
(Closing stock)	(400)	(300)	nil
Cost of goods sold	2,100	2,100	2,100
Fixed cost of period	800	800	800
Total cost	2,900	2,900	2,900
Sales in units	210	210	210
Sales at £20 each	4,200	4,200	4,200
Profit	1,300	1,300	1,300

Profit using absorption costing – profit using marginal costing

	160	–40	–120

Explanation of profit is (change in stock levels) × overhead cost rate

	+40 × £4	–10 × £4	–30 × £4

(a) £1,260 see table
(b) £1,300 see table
(c) +40 × £4 = +£160 see table
(d) £560 see table
(e) £400 see table

Problem solving and evaluation

C5.1

Expected profit per quarter under absorption costing

	Qtr 1 £000	Qtr 2 £000	Qtr 3 £000	Qtr 4 £000		Total £000
Sales	108	132	108	132		480
Production units	1,000	1,000	900	1,100		
	£	£	£	£	£	£
Opening inventory at £90	nil	9	nil	nil		nil
Cost of production:						
At £90 per unit	90	90	81	99		360
Under/(over) absorbed	nil	nil	2	(2)	–	
Closing inventory at £90	(9)	nil	nil	nil		nil
Cost of goods sold	81	99	83	97		360
Profit	27	33	25	35		120

Under-absorbed in quarter 3 = 100 at £20 each
Over-absorbed in quarter 4 = 100 at £20 each

Expected profit per quarter under marginal costing

	Qtr 1 £	Qtr 2 £	Qtr 3 £	Qtr 4 £	Total £
Sales	108	132	108	132	480
	£	£	£	£	£
Production units	1,000	1,000	900	1,100	
Opening inventory at £70	nil	7	nil	nil	nil
Cost of production at £70	70	70	63	77	280
Closing inventory at £70	(7)	nil	nil	nil	nil
Variable cost of goods sold	63	77	63	77	280
Fixed costs of qtr	20	20	20	20	80
Total costs	83	97	83	97	360
Profit	25	35	25	35	120

Comparison of profit, using absorption costing and marginal costing

	Qtr 1 £000	Qtr 2 £000	Qtr 3 £000	Qtr 4 £000	Total £000
Absorption costing	27	33	25	35	120
Marginal costing	25	35	25	35	120
Difference	+2	−2	nil	nil	0

In quarter 1 the absorption costing profit is higher by £2,000. This is because there is an increase in inventory of 100 units, carrying a fixed overhead cost of £20 each.

In quarter 2 the absorption costing profit is lower by £2,000. This is because there is a decrease in inventory of 100 units, carrying a fixed overhead cost of £20 each.

In quarters 3 and 4 the inventory levels do not change and so the profit under absorption costing is the same as that under marginal costing.

Chapter 6

Test your understanding

A6.12

(a) 16 components are charged to the job card and used as part of the value of work-in-progress.
(b) The amount of £600 is added to work-in-progress, split as shown between the two jobs mentioned.
(c) The job card is closed and the record is transferred to finished goods stock.

Application

B6.1

	£
Direct costs	
Materials used:	
500 drums of milk	75,000
Cartons	4,000
Cheesemakers' wages	6,000
Prime cost	85,000
Overhead costs	
Cleaning and hygiene	1,200
Rent, rates, electricity	8,000
Cost of production	94,200

B6.2

Job cost record: Job 801		
3 May	Direct materials 40 × £2,800	112,000 †
30 May	Direct labour £20,000/2	10,000 ♥
	Prime cost	122,000
30 May	Production overhead: (see note)	20,600
	Total production cost	142,600
	To finished goods	(142,600)
	Work-in-progress	nil

Job cost record: Job 802		
3 May	Direct materials (£64,000/20) × 10	32,000 †
30 May	Direct labour £20,000/4	5,000 ♥
	Prime cost	37,000
30 May	Production overhead: (see note)	10,300
	Total production cost	47,300
	Finished goods	(47,300)
	Work-in-progress	nil

Job cost record: Job 803		
3 June	Direct materials (£64,000/20) × 4	12,800 †
30 June	Direct labour £20,000/4	5,000 ♥
	Prime cost	17,800
30 June	Production overhead: (see note)	10,300
	Total production cost	28,100
	Finished goods	28,100
1 May	Work-in-progress	nil

Note on production overheads:

	£
Rent, rates and electricity	18,000 ‡
Stain, varnish, etc.	22,500 ♣
Security	700 φ
	41,200

Labour cost is £20,000 in total so production overhead is £2.06 per £ of labour.

Problem solving and evaluation

C6.1 Frames Ltd

Job cost estimate for 500 single- and 200 double-glazed units:

	Single	Double	Total
Quantity	500	200	
	£	£	£
Direct material[1]	45,000	26,000	71,000
Direct labour[2]	16,250	8,000	24,250
Prime cost	61,250	34,000	95,250
Variable production overhead[3]	19,500	9,600	29,100
Fixed production overhead[4]	20,000	10,000	30,000
Total cost of production	100,750	53,600	154,350

Notes
1 Direct material: single 500 × £90 = £45,000; double 200 × £130 = £26,000.
2 Direct labour: single 500 × £32.50 = £16,250; double 200 × £40 = £8,000.
3 Variable production overhead: single 500 × £39 = £19,500; double 200 × £48 = £9,600.
4 Fixed overhead rates: single 160/4 = £40 per unit; double 100/2 = £50 per unit; applied to 500 units single = £20,000 and to 200 units double = £10,000.

C6.2

430 packages (needs 2 shifts): profit for 1 day

	£	£
Selling price 430 packages at £25.20		10,836
Cost of direct materials 430 at £23.75	10,213	
Cost of labour (£100 + £120)	220	
Supervision £40	40	
Other fixed overheads £280	280	
Depreciation £100	100	
		10,853
Net loss		(17)

880 packages (needs 3 shifts): profit for 1 day

	£	£
Selling price 880 packages at £25.00		22,000
Cost of direct materials 880 at £23.75	20,900	
Cost of labour (£100 + £120 + £160)	380	
Supervision £40 + £40	80	
Other fixed overheads £280	280	
Depreciation £100	100	
		21,740
Net profit		260
Net profit per package		£0.30

1,350 packages (needs 3.8 shifts): profit for 1 day

	£	£
Selling price 1,350 packages at £24.80		33,480
Cost of direct materials 1,350 at £23.75	32,063	
Cost of labour (£100 + £120 + £160 + £100)	480	
Supervision £40 + £40 + £20	100	
Other fixed overheads £280 + £100	380	
Depreciation £100 + £100	200	33,223
Net profit		257
Net profit per package		£0.19

Explanation. The 880-package option is the preferred one because it gives the benefit of a higher volume of profit without increasing the fixed costs. The 1,350-package option takes up more fixed costs and so reduces unit profit.

Chapter 7

Test your understanding

A7.17

Debit raw materials inventory £45,000; credit trade creditors £45,000
Debit direct wages account £16,000; credit cash £16,000
Debit wages account £2,000; credit cash £2,000
At the end of the month
Debit work-in-progress £16,000; credit wages £16,000 (direct wages)
Debit production overhead £2,000; credit wages £2,000 (indirect wages)
Debit production overhead £6,500; credit cash £6,500

A7.18

20 components are charged to the job card and used as part of the value of work-in-progress.
   In the ledger there is a debit of £80 to work-in-progress and a credit to stores of materials.

A7.19

The amount of £600 is added to work-in-progress, split as shown between the two jobs mentioned.
   In the ledger there is a debit of £600 to work-in-progress and a credit to the wages total account.

A7.20

The job card is closed and the record is transferred to finished goods stock.
   In the ledger there is a debit of £3,500 to finished goods inventory and a credit to work-in-progress account.

B7.1 Dairy, ledger accounts

		£			£
			Cash account		
			1 May	Cartons	6,000
			14 May	Wages: Cheesemakers	3,000
			14 May	Wages: Cleaning	600
			16 May	Rent, rates, electricity	8,000
			28 May	Wages:Cheesemakers	3,000
31 May	Balance c/d	21,200	28 May	Wages: Cleaning	600
		21,000			21,200
			1 June	Balance b/d	21,200
			Trade creditor		
2 May	1 drum returned	150	1 May	600 drums milk	90,000
31 May	Balance c/d	89,850			
		90,000			90.000
			1 June	Balance b/d	89,850
			Materials inventory		
1 May	Trade creditor (600 drums)	90,000	2 May	Returned to supplier	150
1 May	Cash (cartons)	6,000	3 May	Work-in-progress (500 drums)	75,000
			4 May	Production overhead (cartons)	4,000
			31 May	Balance c/d	16,850
		96,000			96,000
1 June	Balance b/d	16,850			
			Wages		
14 May	Cash	3,000	31 May	Production overhead	1,200
14 May	Cash	600	31 May	Work-in-progress	6,000
28 May	Cash	3,000			
28 May	Cash	600			
		7,200			7,200
			Production overhead		
4 May	Materials (cartons)	6,000	31 May	Work-in-progress	15,200
16 May	Cash (rent etc)	8,000			
31 May	Wages (cleaning)	1,200			
		15,200			15,200
			Work-in-progress		
3 May	Direct materials	75,000	30 May	Finished goods	96,200
31 May	Direct labour	6,000			
31 May	Production overhead	15,200			
		96,200			96,200
			Finished goods inventory		
31 May	Work-in-progress	96,200	31 May	Cost of goods sold	90,200
			31 May	Balance c/d	6,000
		96,200			96,200
1 June	Balance b/d	6,000			
			Cost of goods sold		
31 May	Finished goods	90,200			

B7.2

		£		£

Transfer production overhead cost of £27,000 to work-in-progress account

| Work-in-progress | Dr | 27,000 | | |
| Production overhead | | | Cr | 27,000 |

Transfer work-in-progress of £12,000 to finished goods inventory account

| Finished goods inventory | Dr | 12,000 | | |
| Work-in-progress | | | Cr | 12,000 |

Pay £1,500 cash for production overhead costs

| Production overhead | Dr | 1,500 | | |
| Cash | | | Cr | 1,500 |

Return to a supplier items of inventory having a cost of £900

| Trade creditor | Dr | 900 | | |
| Materials inventory | | | Cr | 900 |

Transfer finished goods inventory of £31,000 to cost of goods sold

| Cost of goods sold | Dr | 31,000 | | |
| Finished goods inventory | | | Cr | 31,000 |

Transfer cleaner's wages of £500 from wages ledger account to production overhead cost ledger account.

| Production overhead cost | Dr | 500 | | |
| Labour cost | | | Cr | 500 |

Purchase inventory of raw materials on credit, cost of £14,000

| Materials inventory | Dr | 14,000 | | |
| Trade creditor | | | Cr | 14,000 |

Transfer raw materials inventory of £980 to work-in-progress

| Work-in-progress | Dr | 980 | | |
| Materials inventory | | | Cr | 980 |

Pay direct labour wages in cash £1,000

| Wages | Dr | 1,000 | | |
| Cash | | | Cr | 1,000 |

Transfer direct labour wages £1,000 to work-in-progress

| Work-in-progress | Dr | 1,000 | | |
| Labour cost | | | Cr | 1,000 |

C7.1 Bridge Builders Ltd

Contract account
Current transactions section

Year 1		£000	Year 1		£000
May	Materials purchased	91			
May	Equipment at cost	14	Dec	Materials on site c/d	15
May	Architect's fee	7		Equipment on site c/d	9
May–Dec	Wages paid	71			
Sept	Subcontractors	10	Dec	Cost of work certified	203
May–Dec	Direct costs	22			
Dec	Head office charges	6			
Dec	Due to subcontractor c/d	3			
Dec	Direct costs incurred c/d	3			
		227			227

Profit and loss section

Year 1			Year 1		
Dec	Cost of work certified b/d	203	Dec	Value of work certified	280
Dec	Profit and loss account*	51			
Dec	Contract profit suspense c/d	26			
2		280			280

Balances brought forward section

Year 2			Year 2		
Jan	Equipment on site b/d	9	Jan	Due to subcontractor b/d	3
	Material on site b/d	15	Jan	Due for direct costs b/d	3
			Jan	Contract profit suspense b/d	26

*(280 − 203) × 2/3 = 52

Chapter 8

Test your understanding

A8.15
800 equivalent units at £3 = £2,400.

A8.16
1,800 units with respect to materials and 600 units with respect to conversion and overhead.

A8.17
Problem for allocation is the £2,000 of joint costs. These could be allocated by proportion to volume 3 : 1 : 2 or by sales value net of costs, i.e. £(15,000 − 4,000) : £(4,000 − 1,800) : £(6,000 − 2,400).

Application **B8.1**

	Physical flow (units)	Equivalent units of output
INPUT		
Work-in-progress at start	50,000	
Material introduced	80,000	
	130,000	
OUTPUT		
Goods finished this month	100,000	100,000
Work-in-progress at end (20% completed)	30,000	6,000
Total	130,000	106,000
		£
Opening work-in-progress brought forward		42,000
Incurred this month		140,000
Total costs to be accounted for		182,000

Cost per equivalent unit $= \dfrac{£182,000}{106,000} = £1.717$

		£
Value of finished output 100,000 × £1.717		171,700
Work-in-progress 6,000 × £1.717		10,300
Total costs accounted for		182,000

B8.2

	Physical flow (units)	Equivalent units of output	
		Materials	Conversion
INPUT			
Work-in-progress at start	2,000		
Material introduced	6,200		
	8,200		
OUTPUT			
Goods finished this month	7,000	(100%) 7,000	(100%) 7,000
Work-in-progress at end (30% completed)	1,200	(100%) 1,200	(30%) 360
Total	8,200	8,200	7,360

	Materials	Conversion	Total
	£	£	£
Opening work-in-progress brought forward	1,700	1,900	3,600
Incurred this month £14,700 + £12,820	14,700	12,820	27,520
Total costs to be accounted for	16,400	14,720	31,120

	Materials	Conversion
Cost per equivalent unit =	$\dfrac{16,400}{8,200} = £2$	$\dfrac{£14,720}{7,360} = £2$

		£
Value of finished output 7,000 × £4		28,000
Work-in-progress:		
Materials 1,200 × £2	2,400	
Conversion 360 × £2	720	3,120
Total costs accounted for		31,120

B8.3

(1)(a) Allocate joint costs by units of output.

	Liquefied gas £	Refined oil £	Grease £	Total £
Sales	20,000	230,000	8,000	258,000
Cost of crude oil*	2,038	101,942	1,020	105,000
Refining costs**	874	43,689	437	45,000
Additional processing costs	12,000	60,000		72,000
Total allocated costs	14,912	205,631	1,457	222,000
Profit	5,088	24,369	6,543	36,000

*Total output 515,000 units, crude oil cost £105,000, therefore unit cost was 20.39 pence per unit.
**Total output 515,000, refining cost was £45,000, therefore unit cost was 8.74 pence per unit.

(1)(b) Allocate joint costs by sales value.

	Liquefied gas £	Refined oil £	Grease £	Total £
Sales	20,000	230,000	8,000	258,000
Cost of crude oil*	8,140	93,604	3,256	105,000
Refining costs**	3,488	40,116	1,396	45,000
Additional processing costs	12,000	60,000		72,000
Total allocated costs	23,628	193,720	4,652	222,000
Profit/(Loss)	(3,628)	36,280	3,348	36,000

*(20/258) × £105,000, (230/258) × £105,000, (8/258) × £105,000.
**(20/258) × £45,000, (230/258) × £45,000, (8/258) × £45,000.

(2) For decision-making purposes the previous cost allocations should not be used. Instead the extra revenue should be compared with the extra cost.

	Liquefied gas £	Refined oil £	Grease £	Total £
Sales as recorded	20,000	230,000	8,000	258,000
Sales at split-off point	5,000	175,000	8,000	188,000
Additional sales through processing	15,000	55,000	nil	70,000
Additional processing costs	12,000	60,000		72,000

There has therefore been a net loss of £2,000 through processing further.

Problem solving and evaluation

C8.1

(This solution follows the example set out in the chapter in which there is no opening work-in-progress.)

Assembly department

(i) Data in respect of month of July Year 2 (as per question).

(ii) Statement of physical flows and equivalent units of output for the month.

	Physical flow (units)	Equivalent units of output	
		Material	Conversion
INPUT			
Units commenced	80,000		
	80,000		
OUTPUT			
Units completed in month	60,000	(100%) 60,000	(100%) 60,000
Work-in-progress at end	20,000	(100%) 20,000	(50%) 10,000
Total equivalent units	80,000	80,000	70,000

(iii) Ascertain total costs to be accounted for this period.

	Material	Labour & prodn o/head	Total
	£	£	£
Incurred this month	240,000	205,000	445,000

(iv) Calculate cost per equivalent unit.

	Material	Conversion
Total costs to be accounted for	£240,000	£205,000
Number of equivalent units	80,000	70,000
Cost per equivalent unit	£3	£2.93

(v) Apportion cost between finished output and work-in-progress.

		£	£
Value of finished output 60,000 × £5.93			355,700
Work-in-progress:			
Material 20,000 × £3		60,000	
Labour & o/heads 10,000 × £2.93		29,300	
			89,300
Total costs accounted for			445,000

Finishing department

(i) Data in respect of month of July Year 2 (as per question).

(It is necessary to assume that the 60,000 units completed and transferred out of Assembly during the month were all transferred into Finishing.)

(ii) Statement of physical flows and equivalent units of output for the month.

	Physical flow (units)	Equivalent units of output	
		Material	Conversion
INPUT			
Transferred from Assembly	60,000		
	60,000		
OUTPUT			
Units completed in month	50,000	(100%) 50,000	(100%) 50,000
Work-in-progress at end	10,000	(100%) 10,000	(70%) 7,000
Total equivalent units	60,000	60,000	57,000

(iii) Ascertain total costs to be accounted for this period.

	Material	Labour & prodn o/head	Total
	£	£	£
Transferred in from Assembly	355,700		355,700
Incurred this month	88,500	198,100	286,600
	444,200	198,100	642,300

(iv) Calculate cost per equivalent unit.

	Material	Conversion
Total costs to be accounted for	£444,200	£198,100
Number of equivalent units	60,000	57,000
Cost per equivalent unit	£7.403	£3.475

(v) Apportion cost between finished output and work-in-progress.

	£	£
Value of finished output 50,000 × £10.878		543,945
Work-in-progress:		
Material 10,000 × £7.403	74,030	
Labour & o/heads 7,000 × £3.475	24,325	
		98,355
Total costs accounted for*		642,300

*Rounding used where necessary to ensure all costs included.

Chapter 9

Application

B9.1

Contribution is £5.50 − £3.00 = £2.50.
Breakeven point equals fixed cost/contribution = 5,000/2.50 = 2,000 units.

B9.2

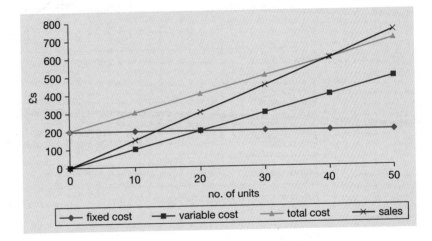

B9.3 Montrose Glass Products Ltd

(a) If Basic closes down there is a lost contribution of [£45 − £(15 + 20 + 5)] = £5. Fixed costs are carried in any event.
(b) If Standard closes down, the variable cost of £37 is saved, compared with revenue of £35. The company will gain £2,000 from closing down the Standard line.
(c) The best advice is to close down Standard but not Basic.

B9.4 Chris Gibson Kitchenware Ltd

(a)

	Dishwashers £000s	Fridges £000s	Ovens £000s	Total £000s
Sales	180	330	270	780
Variable costs	(120)	(150)	(132)	(402)
Contribution	60	80	138	378
Fixed cost				(268)
Total profit				110

(b) Dishwashers should not be dropped, because they make a contribution to fixed cost and profit. If production ceased the contribution of £60,000 would be lost but the fixed overheads would continue at £110,000. Overall the profit would reduce to £50,000. It may be that in the longer term an element of fixed cost can be identified as related to dishwashers alone. If this element were to exceed £60,000 it might be reasonable to discontinue production of dishwashers and discontinue the fixed cost.

B9.5 Capital Tours Ltd

(a) Total costs are £180,000 of which £60,000 are fixed costs. Variable cost is therefore £120,000 over 1,000 tours, or £120 per tour.
Selling price = £200 per person, contribution = £80 per person.
At new offer price of £140 per tour, contribution = £20 per person and so is acceptable in the short term.

(b) The offer is acceptable provided it does not displace any tours for which £200 would be paid. Also there must be no risk of offending existing customers who have already paid £200. If the new lower price became common knowledge, the price might be driven down so that the breakeven point would increase and more tours would have to be sold to achieve the same total profit.

Problem solving and evaluation

C9.1 Dairyproducts Ltd

	Cartons of cream	Aerosol cans of cream	Packets of cheese	Total
Units of output	400,000	96,000	280,000	
	£	£	£	£
Selling price	0.75	1.05	1.30	
Variable cost	0.45	0.50	1.00	
Contribution per unit	0.30	0.55	0.30	
Total contribution	120,000	52,800	84,000	256,800
Fixed cost	60,000	24,000	56,000	140,000
Net profit of current prodn, per week				116,800
Annual profit				5,840,000

Range of demand for aerosol cream cheese

Volume	60,000	80,000	100,000
	£	£	£
Sales price	1.50	1.40	1.15
Variable cost	0.50	0.50	0.50
Contribution per unit	1.00	0.90	0.65
Total contribution per week	60,000	72,000	65,000
Annual for 50 weeks		3,600,000	
Less:			
Additional advertising		(1,000,000)	
Modification cost		(400,000)	
Additional fixed cost		(500,000)	
Net benefit		1,700,000	

Reducing production of cream cartons by 20% per annum will lose £120,000 × 50 × 20%, i.e. £1,200,000.
Reducing production of packet cheese by 25% per annum will lose £84,000 × 50 × 25%, i.e. £1,050,000.
The net benefit of the new product is therefore greater than the loss on either of the options withdrawn.
　　The recommendation is to reduce packet cheese and replace with aerosol cream cheese. The only possible warning here is that there is only £150,000 of difference between withdrawing cream cartons and withdrawing packet cheese. If the growing customer dissatisfaction with cream in cartons is serious, the longer-term view might prevail over the short-term recommendation.

Chapter 10

Application   **B10.1**

Relevant costs are the costs appropriate to a specific management decision. They are those future costs which will be affected by a decision to be taken. Non-relevant costs will not be affected by the decision.

	Decision 1 Buy shop next door	Decision 2 Do not buy	Difference (relevant cost)
Capital costs			
Cost item 1: purchase price	+£140,000	–	+£140,000
Cost item 2: cost of existing shop	Sunk cost	–	–
Cost item 3: Sales value of existing shop	Non-relevant, not to be sold		–
Refit cost	+£20,000	–	+£20,000
Sales of existing fittings	–£5,000	–	–£5,000
Relevant capital cost			+£155,000
Running costs			
Depreciation of shop	+£7,000		+£7,000
Depreciation of refit	+£4,000		+£4,000
Shop manager	+£30,000	£30,000	–
New assistant	+£12,000	–	+£12,000
New heat and light	+£6,000	–	+£6,000
Fixed cost saving	–£1,000		–£1,000
Relevant running costs			+£28,000

Comment. The investment in capital cost will require evaluation for whether the additional cash flows can repay interest on the £155,000 loan required and eventually repay the loan.
The sales from the new shop need to cover the additional running costs of £28,000.

B10.2

Calculation of cost of all options, based on combined probabilities

Condition	Predicted pupil demand (1)	Predicted surplus per pupil (2)	Predicted surplus (3)	Joint probability (4)	Expected cost (5)
Council cuts back funds	5,000	£1.00	£5,000	.4 × .2 = .08	400
		£1.50	£7,500	.4 × .2 = .08	600
		£2.50	£12,500	.4 × .6 = .24	3,000
Normal conditions	6,000	£1.00	£6,000	.3 × .2 = .06	360
		£1.50	£9,000	.3 × .2 = .06	540
		£2.50	£15,000	.3 × .6 = .18	2,700
Schools 'active and healthy' programme	8,000	£1.00	£8,000	.3 × .2 = .06	480
		£1.50	£12,000	.3 × .2 = .06	720
		£2.50	20,000	.3 × .6 = .18	3,600
Total expected cost					12,400

Expected outcomes for decision tree

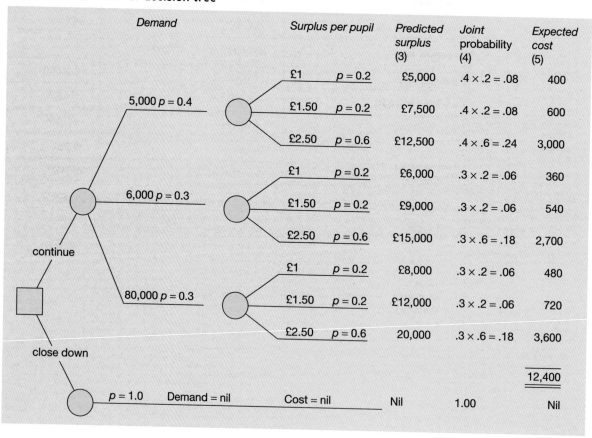

B10.3

Effect of a 1% increase in sales

Note that a 1% increase in sales will be matched by a 1% increase in variable costs.

	£		£
Sales	80,000	+1%	80,800
Variable souvenirs costs	(26,000)	+1%	(26,260)
Variable labour costs	(30,000)	+1%	(30,300)
Fixed costs	(5,000)		(5,000)
Profit	19,000		19,240

Percentage increase in profit = 240/19,000 = 1.26%
So a 1% *increase* in sales and all variable costs causes a 1.26% *increase* in profit.
The sensitivity factor is +1.26

Effect of a 1% increase in materials cost

	£		£
Sales	80,000		80,000
Variable souvenirs costs	(26,000)	+1%	(26,260)
Variable labour costs	(30,000)		(30,000)
Fixed costs	(5,000)		(5,000)
Profit	19,000		18,740

Percentage decrease in profit = 260/19,000 = 1.37%
So a 1% *increase* in variable cost of souvenirs causes a 1.37% *decrease* in profit.
The sensitivity factor is −1.37

Effect of a 1% increase in labour cost

	£		£
Sales	80,000		80,000
Variable souvenirs costs	(26,000)		(26,000)
Variable labour costs	(30,000)	+1%	(30,300)
Fixed costs	(5,000)		(5,000)
Profit	19,000		18,700

Percentage decrease in profit = 300/19,000 = 1.58%
So a 1% *increase* in variable cost of souvenirs causes a 1.58% *decrease* in profit.
The sensitivity factor is −1.58

Effect of a 1% increase in fixed cost

	£		£
Sales	80,000		80,000
Variable souvenirs costs	(26,000)		(26,000)
Variable labour costs	(30,000)		(30,000)
Fixed costs	(5,000)	+1%	(5,050)
Profit	19,000		18,950

Percentage decrease in profit = 50/19,000 = −.26%
So a 1% *increase* in a fixed cost causes a 0.26% *decrease* in profit.
The sensitivity factor is −0.26.

Chapter 11

Test your understanding

A11.16

$$\frac{£100}{(1 + 0.08)^1} = £92.6$$

$$\frac{£100}{(1 + 0.08)^2} = £85.73$$

$$\frac{£100}{(1 + 0.08)^3} = £79.4$$

Use the Appendix to Chapter 10 to check these calculations against the table of discount factors in the column for 8%.

A11.17

Calculate the present value of £100 receivable at the end of five years using a discount rate of (a) 4%, (b) 6% and (c) 8% per annum.

$$\frac{£100}{(1 + 0.04)^5} = £82.2$$

$$\frac{£100}{(1 + 0.06)^5} = £74.7$$

$$\frac{£100}{(1 + 0.08)^5} = £68.1$$

Use the Appendix to Chapter 10 to check these calculations against the table of discount factors in the columns for 4%, 6% and 8%. Note that the present value becomes less as the discount rate increases.

Application

B11.1 Projects Ltd
Payback period
The cumulative cash flows are:

End of year	£
1	10,000
2	25,000
3	45,000
4	70,000

The payback of £50,000 occurs one-fifth of the way into Year 4, i.e. payback is 3.2 years.

Accounting rate of return
Total profit over 5 years is £95,000 less depreciation of £40,000, i.e. £55,000.
Average profit is therefore £11,000 per annum.
Accounting rate of return is 11,000/50,000 = 22%.

Net present value
(Using assumed discount rate of 10%)
Using the formula approach the net present value is calculated as:

$$\frac{10,000}{(1.10)} + \frac{15,000}{(1.10)^2} + \frac{20,000}{(1.10)^3} + \frac{25,000}{(1.10)^4} + \frac{{}^*35,000}{(1.10)^5} - 50,000$$

= 9,090 + 12,397 + 15,026 + 17,075 + 21,732 − 50,000

= 75,320 − 50,000

= 25,320

*Cash flow forecast for Year 5 plus scrap value expected at end.

Using the discount tables the net present value is calculated as:

End of year	Cash flow £	Discount factor	Present value £
1	10,000	0.909	9,090
2	15,000	0.826	12,390
3	20,000	0.751	15,020
4	25,000	0.683	17,075
5	35,000	0.621	21,735
			75,310
Less initial outlay			(50,000)
Net present value			25,310

(Difference from formula-based answer is due to rounding.)

B11.2
Difference = 122 + 58 = 180.
IRR = 22 + 2(122/180) = 23.36%.

B11.3

	Machine A	Machine B
Capital expenditure required	£65,000	£60,000
Estimated life in years	4	4
Residual value	nil	nil
Cash flow after taxation each year	£25,000	£24,000
Payback	2 + 15/25 = 2.6 years	2 + 12/24 = 2.5 years
NPV	79,225 − 65,000 = 14,225	76,056 − 60,000 = 16,056
Profitability index	79,225/65,000 = 1.22	76,056/60,000 = 1.26

On payback, Machine A is preferable; on NPV and profitability index, Machine B is preferable but in all cases the answers are close so that other non-financial factors may also need to be considered.

Problem solving and evaluation

C11.1

Year	Net cash flows £000	Discount factor at 8% £000	Present value £000
1	50	.926	46.3
2	200	.857	171.4
3	225	.794	178.7
4	225	.735	165.4
5	100	.681	681.0
			1,242.8
	Cost		−500.0
	NPV		742.8

Chapter 12

Application

B12.1 Peter Green

	End of year					
	Year 0 £	Year 1 £	Year 2 £	Year 3 £	Year 4 £	Year 5 £
Forecast cash flows		80,000	80,000	80,000	80,000	
Fixed asset cost	(90,000)					
Tax payable at 20%			(16,000)	(16,000)	(16,000)	(16,000)
Tax benefit of allowance		18,000				
Sale of fixed assets					10,000	
Balancing charge						(2,000)
Net cash flow	(90,000)	98,000	64,000	64,000	74,000	(18,000)
Discount factor at 6% (from tables)	1.000	0.943	0.890	0.840	0.792	0.747
Present value	(90,000)	92,414	56,960	53,760	58,608	(13,446)
Net present value	158,296					

B12.2 Foresight

(a)

		Cash flow £m	Discount factor	Discounted flow £m
0	Initial investment	(150)	1.000	(150)
1	Annual flow	55	0.909	+50
2	Annual flow	71	0.826	+59
3	Annual flow	45	0.751	+34
3	Return of working capital	30	0.751	+22
3	Sale of fixed assets	15	0.751	+11
	Net present value			+26

(b)

Yr		Capital invested £	Interest paid at 10% £	Cash flow £	Net of interest paid £	Invest surplus at 10% £	Balance £
0	Investment	150					
1	Cash flows		15	55	40	–	40
2	Cash flows		15	71	56	4	100
3	Cash flows		15	45	30	10	140
3	Return of working capital			30			170
3	Disposal of fixed assets			15			185
3	Return of initial investment			(150)			(150)
3	Surplus						35

The present value of £35 occurring at the end of year 3 is £35m × 0.751 = £26m

Problem solving and evaluation

C12.1 Offshore Services Ltd

	Yr	ALPHA £000s	Disct	BRAVO £000s	Disct	CHARLIE £000s	Disct	DELTA £000s	Disct
Outlay	–	(600)	(600)	(300)	(300)	(120)	(120)	(210)	(210)
Cash flow benefits:									
	1	435	395	–		48	44	81	74
	2	435	359	–		48	40	81	67
	3	–	–	219	164	48	36	81	61
	4	–		219	150	48	33	81	55
	5	–		219	136	48	30	81	50
Total PV			754		450		183		307
NPV			154		150		63		97
Total PV/outlay			1.26		1.50		1.53		1.46
Internal rate of return		28.8%		22.0%		28.6%		26.8%	

All the projects are acceptable because they all have a positive net present value, but the maximisation of net present value from an investment of £1m requires selection of the projects which give the highest net present value per £ of investment. This is most conveniently estimated by comparing the total present value with the outlay (sometimes referred to as the *profitability index*). The order of preference is therefore:

Charlie, Bravo, Delta, Alpha.

The highest net present value within a £1m investment limit would be £309,000 obtained from Bravo, Charlie and Delta. If the additional funding can be borrowed, then Alpha is also desirable.

C12.2 Advanced plc

This question requires evaluation of the investment of £1,150,000 as compared with continuing on the existing basis with no investment.

	Year 1 £000s	Year 2 £000s	Year 3 £000s	Year 4 £000s	Year 5 £000s
Existing sales volume at £10 each	4,000	4,500	5,000	6,000	7,500
Proposed sales volume at £8.50	4,760	5,355	5,950	7,140	8,925
Incremental cash flow from sales	760	855	950	1,140	1,425
Existing production outflow at £7.50	3,150	3,263	3,788	4,575	5,475
New production outflow at £6.20	3,497	3,949	4,309	5,208	6,473
Incremental cash outflow on production	347	686	521	633	998
Excess inflow over outflow	413	169	429	507	427
Incremental scrap value					130
	413	169	429	507	557
Discount factors at 12%	0.893	0.797	0.712	0.636	0.567
Present value	369	135	305	322	316

Total present value = 1,447,000.

Investment required is £1,150,000 but there is scrap value from the existing machine of £30,000, giving a net outlay of £1,120,000.

So compare present value of £1,447,000 with outlay of £1,120,000. Net present value is positive therefore investment is acceptable.

Other matters – is demand sustainable, are production costs controllable at lower level, is scrap value forecast realistic?

Chapter 13

Test your understanding

A13.11

In store = 1,000 + 4,000 – 4,200 = 800

A13.12

	Jan	Feb	Mar	Apr	May	June
	£	£	£	£	£	£
Sales	12,000	13,000	14,000	13,500	12,600	11,100
Cash received – budget	nil	12,000	13,000	14,000	13,500	12,600

A13.13

	£
Goods purchased during January	18,000
Owing to creditors at end of January	13,600
Cash paid for January purchases	4,400
Payment for amounts owed at start	12,500
Total paid	16,900

A13.14

Cost of indirect materials in March £500, split £200 variable and £300 fixed.

During April direct labour hours will be 20% higher and it is known that variable indirect material is proportionate to direct labour hours, so increase variable cost by 20% from £200 to £240. Fixed cost remains constant so total budget is £540.

Application

B13.1 Garden Ornament Company

From the information presented in Tables T 1 to T 5 the various detailed budgets are prepared as shown in Tables T 6 to T 18. These lead to the master budget set out in Tables T 19 to T 21.

Sales budget: sales and debtors

The sales budget sets out the volume of sales expected for each product, multiplied by the expected selling price, to obtain the total sales by value expected for each product. The total sales for the year ahead may then be calculated, shown in bold print in the sales budget.

(T 6)

Sales budget	Ref.	Ducks	Herons	Total for year
Unit sales for year	T 1	8,000	15,000	
Unit selling price	T 1	£30	£45	
Total sales		£240,000	£675,000	**£915,000**

The year-end debtors are calculated as half of one month's sales (one-twenty-fourth of the total year's sales if these are spread evenly throughout the year).

(T 7)

Debtors budget	Ref.	Ducks	Herons	Total for year
Total sales	T 6	£240,000	£675,000	£915,000
		divide by 24	divide by 24	
Debtors at year-end		£10,000	£28,125	**£38,125**

Production plan

(T 8)

Production plan in units	Ref.	Ducks	Herons
Planned sales volume	T 1	8,000	15,000
Add planned closing stock of finished goods	T 3	–	–
Less opening stock of finished goods	T 3	–	–
Planned unit production for year		8,000	15,000

Direct materials budget: Purchases, stock and trade creditors

Once the production plan is decided, the costs of the various inputs to production may be calculated. Direct materials must be purchased to satisfy the production plans, but the purchases budget must also take into account the need to hold stock of raw materials. After the purchases budget has been quantified in terms of cost, the impact on trade creditors may also be established.

The *purchases budget* is based on the units required for production in the period, making allowance for the opening and closing stock of raw materials. The plan is to hold sufficient stock at the end of the period to meet 60 per cent of the following month's production (*see* T 3). The number of units to be purchased will equal the planned production for the period, plus the planned stock of raw materials at the end of the period (shown in the opening balance sheet at T 5), minus the planned stock of raw materials at the end of the period (calculated in T 8).

(T 9)

Purchases budget in units	Ref.	Ducks	Herons
Production volume	T 8	8,000	15,000
Add raw materials stock planned for end of period	T 3	400 60% of (8,000/12)	750 60% of (15,000/12)
Less raw materials stock held at start of period	T 5	400	750
Purchases of raw materials planned		8,000	15,000

(T 10)

Purchases budget in £s	Ref.	Ducks	Herons	Total for year
Volume of purchases	T 9	8,000	15,000	
		£	£	£
Cost per unit	T 1	14	16	
Total purchase cost		112,000	240,000	**352,000**

Trade creditors are calculated as one month's purchases, a relatively uncomplicated procedure in this instance because the purchases remain constant from month to month.

(T 11)

One month's purchases 352,000/12	**£29,333**

The direct materials cost of goods sold must also be calculated at this point, for use in the budgeted profit and loss account. The direct materials cost of goods sold is based on the materials used in production of the period (which in this example is all sold during the period).

(T 12)

Direct materials cost of goods sold	Ref.	Ducks	Herons	Total for year
Production in units	T 8	8,000	15,000	
		£	£	
Materials cost per unit	T 1	14	16	
Total cost of goods to be sold		£112,000	£240,000	**£352,000**

Direct labour budget

The direct labour budget takes the volume of production in units and multiplies that by the expanded labour cost per unit to give a labour cost for each separate item of product and a total for the year, shown in bold print.

(T 13)

Direct labour budget	Ref.	Ducks	Herons	Total for year
Production in units	T 8	8,000	15,000	
		£	£	£
Labour cost per unit	T 1	12	13	
Total cost		96,000	195,000	**291,000**

It is also useful to check on the total resource requirement which corresponds to this total labour cost, since it takes time to plan increases or decreases in labour resources. The average direct labour cost was given in (T 1) as £15,000 per person per year. The following calculation assumes that the employees can work equally efficiently on any of the three product lines.

(T 14)

Resource requirement: Based on an average cost of £15,000 per person per year, the total labour cost of £291,000 would require 19.4 full-time equivalent persons.

Production overhead budget

Production overheads include all those overhead items which relate to the production activity. In this example it includes heat and light, business rates and depreciation. Depreciation is calculated at a rate of 20% on the total cost of equipment held during the year (£190,000 at the start, as shown in (T 5), plus an additional £70,000 noted in (T 4)) (£260,000 × 20% = £52,000).

(T 15)

Production overhead budget	Ref.	£
Heat and light	T 2	8,000
Production fixed overheads	T 2	4,000
Depreciation	T 4	52,000
Total		**64,000**

Total production cost budget

Total production cost budget comprises the cost of direct materials, direct labour and production overhead.

(T 16)

Production cost budget	Ref.	£
Direct materials	T 12	352,000
Direct labour	T 13	291,000
Production overhead	T 15	64,000
Total		**707,000**

Administration expense budget
(T 17)

Administration budget	Ref.	£
Partners' salaries (taken in cash)	T 2	55,000
Rent of premises	T 2	11,000
Office staff	T 2	48,450
Total		**114,450**

Marketing expense budget

The marketing expense budget relates to all aspects of the costs of advertising and selling the product. The information in (T 2) specifies a marketing cost which is dependent on sales, being estimated as 18% of sales value.

(T 18)

Marketing expense budget	Ref.	£
18% of £915,000	T 2 & T 6	**164,700**

Master budget

The master budget has three components: the budgeted profit and loss account for the year, the budgeted cash flow statement and the budgeted balance sheet. These are now set out using the foregoing separate budgets. Where the derivation of figures in the master budget should be evident from the earlier budgets, no explanation is given, but where further calculations have been performed these are shown as working notes.

Budgeted profit and loss account
(T 19)

Budgeted profit and loss account for the year ended 31 December Year 5

	Ref.	Ducks	Herons	Total for year
		£	£	£
Total sales	T 6	240,000	675,000	915,000
Material cost	T 12	112,000	240,000	352,000
Labour cost	T 13	96,000	195,000	291,000
Total variable cost		208,000	435,000	643,000
Contribution		32,000	240,000	272,000
% on sales		13.3%	35.6%	
Production overhead	T 15			64,000
Gross profit				208,000
Administration cost	T 17			(114,450)
Marketing cost	T 18			(164,700)
Net loss				(71,150)

Budgeted cash flow statement

Where expenses are paid for as soon as they are incurred, the cash outflow equals the expense as shown in the budgeted profit and loss account. In the case of cash collected from customers, debtors at the start and end of the period must be taken into the calculation. In the case of cash paid to suppliers the creditors at the start and end of the period must be taken into account. The cash flow statement contains references to working notes which follow the statement and set out the necessary detail.

(T 20)

Budgeted cash flow statement for the year ended 31 December Year 5

	Note	£	£
Cash to be collected from customers	1		908,875
Cash to be paid to suppliers	2	352,667	
Direct labour	3	291,000	
Heat and light	3	8,000	
Production fixed overheads	3	4,000	
Partners' salaries	3	55,000	
Rent of premises	3	11,000	
Office staff costs	3	48,450	
Marketing costs	3	164,700	
Net cash outflow from operations			934,817
New equipment to be purchased			(25,942)
Net cash outflow			70,000
Cash balance at start of year	T 5		(95,942)
Cash balance at end of year			2,500
			(93,442)

Working notes for budgeted cash flow statement

Note 1: Cash to be collected from customers:

	Ref.	£
Sales during the period	T 6	915,000
Less credit sales which remain as debtors at the end of the year	T 7	38,125
		876,875
Add cash collected from debtors at the start of the year	T 5	32,000
Cash to be collected from customers		908,875

Note 2: Cash to be paid to suppliers:

	Ref.	£
Purchases during the period	T 10	352,000
Less credit purchases which remain as creditors at the end of the year	T 11	29,333
		322,667
Add cash paid to creditors at the start of the year	T 5	30,000
Cash to be paid to suppliers		352,667

Note 3: Other cash payments

It has been assumed, for the convenience of this illustration, that all other expense items are paid for as they are incurred. In reality this would be unlikely and there would be further calculations of the type shown in Note 2, making allowance for creditors at the start and end of the period.

Budgeted balance sheet
(T 21)

Budgeted balance sheet at 31 December Year 5

	£	£
Equipment at cost (Note 1)		260,000
Accumulated depreciation (Note 2)		92,000
Net book value		168,000
Stock of raw materials (Note 3)	17,600	
Trade debtors (T 7)	38,125	
	55,725	
Bank borrowing (T 20)	93,442	
Trade creditors (T 11)	29,333	
	122,775	
Net current liabilities		(67,050)
Total assets less current liabilities		100,950
Partners' capital (Note 4)		100,950

Working notes for budgeted balance sheet

Note 1
Equipment at cost = £190,000 + £70,000   =   £260,000

Note 2
Accumulated depreciation = £40,000 + £52,000   =   £92,000

Note 3
Stock of raw material

	£
For 400 ducks @ £14 each	5,600
For 750 herons @ £16 each	12,000
	17,600

Note 4
Partners' capital = £172,100 + (£71,150)   =   £100,950

Comment: Not a promising picture of where the business is likely to be heading but this amount of detail will help identify where action needs to be taken to improve profit and cash flow.

B13.2 Tools Ltd
(Note that in questions of this type there will often be more than one way of interpreting the information given. That is not a problem provided the total column is used to check for arithmetic consistency.)

Sales budget
Selling price £90 per unit

	Year 1				Total
	Quarter 1	Quarter 2	Quarter 3	Quarter 4	
Modified tool units	4,050	4,200	4,350	3,900	16,500
	£	£	£	£	£
Sales	364,500	378,000	391,500	351,000	1,485,000

Production budget for each quarter
By units, production must meet the sales of this quarter and 100 per cent of planned sales of the next quarter:

	Year 1				Total
	Quarter 1	Quarter 2	Quarter 3	Quarter 4	
Modified tool units	4,050	4,200	4,350	3,900	16,500
For sales of quarter	4,050	4,200	4,350	3,900	
Add 10 per cent of next qtr sales	420	435	390	405	405
	4,470	4,635	4,740	4,305	
Less stock of previous qtr	–	420	435	390	
Production required	4,470	4,215	4,305	3,915	16,905

Converting from units of production to costs of production

	Year 1				Total
	Quarter 1	Quarter 2	Quarter 3	Quarter 4	
Units to be produced	4,470	4,215	4,305	3,915	16,905
	£	£	£	£	£
Direct materials	107,280	101,160	103,320	93,960	405,720
Direct labour	134,100	126,450	129,150	117,450	507,150
Fixed overhead*	44,700	42,150	43,050	39,150	169,050
	286,080	269,760	275,520	250,560	1,081,920
*Includes depreciation of	5,288	4,987	5,093	4,632	20,000

(Note that fixed overhead includes depreciation of £20,000 per annum, allocated on the basis of a cost per unit produced. Total production is 16,905 units so depreciation is £1.183 per unit.)

Cash budget for each quarter

	Year 1				Total
	Quarter 1	Quarter 2	Quarter 3	Quarter 4	
	£	£	£	£	£
Cash from customers					
$^1/_3$ current quarter	121,500	126,000	130,500	117,000	
$^2/_3$ previous quarter	–	243,000	252,000	261,000	
Total cash received	121,500	369,000	382,500	378,000	1,251,000
Purchase of fixed assets	100,000				100,000
Payment to suppliers*	83,520	103,200	102,600	97,080	386,400
Wages	134,100	126,450	129,150	117,450	507,150
Fixed overhead (excl depn)	39,412	37,163	37,957	34,518	149,050
Total cash payments	357,032	266,813	269,707	249,048	1,142,600
Receipts less payments	(235,532)	102,187	112,793	128,952	(108,400)

*Schedule of payments to suppliers on one month's credit.

The initial stock of 500 units will be paid for at the start of month 2 together with one-third of the units required for month 1's production. Thereafter the payment is always on a one-third basis because the 500 units of stock remains constant.

	Quarter 1	Quarter 2	Quarter 3	Quarter 4	Total
	£	£	£	£	£
Direct materials purchased	107,280	101,160	103,320	93,960	405,720
Payment for initial stock	12,000				12,000
Two months' purchases	71,520	67,440	68,880	62,640	
One month from previous qtr	–	35,760	33,720	34,440	31,320
Total payment	83,520	103,200	102,600	97,080	386,400

Comment on cash flow statement

This is the type of statement which would be required by someone being asked to lend money to the business. The start-up situation requires cash, but there is a positive cash flow from operations. The lender would want to add to the cash flow statement a schedule of loan repayments and interest payments to see whether the operational cash flows could meet the financing needs of the business.

B13.3 Bright Papers Ltd
Cash from customers
(£000s)

Sales budget	Year 1	Year 2	Year 3	Year 4
Unit sales for year	£800	£950	£1,200	£1,500
Unit selling price	£10.20	£10.56	£11.04	£12.00
Total sales	£8,160	£10,032	£13,248	£18,000

The year-end debtors are calculated on the basis that the sales are spread evenly throughout the year.

(£000s)

Debtors budget	Year 1	Year 2	Year 3	Year 4
Total sales	£8,160	£10,032	£13,248	£18,000
Months/12	1/12	1/12	1.5/12	2/12
Debtors at year-end	£680	£836	£1,656	£3,000

Cash received from customers is equal to the year's sales plus debtors at the start of the year less debtors at the end of the year.

(£000s)

Cash received budget	Year 1	Year 2	Year 3	Year 4
Total sales	£8,160	£10,032	£13,248	£18,000
Debtors at start	–	£680	£836	£1,656
Debtors at year-end	£(680)	£(836)	£(1,656)	£(3,000)
Cash received	£7,480	£9,876	£12,428	£16,656

Cash paid to suppliers
The purchases budget is based on the units required for production in the period (if necessary making allowance for the opening and closing stock of raw materials).

(£000s)

Purchases budget in units	Year 1	Year 2	Year 3	Year 4
Production volume	850	1,000	1,300	1,600
Add raw materials stock planned for end of period	nil	nil	nil	nil
Less raw materials stock held at start of period	nil	nil	nil	nil
Purchases of raw materials planned	850	1,000	1,300	1,600

(£000s)

Purchases budget	Year 1	Year 2	Year 3	Year 4
Volume of purchases	850	1,000	1,300	1,600
Cost per unit	£2.04	£2.28	£2.64	£3.00
Total purchase cost	£1,734	£2,280	£3,432	£4,800

Trade creditors allow different credit periods in different years.

(£000s)

Creditors budget	Year 1	Year 2	Year 3	Year 4
Total purchases	£1,734	£2,280	£3,432	£4,800
Months/12	2/12	1.5/12	1.5/12	1/12
Creditors at year-end	£289	£285	£429	£400

(£000s)

Cash paid to suppliers	Year 1	Year 2	Year 3	Year 4
Total purchase cost	£1,734	£2,280	£3,432	£4,800
Add creditors at start	–	£289	£285	£429
Less creditors at end	(£289)	(£285)	(£429)	(£400)
Cash paid	£1,445	£2,284	£3,288	£4,829

Payments to employees for wages

Direct labour budget

The direct labour budget takes the volume of production in units and multiplies that by the expected labour cost per unit to give a labour cost for each separate item of product and a total for the year, shown in bold print.

(£000s)

Direct labour budget	Year 1	Year 2	Year 3	Year 4
Production in units	850	1,000	1,300	1,600
Labour cost per unit	£0.60	£0.75	£0.90	£0.90
Total cost	**£510**	**£750**	**£1,170**	**£1,440**

Payment for overheads

Production overhead budget

Total production overhead comprises variable and fixed overhead. The variable overhead is calculated using the variable overhead cost per unit multiplied by the number of units produced. The fixed overhead is fixed for each year and is not affected by volume of activity in the period.

(£000s)

Production overhead budget	Year 1	Year 2	Year 3	Year 4
Production in units	850	1,000	1,300	1,600
Variable overhead cost per unit	£0.40	£0.50	£0.60	£0.60
Total variable overhead cost	£340	£500	£780	£960
Fixed overhead*	£5,000	£5,100	£5,200	£5,300
Total prodn o'head	£5,340	£5,600	£5,980	£6,260

*For cash flows deduct £1,500 each year.

Cash budgets for each of the four years

	Year 1 £	Year 2 £	Year 3 £	Year 4 £
Cash from customers	7,480	9,876	12,428	16,656
Cash paid to suppliers	1,445	2,284	3,288	4,829
Wages paid	510	750	1,170	1,440
Variable overhead	340	500	780	960
Fixed overhead*	3,500	3,600	3,700	3,800
Total paid	5,795	7,134	8,938	11,029
Net cash flow	1,685	2,742	3,490	5,627

*Excluding depreciation because that does not involve a cash flow.

Problem solving and evaluation

C13.1 Alpha Ltd

Budgeted profit and loss account

	Original for half-year to 31 March £	Actual for half-year to 31 March £	Note
Sales	7,800,000	6,240,000	down 20%
Cost of sales	(5,226,000)	(4,305,600)	residual
Gross profit (original budget at 33%)	2,574,000	1,934,400	31%
Fixed overheads:			
Selling and advertising	(750,000)	(650,000)	Advtg – £100k
General administration	(547,250)	(492,525)	down 10%
Operating profit	1,276,750	791,875	
Interest payable on medium-term loan	(67,500)	(73,750)	33.75 + 40
Royalties payable on sales	(390,000)	(312,000)	5%
Net profit	819,250	406,125	

(Note the impact of the increase in stock levels has been ignored in this and the next statement because it is a temporary fluctuation which is put right by the end of the year.)

	Actual for half-year to 31 March £	Revised budget for half-year to 30 Sept £
Sales	6,240,000	6,240,000
Cost of sales	(4,305,600)	(4,180,800)
Gross profit (original budget at 33%)	1,934,400	2,059,200
Fixed overheads:		
Selling and advertising	(650,000)	(650,000)
General administration	(492,525)	(492,525)
Operating profit	791,875	916,675
Interest payable on medium-term loan	(73,750)	(80,000)
Royalties payable on sales	(312,000)	(312,000)
Net profit	406,125	524,675

The question asks only for the results at 31 March and the revised budget thereafter but the information may be used to reply to the question asked by the directors in relation to the cash flow impact. You may find this more difficult but it is something which you can at least think out in general terms. First of all the measures taken to restore the gross profit must have an impact. Then the directors are controlling the level of stock so that it is not using up resources in the form of cash. Reducing the period of credit given to trade debtors will improve cash flow (basing the calculation on the lower level of actual sales achieved and expected). Finally the cost of goods sold has been controlled better in the second half. This will reduce the amount owing to creditors, even though the period of credit remains unchanged.

Chapter 14

Application **B14.1**

	Original budget (1)	Flexible budget (2)	Actual for March (3)	Variance (2) – (3)	
Units manufactured	12,000	14,000	14,000		
	£	£	£	£	
Direct materials	48,000	56,000	53,000	3,000	(F)
Direct labour	24,000	28,000	29,000	1,000	(A)
Variable overhead	6,000	7,000	7,200	200	(A)
Fixed overhead	4,000	4,000	4,500	500	(A)
Total costs	82,000	95,000	93,700	1,300	(F)

The direct materials variance is 5.4% of the flexible budget amount and needs investigating even although it is favourable. Two possible questions to investigate are: (1) Did the budget estimates use outdated prices? (2) Has the buying department chosen low price materials without perhaps considering the quality?

The labour variance is 3.6% of the flexible budget amount. Questions that could be asked here are: (1) Has there been a rise in pay rates since the budget was set? (2) Has the apparent purchase of lower cost materials had an impact on labour through using poorer quality materials?

The variable overhead and fixed overhead variances are lower percentages of the flexible budget, but the reasons should be noted to ensure that the variances do not increase in future periods.

Chapter 15

Test your understanding **A15.17**

20,000 blocks require 100,000 kg of material so standard usage is 5 kg per block.
16,000 blocks should use 80,000 kg but actual usage is 80,080 kg. Adverse usage variance is 80 kg at standard cost of £3 per kg, i.e. adverse variance £240.

A15.18

Total variance is £6,000 adverse less £2,500 favourable = £3,500 adverse. So actual costs were £3,500 higher than standard cost, i.e. £39,500.

A15.19

Fixed overhead expenditure variance is £1,500 adverse. Volume variance £2 × 1,000 = £2,000 adverse.

Application **B15.1 Plastics Ltd**

	Budget for May	Actual for May	Variance	
Production in units	42,800	42,800		
	£	£	£	
Direct material	256,800	267,220	10,420	(A)
Direct labour	342,400	356,577	14,177	(A)
Variable overhead	171,200	165,243	5,957	(F)
Fixed overhead	90,000	95,000	5,000	(A)
Total production cost	860,400	884,040	23,640	(A)
Less stock increase at standard cost,				
2,800 units at £21	58,800	58,800		
Cost of goods sold	801,600	825,240		
Sales 40,000 × £70	2,800,000	2,800,000		
Net profit	1,998,400	1,974,760	23,640	(A)

Note on standard cost

	£
Budgeted cost per unit	
Direct material 5 kg × £1.20	6
Direct labour 2 hours × £4	8
Variable overhead 2 hours × £2	4
Fixed overhead £90,000/30,000	3
	21

Analysis of variances
Direct materials (total variance £10,420 adverse):

Price variance = AQ (SP − AP)	Usage variance = SP (SQ − AQ)
= 213,776 kg (£1.20 − £1.25)	= £1.20 (214,000 − 213,776)
= £10,688 adverse variance	= £268 favourable variance

Direct labour (total variance £14,177 adverse):

Rate variance = AH (SR − AR)	Efficiency variance = SR (SH − AH)
= 86,970 hours (£4.00 − £4.10)	= £4.00 (85,600 − 86,970)
= £8,697 adverse variance	= £5,480 adverse variance

Variable overhead (total variance £5,957 favourable):

Rate variance = AH (SR − AR)	Efficiency variance = SR (SH − AH)
= 86,970 hours (£2.00 − £1.90)	= £2.00 (85,600 − 86,970)
= £8,697 favourable variance	= £2,740 adverse variance

Fixed overhead expenditure variance is £5,000 adverse, indicating overspending.

One possible interpretation of the variance analysis is that less wastage of material occurred through buying higher-quality material at a higher unit price. Labour was paid more than expected, which may have been due to an unexpected pay award, but nevertheless worked less efficiently than expected. The inefficient working has a consequence also on the efficiency of using variable overheads although this was more than offset by a lower than expected rate of variable overhead cost.

B15.2
Budgeted and actual costs for the month of May

	Budget £	Actual £	Variance £	
Actual level of output (units)	120	120		
Direct materials	30,000	31,200	1,200	(A)
Direct labour	18,000	16,800	1,200	(F)
Fixed manufacturing overhead	10,000	9,600	400	(F)
Total costs of production	58,000	57,600	400	(F)

Analysis of variances
Direct materials (total variance £1,200 adverse):

Price variance = AQ (SP − AP)	Usage variance = SP (SQ − AQ)
= 1,300 kg (£25 − £24)	= £25 (1,200 − 1,300)
= £1,300 favourable variance	= £2,500 adverse variance

Direct labour (total variance £1,200 favourable):

Rate variance = AH (SR − AR)	Efficiency variance = SR (SH − AH)
= 1,400 hours (£12 − £10)	= £10 (1,800 − 1,400)
= £2,800 adverse variance	= £4,000 favourable variance

Fixed overhead variance is an expenditure variance reflecting less spent than expected.

One possible explanation here is that the company tried to save money by buying cheaper material, but this had the wrong effect because it increased wastage and hence usage was greater. The rate variance indicates that the incentive payment was successful: it had a cost which was more than offset by greater efficiency.

B15.3 Carrypack Ltd – month of April Year 6

	Flexible budget	Actual	Variance
	12,300 units	12,300 units	
	£	£	£
Sales: 12,300 units @ £50 each	615,000	615,000	nil
Production: 12,300 units			
	£	£	£
Direct materials	135,300	136,220	920 (A)
Direct labour	110,700	129,200	18,500 (A)
Variable overheads	73,800	72,200	1,600 (F)
Fixed overhead	48,000	49,400	1,400 (A)
Total cost	367,800	387,020	19,220 (A)
Actual profit	247,200	227,980	19,220 (A)

Direct materials (total variance £920 adverse):

Price variance = AQ (SP − AP) = 27,800 kg (£5.00 − £4.90) = £2,780 favourable variance	Usage variance = SP (SQ − AQ) = £5 (*27,060 − 27,800) = £3,700 adverse variance

*26,400 kg is standard for 12,000 units so proportionately 27,060 kg is standard for 12,300 units.

Direct labour (total variance £18,500 adverse):

Rate variance = AH (SR − AR) = 38,000 hours (£3.00 − £3.40) = £15,200 adverse variance	Efficiency variance = SR (SH − AH) = £3.00 (36,900 − 38,000) = £3,300 adverse variance

Variable overhead (total variance £1,600 favourable):

Rate variance = AH (SR − AR) = 38,000 hours (£2.00 − £1.90) = £3,800 favourable variance	Efficiency variance = SR (SH − AH) = £2.00 (36,900 − 38,000) = £2,200 adverse variance

Fixed overhead expenditure variance is £1,400 adverse, indicating overspending.
Comment: Direct materials needs investigating for controllability of the usage variance and whether low-price goods have been purchased with a consequence of more wastage. Direct labour is the variance of most concern because of its magnitude. If the labour rate has changed then the budget should be revised so that the non-controllable variance of £15,200 is not reported. The inefficiency of labour working is matched by inefficiency in use of variable overhead and the cause of the unexpected extra hours should be investigated.

Problem solving and evaluation

C15.1 Cabinets Ltd
Reconstructed budget for May Year 4

Production units budgeted	1,800
	£
Direct materials £3.00 × (9,600 × 1,800/1,600)	32,400
Direct labour £8.00 × (4,800 × 1,800/1,600)	43,200
Fixed overhead	36,000
Total budgeted cost	111,600

In the following tables, the figures in italics are the items which have been calculated from a knowledge of the other items in the table.

Direct materials (total variance £2,560 adverse):

Price variance = AQ (SP – AP) = 11,200 kg (£3.00 – £2.80) = £2,240 favourable variance	Usage variance = SP (SQ – AQ) = £3.00 (9,600 – 11,200) = £4,800 adverse variance

Direct labour (total variance £12,000 adverse):

Rate variance = AH (SR – AR) = 5,600 hours (£8.00 – £9.00) = £5,600 adverse variance	Efficiency variance = SR (SH – AH) = £8.00 (4,800 – 5,600) = £6,400 adverse variance

Fixed overhead expenditure variance is £3,000 adverse, indicating the budget was £36,000.

One possible interpretation is that cheaper material was bought but resulted in more wastage, the adverse effect on usage exceeding the price saving. The labour rate increased, possibly due to an agreed wage rise, but the efficiency worsened, perhaps because of the cheaper material. The adverse fixed overhead expenditure indicates overspending which is not related to volume effects.

C15.2 Fixit Ltd

	Flexible budget	Actual	Variance	
Production in units	5,500	5,500		
	£	£	£	
Direct materials	22,000	22,764	764	(A)
Direct labour	66,000	75,900	9,900	(A)
Variable production overhead	15,400	14,950	450	(F)
Fixed production overhead	10,000	9,000	1,000	(F)
Depreciation	4,000	4,000	–	
	117,400	126,614	9,214	(A)

Analysis of variances
Direct materials (total variance £764 adverse):

Price variance = AQ (SP – AP) = 54,200 kg (£0.40 – £0.42) = £1,084 adverse variance	Usage variance = SP (SQ – AQ) = £0.40 (55,000 – 54,200) = £320 favourable variance

Direct labour (total variance £9,900 adverse):

PRate variance = AH (SR – AR) = 11,500 hours (£6.00 – £6.60) = £6,900 adverse variance	Efficiency variance = SR (SH – AH) = £6.00 (11,000 – 11,500) = £3,000 adverse variance

Variable overhead (total variance £450 favourable):

Rate variance = AH (SR – AR) = 11,500 hours (£1.40 – £1.30) = £1,150 favourable variance	Efficiency variance = SR (SH – AH) = £1.40 (11,000 – 11,500) = £700 adverse variance

Fixed overhead expenditure variance is £1,000 favourable, indicating underspending.

Comment: More expensive material may have produced better quality and caused some off-setting in less material wastage. However, efficiency of working was lower than expected, affecting both labour and variable overhead costs. The variable overhead rate was lower than expected, suggesting some saving on the cost of overheads, but the labour rate was higher than expected, suggesting an unexpected pay award.

C15.3 Concrete Products Ltd
Heavy paving

	Actual tonnes	Budget tonnes	Flexible budget tonnes	Variance	
Sales volume	29,000	27,500	29,000		
Production volume	29,000	27,500	29,000		
	£000s	£000s	£000s	£000s	
Revenue	720	690	727	7	(A)
Variable cost of sales	280	270	285	5	(F)
Contribution	440	420	442	2	(A)

Garden paving

	Actual tonnes	Budget tonnes	Flexible budget tonnes	Variance	
Sales volume	10,500	8,500	10,500		
Production volume	10,500	8,500	10,500		
	£000s	£000s	£000s	£000s	
Revenue	430	300	370	60	(F)
Variable cost of sales	170	127	157	13	(A)
Contribution	260	173	213	47	(F)

Comment: The comparison between budget and actual must be made on the basis of a flexible budget which allows for the revised levels of production and sales. In both cases the activity has been greater than was expected when the budget was set. Making comparison with a flexible budget shows that heavy paving made a contribution which was £2,000 less than expected while garden paving made a contribution which was £47,000 greater than expected.

Questions to ask:
1 Has there been a change in the sales price of these items? If so the budget should be revised to take account of the new price, and the variance for the period would be £8,000 adverse.
2 Has there been a change in the cost of direct materials? If so the budget should be revised to avoid giving the impression of an adverse variance of £8,000. The usefulness of variance analysis lies in identifying controllable variances, not in relating to outdated budgets.
3 On the presumption that there has been no change in the labour rate, is the supervisory team working effectively? One explanation of the adverse cost variance could be inefficient working in the production department.

Chapter 16

Problem solving and evaluation

C16.1 Furniture Manufacture Ltd
A control report should emphasise the costs which are controllable within the organisation and which are most closely the responsibility of the manager concerned.

Although the power failure was beyond the control of the departmental manager, the company needs to know the cost of that failure. If there was a power failure then there can have been no productive work from direct labour and it is likely that indirect labour, indirect materials and indirect production overhead would not have been incurred during that time. The fixed overheads will have been incurred irrespective but the variable maintenance costs may not have been incurred where there was no activity to maintain. So the budgeted cost should be recalculated at 75% of the expected cost and compared with actual. This may give a better comparison with the actual cost.

	Fixed	Budgeted cost Original variable	Revised variable	Total	Actual cost	Variance (F) = favourable (A) = adverse
	£	£	£	£	£	£
Direct labour	–	36,000	27,000	27,000	30,000	3,000 (A)
Indirect labour	6,000	8,000	6,000	12,000	14,000	2,000 (A)
Indirect materials	–	4,000	3,000	3,000	3,500	500 (A)
Power	3,000	12,000	9,000	12,000	9,000	3,000 (F)
Maintenance materials	–	5,000	3,750	3,750	3,000	750 (F)
Maintenance labour	5,000	4,000	3,000	8,000	15,000	7,000 (A)
Depreciation	85,000	–	–	85,000	75,000	10,000 (F)
Production overhead	–	20,000	15,000	15,000	15,000	–

The revised table suggests that the bench assembly department manager should not be quite so complacent as was indicated from the earlier table. The labour costs appear to be higher than would be expected for a power failure period, unless the explanation is that they have been paid overtime rates to catch up on the work. Questions also need to be asked about the maintenance labour. It may be that the explanation is that additional maintenance was undertaken during the enforced idleness, although this explanation depends on being able to undertake maintenance without an electricity supply.

C16.2
(a) For explanation of responsibility accounting see the chapter.
(b) Manager of distribution division needs:
- area totals for demand (5 columns)
- area totals for running costs of floats
- area totals for drivers' wages and managers' salaries
- area totals for cash collection and note on areas of slow payment problems, with action taken
- copy of area returns as backup if required
- exception report from each area manager highlighting problem areas and action taken
- ratios identifying relationships of key variables.

Area manager needs:
- depot totals for demand (10 columns)
- depot totals for running costs of floats
- depot totals for drivers' wages and managers' salaries
- depot totals for cash collected and note on dealing with slow payers
- copy of depot returns as backup if required
- ratios identifying relationships of key variables.

Depot manager needs:
- delivery demand analysed by driver
- running costs of float analysed by driver
- drivers' wages for each employee
- cash collection analysed by driver
- ratios relating input to output.

Chapter 17

Application **B17.1**
For Division X the new project would bring a ROI of £1.2m on £4m or 30%, appearing unattractive in the context of the existing ROI of 33%. The residual income would be (£1.2m – £0.4m) = £0.8m which is an addition to the profit of the division after rewarding investment and therefore would be attractive on RI measures.

For Division Y the ROI of £0.8m on £4m is 20% which looks attractive when compared with the existing level of 4%. The residual income would be (£0.8m – £0.4m) = £0.4m. This is acceptable but if the company has only £4m to invest it would produce a higher RI in division X.

B17.2

(a) Transfer price = £10 per chair

Supplying division (A)

Output	Revenue @ £10	Variable cost @ £8	Fixed cost	Profit/(loss)
	£	£	£	£
30	300	240	200	(140)
40	400	320	200	(120)
50	500	400	200	(100)
60	600	480	200	(80)
70	700	560	200	(60)
80	800	640	200	(40)

Receiving division (B)

Acquired	Revenue	Variable cost @ £7	Transfer @ £10	Fixed cost	Profit/loss
	£	£	£	£	£
30	720	210	300	60	150
40	920	280	400	60	180
50	**1100**	**350**	**500**	**60**	**190**
60	1260	420	600	60	180
70	1400	490	700	60	150
80	1520	560	800	60	100

Company as a whole

Output	Revenue	Variable cost @ £15	Fixed cost	Profit/loss
30	720	450	260	10
40	920	600	260	60
50	1100	750	260	90
60	**1260**	**900**	**260**	**100**
70	1400	1050	260	90
80	1520	1200	260	60

(b) Transfer price = marginal cost of supplying division = £8 per unit.

Receiving division (B)

Acquired	Revenue	Variable cost	Transfer	Fixed cost	Profit/loss
	£	£	£	£	£
30	720	210	240	60	210
40	920	280	320	60	260
50	1100	350	400	60	290
60	**1260**	**420**	**480**	**60**	**300**
70	1400	490	560	60	290
80	1520	560	640	60	260

Supplying division (A)

Output	Revenue @ £8	Variable cost @ £8	Fixed cost	Profit/(loss)
	£	£	£	£
30	240	240	200	(200)
40	320	320	200	(200)
50	400	400	200	(200)
60	480	480	200	(200)
70	560	560	200	(200)
80	640	640	200	(200)

C17.1
Musical Productions Ltd

	CD £000s	PS £000s
Investment in fixed assets	840	700
Revenue	420	210
Operating expenses	210	140
Profit	210	70
ROI from budget	25%	10%
New investment	140	140
Expected profits	28	28
ROI from new project	20%	20%
Interest payable at 18%	25.2	25.2
Residual income from project	2.8	2.8

In ROI terms the project would be rejected by CD and accepted by PS. The residual income calculation is neutral to the decision, confirming only that the project can meet interest costs and leave a surplus.

The location of the project should therefore be based on other factors such as efficiency of management or suitability of workforce skills.

Chapter 18

Application **B18.1**

	A £m	B £m
During year		
Sales	200	200
Cost of sales	150	150
Gross profit	50	50
At end of year		
Inventory (stock)	12	24
Trade debtors	3	13
Trade creditors	11	11
Stockholding period	12 × 365/150 = 29.2 days	24 × 365/150 = 58.4 days
Debtors collection period	3 × 365/200 = 5.5 days	13 × 365/200 = 23.7 days
Creditors payment period	11 × 365/150 = 26.8 days	11 × 365/150 = 26.8 days
Working capital cycle	7.9 days	55.3 days

Comment. The wholesaler is expecting almost immediate payment from customers (average five days) and is holding inventory for 29 days. Suppliers allow 26.8 days. So the wholesaler's need for working capital support is relatively low at 7.9 days.

The manufacturer has the same amount of credit allowed by suppliers but has a longer stock-holding period (58.4 days) and a longer period of credit taken by customers (23.7 days). That leaves a relatively long period requiring support for working capital (55.3 days).

C18.1
Solution

	At start £	Year 1 £	Year 2 £	Year 3 £	Year 4 £	Year 5 £
Buildings	1,500,000					
Land lease	120,000					
Machinery	500,000	50,000	50,000	50,000	50,000	50,000
LT Loan repayment						250,000
LT Loan interest		50,000	50,000	50,000	50,000	50,000
MT loan repayment		100,000	100,000	100,000	100,000	100,000
MT loan interest		40,000	32,000	24,000	16,000	8,000
Outflows	2,120,000	240,000	232,000	224,000	216,000	458,000
Share capital	600,000					
Area grant		130,000	130,000	130,000	130,000	
Machinery grant		100,000	10,000	10,000	10,000	10,000
Long-term loan	1,000,000					
Medium-term loan	500,000					
Royalties				15,000	40,000	
Inflows	2,100,000	230,000	140,000	155,000	180,000	10,000
Net flow before operating	(20,000)	(10,000)	(92,000)	(69,000)	(36,000)	(448,000)
Operating cash flow (see below)		(618,800)	(113,800)	(858,800)	96,200	301,200
Total	(20,000)	(628,800)	(205,800)	(927,800)	60,200	(146,800)
Cumulative pre int		(650,600)	(914,954)	(1,925,100)	(2,038,159)	(2,368,393)
Overdraft interest 9%	(1,800)	(58,554)	(82,346)	(173,259)	(183,434)	(213,155)
Cumulative	(21,800)	(709,154)	(997,300)	(2,098,359)	(2,221,593)	(2,581,548)
Profit		(200,000)	0	150,000	400,000	1,000,000
Depreciation						
Land		1,200	1,200	1,200	1,200	1,200
Buildings		30,000	30,000	30,000	30,000	30,000
Plant		50,000	55,000	60,000	65,000	70,000
Increase in w.cap		500,000	200,000	1,100,000	400,000	800,000
Operating cash flow		(618,800)	(113,800)	(858,800)	96,200	301,200

Comment. The overdraft facility became inadequate during Year 3. There are two problems with this business plan. One is the level of working capital envisaged, particularly in Year 3 when sales begin to rise rapidly. In relation to sales, the working capital of Year 3 represents a working capital cycle of around 100 days, which is probably capable of being reduced by better management of inventory and debtors. The other problem is the amount of borrowing and the interest payments that begin almost immediately. The owner may need to look for some equity finance source that would be willing to wait for the profits to begin to rise.

Index

Note: terms listed in **bold** appear in the glossary.